THE ELEMENT ENCYCLOPEDIA OF SECRET SIGNS AND SYMBOLS

THE ELEMENT ENCYCLOPEDIA OF SECRET SIGNS AND SYMBOLS

The Ultimate A–Z Guide from Alchemy to the Zodiac

Adele Nozedar

HarperCollins*Publishers*
77–85 Fulham Palace Road,
Hammersmith, London W6 8JB
www.harpercollins.co.uk

First published by HarperCollins*Publishers* 2008

10 9 8 7 6 5 4 3 2

A catalogue record of this book
is available from the British Library

ISBN 978-0-00-785049-5

Printed and bound in India by
Thomson Press (India) Limited

For Adam
and for the seven secrets

'In every grain of sand there lies
hidden the soil of a star'
Arthur Machen

'I do not need a leash or a tie
To lead me astray
In the land where dreams lie'
Yoav

CONTENTS

In Nature's temple, living pillars rise
Speaking sometimes in words of abstruse sense;
Man walks through woods of symbols, dark and dense,
Which gaze at him with fond familiar eyes.

Like distant echoes blent in the beyond
In unity, in a deep darksome way,
Vast as black night and vast as splendent day,
Perfumes and sounds and colors correspond

From "Correspondences," Charles Baudelaire

INTRODUCTION

The wandering woodsman

A couple of summers ago, lost again down a country lane somewhere in the Welsh borders among the timeless hills that mobile phone signals can't penetrate, I stumbled upon a traditional gypsy caravan. Half hidden behind a bank of trees and hedges, the caravan was a really surprising and interesting thing to come across. By now, I was late beyond redemption for my appointment and unable to communicate with anyone so I thought I'd might as well stay for a closer look.

It was like stepping back into another century.

The owner was an itinerate woodsman, making a living during bad times doing odd jobs and in good times by using his skills as a tree surgeon, a carpenter, or as a whittler of trinkets that he sold from the roadside or at country fairs. The caravan was very clean and tidy and reminded me of being on board a boat—everything slotted into place. There was a fire outside, with an enamel bucket suspended over it from a tripod of wooden poles. At first, I thought this was some kind of weird-smelling soup but it turned out to be full of socks and underwear, bubbling away like a soapy broth.

I'd thought that the days of people living like this, apart maybe from some new age travelers, were over, but apparently not. The owner seemed happy to chat and I'm afraid I probably bombarded him with questions; however, he also told me about something that really set my imagination alight and which actually led to the idea for the book that you're holding.

He told me about an ancient language of symbols used by the gypsies and travelers to tell each other where they were headed, essential information to anyone on the road, such as which farmers were friendly, and which were not. Admittedly, he said, this language was disappearing rapidly, not needed any more since apparently even the most impoverished latter-day nomad can afford a mobile phone—even if there's not always a signal.

But the whole incident got me thinking about the need for a kind of symbolic language, not just among travelers, but for anyone who might have to keep certain information safe within the confines of sympathizers. Once you start to poke around, the vestiges of these hidden languages seem to be everywhere, and it's my belief that the images contained within them are easily accessed from our subconscious minds if we can find the key to understanding them.

The aim of this book is to seek a true understanding of the secret signs, sacred symbols and other indicators of the arcane, hidden world that are so thickly clustered around us. During this process, we'll shed light on the cultural, psychological, and anthropological nature of our signs and symbols. We'll also be surprised to discover that many of the everyday things we take for granted can hold hidden secrets, and by having the key to this knowledge we'll gain an insight into the minds and concerns of our forbears who constructed these symbols.

By bringing this ancient knowledge from the shadows and into the daylight of our modern world, we'll have a greater understanding of what we are and how we think, and how we relate to the world around us.

SECRET AND SACRED

But what exactly does "secret" and "sacred" really mean? And what is a "symbol"? These are evocative words worth clarifying.

"Secret" comes from the Latin, *secretus*, meaning "separate," or "set apart."

"Sacred" also comes originally from the Latin *sacrere*, meaning "holy" or "consecrated."

"Symbol" comes from a Greek verb, *symballein*, meaning to "throw together," literally a "coincidence." As an object, the *symballon* (meaning "mark" or "token") appeared on an ancient Egyptian artifact that was used as a sign of identification, like a ticket. However, as a verb, *symballein* was also used by the Greeks to mean a gathering that was occluded or veiled in some way, that could only be understood by the initiate and was therefore camouflaged to the casual observer.

In this sense, we could say that all "symbols" are, by their very nature, secrets of one sort or another. At times during the writing of this book, it has seemed as though absolutely everything in the Universe has a dual meaning, or hides a secret of some kind. And uncanny coincidences have been coming thick and fast during the entire investigation. Some people say there's no such thing as a coincidence, and that even the random factor which sent me down the wrong road to encounter a gypsy caravan was somehow pre-ordained. I can't answer that and in many ways the suggestion is irrelevant.

For the purposes of definition, however, in this book we are investigating the signs and symbols that are set apart from the mundane, or made holy for some reason. Many of these symbols are also objects. Any object that also has symbolic meaning is called a "symbolate." For example, a wine glass might be a handy vessel from which to drink a nice glass of dry white wine at the end of the day, but as the chalice or goblet, it becomes a significant and universal symbol of the feminine and is used as such in ritual. As the Holy Grail, it becomes a symbol of a deeply meaningful quest for the spiritual, a symbol of the feminine part of man and the ultimate search for the Goddess within, the marriage of opposites and one of the ultimate aims of alchemy.

Mercia Eliade, in his book *The Sacred and the Profane*, explains it very well. He says that the sacred is that which manifests itself as a reality different from "normal" realities. But again, this definition begs another question, the answer to which is purely contextual: what is "normal"?

WHAT MAKES A SIGN OR SYMBOL EITHER SECRET OR SACRED?

Arguably, all symbols are, by their very nature, both secret and, in a way, sacred. They all have an element of the mystical and the magical about them since they are our attempt to explain the Universe in a more direct and visceral way than maybe words are capable of, a sentiment expressed perfectly (although admittedly in words) in the title of the song "A Picture Paints a Thousand Words."

However, the definition of a secret or sacred symbol, as opposed to any other kind, is that this symbol hides an inner meaning. The symbol may appear at first glance to be easily understood, but within the symbol is hidden a greater mystery.

Throughout history, there have been occasions when it has been essential to keep certain information hidden. Sometimes knowledge can be a dangerous thing, and yet it would be imperative to be able to recognize other people who were a part of the secret cult or society. In the early days of Christianity, for example, when allegiance to the new faith could result in death, followers had a secret code of recognition, a simple symbol of a fish.

Similarly, as we've seen, gypsies, romanies, and other traveling people were forced to develop an extensive language of symbols by means of which they could keep track of one another, telling friends how far ahead they might be, where they were headed for, which houses had people who were liable to be sympathetic, and which towns and farmsteads might best be avoided. If gypsies are effectively a secret society with their own means of communication, there were other such organizations that needed to keep their secrets, in particular those that were subject to persecution or who had secrets so momentous that we are still trying to unravel the true meaning of their symbols centuries later. These groups include the Cathars and the Knights Templar, who have left visual clues all along the course of their wanderings throughout the world. Deciphering the meaning of these clues with an absolute degree of accuracy is another matter.

There's also a symbolic language used by Native American trackers and hunters, who use signs and symbols invisible to anyone who is not attuned to them, but which carry vital information to anyone who does.

VITAL SIGNS

Symbolism is said to concern man's very knowledge of himself. To be able to understand symbols is to be able to understand an elemental way of explaining the Universe, and gives us a method of interpreting reality in a subtle way which has a way of transcending time, race, culture, our everyday concerns.

J.C. Cooper, in his *Encyclopedia of Traditional Symbols*, puts it like this:

The symbol ... goes beyond the individual to the Universal and is innate in the life of the spirit ... It is the external expression of the higher truth which is symbolized ...

It helps us to understand these mysterious signs and symbols if we can step into the footprints of the primitive person who is still buried deep inside us, the person who is close to the elements and who understands the interconnectedness of all things and who invented these secret signs and sacred symbols in the first place.

Signs and symbols, our invention of them and our understanding of them, transcend the barriers of written language and are at the very heart of our existence as human beings.

It's easy to forget that, once, the ability to write was reserved for the privileged few. Knowledge is power, the ability to wield it affords control, and ignorance is definitely not bliss. The alphabetical symbols that we now juggle so readily are themselves a set of the most magical and potent symbols that you're ever likely to find. But pictorial symbols override literacy; the messages they carry are nothing to do with the ability to read or write.

Of special interest are the signs and symbols associated with the natural world, the stars and planets, the landscape, the flora and fauna surrounding us. Human beings have always attached meaning to things in the natural world. We believe, fundamentally, that the sacred is present in everything. If we decide that a particular tree, or mountain, or stone is sacred, then this object becomes greater than the mere sum of its parts. If something "miraculous" occurs at a certain place—for example, a lightning strike—then that place becomes sacred, and the person associated with the event is also celebrated and may be venerated by being made a saint or its equivalent.

Symbols exist everywhere. They exist, not only on the page or chiseled into rock, but they also live and breathe and are an essential part of the landscape of our understanding. They exist as part of religions and belief systems from all over the world, whether in the lavish iconography of the Catholic Church, for example, or in the elaborate meanings behind the seemingly simple mudras, or hand gestures, of the East.

There are entire coded alphabets said to contain secrets given to us by angels or demons; there are arcane scripts of languages long forgotten which still carry a relevance today for those who would wish to keep their secrets very safe indeed, for reasons we can only guess at.

Throughout this book, there are some constantly repeating themes that go to the very core of man's concerns. Foremost among these are fertility, protection (from the elements and the evil eye), communication with the spirits and the Gods, good health and good luck, a fine time in the Afterlife.

However, at the very heart of this book lies a great dilemma.

THE BUTTERFLY AND THE WHEEL: HOW TO DESCRIBE A SYMBOL

The butterfly's attractiveness derives not only from colors and symmetry: deeper motives contribute to it. We would not think them so beautiful if they did not fly, or if they flew straight and briskly like bees, or if they stung, or above all if they did not enact the perturbing mystery of metamorphosis: the latter assumes in our eyes the value of a badly decoded message, a symbol, a sign.

Primo Levi

As with subsequent flights, Apollo 8 bowled along sideways, like a silver rolling pin, spinning slowly to distribute the sun's intense heat. From the craft's angle of approach the Moon was in darkness, so for the first two days the astronauts saw only the Earth shrinking behind them and a coy black void ahead, bereft of stars and glowing, until finally they were drifting engine-first around the far side, preparing for the "burn" that would slow them

into the lunar orbit. Still they saw nothing—until suddenly and without warning an immense arc of sun-drenched lunar surface appeared in their windows and the three men got the shocks of their lives, as the ethereal disc they and the rest of humanity had known up to then revealed itself as an awesome globe, cool and remote, without sound or motion, magisterial but issuing no invitation whatsoever ... Upon their return, they described a forbidding and hostile world. It was the Earth that sang to them from afar.

Andrew Smith, *Moondust: In Search of the Men Who Fell to Earth* [2006]

This anecdote, taken from Andrew Smith's enthralling page-turning account of the lives of the 12 men who actually stood on the surface of the Moon as part of the Apollo space mission, is an oblique reminder of one of the major dilemmas in writing a book that dares to try to explain secret and sacred symbols.

If mystique is an inherent part of the nature of something, does explaining it demystify it somehow and make it less important, less meaningful, less of itself?

How can it make sense to use words to describe something that was made to avoid the use of words in the first place? Isn't this something of an anomaly, an incongruity? To understand a symbol properly we need to pin it down for a moment, hold it still, see what it looks like from all angles, smell it, feel it, taste it, stick it under a microscope, turn it inside out and outside in again. We need to try to climb into the heads of the people who created it, and understand something of the time that they lived in and their daily concerns. What were their beliefs, their superstitions? How did they get their food? How did they perceive their Gods? How did they communicate with these Gods, and with one another?

And after all this, like a butterfly killed with chloroform, perhaps there's a danger that the outward appearance of the symbol might be preserved, but that its essential nature might somehow be destroyed in the process of analysis.

So, what has all this to do with the Apollo 8 Moon landing?

The Moon, along with the Sun, is arguably one of our most important symbols, visible to everyone, universally acknowledged by humankind. Her pale beauty changes constantly, eternally playing the coquettish and mutable female to the uniform indelibility of the masculine Sun, mirroring the woman's menstrual cycle as well as (allegedly) affecting the tides, the growth patterns of plants and the mating cycles of animals, inspiring myths, legends, songs, poetry, and romances.

The term "lunatic," meaning a crazed person, is derived from the name of the Moon, Luna, whose swollen fullness is meant to draw out the underlying madness that seems to affect many human beings. The constantly changing face of the Moon is said to mirror the changeability of woman herself; it is her prerogative to change her mind, to alter her appearance, to have mood swings. Although this might be a physically distant Goddess, 250,000 miles away in mundane measurement, in the vast scale of things, she's very close, and her influence is profound.

Prior to our physical exploration of the Moon, there was a great deal of panic and superstition about what would happen when man actually stepped onto her surface. Alongside some very real practical concerns

(for example, would the spacecraft, embarrassingly, tip over in front of the collective cameras of the nations of the Earth and sink beneath a miasma of fathomless dust, like some sort of lunar version of the *Titanic*?), other fears were based firmly in a superstitious belief that somehow we would anger the ageless Moon Goddess, or perhaps disturb the ghosts of the generations of dead that inhabited the mysterious shadowy faces and forms that seemed, from the viewpoint of the Earth, to personify her.

The question is this: Did that "one small step," still poignantly embossed in the ageless dust of the Moon's silent vast emptiness as the regulated pattern of a Moon boot's sole, render obsolete her symbolic meaning? Did her pale luminescence become one iota less glamorous, just because of man's proximity, his effective invasion?

The answer is a resounding *no*.

The Moon is no more a simple lump of rock floating in the sky than the woman who gave birth to you is just a female member of the human species with fully functioning reproductive organs.

Instead, the analogy of the "giant leap for Mankind" that Neil Armstrong used specifically to describe the Moon landings but which applies to the entire mission, resulted in a new perspective on the Earth. For the first time, man was able to view his home planet in a way never before possible. In many ways those first astronauts were in the position of the Gods themselves, able to see Earth from above: "tiny, jewel-like, and frighteningly alone." This iconic image has meant that the Earth itself has become a symbol, and our own vital role, as Godlike creatures that can determine its future, has become apparent. A different perspective, another viewpoint, has increased our knowledge and understanding.

Not only that, but the sorcery of a full Moon remains intact.

THE PICTURE WORTH A THOUSAND WORDS

The use of a simple symbol in a film, a book or an advertisement says far more than any wordy explanation ever could, acting as a visual shortcut to that part of our minds that understands them. There are millions of examples; let's take just one, the movie *Blade Runner*, Ridley Scott's interpretation of the Philip K. Dick novel, *Do Androids Dream of Electric Sheep?*. Both novel and movie use symbols to great effect. In the story, replicant human beings have been created to carry out demeaning work in extraterrestrial colonies. However, some of the replicants stage an uprising, which results in their being banned from the planet Earth. The Blade Runners are human beings whose mission it is to exterminate any replicants still on Earth.

One of the methods that the Blade Runner uses to determine the identity of a replicant is to test the responses of their eyes. Here, Scott uses the analogy of the eye as the "mirror of the soul," the reflexes and responses of the pupils reacting according to the emotions. This poses the question; what exactly is a soul? If the replicant is indistinguishable

from the human being in that it has imprinted memories, emotional responses and feelings—i.e. it does not know that it is a replicant and is virtually indistinguishable from a human being—then surely this demands sympathy?

It's important to remember that the meanings of symbols can change, in the same way that the caterpillar changes into the butterfly, as the continuing archaeology of symbols casts a clearer light.

The chameleon nature of symbols also means that any book about them can never hope to be complete.

A good example is the number 666, personified in some cultures as the number of the Beast, which sends a frisson of terror through the very soul. Just before the time of submitting this manuscript, a new theory about the number 666 emerged. It seems that the 666 might originally have been 665, or even 616, the subject of the slip of the tongue or of the pen some thousands of years ago. So, do we hold the presses and start again? No. The fact is that the number 666, whatever the truth, *is* the symbol that's important, imprinted on our collective consciousness after years of being synonymous with the notion of evil, however nebulous that might be in itself.

NO BEGINNING, NO END: ANATOMY OF A SIMPLE SYMBOL

Rodin said, "Man never invented anything new, only discovered things." While it's true to say that some symbols have been manmade for a specific purpose, it's equally accurate to argue that everything is inspired in some way by the natural world around us, by the forms of nature, plants, animals, the elements. Even a reaction against the fluid forms of nature is generally inspired by a desire to provide an alternative. Sometimes the revelation of a natural symbol is immediate; other such discoveries are the result of years of painstaking observation.

One of our simplest symbols has elaborate and arcane origins.

Here is a picture, not of a manmade or computer-generated pattern, but of the shape made in the sky by the Planet Venus. Venus is

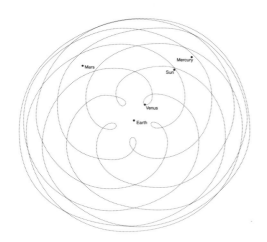

the only planet whose dance around the Sun in the depths of space describes such a definite and distinctive form, and we can only imagine the sense of wonder that must have been felt by the ancient Akkadians who first charted the design. They also realized that the Morning Star and the Evening Star, previously considered to be two separate celestial bodies, were one and the same. This discovery had a profound effect, which has cast such a long shadow over the archaeology of symbols that we are still governed by it today. Here's why.

Because of Venus's proximity to the Sun, its light is often obliterated, and so it is visible only in the early morning or in the evening, either just before sunrise or just after sunset. The Greeks called the morning star Eosphoros, "bringer of the dawn" (later, the star would be called Lucifer, the brightest of the angels cast out of the Heavens). As the Evening Star, it was called Hesperos, "star of the evening" (which gives us the name of evening prayers, or vespers).

It takes eight years and one day for the appearances of Venus to complete an entire pentagram. These days we can plot these movements relatively easily, but for our ancestors the process must have been elaborate and painstaking, as uncertain and laborious a voyage of discovery as the traversing of any great physical ocean. The Goddess that we know as Venus was, to the Akkadians, Ishtar/Inanna, divinity not only of love and harmony but also Goddess of war. Incidentally, Venus is the only major planet of our solar system, aside from the Earth itself, to be designated a feminine spirit.

The Mayans determined their calendrical system from the movements of Venus, and chose propitious positions of the planet to determine the time of a war. The five-pointed star that is still used as a military symbol—stenciled onto tanks, for example, or used in insignia—derives from the stately movement of this great astral Goddess.

Similarly, the apple given by Eve to Adam contained a hidden symbol within it; the pentagram created by the pattern of the pips. Eve offered Adam not only knowledge of the divine feminine—a holy grail indeed—but offered him a symbol of the true marriage of opposites, the feminine number two wedding to the masculine number three. Eve, therefore, personifies Ishtar/Venus/Aphrodite as the Goddess of sensual love (and Venus, incidentally, is the derivation of the word "Venereal"). Further, Ishtar was demonized in the Bible as the Whore of Babylon.

This is the sort of story that fills me with an utter sense of awe. A seemingly simple thing such as the shape made in the sky by the path of a planet, so full of complexities and contradictions, which not only clarifies some aspects of the symbol made by the planet but that also poses further questions. The truth is that the quest to understand the meaning of a symbol is as much a personal voyage of discovery as a collective one, and it is in the spirit of exploration that I hope you will adventure into this book.

WIZARDS AND TRUE STARS

Speaking of celestial bodies, there are several stars that have been involved in the adventure of this book, many of whom, just like Venus, have been out and about in the early morning and in the late evening, working hard to glue together the many disparate elements of a tricky manuscript.

The brightest star in this firmament has to be Katy Carrington at Harper Element, who was not only instrumental in the conception of this book but who has also talked me down from the ledge (metaphorically speaking) several times, probably without even realizing it. She has had an uncanny knack of calling just at the times when I've been feeling like a rabbit in the headlights, alternately dazzled by the array of possible entries and despairing of ever being able to make sense of it all. Her quick-witted humor, ready encouragement and clarity of thought have been utterly inspirational.

Terence Caven, too, has had the monumental task of collating all the illustrations for this book, and has done so with a calm patience and unflappability in the face of my tedious bombardment of emails.

On the editorial team, Simon Gerratt, Charlotte Ridings, Martin Noble, and Mark Bolland have managed to turn what could have been a thankless task into an enjoyable one, their incisive suggestions and gentle diplomacy adding an incalculable value to the original text. Also at Harpers, I'd like to thank Jeannine Dillon and Chris Wold for the enthusiasm that helped drive this project forward. I am also very grateful to Kate Latham, Faith Booker and Graham Holmes.

Finally, credit is due to Laura Summers, always a pleasure to deal with, and also to someone who isn't at HarperCollins any more but to whom I extend my deepest gratitude for all sorts of reasons, Wanda Whiteley.

Any book about symbols would be nothing without the illustrations. Paul Khera has done the bulk of these, with additional thanks to Anat Cederbaum, Myong Hwi Kim, Kruti Sanaija, and Yuki Nakamura for advice and help with some aspects of these pictures. Paul managed to karate chop his way very rapidly through some complex images with calm aplomb and no significant gasping for breath. I am also lucky enough to have Finlay Cowan contribute images to this book.

Other illustrators include David Little, Lyndall Fernie, and Kalavathi Devi. I would also like to thank Willa and Milo Seary for their drawings and for the valuable insight they gave me into how children regard the elements. Gavin and Davina Hogg very kindly allowed me to use the schematics for their amazingly lovely Green Man Maze, designed by David Eveleigh. Contact them at www.penpont.com.

Finally, Sigorour Atlason—who never sleeps—was incredibly helpful in providing information about, and images of, some rare Icelandic rune staves. If you happen to be in Iceland, I can recommend a visit to the Museum of Icelandic Sorcery and Witchcraft in Holmavik, where you can say hello in person to Sigorour, and maybe even look at his necropants (www.galdrasning.is).

Several people have lent me books, made suggestions or given moral support. Many thanks are due to Caroline Danby, Tania Ahsan, Hamraz Ahsan, Carla Edgley, Judy Roland, and Theo Chalmers. Lisa, you wanted a lump of wood for your birthday; here it is. As ever, the lovely people at the Order of Bards, Ovates and Druids have been wonderfully helpful, especially Beith, who gave me invaluable information about some rare early Irish magical practices. Stuart Mitchell at Rosslyn Chapel shared some valuable information about his and his father Thomas' intriguing discoveries. Stuart's work can be viewed at www.stuart-mitchell.com

I am hugely indebted to everyone at Raquetty Lodge, Hay on Wye, who, having met me just once, bizarrely lent me their gorgeous house for nearly a month. This change of scene gave me a new perspective and the invaluable headspace I needed to grapple with the final stages of this book. Special thanks are due to Katy Garratt, who lent me her bedroom. I'd also like to thank Ros and Geoff Garratt and the people who looked after me during my stay; Pammy Gibson-Watt, Aubrey Fry, and Stephanie Smith.

While I was staying in Hay, I was lucky enough to witness the sensational Hay on Fire festival, which handily took place just as I was writing about the elements. A more primal celebration of fire can't be imagined, the whole event being completely sensational and inspiring.

Finally, I could not have written this book without music to drive me through the rougher parts and to celebrate the smoother. The soundtrack has been varied, but the real highpoint has been the debut album by Yoav, *Charmed and Strange*, which I've been playing virtually nonstop (and very loud) since I found it. I am also indebted to the visionary Mike Alway, who has kept me supplied with some awesome and inspirational releases from his El label. I also need to thank Matthew Bellamy, Chris Wolstenholme, and Dominic Howard.

Most of all I have to thank starship commander Adam Fuest for putting up with my obsession about this book and my possible bouts of absentmindedness about anything else during the writing of it.

Part One
SIGNS AND SYMBOLS OF MAGIC AND MYSTERY

This opening part is also the largest single section of this book and deals with symbols from all over the world. They are generally an inherent part of a culture, with religious or spiritual meaning, encompassing Christianity, Judaism, Islam, modern religious practices such as Jainism and Scientology, diverse ancient and modern Pagan beliefs as well as magical and esoteric practices. Objects with a symbolic meaning are also included.

We've tried to present a really comprehensive range of symbols, given the confines of the space available. Underscoring the diversity of these images is a fervent hope that their explanations will add to our greater understanding of each other, while allowing the symbols themselves to retain their inherent mystical aura.

This isn't difficult, since symbolism is a slippery subject. Most of our primal symbols come from a time prior to verbal communication as we know it today, and most certainly predate the written word, which itself obliterates much of the need for diagrammatic symbols. Apart from the very modern signs, whose living inventors can explain their meaning, for the most part these pictorial metaphors must remain open to conjecture. Enigma is, after all, an important characteristic of a mystical or magical symbol. All we can do here is offer possibilities, based on our existing knowledge, with a sprinkling of intuition and deductive reasoning thrown in for good measure.

It is important to bear in mind that symbols are not static objects, but continue to develop, adding to their range of interpretations. Therefore, there can be no absolutely definitive interpretation of any symbol.

The most logical way to understand a symbol is simply to observe it. See what it looks like, listen to what it says. This involves a deal of impartiality and it is essential to be aware of any preconceptions so that we can remove them. An obvious example is the swastika, made sinister after its appropriation by the Nazi regime. However, compare the swastika to this drawing of the Sun by a

FIRST SIGNS: THE BASIC SHAPES OF SYMBOLS

There are certain elemental structures that occur repeatedly, not only as component parts of more elaborate symbols, but also with rich meanings of their own. In fact, it's probably true to say that the simpler the symbol, the more scope there is for interpretation; ergo, the more meaningful it is and, paradoxically, the more complex it becomes. These primary shapes transcend barriers of time, geography, and cultural context, part of a universal language that goes before, and beyond, words. Don't be fooled into thinking that these basic shapes are as self-explanatory as to need no analysis. A true understanding of what they represent can only add to the comprehension of the more elaborate shapes and symbols that follow in this section.

Space

The elements of a symbol are defined only by the space that is a part of its construction. Like the wind, the effect of space is gauged by its effect on the things within it or surrounding it. The concept of space, the void, is a profound part of our experience. To reach a state of "emptiness" is, for many, the ultimate spiritual experience and a way of connecting to the Absolute. When John Lennon wrote "Imagine," whose lyrics gradually strip away the trappings of the material world, it was this idea that inspired him.

six-year old: they are very similar. The swastika is a very ancient Sun Symbol, possibly dating back to Paleolithic times. If the symbol hadn't already enjoyed such a primal place in our collective conscious then it would never have had such a powerful impact.

In the same way that the same word can mean different things to different people, the meanings of symbols are not always straightforward either. The inverted cross, to a practicing Catholic, is a reminder of St. Peter, who elected to be crucified on a cross of this type. To others, it is a popular emblem of Satanism, a religious cult that likes to use inversions and reversals. Therefore, the context in which a symbol is set is of paramount importance.

When you dip into this section, try to look at the symbol first and see what it tells you, before you read the interpretation.

To be aware of the possibility of space within a flat, two-dimensional representation is to give that shape substance and a new kind of reality that lifts it off the page and makes it real. Space is not flat and cannot be confined by lines on a piece of paper. The page and the shape on it do not exist in isolation, but are a part of a greater cosmos. This book and you, the reader, are a part of this equation.

The concept of **zero** is a space. Indeed, the realization that "nothing" can be "something" marked a profound leap forward in man's development. All creation myths begin with a Void, symbolic of potential.

Although attempts to explain the concept of space are inevitably faulty, it might help to think of a blank page. Before a mark is made upon the paper, the potential for what might appear there is so vast as to be unimaginable, a consideration which causes consternation for some artists and writers. Without this space, there is no arena for anything else to exist. This absence of any thing means that no thing is the most important symbol in the World.

Dot

A dot might seem to be an unassuming little thing, the first mark on the pristine sheet of paper. In this case, the dot is a beginning. But see what just happened there? The dot, an essential component in the structure of the sentence, closed it, making it a symbol of ending. Therefore, the dot is both an origination and a conclusion, encompassing all the possibilities of the Universe within it, a seed full of potential and a symbol of the Supreme Being. The dot is the point of creation, for example the place where the arms of the cross intersect.

The dot is also called the bindhu, which means "drop." The bindhu is a symbol of the Absolute, marked on the **forehead** at the position of the third **eye** in the place believed to be the seat of the **soul**.

The presence of dots within a symbol can signify the presence of something else. A dot in the center of the **Star of David** marks the **quintessence**, or Fifth Element. It also acts as reminder of the concept of space. The decorated dots that surround the **doorways** of Eastern **temples** are not merely ornamental devices but have significance relevant to the worshippers. Dots frequently appear in this way, acting as a sort of shorthand for the tenets of a faith. In the **Jain Symbol**, for example, the dots stand for the **Three Jewels** of Jainism. The dots in each half of the **yin yang** symbol unify the two halves: one dot is "yin," the other "yang." Together they demonstrate the interdependence of opposing forces.

Circle

The next logical magical symbol is the circle. Effectively an expansion of the dot, the circle represents the **spirit** and the cosmos. Further, the circle itself is constructed from "some thing" (the unbroken line) and "no thing" (the space inside and outside this line).

Therefore, the circle unifies spirit and matter. The structure itself has great strength—think of the cylindrical shape of a lighthouse, built that way in order to withstand the fiercest attack by a stormy **sea**.

The physical and spiritual strength of this symbol are there because the perfect circle has no beginning and no end; it is unassailable. This power is the reason why the circle is used in magical practices such as spell-casting. The magic circle creates a fortress of psychic protection, a physical and spiritual safe haven where unwanted or uninvited entities cannot enter.

Hermes Trismegistus said of the circle:

God is a circle whose center is everywhere and circumference is nowhere.

Where would ancient man have seen the most important circles? Obviously, in the **Sun** and the **Moon**. As the Sun, the circle is masculine, but when it is the Moon, it is feminine. Because the passage of time is marked by the journey of the Sun, Moon and **stars** in orbit around our Earth, the circle is a symbol of the passage of time. In this form, it commonly appears as the **wheel**.

Because the circle has no divisions and no sides, it is also a symbol of equality. King Arthur's Round Table was the perfect piece of furniture for the fellowship of Knights who were each as important as each other. Similarly, the Dalai Lama has a "circular" Council.

Arc

Perhaps the most prominent arc of the natural world appears in the elusive form of the **rainbow**, which primitive man saw as a bridge between the Heavens and the Earth.

As a part of a circle, the arc symbolizes potential spirit. The position of the arc is important. Upright, shaped like a cup or **chalice**, it implies the feminine principle, something that can contain the spirit. If the arc is inverted, then the opposite is true and it becomes a triumphal, victorious, masculine symbol. As such, the arc can take the form of an archway. The vaulted or arched shape of many holy buildings, from a great variety of different faiths, represents the vault of the Heavens. The arc shape often appears in planetary symbols.

Vertical line

Man, alone in the animal kingdom, stands upright, so the vertical line represents the physical symbol of the number **One**, man striving toward spirit. This simple line is the

basic shape of the **World Tree** or **Axis Mundi** that connects the Heavens, the Earth and the lower regions. It is not only a basic phallic symbol but also signifies the soul that strives for union with the Divine.

The upright line tells us where we are at a precise moment; think of the big hand of the clock, vertically oriented at 12 o'clock.

Horizontal line

The opposite of the vertical line, the horizontal line represents matter, and the forward and backward movement of time. This line also signifies the skyline or horizon and man's place on the Earth.

Cross

Here, the vertical and horizontal lines come together to create a new symbol—the cross. There are of course countless different types of cross, a few of which are covered in this section of the book. Despite any embellishments or devices, however, the basic meaning of the cross stays the same.

The earliest example of the cross comes from Crete and dates back to the fifteenth century BC although it is much older than this, ancient beyond proper reckoning. It is an incredibly versatile and useful sign with many interpretations. As the convergence of the vertical and horizontal lines, it symbolizes the union of the material and the spiritual (think of the sign of the cross given by Catholic priests). As a geometric tool, it has no equal; if you put the cross inside the circle, then you are able to divide the circle equally. Similarly, the cross is said to "give birth to" the square.

Because of its four cardinal points, the cross represents the elements and the directions.

In the West the cross equates with the number **4,** but in China, it is associated with the number **5** since the "dot" in the middle of the cross, where the two arms intersect, is also included.

The cross is sometimes disguised as another symbol, such as a four-petaled flower. All over the world, the cross is a symbol of protection.

Square

Said to be the first shape invented by Man, the square represents the created Universe as opposed to the spiritual dimensions depicted by the circle.

The square represents the Earth and the four elements. Plato described the square, like the circle, as being "absolutely beautiful in itself." Like the cross, the square is associated with the number 4. A square has four corners; to speak of the "four corners of the Earth" is something of an anomaly since the Earth is round, without corners. All the symbolism of the number 4 is encompassed within the square, and it is interesting to note that, just as the square represents the created Universe, in the Hebrew faith the Holy Name of the Creator is comprised of four letters.

The square gives man a safe, static reference point, and a stable, unmoving shape as opposed to the continual motion of the circle.

Temples and holy buildings are often built in the form of a square, solidly designed to align with the four points of the compass. The **Ka'aba** at **Mecca** is a fine example, as is the base of the Buddhist **Stupa**. **Altars**, too, are square. Square shapes define limits and create boundaries; to speak of someone as being "square" means that they are fixed and unchangeable.

Lozenge

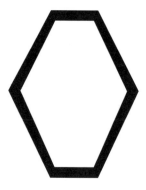

A diamond shape often with rounded rather than pointed ends, the lozenge is often overlooked, but is actually a representation of the female genitalia. As such, its most popular appearance is probably as the **Vesica Piscis**, the sacred **doorway** through which spirit enters the world of matter. In **heraldry**, for example, the lozenge is used in place of the masculine shield, to denote a coat of arms belonging to a woman or a noncombative male, such as a member of the clergy.

Triangle

The triangle shares all the symbolic significance of the number **3**, as a shape, and therefore represents the many things that come in groups of three, from the Holy Trinity to the triple aspect of the Goddess. Triangles appear in lots of different signs and symbols. In ancient times, the triangle was considered synonymous with light, and the meanings of the triangle vary according to which way up it is. When it sits firmly on its base, then it is

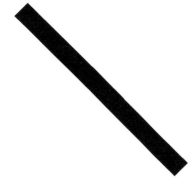

a masculine, virile symbol, representing **fire**. The other way up it becomes the water element, a **chalice** shape, emblematic of the feminine powers. Balanced on its point in this way the triangle also represents the **yoni**, further underpinning the Goddess aspect. The equilateral triangle is a harmonious form, used to indicate the Higher Powers, providing a framework, for example, for the **All Seeing Eye of God**.

As a symbol of strength, the triangle reinforces the corners of the square, both physically and metaphysically. The solid shape of the triangle also makes its appearance in yogic positions, for example in the Trikona Asana or Triangle Posture.

Diagonal

The square can be divided into two diagonal triangles. Because the length of these shapes has no simple relationship to its sides, the Greeks concluded that the diagonal must be a symbol of the irrational. Therefore, the diagonal, or oblique, has come to be associated with the incomprehensible, occult world. In J.K. Rowling's Harry Potter books, Diagon Alley is the hidden part of London that is a magical high street full of occult devices.

Zig-zag

However it is interpreted, the jagged shape of the zig-zag carries with it the idea of heat, energy, vitality, and movement, the archetypal sign for lightning or electricity. The double zig-zag that makes the Astrological glyph for **Aquarius** could be **water** or it could be the life-force itself. The **serpent** that **spirals** up the **caduceus** is a softened zig-zag shape. There is an inherent danger in the zig-zag, and the deities that carry it in their hands do so as a sign of their own authority and power.

AASKOUANDY

Ironically, the first entry in this encyclopedia is a symbol that is impossible to illustrate because it takes various different forms.

An Aaskouandy charm is any object that is unusual in some way, which appears unexpectedly or is somehow out of place in its surroundings. For example, if a **stone** is found in the entrails of an animal that was particularly hard to hunt, then this stone is perceived to be the object that gave the animal its power, and so is eligible for Aaskouandy status.

The Iriquois believe that the Aaskouandy, a magical charm of considerable power, has a mind of its own, so much so that if it is neglected it can even turn against its owner. They also believe that the Aaskouandy has trickster tendencies and can change shape at will, so confusingly it may metamorphose into another object altogether.

Because the Aaskouandy is an independent being, the owner is careful to stay on the right side of it, keeping it happy with gifts and feasts.

If an Aaskouandy appears in the shape of a **fish** or **serpent**, then this is particularly potent because of the inherent power of these creatures. In this case, the Aaskouandy changes its name, too, and becomes an **Onniont**.

ABRAXAS

Depending on your point of view, Abraxas is either an Egyptian Sun God who was adopted by the early Christian Gnostics, or a **demon** from Hell who is closely associated with Lucifer, although there is a case for the

former, since he was not demoted to the ranks of a demon until the Middle Ages.

Abraxas was no ordinary god, however. As Ruler of the First Heaven he had dominion over the cycles of birth, death, and resurrection.

Whatever the case, the symbol for Abraxas is a very unusual one. He has the head of a **chicken**, the torso of a man, and two **serpents** for **legs**. He holds a **shield** in one hand and a flail-like instrument in the other. The image of Abraxas was carved onto **stones** (called Abraxas Stones) and the stone used as a magical **amulet**. Occasionally Abraxas will appear driving a chariot drawn by **four horses**; these horses represent the **elements**.

This Abraxas symbol was adopted by the Knights Templar, who used it on their seals. No one knows precisely why this symbol was of particular significance, but a hidden secret within the name "Abraxas" may provide a clue.

In Greek, the **7 letters** are the initials of the first **7 planets** in the Solar System.

Further, if we apply **numerology** to the name then it adds up to **365**, not only the number of days in a year but also the number of the spirits that those same early Gnostics believed were emanations from God.

Added to the mix is the speculation that the supreme magical word, "**Abracadabra,**" may derive from the name Abraxas, which means "harm me not."

ADRINKA SYMBOLS

Originating in Ghana, Adrinka symbols are now related, in general, to the Ashanti people. There are hundreds of these signs, which were originally printed on the cloth that was used in sacred ceremonies and rituals, **funerals** in particular. "Adrinka" means "goodbye."

The patterns are created using a block printing method. The symbols are cut into a calabash gourd, and then stamped onto the cloth in ink or paint.

The language of Adrinka is rich and varied, embracing philosophical concepts and sociological ideas as well as straightforward words. The symbols take their influence from **plants**, **animals**, the landscape, and the natural world, as well as manmade objects. There is a vast Adrinka vocabulary, with

complex meanings attached to what might appear, at first glance, to be simple little doodles.

AESCLEPIUS WAND

Often confused with the **Caduceus**, the Wand or Rod of Aesclepius is the true symbol of the medical profession. The symbol belongs to the Greek God of Healing whose name it bears. Although the origins of many symbols are indeterminate, there is a theory that the Aesclepius Wand came about due to the method of removal of a certain parasite that was drawn gradually from the body by winding it around a stick. However, the **serpent** is a powerful symbol of healing, despite its toxic nature. In general, the symbol of the serpent rising up toward the top of a pole or **tree** is representative of matter transforming into spirit and of enlightenment.

AGNUS DEI

Agnus Dei translates as the Lamb of God, and is also known as the Paschal Lamb. It is symbolized pictorially as a lamb with a **halo**, proudly trotting along, carrying a banner and a **cross**.

Lambs were commonly sacrificed during the time of the **Passover**, the **blood** sprinkled in the **doorway** or rubbed onto the lintel, so the connection was made because of the sacrifice of Christ.

Part of the Catholic mass includes the plea, repeated three times:

Lamb of God, who takes away the sins of the world, have mercy on us.

AKHET

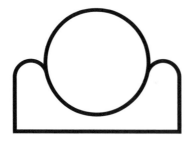

In Egyptian, Akhet means "dawn." This symbol—often made into an amulet by the Ancient Egyptians—symbolized the new **Sun** rising over the sacred **mountain**.

The symbol sometimes features the double-headed **lion**, or Aker, that guards it, and is also related to the glyph used to denote the astrological sign of **Libra**.

AKWABA

This is an African fertility symbol belonging to the Ashanti tribe. The Akwaba is a doll, usually carved of wood, which commands the same attention as a real infant. It is dressed, washed and even "fed" until the human child is actually born, an example of sympathetic magic believed to ensure the arrival of the true baby.

ALCHEMY

Alchemy is an ancient art, at the heart of which lies the manufacture of a mysterious substance called the **Philosopher's Stone,** the highly desirable and legendary object that is said to transform base metals—such as **lead**—into **gold**.

However, the gold in this instance symbolizes not just the valuable **metal,** but enlightenment and eternal life, and Alchemists are concerned with their own spiritual and personal development as well as the pursuit of the seemingly unattainable goal. The Chinese differentiate these different kinds of alchemy as nei-tan (the alchemy of spiritual transformation) and wai-tan (the straightforward "lead-into-gold" type).

The motto of the Alchemists is *Solve et Coagula,* meaning "Solution and Coagulation."

The work of the early Alchemists was necessarily a secretive and clandestine matter, and its secrets are still held within a rich encrustation of symbols, pictures, oblique references, double meanings, and riddles. Alchemical symbolism features animals, birds, colors, and parables as well as archetypal symbols such as the **Cosmic Egg**.

The key tenets of alchemy are encompassed in something called the **Smaragdina Tablet,** or the Emerald Tablet, which is said to have been found by Alexander the Great in the tomb of Hermes Trismegistus (Hermes the Thrice Great) who is the founder of all things alchemical. The Alchemical Tradition exists/existed in Ancient Egypt, China, and India, but its most recent incarnation was in medieval Europe.

Those who dabbled in alchemy include the famous and the infamous, such as John Dee (astrologer to Queen Elizabeth I), Paracelsus, Albertus Magnus, Christian Rosenkreuz, Nicholas Flamel, and Isaac Newton. Some of the chemical treatises are befuddling to even the most learned of scholars, but the very word "alchemy" is almost in itself a symbol, conjuring up images that are magical, mystical, and marvelous.

Alchemical symbols

Although some of the alchemical symbols occasionally varied a little between practitioners, the following lists show the most commonly used interpretations. This list is by no means comprehensive but gives a good cross-section of the "feel" of these mysterious signs. It is interesting to see how many of these alchemical symbols have survived to the present day, and how the meanings of the simpler symbols are so universal that they extend well beyond the reaches of this one system.

THE FOUR BASIC ELEMENTS

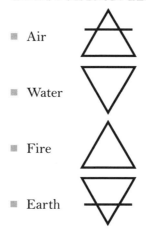

- Air
- Water
- Fire
- Earth

THE FOUR SEASONS

- Spring
- Summer
- Fall
- Winter

THE SEVEN PLANETARY METALS

- Sun
  gold
- Moon
  silver
- Mercury
  mercury or quicksilver
- Venus
  copper
- Mars
  iron
- Jupiter
  tin
- Saturn
  lead

THE ALCHEMICAL SPIRITS

- The World Spirit
- The Spirit of Silver

- The Spirit of Mercury
- The Spirit of Copper
- The Spirit of Tin

ALL SEEING EYE

Probably the best-known use of the All Seeing Eye symbol is as a part of the design of the **Great Seal of the United States of America,** which appears on the **US Dollar Bill.** Set within a **triangle,** a single **eye** is surrounded by rays of light; on the Seal, the whole rests on top of an unfinished **pyramid.**

There is something quite sinister about this disembodied, ever-watchful eye, although its symbolic meaning is simple; it represents

God watching over humankind, and is also known as the **Eye of Providence**.

The eye itself is a powerful and popular symbol, and the All Seeing Eye has its roots in the Egyptian **Eye of Horus**. The addition of the triangle represents all the different aspects of the shape, including the Christian Trinity of the Father, Son, and Holy Ghost.

The fact that the Great Seal was a symbol that belonged to **Freemasonry** and **alchemy** prior to its adoption as part of the Great Seal of the USA has given rise to many conspiracy theories. That the All Seeing Eye is also the symbol of the Illuminati, a secretive organization within the Catholic Church, has further bolstered these theories.

In Freemasonry, God is known as the Architect of the Universe. The first reference to the All Seeing Eye as a Masonic symbol appeared in 1797, although the Great Seal was designed in 1776 and first used in 1782. It is whispered that Masonic influences must have been at work when the Seal was designed; no one will ever know for sure, although those magical symbols that encrust the Seal must have been put there for a reason. What is certain is that when the Eye was adopted as part of the design of the Dollar in 1935, it was as a direct result of the influence of the President, Franklin Roosevelt, who had no reason to conceal his Masonic affiliations.

ALMADEL

This is a particular kind of magical **amulet**, made of wax so that the secret names of **demons** can be written or engraved upon it. The whole is then melted so that its creator need never reveal the secret. The color of the almadel should correspond to its magical intention.

ALTAR

The root of the word Altar means "high" or "high place," and therefore the altar is symbolic of the **Holy Mountain**, given that it is raised above its immediate surroundings and is used as a focus for holy rites and sacred practices. Altars, as such, exist in all religions and cultures, the symbolic meaning remaining unchanged across diverse belief systems. Altars certainly provide the main focus within churches, but they are not confined to large public buildings, many faiths have a small domestic altar in the home.

AMULET

Although it is worn on the body as a piece of **jewelry**, the amulet is different from "normal" jewelry in that it holds a magical significance that is peculiar to its owner or wearer. Generally, the powers of the amulet fall into two specific categories, either to bring luck or to avert evil; either of these qualities arguably reflect a positive or negative attitude on the part of the owner. The **talisman** is effectively the same thing as an amulet although its name derives from an Arabic word meaning "magic picture." Therefore a charm made specifically and inscribed with the names of the spirits, **the Seal of Solomon**, and other mystical symbols is more likely to be referred to as a talisman.

Significant symbols for use as amulets include **birthstones** (or other **gems** according to their magical powers), astrological signs, specific symbols such as the **Hand of Fatima** or the **cornus**, and symbols specific to the religious and spiritual beliefs of the wearer, such as the **cross**, the **star**, words, names, and **numbers**.

Incidentally, both amulets and talismans are referred to as charms; the origin of this word has the same root as the Latin word for "song," indicating the link between a magical sound and a magical intention.

Ankh

Essentially the **tau cross** surmounted by a loop or **circle**, the ankh is a prominent feature of Ancient Egyptian reliefs, artworks, and funerary paraphernalia. Like the tau, the ankh is a letter; specifically, it is a **hieroglyph** meaning "life."

The volume of meaning that can be squeezed from such a simple symbol is awe-inspiring. The Ankh represents the male and female genitalia, the **Sun** coming over the horizon, and the union of Heaven and Earth. This association with the Sun means that the ankh is traditionally drawn in **gold**—the color of the Sun—and never in **silver**, which relates to the **Moon**.

Putting aside the complexities of these separate elements, though, what does the ankh look like? Its resemblance to a **key** gives a clue to another meaning of this magical symbol. The Egyptians believed that the Afterlife was as meaningful as the present one, and the ankh provided the key to the gates of death and what lay beyond.

Powerful symbols frequently stray across into other cultures despite their origins, and the ankh is no exception. Because it symbolizes immortality and the Universe, it was initially borrowed by the fourth-century Coptic Christians who used it as a symbol to reinforce Christ's message that there is life after death. The ankh is used by the Rosicrucians too. Even though its actual invention is shrouded in thousands of years of mystery, the ankh symbol can be bought in any high street jewelry store anywhere in the world. When Elvis Presley was criticized for wearing the "pagan" Ankh among his many other crosses, he commented, "I don't want to miss out on Heaven because of a technicality."

Antimony

See **Gray Wolf**.

APHRODISIACS

The Pomegranate Badge of Katherine of Aragon

The Greek Goddess of Love, Aphrodite, lends her name to an extensive list of foods and other weird and wonderful items that are supposed to increase the libido and enhance the chances of seduction and therefore fecundity. The issue of fertility has always been an overriding concern for humankind, and any substance that either enhances sexual prowess or increases the chance of conception have always been highly sought after.

Ancient man had a limited seasonal diet, and a bad hunt or the failure of a crop could literally be a life-or-death matter. Getting enough food to eat was an overriding concern. Chances of fertility are restricted if nourishment is poor, and so certain foods were given magical powers in the hopes that they might increase both male and female potency despite the limited diet. There is a marked differentiation between the foods that increase fertility versus the ones that enhance sex drive, and given that early man did not know about the chemical constituencies of food, many aphrodisiacs were chosen as such

primarily because of their symbolic significance. The Doctrine of Signatures—the notion that a plant or a feature of an animal that is similar in appearance or quality to a body part could be beneficial to the organ it resembles—had an important part to play in deciding which foods had aphrodisiac qualities. **Rhinoceros** horn, for example, still carries a frisson as a stimulant to sexual appetites, as does Spanish Fly. Both these ingredients, sort of mystical precursors to Viagra, were ingested by men in eager anticipation of increased virility.

Pliny the Elder and Dioscordes documented many of these aphrodisiacs as far back as the first century, and it is likely that they would have been regarded as such for some time prior to this.

The behavior and lifestyle of certain animals made them fertility symbols, too. For example, the **sparrow**, a prolific breeder, was sacred to Aphrodite and its blood was a popular ingredient in love potions. Steak was thought to contain all the virility of the animal it came from, the bloodier the better. Ground **rhinoceros** horn is symbolic of the libido but the power of the rhino is also perceived as the ultimate in male sexual energy.

This ancient, visceral belief in the power of appearances has meant that many of the original foods that were considered to have aphrodisiac powers by ancient man still carry the same meanings today, despite their actual chemical constituency. It is true to say that certain foods actually do have aphrodisiac powers purely because of these old beliefs, and generally owe more to folklore and symbolism than to fact; however, a symbol is a potent force and often the association alone is enough to bring about the desired effect. For example, a dinner date where oysters and strawberries are on the menu will leave no doubt about the intended conclusion to the evening.

To our ancestors, any kind of food that resembled the **penis**, the **vagina**, or constituent parts thereof, carried powerful suggestive meanings, although latterly our ability to analyze certain minerals and trace elements has proven that some supposedly aphrodisiac foods may actually deserve their reputation. For example, the fifty oysters that Casanova reputedly managed to swallow every day for breakfast not only resemble the female sexual parts in scent, texture and form, but it has also been discovered that their high zinc content may indeed help enhance the libido; a large proportion of zinc is spent when men ejaculate.

For ancient man it was not always necessary for the foods to be eaten for them to have the desired effect. Some of the weird and wonderful things considered to have aphrodisiac qualities were toxic, but could work their magic simply by close proximity. The berries of **mistletoe**, for example, were a reminder of the **semen** of the Gods and the little crosses on the undersides were kisses, but it would be unwise to eat them.

Seeds, nuts, bulbs, and eggs, because they are full of potential new life, were considered as aids to fertility; snails, too, were considered to enhance sexual appetites because of the viscous fluid of the trails they leave behind, although slugs are not considered to have any aphrodisiac qualities whatsoever.

Here is a brief list of some of the foods that have been considered, at some time or other, to have aphrodisiac qualities.

Nuts, seeds, and bulbs

ANISEED

Falls into the category of seeds. Also aids digestion and sweetens the breath which could explain why the Romans considered it a useful ingredient for seduction.

STAR ANISE

Because of its shape, the star anise was sacred to the Goddess and therefore a potent fertility symbol.

Fruits

In general, all seed-bearing fruits are aphrodisiacs. Their numerous seeds, their texture, scent, and color make them a naturally sexy foodstuff.

APPLE

Infamous as the fruit that Eve gave to Adam, a symbol of sexual awakening.

CHERRY

Sensuously **red** and juicy, and containing a potent symbol of new life inside the stone. "Popping the cherry" is a slang term for losing one's virginity.

RASPBERRIES AND STRAWBERRIES

Libido enhancing because of their color, their many tiny seeds, and their resemblance to **nipples**.

TOMATO

The tomato is also called the Love Apple and is regarded as an aphrodisiac, because of the prolific number of seeds contained within it.

However, the name itself is the result of an accidental misinterpretation. Because they were originally a **yellow** color they were called Pomo D'or in Italy, the Apple of **Gold**. It was also called the Pomo d'Moro—the apple of the Moors, referring to its Spanish origins. From here, it was just a slip of the tongue to the French, Pomme d'Amour, or Love Apple.

Male genitalia

Many of these are self-explanatory, all considered powerful simply because of their shape. Asparagus, carrots, and cucumber are just a few of the "phallic vegetables."

AVOCADO

The Mexicans called the avocado tree the "testicle tree," since the fruit dangles down in pairs. The sensual texture of avocado adds to its reputation.

BANANA

The banana flower resembles the phallus. Islamic tales say that Adam and Eve covered their sexual parts with banana leaves rather than the more common fig leaves.

CLOVES

Because they resemble little phalluses, cloves were considered to enhance male potency. The clove tree was planted to signify the birth of a baby boy in certain parts of Indonesia, the health of the **tree** reflecting the health of the child as it grew up.

Female genitalia

ALMOND

As well as being the same shape as the **vesica piscis**, the sacred doorway through which matter emerges into spirit, the almond is a nut and therefore carries the potential for new life.

FIG

The plethora of tiny seeds inside the fig is symbolic of fertility, and the moist plumpness of the fruit has a very sensual, feminine element to it.

OYSTER

The oyster's resemblance in form, scent, and texture to the female genitalia is renowned. Oysters have had a long history as an aphrodisiac and their reputation is well known. The **pearl** that is sometimes found inside the oyster was said to increase the powers of arousal, because it resembles the **clitoris**.

Other shellfish, such as mussels, fall into this same category.

Spices and herbs

Anything sharp tasting or pungent is believed to stimulate the senses, so spices are often used as libido-enhancing ingredients.

ASAFOETIDA

This is the ground root of a **fennel**-like plant. It has a powerful odor, and despite its folk name, Devil's Dung, it is used as a sexual stimulant in Ayurvedic medicine.

CINNAMON

The glorious scent of cinnamon was reputedly used as oil by the Queen of Sheba to help her capture the attention of King Solomon.

CORIANDER

Also comes under the category of seeds. Reputed to stimulate appetites of all kinds.

FENNEL

The Egyptians who used this as a sexual stimulant cannot have known that it contains plant estrogens that can help balance female hormones. These estrogens also enhance the **breasts**.

GINGER AND GINSENG

Considered to have aphrodisiac powers because of their sharp sensual taste, and because their roots resemble the human form.

MINT

A Greek legend says that Menthe, a beautiful nymph, was transformed into the herb because Persephone was jealous of the beautiful scent that captivated her husband, Pluto.

Honey

The sweetness of honey made it a rarity for ancient man. It is likely to have given humankind its first instance of alcohol in the form of mead, and its intoxicating effect has distinct aphrodisiac qualities. **Bees** are themselves symbols of fertility, and honey gives its name to the honeymoon period spent by newlyweds immediately after their marriage.

Chocolate

The melting point of chocolate is the same as that of **blood** temperature, and so its mouth-feel alone is a sensual experience. Added to this, chocolate contains mood-lifting substances, including phenylethylamine which, when released into the bloodstream, induces feelings of euphoria. Still arguably the most popular food given as a gesture of love. When the sixteenth-century Spanish *conquistador* Hernán Cortés heard about its reputation as an aphrodisiac, he planted two thousand trees.

APOTROPE

This is a word of Greek origin meaning to "turn away," and refers to a specific kind of **amulet** designed to ward off evil of some kind. The amulet therefore features a protective symbol, such as an **eye** (which wards off the evil eye, by staring right back at it), or the **Hand of Fatima.**

ARC

See **First signs: Arc**.

ARK

There are two famous arks, Noah's Ark and the Ark of the Covenant. Both held extremely valuable objects, and so the ark symbolizes a treasure chest, a secure repository for items of secret or sacred significance. The word comes from the Latin, *arca*. The Greeks described the same item as a chest.

There are also two Hebrew definitions for the ark. One explains it as a wooden chest, the other as a flat-roofed building twice as long as it was high and wide. The ark could also float, and the same word is used to describe the casket that the baby Moses was found in, floating in the reeds.

In the Bible, the Ark that God commands Noah to build has a very specific set of instructions as to size, measurements, and materials used. The momentous treasure contained in this "box" was a breeding pair of every animal in the world, a genetic repository to safeguard the future of all creatures on Earth after the deluge had washed everything else away. The Ark was God's promise of protection to His chosen people. However, as Barbara G. Walker points out in her *Woman's Dictionary of Symbols and Sacred Objects*, the scale of the Ark must have been mind-boggling if its purpose as outlined in the Bible were to be taken literally, since it would have had to hold

7,000 species of worms, 80,000 species of molluscs, 30,000 species of crustaceans, 50,000 species of arachnids, 900,000 species of insects, 2,500 species of amphibians, 6,000 species of reptiles, 8,600 species of birds, and 3,500 species of mammals, as well as food for one and all.

The Ark of the Covenant, similarly, had to be made to strictly detailed plans, as was the building that should house it. **Shittim** wood—the timber from the incorruptible **acacia tree**—was specified for the basic construction. The Book of Exodus also describes the other materials that had to be used; **gold** and **silver**, brass, **blue**, **red**, and **purple** silk, fine linen, **goats**' hair, **spices**, various precious gems, red rams' skins, and "the skins of **badgers**."

Inside the Ark were stored the two Books of the Law, Aaron's Rod, and a pot of the **manna** that the Children of Israel lived on during their time in the wilderness.

There is speculation about what actually happened to the Ark when Nebuchadnezzar destroyed the Temple of David in the sixth century BC. However, Jewish faith decrees that the Ark will be restored to its rightful place with the coming of the Messiah.

ARROW

Symbol of flight, penetration, and direction. As a weapon, the arrow is a symbol of the power of the person who carries it, along with the bow. As a sacred symbol, it is the attribute of the Goddess of the Hunt, **Artemis/Diana**, as well as of **Eros**, who uses his arrows to

pierce the people's **hearts** with love. Here, the arrow also serves as a phallic symbol and an emblem of masculine power. The symbol of the heart pierced with an arrow, popular on **Valentine's Day** cards, is a covert symbol of sexual union.

The arrow as a symbol of direction works on a physical level and a metaphorical level. The arrow that shoots high up into the sky is an emblem of the link between Earth and Heaven, a symbol of an idea, or of a message being carried directly to the Gods.

The arrow is used, too, as an analogy for swiftness and sureness, since the arrow cannot travel in anything but a straight line. The astrological sign of **Sagittarius**, the hybrid creature that is always depicted in the process of shooting an arrow from his bow, has a Latin root, *sagitta*; this means "arrow" and is derived from a verb, *sagire*, that means "to perceive keenly or quickly." Therefore, the arrow is symbolic of quick-wittedness and intuition.

Arrows were used by the ancient Arabians, Chaldeans, Greeks, and Tibetans in a form of divination called Belomancy. This was practiced by shooting arrows in the air and reading a meaning from the direction of the arrows or their positions in relation to each other. For example, crossed or touching arrows meant "no." Later, the arrows had words written on them to make any answers even more definitive.

ASHTAMANGALA

In Sanskrit, Ashta means "eight" and Mangala "auspicious," and the word refers to the eight auspicious symbols of Himalayan Buddhism, although the relevance of eight sacred objects is important in the Hindu faith, too, and also in China. The Ashtamangala of the Tibetan system are, in no particular order, the Vase of Treasure, the Two Golden **Fish**, the **Dharma Wheel**, the Conch **Shell**, the **Endless Knot**, the Victory Banner, the **Lotus** Flower, and the Parasol. These symbols are used both in the home and in public areas and the hidden meanings of the objects are far more significant than their surface value.

The Parasol

Represents the sky, and is not only a symbol of protection but a sign of expansion and learning.

The Two Golden Fish

These are also a symbol of the **eyes** of the Buddha, and act as a reminder to be fearless no matter what fate brings.

The Treasure Vase

Any representation of a vessel is as important for the space it contains as well as for any material objects it might be able to hold. The spiritual treasures within this vase include good health and a long life, good luck, wisdom, and prosperity.

The Lotus Flower

Symbolizes purity of mind, body, action, and speech. The lotus flower rises above the metaphorical "muddy water" of attachment and desire.

The Conch Shell

Because this shell can be used as a sounding horn, it acts as a reminder that followers need to be open to the sound of the Buddha's teach-ings and that they need to stay awake (in a metaphorical sense), remaining aware and alert.

The Endless Knot

Symbolizes compassion and wisdom com-bined, and the need to unite spiritual and material matters.

The Victory Banner

Represents the triumph of a positive mind over seemingly negative obstacles.

The Dharma Wheel

Represents the teachings of the Buddha. It is also a **Mandala** or **Sun** symbol.

Asson

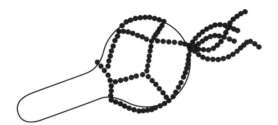

For practitioners of Voudon, the asson is a sacred rattle, made from a large dried-out gourd with seeds inside, and covered with beads and **snake** bones. It is used in important rites and ceremonies and is itself a symbol of the authority of the Houngan, the Voudon priest that is considered the Chief of the Spirits. The asson is the equivalent of the **scepter**. It is a larger object than the musical instrument called the **cha cha**, although they do have a similar appearance.

Astrum Argentum seal

This is the seal that was designed by Aleister Crowley as the emblem of his Esoterical Magickal Order, the Astrum Argentum, or "Silver **Star**." The seal uses a seven-pointed star as the basis of its design. See also **Cancellarius seal**.

Athame

This is the ceremonial knife used by a **witch**. It generally has a **black** handle, and is used to mark a magical **circle**, for example, or to direct energy, but is never used to cut anything. For physical cutting, a **boline** is used.

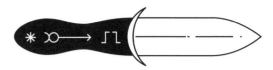

The pointed shape of the blade of the athame suggests the element of **fire,** which it also symbolizes. The athame is balanced by the **chalice**, which represents **water**.

Athanor

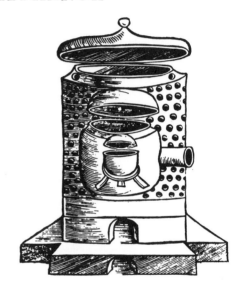

A key symbol of **alchemy**, the Athanor is the furnace of the Alchemists. However, as with everything else in alchemy, the Athanor is no simple piece of laboratory equipment. Regarded as the vessel in which transmutation takes place, the Athanor exists on a metaphysical level, too, as the **Orphic Egg** or as a place of ultimate creation, a kind of universal **womb**.

ATHEIST SYMBOL

Based on the Atomic Swirl, this is the symbol of the American Atheist Association, although it is used by other such organizations too. It represents the idea that science is the only thing that can show the way forward to a better life for everyone. The broken loop at the bottom of the symbol represents the idea that there are questions yet to be asked and yet to be answered.

ATLANTIS CROSS

This symbol, comprised of a **cross** intersected by **three circles**, is a sign of recognition among groups who claim an Atlantean descent; that is to say, people who believe that they are descended, literally or spiritually, from inhabitants of the lost island of Atlantis. The crossed circle that forms a main feature of this symbol represents the **four elements** and the four directions.

AWEN

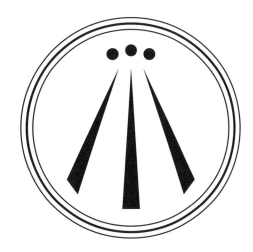

The Awen is related to many new Druid movements. The actual word, which is Welsh, means "inspiration" or "essence." Related to the Breton symbol called the Triban and with a nod to the Trishul, the trident held by the Hindu deity, **Shiva**, the Awen is composed of **three** convergent rays, like paths, leading to a high point, a **dot** (or three dots) similar to the bindhu.

Each ray carries various meanings, which are equally significant and come in sets of three. They stand for past, present, and future: love, knowledge, and truth: male and female energy and the balance between the two, or the three pillars of wisdom. Another interpretation of the symbol is of the three fundamental letters of the name of God, I, O, and U, which, when pronounced contribute to the actual word "Awen," which can be intoned in much the same way as the **Aum** of Eastern tradition, used as a meditative focus.

The Order of Bards, Ovates, and Druids place the three lines and the three dots within three concentric rings, further amplifying the meaning of the symbol as well as placing it within protective, magical **circles**.

AXIS MUNDI

Quite literally, the Axis Mundi translates as the "world axis," the axis around which the world revolves and which links the Heavens to the Earth and the dominions below. It is a universal concept, often defined symbolically as a **tree** or **standing stone**, a **mountain**, the **omphalos**, the **lingam**, the **Vajra**, the **pole star**. The **solstices** represent the World Axis in terms of time.

BA

For the Ancient Egyptians, the Ba was the symbolic representation of the **soul**. It takes the form of a small **bird** with the **head** of a human being. The Ba could fly between its owner and the Gods for as long as the body was intact. The Ba is twinned with the **Ka**. If the Ba represented the soul, then the Ka was the "life-force," the spark of life that animated the body and whose departure resulted in death. The Ka was sustained with offerings of food and drink, although it was the "ka" or

spirit of the food and drink that was consumed. In the Afterlife, the Ba and the Ka would be reunited to form one single entity.

BAPHOMET

The Baphomet we recognize today is a winged **goat** with a masculine torso and **breasts**; he has a blazing torch between his **horns,** and cloven **feet.** Adding to the confusion, one **arm** is male and the other is female, and all in all this has become a real bogeyman of a symbol, inspiring fright and terror.

The image made its first appearance relatively recently, in Eliphas Levi's *Dogma and Rituals of High Magic* (1854). Although Levi intended the creature (also called the **Goat of Mendes**) to be an idealized symbolic form, an amalgam of images from all disciplines including the Kabbalah, he actually created something that looks far more terrifying than he may have originally intended. The picture influenced illustrations of the Devil, not only in **Tarot** card illustrations but also among latter-day rock bands and, as already mentioned, among Satanists.

Baphomet himself was first described at the trials of the **Knights Templar,** centuries before Levi's interpretation. When the Order began in the twelfth century, it was designed to protect pilgrims traveling to Jerusalem. Because the Knights were exempt from taxation, they amassed a huge amount of wealth and, consequently, power. When they became a threat to the establishment, they were persecuted, and part of this persecution included accusations of heresy including the worship of a peculiar looking goat-headed creature.

BECKONING CAT

A friendly little statuette with a warm welcome found all over Japan and China. What the cat is doing with his paws carries a secret message.

The cute little Maneki Neko or beckoning **cat** is ubiquitous in Japan and China where he appears in both homes and offices. This friendly-looking china cat can also be seen in oriental restaurants all over the world and is for many people the ultimate symbol of prosperity and good luck.

The Maneki Neko comes in different colors, each of which signifies a different meaning. For example, a **red** cat will protect from illness, and a **black** one will ward off evil.

The position of the paws also carries a message. With the right paw raised the cat will bring money and happiness to home and workplace. A cat raising its left paw (like the one illustrated here) will attract new customers for a business. And a cat with both paws raised hits the jackpot; both home and business will be happy and profitable, attracting good luck, friends, prosperity, and new clients.

This cat is also the symbol of the small Buddhist temple in Tokyo, where the original incident that shot the cat to fame is said to have happened. Originally the temple was a lowly place, whose impoverished priest would regularly share what little food he had with his pet cat. One day some Samurai were passing and noticed this cat, who had one paw raised as though to say hello. The warriors

stopped, intrigued by the beckoning cat, and went into the temple just as a horrendous rain storm started. They believed that paying attention to the cat's invitation had prevented them being struck by lightning. Thereafter, the fortunes of the priest, the temple, and of course the cat, started to change for the better.

Bell

There is a mysticism surrounding the bell that far transcends its mundane use as a way of getting attention in the schoolroom, for example. The sound of the bell is universally accepted as a way of communicating with the spirits, or as a herald for the arrival of a supernatural, holy power.

The analogy of the bell occurs in language, too, used to symbolize something of sacred origin. In Islam, the "reverberation of the bell" is used to describe the sound of the revelations of the Qu'ran, and in Buddhism, the "sound of the golden bell" is an analogy for heavenly voices. The sound of a bell is a reminder that, like the sound, the world may be experienced, but not possessed.

Pagoda roofs sometimes have hundreds of tiny bells hanging from them, symbolizing, in sound, the concepts of the Buddhist laws as well as frightening away any malicious entities. For the same reason, the church bells of Christian churches, at one time, were peeled not only during processions or as a notice of a ceremony or service, but also during thunderstorms to chase away **demons**.

The bell is also a sacred object. In the form of the Buddhist **Drilbu**, or the Hindu Ghanta, it symbolizes the illusory world, because of the fleetingly resonant nature of its sound. It is the feminine principle paired up with the masculine **vajra**.

The use of these oriental bells largely influenced their European symbolism and use. The sweet reverberation of a bell, rung **three** times in the silence of a large stone church or **cathedral**, has a quality of calming the atmosphere, attracting the attention of the worshippers, welcoming in the spirits and setting the scene for the ritual that follows.

The power of the bell as a way of spiritual communication is carried one step further in the magical bell made of an amalgam of the **seven sacred metals** that are ruled by the **planets**. This bell, engraved with the **Tetragrammaton** and the planetary seals from **alchemy**, allegedly has the power to summon the spirits of the dead. However, this spell calls for the bell to be put into a grave for **seven** days and seven nights before it will work properly.

Bell, book and candle

Singly, these items all have mystical significance. When grouped together, they have a certain frisson, somehow seeming to resonate with dark forces, pagan ideals, and witchcraft in particular. However, this sinister grouping actually comes from the rites of **excommunication** or **anathema** in the Roman Catholic Church. Effectively a powerful curse, this ritual is taken very seriously, reserved only for those whose transgressions against the Church are deemed unforgivable.

After the officiating cleric has verbally declared the excommunication, he declares it symbolically with three actions; he shuts the bible, sounds the **bell**, and then snuffs out the **candle**.

These actions are clear. Closing the bible tells the excommunicant that he is no longer privy to the Word of God. Ringing the bell is symbolic of mourning for the "departed," the excommunicant, who is now effectively spiritually dead to the Church. Snuffing the candle is a universal sign of the "snuffing out" of the **soul**, now doomed because of its banishment from the faith.

BESOM

See **Broomstick**.

BINDHU

See **First Signs: Dot**.

BLACK SUN

The notion of the **Sun** being **black** runs completely counter to what is generally accepted about it; the simplest explanation for a Black Sun is that it describes what happens at night,

when the Sun is casting its light on another part of the planet. However, the Black Sun more sinisterly denotes the idea of the world going wrong, destructive forces, disaster, and even death.

Whether the Nazis were aware of this aspect of the Black Sun is open to conjecture. The symbol reproduced for this entry was also called the "Sonnenrad" or Sun Wheel and was based on the design of early medieval brooches, some of which had a swastika in the center. The "rays" numbered between **five** and **twelve**, with the twelve-rayed symbol denoting the passage of the Sun through the months of the year. The rays bear a great deal of resemblance to the **swastika** and to the lightning flash symbols used by the SS, themselves the same as a **rune** known as "sig," meaning "Sun" or "Victory."

The symbol, used by wartime German occult mystics and still employed by some neo-Nazis, is based on a mosaic set into the floor of the early seventeenth-century castle of Wewelsburg in Germany. Himmler decided that the site of the castle would be the center of the proposed "New World" once victory was achieved. However, the extensive building works planned for the castle were never completed; the ambitious "New World" failed to materialize and the building work that had been started was blasted to the ground in 1945. The mosaic remains, although there is no concrete evidence as to who put it there. The mosaic is of dark **green** marble, set into a cream-colored marble floor.

For neo-Nazis, the symbol has proved a useful one. The single swastika is banned in Germany, and yet the Black Sun symbol hides **three** swastikas within it. Further significance is accorded the symbol since it contains twelve of the aforementioned Sig runes from the Futhark runic system. The circular shape of the symbol implies protection and magical powers. Secret signs, indeed.

Black Sun in alchemy

Alchemists and Hermeticists believe that there are two Suns; one of the pure "philosophical gold" that implies the highest attainment of the Spirit, and the other of the baser "material gold." The Black Sun is the symbol of this material form of the Sun, and symbolizes the unworked, primal matter that needs to be developed.

Blazing star

See **Pentagram** and **Freemasonry**.

Boline

The boline is a **knife** in the **Druid** and **Wiccan** tradition. Its specific symbolism is held within its blade, which is shaped like the crescent **Moon** and **silver** in color. The boline usually has a **white** handle, also in deference to the Moon.

This boline is a practical, ceremonial tool often used for cutting **herbs** either for magical uses or simply for cooking. In the case of the druid, it is also used for cutting **mistletoe** directly from the **tree**.

Book

It might seem as though the book is such a commonplace object that it should not really have much significance as a secret symbol. However, this isn't the case. Take, for example, the **High Priestess** card in the **Tarot**. The Priestess holds a book or scroll, half concealed within the folds of her robe. Here, the book symbolizes knowledge and hidden secrets, and in a wider sense the book symbolizes the very Universe itself. There are also parallels with the book and the **tree of life**; like a tree, the book has "leaves" that represent individual ideas and concepts and that collectively represent the sum total of all knowledge, occult or otherwise.

If we delve into word meanings, we find more analogies between books and trees. The etymology of "book" comes from the Old English *bokiz*, or the Germanic *buche*, meaning **beech**. This is likely to be because **runes** were initially inscribed on beechwood tablets. Similarly, the word "library," originally meant the "inner bark of trees."

A book that is closed is a book that conceals its secrets; sometimes we refer to an inscrutable person as a "closed book." An open book is the opposite, ready to share its information with all and sundry.

The Book of the Dead, for the Ancient Egyptians, was the series of magical charms that were interred with the dead in order that they might journey safely into the next world, and that would provide answers to the questions posed by those casting judgement on the soul. This book, effectively, symbolizes the secrets of the divine that are revealed only to those who have undergone the ultimate initiation: death. The Book of Shadows is a sort of recipe book of spells, charms and rituals, generally belonging to the Wiccan practitioner, written by hand and often in code. This book is the personal property of its owner, and can be a series of traditional texts as well as a personal journal, containing secrets that are passed down from generation to generation.

Brighids Cross

Corn dollies are frequently constructed in the shape of Brighids Cross, and although the symbol itself predates Christianity, it was given the name of the saint in order to ease the passage of acceptance of the new religion.

The symbol is reminiscent of the ancient **Sun** symbol, the **swastika**, its **four** arms pointing to the cardinal points of the compass. They also represent the Elements,

with the point at the center indicating the fifth element or **quintessence**.

Broomstick

The hard and polished elm wood that is traditionally believed to make the handle of the witch's broomstick would help to make it more aerodynamic.

The broomstick, at first, appears to be a simple piece of household equipment. Its form may have changed over the centuries from the traditional dried branch of the **broom plant** (hence the name) but its use seems to have remained unchanged.

However, there's far more to it than that. The very act of sweeping was a sacred task in **temples**, since to be able to clean something properly the person doing the cleaning must himself be both clean and pure.

As well as sweeping away dust and dirt, symbolically the besom or broomstick sweeps away other things too; in parts of France, for example, it's considered bad form to sweep up after dark in case good luck is swept away with the dirt. In Ancient Rome special broomsticks were used by sacred "midwives" or wise women to symbolically sweep away any negative influences from a house in which a baby had just been born. These broom-wielding midwives are the precursor to the **witch** that popularly flies about on a broom-stick, which has to be the ultimate carbon-neutral vehicle.

The broomstick of the female witch is a very handy object to have around. It is often seen as a **phallic symbol**, and in pre-Christian societies marriages were often val-idated by the happy couple leaping together, hand in hand, over the broomstick. It is also a symbol of the liberation of the woman away from domestic drudgery; with her magical broomstick, the witch can fly anywhere, wield her power, and disclose her true identity.

Incidentally, the broomstick is sometimes called a besom; this word originates from the old English *besema*, meaning "woman," and has the same root as the word "bosom."

Bull Roarer

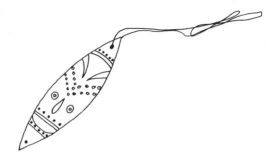

An important ritual object for Native Americans, Eskimos, Africans and the Australian Aborigines, for whom the object is associated with the **Churinga**.

The Bull Roarer is a long, narrow piece of wood with tapering ends that, when attached to a cord and whirled around the head, pro-duces a sound very much like thunder or the bellowing of a bull. It was taboo for woman to see this sacred object, which was used in initiation ceremonies and was regarded as carrying the actual voices of the Spirits.

The Bull Roarer was thought to make men invincible and indeed the noise it produces is quite terrifying, especially if it is not expected. It was also used in fertility rites and as a way of calling for rain.

Bulla

This is a special charm or **amulet** that was given to Roman children when they were born. A sealed locket, the bulla (meaning "bubble" or "knob") contained magical spells specific to the child in question, such as symbols of protection, or wishes for wealth. The bulla was constructed of different mat-erials depending on the wealth of the family,

leather for the poorest families and gold or other precious metals for the wealthiest.

Roman boys put aside their bullae when they reached puberty, and the object was offered to the Gods. Girls wore theirs until the eve of their wedding. In either case it was considered that the bulla belonged to the child, as part and parcel of their personality.

The bulla is the origin of the name of the Papal Bull, the special edict that hails from the Vatican, which is fastened with an oval seal of the same shape as the bulla.

CADUCEUS

A rod, staff, or **wand** generally surmounted with **wings**. Two **serpents** entwine about the staff, forming a **figure-of-eight** shape. The key elements of the construction of this ancient sign are the serpent, the **spiral**, the infinity sign, the circle, wings, and the wand.

The Caduceus is an incredibly ancient symbol, and its earliest recorded appearance is on the goblet of the King of Lagash, dating back some 2600 years BC.

The Caduceus is the emblem of **Mercury/Hermes** and is incredibly rich in meanings: First, the staff or wand is a symbol of power and authority, of magical and supernatural forces, and is the tool of all magicians, medicine men, and shaman. It also represents the **tree of life** or **World Axis.** Then there are the wings on top of the wand.

Wings signify flight (both physical and metaphorical), intuition, the spiritual, communication from the Heavens or the Gods. Mercury is the Messenger of the Gods. The two serpents, twining in opposite directions, represent opposition and equilibrium. They also signify opposites—male and female, day and night, good and evil, and so represent balance. Serpents also remind us of hidden knowledge.

As the serpents scroll around the wand, they form the figure-of-eight shape, or infinity symbol, which stands for completeness and perfection.

Part of the infinity symbol is the circle, ultimately representing the cosmos, the spirit, unity.

All these elements combined make for a powerful symbol that has altered very little over the millennia. Together, they add up to

supernatural power and hidden wisdom, messages from the spiritual realms, authority, the cosmos and infinity, and the pairing of opposites in harmony and unity.

Perhaps the most common use of the Caduceus, both today and since its earliest appearance, is as a symbol of healing and medicine. Aesclepius, the first physician and the God of medicine, had the Caduceus as one of his attributes because he had the power and the intuition (the wand and the wings) to be able to use potentially poisonous or corruptive substances (the serpents) to restore health and, reputedly, to bring the dead back to life.

The Caduceus was not only the instrument of Aesclepius, but of the healing God Ningishzida of Mesopotamia (whose symbol is intertwining snakes), and of the Egyptians Ba'al, **Isis** and Ishtar. It is also found in India where it carries the same meaning.

Cagliostro seal

This curious sigil, the image of a **snake**, impaled by an **arrow** but with an **apple** in its mouth, presses all sorts of symbolic buttons;

all three elements of the seal are powerful emblems in themselves. Is this the snake that tempted Eve with the apple, being punished for its transgressions? The snake also makes a curious S shape; is this significant, and if so, how? In addition, the union of the line of the arrow and the serpent seems to make a **lemniscate**, or figure-of-eight, symbol, meaning infinity. Unfortunately, it seems as though the precise meaning of the seal died with its namesake.

Cagliostro himself seems to be as mysterious as his seal. The self-styled Count Alessandro di Cagliostro was actually born as the much less grand-sounding Guiseppe Balsamo, and lived in Italy in the eighteenth century. The rumors surrounding his life and adventures come thick and fast and there is very little that is known for certain, due in no small part to the dense forest of fantastical stories that Cagliostro seems to have hidden himself within. He said that he had been born into the nobility but for some reason was abandoned on Malta, whereupon he wandered, as a child, throughout Morocco and Egypt where he learned many arcane mysteries, including those of the Kabbalah and alchemical magic. Whatever the truth, he certainly had skills as a pharmacist. It seems that the secure advantages of regular employment held no attraction for the Count, his attention being much more drawn to magical and mystical matters. He became a maker and vendor of magical **amulets** and **talismans**, and later, forgeries, including letters, certificates and a myriad of official documents. He also offered the sexual favors of his beautiful young wife as trade for instruction in forgery.

Cagliostro's Seal has been the result of much analysis and conjecture, its appearance so convincing that it was even incorporated into an early Masonic-style organization called The Brotherhood of Luxor.

CALUMET

For the Plains Indians, the pipe, also called the calumet, is one of the most important and recognizable symbols. Although it is sometimes referred to as the Peace Pipe, shared ceremonially as part of a unifying ritual, the pipe was just as valid a symbol during times of war.

The **tobacco** used in the pipe is also a powerful magical substance originally intended for ritual use only. The **smoke** rising from the pipe signifies a prayer traveling toward the Gods and symbolizes the sacred breath, source of all life. The **fire** that lights the pipe symbolizes the **Sun** and the male element. The pipe itself is equivalent of the prayer that is offered up from it.

The calumet is considered so important that in Native American tradition it is described as though it were a person, and each of its components has the name of a body part. In addition, the bowl is described as an **altar**, and the stem, the passage of the **breath** extending from the human body.

CANCELLARIUS SEAL

This is one of the symbolic seals of Aleister Crowley's Astrum Argentum, or Silver Star order. As the name suggests, it indicates the position of Chancellor. The symbol shows an **Eye of Horus** at the center of rays that are set in **12** groups of **3**.

The Astrum Argentum was started by Crowley in 1907 as an alternative to MacGregor Mather's Golden Dawn. Although he had initially been enamored of the Golden Dawn and its charismatic leader, it is fair to say that Crowley liked to do things his own way, resulting in his expulsion from the Golden Dawn. Crowley believed that his own personal angel, Aiwaz, approved of his decision to supplant Mather's brotherhood. The unusual structure of the Astrum Argentum was typical of Crowley's desire to be different. Each member was supposed to know only his immediate superior and anyone he introduced into the Order. For Crowley, the sole purpose of the Astrum Argentum was to disseminate his own teachings and mystical beliefs. It was assumed that anyone introduced into the Astrum Argentum would already have had a great degree of magical training, in contrast to the Golden Dawn, which was dedicated to teaching.

CANDLE

A candle symbolizes light in the darkness in a way that a lightbulb simply cannot do. A candle represents the element of fire as a benevolent force, made even more powerful if the candle is made of wax, a substance made by a magical creature, the **bee**. The colors of candles are significant in magical practices: for example, **pink** is said to attract love. **Black** candles are used in dark magic.

CAULDRON

In understanding symbols, sometimes it is useful to simply look at the shape and see what it resembles. The traditional cauldron represents nothing so much as the belly of a pregnant woman and, unsurprisingly, the cauldron is an important female symbol all over the world. The circular shape of the cauldron gives another clue; the **circle** is a symbol of never-ending life and regeneration, and these themes recur repeatedly in stories containing cauldron symbolism.

The way the cauldron is used also gives a hint about its symbolic meaning. Things are put into the cauldron, heated, and something different is taken out; the basic ingredients are transformed. Therefore, the cauldron also symbolizes germination and transformation.

Traditionally, cauldrons have three **legs**. The number **3** in this instance represents the triple aspect of the Great Goddess, or the three **fates.** Shakespeare alludes to this when the three Weird Sisters—arguably the most famous witches in literature—cook up trouble at the beginning of *Macbeth.*

In pre-Christian literature, there are countless legends featuring magical cauldrons, and it may be because of this that the cauldron has its witchy associations. Celtic tales tell of cauldrons that contain an unending supply of food or of knowledge. The dead are frequently thrown into a magical Cauldron of Rebirth and climb out the next day, alive once more. Mythical warriors and heroes who died in battle are restored to life in this way. Ceridwen had a cauldron full of

inspiration and magical powers. In India, a magic life-giving food, called **Soma,** was brewed in three huge bottomless cauldrons.

In Greece, there are tales in which an ordeal of initiation involves the person boiling in a cauldron, but after the rite, the initiate emerges with magical powers, including the gift of immortality.

CELTIC CROSS AND SUN CROSS SYMBOL

In the Celtic Cross or Ring Cross symbol, a cross is contained within a **circle**. Very early versions of this cross, found in Ireland, do not show the arms of the cross protruding beyond the circle; the whole symbol is encompassed inside the circle and in this case it becomes the ancient, universal symbol called the **Sun Cross**, the Wheel Cross, or Odin's Cross. This sign first appears at the very start of the Bronze Age. Among other things, it symbolizes the **wheel** and in China represents thunder, power, and energy. It also appears in the Seal of the Babylonian Sun God, **Shamash**.

The Sun Cross symbol also appears in ancient astrology. In modern astrology it still signifies the planet, and element of, Earth; the cross represents the four corners of the planet, the elements and the directions, and the circle is the planet itself.

Because it was the symbol of the Sun, the King and the highest temporal and spiritual powers, it was easy for the early Christians to adopt this pagan sign and incorporate it into the **Latin Cross**. It is still used by Bishops to "bless" a new church, drawn onto the walls in sanctified **water** or oils, at **12** different places around the church.

The Celtic cross is frequently used as a grave marker, or as a war memorial, particularly in Celtic countries.

Incidentally, the Hot Cross Bun, eaten specifically at **Easter** and popularly believed to represent the Christian Cross, is actually of pre-Christian origin. The Greeks, Romans, and Ancient Egyptians all ate wheat cakes to celebrate the coming of spring. These cakes were circular (representing the **Moon** or **Sun**) with a cross that divided the cake into the four lunar quarters or the four seasons.

Celtic knotwork

One of the most distinctive decorative features of Celtic artwork and architecture are the beautiful constructions of Celtic knotwork. It adorns stonework, illuminated manuscripts, **jewelry**; the knotwork has left a distinctive trail that clearly shows all the places in the world that were visited at some point by the Celts.

The knotwork itself would appear to be a purely decorative device. If at one time there were specific symbolic meanings attached, then these have been lost over the centuries. Intertwining shapes and lines, however, generally point toward ideas of connectedness and the harmonious convergence of opposites, male and female, fire and water, Heaven and Earth, for example. In addition, any sign that can be made without the pen leaving the paper tends to have strong protective associations, and knotwork, with its continual looping and spiraling, could have been used in this way, perhaps used for **amulets** and **talismans**.

Existing symbols—such as a **heart**, or birds and animals—are often rendered in Celtic knotwork. In this case, the form of the underlying shape carries the symbolic meaning.

The Celtic Knot that is square in form is a protective symbol, called a **shield knot**.

Cha cha

In Haiti, there are certain seed pods called cha cha that are used to make rattles for ceremonial music-making in Voudon rituals. The rattle is called a cha cha, too, and the dance of the same name also comes from the name of the seedpod.

See also **asson**.

Chalice

This is a cup or **grail** that is generally used in rituals. No matter what the religious or spiritual persuasion of the celebrant, a chalice of some form is used, whether it be the highly ornamented vessel of the Catholic Church or the simpler wooden cup favored by some pagan groups. The chalice itself is symbolic of **water** or of the Spirit, and is used as such in the suit of Cups in the **Tarot**, for example. The chalice is also a universal symbol of the feminine aspect because of its shape, its use as a vessel, and its link with water.

Eastern religions use a kind of **bell**, called a **Drilbu**, in the place of a chalice.

Chaos Wheel

The Chaos Wheel, or Chaos **Star**, is a wheel constructed from eight **arrow**-headed spokes. Representing the notion of infinite possibilities, the symbol is a recent addition to a veritable galaxy of meaningful shapes. Designed

by science fiction writer Michael Moorcock, it has been adopted as an emblem by exponents of Chaos Magic, the contemporary branch of magic inspired by the works of Austin Osman Spare.

CHESS

Chess originated in India. The checkerboard that chess is played on is, in itself, a secret symbol. It is symbolic of the world that we understand, that is composed of opposing forces. Also, the **black** and **white** colors of the symmetrically arranged **squares** stand for male/female, light/dark, positive/negative, good/evil in much the same way as the **yin-yang** sign does. It is no accident that the floor of the **Freemason's** temple has the same construction as the chessboard, a constant reminder of both the harmony and tension between opposites. The pieces, too, are black and white, reinforcing this idea.

The chessboard has a further mystery that can be revealed in the number of the squares. Each side has **eight** squares. Eight is the number of infinity and of completion, and eight times eight makes **64**, the number of cosmic unity. This is the magical number that,

in sacred geometry, is the basis of temple construction.

The **square** shape of the board symbolizes the stability of the **Earth** and its **four** corners, the **directions** and the **elements**.

Superficially, chess might seem to be a relatively straightforward game, a simple series of different moves ascribed to each of the pieces. However, its complexities are only really revealed when the player is so familiar with the rules that he or she can carry them out automatically. Chess is plainly connected to war strategy and the ability to surprise the opponent. A good player will understand the need to sacrifice pieces in order to gain a greater advantage. Although the pawn may appear to be valueless, it is arguably one of the most important pieces on the board, and certainly the most prolific. We even use the word 'pawn' to describe a person that we think is insignificant.

In Ingmar Bergman's film *The Seventh Seal*, the Knight, Antonius Block, invites the hooded figure of Death to join him in a game, despite the fact that Death warns him that he cannot win. Effectively, chess owes as much to chance as choice, and further underlines the dilemma between the concepts of fate versus free will. The Knight knows that he will die, yet he persists in playing the game. Stanley Kubrick, too, believed that his skill as a chess player gave him the discipline to think rationally and to see the bigger picture, an invaluable skill for a film director. The detachment and lack of emotion required by the talented player is synonymous, for many, with an idealized, Zen approach to life.

For the Celts, the game of chess was called "intelligence of the wood." It was the game of kings and the stakes were high. The game therefore symbolizes the intellect of the king, despite the fact that the most versatile piece on the board is the queen.

Chi Roh

See **Labarum**.

Chnoubis

The Chnoubis is a hybrid creature, with the head of a **lion** and the tail of a **serpent**. It was carved onto stones for use as an **amulet**, providing protection against poisons in particular. Amulets featuring the Chnoubis date back to the first century and it is supposed that this odd-looking creature may be related to **Abraxas**, whose image was used in a similar way.

Choku Rei

A symbol of Reiki healers, the Choku Rei is comprised of a **spiral** that culminates in a hooked stick. It looks a little like the treble clef used in musical notation. The symbol is

used by Reiki healers to increase the power available to them, and to help focus this energy. The meaning of Choku Rei is "place the power of the Universe here." Healers draw the sign mentally in the air as a form of meditation, generally before and after giving a treatment.

Cicatrix

A cicatrix is a scar, but not just any scar. It refers to a very specific incision that is scored onto the body and carries secret symbols pertaining to the person's religious or magical beliefs. A very painful process called scarification leaves these raised marks on the **skin**. Until the end of the nineteenth century, Maori men had ritual scarring all over their faces in order that they might look more frightening to the enemy. A cicatrix acts as a permanent **amulet** that is an inherent part of the person. Its purpose is similar to that of the tattoo; the pain involved in the process an important rite of passage. Ritual scarring is popular among dark-skinned people because a tattoo is not particularly visible against the skin.

CIMARUTA

In Italian, this means the "sprig of **rue**." It is an **amulet**, made of **silver** in honor of female energy in the form of the Goddess, comprising a model of a sprig of rue with various charms in its **three** branches. The Cimaruta is a very old charm, which evolved from an Etruscan magical amulet. It dates back as far as 4500 BC, although there are more contemporary versions such as the stylized one illustrated here. The charms featured generally include a **crescent Moon**, a **key**, **stars**, daggers, **flowers**; different regions of Italy produced their own specific symbols. Also known as the Witch Charm, the Cimaruta is favored by witches, and to see one in someone's home might indicate the spiritual persuasion of the owner. It is worn either as a pendant or might be hung over a doorway, a possible reason for the Cimaruta being double-sided. When used in this way as an ornament the Cimaruta is usually quite large in size.

The three silver branches of the Cimaruta relate to the notion of the **Triple Goddess**. The charm itself takes on all the significance of the rue plant as being both protective and a tool of witches, used to cast spells and throw hexes.

CIRCLE

See **First signs: Circle**.

CLADDAGH

The Claddagh is a popular symbol, often incorporated into the design of **ring**s, and worn by people as an attractive piece of ornamentation although they may not know what it symbolizes.

Traditionally used as a wedding ring, the Claddagh is so-called because it was originally made in a Galway fishing village of the same name in seventeenth-century Ireland. However, the elements of the design are much older, stretching back into pre-Christian Celtic history. The Romans had a popular ring design, the Fede, which featured clasped hands. "Fede" means "fidelity."

The Claddagh symbol features a **heart** held by a pair of **hands**. A **crown** usually surmounts the heart. These features represent love, friendship, and loyalty.

CLAVICLE

See **Key**.

CLOTHING

Of all the animal kingdom, man is unique in that he wears clothes. In the Bible, Adam and Eve don **fig** leaves to cover the newly discovered sexual parts that are a reminder of the lower animal nature. Once we had managed to protect our modesty and keep ourselves warm, our attention turned to the use of clothes as an outward sign of status or of certain religious observances. As secret symbols, clothes have an elaborate history, especially when they are connected to religious beliefs; sacred texts from all religions are full of instructions as to the nature of certain clothes and how they should be worn. This section doesn't claim to be an extensive analysis of these ideas, but serves merely to point out the meanings of some of the most common items of apparel.

Cape

The cape has a simple design. At its most basic, it is a piece of cloth with a hole in the middle. Often worn by members of the clergy, when it is called a chasuble, the cape shares the same symbolism as the **arc** or dome that it represents; the vault of the Heavens. This suggests the idea of ascendance. The wearer of the cape becomes a living representation of the **Axis Mundi**.

Cloak

As well as being a symbol of religious asceticism, the cloak is the garment of kings. In addition, the word "cloak" has become synonymous with the notion of hiding something; the invisibility cloak is a very ancient idea. The God, **Lugh**, had such a cloak that enabled him to pass unnoticed through the entire Irish army in order to rescue his son. Effectively, though, the cloak makes the wearer invisible without any need for magical intervention. A cloak, especially a hooded one, is a **mask** for the body, covering the wearer from head to foot. A cloak can help someone change his or her identity while at the same time confirming it. In the Bible, St. Martin gives half his cloak to the beggar. This is not only a material gesture but also a symbol of his charitable nature.

The Khirka, a specific type of cloak, originally meant a scrap of torn material. However, its unworldly nature made it an appropriate garment for the Sufi mystic.

It was originally **blue**, signifying a vow of poverty, in the same way that **brown** and **gray** have the same meaning to Christian believers. The Sufi receives the Khirka after three years of training, a sign that he is worthy of initiation. To wear the Khirka, the Sufi must understand the three levels of the mystic life. These are the Truth, the Law, and the Path.

Footwear

When you put your foot upon the ground, this gesture is synonymous with taking possession of the **Earth** beneath it.

Because the holy ground at **churches** and **temples** is not, effectively, a territory that belongs to man, the jumble of shoes, sandals and boots outside the doors of holy places all over the world may certainly be a sign of respect. However, the owners may not be aware that they are, literally, following in the footsteps of a more ancient idea, that they have no claim to this sacred territory. The footwear is significant because it is removed.

The Children of Israel sealed agreements between two parties by swapping one sandal each. In addition, in Northern China the word for "slipper" and "mutual agreement" is the same. This is why slippers are given as wedding presents.

Shoes also symbolize travel, a meaning that precedes the time of motorized transport. In certain Northern European territories, children leave their shoes out for **Father Christmas** to fill with gifts; not only is Santa himself making an arduous journey, but his gifts help in the "journey" of the coming year.

Shoes are also a status symbol. Slaves generally went barefoot; hence, the wearing of shoes were the sign of the free man.

The slipper that Cinderella lost, that later proved her identity to the Prince, is an example of the shoe as a sexual symbol. In common interpretations of this tale these "slippers" sound uncomfortable, since they are apparently made of glass. However, it was an old European tradition that a potential suitor would show his sincerity by making his intended bride a pair of fur boots. It is likely that the word for fur, *vair*, was confused with the word for glass, *verre*. The sexual symbolism continues with these kinky boots; the old word for fur shares its roots with a word meaning "sheath."

Belt/girdle

Often the very first piece of clothing to be worn, especially in Asian countries, the girdle or belt is circular, and so it represents the union of spirit and matter, and of eternity. It also symbolizes the binding aspect; the girdle is a synonym for the **soul** that is bound to the body. Although the girdle is tied around the waist of a baby at birth in some countries, it appears in various other forms. The belts of the martial arts exponent range through the **color**

CONTINUED OVERLEAF ...

spectrum from **white** to **black** to signify levels of expertise.

The girdle also protects; it acts as a symbolic "wall" through which evil entities cannot penetrate. It's a sort of spiritual utility belt. The girdle, too, represents the idea of chastity. The belt worn around robes of monks and others who are called to a spiritual life carries the greater significance of the girdle. Notably, in the Middle Ages prostitutes were allowed to wear neither belt nor **veil**.

To talk of "girding the loins" means to prepare oneself, whether for a journey or something else. The **Ankh** is called the Girdle of Isis or the Buckle of Isis, and carries the same notions of the **circle** and the **knot** as binding forces.

A sash is also a kind of girdle, used in Freemasonry, for example, as a symbol of office. The knot itself is often used as a reminder, and the knot in the girdle or belt is a reminder of the promise made when the girdle was donned.

Another form of a girdle is the Sacred Thread, or Poonal (in Tamil) that is worn by male Hindus, particularly those from the Brahmin caste. The Sacred Thread ceremony can happen any time after the boy's seventh birthday. The thread is handwoven from **three** sets of three strands, although extra strands are added to represent marriage and children. It measures about 96 times the breadth of a man's **four** fingers; this is roughly the same as his height. Resting on the left shoulder, the thread is wrapped around the body, ending under the right arm. It is knotted only once. Once the Sacred Thread ceremony has been carried out, the thread is never taken off although it is replaced once a year. The single knot represents the concept of Brahman, the unity of all things. The numbers of strands in the thread signify various tenets of the Hindu faith.

Glove

Freemasons sometimes wear **white** gloves, not only as a symbol of work to be done, but also to show purity of thought. White gloves are worn for the same reasons in the Catholic Church. They are given to bishops and kings after their investiture, and here they are a reminder of newborn purity. Gloves—especially the highly ornamented kind—are a relatively luxurious item of clothing, emblems of the nobility who used gauntlets as part of the equipment associated with falconry. Gloves on heraldic shields usually indicate some connection with hunting **birds**.

To "throw down the gauntlet" is still used as a synonym for a challenge, dating back to the days of chivalry, where it was a politer version of a slap but hardly any less shocking.

Headgear

Headgear immediately identifies the status of the owner. The crown, for example, is an immediate recognition of royalty. People in authority wear peaked hats. The beggar goes "cap in hand." Additionally, headgear itself indicates a relationship with the divine, since the top of the head is effectively the first point of contact with the spirit that descends from above. The symbolic nature of headgear is altogether different from its practical usage. In temples, churches, and other holy places, the **feet** might be bare but the **head** is covered as a sign of modesty.

The crown

The open crown, coronet, tiara, or diadem has no practical secular purpose; indeed, the heavier crowns that belong to the sovereignty can be headachingly heavy. The crown is a **circle**, symbolizing the idea of immortality and eternity, but with the added dimension of a connection between the spiritual and material that is cemented by the ritual of coronation itself, which signifies a blessing, benediction, or union with the divine power that comes from above. Crowns traditionally feature jeweled "rays" signifying **Sun** beams, an allusion to illumination in all senses of the word.

For the Ancient Egyptians, only pharaohs and deities were permitted to wear the crown. The double crowns of the Pharaohs consisted of the **white** conical miter that represented Upper Egypt, surrounded by the **red** encasement of Lower Egypt. The **serpent** symbol called the **Uraeus**, again worn only by pharaohs, was incorporated into this sacred crown.

The pope wears a triple crown, or **Triregnum** (see **Papal symbols**). The three parts symbolize different aspects of the Catholic faith and of the papal role.

The crown is not always made of princely materials. The crown of **laurels** is still given as a sign of victory, and for Romans, the highest accolade for a soldier

CONTINUED OVERLEAF ...

was to be given a crown made of lowly **grass**. The Corona Graminea signified the ownership of the territory, the right to the land on which the victory had taken place.

The feathered headdresses of Native Americans not only signify the status of the wearer, but the **feathers** themselves signify the different qualities of the birds they belong to. The most valued of all is the **eagle** feather. These headdresses epitomize the crown as a Sun symbol.

The hat

Which single factor is shared by the old-fashioned policeman's helmet from the UK, medieval Jewish hats, the papal Triregnum, and the traditional witch's hat? They all have a tall, conical shape. This has the effect of making the wearer taller than anyone else, more noticeable, and therefore more authoritative. This kind of hat is also a phallic symbol. In addition, the hat of the witch or wizard contains the essence of her magical power in the form of a spiral of energy.

Skullcap

Orthodox Jews wear the skullcap (also known as *yarmulke or kippah*) at all times; it is stated in the Torah that no man should walk more than four paces without the head being covered. This is because of the belief that the head should always be covered in the presence of God, and since

God is omnipotent, then it makes sense that the *yarmulke* is worn at all times.

The *yarmulke* is not only a recognizable symbol of the faith, but covering the head is in itself a sign of respect for, and fear of, God. Many men also cover their heads for the same reasons.

Covering the head as a sign of respect for God is not restricted to the Jewish faith, although many people tend to restrict this practice to the times that they are actually in the place of worship.

Hood

The wearing of a hood is sometimes viewed with suspicion, because it masks the face of the wearer. Therefore, the hood is a symbol of invisibility, of disguise, of secrecy, and tends to have negative connotations because we assume that the wearer has reason to conceal him or herself. The figure of death, with its **scythe**, often wears a hood, alluding to the fact that no one knows what form death will take.

Helmet

Like the hood, the helmet is a symbol of invisibility. It also denotes power and invulnerability. The Greek King of Hell, Hades, wears a helmet, and epitomizes all these powers. The covered-face helmet shares many of the same qualities as the mask.

Khalsas

The five Khalsas are the dress rituals of adherents to the Sikh faith, and signs by which they can be recognized. The five Khalsas are:

1. Kesa—this is uncut **hair**. The hair remains uncut as a reminder that harm must not be inflicted upon the body. Male Sikhs wear the **turban** as an article of faith, and it also makes a practical garment to cover and contain the hair.
2. Kacha—this is a particular kind of undergarment as a symbol of marital chastity. Men and women wear similar garments.
3. Kanga—a wooden comb, symbolizing tidiness and cleanliness.
4. Kara—a steel bangle, which serves as a reminder of the truth and of God.
5. Kirpan—a dagger, for ceremonial use only, and a reminder to protect those who need it.

The Khalsas are sometimes referred to as the Five Ks.

Robes

Nuns, monks, and priests of all persuasions wear the plain robes called habits. As well as acting as a kind of uniform, the habit also symbolizes the rejection of material values in favor of spiritual virtues. Generally colored gray or brown, the wearer no longer has to worry about a choice of clothes since external appearances do not matter. Effectively, the habit removes the individual personality. The sackcloth robes worn by ascetics are an extreme statement of the renunciation of worldly appearance, often worn as a penance.

Robes in general signify the rank of the wearer, and because they are distinctly different from everyday dress, they tend to be the preferred dress of spiritual or religious people. In China, the Imperial Robes were very ornate and carried specific symbolism as a part of their design. The round collar was the Heaven, the **square** hem, the **Earth**; the wearer of this robe was therefore an intermediary between the two. Latter-day druids of some orders wear **green** robes to signify the bardic grade, **blue** for the ovate grade, and the fully initiated druid wears **white** robes. Indeed, pilgrims of all faiths, including Buddhist, Muslim, and Shinto, wear white robes. Buddhist monks and followers of Hare Krishna wear robes of the sacred **saffron** color.

The robes of a shaman, like those of the wizard, are covered in magical signs. They are also decorated with **feathers** (symbolic of transcendence) and the pelt of the animal whose spirit they wish to connect with.

CONTINUED OVERLEAF …

Shirt

A shirt is a symbol of protection. To "lose one's shirt" means to relinquish the last vestige of dignity as well as material wealth. However, to give "the shirt off your back" is a gesture of great generosity, indicating a willingness to give away the last of your material possessions. The "hair shirt" is an uncomfortable garment worn by penitents who want to inflict punishment on them.

The tunic is an earlier form of the shirt. The Cathars used it as an analogy for the human body. When they said that fallen angels wore tunics, they meant that they were made of flesh.

Veil

The veil symbolizes a distinct separation between two states of being, physical objects, or concepts. However, the object effecting this separation is apparently flimsy. It must be remembered that this is a two-way separation; the nun that "takes the veil" to become a Bride of Christ separates herself from the world, but also removes the worldly from her relationship with the spiritual.

The Greek word for veil is "hymen." The veil that is lifted to reveal the face of the bride at her wedding not only symbolizes her new status, but also alludes to the tearing of the hymen which is the physical outcome of a marriage. The word "revelation" comes from the Latin *revelatio*, to draw back the veil.

Penetrating a veil, therefore, is symbolic of initiation; hidden knowledge is often described as "veiled." This veil protects us too; in the same way that the light from the Sun can illuminate, it can also dazzle or even blind us if it comes too close.

The Qu'ran says that women should be addressed from behind a veil. The hijab is the physical manifestation of this idea. Although the hijab has been interpreted by some as a sign of oppression, devout followers of Islam would argue that not only is the wearing of this veil instructed by the Prophet, but also gives the woman a great level of freedom. Here, a veil of misunderstanding separates two ideas and cultures.

According to Buddhists, Maya is the symbolic veil that separates pure reality from the illusory nature of the world in which we live.

COLOR

Despite the fact that colors have an essential part to play in symbolism and the understanding of it, they are, nevertheless, frequently overlooked. Colors are proven to have a profound effect on the human psyche and on our moods. They resonate with the **elements**, the directions, the seasons, the **planets** and **astrological signs** as well as holding huge significance in their own right, for example, in the **Tarot**. Colors, and particular shades of them, confer an immediate identity and make a strong statement. For example, in the **green**, **purple**, and **white** of the Suffragettes (green for hope, purple for dignity, and white for purity), or in the **red** and white stripes of the old-fashioned barber's pole (where the white represented the color of flesh and the red was the **blood** sometimes drawn by the cut-throat razor).

Territories use colors to represent them on their flags. Sometimes the reasons behind these colors have unexpected origins, such as the bright **orange** that is so strongly linked to the Netherlands; more of this later.

The simple colors used by children generally represent the most elemental meanings; **blue** for the **sea** and the **sky**, green for growth, **brown** for the **Earth**, **yellow** for the **Sun**.

The significance of colors is proven by the high value that our ancestors placed on certain plants or substances that could be made into dyes, such as the Imperial Purple of Rome that was produced from a mollusk that was valued more highly than **gold**, or the **saffron** crocus that produced the sacred color of the same name. Prior to the development of chemical dyes, the creation of colors that did not fade in the Sun or wash away was a combination of art, science, and magic, akin to an alchemical process. The impact of the Sun shining through stained glass, painting the interiors of churches with living colors that shimmered and danced, in a medieval world where color was often a privilege of the wealthy few, can only be imagined. Warriors in Ancient Britain daubed themselves in blue pigments in order to look more fearsome to their enemies. The power of red once was so powerful that corpses were daubed in red ochre in the belief that the color had the same life-giving properties as **blood**.

The **seven** colors of the rainbow—which break down into 700 shades that are visible to the naked **eye**—are associated with the seven planets, the days of the

CONTINUED OVERLEAF ...

week, the Seven Heavens, and the seven notes of the musical scale.

Black

SYMBOLIC MEANINGS: *night, the absence of light; mourning, sobriety, denial; authority; perfection and purity; maturity and wisdom.*

Although it's the opposite of white, both shades are, in fact, due to an absence of color and technically speaking black is not a "color" at all. This doesn't stop it having a wealth of symbolic meaning.

Black often has negative connotations for the reason that it is the color of the night, or the absence of light. It doesn't require a great leap of the imagination to extend this light/dark, day/night symbolism to good/bad. A fundamentally natural occurrence to do with the orbit of the Earth around the Sun, therefore, has had far-reaching consequences, resulting in fear, racism, superstition, and bigotry which even continues today simply because of skin color.

In the West, black is the color of mourning and funerals. In some cultures, white is used in this context, in which case it carries the idea of rebirth. Black, however, is not so sanguine. It is final, conclusive, the denial of life.

Despite the mirthless sobriety of black, it depends how you wear it. The "New Black" is a term applied to anything that is in vogue, since black is also somehow dangerous and sexy as well as practical, therefore always fashionable as a color.

The "black **sheep**" of the family refers to the one who is a bit of a scoundrel, and the "black **dog**" means depression. Conversely, a black **cat** is a very lucky symbol in the UK and other parts of the world. A person who holds a black belt in any of the martial arts is considered to be at the pinnacle of their abilities, and indeed, in Japan, black is the color of wisdom, experience, and maturity. In this instance, black is a color of perfection, an idea shared by the Cathars who also saw black as a symbol of completion and purity.

Black is a secretive, mysterious color and used as such in rite and ritual. A polished black **mirror** provides a perfect, glossy surface for scrying or seeing into the future.

Blue

SYMBOLIC MEANINGS: *truth and the intellect; wisdom, loyalty, chastity; peace, piety and contemplation; spirituality; eternity.*

Blue is the color of the Heavens and is related to the fifth **chakra**. Blue is traditionally worn by the Virgin Mary, the very embodiment of all the qualities described above. Whereas the reds, oranges and yellows carry with them a carnival atmosphere, blue is more sober, even somber, despite its many variations. If we're "feeling blue" then we're depressed or melancholy. And yet the bluebird is a universal symbol for happiness. The color has even given its name to a rich vein of **music**. The "blues" actually refers to "blue notes." These are notes, either sung or played, that are pitched down a little for expressive purposes. An example is Billie Holiday's heartbreaking rendition of "Strange Fruit."

There's something cool and detached about blue that gives rise to its reputation for spirituality and chastity. Above all blue is the color of the sky. Like the sky, blue is infinitely spacious. It contains everything, and yet contains nothing. The color is therefore associated with ideas of eternity. When filmmakers and animators want to place a subject against a different background, they film against a blue screen since the color can be made invisible. In Jewish tradition the city of Luz, where the Immortals live, is also called The Blue City. Similarly, the mythical sacred **mountain** of the Hindus, Mount Meru, is constructed entirely of **sapphire** on its southern face and it's this that is said to tinge the skies with blue.

To put any color out of context can have an alienating and often frightening effect. Knowing this, early British warriors daubed themselves in woad. These blue-skinned savages must have been an alarming sight for Roman soldiers.

Members of the aristocracy or the royalty are described as having "blue blood," but why? The phrase originated with the Spanish, *sangre azul*, and refers to the pale-skinned Castilian ruling classes who prided themselves on never having interbred with darker-skinned races. Therefore, their blue veinous blood was plainly visible underneath the surface of their skin. There's even a particular shade of blue that is meant to represent this color, called Royal Blue.

Brown

Symbolic meanings: *poverty, humility, practicality.*

Brown is the color primarily associated with the **Earth**, soil, the raw element before it is covered with greenery. The word for earth, in Latin, is *humus*, which carries the same root as humility. Religious ascetics wear brown as a reminder of this quality and also of their voluntary material poverty.

Gray

Symbolic meanings: sobriety, steadiness, modesty.

Gray is the midway point between black and white, and tellingly the "gray area" is

CONTINUED OVERLEAF ...

an area of indetermination, indecision, or ambiguity. To be described as gray is rather less than flattering, since gray is such a subdued and neutral color, and implies that the person blends into the background. However, gray is also a color of balance and reasonableness and is the color used, in photography, to balance all others.

Because people's hair turns gray with age, the word is often used to describe elderly people and is also a color of wisdom.

For Christians, gray is the color of resurrection and is worn when people are coming out of the full black of mourning as the midway point on the journey to other colors.

Green

SYMBOLIC MEANINGS: *new life, resurrection, hope; the sea; fertility and regeneration; recycling, environmental awareness; a lucky color; an unlucky color.*

Green is an amalgam of blue and yellow, and is the color of the fourth chakra. Green is the universal symbol for "Go!" to red's "Stop."

In common with yellow, there seem to be several anomalies in the symbolic meaning of green. To call someone "green" means that they are inexperienced or innocent and obviously refers to fresh

young shoots, yet jealousy is also described as the "green-**eyed** monster." This saying is actually Shakespearean in origin. In Othello, he describes jealousy as being like the green-eyed monster, the cat, "which doth mock the meat it feeds on." Probably the same origin gives us "green with envy."

Green is a soothing, refreshing color, so it is interesting to discover why it's sometimes believed to be unlucky. It's still a statistical fact that fewer green cars are sold in the UK than any other color because of this superstition.

In the Middle Ages, green was meant to be the color of the Devil. He's even depicted on a stained-glass window in Chartres Cathedral as having green skin and green eyes, strangely similar to a generally held belief about the appearance of Martians. In this sense the color denotes an alien, nonhuman, possibly threatening being; no surprise, then, that it's the color of the Fairy Folk, and it might well be that the color is lucky or unlucky depending on their attitude toward you. If you dressed in green, it was believed that the fairies could claim you as their own.

In Islam, green is the color of paradise, and Mohammed has a green banner. Paradise actually means "garden," and in the arid desert landscape of the Bedouin, any stretch of lush green land must indeed appear heavenly.

The epitome of the nature God in the Western world is the Green Man, the pre-

Christian deity whose leafy face peeps out from bosky woods and verdant forests and reminds us that Mother Nature is supernal. However, the Green Man is not exclusive to the West. He also exists in Islam, as Al Kadir. Al Kadir is the patron of travelers, and he's said to live on the very edge of the world where the oceans of Heaven and Earth merge. Be mindful if you meet Al Kadir that you should do as he tells you, however outlandish the instructions might be.

In alchemy, full of hidden meanings, the Green Lion itself has more than one meaning. It is a symbol for Vitriol (sulfuric acid) which is created by distilling the green iron sulfate crystals in a flask. But the life-force itself was symbolized as the blood of the Green Lion, blood contained in a green vessel; this was a reference not to real, physical **gold**, but to Philosophers' Gold, far more valuable and elusive.

Motley

SYMBOLIC MEANINGS: *wealth; a chameleon personality.*

Not strictly a color as such, but a combination of many other colors. The word is generally used to describe cloth or clothing. The rainbow nature of motley means that whoever wears it has as many aspects as there are colors, a chameleon personality, and it can indicate the trickster or fool (as worn by the jester, or the **fool** in the

Tarot) as well as kings, emperors, and deities. In the Bible, Joseph's coat of many colors is the subject of much envy.

Orange

SYMBOLIC MEANINGS: *balance between spirit and sexuality; fertility and yet virginity; energy; the Sun; like yellow, orange is believed to be an appetite stimulant.*

Orange has two aspects that we see time and time again, pivoting between the material and spiritual worlds, which is not surprising given that the color itself is a balance between red and yellow. As such, it represents the second chakra, the first being red, and the third, yellow.

Orange is a vibrant, cheerful color that definitely lifts the spirits. The orange blossom is the traditional flower for brides because the fruit and the flower can appear on the **orange tree** at the same time, hence the virginity/fertility symbolism.

Similarly, a Hindu bride has an orange powder smeared on her forehead once she is married, a sign of her status. Hindu places of worship are indicated by an orange flag or banner, which is replaced once a year in a colorful and effusive ceremony.

Why is the color orange so closely associated with the Netherlands? Originally it's because of the Dutch ruling dynasty,

CONTINUED OVERLEAF ...

the House of Orange. Loyal Dutch farmers who gave the world the first orange carrot further cemented the association. It might be impossible to associate the carrot with any other color these days, but originally they came in black, red, or purple and were a much more bitter vegetable than the modern varieties. By the 1700s, the Dutch had succeeded in hybridizing pale yellow carrots with red ones. It might be a coincidence, but a recent Unicef survey showed Dutch children to be the happiest in Europe; given that happiness is one of the symbolic associations with the color orange, could there be a link?

Pink

SYMBOLIC MEANINGS: *femininity, innocence, good health, love, patience.*

Pink is the ultimate feminine color, both flirty, girlish and innocent at the same time. Pale pink is used as the symbol for a baby girl, just as pale blue is used for baby boys. This feminine angle is why the color pink has been adopted as a symbol of gay pride.

Pink is the color of universal, unconditional love.

Purple

SYMBOLIC MEANINGS: *royalty and pomp; power, wealth, majesty.*

Purple, or indigo, is the color associated with the sixth chakra.

Since it was first discovered, purple has been *the* color of choice to denote wealth and power. Emperors, kings, and the more powerful members of the clergy—such as bishops—choose the colour as a way of defining their status. This is because the dye itself was originally available from one source and one source only; the secretions of a certain gland of an unfortunate sea snail called the Murex Brandaris. Therefore, purple was extremely costly to produce and strictly the color of those who could afford it, since the dye itself was more expensive even than gold. The most popular shade of the color is called Tyrian Purple (named for the city of Tyre, where it was manufactured). Heracles' **dog**, which had a predilection for snacking on the snails he found along the seashore, is credited with having discovered the dye after his owner noticed the purple staining around his mouth. It is likely, however, that the Minoans on Crete discovered the purple pigment quite some time before Heracles' dog trotted into the picture.

If the Minoan theory is true then the rare purple dye has been with us for at least 3500 years, so its associations with all things glorious and splendid are well embedded into the human psyche even with the advent of synthetic dye alternatives.

Red

SYMBOLIC MEANINGS: *vitality and life-force; fire, the Sun, the South; blood; good luck and prosperity; power and authority; masculine energy; war and anger; passion, energy, sexuality.*

One of the three primary colors, bright red pops out of whatever environment it happens to be in and grabs our attention more than any other color. Moreover, it is the first actual color that is seen by babies. Because it has a lower vibrational frequency than any other color in our visible spectrum, it is associated with the base chakra and symbolizes passion, sexuality, fertility and animal urges. Red-light districts are so called because of the dim red shades of the prostitutes' quarters.

Red is the color of blood, which means that it is associated with the life-forces and vitality. Hunters daub themselves in the red blood of the kill, which they believe will give them empathy with the spirit of the animal. Red is also the color of fire, the Sun and the Southern direction.

The word for "magic," in German, is directly linked to the word for "red ochre." A recent archaeological discovery provided unusual evidence of the reverence in which the color was held by early man.

Lumps of red ochre, as well as tools stained with the substance, were found in early graves in an Israeli cave, indicating its importance as a symbol of vitality, life, and resurrection.

Pure colors used to be very difficult and expensive to produce, and so red cloth was used by people in positions of power, such as the monarchy and the clergy. Byzantine emperors were dressed from head to foot in red. In Rome, red was the color of nobles and generals, and the Holy Roman Church still dresses its cardinals in pure, bright, cardinal red. To roll out the red carpet for someone is to honor their presence.

Red is a color of protection and has been viewed as such for at least the last 2000 years. **Amulets** made from **rubies** or **garnets** were far more valuable than any other kind, able to make the wearer invincible.

And how about the red planet? **Mars** has a preponderance of iron oxide in its soil that gives it a red appearance that is clearly visible to the naked eye. This color is partially responsible for its association with war and warriors.

In India and China, red is the traditional color for weddings. Indian brides wear saris of red or pink, and the Chinese happy couple will be surrounded by a veritable sea of red; clothing, souvenirs, and gifts. Even the home of the bride and groom are decorated with red banners and ribbons. Roman brides, too, favored red for

CONTINUED OVERLEAF ...

their wedding veil, which was called a *flammeum*. This tradition is shared by modern Greek brides.

In Ancient Egypt red was synonymous with evil, because it was the color of the God Seth, who haunted the arid desert places, the personification of destruction. Seth was called the "Red God," and an Egyptian charm of the time goes like this;

Oh, Isis, deliver me from the hands of bad, evil, red things!

Similarly, in Christian symbolism, the Devil is sometimes depicted as a red creature. Like Seth, he also has a predilection for scorched places.

In alchemy, the Red Stone is mercuric sulfide, a compound of sulfur and mercury that is also called vermilion. The creation of vermilion was a very important primary stage in the process of making the Philosopher's Stone, which is itself disguised as the Red Lion, since this elusive substance was characterized by turning red in its final stage.

Saffron

SYMBOLIC MEANINGS: *spirituality, holiness, good fortune.*

Named for the saffron crocuses whose stigmata create the color, the harvesting of these delicate plant parts is a labor-intensive and time-critical matter and so the actual dye is costly to produce. Saffron is an extremely auspicious color for Buddhists, Hindus, Jains, and Sikhs, and a saffron or orange banner indicates a place of spiritual worship. The foreheads of Hindu deities are daubed with saffron paste to denote their celestial status, and although the Hindu pantheon is vast and complex, the use of saffron is a unifying factor across the many different manifestations of the faith.

Saffron is paler and more golden than true orange, and is said to be the color of wisdom, the rising Sun, and of Mother Earth.

Violet

SYMBOLIC MEANINGS: *knowledge and intelligence, piety, sobriety, humility, temperance; peace and spirituality.*

Violet is the color associated with the seventh chakra.

There are many shades of violet ranging from ethereal pale shades through to the darker mauve, considered the only color acceptable as a relief from the relentless strict mourning convention of black and gray in Victorian times.

Violet is a combination of red and blue, and its association with temperance is indicated in some Tarot suits. Temperance is the 14th card of the Major Arcana and is depicted by a woman holding a jug or vase in either hand, one red, one blue, pouring a clear liquid from one to the other.

Violet is often worn by people predisposed toward psychic matters, and is the perfect symbol of the "higher" mind, combining as it does the earthy, fieriness of red with the cool reasonableness of blue to forge an entirely different hue. It's association with the seventh chakra, at the crown position at the top of the head, that gives violet the power to connect with the world of spirit.

The humble qualities of violet as a color come from the flower. The tiny violet grows close to the ground, hidden modestly in among the **grass**, yet noticeable because of its striking color.

White

SYMBOLIC MEANINGS: *purity, virginity; death and rebirth, a beginning and an end; in the Far East, mourning.*

White is both the absence of any color and the sum of all colors together, so in a sense it can mean everything or nothing. This combination of all colors has given white the name of the "many-colored **lotus**" in Buddhist teachings.

Probably the most telling of both ends of white's symbolic spectrum are reflected in its associations with purity and a fresh start (as worn by brides in the Western tradition, as an optimistic sign of virginity) and as the color of mourning in the East, a use that used to be common in Europe, too. Cadavers all over the world are still wrapped in white shrouds and, as death precedes birth, the white here has an optimistic meaning, since in this instance, white symbolizes rebirth. White is also used to denote initiation, another form of rebirth. Children wear white at their First Communion, and in Africa, boys smear their bodies with white paste after circumcision to show that they are apart from their main society for a time. When they re-enter, it is as men, their bodies painted red.

White is the color of expectation and contains all the potential of the blank canvas. The pristine glory of a fresh fall of snow makes the world look clean and pure but white shows up every mark, hence its usefulness in hospitals and other clinical environments.

White is a symbol of peace, and the white flag is a universal sign of submission and surrender. However, the white feather is a sign of cowardice. This originates in the days of cock-fighting when a **bird** with a white **feather** in its tail was believed to be a poor fighter. The potency of this particular white symbol is such that, just after the Second World War, an "order of the White Feather" was started as a method of goading men into joining the army. Womenfolk were encouraged to hand the white feather of cowardice to any man not wearing a uniform.

CONTINUED OVERLEAF ...

Yellow

SYMBOLIC MEANINGS: *the Sun; power, authority; the intellect and intuition; goodness; light, life, truth, immortality; endurance; the Empire and fertility [China]; cowardice, treachery.*

Yellow is one of the three primary colors and is related to the third chakra which lives in the region of the solar plexus. This is apt, since yellow, like red and orange, is one of the Sun colors. It could be argued that yellow is the most dazzling of the three, so the association makes good sense. The Ancient Egyptians had only six colors available in their pallet, and wherever yellow is used this indicates endurability and timelessness.

In China, yellow is the color of the Emperor. The average man in the street was forbidden from wearing it until relatively recently. It is also the color of fertility, since healthy soil in China is a yellow color. Because of this, all the hangings, sheets, and pillows of the bridal bed were dyed in vibrant shades of yellow as well as red.

However, there are some contradictions with yellow. In the UK and USA, to call someone "yellow" or to say that they have a "yellow streak" means that they are cowardly. There are several theories about why this should be. The one that seems to fit best is that Judas Iscariot wore yellow robes, and his own cowardly act was to betray Christ for thirty pieces of **silver**.

Jewish people were made to wear a yellow **Star of David** during the Nazi regime of the Second World War. Similarly, in 1215 the Lateran Council ordered Jews to wear a yellow circle to identify themselves. It was probably small comfort for these persecuted people that they believed yellow to be synonymous with beauty. In tenth-century France, the doors of criminals were painted yellow. Conversely, in the fourteenth century, the yellow chrysanthemum was worn by warriors as a symbol of courage.

Because leaves turn yellow and then to black with the onset of fall, in several places, including Ancient Egypt, yellow is a color of mourning. A yellow cross was painted on doors as a sign of the plague, possibly for the same reasons, and even today yellow marks off a quarantined area.

THE ELEMENT ENCYCLOPEDIA OF SECRET SIGNS AND SYMBOLS

Compasses

See **Freemasonry**.

Corn Dolly

These days, the corn dolly generally gathers dust in gift shops, an innocuous souvenir for tourists in rural areas, particularly in the United Kingdom. However, its origins as a powerful magical symbol go back thousands of years to pre-Christian times. It may come as a surprise that the corn dolly hanging on the kitchen wall can trace its roots back to a particularly bloody ritual.

In any agrarian culture, the success of the crop is all-important and in Northern Europe the harvest produce was essential to survival during the winter period. It was the generally held belief that the **spirit** of the harvest—in this case, the versatile **grain** crop—resided in the plant, and once the plant was cut down then the spirit effectively became homeless. In order to provide a new home for this spirit,

the farmers made a corn dolly from the very last stalks of the crop. The dolly would spend her time indoors over the winter, waiting to be ploughed back into the ground at the start of the new season. In places where the corn dolly custom was not established, the last few stalks of corn were violently beaten into the ground, thus driving the spirit back into the **Earth**.

The dolly was made into the shape of an old woman, representing the Crone aspect of the Harvest Goddess. She was drenched in **water** as a further propitiation to the Gods and to ensure that plenty of rain would feed the harvest to come. Different areas had different styles of corn dollies.

However, the custom of preserving the spirit of the harvest was not always carried out in such a genteel way. The Phrygians, who lived in central Asia Minor and worshipped the Mother of the Gods, Cybele, carried out a different sort of ceremony. Their "corn dolly" was formed from thickly plaited sheaves of corn formed into a tall column. Any stranger found in the vicinity was captured in the belief that his presence there would mean that the spirit of the harvest had possessed his body and caused him to wander into the area. The hapless stranger was then trapped within this cage of corn and then beheaded in the belief that the blood that fell upon the ground contained the valuable "soul" of the crop.

Cornicello

An **amulet** designed to protect the wearer, the cornicello features the effigy of the **horn**, is made of horn, or is horn-shaped. "Cornicello" comes from an Italian word meaning "little horn."

Cornucopia

Also called the Horn of Plenty, the cornucopia is often depicted in paintings and on friezes where it symbolizes the notion of boundless abundance, as **flowers**, **fruits**, sheaves of **wheat**, and other produce spill out of a hollow horn or a twisting basket woven in the shape of the horn. The origin of the cornucopia is found in the Greek myth of Amalthea. Amalthea fed the infant **Zeus** a drink of goat's **milk** and was given the brimming goat's horn as a reward. Sometimes the infant Zeus is depicted being fed the milk from the horn itself. The Cornucopia, as a symbol of a bounteous harvest, is also associated with **Ceres**, the Goddess of corn, and also with Fortuna, Goddess of good fortune.

The idea of a bottomless, bounteous container has similarities to the symbol of the **cauldron**.

Cosmic Egg

See **Egg**.

Cosmogram

This is a flat graphic symbol that represents

the cosmos, and is often used as a meditative focus. The **mandala** is a Cosmogram, as are the elaborate depictions of tortoises holding up the planet.

Cosmograms commonly feature the most basic shapes of the circle (representing the planet, and unity) and the square (the Earth and the directions).

COWRIE SHELL

More than any other shell, the cowrie has a marked resemblance to the female genitalia or **yoni**. Because of the ancient idea of the Doctrine of Signatures, the shell is therefore

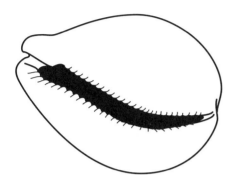

endowed with magical powers of fertility, good luck, and wealth. Originating from the Malaysian area, cowrie shells were used as currency for some time. Their use in decorative masks, headdresses, and other items was widespread, where it had the new addition of being a status symbol because of its use as small change.

The cowrie also represents another body part: the **eye**. Therefore, along with other objects from the natural world that have a similar appearance, the cowrie is considered to protect against evil.

CRESCENT MOON
AND STAR

The crescent Moon is possibly the most distinctive Moon symbol; it shows the changing shape of the Moon and also the return to the same shape. Like the Moon, it is connected to the female principle and the element of **water**.

It is also linked to virginity. Goddesses with a strong Moon connection—such as Diana, or Artemis—are often depicted with the unmistakable crescent Moon shape close by. In Christian iconography, Mary the Virgin, also known by the lyrical epithet **Star** of the **Sea**, appears standing on a crescent Moon with stars in the background, hinting at her Goddess nature. She generally wears the color **blue**, symbolic of spirituality and chastity. The crescent Moon that rests on its "back" looks like a **chalice**.

The crescent Moon with the star is one of the most iconographic symbols of Islam, although the symbol is believed to predate the faith by thousands of years as the symbol of another of the great Moon Goddesses, **Tanit Astarte**, the Queen of Heaven. There are several stories that explain why the symbol was adopted. One is that the founder of the Ottoman Empire, Osman, had a dream in which the crescent Moon stretched across the Earth. Because of this, he kept the existing Moon Goddess symbol and made it the emblem of his Empire.

Incidentally, the croissant—virtually a national symbol of France—is said to have been invented when the Turks were besieging Budapest in 1686 (another account gives the city as Vienna three years earlier). They dug underground passages with the idea of reaching the center of town without attracting attention. However, a baker, working through the night, heard the noise and raised the alarm. As a reward for saving the city, the baker was given the right to bake a special pastry in the form of the crescent Moon that was featured on the Ottoman flag.

CROSS

See **First signs: Cross**.

CROSS AND CROWN

A Christian symbol, the Cross and Crown is a reminder of the rewards that come in Heaven (the crown) after the tribulations of life (the cross) are over. Some latter-day Knights Templar organizations use this symbol.

CROSS LORRAINE

Essentially a heraldic device used by the Dukes of Lorraine, the Cross Lorraine is a vertical bar with a horizontal bar equally spaced at either end. However, this cross is used elsewhere too. In the Catholic Church the cross signifies the rank of cardinal, and in renaissance **alchemy** it was used as a symbol of **spirit** and matter.

Additionally the Cross Lorraine is used to denote one of the degrees within Freemasonry. During the Second World War it was adopted by the French Resistance as their secret symbol, an emblem to stand in opposition to the **swastika**, which had been rendered sinister by the Nazis, and lost for a time its meaning as a positive **Sun** symbol.

CROSSROADS

In fairy stories and myths, it is often at the crossroads where mischief awaits, usually in the form of otherworldly spirits. Effectively, the crossroads symbolizes the intersection of **two** paths, making **four** potential routes, and a place where a decision must be made, not only practically, but metaphorically too. The

X of the crossroads marks a spot where two worlds meet.

One of the more recent tales about an encounter at a crossroads concerns the renowned blues guitarist and musician, Robert Johnson. Johnson is alleged to have met the Devil at a crossroads, and to have exchanged his **soul** for his remarkable talent as a musician and songwriter. Johnson exacerbated this devilish reputation when he recorded a track called "Cross Road Blues," based on a myth from the Deep South. This legend tells that a daring person who fancied striking a deal with Satan should wait for him at a crossroads late at night. The origins of this story go back to African folklore, where a deity called Esu was the guardian of the crossroads. When Christianity took over, these old Gods were, quite literally, demonized, and Esu was transformed into the Devil. **Hecate**, too, personified as the Queen of the Witches, was called the Goddess of the Crossroads.

In Celtic mythology, corpses belonging to those considered "unholy" were buried at crossroads in order to prevent them coming back to life and because the crossroads was a Gate to the Otherworld. Gibbets were placed at crossroads for the same reason.

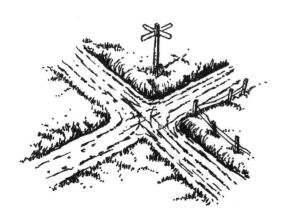

CROW'S FOOT

The crow's foot is also known as the Witch's Foot, and was feared as an indicator of death, used in casting spells against enemies. Crows, like ravens, were associated with the witches and warlocks who were believed to be able to transform themselves into these black birds so that they could travel unnoticed to their sabbats.

The name crow's foot is also given to the lines that radiate around the outer corners of the eyes with the coming of age and the inevitable approach of death.

CRUCIFIX

A **Latin Cross** with a model of the body of the Christ fixed to it. It is used in the Christian tradition as a reminder of the sacrifice that Christ made for humankind.

CRUX DISSIMULATA

In third-century Rome, early Christians were persecuted to such a degree that their lives were threatened and the symbols of their faith had to be disguised. One of the ways they recognized one another was by the sign of the **fish** or **ichthus**; another way was to disguise the Cross cleverly as something else. The

meaning of Crux Dissimulata is "disguised" or "dissimilar" cross.

One of the more ingenious forms of this secret symbol, shown here, was the anchor. The top of the anchor is formed like a cross and, in addition, the anchor is plainly a symbol of stability. Because anchors are associated with the sea, too, the fish symbol could easily be incorporated into it. The Crux Dissimulata was used as secret symbol and a rallying call for adherents to the new and dangerous faith.

CRYSTAL BALL

Combining the sphere's perfection and totality with the clarity and brilliance of **crystal**, the crystal ball is a part of the toolkit of the professional clairvoyant or seer. The clarity of the crystal matches the "clear sight" of the psychic. When used for scrying, the crystal ball acts as a focus for meditation, enabling the adept to access a place that is out of time in order to be able to see into the future.

This practice of scrying is carried out in various ways. Instead of an expensive crystal, cheaper methods are apparently just as effective for the talented psychic. A bowl of water, a mirror, a drop of blood, or a pool of ink can be used. However, the glamor of the genuine crystal ball is hard to beat.

CUBE

The cube carries all the symbolism of the **square** (at its most basic, the material world and the elements) except that it is, of course, three-dimensional. The cube is solid, stable, reliable, and often forms the basis of other buildings. It is also a symbol of moral perfection. The cube is a symbol of material eternity. One of the most famous cubes is the **Ka'aba** that stands at the center of the Grand Mosque at **Mecca**, and which is a symbol of power and eternity.

If the cube is unfolded, it turns into a cross; this cross gives us the standard floor plan of Christian churches and further reinforces the idea of stability and eternity.

One of the five **Platonic solids** and one of the **Tattvas**, the cube represents the element of **Earth**.

Daruma

This is a small doll intended to resemble the founder of Zen Buddhism, The Bodhidharma Daruma. Daruma brought the teachings from India to China in the sixth century. The dolls are ubiquitous in Japan as a good-luck symbol par excellence as well as a reminder of the need for patience.

The dolls are rounded and chunky, reflecting the story that the Bodhidharma spent such a long time (reputedly nine years) meditating motionless in a **cave** that his limbs atrophied. A weight inside the base of the rotund little figure means that it may wobble but it never falls over, and this feature symbolizes Daruma's persistence in his meditative process as well as illustrating the Buddhist tenet that you can fall over seven times but still get up again on the eighth. He was so zealous that he is even reputed to have cut off his eyelids so that he could not fall asleep, and this is why the dolls also have wide, staring **eyes**. Coincidentally, the gift of tea was given to Daruma by God to help him keep awake.

Given as a gift at the New Year, each of the eyes of the Daruma doll are colored with a marker when certain goals are achieved.

When both eyes are colored the little doll is burned on a shrine as an offering.

Dearinth

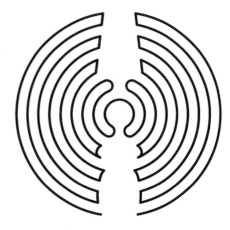

A relatively new sign, the dearinth was invented by Oberon Zell as the symbol for his Church of All Worlds. Zell is credited with inventing the term "Neo-Pagan." The symbol represents a **labyrinth** but also cleverly includes the figure of the God and Goddess. The **nine** concentric circles of the Dearinth relate to the nine levels of initiation within the Church.

Degrees of witchcraft

Witches and wizards might write their names, followed by a symbol that denotes the level of his or her initiation into the Craft.

First degree [inverted triangle]

This shows the neophyte that has been introduced to the most basic teachings and traditions. The shape of this inverted **triangle** is also drawn in the **air** as the "threefold salute," and is drawn in the sequence of **breast**, breast, **genitals**, breast.

Second degree [1]

The second stage of witchcraft, and a deeper level of knowledge is also represented by a gesture that emulates the shape of the upright triangle; **mouth**, breast, breast, mouth.

Second degree [2]

The Fivefold Salute describes the shape of an inverted **pentagram** by tracing a line from genitals to right breast, then left hip to right hip and back to genitals.

Third degree

This is the sign used by fully fledged witches and wizards. Formed of a pentagram surmounted by an upright triangle, it is traced in the air from mouth to breast, then back to the mouth, genitals, right **foot**, left **knee**, right knee, left foot and back to the genitals.

DHARMA WHEEL

The Dharma wheel or Dharmachakra is used as a symbol in both Hinduism and Buddhism. It is an **eight**-spoked wheel, sometimes rendered quite decoratively. Each spoke of the wheel represents one of the pillars of belief that applies to these Dharmic religions.

1. Right faith
2. Right intention
3. Right speech
4. Right action
5. Right livelihood
6. Right thought
7. Right meditation

The wheel symbol in general is complex and is covered elsewhere; this particular wheel represents the notion of overcoming obstacles, difficulties, and challenges.

Djed

An Ancient Egyptian symbol of stability, the djed is an image of a pillar with **four** platforms piled on top of it. As with other pillar-like symbols the world over, the djed also signifies the **World Axis**, the **World Tree**, and the **phallus**.

Doorway

The simple doorway—an everyday object that goes unnoticed most of the time—is symbolic of a transition between one world and the next. Such a doorway may take different forms, as a **dolmen**, a **torii**, a gateway, but the meaning remains the same. In C.S. Lewis's Narnia novels, the wardrobe into which the children step to enter the magical world of Narnia is a good example of this symbol. Both Heaven and Hell lie beyond gates or doorways, and the threshold of such a place is seen as the place where two worlds meet and sometimes collide. Many rituals involve the initiate stepping through a doorway of some kind. The **Vesica Piscis** represents a doorway where the world of **spirit** enters the world of matter.

Dorje

See **Vajra**.

Dot

See **First signs: Dot**.

Double Happiness

This good-luck symbol, ubiquitous in China or in places where there is a strong undercurrent of Chinese culture, comprises the character meaning happiness, repeated twice, hence the name, Double Happiness. The meaning of the sign is inferred in its name, and it is a popular symbol for practitioners of Feng

gn is effective if placed in the
 home that relates to relation-
so said to be particularly lucky
ls.

DREAMCATCHER

The forerunner of the Dreamcatcher was a
Native American spiders' web of **feather**s and
beads, a simple little charm made from a small
hoop of flexible wood, such as **willow**, with
an interlacement of plant fibres designed to
look like a **cobweb**.

This little amulet was used particularly as
a protection for babies and small children.
Hung over their cradles and beds, it was
thought to entrap any negative spirits that
came in the form of nightmares. These malevolent entities, entangled in the web, were
sizzled in the heat from the rising **Sun**. The
spider's web shape gave homage to
Asibikaasi, the mythical Spider Woman,
whose magical webs could catch anything.

The elaborate Dreamcatchers of today, an
essential part of the kit for any self-respecting
New Ager, were invented in the 1960s and
'70s as part of the resurgence in Native
American culture and belief.

DREIDEL

During the Jewish holiday of Chanukah, the
usually strict rules forbidding any kind of
gambling are relaxed slightly. The Dreidel is
a wooden spinning top, its four sides inscribed
with letters. These letters form an acronym
that reminds the players of the meaning of the
holiday. The initial letters, *nun, gimel, heh,* and
shin, stand for a phrase which, when translated, means "A great miracle happened
there," and the top is spun to win small treats
such as sweets and **chocolate** coins. The
Dreidel is symbolic of fun and of the holiday
period but carries a serious message at the
same time.

DRILBU

The Drilbu is the bell-like object that appears sometimes in the right hand of Buddhist statues, and is the female counterpart of the male **Vajra** or **Dorje**. Its Sanskrit counterpart is called the **Ghanta.**

The Drilbu symbolizes knowledge, emptiness and wisdom, and the notes of its bell are a reminder of the transient nature of everything. The actual object is made of an amalgamation of **seven** different **metals**, each of which is associated with the **planets** and is a magical symbol in its own right. The Drilbu is a musical instrument as well as a ritual object. It is chimed **three** times to focus the attention of the people attending any ceremony. Its sweet-sounding resonant note also welcomes in good spirits and drives away any evil ones.

The Drilbu has the same feminine symbolism as the **chalice** in the Western tradition. It is called the Ghanta in the Hindu faith.

DRUZE STAR

This **five**-pointed upright star, comprised of five distinct diamond shapes, is the emblem of the Druze faith, an offshoot of Islam. Each segment is often colored according to its meaning.

The five points of the star remind followers of the religion of the five universal principles of the faith:

1. The masculine element, the **Sun** and the mind. This segment is often colored **green**.
2. The feminine element and the **Moon**, colored **red**.
3. The Word, considered the mediator between the Divine and humankind, colored **yellow**.
4. Will and the realms of possibility, colored **blue**.
5. Finally, the white segment of the star represents actualization, the manifestation of the Word and the Will.

Egg

The egg is as powerful in its symbolism as it is potent as a life-force. The **World Egg** is a ubiquitous symbol for the egg from which the Universe is said to have hatched, an idea that appears in creation myths from all parts of the world. The Celts, Hindus, Egyptians, Greeks, Phoenicians and many more all agree about this idea.

The form this cosmic hatching takes is variable though. Often, the egg rises from primeval waters and is incubated by a **bird**; in Hindu belief, this is the Hamsa, a **goose**. When the egg hatches, the yolk and the white become Heaven and Earth.

The Shinto tradition says that the Universe resembled a giant hen's egg that broke open, with the heavier parts becoming the Earth and the lighter, the Heavens. There is also a theory that the entire Universe is contained in a huge egg that stands upright.

The egg is a symbol of new life, and this idea is borne out with chocolate eggs at **Easter**, which in itself is a celebration of the pre-Christian fertility Goddess, **Eostre,** who also gives her name to the hormone Estrogen. The subsequent celebration of

Christ's death and resurrection meant that the egg kept its significance as a symbol of new life and hope. Archeologists have found clay eggs in Russian burial sites, reinforcing the belief in the egg as a symbol of immortality and of rebirth.

In **alchemy**, the Philosopher's Egg symbolizes the **seed** of spiritual life, and depicts the place wherein a great transformation takes place.

The ancient riddle of what came first, chicken or egg, was deftly if disappointingly answered by Angelus Silesius, who said:

The chicken was in the egg and the egg was in the chicken.

Elven star

This seven-pointed star has several different names and occurs in many different magical traditions, including **Sacred Geometry**. Most prosaically, it is known as the septagram. For wiccans and pagans it is also called the Faerie star, for others it might be referred to as the star of the Seven Sisters since it is associated with the cluster of seven astro-nomical stars called the **Pleiades** (or Flock of Doves). These celestial sisters were believed to guard the **Axis Mundi** as depicted by the **Pole star**.

Wherever it occurs and by whatever name it is known, the Elven star is a reminder of the sacred significance of the number **7**; the seven days of the week, the seven **planets** of the ancient tradition, the **seven magical metals**, and the seven pillars of wisdom. For the Egyptians this star represented the seven spheres of the Afterlife and the seven wise people that the soul would meet on the journey.

The septagram is also an important symbol in the **Kabbalah** where it corresponds to the sphere of **Netzach** or Victory. Here, too, it acts as an aide memoire for all the things that come in groups of seven.

Like the **pentagram**, the Elven star can be drawn without the pen leaving the paper, a tell-tale quality of a protective symbol. Specifically, the Elven star is said to defend secrets from the outside world.

Aleister Crowley adopted a seven-pointed star as the seal for his **Astrum Argentum** (Silver Star) Order.

Emerald tablet

See **Smaragdina Tablet**.

Endless Knot

Different interpretations of the Endless Knot occur in different cultures, including Celtic, Chinese, and in Tibetan Buddhism where it is one of the Eight Auspicious Symbols, or **Ashtamangala**. The knot can be drawn without the pen leaving the paper—this is generally a clue that the symbol is one of protection.

Philosophically, the knot is constructed of "something" (the rope, representative of matter) and "nothing" (the spaces in between), symbolic of **spirit**. These two elements represent the co-dependence of wisdom and compassion, male and female, night and day.

Since the knot has no beginning and no end, there are also comparisons to be drawn with the **circle**.

ENNEAGRAM

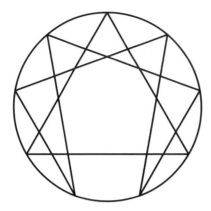

ENSO

This **nine**-pointed geometric figure, with an open side, is an ancient sign that, in Kabbalistic mysticism, is described as "the essence of being." It was revived by G.I. Gurdjieff, the mystic/teacher whose teachings have had a far-reaching effect on the last few generations of esotericists. Gurdjieff used this deceptively simple shape to demonstrate his theories about certain cosmic laws. The primary law that the Enneagram demonstrates is the natural "highs" and "lows" of any aspect of life, whether emotional, mechanical, commercial. Those who have studied the Enneagram in depth believe that it helps them to accept these fluctuations as part of the natural order.

The Enneagram of Personality sees the symbol used as a way to define the nine different personality types identified by Gurdjieff.

Belonging to Zen Buddhism, the Enso is a **circle**, drawn quickly and simply with a brush stroke although years of practice in the art of calligraphy are likely to have preceded the ease with which the symbol can be drawn. The Enso symbolizes eternity, the perfect meditative state, the "no thing," and enlightenment.

EVANGELISTS' SYMBOLS

The **four** evangelists—Disciples of Christ who witnessed and wrote about the events in the life of the Messiah, which comprise the four main books of the New Testament—are often represented not as men but as hybrid creatures. Not only that, but the four men—Matthew, Mark, Luke, and John—are each associated with the four points of the compass, the elements, the winds, and with the four rivers purported to run through Eden. Each evangelist is also ascribed a sign of the **Zodiac**. Collectively, they symbolize stability and the four pillars of the faith.

The angel is the symbol of Matthew. Mark is the **Lion**, whose symbol in stone proliferates around St. Mark's Square in Venice. The **bull** is the symbol of Luke, and the **eagle** represents John. Wherever they are represented, these creatures have wings, as a sign of their divine nature as messengers from God. These hybrid animals are also called the **Tetramorphs.**

EVIL EYE

This is a gaze or stare which is believed to cause actual harm. There are numerous **talismans**, **amulets**, and **charms** intended to counteract the affect of such a deadly gaze. See **Eye** (Part 9).

FALUN GONG SYMBOL

The symbol for the philosophy or spiritual practice of Falun Gong is an amalgam of **two** ancient Eastern signs. Two concentric **circles** encompass a central **swastika**, while **four yin-yang** signs and four further swastikas are evenly spaced around it.

Falun Gong itself is a relatively new movement—it was founded as recently as 1992 by Li Hongzhi—although its practices are based on the ancient art of Qi Gong. Falun Gong relies on certain physical movements and meditation techniques to promote health, harmony and the balance of mind, body, and spirit although the Chinese government denounced Falun Gong as a "cult."

"Falun" means "Wheel of Law/Dharma" in Chinese Buddhism, and the **wheel** symbol itself (the "Falon") replicates the energy wheel that adherents of the practice say is located in the center of the body, akin to a **chakra.** This wheel, once "installed" or awakened, turns continuously, when clockwise absorbing energy from the cosmos, or when anticlockwise, getting rid of waste matter from the physical body. Adepts say that meditation and repetition of the set exercises of the Falun Gong discipline result in them actually being able to see the Falun. The Falun Gong emblem also acts as a **mandala** or also as a **Cosmogram**, a miniature schematic of the Universe.

FAROHAR

A version of the winged solar disc, the Farohar is a Zoroastrian symbol whose name means "to choose." The symbol represents some of the philosophical facets of the religion.

The **three** layers of **feathers** on the **wings** represent the three main tenets of the faith;

good thoughts, good words, good deeds. The disc itself symbolizes the **Sun**, and the notion of eternity. The two banners are a reminder of duality (good and evil, **black** and **white**, spirit and matter, male and female) and the need for balance between opposing elements.

The man seeming to sit on the top of the disc represents Zoroaster himself, and serves as a reminder for his followers to live a morally upright life.

FASCES

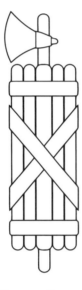

A symbol of Roman Imperial power, the Fasces was originally an axe or an **arrow** with a bundle of **birch** sticks tied around the handle with **red** cords. The numerous sticks represented unity and strength in numbers, but as a symbol of authority, it also implied punishment for those who failed to adhere to the rules. The birch rod itself is synonymous with the idea of punishment, its wood used for the schoolroom canes that inflicted on children in less enlightened times.

The symbol of the Fasces carried great resonance for the Italian people and was revived by Mussolini as the emblem of his political party in the 1930s. Hence, the Latin word for "bundle" became the origin of the word Fascist, which carries far more sinister connotations than a simple collection of sticks.

FEATHER

The Egyptian Goddess of truth, **Ma'at,** has the **ostrich** feather as her attribute. There is a very specific reason for this. Because the ostrich is a flightless **bird**, the design of its feathers is different to those of other birds where one side is larger than the other. The ostrich feather, however, is perfectly balanced and symmetrical, and so is a fitting emblem of justice.

The symbolism of feathers is closely aligned to that of **wings** and birds. They stand for ascendance, flight, communication with the spirit realms and the element of **air**. Shamanistic use of feathers is for all these reasons; the feathers enable the **soul** to become as light as the feather and transcend the boundaries of gravity, time, and space.

Shaman of all nationalities wear feathers as a part of their ritual apparel.

The **eagle** feather is the most valuable of all feathers. In some parts of the world, this feather, synonymous with all the power of the bird, is considered so sacred that only card-carrying Native American tribal members may own them. Eagle feathers that are found in the wrong hands are subject to heavy fines.

The swan's feather appears in the cloaks of druids; because the **swan** is the bird of poetry, its feathers magically confer these powers on the bard.

Used at the end of the **arrow** as a "flight," feathers have a practical as well as symbolic use. Additionally, feathers are a symbol of sacrifice. This is because, when chickens and other birds were ritually slaughtered, all they left behind was a few feathers, fluttering to the ground.

The other major symbolic meaning of the feather associates it with vegetation and with **hair**, primarily because of a similarity in appearance.

FETISH

Although, latterly, the fetish has erotic connotations, the origins of the word are from the French *fetiche* and the Portuguese *fettico*, meaning charm. In sorcery, a fetish is something that is believed to have a spirit of its own, used for magical purposes. It is likely that the first fetish objects were stones of some kind, not necessarily small ones. The **Black Stone** at **Mecca** and the **Stone of Destiny** are good examples of fetish objects whose power, as such, has accumulated over the centuries that people have revered them.

"Lucky" or "unlucky" numbers are fetishes, as are "lucky" or "unlucky" days of the week.

Bodily fluids or parts such as **fingernails** and **teeth** are fetish objects, considered to contain the energy of the creature of origin. Smaller fetish objects were carried in pouches or bags, a practice that continues today in many forms. These fetish or medicine bags should never touch the ground. The reason for this is that contact with the **Earth** is sacrilegious in some way for these empowered objects. It is for exactly the same reason that flags, symbols of national identity, also never touch the ground.

FIRE WHEEL

See **Tomoe**.

FIVE PILLARS OF WISDOM

Islam is conceptualized as a building, which is raised on **five** "pillars." These are: the tenets of the faith, prayer, almsgiving, fasting during the month of **Ramadan**, and the pilgrimage (or Hajj) to **Mecca** (which each adherent of the faith must carry out at least once in his lifetime.)

FLEUR DE LYS

Seen regularly as a heraldic symbol, the stylized **flower**-inspired Fleur de Lys is much older than many people may realize, appearing in Mesopotamian art, on Ancient Egyptian reliefs, and even on Dogon objects.

The literal translation is the "flower of the **lily**" and it is a symbol of purity, being associated with the **dove** and the Virgin Mary. At **Rennes le Chateau,** the Fleur de Lys is a prominent symbol, too, in the Church of Mary Magdalene.

FLOWER OF LIFE

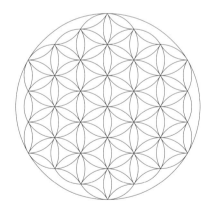

The ubiquity of this beautifully satisfying geometric symbol is astonishing. It appears at the Golden Temple in Amritsar, in a Buddhist Temple at Ajanta, India, in the Louvre and at Ephesus. It has been embroidered onto the robes of Sultans. It can be seen in Cordoba, in Marrakech, in Beijing, the Lebanon, in Egypt, and Japan. It is chiseled into wood in Holland and carved into stone in Scotland and Austria. The oldest example of the Flower of Life is believed to be 2500 years old.

The Flower of Life design is deceptively simple. It consists of a series of evenly spaced interlinking **circles**. As more circles are added, the pattern emerges. The design has been favored by religions, architects, and scientists alike.

Despite the seeming simplicity of the design, hidden within it are subtle complexities that have such a profound meaning for some that they believe the Flower of Life depicts the fundamental forms of time and space.

The most obvious symbols inherent within the Flower of Life are the **circle**, the hexagon or **six-pointed star**, and the **vesica piscis**. Furthermore, three intersecting circles alone form a Borromean Ring which is also known as the **Tripod of Life** symbol.

Some important symbolic sequences can be derived from many-circled versions of the design, for example **Metatron's Cube** can be derived from the Flower of Life, and the **five Platonic solids** can then be "extracted" from

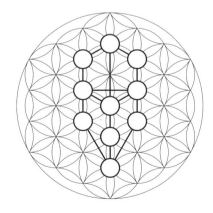

Flower of Life showing Kabbalistic tree of life

THE ELEMENT ENCYCLOPEDIA OF SECRET SIGNS AND SYMBOLS

Metatron's Cube. As if these fundamental principles of sacred geometry were not enough, the **Kabbalistic tree of life** can be discerned within the Flower of Life, as can the **Seed of Life**.

For many, the Flower of Life is an object of mystery which may well unlock the secrets of the Universe, since they believe that it contains a record of information about all living things. The Flower of Life is used as a focus both for study and meditation.

FORKED CROSS

See **Y of Pythagoras**.

FRUIT OF LIFE

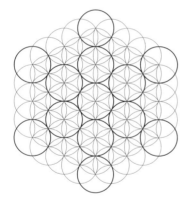

The **Flower of Life** pattern, if constructed of at least **five circles** down and across, holds another symbol within it. This is the Fruit of Life, formed from a **six-rayed star** of five circles in all directions. There are **13** circles in total. This **star** shape then gives the foundation for the construction of **Metatron's Cube**, from which, in turn, the **five Platonic solids** can be made.

FU

In China, the Fu is an ancient symbol of good luck, and is still popularly used in **talismans** and charms. The word Fu sounds like the word for **bat**; so, by association, bats are auspicious, too, especially if they are **five** in number. The actual ideogram of Fu shows a God blessing a farm, which is an analogy for the Earth; the farm is split into **four** parts, the four parts resembling the four directions and the four elements.

FURKA

See **Y of Pythagoras**.

GAMMADION

The gammadion is a form of **swastika**, but with shorter arms, and is so-called because it is constructed from **four** Greek "gamma" letters. This sign was widespread, appearing across Europe and through to India. Like the swastika, it is a solar symbol, and the four arms of the symbol represent all the universal objects and concepts that come in groups of four: the directions, the seasons, the elements, the solstices, and the equinoxes.

FOOD MAGIC

Every week of the year, on most continents around this planet, millions of people participate in a profoundly magical ritual whereby two very basic everyday foodstuffs, which are available in supermarkets or on stalls pretty much anywhere you care to mention around the world, have a spell cast over them by means of a sacred incantation. The person officiating over this ceremony makes symbolic gestures with his or her **hands** and **arms**. This spellbinding usually takes place in a language very few fully comprehend, a language full of secrets, and as a result these mundane objects are transformed into something as mystical, sacred, and awe-inspiring as anything you could ever imagine.

In addition, this ritual generally takes place in a building whose architecture and design has been informed by knowledge of the directions, shapes, and patterns that link the Heavens with the Earth in an arrangement of the sacred symbols which some say were dictated to man by the very **angels** themselves.

When the Holy Communion of the Roman Catholic Church takes place, the simple ingredients of **bread** and **wine** are transformed, many believe, into the actual **body** and **blood** of the Christ. This is not just a symbolic representation, some say, but a very real and profound belief that underpins the foundations of the religion. By eating this holy, sacred food, imbued with magical intent, the recipient voluntarily absorbs the spirit of the Messiah.

The ritual and perceived reality of this act are inseparable, but bread and wine are not the only sacred foods we absorb as part of our everyday lives. We need food to live, so it comes as no surprise that we have accorded many ingredients with magical powers. Indeed, some of the things we eat every day carry both constituent elements and meanings which go far beyond mere nutrition. Many other foods—**nuts**, **apples**, and other **fruits** and vegetables— are covered in other sections of this book, and this is by no means an exhaustive inventory, but a look at some of the foods, real and mythical, which have become symbols in themselves.

Ambrosia

For the Greeks, Ambrosia was the food of the Gods. Given that it conferred immortality, the **Deities** on Mount Olympus guarded it jealously. As well as ensuring eternal life, Ambrosia could be used as an ointment that could heal any wound. However, for a mortal, eating Ambrosia was a big mistake. Take the story of Tantalus, for example. He was invited to eat with the Gods, and so, presuming that he was accepted as one of them, he ate ambrosia. In the tradition of all good dinner party guests, he decided to return the favor and invited the Gods round to his place. Deciding somewhat sycophantically that they should feast upon all the good things that they had given him, he served up the flesh of his own children, and was banished to Hades.

Chocolate

Long before the discovery of the Americas, the natives of Brazil, Mexico, the West Indies, and South America used the **seeds** of the chocolatl **tree** to make a stimulating drink. These bean-like seeds were cacahuatl, or cocoa. Primarily symbolic of love, chocolate is a sensual food with **aphrodisiac** properties that are due, in part, to association. However, its melting point is the same temperature as blood, a very satisfying sensation.

The botanical name of the plant gives a clue as to its sacred status. Theobroma Cacao means "food of the Gods," from the Greek "Theo," meaning God and "Broma," meaning food.

The beans were so highly valued that the Mayans used them as currency. Possibly the world's first chocoholic, their ruler Montezuma was completely addicted to the beans. He drank them infused in cold **water** with no seasoning. He served this sacred drink in goblets of beaten **gold**, and at the coronation of Montezuma II in 1502 a concoction of chocolate and psilocybin **mushrooms** was served to the guests. This must have been a heady mixture.

Cortés cultivated the plant primarily because of its reputation as an aphrodisiac; this secret was divulged by one of the nineteen young women given to him by Montezuma as a tribute. Perhaps the 2000 chocolatl trees that he consequently planted were testimony to the efficacy of the beans in keeping the ladies satisfied.

By 1550, chocolate factories were operating in Lisbon, Genoa, Marseilles, and other European cities. The recipes became more and more refined. Catherine de Medici slowed down the progress of chocolate for a while because it was so good that she wanted it all to herself. However, although the Church tried to ban many of the foodstuffs that had been discovered in the New World, especially those that were considered as stimulants, their advice was largely ignored and it is possible that this disapproval increased the popularity of this illicit substance. Neither Catherine nor all the forces of the Church could stop the world becoming chocolate coated.

CONTINUED OVERLEAF ...

Today, the form of chocolate has changed so much that Montezuma would probably find it unrecognizable, both in taste and form. However, it is still unrivalled as a token and symbol of love.

Honey

Legislation decrees that all packaged food carry a "best before" date, but this seems to be particularly unnecessary in the case of honey, since jars of the stuff found in the tombs of Egyptian kings several thousand years ago has proved to be perfectly edible even now. It could well be because honey is so long lasting, and because it is used as a preservative, that it is a symbol of immortality and is used in funerary rites. The **bees** that make the honey have their place in the realms of magical creatures accorded with supernatural powers, but more of that in the **fauna** section. The Promised Land is said to "flow with **milk** and honey" as being the very best that the Gods can offer.

The sweetness of honey is believed to confer gifts of learning and poetry. We'll never know if the story that Pythagoras existed on honey alone is true, but the fact that the rumor exists is in accord with his God-like status. As well as being edible and fermentable, honey has healing and antiseptic qualities, and a dollop of honey smeared onto a wound will soon draw out any impurities and speed the healing process.

Honey is said to be an aphrodisiac and to encourage fertility and virility, wealth and abundance, and is a symbol of the **Sun**, partly because of the flowers from which it is made but also because of its **color.**

Manna

When the Children of Israel were struggling to survive in the wilderness, manna appeared, miraculously, overnight, and so they could eat. Precisely what manna was—or is—is debatable. Some believe it might be a kind of fungus, others believe that it might be sap or resin exuded from the **tamarisk tree.** The symbolic meaning of manna is of something provided freely by the Universe or by God and is the ultimate reminder that we have everything we need. Manna is also associated with the Bread of Life or the Eucharist.

Mead

Like honey, mead also carries the gift of immortality. The Celts believed it was the favored drink of the Gods in the Otherworld. Mead is a sacred drink in Africa, too, where it is believed that drinking the stuff will make you more knowledgeable. Worth a try! Mead is very simple to make—it's simply honey mixed with water and allowed to ferment—and this process of fermentation is akin to a magical process in itself, which is akin to transmutation in **alchemy.**

Milk

Given that milk is the first food, it's not surprising that it is associated with many stories of the Creation, and is a symbol of divinity. Amrita, or **Soma**, the absolute nectar of life for Hindus and the equivalent of **Ambrosia**, was created as a cosmic **sea** of milk was churned. The curds that were created by this epic stirring formed the Earth, the Universe, and the stars. Along with **honey**, there is an abundance of milk in the Promised Land, and Indian myths tell of a magical milk tree in Heaven. Because of its color and its association with the feminine, milk is a symbol of the **Moon**.

The main food source for milk for us human beings (once we're weaned) is the **cow**. The cow is sacred in India because during times of famine it made far more sense to keep the animal alive for its milk rather than slaughter and eat it purely for its meat, so all parts of the cow are accorded sacred status and are ruled over by one or other of the Gods or Goddesses.

In the hidden symbolic language of alchemy, the **Philosopher's Stone** is sometimes called the Virgin's Milk.

Nectar

Nectar is often referred to as **ambrosia**, but has secrets of its own to tell. Flowers create it, and its scent attracts the **bees**, which then transform the nectar into honey. Seemingly insignificant, nectar is nevertheless a very magical ingredient, created from flowers, sunshine, and bees working together in a collective consciousness known as the "hive mind" in an environment which itself is constructed from one of the key shapes in **sacred geometry**, the **hexagon**.

Soma

Like the Greek Olympians, the Indian deities had a type of food, like **ambrosia**, that ensured their immortality. This was Soma, or Amrita. Whereas dire consequences befell any mortal that dared to partake of ambrosia, the Indian Gods were more generous with their Soma, and any mortal that ate it was immediately given immortality and access to Heaven. The ancient Indian Vedic scriptures, the Ramayana, tell the story of Rama, an epic hero, the perfect man. Rama was born after his father was visited by an **angel**. This angel brought with him some magical food. Eating this Soma meant that Rama's father was able to sire offspring that were the human incarnations of the God, **Vishnu**.

CONTINUED OVERLEAF ...

Wine

The symbolic meanings of wine are generally attached to the red variety; it seems that a nice dry white or a sweet rose carries no hidden mystery. Here are some things to think about next time you open a nice bottle of claret.

The red color means that wine is often linked to **blood**, particularly since the wine is the "blood" of the grape. Because it looks like blood, wine is often used in rituals where blood would otherwise be called for, and because ceremonial wine is often drunk from a shared **chalice**, it is seen, like **bread**, as a unifying principle. Wine is male, and bread is female. As a partner to bread in the ritual of the Eucharist, the consecrated wine is transformed into the blood of the Christ, a reminder of both sacrifice and immortal life, and it's this transformative power that accords wine with much of its mystique. When the water is turned into wine in the story of the Marriage at Cana, what is really being shown here is the transformation of the mundane into the magical, the Earthly into the Heavenly. It is this magical process of fermentation at work that explains why wine is associated with the **Bacchus/Dionysus**, and the intoxicating power of wine is symbolic of divine possession.

The phrase, "In Vino Veritas" links wine to the truth and is a reminder that those intoxicated by perhaps a little too much of that nice claret will be more likely to speak the truth than most, which can be good or bad, depending on the circumstances.

Gar

See **Gungnir.**

Ghanta

See **Drilbu.**

Globus Cruciger

This is the globe surmounted by a **cross**, which is one of the Christian symbols of authority, and its symbolism is obvious. The orb represents the **Earth**, and the Cross, that major symbol of the faith, is Christ's supremacy over it.

The Globus Cruciger is often depicted as an actual object but was also used purely as a symbol on Roman coins from the time when Christianity became the prominent religion, round about the fifth century AD. Prior to this, the lone orb had been used in the same way, to imply authority. The addition of the cross brought the well-known emblem into the Christian domain. In Britain, the Globus Cruciger appears as a physical object that is used during the coronation of the monarch. It is called the Orb and is part of the Royal Jewels.

Goat of Mendes

Also called the Sigil of **Baphomet** or the Sabbatic **Goat**, this sinister-looking symbol features an inverted **pentagram** containing the head of a goat, the upward V of the **star** framing the **horns**. This symbol has become an icon of modern occultism, believed to be the very representation of the Devil himself, which was exacerbated when Anton La Vey adopted it in the 1960s for his Church of Satan.

Sometimes the symbol is encircled with a double ring, containing the Hebrew letters spelling "**Leviathan,**" the mythical sea monster that features in the Old Testament.

Gopura

The ornately elaborate gateway into the Hindu temples, the Gopura carry the same significance as the Japanese **Torii**, marking a transition between the world of matter and the world of spirit.

Gray Wolf

Otherwise known as Lupus Mettalorum, in **alchemy** antimony is disguised as the Gray Wolf. This Gray Wolf is the penultimate

Signs and symbols of Freemasonry

Although many of the entries in this encyclopedia have an association with Freemasonry, many secret signs and sacred symbols belong specifically to this discipline, hence the need for a separate entry dedicated to the Craft.

The Catholic Encyclopedia describes Freemasonry as

a system of morality veiled in allegory and illustrated with symbols.

Many of the signs and symbols associated with this ancient brotherhood are necessarily to do with building and architecture, and the instruments of these disciplines are used to carry analogies. One of the central tenets of Freemasonry, however, is that there should be as little dogma as possible, and so the meanings of many of the associated symbols are deliberately oblique and can remain open to personal interpretation.

1. *Acacia*

Represents the idea of initiation, and is also used in Masonic funerals as a symbol of rebirth. The martyred master mason who designed the **Temple of Solomon** at Jerusalem, **Hiram Abiff**, had his burial place marked with an acacia branch. See **Acacia** in Part 4.

2. *Blazing star*

Freemasons give this name to the **Pentagram**. Freemasons, like Pythagoras, regard the number **5** as sacred.

3. *Column*

Many of the symbols within Freemasonry take their inspiration from the Temple of Solomon, the first temple in Jerusalem.

The structure of the Masonic Hall generally has two columns at either side of its main door that relate to the original columns set by the architect, Hiram, in the porch of the temple. These original columns were made of brass or **bronze**. The pillars are known by their Hebrew names and are also referred to in the **Kabbalah**; on the right is Jachin (meaning stability) and the left is Boaz (meaning strength). The columns also have a male/female polarity, Jachin often painted **red** to symbolize the **Sun** and fiery qualities of the active male principle, and the female Boaz painted **white** for the **Moon** and the passive feminine virtues. In rites, the columns are used to denote the grade of mason. Apprentices stand before the red column, Masons stand in front of the white column, and the Master Masons in the central space between the two.

4. Compasses

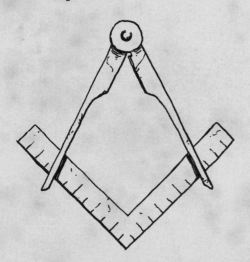

One of the foremost symbols within Freemasonry, the compasses combine with the **Masons Square**. The letter **G** might be incorporated into the design, especially in older representations, and other elements might be added; a Sun and Moon, for example.

Although Freemasons prefer to leave many of their associated symbols open to interpretation, we can make some assumptions about this particular emblem simply by looking at its form and by bearing in mind how the tools are used.

Both the compass and the **square** are mathematical tools, used for precise measurements in disciplines that can leave no room for error: building, construction, and architecture. There is a natural symbiosis between these tools, since the **circle** is used to form the square, and the square can be used to give form to the circle; this is called squaring the circle and is a fundamental rule applied to geometry, sacred or otherwise. Any instruments used for measuring must, ergo, be symbols of judgement and definition.

Further, in this Masonic pairing, the feminine circle (which it is the sacred task of the compasses to create) forms a perfect union with the masculine square; therefore the spiritual combines with the material, Earth with Heaven. Another aspect of the compasses and the square delves even further into the symbolism of the circle and the square, with the former representing space and the latter, time. The mason, as "architect," rules over all these aspects and dimensions.

CONTINUED OVERLEAF …

Because they are used to draw a perfect circle, the compasses themselves have significance as a tool used by God as the "architect" of the Universe. This idea is represented perfectly in the William Blake painting *The Ancient of Days Measuring Time* in which God stretches toward Earth, compasses in hand, with the golden disc of the Sun behind him.

Compasses work by turning on a central axle or pivot. This means that they are also a symbol of the **Axis Mundi**, of the circular nature of time, and of the **ouroboros**, the **serpent** which continually swallows its own tail.

4a. The square

There's a common phrase, "on the square" or "on the level." This means to be open, honest, proper, and above board, and springs directly from Masonic practice and ritual.

All the symbolism of the square and of the number 4 is applicable to this tool; it stands for solidity, respect, security.

4b. The angle of the compass

Accounts differ as to whether the angle of the compass carries any special significance. The Masonic Compass is certainly drawn in different degrees. Some say that this represents the different degrees within Masonry, but again this is a matter for the inner sanctum of Masons.

4c. The triangle

Both the square and the compasses form a triangle, a symbol both of stability and of the spirit world.

4d. The six-pointed star

Hidden within the square and compasses symbol is another magical sign, the **Seal of Solomon**, the **hexagram** or six-pointed star. This can be made if a line is drawn across the open point of the square and compasses. The seal is formed of two interlocking triangles and is one of the most ancient and universal magical symbols, also used in **alchemy**. Among other meanings, this star can be interpreted to mean "as above, so below."

4e. The letter G

This does not always feature in the symbol of the compass and the square, and when it does there is ambivalence as to its meaning. Some say that it stands for God, others argue Geometry. Other interpretations including the notion that the G stands for Generation or possibly Government or even the **Great Bear**, the star that signifies the celestial pole or center, not only a physical center but a philosophical one. However, Masons agree that there is no definitive answer.

5. Hiram Abiff

The legend of Hiram Abiff is the central core and inspiration for Freemasons. Hiram was a Master Mason who specialized in metalwork, and was one of the prime designers of the Temple of Solomon in Jerusalem. Here is the legend.

After the temple was completed, three of the other workers decided that they wanted to extract the secrets from Hiram that would qualify them to be Master Masons. They positioned themselves at the doors of the temple and individually demanded to know these secrets. Hiram refused each one in turn, telling them that the knowledge they desired could be gained only by experience. The three turned on Hiram and killed him; one struck a blow to his **throat** with a **rule**, the next hit him on the **chest** with an **iron** measuring square, and the third finished the job by hitting him on the forehead with a **hammer**. Full of remorse for the crime that they quickly realized was a fruitless murder, the "three ruffians," as they came to be called, buried Hiram and placed an **acacia tree** over his grave.

However, although Hiram was effectively dead, his memory lives on and so effectively he is reborn. The **initiation** of the grade of Master Mason re-enacts the ritual of the death of Hiram. In as much as there are any hard and fast rules which apply to the symbolism inherent within Freemasonry, the three blows symbolize three different kinds of death: the death of the body (the blow to the throat) the death of the feelings (the strike on the chest) and the death of the mind (the blow to the forehead). Thus, the would-be Master Mason leaves his old self behind, the initiatory process symbolizing his rebirth into the higher moral values that were held by Hiram, of integrity, knowledge, and detachment. In other words, the mason is reborn as a better individual, having risen above the ignorance, hypocrisy, and envy personalized by his murderers.

6. Hammer and chisel

The hammer, in use at Masonic meetings, is not used simply to gain the attention of the gathering. Effectively, it represents the powers of the intellect that drive the thoughts and the will of the individual. At

CONTINUED OVERLEAF ...

Lodge meetings, the hammer is the symbol of the authority of the Worshipful Master who presides over the meeting.

The chisel is only useful if it is directed by the will of the hammer, and so represents the intellect and finer discernment.

7. *Level and plumbline*

Again, the level and the plumbline attached to it are inseparable items of practical building equipment that serve a deeper symbolic meaning within Freemasonry. The level comprises a set square, from the center of which hangs the plumbline. The plumbline is used to define both the vertical and horizontal lines, so it takes on the symbolism of the **cross**, too. The vertical level symbolizes the apprentice, and the horizontal, the degree of Fellowcraft.

It is also worth bearing in mind the philosophical meanings of the word "level," meaning steady and honest, as well as its practical application as a tool. These two meanings are inextricably linked from the actual symbol of the tool itself.

8. *Rule*

Correct measurements, defined by the rule, are essential to the physical construction of a building, and ensure that the design concept will work in the real world. Also of significance are the degrees of measurement that are depicted on the actual ruler itself; in the imperial measurements, these degrees of 12 and 24 correspond to the daily cycle of the Sun. In this sense, the rule represents the macrocosm. The rule also keeps everything in order, and acts as a guide.

9. *Triangle*

To Freemasons, the triangle symbolizes the Greek capital A, which they call the "shining Delta." The triangle also indicates the meanings of things in triplicate, such as "right thinking, right speaking, and right doing." On a microcosmic scale, the base of the triangle represents duration, and the two sides symbolize the qualities of light and darkness, male and female, etc. Possibly the most famous symbolic use of the Masonic triangle—which traditionally has an angle of 36 degrees at the apex and two angles of 72 degrees at the base—is the one that includes a **blazing star** and also a pentagram as seen on the **Seal of the United States** and on the **United States Dollar.**

10. *Tracing board or trestle board*

As with many of the symbols inherent within Freemasonry, the tracing board itself is a symbolic representation of an important piece of practical equipment used in masonry.

The tracing, or trestle, board has its origins in the flat piece of wood or cloth that was used as a drawing board by the Master Mason, on which he sketched the diagrams, schemes and measurements needed for the building work in question. Initially represented as a piece of cloth which was rolled out on the floor at the beginning of a Masonic meeting, the tracing board is now a piece of wood that contains the signs and symbols relevant to the Brothers within their degrees of Masonic hierarchy. The boards are elaborate works of art, with the symbols woven into the whole in a pictorial, allegorical way. The symbols that are already mentioned in this section all take their place. The seemingly simple builders' tools serve to remind the initiate of their more esoteric spiritual meanings that amount to the betterment of the person and personal enlightenment.

There are hundreds, if not thousands, of different sorts of tracing boards, all usually the work of individual artists. Different tracing boards show the different degrees of the Craft.

As well as showing pictures of the tools involved with practical masonry, tracing boards might tell the story of Hiram Abiff's murder or perhaps show pictures of the ritual re-enactment of this crime as part of initiation ceremonies. Tracing boards also represent features of the actual temple: the pillars, the **checkerboard floor**, the porch with its two columns.

11. *Masonic apron*

The humble apron of the working Mason is elevated to almost religious status by the Freemasons. Generally made of leather, the way the apron is worn symbolizes the status of its wearer, with the bib worn up for the apprentice, or down by superior grades. Wearing the apron is representative of work and the necessity to be busy and industrious, and also of the **fig leaves** worn by Adam and Eve; as such the apron preserves the modesty of the wearer. Like the tracing board, the Masonic Apron has the signs and symbols of the Craft embroidered on it.

One of the most famous of the many Masonic aprons is that which belonged to

CONTINUED OVERLEAF ...

George Washington. Given to him in 1784 by the Marquis de Lafeyette whose wife embroidered the apron, it displays many Masonic symbols. Nothing is left to chance; the border colors of red, white, and blue are not only the national colors of France but also of the USA. Other symbols on this historic apron include:

- **the All Seeing Eye**—watchfulness, the Supreme Being;
- **rays**—show the power of the Supreme Being to reach inside the hearts of men;
- **rainbow**—symbolic of the arch of Solomons Temple that is supported by the two pillars, Jachim and Boaz;
- **Moon**—the female principle;
- **globes** on top of pillars—peace and plenty;
- **the three tapers**—symbolize the three stages of the Sun; rising in the East, in the Southern sky at noon, and setting in the West;
- **trowel**—symbolic of spreading love and affection, the "cement" that binds the Brothers of Freemasonry;
- **five-pointed star**—represents friendship;
- **checkered pavement**—often a feature of temples and again is based on the floor of Solomon's original temple and represents the duality of opposites, male and female, and so on;
- **steps**—represent the degrees of masonry;
- **coffin**—represents death and therefore rebirth and is a recurrent motif in Freemasonry;
- **skull and cross bones**—symbols of mortality but also of rebirth;
- **acacia**;
- **compasses;**
- **the square and level**;
- **the ark**—safety and refuge;
- **tassel and knot**—the ties that bind the Brothers;
- **the Sun**—the Light of God, the male principle;
- **sword and heart**—symbolic of justice being done; nothing can be hidden from the eyes of the Great Architect;
- **seven six-pointed stars**—here, seven stands for the seven liberal arts and sciences;
- **beehive**—a symbol of industry and a reminder that man should be rational and industrious at the same time.

12. 47th Problem of Euclid, also known as the *Bride's Chair*

This mathematical theorem has been called one of the foundations of Freemasonry. It is called the 47th Problem for no more esoteric reason than Euclid published a book of theorems, of which this was number 47.

Its significance within Freemasonry is somewhat nebulous. However, the beginnings of the Fellowship in architecture and construction, and the usefulness of the 47th Problem as a measuring device, might give us the answer. The design features in Masonic regalia including lodge decorations and Masonic "jewels."

The 47th Problem is also called the **Egyptian string trick**, and a practical demonstration in making of the shape illustrates its efficacy perfectly. Take a piece of string and tie 12 knots at exact intervals along the string. Then join the ends of the string, again making sure that the knots are evenly spaced. Hammer a stick into the ground. Put one of the knots over the stick. Stretch three divisions of knots and sink another stick into the ground at the point of the third knot. Then take a third stick and skewer it into the ground at the point where a fourth knot falls. This gives a triangle in the proportions of three, four and five, and further, the lines of the string can be extrapolated to make three squares of 9 parts, 16 parts, and 25 parts.

This simple device enabled the Egyptians to remeasure their fields after the Nile flooded every few years, washing away the boundary markers. The Egyptian string trick results in a perfect right angle, an essential device in the construction of a building, and as essential today as it was thousands of years ago,

although methods of constructing the angle may have changed. Pythagoras traveled to Egypt and may have discovered it there, or he may have discovered it alone. Whatever the case, it is this geometrical solution that caused him to shout "Eureka." In addition, it is said that 100 **bulls** were sacrificed in honor of the importance of this seemingly simple discovery, indubitably one of the secrets that was part of the hidden knowledge of the Master Mason; it may well have been one of the pieces of information for which Hiram Abiff was murdered.

13. *Ashlar*

In material terms, ashlar is the rough **stone** that comes straight from the quarry. In philosophical terms, to the Freemason, ashlar symbolizes the rough and imperfect state of man before he is rendered smooth and perfect in his ideally realized state. It relates to the alchemical idea of base matter that can be perfected through intellectual and spiritual realization.

14. *Point within the circle*

A seemingly simple symbol, the circle with a dot at its very center is a sign of birth and resurrection dating back to Egyptian times when it was used as an

CONTINUED OVERLEAF ...

emblem of the Sun God, **Ra**. The symbol is associated particularly with the days of St. John the Baptist and St. John the Evangelist, which fall on the summer and winter solstices respectively.

15. *The temple floor*

Although it is stated time and time again that the symbols inherent within Freemasonry are nondogmatic and are as such open to interpretation, it is safe to say that the features of the actual temple form an important part of the secret signs of the Craft. The floor of the temple is no exception.

It is constructed of checkered tiles of black and white. These colors represent the duality of opposites; night and day, dark and light, male and female, fire and water, Earth and air, and all the other manifestations of this concept. In Ancient Egypt, the colors were used as a reminder of the need to unify spirit and matter.

16. *GAOTU*

Abbreviated words, initials and acronyms form a large part of Masonic ritual, since the pronunciation of certain words is believed to dilute their power and abbreviations are used instead. The abbreviation of GAOTU stands for Great Architect of the Universe, which in turn refers to God. Here there is a parallel to the nature of God as the builder or designer of the **macrocosm**, and the role of the Freemason as the designer of the **microcosm**.

stage in the making of the **Philosopher's Stone**, so in terms of the spiritual and psychological development of man it symbolizes the condition that brings him very close to the enlightenment he seeks; however, both physically and metaphorically speaking, the final stage of making **lead** into **gold** is yet to come, so the gray wolf can symbolize either success or failure.

GREAT SEAL OF THE UNITED STATES OF AMERICA

See **United States dollar bill**.

GREEN MAN

The symbol of the Green Man could be said to lurk in the subconscious minds of anyone with an affinity for leafy, wooded, and bosky places, although the term was not coined in the UK until the 1930s. Such a character—latterly interpreted as being the raw spirit of Nature—exists not only in the British Isles but in India, Asia, and Arabic countries too.

With a head seemingly constructed of leaves and **vines**, the Green Man is sometimes depicted as human, and sometimes as an animal. Despite his popularity as a garden ornament and its proliferation in garden centers, one of the oldest Green Man symbols discovered thus far is a piece of stonework on an Irish obelisk that dates back to 300 BC. Irish myth features a character called a Derg Corra, meaning "man in the tree," and it may well be the case that he and the Green Man

are one and the same. See Section 6, "Sacred Geometry and Places of Pilgrimage," for an example of the Green Man made into a living **maze**.

GUNGNIR

This is the magical weapon known as Odin's Spear or Javelin. Like **Mjolnir**, the magical hammer belonging to Odin, Gungnir—whose name means "The Unwavering One"—has two very practical qualities that render it an essential tool in the arsenal of the powerful thunder god; it always hit its mark, and it always returns, like a boomerang, back to the thrower. As well as being a sacred object, there is a runic symbol, Gar, that also represents the Gungnir.

HALO

The halo, aureole, or aura all refer to an emanation of light, generally depicted appearing around the head. The halo is a symbol of spiritual sanctity or of divine grace, used in Christian iconography, for example, in pictures of saints. Although the halo is the sign that a person is blessed by the Divine, some people claim that they can actually see this phenomenon, and that the many **colors** of the aura that surrounds the entire body can be used as a diagnostic tool.

HAND OF FATIMA

Also known as the Khamsa, the Hand of Fatima is named for Fatima Zahra, the daughter of Mohammed. It is a very ancient symbol, often used as a **talisman**, and in the Middle East it is ubiquitous, appearing in houses, shops, in taxis, and hotels. The hand is not really shaped like a normal human hand, but has two balanced **thumbs** and no little **finger**. The **eye** in its palm wards off the evil eye, so the Hand of Fatima is a double symbol of protection since the **palm**, held up, is a forbidding gesture. Khamsa actually means **"five"** and has relevance for both Muslims and Jews. Peace activists have adopted the Hand of Fatima in recent years; a reminder that the two faiths have many commonly shared beliefs.

HAND OF GLORY

If magical charms have more efficacy the harder they are to construct or come by, then the Hand of Glory must be powerful indeed. Noticeably absent from New Age emporia, the Hand of Glory was popular with thieves during the sixteenth century. It was a light, or **candle**, made from the severed **hand** of a hanged convict. After this grisly relic was mummified by being embalmed in oils and special **herbs**, it was turned into a candle using tallow also made from a hanged corpse.

The Hand of Glory was the favored tool of thieves because, once alight, it was said to render household members unconscious. Therefore the thief could go about his nefarious activities undisturbed.

HEX SYMBOLS

In the south-eastern part of Pennsylvania lives a population of European settlers, primarily from the Rhine area. These people come from different religious communities including Lutheran, Moravian, Quakers, Mennonites, and others. Some of these

groups, despite their deeply held religious beliefs, are united by one thing; a thriving belief in witchcraft, also known as Hexerie, from the German, Hexen, meaning "witch."

Despite their godliness, these are a very superstitious people. One of the popularly held beliefs is that a **cross**, drawn on the door-latch, will prevent the Devil from entering the house.

There is a whole series of magical protective symbols that the community paint or carve onto the sides of their barns or houses. Called Hex Signs or Barn Signs, these magic symbols are used for a variety of reasons, including averting evil, bringing fertility and prosperity, promoting health, and control of the weather. Many of these signs, which are individually designed, become closely inter-linked with a specific family, akin to a coat of arms, and are even tooled into the leather covers of the family bibles.

These hex symbols are beautifully decorative and use universally familiar symbols in their design, including **hearts** for love, **stars** for good luck, **oak** leaves and **acorns** for strength and growth. They also use the image of a **bird** called a distelfink, a type of finch that lines its nest with thistledown. This bird is particularly associated with good fortune. The "double distelfink" brings double the luck.

HEXAGRAM

See **Seal of Solomon** and **I Ching**.

HOLY GRAIL

To say that something is like searching for the Holy Grail implies that the search is for a highly treasured and elusive object that might never be found. If there is a genuine Holy Grail, like the **Philosopher's Stone**, it has retained its hard-to-get status.

The Holy Grail legend has direct links with two mystical pre-Christian items; the magical **cauldron** of the Celtic Gods that never emptied and kept everyone satisfied, and the magical **chalice** that represents spiritual authority and kingship. However, received information about an actual physical Holy Grail says that it is either the cup that Christ drank from at the Last Supper or the vessel that caught his blood during his cruci-fixion. The sacred vessel subsequently went missing.

There is a rumor that a fragment of the true Holy Grail, known as the Nanteos Cup, is secreted somewhere in the United Kingdom, specifically in Wales. The cup, made of olive-wood, is reputed to have been brought to Glastonbury by Joseph of Arimethea, where it was looked after by the monks who lived at the Abbey. The Dissolution of the Monasteries in the sixteenth century, in which monasteries were abolished and their valuable property

HERALDRY

❖

The symbols and signs of heraldry act as a sort of historical shorthand, encoding the attributes of the families to whom the heraldic crests belong. The various coats of arms, still in use today, originated in the need to be able to identify opposing armies and single combatants. This necessity dates back to the time of hand-to-hand combat, almost 1000 years ago, although soldiers of much earlier times painted images on their shields that held significance for them, personally, as well as being a sign of identity. Although the blazes, escutcheons, badges, mottos, and crests may at first appear to be a dense forest of impenetrable symbols, their secrets can be interpreted easily. This entry does not pretend to be an exhaustive analysis of the elaborate heraldic codes, but gives a general overview of some of the most commonly used emblems.

The Great Seal of the United States of America

The Great Seal that is featured on the **United States dollar bill** contains many heraldic attributes. Here are some features to look out for.

1. SHAPE—THE SHIELD VERSUS THE LOZENGE

Since women didn't go to war, women's heraldic designs are depicted on a lozenge-shaped framework (which looks like a diamond tipped onto one point), as opposed to the shield of the male. The lozenge itself, suggestive of the **vesica piscis**, is a feminine symbol. Although the shield shapes vary, the difference between the two shapes is easily recognizable. Similarly, members of the noncombative clergy use the lozenge or oval shape.

2. COLOR

The colors used within heraldry are called tinctures. There are also fields of patterns known as Furs, the most common of which is called "**ermine,**" and resembles the fur of the ermine **stoat**; the other is called "vair" and comes from a variegated gray-blue colored squirrel. The names of the colors are different, too, retaining their archaic (primarily French) origins.

Gold = Or
Silver = Argent
Red = Gules
Blue = Azure
Purple = Purpure
Green = Vert
Black = Sable

In order that they may remain as clear and visible as possible, a color is rarely laid on top of another color, and the same rule applies to the metallics.

3. DIVISIONS

The shield, or lozenge, can be divided in a number of ways. Split in half horizontally it is called "party per fess." Vertically, it becomes "party per pale." When it is divided diagonally from left to right, it is "party per bend." The opposite direction gives "party per sinister." The "field" of the lozenge or shield can also be split with a **saltire** cross, or a "normal" one. It can be divided by a chevron, or into three with a Y-shape. There are other variations; lines can also be wavy or curved.

4. CHARGES

A charge is, effectively, a picture. It can be any object, a symbol, an **animal**, a **plant**. Exotic creatures have a large part to play in heraldry; **unicorns** and **dragons** join their more realistic counterparts, **boars, lions, eagles**. The symbolism of these creatures is explored elsewhere in this book, but there may also be a specific link belonging to a family coat of arms, which will have passed into the annals of the family history. The Fleur de Lys has its place as the symbol of the French ruling classes, for example.

5. CREST

This is the element that rests on top of the emblem, effectively crowning it. It tends to appear above the shield, and is the symbolic counterpart of the plume of **feathers** that knights once wore on their helmets as a sign of distinction and recognition. Because women did not have any occasion to wear a helmet, then the lozenge generally has no crest.

6. MOTTOES

This is a phrase that describes the bearer of the heraldic emblem. It acts as a sort of historic mission statement; the name of

CONTINUED OVERLEAF ...

the family might be used in the motto as a pun or play on words. The motto can be in any language although Latin and French are possibly the most popular.

7. SUPPORTERS

The shield or lozenge is sometimes supported, generally by animals that stand upright and appear to hold the shield. Again, these creatures bear a relevance to the owner of the heraldic device.

Other heraldic symbols

Symbols used within heraldic devices generally are concise shorthand for the qualities of its owner, and the individual

meaning can be found in other parts of this book. The **lion**, for example, signifies valor, the **fox**, a wily intelligence.

Heraldic devices have meanings of their own; the "mullet," for example, is not a **fish**, but a **star** that denotes the third son. Other curiosities include the Bezant, or gold coin, meaning that the owner can be entrusted with treasure; the escutcheon, a small shield that shows a claim to, or descent from, royalty; a talbot is a hunting hound. A martlet is a symbol of a small **bird** with no feet, the mark of the fourth son who will have to rely on his own resources since he will not be able to rely on an inheritance. The stirrup signifies action.

seized by the Crown, meant that the sacred relic had to be removed. It allegedly ended up at Nanteos Mansion near Aberystwyth. Although it is now just a small fragment of wood, **water** drunk from it is claimed to have healing powers. Sadly, this marvelous story currently has no forensic evidence to support it and so the Holy Grail remains true to its symbolic meaning, tantalizingly beyond our grasp, for the time being at least.

The Grail Legends of the Arthurian Tales also symbolize the quest for something beyond reach. The knights, galvanized into action to find this object of desire, soon realize that they are seeking something much more than a cup; given that the shape of the grail is a feminine symbol and a powerful emblem of the spirit, according to Jung it symbolizes "the inner wholeness for which men have always been searching." As such, the Holy Grail has marked parallels with the **Philosopher's Stone** of the Alchemists, and an equally elusive nature.

HORIZONTAL LINE

See **First signs: Horizontal line**.

HORNED SHAMAN

This symbol has a deep resonance for many, and was first discovered in the cave paintings of Ariege in France. These paintings date back to 10,000 BC. The figure may be the precursor to **Cernunnos** and other antlered deities. The horned shaman is also called the Dancing Sorcerer, said to represent a shaman performing a ritual ceremony. However, this theory cannot be proven conclusively.

HORNS OF ODIN

Norse legends tell of a magical **mead** that was brewed from the blood of a wise God, Kvasir; to drink this mead would be to benefit from the wisdom of the God. **Odin** managed to find this drink, and the triple **horns** represent the three draughts that he drank.

The horn itself is both a masculine and phallic symbol, but because it can be used as a container, it encompasses the female aspect, too. The triple horn appears in stone carvings, over the heads of warriors, implying rewards in Valhalla, the Hall of Slain Warriors that is the home of Odin.

Today, the symbol is used as a sign of identity by followers of the Asatru faith. Asatru is a relatively modern religion that acknowledges the much more ancient pre-Christian Norse beliefs.

HORSESHOE

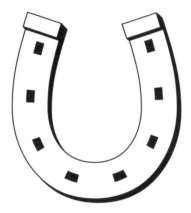

The horseshoe has acquired symbolic significance not because of its function, but because of its shape and the **metal** used to make it. It is shaped like the **arc**, one of the first sacred symbols that represents the vault of the Heavens. When it is "upside down" it is also shaped like the last letter of the Greek alphabet, the Omega.

Flip the horseshoe the other way up, however, and it resembles the crescent **Moon**, therefore invoking the protection of the Moon Goddess. The **iron** that the horseshoe is made from further enhances this protective quality. Iron is a protective metal, which evil entities will go out of their way to avoid. The horseshoe also looks like the **yoni**, further strengthening its links with the Goddess.

The horseshoe is a well-known good-luck symbol and appears on greetings cards, wedding souvenirs, and the like. People nail them up over doorways for the same reason,

although there is some controversy as to which way up the horseshoe should go. One school of thought says that it should rest on its curved end to hold in the luck, which, if the horseshoe were reversed, would pour away. However, pre-Christian superstition says that the horseshoe should be positioned so that it looks like the **sky**, and also like the yoni.

HOURGLASS

The function of the hourglass is to mark the passing of time, as sand trickles through the narrow waist in the middle of the transparent glass container that is the same shape as a **figure of eight**. Therefore, the hourglass is often used as a motif to show the inevitability of death.

However, the shape of the hourglass, as well as being a visual symbol and a word used to describe the figure of a shapely woman, is a lemniscate, or **infinity sign**. This indicates eternity. That the hourglass can be turned upside down to start the cycle all over again makes it an optimistic symbol of rebirth.

I Ching

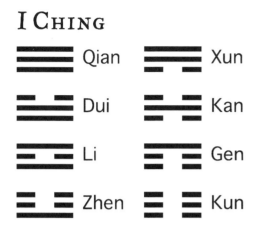

Qian   Xun

Dui   Kan

Li   Gen

Zhen   Kun

The I Ching is an ancient Chinese system of philosophical divination, possibly dating back to the eighth century BC, which is still in use today.

The I Ching, or Book of Changes, was the only book that escaped destruction when all the Chinese philosophical works were burned in the third century BC. Either dried **yarrow** stalks or special coins, usually with square holes in the center, plus knowledge and a fair sprinkling of intuition, are the tools of the I Ching.

The basis of the system is just two simple lines, one continuous, one broken. The most profound symbols are usually the simplest, and these two lines encompass the universal source of all things, also known as the tau (as in Taoism).

The unbroken line represents all aspects of the positive; male, **Sun**, fire, heat, action, odd numbers, **yang**. The broken line represents the opposites.

These lines combine to make **64** possible combinations.

The lines also form a set of **eight** trigrams that represent the elements of **air, water, fire**, and **earth**, with the four sub-elements of breath, sea, thunderbolt, and mountain.

The interpretations of the I Ching are beautifully oblique; the philosophy behind this system is about finding balance. Both the flags of Vietman and of South Korea feature trigrams from the I Ching.

Icelandic Stave Symbols

Early Icelandic grimoires (magical texts full of spells and occult information) contain long lists of curious, angular-looking symbols, all intended for a specific purpose. Their origins go back to the ancient rune system, with a sprinkling of later medieval and renaissance magic thrown in for good measure. The purposes of the symbols tell the story of the lifestyles and concerns of the people down the passage of the years; the importance of a good catch for fishermen, protection against thieves and ghosts, how to frighten away enemies.

The intentions of these ancient symbols are extremely varied and there seems to be one for almost every conceivable occasion. The lists read a little bit like a magical book of household management. There are staves included to help ensure the quality of butter, for lock breaking, and even for raising the dead.

Popularly referred to as Magical Staves, these signs are sometimes comprised of several runic symbols merged together (a bind rune) and others stand alone.

Aegishjalmur

One of these stave symbols is called the **Helm of Awe** or Aegishjalmur. It looks like a snowflake, except it has eight arms radiating from the central point instead of six.

Its purpose, as the name suggests, was to instil fear in the hearts of enemies and to guard the wearer against abuse of his own power. To work properly it needs to be engraved onto lead and then pressed into the forehead.

Latterly, followers of the Asatru belief adopted the Helm of Awe as one of their cornerstone symbols.

Hulinhjalmur: to make yourself invisible

Although invisibility is likely to be an incredibly useful asset, the construction of this stave is particularly tricky. It might not seem too difficult to engrave it on a piece of lignite using magnetic steel that has been hardened by soaking in human blood, but the instructions for blending of the ink could be a real nuisance. The recipe calls for three drops of blood from the index finger of the left hand, and three from the ring finger of the right hand; two drops of blood from the right nipple and one from the left. To this is added six drops of blood from the heart of a living raven. All this blood needs to be melted down with the raven's brain and parts of a human stomach. Voila. Now you see me …

DISCLAIMER

Hulinhjalmur, it will be noted, has no counter stave to restore visibility. Neither the authors nor the publishers of this book accept any responsibility for misuse of rune staves.

ICHTHYS WHEEL

At first glance, this looks like a simple **six**-spoked wheel. However, the name of Christ is cleverly hidden within it, and like the **vesica piscis**, was a way for early, persecuted Christians to recognize one another. The Greek letters I X O Y E can be laid over the circle.

IHS

These initials form a symbolic monogram for Christ. The monogram comprises the letters *iota*, *ete*, and *sigma*, which are the first three letters of the name of Jesus in Greek, *Iesous*. The letters also stand for the Latin phrase, *Iesous Hominum Salvator*, meaning Jesus, Saviour of Man.

Later, the symbol became a sign of peace.

The IHS symbol is generally embossed onto the communion wafer, and the initials surrounded by the rays of the Sun.

Incense

Its origins in *incendere*, the Latin word for **fire,** the importance of incense as a magical symbol lies in the resins and spices that it is made from, its perfume, and the action of its smoke that rises up toward the sky. This smoke is believed to conduct prayers, messages, and devotions toward the deities. The scent is said to please the Gods as well as lifting the spirits of worshippers, and the fact that frankincense was one of the **three** gifts given by the Wise Men to the infant Christ is a reminder of its significance. In Christianity, incense was first used in burials as a symbol of purity that would drive away demons and to carry the soul up to Heaven. However, its use soon expanded, and today, incense has a prominent part to play in rites of all kinds, especially within the Roman Catholic Church and the High Church of England. Neopagan groups, too, use incense for the same reasons.

Burning of incense transcends faiths and cultural boundaries. For Native Americans, the fragrant smoke given off by **tobacco** and other herbs when they share the **calumet** or pipe carries exactly the same significance as the incense that is burned in churches and the "dhupa" (or dhoop sticks) of Hindu ritual. For Hindus, incense represents the element of air and the perception of the consciousness.

The tower of smoke that rises up from the incense is symbolic of the **Axis Mundi.**

Practitioners of ceremonial magic might use incense so that disembodied entities, such as **elementals** or other spirits, might use the smoke to make themselves manifest.

Indalo

This is a prehistoric symbol of magical significance, found in **caves** in the Almeira region of Spain and known to have been created about 5000 years ago.

The symbol is very simple, showing a stick man holding an **arch** above his head. The arch represents either a **rainbow** or the vault of

object, the camera where it appears as the infinity lens focus.

To get the sense of what the infinity sign is and how it feels, find something circular and flexible—an elastic band will do. Then twist it once. That is the lemniscate. The flat, one-dimensional **circle** is suddenly lent a new dimension by this simple twist.

As a mathematical device, the infinity sign was first "discovered" in 1655 by John Wallis, but its significance as a religious symbol is much older.

The infinity sign has its origins in the Arabic numerals that actually came from India in the first place. The sign can be drawn in one continuous movement, making a seesaw movement of clockwise and counter-clockwise loops. These loops reflect the balance of opposites; male and female, day and night, dark and light. Because the circles of the lemniscate sit side by side, the sign implies equality between these opposing forces, with the connecting point in the center the convergent point. The sign epitomizes the idea of sexual union and of "two becoming one." The infinity sign stands for wholeness and completion.

The lemniscate appears in the elaborate curlicues in Arabic calligraphic renderings of the Name of God; the elegant loops providing a decorative device as well as pointing toward the idea of eternity.

The symbol appears in the **Tarot**, as part of the **Magician** card. In the Pamela Colman/Rider Waite version, the magician has the lemniscate floating boldly above his **head**; in other decks, the brim of his **hat** conceals the shape. Disguising the symbol in this way is a suitable device for such a mysterious character.

the Heavens. Indalo was perceived to be a go-between between man and God, the rainbow providing a bridge between Heaven and Earth. This sign, which looks like a child's drawing, serves as a reminder of the complex belief of man as the microcosm and the Universe as the macrocosm.

The Indalo figure has become a logo for the village of Mojacar in particular and for the whole area in general. Sometimes he is called Mojacar Man.

INFINITY

Often the simplest symbols are the ones with the richest meanings. The infinity sign, the **figure of eight**, and the **lemniscate** all refer to the same shape that contains a wealth of complex meaning within its fluid lines. This mysterious symbol is found on an everyday

INVERTED CROSS

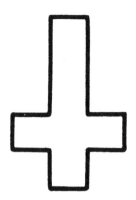

The "upside down" crucifix, or **Cross** of St. Peter, has become a sinister symbol purportedly belonging to Satanists, whose penchant for reversing certain aspects of the Christian faith (such as the **Mass** and the Lord's Prayer) is well documented. In horror movies the inverted cross represents the Devil. However, the inverted cross originated as the type of cross upon which St. Peter chose to be executed since, like St. Andrew, he felt unworthy of being crucified on the same type of cross as Christ. Devout Catholics view this particular cross as a sign of deep humility and unworthiness in the sight of the Messiah. The Pope is said to be the successor of St. Peter and so, logically, has been photographed with this type of cross in the background, giving rise to hysterical conspiracy theories about satanic influences within the Catholic Church.

IRMINSUL

This early Anglo Saxon symbol has been adopted as one of the cornerstone signs of the Asatru religion. It takes the form of a single pillar, with an ornamented cross bar or a **Sun wheel** surmounting it.

The word itself means "great pillar" and it is connected to the Nordic **World Tree**, or **Yggdrasil**, that connects the Earth with the Heavens. The root of its name is shared not only by Yggdrasil but also by the God, Odin, and a clue to the close connection between the **three**.

JAIN SYMBOL

Also called the Parasparopgraho Jivanam, this sacred symbol of the ancient Jain faith (an offshoot of Hinduism) is constructed from several other signs and symbols.

First, the outline of the symbol is called the Lok and is representative of the Universe. The lower part reminds Jains of the concept of **Seven** Hells. The central part represents the Earthly plane, and the upper portion represents the Heavens. Then, working from the top down, the curved **arc** represents not only the **Moon**, but is called the Siddhasila, the final resting-place of souls that have been liberated from the karmic **wheel** of death and rebirth. These souls are called Siddhas.

The **dot** or bindhu within the arc is indicative of the zero, the every thing and the nothing combined. It is also representative of the Siddha.

Below the arc are three further bindhu. These represent the **Three** Jewels of Jainism, namely, the rules for attaining the desired liberation of the soul. These rules are:

- Right Faith (Samyak Darshan)
- Right Knowledge (Samyak Jnan)
- Right Conduct (Samyak Charitra)

Below these three sacred dots is the **swastika**, the very ancient solar symbol. Here, the **four** arms of the swastika symbolize the four realms into which a soul may be reborn; a soul can become a heavenly being, a human being, an animal being, or a hellish being.

Underneath the swastika is the upraised **hand**, a universal symbol meaning "stop." Inside the hand is the word Ahimsa, one of the tenets of Hinduism and Jainism, which is an offshoot of this faith. Ahimsa means "nonviolence" and the word itself is contained within a wheel. The combination of the hand and the word within the wheel are a reminder to stop and think before acting, to do nothing which could harm any creature, otherwise the wheel of birth and rebirth will keep on turning and the soul will never be liberated.

Japa Mala

See **Rudraksha**.

Jerusalem Cross

This is one large cross with smaller crosses in between the spaces. Originally used by the Crusaders, hence its name, the **five** crosses symbolize the five wounds of Christ.

Jewelry

The precious metals and beautiful gems that make up jewelry spring from the **womb** of the Earth. Legends tell us that these gems are mined by dwarves and that jewelry is constructed by **elves** and **goblins**. Metals and gems are themselves full of hidden meanings. Gems symbolize not only material wealth but also wisdom and the riches of the mind and spirit. Buddhist doctrines are called "jewels." And, as the song says, **diamonds** really are forever! Not only the stones, but also the precious materials that go into the design of jewelry, are eternal and incorruptible. Ancient jewelry often looks as new as the day it was made and was worn by royalty as well as the common man.

There is evidence that man adorned himself with jewelry as long ago as 40,000 years, and the very earliest kind was made of **shells**, animal **bones** and **teeth**. The importance of this jewelry was such that people were even buried with it.

Jewelry is not only decorative: it can be functional, too, for instance, to hold clothing together (buckles, brooches, pins, and clips). It stores wealth (think of the archetypal gypsy, dripping **gold**—this jewelry is the same as money in the bank). Jewelry can take the form of protective **amulets** and **talismans**, with countless designs intended specifically to avert the **Evil Eye**. It also denotes status or membership of a group or tribe, or can give information about the wearer, for example, the wedding **ring** as a symbol of binding, or the **jet** mourning jewelry worn by bereaved Victorians. In Rome, the Sumptuary Laws gave instructions as to who had the right to wear specific sorts of jewelry.

The wearing of religious symbols, like the **crucifix** or **Star of David,** may sometimes be the cause of contention because of a lack of understanding of religious and cultural values. For example, a woman working at a major airport in the UK was told that her crucifix could be offensive. In addition, there have been instances where the facial jewelry of some Hindus has been looked at askance by people who do not understand the reasons for this adornment. A deeper understanding of the reasons that people choose to wear certain jewelry can only help to bring more harmony between diverse cultures. The nose ring, for example, is a practice copied from Indian cultures where piercing is believed to enhance fertility.

Ring

Wearing a ring indicates a link or bond; the wedding ring is the perfect example of this. In J.R.R. Tolkein's *The Lord of the Rings*, the mystical ring bears the inscription "one ring to bind them." The **Fisherman's Ring,** which is exclusive to the Pope, is used as his personal seal, being broken when he dies.

The ring, of course, is a circle, and so it carries all the symbolic significance of the shape; eternity and unity. The signet ring has a personal seal or other hieroglyphic device engraved on it used as a sign of identity.

Solomon had a particularly magical ring, the possible source of all his wisdom. He used it to conjure up the **demons** that then became his slaves, but when he lost the ring all his wisdom disappeared too, until it was returned to him.

Plato describes a ring that belonged to the shepherd, Gyges. His ring had a rotating bezel that, if turned inward, made him invisible.

The fingers on which rings are worn also have significance. The fourth finger of the left hand that is traditionally designated for the wedding or engagement ring has a direct link to the **heart**. Archers in China and Persia wore rings to protect their **thumbs**, so the thumb ring indicated military rank. A ring worn on the index or "pointing" finger indicates authority.

In India, **toe** rings, or bichiya, also denote status. Worn on the second toes of both **feet** they are a sign of marriage. Hindus traditionally consider it disrespectful to wear gold below the waist so these rings are usually, but not always, made of **silver**.

Necklace

A necklace is a sign of identity, more visible and more immediately obvious than the ring. For example, it can signify a chain of office (as in the ornate mayoral necklace) or a chain of bondage, like the collars worn by slaves. The Goddess Kali is immediately identifiable by her necklace of human **skulls**, and witches traditionally wear a necklace of **acorns**. Amulets and talismans often appear as pendants, and lockets of all kinds secrete hidden information.

JIZO

This is a Japanese Buddha symbol. Almost cartoonlike, Jizo is depicted as an innocent, childlike character, venerated as a protector of the souls of children and unborn babies.

Jizo is ubiquitous in Japan, often appearing as a statuette dressed in robes. People also surround the Jizo statuette with offerings of **food**, sweets, **incense**, and pebbles.

KABBALAH

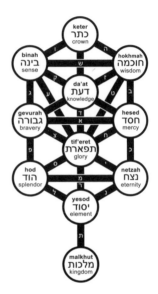

YAH, the Lord of Hosts, the living Elohim, King of the Universe, Omnipotent, the Merciful and Gracious God, Supreme and Extolled, Dweller in the Height whose habitation is Eternity, who is Sublime and Most Holy, engraved His name and ordained the Universe in thirty-two mysterious paths of wisdom, by the three Sephariam, namely, Numbers, Letters and Sounds, which are in Him and one and the Same

[from the Sefer Yetzirah]

A very short history

Most systems of faith have an exoteric, or external level of understanding that is aimed at the masses, and an esoteric, or inner level of meaning that is the reserve of the priests and initiates. The deeply mystical Kabbalah is the enigmatic aspect of the Jewish doctrine. The word has its root in Hebrew, QBL, meaning "to receive" or alternately "mouth to ear," or "the unwritten law," and like most mystery traditions its secrets were originally communicated orally. It shares the same root as the word Cabal, meaning "secret intrigue."

These secrets, so the story goes, were given directly from God to the Archangels who then passed the information on to Adam after his expulsion from the Garden of Eden, in order that he might regain his former favor in the eyes of God. The secrets passed through Noah to Abraham, who shared the mysteries with the Egyptians. From here the Kabbalah spread to other parts of the world. Moses, too, had kabbalistic instruction directly from God. According to Jewish mystics, the third time he climbed Mount Siani he spent forty days learning its secret doctrine from the angels while he was wandering in the Desert. Thereafter, Moses concealed the teachings that appeared for the first time in written form in the first four books of the Old Testament.

In the first century, Rabbi Simeon Ben Jochai had to hide in a cave with his son for twelve years, avoiding execution because of his criticism of the Roman Empire. During this time, the Rabbi taught the secrets of the Kabbalah to his son, and these teachings appeared as a book, published in thirteenth-century Spain, called the Zohar. It is this book which is the cornerstone of the Kabbalistic doctrines.

The universality of the ideas within the Kabbalah means that it has been adopted by numerous different religions. Not surprising, since the beauty and logic of its construction is awe-inspiring and all-encompassing. There was a general upsurge of interest in esoterica in the Middle Ages and this time saw the development of a Hermetic Kabbalah, a combination of Kabbalistic teachings and Greek Hermeticism. In turn, alchemy and Rosicrucianism were influenced by its secrets as was Freemasonry. The Tarot takes its influence from the Kabbalah. The Golden Dawn based its symbolic language on that of the Kabbalah. Its influence has been all pervasive, thousands of years after the angels imparted its intricacies to the First Man.

The doctrines encompass **The Four Worlds** and **The Tree of Life**, while the latter, in turn, encompasses **The Ten Numbers** and **The 22 Letters**.

The Four Worlds

The **Greatest Name**, Jehovah, or IHVH, has an element attached to each letter. Further, the letters also represent the Four Worlds. These are Atziluth (emanation), the world of pure spirit, an archetypal world where there is no separation or division. This is the world of the Gods. Atziluth is associated with the element of fire and the letter I, and from it the other three worlds are "born."

Briah, "cosmos" or "creation," is the next world, represented by the letter H and the water element. This is the world where separation begins, where one idea might separate from others, although this world is still formless.

Yetzirah, represented by the V and the element of air, is the next world born from Briah. This is the domain of imagination and thought, corresponding to the astral world, a level of consciousness that immediately precedes the physical.

The fourth world is Assiah, which means "to do." Assiah is the material world, represented by the final letter H and the earth element. It is the here and now, our physical reality, the world of separation that is constructed from the finer elements that precede it.

The Tree of Life

This is the most famous graphic representation of the Kabbalah's diverse unfolding of ideas. All of nature is enclosed within its relatively simple form that has multi-layered dimensions of significance that belie a straightforward graphic representation. Its ten spheres or sephiroth represent the ten numbers, and are connected by 22 paths or branches that also represent the 22 letters of the Hebrew alphabet. The letters and numbers comprise the 32 paths of wisdom that are written about in the Sefer Yetzirah, the very early kabbalistic text said to have been written by Abraham.

The three columns of the tree are symbols in themselves. The central one represents balance or equilibrium. The one on the right is called Jachin, male energy; on the left is Boaz, female energy. These are the pillars that were represented in the Great Temple in Jerusalem and which also influence the design of Masonic temples. They also appear in the **Tarot**. Here are the component elements of the tree.

THE TEN NUMBERS

Behold! From the Ten Ineffable Sephiroth do proceed the One Spirit of the Gods of the Living; Air, Water, Fire, and als Height, Deoth, East, West, South and North

[from the Sefer Yetzirah]

In the diagram, these are represented by the spheres or sephira.

ONE

The uppermost sephira of the tree is One, the Crown (Keter). It is the start of manifestation, positive, but undefinable because it as yet bears no relation to anything else.

TWO

To the right of Keter, just below it, is the sephira of Hokhmah or Wisdom, the number two. It enables a line to be made between it and the number One.

THREE

To the left of Hokhmah is Binah, meaning "understanding." It makes a triangle and all three numbers give definition to one another.

These first three sephiroth represent Atziluth, the element of fire and the first of the four worlds described above.

FOUR

Next, moving down the Tree, beneath Hokhmah, is Hesed, or Mercy. Now the Universe contained within the Tree can have four elements and four directions, and can form a square.

FIVE

To the left of Hesed is Gevurah, meaning strength. This implies the idea of time, without which nothing can happen in the Universe as we experience it.

SIX

With Tif'eret, meaning Beauty, another dimension is added; as well as the four elements and "above" and "below." The number six contributes the notions of past and future and consciousness of the self.

SEVEN

Netzah, or victory, is the next of the sephira. It sits below Hesed. It represents the notion of the emotional nature and the pure joy of existence. Despite the possibility of suffering, the soul is happy to be made manifest in human form.

EIGHT

Hod, or Splendor, symbolizes the intellectual nature, or thought.

NINE

Yesod, the Foundation, brings the notion of Sense of Being, adding to the emotional and intellectual natures of Tiphareth and Netzach to give man a sense of reality.

TEN

The final sephira, sitting at the bottom of the tree, is called Malkhut, or the Kingdom. Here, the void represented by the zero has become manifest, and self-consciousness is fully developed within a physical world. It is appropriately sited at the base of the tree since it is the sphere of all life on Earth.

THE TRIPLE VEILS OF THE NEGATIVE: THE THREEFOLD NATURE OF ZERO

In the Kabbalah, the concept of nothing, or zero, is called Ain, the void. This concept embraces two further ideas: firstly Infinite Space, called Ain Soph (without limit). This concept is represented by the **dot**, or bindhu, which contains the seed of everything within it. There is also the concept of a time–space continuum, Ain Soph Aur, The Limitless Light. These abstract ideas are the Triple Veils of the Negative.

THE 22 LETTERS

Like other magical alphabets from different traditions, the characters of Hebrew are thought to be the magical symbols with which God created the physical world by means of the sounds they represent.

These letters are generally split into three groups. There are three "mother" letters that correspond to the elements of air, water, and fire. The seven "double" letters correspond to the seven traditional planets, and the 12 remaining "simple" letters are linked to the signs of the Zodiac. Again in common with other alphabets, the letters also correspond to numbers and so have a double meaning. The letters are represented in the tree diagram by the 22 paths that link the spheres that contain the numbers.

Kabbalists also link the five parts of the human soul to the four elements, plus the fifth element, ether, or the quintessence. Earth is the "animal soul" named Nephesch. This is the domain of the instincts and the senses. Air symbolizes the intelligence and is called Ruach. It corresponds to the breath, too, and has the same meaning as Prana in Sanskrit philosophy. Water is called Neshamah, and in common with other traditions this element corresponds to the intuition. The fiery part of the soul is called Chiah, and has the same meaning as Chi, the essence of life. Finally, Yechidah encompasses the whole, the Highest Self, symbolizing spirit.

These further intricacies and connections within this fascinating system are far too elaborate to explain within the confines of this book, in the vigorous depth that they deserve. Hopefully this brief description of the concepts used within the Kabbalah will provide a fundamental grasp of its mysteries.

KAPALA

The kapala, or Thod Pa, is one of the "charnel ground" implements used in sacred rites in Tibetan Buddhism. It is a bowl or **chalice** made from a human **skull**, highly decorated and extremely valuable.

It is thought that the use of the skull may originate from much earlier times, from the practice of human sacrifice. The kapala is a symbol of the triumph of good over evil. Each skull is carefully selected, washed, and sanctified before use.

A kapala made from the skull of a child that died prior to puberty is particularly desirable, because of its purity. The object is usually held with the left **hand**.

KERUB

The original Kerubim are very different from the chubby-cheeked little creatures that seem to pop up everywhere these days, which are

in fact completely different creatures known as putti. The "true" Kerubim are imposing, winged creatures who guard the thrones of Gods and kings as well as the Mesopotamian **tree of life**. The book of Ezekiel in the Old Testament of the Bible describes the four Kerubim, each of which have a different head; the **lion**, the **bull**, the **eagle**, and the human **head**. These were later absorbed into the symbols of the four **evangelists**, Matthew, Mark, Luke, and John, of the New Testament.

These mighty Kerubim are also the embodiment of the energy in the **tetragrammaton**, the Name of God in symbolic form.

KEY

The key, or **clavicle**, is symbolic of access to something that has been hitherto kept hidden or which is a secret. However, keys are used for locking as well as for unlocking, and deities that are depicted holding keys, for example, may symbolize the need to keep something private or occluded. A key need not be a physical object, and the act of unlocking is not restricted to mundane artifacts. A code, for example, may hold the key to understanding a secret language or cipher. Holy and sacred words were considered such powerful locking/unlocking mechanisms that they were rarely used; for example, the words "Open Sesame" were a key that unlocked the door into the treasure cave.

Our ancestors used the physical key as a magical charm or talisman, an example of sympathetic magic, when something needed to be unlocked in some way. For example, Jewish midwives put the key to the synagogue into the hand of a woman who was about to give birth, in the hopes that the association would help the baby "unlock" the door of the womb. Keys were buried with people in order that the gates to the Underworld would open easily.

St. Peter, one of the apostles of Christ, holds the keys to the "pearly gates" of Heaven. These **crossed keys** have become a **Papal symbol** and represent the powers given by Christ; one key is **gold** (the **Sun**, and male energy) and the other is **silver** (feminine energy, the **Moon**). The golden key signifies the power to bind or release in Heaven, and the silver represents the same powers on Earth. Prior to their adoption by the Pope, these gold and silver keys were the attribute of the Roman God, **Janus**, whose two faces mean that he can look in two directions at the same time. These keys symbolically unlocked the gates of the solstices.

Initiation, too, provides a key that unlocks secret knowledge or information. The key is a symbol of power, a visible sign of this initiation. Being given the keys to a town or city is a great honor, with implications of power and ownership and has parallels with the medieval custom of handing over keys as a way of granting power. The "key of the door" that is given on the 21st birthday signifies the coming of age into adulthood, and the **Tarot** card that is numbered 21 is the card of the World.

KHANDA

A symbol belonging to the Sikh religion, the Khanda symbolizes the **four** aspects of the Sikh faith as well as encompassing the four sacred weapons within its shape.

The double-edged sword that gives the Khanda its name is in the center of the symbol. It stands for the creative power of God and the knowledge of divinity.

The **circle** around the edge of the Khanda dagger is called the chakkar, or **wheel**, and the word shares the same root as **chakra**. This is also a medieval weapon, and like all circular symbols, it represents eternity and unity.

The daggers at either side of the symbol, which cross over at the bottom of the symbol are called Kirpans. These knives belonged to the guru Hargobind and symbolize the balance of spirit and matter.

KNOT OF ISIS

See **Tyet**.

KNOT

Knots, because they symbolize the act of binding, hold powerful symbolic and magical significance. The notion of binding extends to the spirit, as well as material things. In some pagan **wedding** rites the hands of the bride and groom are bound together, physically, as a symbol of the vows that bind them together, body and soul. For Buddhists, the untying of a knot signifies an unbinding from material things, to become liberated from them, and is therefore symbolic of death.

Knots hold a great significance for fishermen, not a surprise considering that fishing nets are constructed from knots. Any person who risks his life by putting themselves at the mercy of the elements tends to have an under-

standably superstitious approach to life. Some fishermen still carry a piece of rope with three knots in it, although they may have forgotten what these knots symbolize. The first knot, if untied, brings fair winds; the second, storms; and the third keeps these storms in check. Arabic men believe that the knot is a powerful talisman against the Evil Eye, so they tie a knot into their beards. However, it is forbidden for pilgrims to **Mecca** to wear any knots in their clothing.

The Qu'ran mentions a specific charm for the making and using of knots. It reads:

Say thou: "I take refuge with the Lord of Daybreak
From the evil of all He hath made
And from the evil of the dark on when it spreads
And from the evil of those who blow upon knots
And the evil of the envious when he envies."

This refers to the magical practice of using the breath to charge an item with magical powers.

Because weaving and knitting are female crafts that involve a complicated series of knots, and because women "knot" their **hair**, knots and knot magic are closely associated with witches. In the Qu'ran, for example, there is a warning against "those who breathe on knots." This refers to the witches that were supposed to cast spells in this way. The Three **Fates** of Greek mythology weave and knot the threads of existence. Midwives ensured that birthing mothers had no knots about their person that might hinder the birth of the baby.

Egyptians believed that the knot symbolized eternal life. They tied their sandals in such a way that the knot made an imprint on the ground, a reminder of the **Knot of Isis**.

Kokopeli

Kokopeli, in Hopi Indian, means "wooden backed." It is the name of a symbol that first appears in prehistoric rock carvings, a hunchbacked little figure with antlers on his head, playing a flute. Although the true age, provenance and explanation for this curious symbol are indeterminate, Kokopeli is believed to be a fertility symbol (hence the antlers), and the small bag (possibly containing **seeds**) which he sometimes carries. Kokopeli represents the essence of the creative force, whatever form it might take.

There is a Hopi legend which says that Kokopeli traveled from village to village playing his flute. Wherever he went, he was welcomed with a huge party, the villagers singing and dancing all night. In the morning, presumably through the haze of a terrible hangover, Kokopeli had evidently shared his magical powers of fecundity since all the fields were full of healthy crops and all the girls would shortly find that they were pregnant. Kokopeli also symbolizes the end of winter and the coming of **spring**, hope, and new life.

Kundalini Serpent

This is the symbol used to describe the vast reserve of physical and spiritual energy that lives, half-dormant, at the base of the **spine**. Derived from a Sanskrit word meaning "spiral" or "coil," the Kundalini Serpent is coiled into **three circles,** with its tail in its mouth, similar to the **ouroboros**. Kundalini energy is female, and when awakened systematically by techniques such as yoga and meditation, she spirals up the spine via the **chakras** toward the top of the head, where she joins the male energy that comes down to meet it from above. This descending masculine energy symbolizes the consciousness of the unity of the Universe.

Labarum

The earliest Christian symbol, prior to the adoption of the **Latin Cross,** was the **Labarum.** This symbol has a very early provenance, since it is believed to have been an adaptation of the Egyptian **ankh** and was also a symbol of the Sun God, Mithras. In this case, it appears enclosed in a **wheel**. The Labarum proved a handy device for bridging the gap between Mithraism (the favored religion of the Roman soldiers) and Christianity.

Not only does the symbol contain the first two Greek letters of Christ's name (hence it is also known as the "**Chi Roh**" or the "Monogram of Christ") but it was given immediate prominence when Emperor Constantine saw the symbol in a dream.

Constantine was a major figure in the spread of Christianity, the first Imperial Emperor to adopt the new religion. Some accounts of his vision of the Labarum say that his entire army saw the symbol hanging in the **sky**. This anecdote, incidentally, has parallels to the story of the **crescent Moon** and **star** symbol, also seen in a dream by Osman, founder of the Ottoman Empire.

Like Osman, Constantine's dream told him that the sign would bring victory, and so he had it painted onto his soldiers' shields.

It may have been coincidence that shortly afterwards Constantine's forces won the Battle of the Milvian Bridge, but nevertheless the Labarum's place as a hugely important symbol was determined, adopted as the emblem of the Empire in AD 324, 12 years after the decisive victory.

LABRYS

Although the word *labrys* is Greek and refers to the double-headed **axe** or hatchet, the symbol exists all over the world, in India, Africa, and England as well as in the European countries.

The single-headed axe is symbolic of the power of light (because it sometimes makes sparks) and of thunder and lightning. It is often seen as the favored weapon of various Gods, such as **Thor**.

The double-headed axe is more complex. The first instrument of its kind is believed to have been made 8000 years ago, and it was the favored tool of the Amazonians who lived in central Asia, specifically in the Kazakhstan area. Because of its shape, it carries much of the significance of the **tau cross**. Its name suggests that it is connected to the **labyrinth**; both were powerful symbols in the Minoan culture of ancient Crete, as was the **bull**. The Labyrinth at Knossos used the image of the Labrys as a decorative device. The double-headed axe is sometimes seen over the head of the bull or ox, whose horns it resembles. In addition, the bull was ritually slaughtered using the Labrys.

The Minoan Culture was predominantly matriarchal and because of this, and because the Labrys has strong links to the female Amazonian warriors, with the Amazons, the term "battleaxe" has come to mean a ferocious woman. Various Lesbian groups adopted the symbol sometime in the 1970s, and some women wear it as a piece of **jewelry** to indicate their sexuality.

LABYRINTH

The earliest recorded instance of the word "labyrinth" is in descriptions of the labyrinth that housed the **minotaur** in Greek myth. The name means "house of the double **axe**," a reference to the **Labrys** that was a powerful emblem of the Minoan culture. Although the labyrinth and the maze are often referred to as the same thing, a **maze** has lots of different paths, including branches that lead to dead ends, whereas a labyrinth has only one winding path that leads ineffably to the center and offers no possibility of choice. The space available within the labyrinth is used ingeniously to ensure that the path is as long as possible.

The most significant symbolism of the labyrinth is that of the journey of the **soul** to its center and then back toward the outside once more, the cycle of death and rebirth, a metaphysical pilgrimage of the spirit. The center of the labyrinth represents the **womb**, and to reach the center of the "labyrinth of life" is initiation and enlightenment. In this sense the labyrinth has parallels with the **mandala** as well as with the **spiral** patterns of the Celts, a good example of which can be seen on the massive stones in front of the entrance at **Newgrange** in Ireland.

Labyrinth patterns are universal, and earlier than the mythical labyrinth. They appear on fragments of **amulets** from Ancient Egypt, on Mycenean seals, and on Etruscan vases.

Labyrinth patterns were adopted by Christian churches, the earliest of which is in Algeria, at the Reparatus Basillica, dating back to the year 324. There is generally held to be significance in the number of concentric shapes or layers of the path, and also its length; the famous labyrinth at **Chartres Cathedral**, for example, has **11** concentric circles and is exactly **666** feet long. Because the number 666 is usually misconstrued as having evil origins, this has led to some wild conspiracy theories about the designer of the labyrinth, but 666 is a sacred number, the number of humankind. In the center of this particular labyrinth is a six-petaled flower that conceals the **hexagram** or **Seal of Solomon** within it, a reminder that labyrinths are sometimes called Solomon's Maze.

Because the winding trail of the labyrinth moves both in a clockwise (deosil) and an anticlockwork (widdershins) direction, it symbolizes the course of the **Sun** and the waxing and waning of the **Moon**.

LADDER

An everyday object, the ladder nevertheless has esoteric meaning as an aspect of the relationship between Heaven and Earth. At its most basic, the ladder is symbolic of ascension, transcendence, and the fulfilment of

LATIN CROSS

potential; the Greek word for ladder is "climax." A ladder is also synonymous with the idea of communication between the worlds. The notion that the material and spiritual worlds used to be connected by a ladder, that was either removed or broken, is a common symbolic thread running through many cultures, although the Shinto faith says that the Goddess Amerasatu, who borrowed the magical ladder, kept the connection. The ladder sometimes depicted on the tracing boards of **Freemasonry** signifies initiation and a penetration of the higher levels of the cosmos. A **rainbow** also serves as a ladder, or bridge, between the celestial realms and the ones below.

The number of rungs on this symbolic ladder is important, too, The Buddha has a ladder of **seven** colors, and in the Mithraic religion, there was a ceremonial ladder of seven rungs, each made from a different **metal** that corresponded to each of the known seven **planets**, from **lead**, the base metal, to **gold**, considered to be the most sublime. Climbing this ladder was a physical representation of the ascent through the Seven Heavens.

The ladder is also one of the many vertical items that signify the **Axis Mundi**.

The Latin Cross (or Christian Cross) is the typical **cross** shape that is the major symbol of Christianity, no matter what form the faith takes. When the body of Christ appears on the Cross, it then becomes a **crucifix**. Such has been the impact of this symbol on the religion that its major places of worship are built in the shape of a cross as seen from above.

The Latin Cross is symbolic of the victory of life over death, and in a happy coincidence, the benediction made when the sign of the Cross is drawn in the air not only indicates the "Father, Son and Holy Ghost," but coincides with a much earlier use of the cross; as a symbol of protection.

The Christian Cross as we know it today was not always the symbol of the Church, and it may not even be the case that Christ was crucified on this sort of cross. Accounts vary, but a **tau** cross, a simple straight beam, or perhaps even a living **tree** might have been used. Logic dictates that, because it was used as a particularly gruesome torture implement, this kind of cross would not have been an encouraging symbol for what was then a new religion. The **Chi-Roh** or **Labarum** was used instead, but by the third century the cross had been accepted.

The form of the cross itself holds an intriguing hidden secret. If its measurements are drawn correctly, that is, **four** square parts in the vertical to **three** square parts in the horizontal (making **six** parts in total since the square that links the upright and the cross part can be shared by both) then this shape can be folded into a neat cube. Further, other geometric shapes can be made from this versatile cross if diagonal folds are included.

The Freemasons have explored some of these shapes.

LEMNISCATE

See **Infinity sign**.

LEVIATHAN CROSS

The Leviathan Cross is also sometimes referred to as the Crux Satana, since it was adopted by Anton LaVey as a symbol for his Church of Satan. However, there is no record of this particular cross having any other satanic connections prior to this. The cross was used by both the Knights Templar and the Cathars.

In **alchemy**, the Leviathan Cross is the symbol for sulfur, which is one of the three essential elements of Nature along with **salt** and **mercury** (quicksilver).

The symbol itself is quite elaborate. There are two bars on the upright part of the cross, symbolizing double protection and a balance between male and female. At the bottom of the cross is the infinity sign or lemniscate, which also becomes the double **ouroboros**. The cross also carries phallic connotations.

LINGAM

In the Hindu faith, the lingam is a ubiquitous symbol whose name also means "sign." This Sanskrit word shares its root, however, with the words for both "plough" and "phallus." The lingam is symbolic of the phallus and procreation, but with the emphasis on creative energy and the spirit of life, rather than eroticism. The lingam is the symbol of the great Hindu deity, **Shiva**.

In yoga, the lingam is envisaged as a tower of light that rises up from the base of the spine. The **Kundalini Serpent** of energy rises up this tower of light, which represents the power of knowledge.

Lingam symbols occur naturally in the landscape as certain standing stones and rocks, but the linga that are a fundamental feature in temples are manmade, carved from stone. The base of the object is **square**, symbolic of the Earth, stability and security, and the upper part is cylindrical.

The lingam, on its own, effectively belongs to the world of theory, of untried and untested things. In conjunction with the **yoni**, however, the lingam becomes empowered. The yoni is symbolic of the **womb**, female energy and creativity. The pair are inextricably linked, the yoni symbolized as the shallow basin that surrounds the lingam.

The temple lingam is anointed with oil and **water** and decorated with flowers. It is one of the many objects that represent the **Axis Mundi**.

LION OF JUDAH

This is not only the symbol but also the honorary title of the Ras Tafari, the Emperor Haile Selassie. According to followers of the Rastafarian faith, Haile Selassie was the Messiah.

Legend says that the Emperor was descended from the Tribe of Judah, whose emblem was the **lion**.

The Rastafarian Lion of Judah carries the Flag of Ethiopia in his mouth and the crown of the Emperor on his head.

MAGEN DAVID

See **Seal of Solomon**.

MAGIC CIRCLE

The **circle** is a powerful symbol, standing for strength, union, protection, eternity. A magic circle signifies all these things, and has the added benefit of being "charged" by various rituals. A magic circle is generally inscribed on the floor or ground as a way of delineating the area in which magical activity will take place.

Prior to occult activity, the circle is "cast." Different practitioners of magic have different methods of doing this. However, **salt** is popular in constructing the circle because of its protective qualities. Candles and incense are used too. Due respect is given to this magic circle as a sacred space, symbolic of the microcosm.

Practitioners of the occult arts set great store by the correct construction of a magic circle. Aleister Crowley, for example, who liked to call up various otherworldly spirits, found at one time that the only thing standing between him and imminent demonic destruction was a circle of sand and some powerful magical intention.

MAGIC KNOT

Also called the Witch's Knot or the Witch's Charm, this symbol is comprised of four interlocking **vesica piscis** shapes, sometimes with the addition of a central circle. Because it can be drawn in one continuous line without the pen leaving the paper, it is a symbol of protection, and despite its name was often used in the Middle Ages as an anti-witchcraft symbol; however, it was also used by witches to control the weather or as a love charm, which indicates that the symbol was used homeopathically. There are lots of different magic knots.

MAGIC SEAL

This symbol uses **numbers** and shapes to make a magical symbol said to help the magician harness the powers and qualities of a planetary deity. Each planet has its own magic square and the size of this **kamea** and the order of the numbers in it are particularly significant. A shape is then overlaid on top of these numbers, connecting them together to make a **sigil** for the planet.

MAGICIAN, SIGNS OF

There is an ancient African belief in certain give-away signs that describe a practitioner of the magical arts. The description is rather generalized, but here it is. The ideal sorcerer can be male or female, of average height, aged between 22 to 26 or, alternatively, between 30 and 55. Fair-haired magicians are allegedly more powerful than dark, and fuller lips are better.

MALTESE CROSS

See **Templar Cross**.

MAN IN THE MAZE

A symbol belonging to the Native Americans, found both in basketry and in Hopi Indian **silver** work.

The symbol shows a **maze**, with the figure of a man either about to leave or enter it. The symbol represents the choices and decisions that a person has to make during the journey of their life. The center of the **labyrinth** is dark, signifying the unknown world and the mysteries of initiation, and the outer area is light, the known world, and familiar things.

MANAIA

For Maoris, the Manaia was a mythical **bird**-like creature, a protecting spirit and a messenger from the Gods, hence the resemblance to the bird. This stylized symbol is frequently seen as an **amulet**, made from a type of Maori **jade** called **Greenstone**.

MANDALA

The word mandala is Sanskrit, and means "**circle**." The mandala itself may be enclosed in a **square** or might contain squares and other shapes, such as the **triangle**, within it. They can also contain animals, flowers, plants. Despite its name, it is not always necessary for the mandala to be circular in shape.

An important symbol within the Hindu tradition, the mandala is now recognized everywhere for its beautiful **colors** and pleasing patterns even where its significance as a piece of religious design may not be understood.

The mandala can be as simple or as complex as the designer wishes it to be. Monks created the original mandalas, at least 2500 years ago, as a part of their traditional spiritual training. The mandala is a mystical and magical map of the Universe, constructed in such a way that the focus of attention is drawn continuously to the center and then back to the outer frame.

As a focus for meditation, the shapes and patterns of the mandala can be open to interpretation by each individual. However, every individual element, including the colors that are used, has significance.

The image of the unfolding petals of the **lotus** flower, in the center of which yogis envisage themselves sitting, is a mandala. A perfect physical representation of the shape is found at the **Temple of Borobudur**, in Java. The entire temple, viewed from above, forms the traditional circular mandala, sitting in a square framework with gates at each quarter. Walking around this three-dimensional mandala, in the correct sequence, is a meditative process.

Carl Jung recognized the usefulness of creating mandalas as part of his psychological explorations, and described them as "a representation of the unconscious self."

MANDORLA

See **Vesica Piscis**.

MANEKI NEKO

See **Beckoning cat**.

MANIKIN

Also known as the poppet (hence the word "puppet") or sometimes the Voodoo Doll, the manikin, in magical symbolism, is a model of a human being, a representation of a real person, and not a child's toy. Constructed by a practitioner of magic, the idea is that what-ever happens to the doll also happens to its human counterpart. The doll only "works," though, if its constituent parts include some physical substance from the person it is supposed to be; **hair**, **blood,** or **spittle**, for example. The doll is "dressed" in a scrap of the intended person's clothing.

These items seem to be universal.

The uses of such dolls generally have a sinister twist, malevolent rather than benevolent. The common perception is of the manikin used as a sort of psychic pincushion, each pin believed to inflict a similar wound in the unfortunate person that it represents. They are also used to attract love, in which case the manikin is made to represent the person that is the object of the maker's desire, with emphasis placed on the sexual parts. Then the doll has to be blessed, buried, and dug up again, when a pin is used to pierce the **heart** in much the same way as cupid's **arrow**.

However, possibly the most sinister kind comes from the Amoy region of China. **Peach** wood—itself a magical substance—is collected, in secret, in the dead of night. This raw wood is hidden somewhere close to a pregnant woman, but it is important that she should not know of its presence. As soon as possible after the baby is born the wood is retrieved and carved into a doll that resembles the baby in gender and in any other possible way. Various spells follow, so that the doll becomes animated with a part of the unfortunate infant's spirit. Allegedly, this can damage the soul of the baby in such a way that it may be impaired or even killed.

The manikin is a fine example of sympathetic magic, the idea that a part of something extrapolates to encompass the whole.

Manji

The meaning of this word is simple; it means the "Chinese symbol for eternality." It is essentially a **swastika**, the ancient solar symbol. However, in the Buddhist belief system it signifies the balance of opposing forces, harmony, and dharma (proper conduct, doing the right thing).

The Manji can face either way, and like the swastika (despite some superstitious beliefs about it) both directions have positive connotations. Facing to the left and turning clockwise, it signifies love and mercy. Facing to the right and turning counter-clockwise, the Manji stands for intelligence and strength.

Mankolam

See **Paisley**.

Mark of the Beast

Created by infamous ritual magician Aleister Crowley, the self-styled Great Beast, the Mark of the Beast became, effectively, his own personal sign. It cleverly combines the

ancient **Sun symbol** (the **circle** with the dot) with the emblem of the **crescent Moon**, all comprised of three overlapping circles. It does not need an expert in hidden signs to be able to discern the overall image created, which reveals Crowley's overarching fascination with sex magick.

Mark of the Bustard

This is a three-branched symbol that appears on the **cloaks** of shaman. It represents communication between the world of death and the world of resurrection. The same symbol, if seen in the dust around the bed of a recently deceased person, says that the soul of the person has left the body and taken wing.

The bustard itself, although it seldom flies, symbolizes the union between Earth and Heaven.

MASK

A mask covers the face of the individual, effectively blocking out his or her own identity and replacing it with the spirit or personality represented by the mask. Many people who have worn masks describe the ease with which their own personality dissolves when the face is hidden or disguised. There are three main categories for the use of masks: in theater, in carnival, in funerals. In addition, shaman use masks to help him or her take on the spirit of an **animal** or a **deity**.

In Ancient Greece and Rome, the Chorus was the name given to the actors that described the events taking place. They wore masks that represented archetypal human emotions; the classical "comedy" and "tragedy" masks come from this tradition. Similarly, the masks of the Japanese No Theater convey universal archetypes: old man, young girl, mother, father, for example.

There was a Persian sect called the Maskhara, who wore animal masks or else blackened their faces, making themselves unrecognizable during their henbane-fueled rituals. This anonymity probably meant that they felt more able to give in to the effects of the drug, sublimating their human personalities.

The very real possibility that a seemingly inanimate object such as a mask can sublimate the ego means that the ritual use of a mask is a dangerous practice. Wearing a mask that symbolizes the "dark" side or the base tendencies can cause those qualities to manifest in the person. Additionally, because the skin or head of an animal is believed to retain the essence of the creature, it is a distinct possibility that the spirit could possess the wearer of such a mask, the human body possessed by this spirit.

The Konoga masks of the Dogon, an African tribe from Mali, are worn during the masked dances that replicate the actions of God when the Universe was made. These dances possibly started out as a way of encouraging the Spirits to bless the hunt, but have evolved into something with a wider breadth of meaning that is described in the actual name of the mask; Konoga means "hand of God."

The Kachina masks of the Hopi Indians are worn to welcome back the benevolent spirits that spend time with these people for six months in every year.

MAYPOLE

The maypole used to be a very common site in many Northern European countries, where it was a symbol of the phallus of the May King as well as a representation of the **World Axis** or **World Tree**. Although we tend to think of the maypole as a rural phenomenon, they

resurgence in the popularity of the maypole, which became a symbol of defiance. At this time there were over a hundred maypoles freshly erected in London, hard to believe for a modern-day dweller in the city.

The pagan origins of the maypole were effectively forgotten, as the pole became a quaint symbol of rural pursuits and an archaic relic of a Merrie England that has become a thing of the past.

were erected in cities, too. Traditionally, the pole was decked with flowers, with several long ribbons attached to the top. During pre-Christian **Beltane** ceremonies, the girls would each take one of the ribbons and dance in an anti-clockwise direction, while the boys took the other set and danced clockwise. This deosil/widdershins dance represented the male/solar powers interweaving with the female/lunar qualities, a celebration of the harmony inherent within the Universe that was also a powerful fertility ritual.

However, evangelical Protestants considered the maypole an anti-Christian object that could lead to lewd behavior and even, God forbid, merrymaking on a Sunday. The consequence of this change in attitude was a general maypole ban; many were chopped up and burned. However, there were pockets of insurrection where people refused to remove the maypole, since it provided a useful focus for other sociable activities, too. During the Restoration in 1660, there was a general

MAZE

The maze carries similar symbolism to the **labyrinth** in that it represents a metaphorical journey. However, whereas a labyrinth consists of one long path that maximizes the use of the space available and is as long as possible, the maze generally has meandering twists and turns and many dead-ends. See Section 6, Sacred Geometry and Places of Pilgrimage, for an unusual example of a living maze constructed in the image of the **Green Man**.

Medicine wheel

The "genuine" medicine wheel is a Native American construction, a three-dimensional, physical object that is made from stone, laid out in a circular pattern, generally in North America. They are investigated in depth in section 6. However, the medicine wheel is also drawn as a form of meditation. The medicine wheel is a symbol of Native American spiritual belief, the **circle** representing the ideas of infinity, rebirth, motion. Ultimately the circle is the symbol of the **Zero** Chiefs, the notion that the Zero is not "no thing," but "every thing."

The individual elements within the wheel vary according to the preferences of the designer; **feathers**, **Sun wheel** symbols, animal **totem** emblems, signs for the elements and the directions, and many others.

Mehendi

This is the ancient art of adorning the **hands** and **feet** with henna paste. It is carried out as a ritual in any part of the world where the henna-producing *Hawsonia inermis* plant grows, although it is safe to say that India is most closely associated with this symbolic art form. Formerly the paste was made at home in quite an elaborate process, but these days the paste can be bought in tubes that make it easier to apply.

Its most popular use is in decorating the bride for her **wedding**. Less wealthy brides use the mehendi as a substitute for expensive **gold jewelry**.

The style of the designs and the use of the symbols vary from country to country and from region to region, and many of the meanings of the traditional patterns that are still in use have been lost over the years. Unsurprisingly, most of the patterns bring wishes for fertility, prosperity, and a happy life. Sometimes the names of the bride and the groom are secreted in the curlicues of the design. Traditionally, the bride is not allowed to do any housework until her wedding mehendi designs have faded away.

Menorah

This is the **seven**-branched candelabra of the Jewish tradition. The Bible is very specific as to the construction of the golden Menorah that was made for the Holy Temple in Jerusalem, and it is described as **three** branches that come out from either side of a candlestick. The seven lights are significant since they number the seven days of creation and were originally lit, one day at a time, until all seven lights were glowing at the end of the week. The lights also signify the seven planets, and accordingly the seven archangels of the celestial spheres that relate to these planets.

The Menorah has become an instantly recognizable emblem of the Jewish faith, and appears on the coat of arms of Israel among other places.

Merkabah

In the Kabbalistic tradition, all **ten** of the qualities of the **tree of life** are collectively referred to as the Merkabah, or Chariot of God. This mystical chariot gives God the power to

descend from Heaven to enter the souls of men. The symbol shown here is used as a meditative focus, to attain the state of mind and spirit necessary to achieve union with the elements of the **tree of life** and so become part of the collective spirit of the cosmos.

Mesopotamian tree of life

Believed by some to be the "original" tree of life, the symbol which is universal, appearing in all cultures, the Mesopotamian one was said to be a colossal tree which grew in the center of the world, and from whose roots flowed the Apsu, the primordial water from which all life emanated.

Messianic seal

Comprised of a string of **three** symbols, starting with the **Vesica Piscis**, then the **Star of David**, and topped by a **Menorah**, this seal is the insignia of the Messianic Christian Movement, a group that has adopted some Jewish practices into their rituals, possibly in an attempt to persuade Jewish people to convert to Christianity.

The symbol is believed to have been used by very early followers of Christ, and is found carved onto stone that dates back to the first century AD.

METATRON'S CUBE

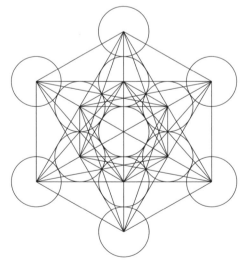

In Christianity, Judaism, and Islam, Metatron is said to be one of the most powerful angels in Heaven. It is testimony to this power that Metatron was allowed to be seated in Heaven, a privilege that was reserved only for God. However, Metatron was seated because it was his role, as scribe, to record the history and deeds of humankind.

Metatron's Cube can be formed from the **Fruit of Life** symbol, by using the points of intersection to make the shape geometrically correct. The power of this complex geometric symbol lies in the shapes of the **five Platonic solids** hidden within it.

Early Kabbalistic documents say that Metatron formed this "cube" from his **soul**.

Apart from its geometric significance, the cube is a powerful symbol of protection, able to keep away demons and other unwanted influences.

MEZUZAH

In Hebrew, Mezuzah means "doorpost," but the word refers, in this case, to the small container that is attached to the doorposts of any Jewish buildings, be they homes, government offices, shops, etc. This small case contains a piece of paper or parchment with two verses from the Bible, from the Book of Deuteronomy. Jewish religious law requires that a Mezuzah is attached to every doorpost.

Written on the reverse side of the paper is the word Shaddai, which is one of the names of God believed to be a **notarikon** for a phrase which, in translation, means "Guardian of the Doors of Israel."

Since the **doorway** is symbolic of a move between two states of being or between this world and the next, it makes sense that they should need to be protected. The Mezuzah, when it is constructed properly and affixed with due reverence, is a powerful tool of protection. It is customary for Jewish people to touch or **kiss** the Mezuzah when they pass by.

Miraculous Medal

This is one of the many symbols, called Marian Symbols, adopted by followers of the Virgin Mary within the Catholic Church. This particular symbol is said to have come in a vision to St. Catherine Laboure in 1830.

In the vision, Mary herself directed the design of it. It is intended as an emblem of charity.

The symbol consists of an intertwined M and a **cross**, and 12 **stars** that represent the Twelve Tribes of Israel. The **hearts** signify the Sacred Heart of Jesus and the Immaculate Heart of Mary.

Mirror

The belief that a reflection can somehow be an actual part of the **soul** may be a primitive one, but it reaches far into our collective conscious. The mirror is somehow regarded as a mystical gateway into another world. Lewis Carroll plays with this idea to great effect in *Through the Looking Glass*. Here, the mirror is a window to a parallel Universe of opposites, a sort of negative image of reality. The mirror is used as a magical object, again, in the fairy tale of Snow White, where the mirror of the evil Queen has a spirit of its own that can see what is going on elsewhere in the world. The mirror can tell the Queen "who is the fairest in the land." Like the mirror in this fairy tale, the mirror always reflects the impartial truth, and so is symbolic of honesty and purity.

The Buddhist Mirror of Dharma reveals the causes of past actions, so here the mirror symbolizes not only truth but also enlightenment. For Tibetan Buddhists, the "Wisdom of the Great Mirror" teaches a secret similar to that of Plato's **Cave** of Shadows; that the things reflected in the mirror are just another aspect of the Void. In Japanese mythology, the mirror that belongs to the Goddess, **Ameratasu**, draws light from the darkness of a cavern and beams that light back out into the world.

The ancient Celts believed, too, that the mirror could capture the souls, and their women were buried with a mirror to keep the soul safe.

Mirrors appear repeatedly in myths and legends from all over the world. A broken mirror is a symbol of doom, the archetypal bad omen, and popular superstitious belief says that the person breaking the glass will suffer **seven** years' bad luck, although there are certain unusual measures that can be taken to minimize this. These include burying the mirror in a piece of thick cloth deep in the ground, presumably so that the reflection of the "bad luck" is hidden in the dark.

A **black** bowl filled with water makes a reflective surface; the water is associated with the **Moon**, itself a mirror of the **Sun**, and for those with the talent to move outside the confines of linear time this scrying bowl provides a magical mirror that can be used as a divinatory tool. The use of reflective surfaces is one of the most ancient forms of divination. **Pythagoras** had a magical mirror, which he placed in moonlight in order to "charge" it with lunar, occult powers. He then used the mirror to divine the future.

The reflective surface of the **Witch Ball**, hanging in a window, wards off evil spirits by reflecting their malevolence right back at them. In this sense, it has a similar use to the hexagonal mirror used by practitioners of Feng Shui. This mirror is fixed above the doorway of the home, the **eight** sides of the frame repelling bad influences from all directions, a protective symbol.

There is a primitive idea among some people that a photograph somehow captures part of their soul. Effectively, a photograph is a reflection created by the mirror reflexes inside the camera. If the mirror reflects the soul, then the well-polished mirror is symbolic of the purity of the soul as well as of knowledge, consciousness, and self-awareness. The **eye**, itself a reflective surface, is called the Mirror of the Soul and is believed to be able to convey what is hidden inside the conscience of its owner.

The ancient Celts believed, too, that the mirror could capture the soul, and their women were buried with a mirror to keep the soul safe. Everyone knows from horror movies and gothic tales that vampires have no souls; sometimes this is indicated by its lack of reflection in a mirror. In Bram Stoker's *Dracula*, the evil count throws Jonathan Harker's shaving mirror out of the window in case his secret is revealed.

Mjolnir

Also known as the Hammer of the Gods or Thor's Hammer, the Mjolnir symbol owes its significance to its long history as a supernaturally powerful object.

The word carries with it connotations of crushing and grinding, both in the agricultural sense (it shares its root with the word "meal") and in the destructive sense. Both the hammer and the **axe** are associated with **lightning**, because, like lightning, they strike fast and hard. Thor, as the God of Thunder, found lightning to be a useful and appropriate weapon.

The origins of this particular hammer are steeped in myth. One of the legends describes it as having fallen to Earth as a meteor; other sources state that the trickster God, Loki, manufactured it. Its power was legendary, too. Mjolnir was able to destroy **mountains** or topple giants with a single strike. A particular feature of the hammer, which made it especially useful, as a weapon of war, was its boomerang-like quality of returning to whoever threw it.

As an **amulet**, the Mjolnir offers protection, and despite origins that are squarely placed within the pagan realms, it has managed to slip the wide net cast by Christianity. It continues to be popular today as a major symbol of the Asatru faith.

MONAD

The Monad, in essence, refers to the upright symbol of a **vertical line**, but is also taken to mean The One, the Godhead, the intellect.

The root of the word is Greek and it shares its origins with the word for Monastery as well as Mono.

Dr. John Dee was an occultist and astrologer and most famously was advisor to Queen Elizabeth I. He devised a magical sign that he called the Monad, which is illustrated here. Published in 1583, the Monad of Dr. John Dee is an amalgam of the **four** symbols that represent the **Sun**, the **Moon**, the **Elements** and **Fire** (since this related to **Aries**, the first sign of the **Zodiac**). This Monad carried such logical symbolic meaning that it was adopted by the **Alchemists** and the **Rosicrucians**. Dee also pointed out that his Monad contained the constituent symbols of all the **planets** too.

NAVAJO SAND PAINTING

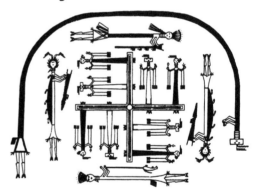

Bearing some relation to the **rangoli** patterns of India, sand painting is not restricted to the Navajo people but is also practiced by Australian Aborigines and Tibetan Monks. The Indian and Tibetan drawings serve to remind of the impermanence of life.

However, the Navajo version of this very ancient art is carried out specifically for healing purposes. There are numerous different traditional designs, created painstakingly like the rangoli, by letting the fine sand run through the fingers, accompanied by prayers and chanting. The symbols in the picture include representations of the Gods to whom the appeal is made.

Once the painting is finished, the "patient" destroys the image by sitting in the middle of it where he not only absorbs the energy of the symbols but also releases his "illness" into the sand. This sand is disposed of with care, considered toxic after it has been used in this way.

The authentic ritual sand paintings are a closely guarded secret. Any paintings likely to be seen by the outside world will have been created in a different way, using incorrect **colors** or sequences of shapes to ensure these sacred symbols retain their potency.

NAZAR

This is an **amulet** designed specifically to repel the **Evil Eye**. Originating in Turkey, the Nazar is found in shops frequented by tourists. It is a pretty piece of circular **blue** glass, with additional dollops of glass set in a concentric **circle** of blue and white to represent the eye. Traditionally, the nazar is hung in windows or **doorways** to repel undesirable influences.

NER TAMID

The Ner Tamid is the Hebrew name for the sanctuary lamp, which burns constantly in both synagogues and Roman Catholic churches and chapels. Other names include the Altar Lamp or Eternal Flame.

The lamp is a sacred symbol of the omnipresence of God (in the Tabernacle) or Jesus (in the Church), and the flame itself equates the spirit of God or Jesus to the power of light and the **Sun**, which also burns constantly. The lamp is made from **red** glass to differentiate between other candles. Keeping such an important symbolic flame alight is an important task; however, this is much easier now, since electric versions are available.

Omamori

These **amulets** are given to devotees of the Shinto religion when they make an offering or donation to a **shrine**. Omamori, in Japanese, means "blessed protector." The charms are generally made of paper or fabric that is made into small packets or pouches and then consecrated in a **temple** ritual. They usually have the name of their temple of origin on the front and a symbol of good luck or prosperity on the other side. Sometimes, Omamori are made with more permanent materials, such as wood or metal.

Omphalos

Omphalos is a Greek word meaning "**navel**," although the concept is not restricted to Greece but is an archetypal symbol found all over the world. Because the navel, in the human being, is the point of contact with the life-force generated by the mother, the omphalos, similarly, connects the **Earth** with the life-force generated by the Godhead.

Usually symbolized by a great **stone**, the omphalos is representative of both the physical navel and spiritual navel that is the center of the world. The idea also equates to other symbols including the **Lingam**, the **World Tree**, and the **Axis Mundi.**

The most famous omphalos stone in the world is the one at **Delphi** in Greece. Ancient Greeks considered this omphalos to be the center of the Earth; not only that, but this particular omphalos stone was a channel of communication between **three** worlds; the mortals living on the Earth, the Deities in Heaven, and the dead in the Underworld. Legend has it that **Zeus** sent out two **eagles** from opposite ends of the Earth to determine the exact position of this auspicious spot. The omphalos was situated at the point where the **birds** crossed in flight.

There are many other omphalos symbols scattered around the globe. The stone that the **Ark of the Covenant** rested on, in the Inner Sanctum of the **Temple at Jerusalem**, is an omphalos. For Buddhists, it is symbolized by the **tree** that the Buddha sat under when he achieved enlightenment. The Celts have several single standing stones, called **Menhirs**, that are phallic symbols as well as omphalos symbols.

Onniont

For the Iriquois an Onniont is a particularly potent form of **Aaskouandy**, which itself is a magical charm believed to have a mind of its own. The Aaskouandy generally comes in the form of a **stone** or similar object that is found unexpectedly.

The Onniont comes in the shape of a **fish**, or **serpent**, and gives its owner the power to pierce anything in his way, such as trees, rocks, or wild animals, in order to reach the object of desire.

Orphic egg

This is the symbol of an **egg** encircled by a coiled snake, and depicts the Greek myth that the world was hatched from a silver egg; this silver egg sat in the darkness, an image that is closely associated with the Moon. It is sometimes called the **Cosmic Egg**.

Orthodox Cross

This is a **Latin Cross** with two additional crossbars at the top and a slanting bar at the bottom that resembles the footrest that, some people argue, was a feature of the cross upon which Christ was crucified. The additional bar at the top of the cross represents the initials I.N.R.I., meaning "Jesus of Nazareth, King of the Jews," a phrase designed to taunt Jesus.

Because the lower footrest slants diagonally, it symbolizes two directions, Heaven and Hell. The thieves who were executed at either side of Christ have their destinies sym-

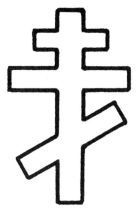

bolized by this slant. The repentant thief takes the upward path toward Heaven, while the other, not at all repentant, goes to Hell.

Ouroboros

The **circle** and the **serpent** are both symbols that are potent with mystical meaning, and they come together in the ouroboros.

The serpent that constantly revolves, swallowing the end of its own tail, most commonly forms the circular or oval shape of the ouroboros. However, sometimes the symbol is constructed of a **dragon** rather than a serpent, or a pair of snakes that swallow one another's tails. The dragon and the serpent are closely connected; both creatures often guard treasure of some kind.

The ouroboros is a primal symbol of great antiquity. Although it makes its first appearance in Ancient Egypt around 1600 BC, it is likely to be even older than this. The ouroboros was named by the Greeks, and means "self-devourer." The ouroboros speaks of motion, continuity, and self-fertilization.

Although the name is Greek the ouroboros as a concept appears elsewhere; for example, in Norse myth the great serpent Jormungandr is so large that he can hug the planet and still be able to grasp the end of his tail in his teeth. It also appears in Hindu myth as the serpent Goddess, Nahusha, which creates the world. It also hints at the image of the **Cosmic Egg** that is encircled by the spiraling snake.

The most obvious explanation for the ouroboros is that it symbolizes not only the cyclical nature of time and the seasons, but also the eternal cycle of rebirth. This idea makes sense because the serpent's habit of shedding its skin makes it an ideal symbol of rebirth and renewal. For the Gnostics, the ouroboros symbolizes eternity. At the same time, it serves as a reminder of the confines of the material world, and yet of aspiration to a higher state of being.

The serpent is a creature of the **Earth**, close to the ground. The circle is a symbol of completion and spiritual perfection, and in this sense, the ouroboros demonstrates a union of opposites, Heaven and Earth working in harmony.

There is also a double ouroboros, where the serpent twists into the **infinity symbol.**

In **alchemy**, the symbol speaks of purity, wholeness, and infinity.

PA KUA

This is a hexagonal shape formed by the **eight** trigrams of the **I Ching**. These trigrams are sometimes carved onto wood and used to frame the **mirror** of the same name that is said to be an effective tool belonging to the ancient discipline of Feng Shui.

PAISLEY

The name Paisley might seem incongruous for a design motif which is of Eastern origin. The original pattern, known as the "buta" in Persia and as the "mankolam" in India, made its way across the continents in the form of shawls and fabrics brought back by Scottish soldiers returning from the colonies in the nineteenth century. The weavers in the small Renfrewshire town of Paisley, already known for its woven and printed fabrics, copied the designs; hence the name.

There are several theories as to the inspiration for the familiar, curving teardrop design but it is generally believed to have been inspired by plant or fruit forms. The mango that inspired the mankolam is an emblem of fertility and good luck. It may also be a derivation of the shape of the leaf of the sacred **Bodhi tree** that the Buddha was sitting underneath when he gained enlightenment.

PALAD KHIK

The Palad Khik is a very specific kind of **amulet** that originates in Thailand. The phrase means "Honorable Surrogate **Penis**" and this accurately describes the form of the charm. The Honorable Surrogate Penis is secreted underneath the clothes of Thai males, offset from the real thing, in the hopes that it will absorb any evil spells that might be directed by malicious people against the genuine penis.

The Palad Khik originated in India and was brought to Thailand 1200 years ago. These ancient amulets once featured inscriptions to Shiva, then to Buddha. The idea of

protecting the sexual parts naturally transcends any religious boundaries. However, modern Palad Khik amulets bear inscriptions written in an ancient style of script that is impenetrable to most latter-day Thais, but which no doubt lends an enticing antique appeal to the tourist market.

PALM CROSS

The **Palm** Cross is traditionally made and given to Christian churchgoers on Palm Sunday, just before **Easter**, to commemorate the victorious entry of Christ into Jerusalem not long before he was crucified. Palm leaves—a symbol of victory—were strewn on the ground along the route taken by Christ, hence their use in the manufacture of the crosses.

PAPAL SYMBOLS

The regalia, insignia, symbols, and emblems belonging to the Pope, the Roman Catholic Church, and the Vatican City State are so numerous that they merit a separate entry. These symbols tend to be occluded in mystery, often subject to conjecture and confusion. However, any mysteries can be clarified with a little analysis.

Most importantly, the Pope himself is a living, breathing symbol, the human representation of God on Earth.

Triregnum

Also called the tiara or Triple **Crown**, the Triregnum has not been in use since the early 1960s but prior to this time was used in the coronation of the Pope and subsequently in important processions. In appearance, it looks similar to some of the headgear depicted in Ancient Egyptian reliefs and statuary and it fulfils many of the functions associated with ritual headgear and crowns; it enhances the status of the wearer, making him taller and more noticeable. The Triregnum brings the wearer closer to Heaven; the shape can emulate the **halo** or a similar sign of sanctity. There have been several of these "crowns," and 22 are still in existence today. Since 1342 when the third part was added, the symbolic aspects of these tiaras have been the cone shape, the rich encrustation of **jewels**, and of course the three levels that give the Triregnum its name. When Pope Paul VI decided to simply lay the crown on the **altar** in St. Peter's Basilica after the Second Vatican Council, the very act itself symbolized an acknowledgement of a new time for the Vatican, a time of humility and, effectively, a new start cognizant with changing times.

There are numerous theories about the symbolic meanings of the three parts of the crown; moral, temporal, and spiritual authority; the Holy Trinity; the acknowledgement of the wearer as being Father of Princes, Ruler of the World, and Jesus Christ on Earth; also, the Heavenly, Earthly, and Human aspects of the Universe.

The Triregnum, although currently not in use as a physical object, appears on the flag of the Vatican City.

The Fisherman's Ring

This is a **gold** ring with a depiction of St. Peter casting his nets from a boat, also known as the Pescatorio. A new ring is cast for each

pope, including his name around the edge of the picture, and the ring that belonged to the old Pope is smashed. This means that there is only ever one of these rings in existence. The destruction of the ring had a practical purpose as well as a symbolic meaning (signifying the end of the old reign). The ring was used by the Pope to seal private correspondence, so destroying it ensured that no one could use it in the interregnum, the period where there was no pope. The image on the ring is now represented as a stamp, although the kissing of the ring is still a mark of respect for the Pope.

The Crossed Keys

Another of the symbols of the Vatican flag and other papal insignia is that of the crossed keys of St. Peter, to whom Christ gave the **keys** to the Kingdom of Heaven. One key is **silver**; one key is **gold**, the two bound together by a **red** cord. The silver represents the authority of the Pope on Earth and the Gold, his authority in Heaven. The keys are crossed in a **saltire cross**.

The Umbraculum

Traditionally, the Pope was always shaded in some way, and the Umbraculum, or Umbrella, which appears on papal insignia, signifies not only this idea but also the notion of protection. At one time a man would walk along with the actual object ensuring that the Pope was shaded and protected at all times. This practice no longer continues but the emblem remains. It has parallels to the parasol that is one of the **eight sacred symbols** of Tibetan Buddhism.

Papal Cross

This cross has three cross bars, of graduated lengths. Like the **Triregnum**, the symbolism of these three bars is open to conjecture, but it is generally held that they represent both the Holy Trinity and the three aspects of the power of the Pope. This cross also looks rather like a **ladder**, and so it represents a symbolic stairway to Heaven.

PARASPAROPGRAHO JIVANAM

See **Jain symbol**.

PAX CULTURA

The symbol of the International Banner of Peace, or Pax Cultura, was designed with the intention that it would act as a kind of cultural **Red Cross** symbol, to protect sites or areas of universal cultural heritage or importance during time of war. This symbol comprises three **circles** (representing art, science, and religion) formed into a **triangle** shape, surrounded by a further circle, representing the idea of unity.

PEACE SIGN

This circular sign, with its upside-down forked **cross** shape, is ubiquitous as a peace sign and, specifically, as the symbol for the Campaign for Nuclear Disarmament. Although the sign is not strictly secret or particularly sacred, it is a good example of how a sign is designed and how the elements of symbols can be misinterpreted.

Some Evangelical Christians have supposed that the cross-type symbol inside the **circle** is a nod to the cross that was used for upside-down crucifixion at the hands of the

Although it started out as being the emblem of the CND movement, the symbol is now universally accepted as a sign of peace.

PENTACLE

Sometimes there is confusion between the pentacle and the **pentagram.** For the record, the pentagram is the five-pointed star symbol, whereas the pentacle is a more generic term for a mystical or magical symbol.

It is likely that the word "pentacle" originates from the Latin root, "pend," to hang; hence "pendant." A pentacle is often designed to hang around the neck.

The pentacle can be made of any material, although Trithemius (a fifteenth-century abbot with a great knowledge of the occult) recommended "virgin parchment" or a square plate of **silver**. Various symbols and signs that are appropriate for its intended use are then drawn or engraved on the pentacle, including the signs belonging to the forces or spirits that the magician decides to invoke. Sometimes the reverse of the pentacle features the **Seal of Solomon**, adding even more magical kudos to the object.

For more complex magical endeavors, such as raising spirits, a series of powerful pentacles are designed, which the adept reveals one at a time to the spirits in question until the object of the exercise is accomplished, at which point the pentacles are all covered up again.

Emperor Nero, called the Cross of Nero or the Cross of St. Peter. This particular cross has unfortunate connotations of Satanism because of their reported penchant for turning Christian symbols or prayers back to front or upside down. The cross shape also resembles a particular runic symbol that is used by some neo-Nazi groups, although here again there is a gross misunderstanding. The symbol actually means "elk," a creature that has no shady symbolic meaning whatsoever. However, this was misinterpreted as meaning "life." Therefore, if inverted it should, in theory, mean "death." All the neo-Nazis got for their pains was an inverted elk, which is more comic than sinister.

The actual invention of the symbol has a simple story. Gerald Holtom, instrumental in the Campaign for Nuclear Disarmament, created it. A Christian, Gerald originally used the **Christian Cross** within the circle, but there were objections from parties who felt that this could be misinterpreted or might alienate some parties. So Holtom thought about the shape of a human being in despair, with arms outstretched downwards in a pleading gesture, and the sign was born.

PENTAGRAM

It is possible that the pentagram was discovered by very early astronomical research, in the Tigris–Euphrates area, some 6000 years ago. Archaeologists have found fragments of pottery with the symbol, dating back to 4000 years ago, but it was Pythagoras who really brought the five-pointed star to the prominent position it holds today.

If an **apple** is cut in half across its "equator" then the pattern of the seeds is revealed, a perfect five-pointed star or pentagram. The repercussions of this hidden magical symbol are far-reaching. **Five**, comprised of the feminine number **2** and the masculine number **3**, is the number of harmony, of the union of opposites (for example in sexual congress), and of marriage. It is also the number of humankind because of the five points of extremity of the human body. When Eve gave Adam the Apple of Knowledge in the Garden of Eden, therefore, it was not just a piece of **fruit** she was offering him, but a potent symbol of wisdom.

Eating the fruit that contains the pentagram resulted in a profound awakening for Adam and Eve. They became not only aware of their own sexual natures, but they realized that they could make their own choices.

Not only is the pentagram a symbol of power, but it is imbued with actual power and is used in spell casting and the revelation of secrets.

The pentagram is either pentagonal or **star**-shaped. Earliest representations of it appear scratched on the walls of **caves**, and it is understandable that ancient man would have a natural and automatic reverence for the stars; this is as relevant today as it was then.

The ubiquity of this sign can't be stressed enough. It has associated not only with pagan practice but also with Christian mysticism, **druidry, magic, sacred geometry, alchemy, the Kabbalah**; it appears in the **Tarot** where it can represent the suit of Coins, and it is an important symbol in **Freemasonry**, where it is called the **"Blazing Star."**

One instance of its use was as a secret symbol whereby followers of **Pythagoras** could recognize one another since, as Adam had discovered, it was the **key** to higher knowledge.

Pythagoras held that 5 was the number of Man, because of both the division of the soul and of the body into five parts each. Further, the five points of the pentagram represented the **elements: earth, air, fire, water,** and psyche, or **ether** in the Eastern tradition. The followers would describe the sign of the pentagram upon themselves in exactly the same way as do **pagan** people, who use it as a sign of protection, in much the same way that Christians use the **Latin Cross**.

If you want to try it, here's how. The sign starts at the left **breast**, and then goes to the **forehead**, then to the right breast, then the left shoulder followed by the right shoulder, and back again to the left breast. Pythagoreans would accompany this with a greeting of "good health," because another hidden meaning within the pentagram is that the initials of the five elements which each of the points represented were an anagram for the name of the Goddess of healing, Hygiea.

In the **Kabbalah**, the pentagram represents the upper five **sephiroth** on the **tree of life**, whose qualities are justice, mercy, wisdom, understanding, and transcendent splendor.

Freemasonry draws upon much of the Pythagorean symbolism of the Pentagram, although it is also seen as a reminder that Christ was spirit descended into matter, and as such represents the Star of Bethlehem.

The inverted pentagram has been accorded a more sinister interpretation than was ever intended; up until relatively recently it didn't seem to matter which way up the star landed, after all this symbol is like the **circle** in that it has no beginning and no end. However, the symbol of **Baphomet** makes use of the upside-down pentagram.

The Pentagram is the sign of Venus, both the planet known as the morning star, and the Goddess. Over the course of four years and one day, the planet describes the shape of a pentagram in the sky. Uniquely, Venus is the only planet whose movements trace such a graphically recognizable symbol, a secret sign written in the sky.

PERSIAN RUGS

If you have a Persian rug in your house, then every day you unwittingly walk over an ancient series of elaborate secret symbols whose colorful intricacies hide a wealth of information.

No two Persian rugs are ever the same. Despite the fact that some of the patterns may have been copied for centuries, the makers weave in a deliberate "mistake" so that the pattern is never perfect; this is an acknowledgment that only Allah is perfect.

The rugs themselves divide into two general categories; those with curving, floral patterns, and those with a more geometric design.

Some of the inspirations for these patterns include the architecture of mosques, **flowers**, **trees**, and other vegetation, **animals**, spirals, and the curious paisley design. Some patterns were drawn by the original designer without his **hand** ever leaving the page.

The patterns of the rugs also tell of their provenance and the tribes that designed them, each tribe having its own unique patterns.

Some of the hidden patterns within Persian rugs have specific meanings. These include the **parrot** (love), the **pomegranate** (abundance), the **tree of life** (eternity) the carnation (happiness), and the **camel** (wealth).

PHILOSOPHER'S STONE

There are few symbols so crammed full of esoteric meaning or arcane mystery as the Philosopher's Stone. It is so elusive that it has no actual pictorial emblem, but is hidden within a series of cleverly veiled clues and linguistic ambiguities from the realms of **alchemy.**

The process of making the Philosopher's Stone reputedly requires just **seven** steps, and oblique instructions for these steps are described in **The Emerald Tablet**. However, like the Holy Grail, the Philosopher's Stone exists on a metaphysical level as well as any supposed physical level, so analysis of these instructions has to be carried out on many levels. This is the stone of the Philosophers for a very good reason.

Essentially, to the Alchemists, the Philosopher's Stone was a substance that could effect the transmutation not only from **lead** into **gold**, but could turn any substance into something else, seemingly having the same power as a **magic wand**. The Stone was also able to restore youth and so had the power of eternal life.

Reputedly, the ingredients needed to make this stone would not necessarily come about by hard work, but would be revealed to a very few "chosen ones" by the angels; angelic intervention itself is often a synonym for a stroke of inspiration or intuition that goes beyond logic.

There have been a few characters throughout history who have claimed to discover the Philosopher's Stone, including Paracelsus. In the sixteenth century, he put forward the theory that the Philosopher's Stone was an undiscovered element, which all the other elements were made from. Sir Isaac Newton was intrigued by alchemical processes and delved deeply into the mysteries of the Philosopher's Stone. Perhaps the bruising stroke of inspiration he received when the **apple** fell on his head and he "discovered" the Universal Law of Gravity was his own personal Philosopher's Stone, won not by hard work but by deductive reasoning and a timely knock on the **head**.

Phurba

This is a sacred knife, used only in ritual practices by Tibetan Buddhists. Like the **Athame** of the Western tradition, it is employed to create the sacred spaces that are used for rites and ceremonies. Its design is based on a stake used in ancient times to tether sacrificial animals, and it is used to describe a **magic circle** in the same way as a **compass**. The phurba can only be owned or handled by initiates.

Prayer flag

Belonging to the Tibetan Buddhist tradition, these are lengths of colorful flags that bear images and **mantras** or prayers. The flags take two forms, either horizontal strings of many flags, or single, vertical flags. Both kinds traditionally punctuate the sacred landscape, fluttering in the breeze among the **mountains, temples, stupas,** and **monasteries** of Nepal and Tibet although they are now seen in other places.

Typical prayer flags come in a series of five differently colored cloths with woodblock designs that represent the five elements. The order and significance of the colors is **blue** (space), **white** (water), **red** (fire), **green** (air), and **yellow** (earth). The designs include mantras and depictions of auspicious symbols such as the **Triratna**.

Tibetans believe that the prayers printed on the flags are carried to the Gods, hence their appearance in high places. As the colors fade, so the prayers become a permanent part of the Universe. Pristine strings of new flags join the faded and tattered older ones, symbolic of the continual renewal of life. In common with other sacred items, prayer flags should not touch the ground.

PRAYER STICK

A fetish object belonging to the Native American tradition, prayer sticks vary in size and materials but all of them share the same intention, that of carrying prayers to the Gods by means of the **feathers** that are attached to the stick in such a way that they flutter in the breeze.

PRAYER STRING

Effectively a string of beads of a number that is significant to individual belief systems, despite their different names or different numbers of beads, effectively they all fulfil the same functions, as an aid to meditation or prayer and a reminder of the tenets of the faith.

For Catholics, the prayer string is called the Rosary, from the Latin, Rosarium, so-called because of its association with the Virgin Mary, for whom the rose is an attribute. Today's rosaries most frequently contain **fifty** beads grouped in sets of **ten** with a larger bead between each set and a **cross** at the very end. Each group of ten is called a decade. The beads are "told," that is, they are passed through the **fingers** with each repetition of a selected group of prayers.

For Buddhist and Hindus, the prayer strings are called Mala, and have **108** beads. One hundred and eight is a sacred number in the Dharmic religions, corresponding to the stages of development of the World, the number of manifestation. The Goddess **Sarasvati** holds a Mala with **50** beads; as Goddess of learning, she is also Goddess of the alphabet, and each of these beads corresponds to the 50 letters of the Sanskrit alphabet.

For Muslims, the prayer string is called the Tasbih, and has **99** beads that correspond to the 99 names of Allah.

Sikhs use a piece of woolen string as a Mala, with 99 **knots** rather than beads.

Lestovka

This is an unusual Russian form of prayer string, generally made of leather and belonging to "old" believers such as the Russian Orthodox Old Ritualists. The 99 "steps" are made by looping the leather strip around twigs or sticks of wood and the whole is completed with **four** flaps—generally triangular in shape, which represent the four Gospels.

Komboloi

Not strictly a rosary, the Komboloi is the string of worry beads that are often seen in the hands of Greek men. The Komboloi looks similar to the rosary but has no religious significance.

PRAYER WHEEL

Also known as Hkhorlo, or Mani Wheels, prayer wheels are an inherent and essential part of Tibetan Buddhism.

The actual prayer wheel itself comes in many different sizes. Some are small enough to be held in the hand, others are large enough to be placed in streams where the action of the flowing **water** keeps the wheel turning. Wheels a meter or more high can be seen at **temples**. Whatever the size, the basic construction of the prayer wheel is the same. A central axle has a long strip of paper wound around it. On this paper is written, over and over, the words of the mantra "**Om Mani Padme Hum.**" The paper is encased in a drum, and in the smaller handheld wheels, the protruding axle acts as a handle so that the wheel can be turned.

Sometimes prayer wheels are constructed with a piece of human skull **bone** secreted in the handle.

Symbolically, the **wheel** itself used to be so sacred in Tibet that it was never used for such a mundane purpose as transport; and any carts or vehicles there were usually not of Tibetan origin.

Prayer wheels are always turned in a clockwise direction, following the path of the **Sun** and to ensure that the words written on the paper are traveling in the right direction.

Symbolically, it is believed that the combination of the elements of the prayer wheel and its turning action produce a powerful energizing spell, which connects the microcosm (the person doing the turning) with the macrocosm (the Gods and the Universe). Both the written and spoken forms of the syllables of the **mantra** carry a sacred power that is further enhanced by motion.

It seems that the symbolic purpose of the prayer wheel is far more powerful than its physical form, however, and it is now possible to get electronic prayer wheels (called Thardo Khorla) or digital prayer wheels, which will download onto a computer.

Q

See **Quintessence**.

QUESTION MARK

This sign is used every day, isn't it? Therefore, it may not be thought of as a symbol of mystery, but that is just what it is. It also resembles the sacred staff of augurs, the lituus that ended with a spiral. Its component elements are the wave, turned on its side. The wave is emblematic of the area between the spiritual and material worlds, that is, between what is a possibility and what exists in actual reality. The **dot**, or bindhu, below, is synonymous with either the seed of potential, or actual reality.

The question mark is used to describe uncertainty or apprehension, but the element of the dot means that the symbol acts as a reminder that the person asking the question has the possible answer within himself.

QUINTESSENCE

Quite literally, the quintessence stands for the "fifth essence" (from the Latin "Quintus," meaning five), and while not strictly speaking a symbol, it forms an important philosophical key to the understanding of many of our secret signs and sacred symbols. It is the element or feature that binds the different parts of a symbol into a harmonious whole, and can often be found in the center of a symbol, where it may be indicated with that most deceptively humble of symbols, the **dot,** or sometimes the letter **Q**.

RAELIAN STAR

If you should happen to see this particular symbol on the car bumper that is ahead of you, then you will know that you are likely to be following the vehicle of a Raelian cult member. The Raelians believe that the planet Earth was created by a people who came from the sky, but not from a God. These people are called the Elohim, and are extraterrestrials.

The symbol used to be comprised of a six-pointed **star** whose arms cleverly morphed into the ancient **Sun** symbol, the **swastika**. However, the symbol was adapted and the swastika removed lest it should inadvertently cause offence. The Raelian Star resembles a spinning galaxy.

Rangoli

Rangoli patterns are known by various different names throughout India according to the region. The word describes both an ancient Hindu tradition and a form of folk art. Known as the **Kolam** in Southern India, this is a beautiful, colorful, and elaborate design that is generally drawn on the floor or on the ground with dyed **rice** flour. Rangoli drawing is not restricted to high days and holidays but is a part of everyday ritual, even in the villages where, at the **doorway** of the house, the pattern welcomes not only visitors but is said to attract the Goddess of Abundance, Lakshmi.

Rangoli drawing started, it is said, when the son of a High Priest died. All the Priests' friends and relatives prayed to the Lord Brahma, who told the King to draw a picture of the boy on the floor. Brahma then brought the drawing to life, so restoring the Priest's son.

The patterns are initially constructed with a series of geometrically placed **dots**, which help the artist to define the shape. The fine rice powder is held with the **finger** and **thumb.** The dots are then joined up by trick-ling the powder with the fingers, requiring concentration and a steady hand. Finally, the pattern is colored with dyed rice powder.

Despite the care and attention that goes into the drawing of the rangoli patterns, it is considered right and proper that footprints destroy them during the course of the day. This in itself symbolizes change and mortality, and is a reminder not to value material possessions, or the works of man, above the world of spirit and the Gods.

The same conceptual celebration of the impermanence of life is celebrated in the finely wrought powder **mandalas** created by Tibetan monks.

Rebis

The Rebis, or Twofold Matter, is just one of the symbols used to denote the idea of the hermaphrodite. It is a perfection of being, comprised by a perfect balance of opposites. The **yin yang** from the Chinese tradition and the **yab yum** from India are among the other symbols that reflect the same idea.

The Rebis illustrated here comes from the rich Alchemical tradition. It is taken from Basil Valentine's *Theathrum Chemicum* (1613).

This particular rendering of it is crammed with symbols, as are many of the drawings of **alchemy**.

The oval shape of the frame suggests the **egg**, symbol of the cosmos and of new potential. Inside the egg is a human figure with one body and the two heads of a man and a woman. The figure stands on a winged, fire-breathing **dragon** that in turn is crouched on the orb of the planet. The dragon symbolizes manifestation, the **fire** that shoots from its mouth is symbolic of the spirit. The planet has **wings**, too, denoting the marriage of the Earth with the Heavens. Inside the planet, there is a **cross**, its **four** arms denoting the four directions and the four elements. In the center of the circle is the **dot**, indicating the fifth element or **quintessence**. There is also a **square** inside the **circle**, and a **triangle**.

Five **stars** surround the figures; **5** is the number of the union of the feminine **2** with the masculine **3**, the union of opposites and the number of marriage. Each star has **six** points; here, the number 6 stands for the male element of fire as depicted by the upward triangle, joining with the female element, **water**, the downward-pointing triangle. The star also alludes to the notion "as above, so below." Above the head of the man is the **Sun**; above the head of the woman is the **crescent Moon**.

RED STRING

You may spot someone wearing a piece of **red** thread or string around the left wrist. This symbol will tell you that you are looking at someone who follows the teachings of the **Kabbalah**, an esoteric area of Jewish mysticism. The red string itself is said to protect the wearer from the **Evil Eye** or from others' envy. The red string itself is an assuming item, and reminds the wearer of our humble origins and that to be human is to be fallible. It is worn on the left side of the body since this is the side that is believed to receive energy first.

Red string is tied around the tomb of Rachel, the great Jewish matriarch. This string is then cut up and given as **amulets**. Each string is tied with **seven knots**, and as each knot is tied, it is a reminder to the wearer to refrain from thinking negative thoughts about others. As a charm, it is full of positive intentions.

Although the piece of red string is as humble an object as its symbolic meaning, it is ironic that some people choose to pay a lot of money for one.

RINGSTONE SYMBOL

This is a sacred symbol of the Baha'i faith, and is so called because it frequently appears on **rings** or other **jewelry**, and is an identifying feature of followers of Baha'i.

Each part of the symbol has significance.

The upper line is the World of God; the central line is the world of manifestation of God's ideas, and the lower line stands for the World of Man.

The vertical line is the element that connects all three, and as such has the same significance as the **World Tree**.

The two **five-pointed stars** that stand at either side of the symbol represent the two messengers of God for this particular age, Bab, who called himself "the gate," and Baha'u'llah, a follower of Bab, who founded the Baha'i religion in the nineteenth century.

The official symbol of the Baha'i faith is an elongated five-pointed star, called the "Hakyal," meaning "temple." Baha'u'llah's writings sometimes appear in the shape of this star.

Roma [Romany]
Chakra

A relatively new symbol, the Roma chakra was adopted as recently as 1971 at the first Romany Congress. The symbol is a neat reminder not only of the origins of the Romani in India, (hence its similarity to the **chakra wheel**), but it also points to the wandering nature of these nomadic people because it looks like the wheel of the Vardo, the special caravans which they have used for centuries. The wheel has **sixteen** spokes.

Rosy Cross

The Rosy cross or **Rose** cross is believed to have been adopted by the Christian Church in its first century, and combines the masculine principle, the material world and the cycle of birth and death (the **cross**) with that of the feminine principle and spiritual unfolding (the **rose**). The rose also signifies the blood of Christ and the power of redemption, and represents Christ's mother, Mary, in her guise as the Goddess, and with whom the rose has always been closely associated.

However, the Rose Cross is known most famously as the symbol for the Rosicrucian Society, and the illustration shown here is based on the Rose Cross Lamen that belongs to the organization.

The Rosicrucian Order was founded by Christian Rosenkreuz, an alchemist traveling in the East in the fourteenth century when he stumbled upon ancient teachings that he passed on to seven other men. They swore that the knowledge would remain hidden for one hundred years.

This legend was written about in two documents, the "Fama Fraternititis" and the "Confessio Fraternititis," published in 1614 and 1615 respectively. Like the Alchemists, the Rosicrucians kept their knowledge veiled and clouded in riddles. However, the Rosy Cross symbol is said to hold the entire bundle of Rosicrucian philosophical secrets within it, providing it is correctly analyzed.

The Golden Dawn also made good use of the versatile Rose Cross, making it into a sort of one-stop dictionary of meanings and reminders. The **Zodiac** and **planets**, the Hebrew **alphabet**, the **Kabbalah** and a whole slew of other elements were heaped into this one intriguing symbol.

Ru

See **Vesica Piscis**.

Rudraksha bead

The Rudraksha **Tree**, or Eleacarpus Ganitrus, grows in the Northern part of India and Pakistan, and the bead is actually its **fruit**, that shrivels to a hard, woodlike texture.

These beads are highly revered as sacred items, since they symbolize the tears that Shiva shed for humanity. Legend says that the first tear that dropped on the ground became the first rudraksha tree, the word itself meaning either "red eyed" or alternatively Rudra (shiva) and Aksha (**eye**)—the Eye of

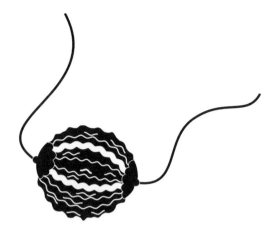

Shiva. The bead is a powerful symbol of protection against the **evil eye**, and symbolizes the eye of Shiva.

Rudraksha beads vary in price according to their perceived power, which is dictated in part by the number of "mukhtis," or facets, which comprise the bead. The most valuable and therefore the most efficacious, is the Ek Mukhti Rudraksha, or one-faceted bead, which is flat and generally has the oval eye shape, reinforcing its symbolic meaning.

Rudraksha beads are used as sacred ornamentation and there are numerous rules as to how, when and by whom they should be worn. For example, it is considered bad form for a menstruating woman to wear her rudraksha beads. The beads are cleaned, blessed, and then charged with power before use.

These holy beads are also used in the japa mala or sacred **prayer strings** of the Hindu monks. These japa mala consist of **108** beads, since 108 is a sacred number in the Dharmic religions.

SACRED HEART

The Sacred Heart symbol was revealed in a vision to a nun, Mary Marguerite Alacoque, in seventeenth-century France. The **heart** is encircled around the center with a **crown** of **thorns**, has flames shooting from the top, and the whole is surmounted by a **cross**. The actual elements of the symbol are self-explanatory, but the symbol rose to prominence when the Bishop of Marseille consecrated his diocese to the Sacred Heart to try to avert the plague that was rampaging through the town. Somehow, the area remained immune from the disease and so the Sacred Heart gained a reputation as a symbol not only of good luck but also of divine intervention.

ST. ANDREW'S CROSS

See **Saltire**.

ST. JOHN'S CROSS

See **Templar Cross**.

ST. PETER'S CROSS

See **Inverted cross**.

SALTIRE

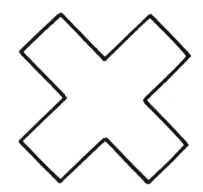

The Saltire is also called the **St. Andrew's Cross**. Legend has it that when Andrew (one of Christ's disciples) was going to be crucified, he deemed himself unworthy to be executed in exactly the same way as his messiah, so the **diagonal** cross was used.

How, then, did Andrew become the Patron Saint of Scotland and the Saltire come to be adopted as the flag of the country, given that Andrew was born near Galilee more than 2000 years ago? Apparently it was an accident. Legend has it that a Greek monk was warned that Andrew's remains were going to be moved from their burial place, and that he should take them "to the ends of the Earth" for safekeeping. This determined monk (possible St. Rule) managed to make it all the way to Scotland, where he was shipwrecked at a place that was later renamed St. Andrews. A **chapel** was constructed to contain the relics; later a **cathedral** would be built on the spot.

The Scottish flag, which shows the **white** saltire of St. Andrew on a **blue** background, is one of the oldest national flags in the world, and dates back to the ninth ceentury.

Scales

Wherever scales or balances appear in mystical symbolism, they are generally used to denote a metaphorical kind of weighing rather than a physical one. Maat, the Egyptian Goddess of Truth, balances the **heart** (representing the conscience) on one side of the scales against justice (the **ostrich** feather) on the other. The ostrich feather is a useful analogy for justice since, unlike other **feathers**, its two sides are perfectly balanced. Other mythological and religious characters that hold the scales as a symbol of judgement and authority share the iconography of Maat. These figures include St. Michael, the archangel of the Day of Judgement. The astrological sign of **Libra**, too, is symbolized by the scales.

The notion of finding balance between opposing forces is a common thread running through esoteric beliefs including **alchemy** and the **Kabbalah**. The pivotal part in the center of the scales is itself symbolic of this point of perfection, a return to oneness between male and female, darkness and light, matter and spirit.

The scales and the sword together stand for truth and justice combined.

Scallop shell

The scallop or mussel shell used to be worn on the caps of pilgrims, particularly those that had completed the pilgrimage to Santiago de Compostela. To find out the reason for this a little backtracking is necessary.

The scallop shell is home to the mussel, a marine creature that, like all other animals that inhabit a watery environment, is associated with the **Moon** and the eternal feminine. The personification of this idea is found in Botticelli's **Venus**, the painting of the Goddess rising up from the **ocean**, standing on the shell, covering her modesty with her luxuriant tresses. The shell is shaped like the female sexual organ; indeed, in France the word *moule* means the same thing. **Pearls** also grow within these shells. Mary, the Mother of Jesus, carried a "precious pearl" within her womb. Hence, the symbol of the shell on the cap of the pilgrim.

Scepter

The scepter takes many forms, effectively a shorter and much more ornamental version of a **staff**. It is an emblem of authority and royalty, a phallic symbol. Breaking the scepter indicates a symbolic castration, an abdication of power. In times of antiquity, the scepter was made of reeds, but it gradually became more permanent and decorative. The **orb** is the female counterpart to the scepter.

Scientology cross

Invented by L. Ron Hubbard, the founder of Scientology, this is a **Latin Cross** with **four** rays emanating diagonally from the intersection. Each of the eight directions of this cross stand for a different feature of the faith; the self, creativity, community, survival of the species, life forms in general, matter, spirit, and the Supreme Being.

Scientology symbol

This symbol is composed of a letter S that links two triangles (which point in the same direction). The S stands for Scientology, and each of the triangles represent three tenets of the philosophy of Scientology; the upper **triangle** is called the KRC and stands for Knowledge, Responsibility, and Control, and the lower ARC triangle represents Affinity, Reality, and Communication.

The symbol was first used in 1952.

Scythe

One of the most common symbols of death, the scythe is the tool used by the Grim Reaper as he reaps his harvest of souls. This tool was also the attribute of the God, **Saturn**, who also appears as Chronos, the God of Time. The scythe of these ancient Gods is not quite the doom-laden instrument as it appears in the skeletal hands of the hooded Grim Reaper; it was more a reminder of the cycle of life.

SEAL OF SHAMASH

Shamash was the Sun god in Mesopotamia. This symbol was used for a few centuries either side of 1000 BC in the Euphrates/Tigris region. Its foundation is the **Sun symbol,** the simple **circle** with a **dot** in the centre, but here the foundation shape has the addition of **four** sets of **three** "rays," whose wavy lines look very like those used even today, by children, when they draw the Sun. The vertical and horizontal beams were probably meant to represent the jurisdiction of Shamash over the four directions.

SEAL OF SOLOMON

Also known as the **Star of David** or the Magen David, the Seal of Solomon is a **hexagram,** a symbol whose outward simplicity hides a complex and layered inner meaning. There are several different versions of the Seal of Solomon, but in its most basic form it consists of two interlocking equilateral **triangles,** forming a **six**-pointed **star.**

The easiest way to understand many symbols is simply to look closely at its component parts and see what they appear to be. The upward-pointing triangle looks like a flame, and this is exactly what it represents. In its most basic form, this triangle is the elemental symbol for **fire**. The Western Tradition, the Eastern Tradition, the Kabbalah, alchemy; all are agreed. There is also agreement about the other triangle that balances on its point; it represents **water**.

Fire is the male element, and water is female. The inverted triangle is also the symbolic representation of the **yoni**. In India, the hexagram is called the **Shatkona** and represents the energies of **Shiva** and **Kali** locked in a constant embrace.

Imagine that the star is cut across the middle. On the left side is the element of **air** and on the right is **earth**. Further, the qualities of fire and water are represented; hot and dry, and moist and cold. Already this simple symbol is taking on a different dimension as the star becomes a map of opposing forces which combine to make all living things and is the symbolic epitome of the phrase "as above, so below." More prosaically, the Star of David has been used as the symbol for alcohol, quite literally, "fire water."

In **alchemy**, the Star of David is a reminder of the **seven** planets and the seven basic **metals**. At the top is **silver**/the **Moon**,

then moving around the points of the star in a clockwise direction are **copper/venus**, **mercury**/mercury, **lead/Saturn, Jupiter/ tin**, and **mars/iron**. In the central space, also called the **quintessence**, are the **Sun/ gold**. Sometimes the Seal will acknowledge this central space with a **dot** or the **tau** symbol.

Alchemists are very fond of concealing their symbols in some way, and sometimes the star is disguised as a six-petaled **flower.** It is hidden in this way in the curious alchemical tome, the Mutus Liber; as its name implies, this "Silent Book" has no words but consists of a series of pictures that describe the process of making the **Philosopher's Stone,** the primary ingredient in the Elixir of Life. Elsewhere, the star is concealed as a flower at the center of the maze at **Chartres Cathedral** and even in the **US dollar**, itself a seething mass of hidden secret symbols.

This incredibly versatile symbol is called the Seal of Solomon because, so the story goes, it featured on a magical signet ring belonging to King Solomon. Supposedly, the ring gave him the power to understand the language of **birds** and **animals**, and to conjure up spirits to do his bidding.

The Star of David as a symbol of the Jewish faith—when it is also known as the **Shield of David** or the **Magen David**—only gained common use as recently as 1897. During the Nazi persecution of the Jewish people, stars made of **yellow** cloth were attached to their clothes. Although it had been intended to be a symbol of persecution, after the war this skewed meaning of the symbol was itself flipped over, and took on the opposite meaning, becoming a badge of honor and pride.

In Tibetan Buddhism, this universally important sign makes its appearance as the Dharmodaya of Vajrayogini. This is a three-dimensional hexagram with the **vajra** at the center. The interior of the symbol is **red**, symbolizing bliss, and the exterior is **white**, signifying emptiness. The **three** angular corners of the triangle represent the "emptiness of cause, effect, and phenomena." The six smaller triangles stand for the six perfections; generosity, wisdom, concentration, effort, patience, and discipline. The smaller triangles at the top and bottom are empty, a reminder of the selflessness of all beings. Each of the four triangles at the sides has small "**wheel of joy**" symbols inside them. These Four Joys are joy, perfect joy, the joy of cessation, and innate joy.

SEAL OF THE KNIGHTS TEMPLAR

The Knights Templar was founded in 1118, with the mandate of protecting pilgrims on their way to Jerusalem. They were granted permission to quarter themselves on the **Temple Mount** itself. There are several seals associated with this venerable order, and the "traditional" seal is the one described here. The seal can be found engraved into stonework, particularly in churches and chapels, for example in **Rosslyn Chapel** in Scotland. The seal, wherever it is found, indicates the presence of the Templars.

The seal has images on both sides. On the front is depicted the image of two knights astride a single, galloping **horse**. This symbolizes several things. First, unity in action or a common purpose; the two men are on one horse, heading together in the same direction. Secondly, that fact that the two Knights share one horse is a reminder of the vow of poverty taken by the Knights. Thirdly, the symbol indicates the Spirit of Christ, a reminder of the message in Matthew's gospel that says that wherever two or more believers are gathered together, then Christ will be there too.

The reverse of the seal shows the dome of the Church of the Holy Sepulcher in Jerusalem.

SECRET OF HERMES

See **Smaragdina Tablet**.

SEED OF LIFE

The seed of life forms a part of the construction of the larger **Flower of Life** geometric pattern. Its creation is simple but the hidden meanings within it are complex. Like the Flower of Life, it contains the **circle**, the **vesica piscis**, and the points of the **hexagon** or six-pointed star.

The **seven** circles that form the symbol signify the **six** days of creation, and the central circle represents the seventh day of rest.

SEFER YETZIRAH SYMBOL

The Sefer Yetzirah is a **Kabbalistic** work known as the Book of Creation, the earliest Kabbalistic work reputedly written by Abraham. The symbol associated with it essentially describes the order of Creation. Because the alphabet itself is a collection of secret symbols that contain the secrets of the Universe within them, each component of the symbol also represents the 22 letters of the Hebrew alphabet.

The symbol consists of an upright equilateral **triangle**, surrounded by a **seven**-pointed **star**. This star is further surrounded by a large **12**-pointed star.

Inside the triangle are **three** letters, the "mother" letters that represent the elements of **air**, **water**, and **fire**. The seven-pointed star represents the seven "double" letters. The largest star symbolizes the 12 "simple" letters.

The Sefer Yetzirah also indicates the symbolic **tree of life**, or Otz Chiim, of the Kabbalah. The three "mother" letters are the three horizontal branches of the tree. The seven-pointed star symbolizes the seven vertical paths, and the 12-pointed star indicates the 12 diagonal paths.

SERPENT CROSS

The **Tau Cross** or the **Christian Cross** with the serpent draped around it is an ancient symbol that has several meanings. It was adopted by the Christian faith to signify the triumph of the cross over the **serpent**, that is, the victory of good over evil, and as such, points toward the serpent that twined around the **tree** in the Garden of Eden. It also represents the transformation of the material into the spiritual as the serpent abandons its usual position on the ground and slithers upwards, toward enlightenment.

The Book of Numbers in the Old Testament of the Bible describes an incident when Moses is leading the Children of Israel through the desert. Their numerous complaints and lack of faith led God to punish them with a plague of snakes. Moses counteracted this curse by following God's instructions to make a "brazen serpent," which he put on a pole, a charm against snakebites. This magical serpent was called Nehushtan, and worshipped as an idol.

The Serpent Cross also appears as an alchemical symbol, indicating the elixir of **mercury**, an effective healing substance once the toxin, represented by the snake, had been "killed."

SHATKONA

See **Seal of Solomon**.

SHEELA NA GIG

A surprising and even shocking symbol when seen for the first time, Sheela na Gig is a Celtic symbol that is often carved into stonework. A grotesque sight, Sheela na Gig is a squat little figure with marked exhibitionist tendencies that seems to smile cheekily as she pulls open the lips of her vulva to reveal a gaping hole. It is possible that, like gargoyles and other frightening figures, Sheela was there to protect; also, in view of her position it might be assumed that she is a symbol of sexuality and fertility.

SHIELD KNOT

The Shield Knot is a universal symbol of protection, seen in all cultures around the world. Although it takes different forms, the distinctive features that make it a powerful protecting charm are the **square** shape and the interlacement pattern. One of the earliest known forms is from Mesopotamia and simply consists of a square with a loop at each corner. The same symbol appears in the **Kabbalah** as the "Shema," used to invoke the **four** Archangels.

SHOFAR

This is a musical instrument that is made from the **horn** of a **ram**. It is based on the Biblical horn that is reputed to have had such power and resonance that it blew down the walls of Jericho.

The Shofar is used ritually, sounded to

signal the beginning of the Jewish New Year, **Rosh Hashanah**. The horn is blown one **hundred** times on this occasion. It is also used to signify the start of **Yom Kippur**, the Day of Atonement.

The use of the horn on this occasion follows an instruction in the Book of Leviticus, which directs a "blast" to be sounded "throughout the Land."

SHOU

The Shou or Chou symbol, is frequently seen but not often understood, by anyone not able to understand Chinese. The symbol is an ancient ideogram meaning "long life."

Despite its antiquity it still appears in many places; on furniture, woven into fabric, made into jewelry. The symbol looks a little like a **peach** stone. The peach was the symbol of the God Shou Hsing, who controlled events in the lives of human beings. The peach belonging to the God conferred the gift of immortality.

SIGIL OF AMETH

Also called the Seal of the Truth of God (*ameth* means truth in Hebrew), the Sigil of Ameth is an elaborate symbol, containing an unusual **six**-pointed **star**. The **hexagram** is normally constructed of **two triangles**, one upright and one upside down. The star in this sigil is made using one line. This would imply a powerful protection. In the center of the symbol is a **five**-pointed star, and written in various places are names of angels and of God. The sigil is connected to Enochian magic, since Dr. John Dee saw the sign in a vision, which he believed had been given to him by angels, although the symbol predates the time of Dee by about three centuries.

SIGIL OF LUCIFER

Dating back to a sixteenth-century Italian Grimoire called the Grimorium Verum or "Grimoire of Truth," this sigil is part of a "set" of secret signs which are said to help in invoking Lucifer. The origins of the sign have been lost in the mists of time although the pointed V shapes do represent the "**horns**"

which are a tell-tale symbol of anything Devilish.

SKULL AND CROSSBONES

A grinning **skull** sits above **two bones** which are crossed diagonally. At first this might seem almost like one of those everyday symbols we take for granted, but another look again at the skull and crossbones makes it start to seem very peculiar.

We recognize it primarily in its form as the Jolly Roger, the wickedly grinning skull with the crossed bones underneath which is the universal emblem of the pirate.

But where did this symbol originate?

As with many of these signs, the history of the skull and crossbones is shrouded in mystery. We know that it is very old (it has been used over the entrances to Spanish cemeteries and graveyards for centuries) and as a symbol of death it has no rival; indeed it has become the universally acknowledged symbol for poison.

It seems that the Knights Templars and the **Freemasons** may hold the key to the inner meaning of this symbol. The Jolly Roger started life as the "Jolie Rouge," the name given by the French branch of the Templars to the flag flown by their warrior ships, and which was later adopted by pirates.

In Freemasonry, the symbol is repeated **six** times on the **Tracing Board** which is spread on the floor of the **Temple** prior to any rituals. Here, the skull and crossbones represents both death and life; by analyzing the symbol we see that the crossed bones form a **saltire**, a diagonal **cross**, which is symbolic of an evolutionary change.

So the symbol of death in the form of the skull is given another aspect, that of hope, progress, reincarnation, and of life after death.

It comes as no surprise, knowing this, that the Templars would bury their dead with the **legs** removed from the body and placed in the shape of the cross.

SMARAGDINA TABLET

A cornerstone of the tenets of **alchemy**, the Smaragdina Tablet (also known as the **Emerald Tablet** or the **Secret of Hermes**) is an ancient text, said to contain the teaching of Hermes Trismegistus, the founder of all things alchemical. The legend goes that Alexander the Great found the tablet in the tomb of Hermes. Inscribed on it, in Phoenician characters, were the instructions for making **gold**. The tomb is reputed to have been near Hebron, and the earliest translations of this mysterious recipe are in Arabic.

The use of **emerald** lends further exoticism to the story; however, at that time any green-colored stone was referred to as emerald and it is likely that the Smaragdina Tablet was made of **green jasper**. Whatever its material construction, the instructions on it have attracted the consideration of many illustrious characters over the centuries, including Roger Bacon, Albertus Magnus, Aleister Crowley, and C.G. Jung. Alchemy is full of hidden secrets and relies heavily on symbols, wordplay, and double meanings to hide its mysteries from all but the most perceptive and adept of interpreters. The words on the Emerald Tablet are no exception. There are several translations. Isaac Newton, who is described as an Alchemist, provided the following interpretation that was found among his papers after his death in 1727.

'Tis true without lying, certain and most true

1. That which is below is like that which is above and that which is above is like that which is below to do the miracles of one only thing.
2. And as all things have been and arose from one by the meditation of one: so all things have their birth from this one thing by adaptation.
3. The Sun is its father, the Moon its mother.
4. The wind hath carried it in its belly, the earth its nurse.
5. The father of all perfection in the whole world is here.

6. Its force or power is entire if it be converted into earth.

7. Separate thou the earth from the fire, the subtle from the gross sweetly with great industry.

8. It ascends from the earth to the heaven and again it descends to the earth and receives the force of things superior and inferior.

9. By this means you shall have the glory of the whole world and thereby all obscurity shall fly from you.

10. Its force is above all force, for it vanquishes every subtle thing and penetrates every solid thing.

11. So was the world created.

12. From this are and do come admirable adaptations where of the means (or process) is here in this.

13. Hence I am called Hermes Trismegistus, having the three parts of the philosophy of the whole world.

14. That which I have said of the operation of the Sun is accomplished and ended.

SOLOMON'S KNOT

This symbol looks like two links of a chain, set at right angles to one another. The sign is particularly ancient and does not belong to one particular people, although the Italian stonemasons called the Comacines, said to be the forerunners of the Freemasons, adopted it as their hallmark and imbued it with mystical symbolism.

The designs of King Solomon's Temple remains a great influence on Freemasonry, so it may be that the Comacines named the symbol. It appears in the abstract patterns inside synagogues so this may be the reason for the name.

Solomon's Knot, like many knot symbols, provides protection. It also resembles the ancient **Sun** symbol, the **Swastika**.

SPEAR OF DESTINY

As a possibly mythological artefact of Christ's last time on Earth, the Spear of Destiny, or Holy Lance, shares some similarities with the **Holy Grail**, in that it is a mystical object said to confer marvelous, if dark, powers upon the owner. However, whereas the associations with the elusive Grail are positive, the Spear carries largely negative connotations, as befits the weapon used to assure the physical death of Christ after the crucifixion. Effectively the Spear is the counterpart to the Grail, not only because of their respective feminine/masculine polarity.

The Spear is mentioned only once in the Bible, in the Gospel of St. John. However, a fourth-century testament, The Gospel of Nicodemus, mentions the name of the soldier, Longinus, who used the Spear to pierce Christ. Therefore the spear is sometimes called the Lancea Longini, after this centurion.

Like the Grail, the Spear (or relics of it) has been the subject of a similar unprovable provenance wherever it has appeared in the millennia since its initial sinister use. It seems to have multiplied since its original appearance in Jerusalem, and among the cities that have laid claim to ownership of the Spear are Rome, Armenia, Paris, and Vienna. The Viennese Lance, known as the Hofburg Spear, was taken by Adolf Hitler although it was restored to Vienna after the war.

Hitler's brief ownership of the Spear has added to its reputation as an object—and a symbol—of evil influence. As such, legends of the Spear of Destiny have influenced books, comics, and films.

Spiral

The spiral shown here comes from the Tibetan tradition, and is the symbol used to describe the origins of the Universe. The spiral shown here turns in a clockwise direction, following the path of the **Sun**, symbolizing the seed of potential energy; a good way to understand the power and movement con-

tained within the spiral is to think of a coiled spring.

This particular emblem looks like a drawing of a snail shell; indeed, the spiral crops up in many places in the natural world, in both flora and fauna and in other phenomena, and has inspired not only artists but also mathematicians and philosophers. The unfurled fronds of the tree fern, in New Zealand, inspire the spiral motifs in Maori art. The tremendous energy of the **whirlwind** or twister is a physical example of the energy and power that can be contained within the spiral.

The spiral is rich in symbolic meaning. It radiates optimistically out from its center, ever expanding, full of endless possibilities. It has a three-dimensional quality that speaks of a journey in time, too, from past to future. The spiral represents the cyclical phases of evolution, and somehow inspires a curiosity about what is coming next.

Spiral motifs appear all over the world, from Neolithic cave complexes in Europe, on carvings of the Goddess from the Paleolithic era, on Celtic stone carvings such as the ones at **Newgrange**, in the Hindu pantheon where it appears, for example, as the **Kundalini**

Serpent, woken up from its tightly coiled state, spiraling up from the base of the **spine**. In Africa, the symbol for the Sun shows a cooking pot surrounded by three **red** spirals. The Aztec Feathered Serpent God, Quetzalcoatl, shared the same symbol as the Tibetan seed of life; their warrior God, Huitzipotchli, has a coat of arms featuring **five** spirals contained within a **circle**.

The double spiral weaves in one direction and then in the next, a reminder of death and rebirth.

In Hindu **temples**, pilgrims walk in a circular path around the various shrines, taking an additional spiral around ritual objects such as the **lingam/yoni**. This clockwise journey is not only a meditative process but "charges" the energy of the place. There is also a (possibly apocryphal) story that Britain managed to repel a possible German invasion during World War Two when a massed group of **witches** met together to protect the country by concentrating on creating a huge spiral-shaped pillar of energy. There are dances and movements, too, which recreate the energy of the spiral. Perhaps the most dramatic instance of this is the Turkish whirling dervish. A more sedate example is the folk dances that involve a spiral line of dancers circling in and out from a central point. The same idea is echoed in the spiral dances of Native Americans.

Spiraling back to the symbol on the snail shell, it is fascinating to note that, for the Mayans, the **winter solstice** was considered the start of the year, the time just before "real" time began. The symbol that represented this concept was the snail; the spiral on its shell inspired the Mayan sign for **zero**.

SQUARE

See **First signs: Square**.

STAFF

The staff is not only a weapon, but serves as a guide and as a support. It is a phallic symbol that also represents fire.

The staff takes many forms, as the Lituus of the augur, as the Bishop's Crozier that also looks like a shepherds' crook, and as the Khakkhara of the Buddhist Monk that supports his steps and fulfils the same role as the staff of a pilgrim. The magic **wand** is another kind. The staff that Joseph of Arimethea pushed into the ground at **Glastonbury**, that sprouted into the mystical **tree** known as the Glastonbury Thorn, is a good example of the staff as a symbol of the **World Tree** and hence the **Axis Mundi**. The staff is a phallic symbol, connecting the Heavens to the Earth via the intermediary of the person that wields it and directs that power. Hence, it is also a symbol of authority.

STAR AND CRESCENT

See **Crescent Moon**.

STAR OF DAVID

See **Seal of Solomon**.

Star of Lakshmi

A Hindu symbol, this **eight**-pointed star, or Ashtalakshmi, is comprised of **two** interlocking **squares**. Each point of the star represents the **eight** kinds of wealth bestowed by the Goddess.

Star

The star is universally accepted as a symbol, and a part of our everyday language. To call someone a "star" is a great compliment. Our ancestors believed that each star had its own spirit, maybe that of the deity, an unborn soul, or the soul of a dead person that had a partic-ularly notable life, an idea that is completely in accord with our use of the word to denote fame; however, there are always positive connotations surrounding the word. The light of a star is only visible in juxtaposition to the darkness surrounding it.

The appearance of a particularly unusual star in the sky heralds an important or auspicious event, for example, the Three Wise Men knew of an ancient prophecy, recorded in the Book of Numbers book in the Old Testament that "there shall come a star out of Jacob." However, it was not only the birth of Christ that was heralded by a star. The Buddha shared this privilege as did the **fire** god, Agni, from the Hindu pantheon.

In terms of astronomical significance, the Pole Star provides a reliable aid to navigation and its unmoving position, static at the center of the great **wheel** of the Heavens, makes it a symbol of the **world axis**. This star is also, for many, a reminder of the constancy of God.

The Yakut tribes of Siberia believed that stars were the windows of the Universe, alternately opened and closed to ventilate the spheres of Heaven. It's easy to imagine a **black** sky full of windows through which shines the powerful, illuminating light of Heaven.

There are hundreds, if not thousands, of different star symbols. The **number** of points in the star is an important part of the design. The **eight**-pointed star might represent the idea of eternity and regeneration, in accordance with the number 8. The **nine**-pointed star might be a reminder of the nine muses, the Nine Worlds of Norse myth, or other aspects of the number nine. The **pentagram**, the **hexagram**, and the **Elven star** (or septagram) are explored under their own entries.

Sufi Winged Heart

Similar to the **Solar Winged Disc** except with a **heart** in the place of the **circle**, the Winged Heart is the symbol of Sufism, the mystic branch of Islam.

Inside the heart is a **pentagram** with its point uppermost. Beneath the star is the **crescent Moon**. Together these symbolize Islam, with the added dimension that the star itself symbolizes divine light and the shape of man, whereas the **Moon** represents the reflection of this light and the notion of the responsiveness of the heart.

The heart represents the transition point between spirit and matter and is a reminder that man's heart can be attracted to material things, or it can be drawn toward matters of the spirit. Therefore, the **wings** symbolize the spirit and the notion of ascendance.

Sun Cross

See **Celtic Cross**.

Sun sign

The Sun is arguably the most prominent feature of our natural world—after all, without it nothing would exist. Therefore it is natural that this bright **star** should be venerated as a deity and that its influence should be so universally pervasive.

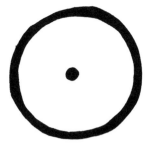

The Sun as a symbol takes many forms, but one of the simplest is the simple **circle** with a **dot** inside which is so simple and obvious as to require almost no explanation.

The Sun is also represented as a **wheel**, turning in the sky from the eastern horizon to the western one. The most famous symbolic representation of this idea, and one of the most ancient is the **swastika**. See **Celtic Cross and Sun Cross Symbol**.

Swastika

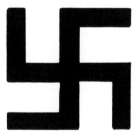

For many people the swastika has been rendered sinister since it was adopted by Adolf Hitler's Nazi regime. They believed, mistakenly, that it was a symbol of a pure Aryan race. In fact, the swastika is a very old **solar symbol**, going back to Neolithic times, revered in many cultures, and found in many different forms, including being a sacred symbol in the sand paintings of the Navaho Indians. It is one of the few symbols that have almost universal meaning, significance, and distribution, and its spread extends throughout India and Northern Europe to Central

America, and as far as East Asia. The name comes from the Sanskrit word, Swasti, meaning "well being" or "so be it," and there is a theory that it may have first been "invented" by basket weavers, since the swastika shape is produced during the weaving process.

In examining the component elements of the swastika, the first thing to notice is that the shape of the **four** arms resembles a **wheel**. Like a wheel, the swastika can rotate in either direction. Officially, if the arms are pointing in a clockwise (deosil) direction, then it symbolizes the **Sun**, the male principle, the overt; if it is pointing counterclockwise (or widdershins) then it resembles the **Moon**, the feminine principle, the covert. In this case, the swastika is sometimes called the "sauvastika." However, there is generally no differentiation in the direction of the swastika that can be discerned from its usage as a religious symbol, and it is certainly not the case—despite popular belief—that the left-oriented swastika is somehow "evil" or that this was the only swastika employed by the Nazis. For the Hopi Indians, the clockwise swastika stands for the **Earth**, and the "reversed" one, the Sun.

The wheel is a major symbol of the Dharmic religions, and so is the swastika. When used in Hindu temples, homes and other places, the swastika is often decorated with a bindhu or **dot** in the center of the space between each arm. The swastika is one of the **108** sacred symbols of the Lord Vishnu.

The next thing to notice is that the swastika has **four** arms, which are jointed, giving further reinforcement to the significance of this number. The number 4 stands for solid, material objects, the constructed Universe, order and discipline, and for the four corners of the world. It also indicates the four winds, the four cardinal directions, the seasons and the elements, with the very center of the swastika representing the **quintessence**, also known as the fifth element. This central hub, the still center, points to the swastika as a symbol of the **Axis Mundi**.

In **Freemasonry**, the hub of the swastika resembles the Pole Star.

TALISMAN

Similar to an **amulet**, a talisman is more likely to be made specifically as part of a magic ritual designed with a particular intention in mind.

The aim of any good maker of talismans is to load the odds in favor of the desired result, by adhering to a strict set of rules when making the object. The complexities of these rules include making sure that the intention of the talisman is coordinated to the day of the week, its ruling angel, its ruling planet, and the hours that the influence of the planet is at its strongest.

Sunday	Monday	Tuesday	Wednesday	Thursday	Friday	Saturday
Michael	Gabriel	Camael	Raphael	Sachiel	Ana'el	Caffiel
name of the 4 Heaven Machen.	*name of the 1 Heaven* Shamain.	*name of the 5 Heaven* Machon.	*name of the 2 Heaven* Raquie.	*name of the 6 Heaven* Zebul.	*name of the 3 Heaven* Sagun.	*No Angels ruling above the 6 Heaven*

Making your own magical talisman

The contents of this book should provide enough guidance in providing the right symbols for your talisman. The chart above gives the correspondences between angels, days of the week and the sigils and planetary symbols of those angels.

This "Talisman for Health" is taken from Sepharial's *Book of Charms and Talismans*. It was chosen because health is the best thing that anyone could wish for. The instructions below should give you the general idea for making talismans with other intentions. Here are the instructions.

1. This particular talisman needs to be made on a Sunday. This is because the Sun is the planet of fire, vitality, and the life-force. If you can make the talisman from **gold**, the metal of the **Sun**, so much the better. If not, make it a golden color.
2. All talismans, no matter what their intention, should be made in the first, eighth, 15th or 22nd hour of the day; these are the hours that the influence of the ruling star or planet is at its strongest.
3. All talismans need to be enclosed within a **circle**.
4. After making, the talisman can be worn or carried in a purse or bag.

THE TAROT: PICTORIAL KEY TO THE UNIVERSE?

Despite the opposition of Christian authorities to these cards, referred to by Scottish clergymen as the Devil's Picture Book, the Tarot is an evocative and intriguing set of symbols that are supposed to be linked to various mystery traditions such as the **Kabbalah**, witchcraft, paganism, and **alchemy**, and have always retained their mystical charisma as a form of divination. The Tarot is connected to the **Zodiac** and the planets, and Jung expounded the notion that the images held within the cards indicate archetypal personalities and symbols. "Normal" playing cards have their origins in the **78** cards of the Tarot, after the removal of the **22** cards of the Major Arcana and the knights of each of the four suits. The two "spare" jokers in the pack are the only remnant of the profoundly important Tarot card called **The Fool**.

"Arcana" means a mystery or a hidden secret, so it is apt that the origin of the cards, as befits any symbol system of such significance, is also cloaked in mystery. That the cards act as an oblique way of disseminating occult teaching is agreed, though. The Tarot's origins have been variously attributed to Hermes Trismegistus, the God and founding father of alchemy, also to the Egyptians, to the Indians, to the Arabians, and to the Chinese.

It is possible that the Knights Templar were responsible for introducing the cards to Europe, using the images to conceal the magical lore of the Saracens from a suspicious Church that was eager to persecute the demonic influences of the heathen East. It is also possible that "normal" playing cards had the Knight removed to disguise the Templar involvement with them. Nevertheless, the medieval church viewed the still cards with great alarm and believed that the heretical sect, the Cathars, were using them to disseminate their wicked Gnostic ideas. Between 1378 and 1450 the cards were banned in Regensburg in Germany, Marseilles, Paris, Siena, Venice, and Northern Italy. Later, however, the Church would try to adapt the cards to suit the Christian doctrines in the same way that they tried to absorb the mythology of the Zodiac.

There's another theory that the Tarot cards were spread by the nomadic Gypsy people. Count de Gebelin, renowned for his analysis of, and research into, the Tarot, said that the word had Egyptian origins, Tar ("road") and Ro ("royal"). Therefore, he posited that the name signified the "royal road to wisdom." Another interesting theory as to the provenance of the name is found in the curious palindrome, ROTA TARO ORAT (TORA) ATOR, which translates as the "Wheel of the taro speaks of (the law of) Hathor."

Whatever its origins, these cards are an evocative embodiment of many of the most significant symbols; they carry a language of their own, which transcends the many words that are used to describe them. The Tarot reaches deep into our subconscious minds. The opulence and prolific imagery of these cards, in particular the Major Arcana, makes their use as a mere divinatory tool seem somehow irrelevant. Although there are thousands of different Tarot sets that are all as diverse as the interests of their designers, each card has fundamental elements that contribute to its archetypal meaning. Every tiny element within a card is significant, from the colors used to its number and its relationship to the card that falls before or after. Which way do the figures face? How do they hold themselves and what is their appearance? Are they young or old? Sallie Nichols, in *Jung and Tarot*, describes the system as "an effective bridge to the ancestral wisdom of our innermost selves." This is a bridge of symbols; what follows is a brief analysis of some of those symbols.

The Minor Arcana

The "lesser secrets" are split into four suits of 14 cards, making 56 cards in total. The first thing to notice is that each group corresponds to the elements and the male/female energies. The **Wands** are **fire**, and Swords are **air**, both male elements. The suits of Coins and Cups represent **earth** and **water** respectively, female elements. These cards run in a sequence from ace to **ten** followed by **four** picture cards, the jack, the knight, the queen and then the king. Barbara Walker draws an interesting parallel between these cards and four stages of life as outlined by the Tantric philosophies.

1. Sambhoga, the Life of Pleasure, the beginning of life and the time when the child has its every need fulfilled by its parents, represented by the Cup of Life, which begins to fill with experience.

2. Nirmana, the building process, is the period of young adulthood, represented by the wand, scepter, or **vajra** as a symbol of the assertion of power.

3. Artha, or earth, stands for the gathering of material possessions, the fruition of efforts, the suit of coins or pentacles that represent riches of all kinds.

4. Moksha means liberation, effectively the "art of dying." The air element represents the soul or breath that leaves the body. This is depicted by the sword, symbol of release. This suit generally has a feeling of danger or calamity about it.

Until Pamela Colman, working with A.E. Waite, revolutionized the minor arcana by giving each one an individual pictorial representation, they were simple sets listing the number of appropriate emblems.

The Major Arcana

These 22 cards form the suit that was abandoned to create the deck of regular playing cards. This short sequence of pictures has been called the "quintessence of occultism," and parallels are drawn between their symbols and the letters of the Hebrew alphabet. Twenty-two is the same as the number of paths between the Sephiroth in the tree-of-life diagram, each one an aspect of the Creator. Ten of the cards also seem to match the aspect of the Sephiroth, too, from the Fool that represents the formless void of the Ain Soph, to the **Wheel** of Fortune that represents the Kingdom, the final Sephiroth.

The symbols used in the Major Arcana also correspond to certain aspects of the Zodiac. For example, the Lover card equates to **Gemini**. The card of the **Moon** also shows a **crab** or a lobster, emblem of **Cancer**. The card for Strength shows the **lion, Leo**. In short, there are as many interpretations of the Tarot as there are people to interpret them.

In a sense, the cards are a sort of mystical **mirror**, reflecting back whatever the individual wants to see. Having said that, the decks used here in the descriptions of the cards include the Marseilles Deck, the first pack of Tarot cards to gain prominence. It first appeared in 1748 and is still widely used today. The A.E. Waite/Pamela Colman deck is also examined. The following descriptions are only a suggestion of the hundreds of different interpretations of the signs that are secreted in the cards.

The 21 numbered cards are often put together in three groups of seven; the first seven cards of the sequence signify the realm of spirit; cards 8 to 14 represent the soul, and the last seven are the material realms. The Fool has no number.

The Fool: Zero

The Fool

The Fool is commonly depicted as a young man in **motley** clothing, striding along without a care in the world, a bundle over his **shoulder**, **staff** of the traveler in hand. A **dog** jumps up at him and rips his clothes, exposing his buttocks. The Fool appears to be dangerously close to the edge of a cliff. The numberless nature of the card indicates that the Fool is somehow outside of society, and to the observer, the Fool appears to be aptly named.

However, there are other aspects to this character. The limp bundle he carries is generally **white**, the color of initiation and secrets. His cap has a **feather**, symbolic of transcendence and truth. The motley of his clothes is the same color worn by kings and priests as well as the jester, and the Fool ignores the animal, material world (the **dog**) in favor of his spiritual quest, no need for a companion on this particular journey. The staff he carries is not only a useful tool, but is similar to the **wand** that connects the Earth with the Heavens.

The image on the card suggests someone at the start of the journey. His bag is empty, ready to be filled with the wisdom he will acquire. This lack of possessions indicates the philosophical ascetic in many religious traditions, who trusts the Universe to provide him with whatever he needs.

The Fool is striding forward into the unknown; the **zero** speaks of potential as well as of completion. The Fool is the only character from the Major Arcana that retains a place in the more mundane playing cards, appearing as the card that can replace any other (his multi-hued clothing gives him a **chameleon** aspect) or else upset the balance. He is a reminder of the spiritual nature of life's journey, and his story unfolds throughout the rest of the Tarot cards.

The Magician: number I

The Magician

The first numbered card of the Major Arcana, The Magician, or Juggler, shows a man standing in front of a table. The table has **four legs** firmly upon the ground, representing the reality of material world, a stable base. On top of the table are the symbols that donate the suits of the minor arcana as well as the elements; the cup, the sword, the wand and the coin or **pentacle**. These, however, do not symbolize reality; the trickster nature of the magician means that they are illusory. The magician, like the fool, wears the motley clothing of the priest or adept.

Somewhere in this card appears the lemniscate, the figure-of-eight or **infinity symbol**. In some cards it is concealed in the swirl of his **hat**; in the Pamela Colman/A.E. Waite Tarot, it floats above his **head** and no attempt is made to disguise it. In this interpretation, the magician points with one hand to the Heavens and with the other, to the Earth; this posture says "as above, so below," the physical form of the meaning of the **Seal of Solomon**.

Whereas the fool has a happy-go-lucky approach to life, the magician is far more serious, full of intention. He holds a wand in one hand and a coin in the other. Because magicians traditionally use tricks to direct our attention elsewhere, it could be that he intends the coin (the world of matter) to be the focus of our attention, or he could be distracting us from it, alluding to the illusory nature of our interpretation of reality. The Magician effectively opens the game of life.

The High Priestess: number 2

The High Priestess

As the Magician has the male number, the Priestess has the number of the female. She's sometimes called the Popess. The Pamela Colman card shows her sitting between the two columns, Boaz (female) and Jachin (male) that are not only the columns of the **kabbalistic** tree of life but also the pillars that were used at the Temple of Solomon and which still influenced the design of Masonic temples. Other elements to note in this card are the **book** or scroll, symbolic of wisdom and the secrets of the Universe that she holds. There

is a **veil**, indicating secrets that are revealed only to the initiate; the **crown** showing heavenly authority, and a throne, symbolic of earthly power. The seated posture of the High Priestess is reserved for those who hold a position of great power. Apart from Hermes, the Scribe of the Heavens, the only character in Heaven who is seated is God.

There may also be a representation of the phases of the **Moon**. Anything with three parts, symbolizing the triple aspect of the Moon, can serve this purpose. The crown of the Priestess sometimes has three layers, or in some decks the symbol may be more obvious. In the Pamela Colman interpretation, the Priestess not only has a crescent Moon at her feet but her crown is in the shape of the **Akhet**, the Egyptian symbol for the **Sun** coming over the horizon that also looks like the "balancing scales" glyph of **Libra**. The Priestess symbolizes balance between two opposing forces. A **cross** is also part of the imagery of this card, generally appearing on the **breast** of the Priestess, indicating her sacred status.

The Empress: number 3

Like the Priestess, the Empress is also a seated, powerful female figure. Many of the clues on this card shout "authority," from her posture to the items that she holds or that surround her. She wears a **crown**, and holds a **scepter** and a shield that has an **eagle** on it. Whereas the Priestess has an air of mystery about her, the Empress holds much more worldly authority while retaining a feminine softness that is denied the Priestess. Her clothing is less rigid, and she is generally depicted in a setting of daytime and openness,

The Empress

Stone. The Emperor also has a shield that shows an **eagle**, but whereas the Empress and her bird face to the right and the conscious realms, the Emperor and his bird face the opposite direction, embracing the unconscious. Effectively, the cards face one another, opposite sides of a pair, balancing and reflecting. The fact that the Emperor shows his hidden side reveals his confidence. He also carries the **scepter** topped by the crossed orb, but whereas the Empress carries hers quite casually, the Emperor holds his firmly in an upright position, a phallic symbol of male authority. The emperor holds his **belt** or **girdle** with one hand, another authoritarian, confident gesture, prepared for defence.

The practical nature of the Emperor is emphasized, too, by his posture. His **legs** are crossed casually and he appears to be leaning against his seat, ready for action, in contrast to the Empress who sits firmly in her throne. His crown, too, is not the elaborate headbear of the Empress but is a **helmet**, a more appropriate piece of headgear for a man that rules actively rather than passively.

rather than in the dark. The scepter she holds looks like the **globus cruciger**. The globe is the material earth and the **cross** is the spirit. This spirit symbolism is further underlined in some instances where the Empress is given a pair of **wings**.

Whereas the Priestess's **arms** are closed, the Empress's arms are open, indicating a maternal or outgoing nature. The Priestess guards something whereas the Empress reveals something. The Empress is a figure of maternal love as well as authority; in the Colman interpretation her shield is **heart**-shaped and instead of the eagle, it shows the alchemical symbol for the female. This Empress has a field of **wheat** before her, symbolic of fertility, and a nod to the Goddess, **Demeter.**

The Emperor: number 4

All the empirical qualities of the number **four** are represented here; strength, solidity, foundation. If the Empress is the archetypal mother, then the Emperor is the Father. Sometimes this fourth card is called the **Cube**

The Emperor

The Hierophant: number 5

The Pope

Also called the Pope, the fifth card of the Major Arcana shows a male figure seated between two pillars, which carry the same symbolism as the ones in the Priestess/Pope card, namely, the pillars of the Temple of Solomon that represent the pillars of the **Kabbalah**, Jachin and Boaz. Positioned in the center of these pillars, the Pope is the balancing factor between two opposing forces and an interpreter between the two worlds, not only the mouthpiece for God on Earth but also the one who intercedes between Man and God. The Pope wears the ancient triple crown, the **Triregnum**, and holds a scepter with a three-barred **papal cross** on the top of it. The hand that holds this scepter wears a **white glove**, a symbol of religious and papal authority and a sign of purity that has been adopted within **Freemasonry**. His right hand is raised in the traditional gesture of **benediction**, with two extended **fingers**. Before him, two people kneel to receive this blessing. They have shaven circles or tonsures indicating that they too are of a spiri-

tual persuasion, likely to be monks. One points to the Earth, the other toward Heaven, symbolic gestures that define the way their blessings will be applied; one accepts the benediction as a spiritual boon, the other applies it in a practical way. Again, the "as above, so below" tenet is indicated by these **arm** positions.

The Lover: number 6

The Lover

This is the sixth card of the Major Arcana. The card is sometimes misinterpreted as the lovers, plural, but the image depicts one lover, the man, who must choose between two ladies. This card is about choice, echoing the forked path of the **Y of Pythagoras**. It is interesting to note that the character portrayed on this card, for the first time, appears as an ordinary human being; he seems to have no mystical or magical attributes and is faced with a very human dilemma. Above the **head** of the lover and invisible to him is the **winged** figure of cupid, bow and **arrow** poised to strike, indicating that in this case the choice may be made by external influences that are beyond the remit of the man himself; the powers of destiny at work.

The two ladies who seek his attentions represent two very different aspects of the feminine personality. One, wearing a head-dress and seemingly more dignified, touches his **shoulder,** indicating a more spiritual relationship than the other, a loose-haired temptress whose hand hovers above his heart. The lover is pulled between reason and the intellect (the head) and the passions of sexuality (the **heart**); his head is turned to the woman on his right, whereas the rest of his body swings to the left.

The number **six** is the number of sexual union, depicted perfectly in the six-pointed star, as the **Shatkona**, the union of opposites. It may be that the young man has to reconcile both aspects of the Divine Feminine within himself in order to become a fully-rounded individual.

The Chariot: number 7

Here, the Lover of the former card is crowned with **gold**, showing that he has resolved the conflict he was faced with. Here, the gold symbolizes the alchemical endgame of enlightenment and transcendence. The man appears to be driving the Chariot, symbolic of control. However, there's a twist that illustrates the need to examine every aspect of each card very closely. Significantly, the **horses** have no reins and the "driver" does not steer the chariot but they appear to be as one. The **scepter** is held in one hand and the other rests lightly on his waist, a casual but powerful gesture. He is secure, in the **four-**posted canopy, to enjoy the journey no matter where he is carried.

The Chariot

The card carries none of the ambiguity of destiny, but rather shows it as an unassailable force, depicted in the **wheels** of the vehicle. Nevertheless the figure is now master of his destiny. The chariot is pulled by two horses, one **white** and one **black**, symbolizing harmony between opposing forces despite the fact that they seem as though they are pulling in opposite directions.

That the character now holds a scepter signifies a spiritual dimension as well as mastery of the material world. However, the name of the card is not the "charioteer" but the "chariot," already giving a clue as to its emphasis. The chariot is not only a physical vehicle but a spiritual one; the body is the "chariot" of the **soul** that carries us where we need to be, directed by the conscious mind.

Seven itself is a sacred number of great significance that occurs time and again; the seven planets, the seven days of the week, the seven Heavens.

Justice: number 8

Justice

This is the eighth card of the Major Arcana, and the first of the second group of **seven** cards that represent the soul and the notion of equilibrium.

The image is of an authoritarian-looking female figure, powerful and assured as she sits in her throne. Her seated posture further underlines her authority. The significant symbols of this card are, first, the **sword** that she holds firmly in her right hand, almost using it in the same way as a **scepter**, a link between the Heaven and the Earth. This implies divine justice as well as the earthly kind. The second significant symbol is the scales that she grasps in her left hand. Together the sword and **scales** have become universal symbols for justice. The card is the eighth, implying symmetry, a reminder of the symmetrical lemniscate shape that is the infinity sign. The pillars of Jachin and Boaz appear once more, in the upright parts of the throne that Justice is seated upon. Sometimes the figure wears a blindfold, implying impartiality.

Finally, the figure wears a crown or helmet that depicts a solar emblem, signifying the light of truth.

Incidentally, A.E. Waite reversed the positions of the Justice card that appears traditionally in the eighth position, and the card for strength, or force, that appears at number 11.

The Hermit: number 9

The Hermit

The ninth card of the numbered sequence of the Major Arcana shows an old man, his **beard** a sign of wisdom and experience, carrying a **staff** in his left hand and a lighted lantern in the other. That he is holding the lamp up as though lighting a path signifies darkness; however, the lantern carried by the hermit, generally a person of spiritual persuasion, may refer to internal as well as external illumination. The figure is hooded and he faces left, looking back toward the cards that precede him almost as though he is lighting the way ahead for all the characters that precede him. The Lover that appeared in the sixth card reappears here, in the ninth position, effectively turned round by 180 degrees, no longer in a quandary about the choices he needs to make but assured in himself and happy to be alone, seeking the path of spiritual enlightenment. The staff he uses as a tool, signifying the journey that is not yet at an end despite his age and experience. When the God, **Woden**, appears in human form it is often as a shabby old man wearing a battered **hat**; the hermit signifies wisdom and the dedication of a life to a higher authority.

The Wheel of Fortune: number 10

The Wheel of Fortune

This is the tenth numbered card, indicating the closing of a **circle**. The **wheel** is a symbol of completion.

Whereas the Hermit indicates the solitary, unworldly life, the Wheel of Fortune is very much a card of the world, representing all its challenges and changes. There are two strange-looking creatures at either side of the wheel that is "crowned" with a **sphinx**-like figure bearing a sword. This figure, which has an alarming appearance, is completely disassociated from the travails of the creatures below.

All the symbolism of the wheel is contained in this card. It stands for the alternation of good luck or bad, dharma, the passing of time and the need for life to have a balance of positive and negative experiences. The wheel is a solar symbol, representing the turning of the **Sun** on its cartwheel journey through the Heavens, a relentless life-force.

The two creatures can be interpreted as opposing forces and the dynamic of the wheel itself. The one on the right appears to be rising with the motion of the wheel, the one on the left is heading, at least temporarily, downwards. The A.E. Waite deck depicts this creature as a **serpent**. The opposing forces are also a reminder of the **yin yang** symbol.

As the character in the Chariot does not need to steer his vehicle but is as one with it and the horses that pull it, the Wheel of Fortune is in some sense a representation of the continuation of that journey. The Wheel of Fortune is an impartial force of nature and a reminder that freedom of choice also means the freedom to rise to challenges, all a part of the rich breadth of experience that life has to offer.

Strength: number 11

This card is sometimes called Necessity. In the picture, a fair-haired woman opens the jaws of a **lion**. However, she does not seem to be exerting any undue strength; she does not wrench open the **mouth** of the **lion**, but uses her fingertips, and the lion does not struggle. Her approach is gentle. The lion might be the

Strength

The Hanging Man: number 12

The Hanged Man

more powerful creature physically, but he is no match for the human character. The card symbolizes the power of moral and spiritual strength versus pure brute force, or victory of the spirit over the flesh.

The **hat** of the woman, like the hat of the magician, has a **lemniscate** or figure-of-eight shaped brim. This implies magical or super-human powers. Unlike the magician, however, she is not surrounded by elemental symbols and she carries no **wand**. All her powers are internal, a part of her being, not reliant on external forces. In the gentleness of the woman's approach toward the lion she uses a subtle power that is the premise of the female. Her strength is the strength of com-passion, not physical muscle. The lion itself is a powerful symbol, of the Sun and the divine powers as well as an uncontrolled animal nature. This animal nature needs to be approached with gentle strength and under-standing to become refined.

Although this card initially appears sinister, first appearances can be deceptive. The char-acter is not hanging from his **neck**, but from his **foot**. In the Middle Ages the practice of hanging someone in this way was called "baf-fling," a punishment intended to humiliate. The word itself now means to "confuse" or "frustrate." The man does not appear to be unduly worried about his strange position. The hands behind his back might be tied together but could also be clasped. It is almost as though his dilemma is self-imposed, and the pose brings to mind the nine days and nights that the God, **Odin**, hung in the great **World Tree**, Yggdrasil, as part of an initia-tory rite so that he might receive wisdom; the secrets of the **runes** were revealed to him during this time. Further, the casually crossed legs of the man make the shape of the figure four, the alchemical symbol for **Hermes** and for **Jupiter**.

In Yogic practice there are head-standing positions or asanas designed in part to provide another view of the world. The

Hanged Man is symbolic of the initiate who puts himself through a difficult process in order to attain enlightenment, a purifying ritual. The character is not only suspended physically, but mentally and spiritually too. He has no way of releasing himself from his fate but must wait patiently for an intervening force to release him. The old name for this card was "prudence."

Death: number 13

All the typical symbolism that we associate with death appears in this card. A skeletal figure, **scythe** in hand, strides across a field. Across the ground are scattered **bones**, a **hand**, a **foot**, the severed **head** of a crowned man. The skeleton's right foot rests on the head of a woman; he has no respect for those he strikes down. However, there are also new shoots appearing in the muddy field, signifying new hope and revitalization despite the apparent massacre all around. The number **13** is often seen as extraneous to the perfect number, **12**, somehow outside of society. It makes sense, then, that the sum total of the 12

needs to be cut back to make way for what comes next.

Although the sight of this card in a Tarot spread can be alarming, it does not signify a physical death but rather a change, an ending or a new beginning. The Death character is a harvester, an essential process that signifies a gathering of sustenance for the winter months ahead, also a way of clearing the ground for the new crops to come. Death is an essential part of the cycle of life. The 13th card, therefore, symbolizes regrowth, reincarnation and renewal, a continuance of the idea of initiation started by the Hanging Man. The **skeleton** itself symbolizes the inner part of ourselves that is rarely revealed. In order to make progress, sometimes that inner part needs to be examined closely to understand its mechanisms.

Temperance: number 14

Temperance is one of the cardinal virtues. It speaks of self-restraint, carefulness and moderation. It also implies an easy-going nature, a sensible person that is wise enough not to be caught up in petty concerns, who can see the bigger picture.

The card shows a female figure, often **winged**, signifying a messenger from God. She wears a five-petaled flower in her hair that is often a hidden symbol for the five-pointed **star** or **pentacle**. The key feature, however, are the **two** jugs that she holds, pouring liquid from one to the other. One jug is **blue** and the other **red**; an alchemical process is at work here, because blue, a feminine color, mixing with the masculine red, produces **violet**, the color of the spirit. Knowing this, the **flower** is suddenly more than mere decoration, since **5** represents the idea of marriage or the union of opposites, is the sum of the female number **2** wedded to the male number **3**.

The similarity to the imagery of this card to the astrological sign of **Aquarius** is quite striking. The sign is linked to the element of air and the circulation of the **blood**, the life-forces. The Temperance card may well be a reminder of rebirth and reincarnation; it is not just liquid that the woman pours with such care from one vessel into the other, but, symbolically, the soul.

The Devil: number 15

The Devil card shows a winged figure, with distinct male genitalia as well as the **breasts** of a woman. His **fingers** and **toes** end in claws. His peculiar headgear includes a pair of antlers or **horns**.

His right hand is raised, and his left holds what appears to be a sword, although it has no hilt; this sword is all blade. The Devil stands on a small plinth that looks like an anvil. This is connected to a rope, and either

XV

The Devil

end of the rope is knotted around the necks of a male figure to the right, and a female figure to the left. These characters are not straight-forward, though. They wear hats with antlers, have the pointed ears of animals, long tails and cloven feet.

The Devil is an archetypal figure of evil, of great antiquity, who existed long before the Christian Church "demonized" the old Gods and spirits. The figure often appeared as a destructive spirit that was carried on the disease-ridden and pestilential winds of the deserts of Mesopotamia. It made sense for our ancestors to personify this natural phenomenon in order to control it somehow. Although we might think we know better, the Devil archetype still carries a powerful symbolic punch. The usual image of the Devil that resonates even today is of an androgynous, hybrid creature, whose animal nature is at conflict with the spirit, and this gives rise to the most basic interpretation of this card. It speaks of ill-gotten gains, giving in to the desires of the flesh, corruption.

At its most basic, this card is a reminder that man is effectively shackled to the material world, and can be corrupted (reverting back to a raw animal state) by these shackles.

The Tower: number 16

The Tower

This dramatic card shows a tower, its crowned top falling toward the left as it is struck by a **thunderbolt** from the right. Two people are thrown toward the ground. In the sky are a number of circles that could be debris, **hail, rain**, or **stones**.

At first glance, this appears to represent some sort of divine retribution, following, as it does, the card of the Devil that warned against the temptations of materialism. The tower should be the safest sort of fortified home. The card also brings to mind the collapse of the Tower of Babel, again an instance of Godly punishment. However, the entire tower is not decimated; the body remains intact, only the turret is damaged. The card represents the sudden turn in fortune that appears to be disastrous but which ends up being a positive force for change. It can also signify a sudden illumination (the **lightning**

bolt, that strikes suddenly and unexpectedly, illuminating all around) that presages a leap forward in consciousness. The pinnacle of the tower represents the ego that sometimes has to be destroyed in the process of enlightenment.

This card symbolizes the unpredictable stroke of fate, the Act of God or destiny, that shakes everything up, but that nevertheless carries benefits in its wake.

The Star: number 17

The Star

The Star depicts a young girl, naked, pouring **water** from two jugs into the river that she kneels at the edge of. One foot is in the water. Above her head is a large **16**-pointed **star** made of two **eight**-pointed stars overlapping each other. Surrounding it are **seven** smaller symmetrically arranged eight-pointed stars. This is the first appearance of stars on a card, but not the last. They represent the mingling of the Earth with the sphere of the Heavens. The surrounding landscape is fertile, and a **bird** sits on top of the **tree** on the left of the card, observing the scene. The bird is a symbol of the soul, as well as a messenger from the Gods.

The jugs, like those in the Temperance Card, are **red** and **blue**. They seem to pour endlessly, one splashing its contents onto the Earth, the other adding to the water in the river. Therefore the girl nourishes the Earth while replenishing the "waters of life" of the spirit, symbolized by the river.

Although this figure appears to have the same sort of angelic nature as Temperance, she has no **wings**, and the jugs are both red, signifying earthly life. The giant fixed star—around which the others seem to orbit—signifies enlightenment, a further step in the progress of the human psyche. This tranquil, vulnerable and human figure stands firmly with one **foot** upon the Earth that is the material world, the other in the water that is the domain of spirit, nourishing both with the divine power that is continually replenished, celestially, from above. This card represents hope and divine inspiration.

The Moon: number 18

At the lower level of the **three** layers that comprise this image, is a **square**-edged lake with a crayfish in it. Above, there are two dogs—or possibly a **wolf** and a **dog**—that up to the Moon, jaws open, possibly howling. To their left and right are the corners of two buildings, both slightly different; one has a roof, the other appears to be open to the sky and is reminiscent of the tower that was struck by **lightning** in card **16**. In the sky at the top of the card is the full **Moon**, with a face that points to the left and with a halo of rays, like moonbeams, surrounding it. There are teardrop shapes surrounding it that seem to

The Moon

either emanate from the Moon or, alternatively, are sucked into it.

The dogs are a reminder of the hounds that accompany the Moon Goddess. Dogs also act as psychopomps, guardians of souls in the spirit world. There is a nightmarish aspect to this card. The surrounding landscape is barren, only two small plants appear in it, a sort of no-man's land. This card represents the "dark night of the soul." However, the preceding card signifies hope, and the Moon provides the light that is reflected from the Sun, illuminating the way ahead, indicating that guidance will come from above.

The Sun: number 19

Here, the Sun beams directly over the heads of twin human figures of indeterminate sex, possibly children. Whereas in the card of the **Moon** the droplets were absorbed by the planet, in the Sun card the droplets are generously falling to Earth. Behind the twins is a wall constructed from four levels of bricks. The twins remind us of the astrological sign of **Gemini** and it has been said that one

XVIIII

The Sun

XX

Judgement

represents the soul, the female, lunar element, and one the spirit, signifying the Sun, and male energy. Again, a Tarot card indicates the union of opposing forces. The hope of the **Star** that had to be held close to the heart during the tribulations of the lunar landscape in card 18 comes to fruition in this card; the Sun heralds the dawning of a new and better day, nightmares dissolved in the heat of its rays. The children play innocently in the full light of day, bounded by the solidity of the material world (the wall) and bathed in heavenly blessings. The children are symbols of the natural self, Adam and Eve, effectively, in their state of innocence before they ate the fruit of wisdom. This is the blessed state that all of us are born into. The Sun card signifies harmony, happiness, a promise fulfilled and the moment of completion that defines enlightenment.

Judgement: number 20

Here, the dominant figure is the winged trumpet-blowing **angel** that appears in a framework of clouds and beams of light, a truly apocalyptic vision. Below, in front of a mountainous landscape, two figures face a third that is climbing out of a trench in the ground. The third figure has its back to us but the tonsured **hair** is the same as that of the character that appeared before the Pope in card **5**. The other two figures are a woman and an old man; they are praying.

This card represents Judgement Day, the resurrection or awakening of the dead. The figures are naked, stripped of all worldly goods, reborn. The trumpet symbolizes the voice of God that awakes them, but this symbolism is not a straightforward biblical revelation; it can also be the trumpet of enlightenment as we are reborn as fully integrated human individuals. Self-awareness and the ability, as adults, to throw off earthly concerns, means that we can become as innocent and alive as the two children in the preceding card. The Judgement card is a call for truth, and a promise to the self to maintain and look after this born-again consciousness. The idea of a "call" from the trumpet also indicates another kind of call, the call toward a vocation or an external driving force that causes us to place the material world in second place.

The World: number 21

The World

This is the last of the cards of the Major Arcana. The number itself signifies the coming of age when the "world" is given symbolically by the key when a person reached his or her 21st **birthday**.

The card shows a young woman, whose sex is concealed by an artfully placed scarf. Her legs make the 4 figure, in common with the hanging man's posture. She looks to the left, **wands** in both **hands**.

The girl is enclosed in a laurel wreath in the shape of the **vesica piscis**, and surrounding her are the four **Tetramorphs**; human/hybrid figures that rule over the elements and the four corners of the Earth. These figures are winged. Working clockwise from the upper left-hand corner they are the man, the **eagle**, the **lion**, and the **ox**.

This is the card of victory and rebirth. The vesica piscis that the girl emerges from is a magical **doorway** from the spiritual world to the material world. Here, the wreath seems to be comprised of two halves that are joined together at the top and bottom, and it also represents the **egg** that itself is a symbol of creation. The **laurel** leaves are symbolic of victory, given to great heroes. The presence of the tetramorphs not only witnesses this victory but signifies the four corners of the world that now belong to the girl. The two wands imply a perfect balance of opposites, conscious and unconscious, matter and spirit, the harmony of the Universe.

TATTVAS

The Tattvas are a series of basic shapes, which contribute to the Hindu system of classifying the elements by giving them a recognizable form. The shapes themselves have influenced holy buildings, particularly the **Stupa**. The Tattvas are described as the building blocks of the Universe and compare in many ways to the **Platonic solids**. In Sanskrit, the meaning of the word equates to "thatness" or "essential nature of."

The shapes, then, and their associations, are as follows.

1. The **crescent Moon**, or "apas," defines the element of **water**. It is colored **silver** or **white**.
2. The **circle**, "vayu," is represented by a **blue** circle.
3. The upright **triangle**, or "tejas," symbolizes **fire**, in common with other systems for symbolizing the elements.
4. Prithvi is a **yellow diamond** that stands for earth.

5. The fifth element—the unifying factor, which in Greek is referred to as "ether," is called Akasa and is symbolized by a **black egg**.

The names of the Tattvas also correspond to the names of the deities that rule the elements. In the same way that the elements have given rise to everything on our planet, all other colors can be made from the colors chosen for the shapes.

Tau Cross

Instantly recognizable as a capital letter T, the tau cross forms the basis for another well-known symbol; the **ankh**.

The Tau is a very ancient symbol indeed, being the sign of three major deities; the Sumerian Sun God, Tammuz, the Roman God Mithras, and the Greek God Attis.

The name comes from the word for the Greek letter T, and it is the last letter of the **Hebrew alphabet**.

There are similarities between all these deities. They all died and were resurrected, and so carry analogies with the Sun that dies every night and is resurrected every morning. The T shape was daubed in ashes onto the foreheads of Tammuz followers; the symbol represents resurrection, reincarnation, life, blood sacrifice, symbolic death, and a gateway.

The tau is also known as the Robbers Cross, because the thieves that were crucified at either side of Christ are believed to have been hanged on a cross of this shape and although it's commonly held that Christ went to his death on a cross with the upright post extending beyond the cross-bar (the **Latin Cross**), it is likely that a tau cross was used.

St. Francis was particularly fond of the tau, and used it almost like a personal signature. In addition, the Egyptian hermit, St. Antony, put its power to good use when he used it to frighten away a hoard of demons. There are very few tau crosses left in the world, but there is still an intact one on Tory Island in Eire dating back to the sixth century. This remainder provides a clue that early Egyptian Coptic Christians may have landed there.

Templar Cross

This cross also goes by the name of the **Cross of St. John**, the **Maltese Cross**, the **Campaign Cross**, the **Iron Cross**, the **Regeneration Cross**, or the **Fishtail Cross.**

The sheer numbers of names that belong to this symbol give a hint as to its ubiquity, but what features set it aside from other crosses?

The Templar Cross has the distinctive curved or pointed ends (hence the "fishtail" epithet) drawing attention to these end bars and giving the cross **eight** points rather than the straightforward **four** of most other

It is both a mathematical idea and a metaphysical symbol that embraces within itself the principles of the natural world, the harmony of the cosmos, the ascent to the divine, and the mysteries of the divine realm.

Starting from the base and working up, then, the **four** dots forming the foundation of the shape represent the four elements; the Earth; the seasons; the cardinal directions **North, South, East** and **West**. The next three dots above stand for Earth, Heaven, and Hell, and also mind, body, and spirit. The next two dots are male and female, light and dark, **yin** and **yang** and so on; and the final dot at the top of the triangle is the Godhead.

Further, working down the pyramid this time, Pythagoras said that the first dot indicated the intellect; the second two, science; the third row, opinion; and the final, base row of four dots, sense.

In total the Tetraktys is comprised of ten dots; these ten simple dots symbolize the totality of the Universe which exists in the now, and also the Universe which is as yet uncreated.

crosses. Eight is the **infinity sign**—standing for the cycle of life, death and rebirth—seen in the **lemniscate** or **figure-of-eight** shape. Christ rose from the tomb eight days after being interred there, so this number also holds significance for Christians, and hence the name "Regeneration Cross."

The cross is the emblem of the Knights of St. John, an ancient chivalrous order that originated during the time of the Crusaders. Also known as the Knights Hospitallers, the Knights set up a hospital in Jerusalem in 1080 to care for pilgrims. This is why the cross is still used as its emblem by the latter-day St. John's Ambulance Brigade.

Tetraktys

The Tetragrammaton—or the four-letter code word for the secret name of God—is sometimes drawn as a Tetraktys, which in Greek means "fourfold." This is a mystical Pythagorean symbol whose simplicity belies a complex meaning. It is comprised of **ten dots** which form a **pyramid** and this unassuming emblem actually symbolizes the Universe. Pythagoras described it thus:

Tetramorphs

Ezekiel had a vision in which he saw **four** figures that the Book of Revelation calls The Four Beasts. These beasts are the **bull**, the **lion**, the **eagle**, and the man. There are several interpretations given to these four creatures that are collectively referred to as Tetramorphs.

Possibly the most common symbolism of the Tetramorphs is their relation to the **four evangelists**. St. Matthew is the man, the lion

THEOSOPHICAL SOCIETY

is St. Mark, the bull is St. Luke, and the eagle is St. John.

However, the animals also represent the four pillars of the Christian faith and the omnipotence of God.

The Tetramorphs are not restricted to the Christian tradition, though. The creatures that appeared to Ezekiel have universal resonance, proved by their depictions in prehistoric cave paintings. The man, the bull, the lion, and the eagle are universal symbols for the four points of the compass and the four elements. The eagle is **air**, representing all the aspects of the mind and intellectual activity; the lion is the element of **fire**, signifying action and strength; the bull is the **earth** element, representing labor and tenacity; and the figure of the man represents **water** and the idea of spiritual intuition.

The emblem of this mystical society, founded by Helena Blavatsky in 1875, is an almost overwhelming smorgasbord of some of the most significant sacred symbols. Blavatsky had an overarching interest in, and an extensive knowledge of, the importance of sacred signs and symbols and so they were all chosen carefully as being significant to the organization, which has headquarters in countries all over the world.

Many of these symbols are themselves comprised of other symbols, such as the **Seal of Solomon** that is made from two interlocking **triangles**. To examine the emblem closely is to unravel an extensive symbolic puzzle, and a more detailed explanation of its component elements are found under their separate entries.

The component elements of the society's symbol include the Seal of Solomon with the **quintessence** indicated at the center, the **swastika**, significant letters from the

Hebrew alphabet, floral devices, the **circle**, the **ouroboros**, the **crown**, and various strategically placed bindhu or **dots**. Additionally, the symbol is said to contain within it all the possible **numbers** from one to ten; these numbers contain all possible numbers. There is a rectangle as part of the design of the base of the crown; however, the square does not appear as a symbol though it could be indicated in the many representations of the number four.

THREE JEWELS OF BUDDHISM

See **Triratna**.

THREE-PRONGED CANDELABRA

In Wicca, the **three**-forked candelabrum is a part of the equipment needed for the ritual **altar**. It holds three candles—**white, red,** and **black**—that symbolize the three aspects of the **Triple Goddess**, as Maid, Mother, and Crone.

THYRSUS

The Thyrsus was a sacred implement used in rituals and festivals during the time of the Ancient Greeks. It was a **staff**, standing about as high as its owner, made from a giant **fennel** stalk topped with a **pine cone** and wrapped with **vine** leaves.

As a phallic symbol, it was combined with a goblet or **chalice**, symbolic of female energy and used to counterbalance the staff. As well as being a symbol of male energy, though, staffs or long poles of some description have a universal use as a sacred instrument to connect the Heavens to the Earth, a conductor for the divine spirit.

TILAKA

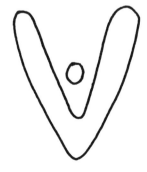

Tilaka is a Sanskrit word, meaning "red," and is the name for the symbols worn on the head, face, and other parts of the body by Hindus. The Tilaka is a sign indicating affiliation to various Hindu deities, each God or Goddess having its own Tilaka.

Tilakas are drawn onto the body, and the forehead in particular, with colored pastes made from ashes (vibhuti), **sandalwood** paste, clay, or other substances such as kumkum or sindhoor.

Perhaps the most basic form of the Tilaka is the red **dot**, or bindhu, worn on the **forehead**. This indicates the third eye and the rising **Sun**.

Generally, men wear the largest Tilakas.

A man sporting a Tilaka made of three horizontal lines that are made from **gray** or **white** ashes is a sign that the person is a Shivaite or follower of Shiva. The three lines are called the tripundra. Followers of Vishnu wear a Tilaka in the form of a **yellow** paste that is made from the clay of a holy river, such as the **Ganges,** melded with **sandalwood** paste. The symbol is two vertical lines that are sometimes joined at the bottom.

Women also wear Tilakas as a sign of beauty, or to indicate their marital status; in this case, they are marked with a yellow line just below the hairline.

Babies also wear Tilakas, but in this case, the **black** dots dabbed onto the face of the baby are put there to make the baby ugly, and therefore of no interest to any passing evil spirit.

TIRATANA

A Buddhist symbol, the Tiratana is also known as the **Three Jewels** of Buddhism. These concepts are depicted as a flame that holds three **circles** protected within it. The flame is symbolic of eternity, and the three

circles are the Buddha, his teachings or Dharma, and the Sangha, his followers.

TOMOE

This word means "turning" or "**circle**" and the symbol shows **two**, **three** or **four** comma-like shapes making a **spiral**. These shapes are emblematic of flames; hence, the symbol is sometimes called the **fire wheel**. It belongs to both Shinto and Buddhist faiths and can be seen in temples of both denominations. It was also used in Japanese Samurai heraldry.

The Tomoe with two flames looks very like the **yin yang** emblem and symbolizes the same concepts. When it is drawn with three flames, the tomoe represents the Earth, Heavens, and humankind, which are the three foundations of the Shinto philosophy.

Torah

This is the Book of the Law of the Jewish faith, comprising the first **five** books of the Old Testament. It appears as a sacred scroll in **synagogues**, where it is called the Sefer Torah. The power of the sacred words on this scroll means that it is used as a magical amulet, believed in particular to heal children or pregnant women.

Torii

In Japan, the Torii is a gate, but this is not a common or garden Western-style opening. The Torii is a Shinto symbol that marks a liminal place, the threshold between this world and the next, between the sacred and the profane, between the material world and the spiritual realms. The Torii tells the pilgrim that he or she is entering a sacred place, and ritual washing of the **hands** and rinsing of the **mouth** takes place before stepping through this holy **doorway**. Buddhist temples sometimes have these sacred gates too.

Torii are now found everywhere and have even found their way into modern architectural use, where they may be rendered in various **metals** rather than the traditional wood or stone. However, its origin as the entrance to the Shinto shrine is where the Torii is seen at its most meaningful.

The word Torii is believed to come from the Shinto words for "**bird**" and "place," and the kanji (Chinese pictorial character) for Torii is the same as that for "bird." Birds are universally accepted as being able to carry messages between man and his Gods and so this theory fits with the idea of the Torii marking a boundary between two worlds.

Totem

The idea of a totem as a sort of spiritual mascot that protects and guides a single individual or an entire clan has transcended its origins as an ancient shamanistic concept. Originally an Algonquin term, a totem is an **animal** or **plant** whose attributes are shared by the person to whom it belongs. A totem belonging to a tribe provides a vital part of its identity as well as a means of understanding the workings of the physical world.

Although we generally think of a totem as belonging to Native American spirituality,

trident wields great power, although this power might take different forms.

The trident is the symbol of the Hindu God, Shiva, whose followers wear a trident-like **Tilaka** symbol on their faces. In the hands of Shiva, the trident represents the three phases of time, past, present, and future, or possibly Heaven, Earth, and Hell. The trident has its own hand gesture or **mudra**, too, called the trishulahastra.

In the hands of Poseidon or Neptune, the trident has a practical use, since it emulates the shape of one of the earliest fishing implements. Poseidon uses it to control the seas, so it is a symbol of authority. Because of its association with **water**, the trident is the alchemical symbol for this element.

Where a trident has three prongs of even length, it is a secret symbol of the Cross of Christianity. However, Satan is often seen harrying the souls in hell with a trident. It is likely that he is depicted with it in order to associate him with the pre-Christian Gods who also used it.

This versatile three-pronged tool is also a **fire** symbol—the prongs look like flames—and it is therefore a symbol of thunderbolts and **lightning**. As such, many of the sky Gods carry a trident, too. These include Thor or Woden of Norse mythology.

they are found in different cultures all over the world.

The revelation of the totem is generally part of an initiatory ritual. For some this takes the form of a shamanic ceremony forming part of the rite of passage at puberty.

A shared totem is a strong bond of kinship or brotherhood; the word itself carries this meaning.

Totem poles are the physical manifestation of a spiritual idea, tall trees carved with birds, animals, fantastical creatures, and other symbols that tell the story of the people they belong to. Because the poles are made of wood, they rot easily and so it has proven difficult to pinpoint their origins precisely.

TRIANGLE

See **First signs: Triangle**.

TRIDENT

The Trident, or Trisula, is a long staff or pole topped by **three** prongs. Whoever wields a

THE ELEMENT ENCYCLOPEDIA OF SECRET SIGNS AND SYMBOLS

TRIPLE GODDESS

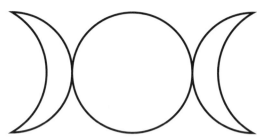

There are numerous symbolic representations of the notion of the triple aspect of the Goddess, but one of the most popular and arguably the most symbolically eloquent is the one illustrated here, which shows the **circle** (representing the full **Moon**), flanked either side by waxing and waning **crescent moons**. This symbol not only associates the Goddess with her Moon, but shows the changing nature of her three aspects as maiden, mother, and crone. The symbol is often fashioned into pendants, some of which have the added lunar significance of a **moonstone** set into the central disc.

Another example of the symbol also uses the Moon, solely in its crescent form. The triquetra is made of three of these crescents.

TRIPOD OF LIFE

Also known as the Borromean Ring, this is a simply constructed symbol that consists of **three** rings which intersect evenly. An extension of a smaller design called the **Vesica Piscis**, and part of a larger design of great symbolic importance called the **Flower of Life**, the Tripod of Life symbolizes the many aspects of the number 3. It also acts as a reminder of all the qualities that come in triplicate, such as the Body, Mind, and Spirit, as

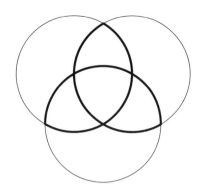

well as the Father, the Son, and the Holy Ghost, i.e. the Holy Trinity of the Christian faith.

TRIQUETRA

A very ancient symbol which in Latin means "three cornered," the triquetra (or triqueta) is comprised of three interlocking **vesica piscis** shapes, sometimes linked together with a **circle**. It is similar to the Nordic **valknut** in its construction and although the sign predates Christianity it has been used as a symbol of the Holy Trinity; in fact, it has been adopted anywhere where a symbol for three connected items or concepts needs to be indicated.

A clue as to the magical, protective nature of the triquetra is that it can be drawn without the pen leaving the paper.

TRIREGNUM

See **Papal symbols**.

TRISKELE

The triskele or triskelion belongs to both Buddhist and Celtic traditions, and appears in various forms in many artworks and carvings. It is comprised of one shape repeated **three** times to produce a **wheel**-like pattern. Traditionally the triskele can appear as three teardrops, three **fishes**, three interlocking **spirals**, or the three **legs** that gives it its Greek meaning (as in the symbols for both the Isle of Man and Sicily). There is also an intriguing version called the Three Hares Triskelion, which again features in both Buddhist and Celtic belief. The **hare** triskelion in particular is the source of much conjecture. Given that the hare is a nocturnal animal and a lunar symbol (the shape of the animal

can be picked out from the craters and ridges of the surface of the **Moon**) it also stands as an emblem of the Goddess.

The triskele is a symbolic representation of the importance of the number 3, and a **Sun** symbol similar to the **swastika**.

TRISULA

See **Trident**.

TROLL CROSS

An early **amulet,** said to give protection against **trolls**, this cross was made of **iron**, a **metal** that further reinforced the aspect of safety since it is generally avoided by mischievous entities. The sign is not really a cross as we know it, rather a **circle** with a C-shaped base.

TSA TSA

In Tibetan Buddhism, the tsa tsa is a small votive statuette of the Buddha, or of other deities, or meaningful objects such as the **stupa**. They are formed in a mold, or stamped out from clay or plaster. Making tsa tsas is both a meditative process and a vocational task that brings favor from the Gods, and making them is an obligatory skill taught to Monks. Tsa Tsas can be worn, or carried as an **amulet**, in which case they are carried about in a little portable shrine called a Gau.

Tsa tsa figurines have special ingredients added that further empower the figure. These additions include **herbs**, **flowers**, or even the funerary ash of llamas or other holy people.

These little statuettes can be seen everywhere, in homes, **temples**, in **caves**, or beside mountains, although they are only considered to be sacred objects after they have been empowered by being blessed.

TYET

The Tyet is a symbol from Ancient Egypt, also known as the **Knot of Isis** or the Blood of Isis.

The Tyet is reminiscent of the **ankh** (except with the cross bars brought down to the sides) and so carries some of its symbolism as a sign of eternal life. However, the Tyet also resembles the knotted piece of cloth that was used during menstruation. The **knot** in itself is of significance, since the Egyptians, in accord with other peoples around the world, believed that knots could both bind magic or let it loose.

The Tyet was used as a funerary symbol, when it was made from a blood **red** stone such as **carnelian** or **red jasper**. It was tied around the neck of the corpse, as a symbol of protection for the spirit in the life to come. The Blood of Isis was a powerful substance, containing blood from the **womb** of the great Goddess.

UDJAT

See **Eye of Horus**.

UNICURSAL HEXAGRAM

Any sign, symbol, or shape that can be drawn in one continuous line without the pen leaving the paper can be described as unicursal. The **five**-pointed star or **pentagram** is a good example. Generally, the **six**-pointed star is drawn as a separate pair of interlinked opposing **triangles**, but the unicursal variety was adopted by Aleister Crowley who perceived it to be important as a personal symbol. It was likely that he knew that unicursality is frequently an important feature of any magical symbol that has protective properties, because the unbroken line of construction means that there are no openings that an unwanted entity might be able to use to gain access to the safe place in the center. It is also sometimes called the Magic Hexagram.

Crowley further added to the power of this symbol by adding the five-petaled **rose**, itself symbolic of a hidden secret that conceals the pentagram within it, if the central point on the outer edge of each petal is joined together. The pentagram is the emblem of the Divine Feminine. In this instance the star secreted within the rose balances on its point, becoming an inverted pentagram that can imply the superiority of matter over spirit or, the need (according to the renowned witch Gerald Gardner who was a contemporary of Crowley's) to be able to face the darkness in order to understand it.

The points of the hexagram and the pentagram add up to **11**, which signifies divine union.

UNIFICATION CHURCH SYMBOL

Members of the Unification Church are popularly known as Moonies, after the organization's founder, the Korean Sun Myung Moon (born Mun Myong Mong). When Moon founded the Church in 1954, he called it the "Holy Spirit Association for the Unification

of World Christianity." Although Moon's original vision was that the Church should unite all the disparate Christian denominations (these tenets are outlined in a book called *The Divine Principle*, which amalgamates the Bible with various Asian spiritual traditions), the more established churches opposed Moon's vision, with the result that the Unification Church became a separate religion.

Some of the practices and beliefs of the Unification Church mean that it is viewed with suspicion as a cult, its members seemingly held in the thrall of its charismatic, and possibly eccentric, leader. Included among the more unusual practices of the Church are the mass weddings of partners that are chosen apparently at random.

Disregarding any outside opinions about the teachings of the Church, its symbol is distinctive and was invented by Moon himself. This is one of the relatively rare occasions where the meaning of a symbol is described by its living inventor.

The central **circle** is God, truth, life, and light, and is believed to be based on an ancient Japanese symbol called the Kuruma, a "mon" symbol, that is, a Japanese heraldic device enclosed within a circle. The Kuruma represents a carriage **wheel** and carries all the symbolism of the wheel in general.

Four main arms radiate from this central **circle**. These represent the four ideals of the central circle reaching all four directions. The circle is further divided to make **12** segments that symbolize the 12 parts of the human character, the 12 disciples of Christ, etc.

The outer circle represents the harmony of the Universe and giving/receiving. The arrowhead notches in either side of this outer circle give a feeling of movement.

UNITED STATES
DOLLAR BILL

If you ever find yourself hanging around in an airport, say, at a loose end, then get hold of a dollar bill and have a close look. It's so crammed full of arcane imagery that a close scrutiny of it will pass the time as effectively as the most gripping novel.

It is a wonderful example of symbolism in action and shows just how powerfully these ancient magical symbols still resonate in a modern world. Although the design of the dollar has changed several times, some

elements have remained constant. Here, then, are those magical symbols.

On the reverse of the dollar, the most noticeable emblem is that of the **Great Seal of the United States**. This takes the form of a **pyramid** with its cap severed and replaced by a triangle with an **eye** inside; this is the **All Seeing Eye**.

This symbol has been associated with the Illuminati and with **Freemasonry** and its appearance on the dollar has given rise to all sorts of conspiracy theories. The phrase "Annuit Coeptus," which is written around the top of the seal, translates as "[we] favor the things which have begun" and indicates that there is work yet to be done. The banner around the bottom of the seal reads "Novus Ordo Seclorum," which means, roughly, "A new order of the Ages."

Although Latin is not actually understood by many people and is officially designated a "dead" language, the use of Latin is a secret sign in itself and lends gravity to the statement, belying the youth of the American Nation whose Declaration of Independence was signed in 1776.

Also featured on the dollar is the Bald **Eagle**, which is the official **bird** symbol of the United States. The Eagle holds the **olive branch** of peace in its right talon, but it is prepared to fight, too, as indicated by the **arrows** in its claws. There are **13** fruits in the olive branch, perfectly balanced by the 13 arrows. It is worth noting here that the covert bird symbol of America is the **dove**—aptly, the Latin name for the dove is Columba. The dove is the bird of peace and conciliation and so provides a nice counterbalance to the eagle, although it does not actually appear on the dollar.

Another bird appears on the dollar, too, but it is hard to find. An **owl**—symbol of wisdom—is supposed to appear on the note.

Above the eagle is a crown of **stars**, again, 13 in total. This represents the number of the States that first joined the Union. The stars can be joined to create **Solomon's seal**, one of the most powerful of all symbols. That the stars combine to create another symbol is a clever nod to the phrase, which streams along on a banner underneath; E Pluribus Unum means "Out of many comes one" and refers to the many States that make one Union.

URAEUS

This is the Egyptian symbol of an upright cobra, head reared in readiness for attack. The Uraeus was the guardian of the **Sun** God, Ra, permanently ready to spit poison at his enemies.

The Uraeus was the definitive symbol of royalty, sovereignty, and divinity. Horus and Set are depicted wearing the Uraeus, and it was the only symbol worn by the Pharaoh that actually legitimized his status as ruler. Worn as a headband, with the rearing cobra sitting at the point of the **third eye**, the Uraeus has parallels with the **Kundalini serpent**.

The Uraeus was initially the symbol for the Divine Goddess in all her aspects, in particular Wadjet, a very early deity that was the protector of Lower Egypt. The protector of Upper Egypt was Nehkbet, the Mother Goddess whose symbol was the **vulture**; together, these Goddesses were called the Two Mistresses.

The rearing cobra is also a **hieroglyphic** sign, meaning "Goddess" or "Priestess."

URIM AND THUMMIM

So charged with mystery and secrecy are the Urim and Thummim that there is debate as to what exactly they were. What is known for sure is that they were connected to the **breastplate of the High Priest** of the ancient Hebrews.

The Urim and Thummim were contained in a secret pocket behind the "essen," or breastplate of the priest. It is possible that they were knucklebones or small stones which had been brought out of Egypt by the Israelites; another theory asserts that they were sacred names written on plates of **gold** to act as **talismans**. It has also been posited that the Urim and Thummim were not objects at all, but the name for a process of divination whereby God could be contacted, enabling decisions to be made; a form of augury. What is agreed is that the names translate as "light and perfection" or "light and truth."

When a slip of paper with the Tetragrammaton (the name of God) written on it was slipped underneath the Urim and Thummim, then the **12** jewels of the breastplate apparently started to glow. This glowing meant that the breastplate was turned on and tuned in, acting as a sort of radio transmitter for messages from God to His people.

The last Priest that was able to access these divine messages from God was Eleazar, who allowed Moses to communicate with God directly. After that time, it seems as though the ability to talk to God in this way was somehow lost, and the Urim and Thummim were used purely as a divination tool, a more indirect form of higher communication.

Vajra

Some Buddhist statues are seen holding an object that looks like a double-headed scepter in one hand, and a bell in the other. These objects are the vajra and the **ghanta**, respectively, male and female.

Vajra is a Sanskrit word, literally meaning "**diamond**-like" and "the hard and mighty one," although the meaning goes deeper than this, carrying metaphysical significance. It is also known as the Thunderbolt, because it is the destroyer of ignorance. The Vajra is an important symbol, and carries complex meanings within its shape.

The central space inside the Vajra indicates the **dot** or bindhu, that apparently most insignificant of symbols that is also possibly the most important. The bindhu represents the sphere of actual reality.

On either side of the bindhu are **lotus** flowers, symmetrically balanced, representing the material world and the spiritual world. The flowers each have **eight** petals.

The lotus flower itself symbolizes the plight of the human being, born into the mud or mire of the material world, but attaining spiritual realization by striving beyond these origins

From the lotus flowers spring flames or spokes, generally **five** in number. This number might vary, but both sides are always symmetrical. The number five in this instance represents the five Buddhas and their wives, and their collected energies and qualities. It is also symbolic of the five wisdoms, which are:

- the wisdom of individuality
- mirror-like wisdom
- reality wisdom
- wisdom of equanimity
- all-encompassing wisdom

Collectively, the ten prongs are a reminder of the ten perfections, which are:

- Generosity
- Proper Conduct
- Renunciation
- Insight
- Diligence
- Tolerance
- Truthfulness
- Determination
- Kindness
- Serenity

The prongs are also a reminder of the steps on the journey to enlightenment and of the ten directions; north, south, east, west, north-east, north-west, south-east, south-west, and finally, Above and Below.

These prongs either curve together to form a point, representing the **Holy Mountain, Mount Meru**. The closed ends of the vajra makes it a symbol of peace; however, sometimes the vajra has open ends. This is a sign of the wrath of the deity who holds it. This is the type of wrath, though, that can destroy all illusions or negativities. The open-ended vajra sometimes has the addition of flames shooting out of the ends.

Incidentally, the Tibetan name for the vajra is the dorje.

The Indian city of Darjeeling, famous for the **tea** that grows in the area, is named after this concept. The name is corrupted from the original Dorje **Lingam.**

VALKNUT

The valknut consists of **three** interlocking **triangle**s and has some similarity to the **triquetra** or the **triskele.** The Valknut is of Viking origin and is seen on **rune** stones and in carvings, and is connected with the God, Odin. The name means, roughly, the **Knot** of Death or the Knot of the Slain.

The knot is likely to have been a protective device, a quality shared by other knot symbols. It carried a promise that Odin would protect the spirit of the Warrior who died in his name, and a reassurance that the warrior would soon be reincarnated.

VERTICAL LINE

See **First signs: Vertical line**.

VESICA PISCIS

Sometimes, a clue to the meaning of a symbol is given in its name. The Vesica Piscis translates as the Vessel of the **Fish** and this information, in combination with its shape, means it takes just a short leap of deductive reasoning to suppose that it refers to the **vagina**. The shape is constructed from the shape made by the intersection of two circles and Pythagoreans believed it represented a similar intersection of the spiritual and material worlds, a sacred **doorway** between two states of being. The Vesica Piscis is one of the most important shapes in **sacred geometry**.

The Egyptian representation of the Vesica Piscis the Egyptian Ru symbol, which similarly represents the vagina as a doorway through which a spirit entered the material world, is an apt metaphor that supports the Pythagorean theory.

The Vesica Piscis is also known as the **Mandorla**, referring to its **almond** shape. The symbol is often used to frame figures in religious iconography. It also appears in the 21st card of the **Major Arcana** of the **Tarot**, which depicts the World.

Also any place where the Goddess is worshipped will generally have a representation of the Vesica Piscis; for example, it is seen on the cover of the **well** at **Glastonbury**.

V.I.T.R.I.O.L.

To call someone "vitriolic" means that they are cruel or that they have a caustic turn of phrase. However, the word has its origins in **alchemy**.

Vitriol itself used to be called Oil of Vitriol and refers to sulfuric acid; this name was given by the eighth-century alchemist, Jabir Ibn Hayan. Sulfuric acid was considered a prime constituent in the making of the **Philosopher's Stone**, and further, a clue to the manufacture of this elusive substance—which was reputed to give the gift of immortality—is held in the initials of the word. The initials of the word, then for Alchemists means:

Visita Interiorem Terrae Rectifando Invenies Operae Lapidem.

Translated, this means:

"Go down into the bowels of the Earth; by distillation you will find the stone for the Work."

As with all things alchemical, there can be more than one meaning to this hidden phrase. Not only does it refer to the manufacture of the Philosopher's Stone, but also it has a philosophical and metaphysical meaning regarding man's own enlightenment and how to attain it.

VOUDON VEVES

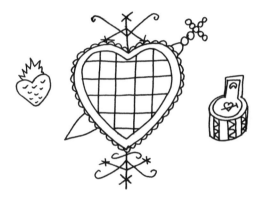

Voudon is an intriguing religion. Brought by African slaves to the Caribbean toward the end of the seventeenth century, the primary tenet of Voudon is that the spirit that animates the physical body during life continues to survive after the death of that body. The spirit develops and grows until it takes on the status of a divinity, or **loa**.

Catholic missionaries were keen to stamp out any traces of the native religion, but Voudon is a powerful force and its followers gradually started to morph some of their own deities with the Catholic saints. The syncretism was almost perfect; any Catholic priest visiting a home of the Voudon was pleased to see a household shrine full of the "correct" statuary of the Catholic faith; the householder, however, saw his preferred spirits and deities in a slightly different form.

Even elements of the liturgy appear in Voudon ceremonies.

An important feature of the Voudon faith is communication with the Ioas. To accomplish this, the Ioa is encouraged to possess the body of a living human being, and much ritual and ceremony is designed with this aim in mind.

Each deity has its own symbol, or veve. The mambo, or priestess, draws the symbol onto the ground in fine cornmeal. The veve is effectively a welcome call to the spirit in question and it is essential that the mambo render the symbol correctly, despite the fact that many of them are very elaborate.

As well as veves for deities, there are veves that call for specific requests. There is a huge range of these symbols that cover all eventualities from debt collection to increasing potency and all things in between. The veve shown here is dedicated to **Erzulie Freda Dahomey**, the Ioa of dreams and love.

WAND

It's likely that the wand belonging to the fairy at the top of the **Christmas tree** will only work in the correct hands, but if not, what an enviable tool it would be. But it's not only fairies who carry wands or similar objects.

The wand is an essential tool for anyone who aspires to a position of authority and power: witches and wizards, druids, bishops, the monarchy. If it sounds strange to think of a bishop holding a wand, think of his crozier, the highly decorated **staff** with a bend in the end like a shepherds' crook; the crozier is his wand. Similarly, the **scepter** of the monarch fills the same role. Essentially, the wand con-

nects the user to the spirit world or to magical powers.

The wand itself is a thin stick or rod, held in the **hand**, and signifies both the power of the person holding it and the extension of that power. The baton of the conductor concentrates the attention of the orchestra to where it's needed; the stage magician uses his wand to direct our attention away from something else.

Wandlike tools have a long history. Wands were found in Egyptian tombs where they would have enabled the soul of the deceased to use the other items laid out for use in the Afterlife. Moses carried a wand of **hazel**, and hazel or **willow** is also the preferred wood for the construction of dowsing rods, another kind of wand. Indeed, the material from which a "magical" wand is made will have great significance, too; druids, for example, use a staff made of **yew** wood to divine the future.

Aesclepius, the son of Apollo, carried a wand around which two **serpents** were entwined; this is a wand which carries healing powers, called a **caduceus**.

In the **Tarot**, the suit of wands is related to the element of **fire**.

WHEEL

The influence of the wheel in symbolism is profound and far-reaching, and nowhere in the world is untouched by its influence. The Tibetans, for example, considered the wheel so sacred that it was never used as a simple means of transport. Native Americans built **medicine wheels**, a representation of the cosmos, in their deserts.

The number of spokes of sacred wheels is significant. The Buddhist Wheel of Dharma, for example, has **eight** spokes, because eight is the number of renewal and regeneration. The Wheel of Life, however, has **six** spokes that represent the six states of being.

The wheel carries much of the same symbolism as the **circle**, however, the primary difference is the turning action of the wheel that rotates continuously, reflecting the cycles of the Sun and the Moon, the planets, the seasons, the highs and lows of man's existence, and time itself. The wheel, naturally, symbolizes death and rebirth. Our ancestors saw the Universe as a vast wheel that turned relentlessly, encompassing everything within it. The **Zodiac**, too, is the celestial "wheel of animals."

The Wheel of Fortune is named for an Etruscan Goddess, Vortumna, meaning "she who turns the year." The Romans renamed her Fortuna. This wheel holds the idea that the destiny of man is symbolized by a wheel, sometimes bringing good fortune, sometimes bad, but always balancing in the end since the **eight** segments of this wheel carried a balance of opposing situations or ideas. Traditionally, these are passion and patience, riches and poverty, glory and humility, war and peace. This wheel reappears in the **Tarot**, depicted in the aptly named Wheel of Fortune card.

Unsurprisingly, the wheel is a powerful solar and lunar symbol. During the time of the winter **solstice**, blazing wheels of **fire** were rolled from the tops of hillsides to symbolize the turning of the seasons, the planetary Sun symbolically represented as it rolled down the "hill" of time and into the darkness of the winter season. The symbol of the wheeled chariot is ubiquitous, and represents the idea of the cycling of the planets. The Sun God frequently appears in a golden chariot pulled by **lions**.

The still point at the center of the wheel gives another symbol, that of the **Axis Mundi** or **Omphalos**, the center of the Universe.

Hindu and Celtic beliefs about the wheel coincide, both sharing a notion that a mystical person was in charge of the turning of the wheel. In Hindu, he is called Chakravarti, meaning the Lord of the Wheel, the same name given to the Druid Mag Ruith. The wheel of the Mag Ruith is made of **yew** wood, appropriate because the yew is the tree of death and rebirth. Legend says that if this wheel ever appears on Earth it will signify the end of the World.

The wheel symbol is disguised in the so-called Rose Windows that appear in cathedrals, such as the one at **Chartres**. In the Middle Ages, they were called "rota," which means wheel. Effectively a form of mandala, Jung called them "representations of the Self of Man transposed onto the cosmic plane."

In **alchemy**, the wheel represents the time needed for the alchemical matter to be decocted or brewed. The fire that had to keep the potion at a constant temperature both day and night was called the "fire of the wheel."

WINGED DISC

This is a very ancient symbol, seen in varying forms around the world. It is a solar symbol, resembling a winged **Sun**. Ancient Assyrians saw it as the symbol of their Sun God, Shamash; the combination of the **wings** and the disc indicate eternity, the Sun, and the communication between man and Gods.

WINGS

Naturally, wings are symbolic of flying, weightlessness, release. Wings signify an ability to rise above the constraints of gravity, and by association, the limitations of the material world. Wings are an expression of the sublime, the desire to transcend everyday reality.

In symbolism, any creature that is given wings as an attribute has some connection with the spirit world, either as a deity or as a

messenger between Earth and Heaven. **Birds** are the supreme manifestation of this idea in the natural world as are **angels** in the idealized world. The Taoist Immortals, who had wings so that they could fly to the Isles of the Immortals, had other birdlike qualities too, including a special diet that made downy **feathers** grow on their bodies.

Wings also symbolize knowledge, enlightenment and the freedom that these can bring. There is a saying in the Rig Veda, "He who understands has wings." Inspiration also appears in the form of wings.

WISDOM EYES OF BUDDHA

This symbol, of the watchful eyes of the Buddha, is to be found on **stupas**, in the position where the actual eyes of the Buddha would be if the building were a statue of the God himself. These eyes are painted on every side of the building, a reminder that the Buddha is able to watch over all **four** corners of the **Earth** in his omnipotence.

The Wisdom Eyes have a bindhu above and between them at the point of the third **eye**, signifying enlightenment. Underneath the eyes is a squiggle that looks a little like a **question mark**. This is the Sanskrit character for the number **1**, and symbolizes the unity of all things.

The Wisdom Eyes of Buddha are so prevalent in Nepal that they have by default become a symbol of the country itself.

Witch ball

The witch ball is a large, hollow glass ball, often with mirrored or otherwise reflective surfaces. The first recorded use of a witch ball comes in 1690 and they gained in popularity during the eighteenth century, hung in windows to repel witches and other malevolent forces, who would presumably be frightened off when they saw their own hideous faces staring back at them.

Some witch balls had strands of **hair** contained inside the hollow interior. These kinds were designed to absorb the evil spirit that would then be ensnared in the strands of hair and be unable to leave. In this sense, the witch

ball fulfils the same purpose as the Native American **dream catcher**, with its net that entangles the nasties that come disguised as nightmares.

The witch ball is probably the precursor to the brightly colored reflective balls that are hung on **Christmas trees**.

World Axis

The notion of an axis that runs through the center of the world and connects the Earth with the Heavens and the Underworld is common among many peoples. This concept is symbolized in various ways, for example as the column or pole, as the **mountain**, as the **World Tree**, and even as columns of **smoke** rising into the air. The **spinal column**, too, is symbolic of the World Axis as are **obelisks**, **towers**, **Menhirs**, **staffs**, standards, and similar objects and symbols.

The **Omphalos**, or **navel**, also represents the same concept.

Wreath

This is a garland of **flowers** and leaves, too large to wear on the head, but often used to denote victory or triumph in games, in war, in competitions of all kinds. **Laurel** wreaths are a particular sign of distinction; the word "laureate" has the same root as the word laurel. Wreaths are also used as a funerary tribute, since the solid outer layer of the object represents the material world, and the space in the center, the world of spirit. The **circular** shape symbolizes eternity.

bolizes adulthood. An important concept in classical philosophy was that of free will to make choices, and Pythagoras' Y symbolizes this concept perfectly.

In the Middle Ages, this type of **cross**, also called the Forked Cross or Furka—was the sign of a thief, because it also resembles the forked tongue of the **serpent**.

Y OF PYTHAGORAS

Pythagoras his forked letter does
Of human life a scheme to us propose;
For virtue's path on the right hand doth lye
An hard ascent presenting to the eye;
But on the top with rest the wearied are
Refreshed; the broad way easier doth appear;
But from its summit the deluded fall;
And dashed among the rocks, find there a funerall ...

It was noticed by Pythagoras that the Greek letter Y, or upsilon, resembles a forked path. To the cognoscenti, therefore, such a simple symbol became laden with hidden meanings. Effectively, the two "paths" of the Y represent earthly wisdom to the left (vice), and divine wisdom to the right (virtue). The traveler must choose which path he shall take when he meets the point of convergence, which sym-

YAB YUM

In Buddhist and Hindu symbolism, Yab Yum means "father mother" and consists of a male and female figure in an overtly sexual embrace. What might seem shocking to prudish Western sensibilities is a symbol of the unity of male and female, wisdom and compassion, spirit and matter, and is seen as a natural part of the cycle of life. The Yab Yum symbol takes many different forms according to which deity/consort pairing is represented.

The Yab Yum carries much of the same symbolism as the **yin yang** sign, or the **Shatkona**.

Yantra

The yantra, in Hinduism and Buddhism, is a linear geometric figure that effectively embodies, in a symbol, the spoken chant or mantra. In essence, it is a symbol of the cosmos. The tradition of drawing and contemplating yantras goes back over 2000 years and is the Hindu equivalent of the Buddhist mandala.

The yantra is used as a focus for concentration and meditation, and it contains some basic elements which are rich symbols in themselves.

The yantra usually contains a **triangle**, either upright (representing male energy) or inverted, representing female energy. Sometimes the yantra contains the interlocking triangles of the **Shatkona**. It will include a **circle** and a **lotus** flower, and the whole is encompassed within a **square** that has "gateway" points, symbolic of the solidity of the **Earth**.

Sometimes the yantra contains Sanskrit letters that not only give definition to the shape but also describe what it represents.

The most important of yantras is called the Sri Yantra, the "Mother of all yantras." The Sri Yantra consists of **nine** interlacing triangles; the space in the center implied as the **dot** or bindhu. Contemplation of the Sri Yantra is in itself a symbolic pilgrimage, with each step in the construction of this intriguing geometric shape taking us to the center, toward the spiritual goal of unity.

If sand is placed on a taut surface and the "aum" sound is chanted, then the resulting shape made by the vibrating sand is in the shape of the yantra, illustrated here.

Yin-yang

Also called the Ta Ki, the yin-yang symbol is Chinese in origin, from the Taoist tradition, although its meaning has extended throughout the World.

Two identical shapes fit snugly inside a **circle**. These shapes are formed by an S-shape that divides the circle. In the fatter part of each shape is a **dot**. Sometimes the shapes are drawn in opposing colors.

The shape of the yin-yang represent the interaction and interplay of opposing forces; yin represents the female, the **Moon**, coldness, passivity; yang is the male element, the **Sun**, heat, and action.

The bindhus or dots inside the fatter part of each shape borrows a color from its partner, and signifies balance and harmony despite seemingly opposing forces.

ZIA PUEBLO SUN SYMBOL

This is an ancient, magical symbol of the Pueblo Indians. It combines one of the most sacred signs, the **circle**, with **four** sets of four stripes. The whole is a symbol of the **Sun**, which is the meaning of the word "Zia." Four is a sacred number for the Zia Pueblos, and here it serves as a reminder of the four seasons, the directions, the **Earth** and its four corners, and the four elements, with the **fifth** element being contained within the whole. The symbol often features on pottery.

The Zia Pueblo symbol is used on the flag of New Mexico.

ZIG-ZAG

See **First signs: Zig-zag**.

THE ZODIAC

The true Zodiac is a conceptual division of space into **12** equal segments, which radiate out from the ecliptic, that is, the apparent path of the **Sun**.

However, the Zodiac also refers to the 12 constellations of **stars** that nowadays symbolize different human personality types. The term "Zodiac" has Greco-Roman origins and means "**circle** of animals," although these "signs" are not restricted to zoological beasts but encompass human forms, too. The Chinese Zodiac bears no relationship to any constellations.

The Zodiac is both a symbol in its own right as well as a collection of symbols. These symbols are totems for each of the 12 astrological signs. It is a **circle** of completion, a continually turning **wheel**, divided into a spiritually perfect number, 12. Each of the different segments expresses a phase of development in the cycle of the Universe as well as in humankind collectively and for each individual, singularly.

If we assume the stars that form the constellations have always been there, then the actual origins of the Zodiac are open to conjecture. Manly P. Hall states "one author … believed man's concept of the Zodiac to be five million years old" although the identity of this author is not given. However, it is probably safe to say that the Zodiac as we know it today has its origins in ancient Babylonia, although this antique Zodiac consisted of **18** segments.

By 2000 BC, the Mesopotamians and the Egyptians were using **four** particular constellations as markers for the changing seasons. These four star clusters are the ones that we still call **Taurus, Leo, Scorpio,** and

Sagittarius. These signs make logical sign-posts in the path of the year, falling as they do between the solstices (June 21 and December 21) and the equinoxes (March 21 and September 21).

A key character in the development of astrology was Ptolemy, a Greek mathematician, astrologer and astronomer who lived in the second century AD. Ptolemy wrote a treatise called the Tetrabyblos, or Four Books. In this, he described the names of the entire set of 12 Zodiacal constellations that we still use today. At this time, astrology and astronomy operated in tandem.

An Arabic mathematician, astronomer and astrologer called Mohammed ibn Musa al Khwarizmi, also mentioned as having discovered algebra, expanded upon Ptolemy's ideas.

The Zodiac and religion

Given that the early Christian Church did its very best to smother anything that smacked of paganism or what they perceived as ungodliness, the fact that belief in the Zodiac not only remained powerful but was allowed to develop seems unusual. Put simply, this is down to man's overwhelming desire to peek into the Book of Fate no matter the strength of his trust in the will of God or Allah.

Despite this, it is true that the early priest-hood did try to destroy astrological theory. For them, the fatalistic nature of the Zodiac ran counter to the idea of divine intervention and the teachings of Christ. However, the Arabic interest in the Tetrabyblos coincided with a period of intense study of the stars. They not only expanded on the Greek theories of astronomy and astrology but also developed equipment, such as the astrolabe,

that could measure the altitude of the stars and their distance from one another.

In the meantime, Christianity was going through a difficult period and needed a shake-up. The Second Coming of Christ, predicted for the year 1000, never happened. Blind faith was all very well, but information was vital. Knowledge from the East was traveling toward the West because of the Crusades. The new centers of learning in Spain were real melting pots of ideas from Sufi mysticism to the **Kabbalah** as well as mathematics and theology.

In the thirteenth century, Thomas Aquinas managed to fuse Christian mystery with some of the beliefs of Aristotle. He threw in a great deal of Sufi influence for good measure. These new teachings, and the new, open-minded attitudes that they portended, provided an open door for astrological ideas. They included the notion that the Universe was akin to a **ladder** stretching between Heaven and Earth, with angelic beings governing the stars and the planets, which themselves influenced all the elements of the Earth. There was a great deal of ambivalence about the Zodiac; there still is. Then, as now, some Christians condemned it as the work of the Devil, whereas others embraced it as part of the bigger picture ordained by God. Cathedral builders in the thirteenth and fourteenth centuries, excited by the "new" astrological ideas that were coming into Europe, used these ideas as inspiration for the design of several key buildings, including **Chartres Cathedral**. Symbols from the Zodiac are not only beautiful to look at, but evocative, and lent themselves well to an overlay of Christian analogy, even if the veneer was particularly thin.

The Celestial Mirror, the Heavenly Wheel

In the same way that early man believed that his **body** was a microcosm of the Universe, made in the shape of God, then it was a logical conclusion that the Zodiac, as a series of constellations with their own meanings and mythologies, was a celestial **mirror** that reflected the important events in the life of man down on Earth. Therefore, it made sense that if the patterns made by the astrological conjunctions could be "decoded" then they could be used as a tool of divination for forecasting future events.

The fact that the positions of the Zodiac signs have shifted in the 3000 years since they were first discovered is often ignored, if it is realized at all. In her *Woman's Dictionary of Myths and Secrets*, Barbara G. Walker states that each sign is skewed by a month; that is, anyone born under a particular sign really belongs to the sign ahead of it, according to the original theory. In effect, this means that anyone currently born under the sign of Scorpio, for example, would have been closer to Capricorn when the Zodiac signs were first "discovered" although there are some areas of overlap.

The Great Wheel (or Rsai Chakra in Hindu belief) of the Zodiac has been interpreted in many different ways. For Egyptians it was the heavenly representation of the **Holy River**, the Nile. For Zoroastrians the Zodiac represented the 12 chiefs of the Sun God, Ahura Mazda. The Akkadians, in 2000 BC, saw the Zodiac as the furrow of the great **Bull** God, El, as he ploughed his way, slowly but surely, through the year.

The cycle of life

Whatever people choose to believe or disbelieve about the Zodiac, its influence is pervasive. Everyone recognizes what it stands for. It is likely that even the most hardened cynic will know his or her own astrological sign and what it means. Emperors, kings, presidents, and world leaders often have their personal astrologers; some are open about this, others are coy. During the Second World War, British Intelligence had their astrologer, Louis de Wohl, as did Hitler.

Each sign is linked to one of four elements and is ruled by a planet. In addition, each sign itself governs a wide variety of things including **flowers**, **trees**, **herbs**, cities, countries, **metals**, **colors**, and parts of the body. Every sign has a basic conceptual meaning that collectively tells the story of a series of developmental steps. Each individual Zodiac symbol is investigated in greater depth below under its own entry.

Although the astrological signs generally start with **Aries**, the circular, wheel-like nature of the Zodiac means that there is really no beginning or end to the signs.

Dates and basic meanings ascribed to the signs of the Zodiac

Sign	Dates	Ruling element	Ruling planet	Basic meaning
Aries	Mar 21–Apr 20	Fire	Mars	Impulsion; the urge to act, will
Taurus	Apr 21–May 20	Earth	Venus	Perseverance, consolidation
Gemini	May 21–June 20	Air	Mercury	Polarity, adaptability
Cancer	June 21–July 22	Water	Moon	Passivity, attachment
Leo	July 23–Aug 22	Fire	Sun	Creation, life
Virgo	Aug 23–Sep 22	Earth	Mercury	Differentiation, diligence
Libra	Sep 23–Oct 22	Air	Venus	Balance, harmony
Scorpio	Oct 23–Nov 22`	Water	Mars/Pluto	Passion, endurance
Sagittarius	Nov 23–Dec 21	Fire	Jupiter	Cultivation of spiritual side, expansion
Capricorn	Dec 22–Jan 20	Earth	Saturn	Elevation, conservation
Aquarius	Jan 21–Feb 19	Air	Saturn/Uranus	Transition to higher states, adaptability
Pisces	Feb 20–Mar 20	Water	Jupiter/Neptune	Intuition, self sacrifice

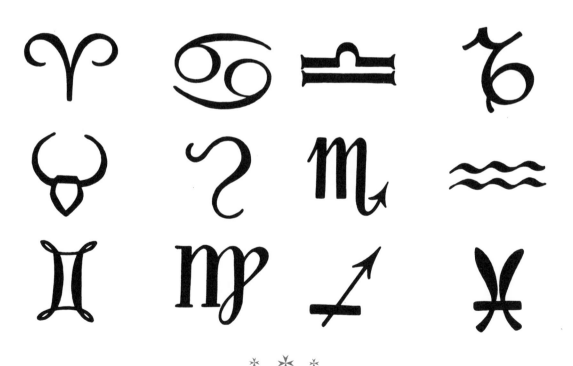

Aries

Polarity:	Positive, Male
Quality:	Cardinal
Ruling planet:	Mars
Element:	Fire
Body part:	The Head and Face
Color:	Red
Gemstone:	Diamond
Metal:	Iron
Flowers:	Honeysuckle, thistle
Trees:	One with thorns
Herbs and spices:	Mustard, cayenne pepper, capers
Food:	Onions, leeks, garlic
Animals:	Sheep and rams
Countries:	England, France, Germany
Cities:	Naples, Florence, Krakow, Birmingham (UK)

Although the Zodiac is an unending wheel, Aries is often referred to as first in line in this herd of astrological creatures. This is because the sign is associated with the vernal equinox and the seasonal start of the year when everything begins to grow again. Aries represents the seed of life, potential, and possibility.

THE RAM

To the Greeks, Aries was a ram called Krios. Indians called it Mesha, the ram, or Aja, the goat. For the Persians, it was a lamb called Varak. To the Babylonians, however, it was either Zappu, meaning hair, or Hunga, the worker.

THE GLYPH

This is the kind of shorthand symbol that belongs to each of the signs, used by astrologers, for example, when compiling astrological charts. These squiggles can be interpreted in a number of different ways. The glyph for Aries distinctly resembles the **horns** of the ram; horns themselves stand alone as a synonym for lust and sexuality. However, they could also represent an upward-shooting fountain of energy or even a flame. Because Aries rules over the face and the head, sometimes the glyph is superimposed over the face of a human figure to show Aries' influence. Again, because it governs the head and the mind, the horns are interpreted as reaching toward the spiritual world, another quality ascribed to Aries. It is interesting to see how the glyph, a simple sign, can start to qualify many different aspects of the sign itself.

QUALITIES

As we've seen, the stellar circle of animals as it exists today was slightly different and the sign that used to occupy the place now taken by Aries was Taurus, and there is a residue of the "bull in a china shop" notion about this position. The spring equinox is a time when new growth is prodigious, everything fighting to burst out of the ground after the barren winter months. The unharnessed energy and vitality of the ram or the bull is appropriate.

Ruled by the planet **Mars** which also rules the God of War, Aries' qualities include energy and vitality, determination, stubbornness, impulsiveness. Aries can also be quick-tempered and aggressively ambitious. The

fire element of Aries is the fire of creation, burning erratically in all directions, an explosion of flame that can be creative or destructive, depending on how it is applied. The brute force and impulsion of the Ram epitomizes this sign; as the first sign of the Zodiac it has a childlike bluntness, and an honest, straightforward approach.

Taurus

Polarity:	Negative, female
Quality:	Fixed
Ruling planet:	Venus
Element:	Earth
Body part:	Throat and neck
Color:	Pink
Gemstone:	Sapphire or emerald
Metal:	Copper
Flowers:	Rose, poppy, foxglove
Trees:	Ash, apple, cypress, vines
Herbs and spices:	Cloves, sorrel, spearmint
Food:	Wheat, berries, apples, grapes
Animals:	Cattle
Countries:	Ireland, Switzerland, Iran
Cities:	Dublin, Lucerne, Mantua, Leipzig

THE BULL

Second in line in the parade of Zodiacal creatures, Taurus symbolizes the bull and has changed in form very little over the millennia. Sometimes he looks ahead, toward Aries, sometimes he looks backwards to the animals in his wake. Astrologers from Persia, Greece, India and Babylonia all agreed that the Taurus constellation was a bull. Aldebaran, the brightest star in the Taurus constellation, was called the **heart** of the bull. Persians referred to the constellation as the Bull of Light. Taurus comes over the horizon at a time between the vernal equinox and the summer solstice, a time in the life of man that requires hard work, concentration and consolidation in order to direct the seed of raw energy sown by Aries.

THE GLYPH

The glyph for Taurus resembles the head and horns of the bull; whereas the horns of Aries signify the brute force of the ram, the horns of Taurus point toward the bull as a beast of burden, and even look a little like a yoke. The planet Venus and the element of earth rule Taurus, and the bull moves the earth as he ploughs its furrows. Despite being the epitome of male power, the bull is aligned to female energies and represents earth-mother qualities. Taurus rules over the throat and so is closely linked to sounds and **music**, and the glyph is interpreted as the larynx, situated in the throat, with the eustacian tubes running from it.

QUALITIES

All the archetypal bull-like qualities are given to people that are born under the sign of Taurus; an immense capacity for hard work, resilience and stubbornness, stability, reliability and domesticity. Added to this are acute sensitivity to all the sights, sounds and scents of the material world, which leads to a great pleasure in sensual delights. The bull rules over the neck and throat, indicating a love of music and the spoken word. When this is added to the other sensory qualities then the bull's sensitivity to beauty is highlighted. The earthiness of the bull is reflected in a lust for all the pleasures of life, and also means that the bull is warm-hearted, generous and energetic.

Gemini

Polarity:	Male, positive
Quality:	Mutable
Ruling planet:	Mercury
Element:	Air
Body part:	Arms and hands, shoulders, collarbone and lungs
Color:	Yellow
Gemstone:	Agate
Metal:	Mercury
Flowers:	Lily of the valley
Trees:	Nut-bearing ones
Herbs and spices:	Aniseed, marjoram, caraway
Food:	Nuts, vegetables that grow above the ground except for carrots
Animals:	Small birds, butterflies, monkeys
Countries:	Wales, Belgium, USA
Cities:	London, Cardiff, Plymouth (UK), San Francisco, Melbourne

THE TWINS

There is agreement among the various astrological disciplines that the constellation representing Gemini is two people generally embracing or holding **hands**, but the sex and the relationship of the pair are debatable. For Egyptians, the pair was a man and a woman. Romans thought that the sign represented **Apollo** and his twin sister **Diana**. The Persians and Greeks had them as twins called Dopatkar and Didumoi. Babylonians thought that they were twins but did not define the gender; and in India, they were called The Lovers, or Mithuna. Gemini could be physical twins, or lovers, or simply androgynous; it doesn't really matter. Whatever their gender, the sign represents duality both in outward appearance and identity, the concept of soul mates. Early representations of Gemini show a couple making love, signifying the union of opposites in harmony that is also indicated by the **yin-yang** or **yab-yum** symbols.

THE GLYPH

The glyph for Gemini, appropriately, looks like the Roman numeral for **2**. The two upright figures are effectively joined both at the **head** (the world of spirit, communication and ideas) and at their **feet** (the world of matter, quite literally, common ground).

QUALITIES

Gemini arrives just before the Summer solstice, the halfway point of the year. The symbolic twins speak of the need for contact with another person, the importance of establishing and maintaining a relationship and the idea that two can make a perfect whole while each struggles to retain its own identity as a single person. Gemini is representative of opposing forces, material and spiritual; sometimes one of the twins is mortal (indicated by a **scythe**) and the other is immortal (holding a lyre).

Belonging to the **air** element and ruled by Mercury, Gemini is communicative, idealistic, inquisitive, versatile and inventive.

Gemini is frequently associated with mythological twins such as the founders of Rome, Romulus and Remus, or the heavenly twins, Castor and Pollux. They also appear in the **Tarot** as the Lovers. People born under the sign of Gemini are supposed to be dualistic in their interests and lifestyles, restless, impatient and easily bored. It is their life's quest to reconcile the opposing forces within and to bring about internal harmony.

Cancer

Polarity:	Negative, female
Quality:	Cardinal
Ruling planet:	Moon
Element:	Water
Body part:	Heart, lungs and stomach
Color:	Silver gray
Gemstone:	Pearl
Metal:	Silver
Flowers:	White flowers in general
Trees:	Ones that are rich in sap; birch, maple, pine.
Herbs and spices:	Saxifrage, verbena, caraway
Food:	Milk, fish, and fruit and vegetables that have high-water content
Animals:	Creatures with shells
Countries:	Holland, Scotland
Cities:	Manchester (UK) Amsterdam, Tokyo

THE CRAB

The constellation known as Cancer was not always depicted as a crab, but whatever its form the shell has always been consistent.

Early European astrologers depicted Cancer as a crayfish. For the Egyptians it was the scarab beetle, a sacred creature representing death and rebirth that was also the sign of the God, Khepera. However, the Persian, Greek, Sanskrit, and Babylonian words for the constellation all mean the same as "crab." The constellation itself was possibly the most important one in the Zodiac, since it contains more fixed stars within the arc of its influence than any other sign. It was not only the Mayans who predicted the world would end when these planets aligned within the constellation. The Romans, too, believed that Cancer had been placed in the sky by Juno to signal the end of all things whenever she decided this should happen.

THE GLYPH

The distinctive "69" glyph that is the astrological shorthand for Cancer can be interpreted in a number of ways. The symbol is constructed from two separate parts that are identical, but polarized by their position. For some this "see-saw" symbol shows the up and down nature that is commonly held to be a Cancerian trait. Because the constellation appears just after the Summer solstice when the seasons are changing, the two spirals could represent this shift. Some see it as two spermatozoa, coming together to make one seed, and again, conception and birth are linked to the sign. Following the theme of nurturing and fertility, the sign might be a pair of breasts. Others see it as representing some of the fixed stars within the constellation itself, one pointing up, and one down, demonstrating the concept "as above, so below."

QUALITIES

This constellation appears just as the seasons begin to change, and the Sun's movement teeters from ascent to descent. A lunar symbol, Cancer belongs to the **water** element and is known to be passive, domesticated, imaginative, romantic and sometimes self-absorbed. The influence of the **Moon** points to a vivid imagination and inner depth, both qualities consistent with the sign. All the creatures that have been identified with this constellation share one common feature: the shell. This symbolizes self-protection and points to the withdrawn nature of some Cancerians. Cancer rules over the parts protected by this shell: the heart, the **lungs** and the **stomach**.

Leo

Polarity:	Positive, male
Quality:	Fixed
Ruling planet:	Sun
Element:	Fire
Body part:	The heart, the back
Color:	Gold
Gemstone:	Ruby
Metal:	Gold
Flowers:	Sunflowers, marigolds
Trees:	Bay, palm, citrus, laurel
Herbs and spices:	Saffron, peppermint, rosemary
Food:	Rice, honey, grapes
Animals:	Cat family
Countries:	Italy, Romania, Sicily
Cities:	Bath, Rome, Prague, Bristol, Los Angeles

THE LION

The constellation known as Leo has always been represented by the lion; the Babylonians sexed the lion as female, and named her Urgula, the lioness. The Romans called this star Regulus, meaning Heart of the Lion; the word also means "little king" or "paw of the lion." One of the first names for Leo was Babylonian and means "Great Light" and indeed the sign's first name was the Great Light, a reference to its ruler, the **Sun**.

Leo is the only sign in the Zodiac that is ruled by the Sun, a star, in contrast to the other Zodiac signs that are all ruled by planets.

THE GLYPH

The sigil for Leo could be the tail of the lion. Alternatively, the circle can be seen as the heart (ruled by the lion) with the scooped curve symbolizing the excitement and the uplift in emotions that the Leo feels when something particularly beautiful or inspiring is experienced. The downward slope, however, signifies the unfinished projects that so often litter the life of the Leo personality. The glyph may also signify the lion's mane.

QUALITIES

Leo appears over the horizon at the height of summer, and like the Sun, the Leo has a passionate and extrovert nature. Generosity and nobility are said to be a major attribute of the sign along with dominant powers of leadership.

The fire element of the Leo makes it theatrical, flamboyant, creative and hospitable, with regal or noble tendencies that can come across as condescension. The fire is the controlled heat of the Sun, though, as opposed to the untamed flames belonging to Aries. The lion is the symbol of power, royalty and pride, the symbol of emperors, which can be used to good or bad effect. The mane of the lion symbolizes the rays of the Sun, and an attribute of the Leo person is said to be manelike hair. The Egyptian Zodiac, the Dendera, shows an image similar to the card called **Strength** in the Tarot. A woman tames a lion, holding open its jaws with apparent ease.

Leo rules over the **spine** and the heart. St. Mark is represented by the winged Leo, which is seen carved in stone, striding majestically around St. Mark's Square in Venice.

Virgo

Polarity:	Negative, female
Quality:	Mutable
Ruling planet:	Mercury
Element:	Earth
Body parts:	Solar plexus and bowels
Color:	Dark brown, green
Gemstone:	Sardonyx
Metal:	Mercury or nickel
Flowers:	Brightly colored small flowers
Trees:	Nut-bearing trees (like Gemini)
Herbs and spices:	Turmeric, saffron and all others with a strong yellow color
Food:	Vegetables that grow in the ground
Animals:	Domestic pets
Countries:	New Zealand, the West Indies, Turkey, Greece, Brazil
Cities:	Paris, Athens, Heidelberg, Boston

THE VIRGIN

Despite her name, over the course of the millennia since the signs of the Zodiac were first defined, Virgo has been portrayed as the prudish virgin, the wanton temptress and all other aspects of the feminine in between these two extremes. She has been identified as many different Goddesses. For the Romans she was **Ceres**, holding a sheaf of corn, symbol of fertility and the harvest; Virgo also appears at the time that the crops are being gathered together. Egyptians linked her with **Isis** and with **Maat**, the Goddess of Truth. All of the names for Virgo refer to her as the Virgin or the Maiden.

A Greek legend links Virgo to **Astraea**, the Goddess of Truth and Virtue who lived with the other Immortals, among human beings on Earth. However, when Pandora opened the box and released all manner of nasties into the world, the Earth became unbearable. Astraea stayed for as long as she could bear it, although she eventually left the Earth, the last of the deities to do so, her finer sensibilities offended by the behavior of humans. It is said that Astraea will return to Earth when humankind is ready for her.

For Christians, she is personified as Mary, the virgin mother of Christ, sometimes portrayed with a **five**-petaled Marian Flower that conceals the five-pointed star or **pentagram**. Early depictions of Virgo show her as a winged angel.

The glyph

The glyph for Virgo links it with the signs for Scorpio and Libra, and has also been proposed to stand for MV, Maria Virgo, referring back to the Virgin Mary. Sometimes the final loop of the triple arches is depicted as the fish or vesica piscis shape, that symbolizes the world of spirit entering the world of matter and further underlines the connection with the Christian virgin.

Qualities

The qualities of Virgo, ruled by the element of earth, are tranquility, discrimination, efficiency, grace and intelligence. Self-control and self-discipline add to the equation, as well as methodical diligence and tidiness. Virgo is

a spiritual sign, and this has been shown by depicting her with the **wings** that signify ascension of the soul. Appearing during the time of the **harvest**, Virgo is maternal, fertile, nurturing and prepared for whatever might come her way.

Libra

Polarity:	Positive, male
Quality:	Cardinal
Ruling planet:	Venus
Element:	Air
Body part:	The back, kidneys and ovaries
Color:	All shades of blue
Gemstone:	Sapphire, jade
Metal:	Copper or bronze
Flowers:	Blue-colored flowers; roses, hydrangeas
Trees:	Ash, poplar
Herbs and spices:	Mint, arrack, cayenne
Food:	Pear, tomato, asparagus, beans
Animals:	Lizards and other small reptiles
Countries:	Austria, Burma, Japan, Argentina, Canada, Upper Egypt
Cities:	Copenhagen, Johannesburg, Lisbon, Vienna, Frankfurt

The scales

The distinctive symbol that represents Libra, the seventh sign of the Zodiac, is the set of **scales**, the only inanimate object that represents a Zodiac sign (although they are often shown in the hands of a human figure). Some schools of thought say that Libra was the last Zodiac sign to be officially recognized, and was formerly a part of the proceeding sign, Scorpio. Others contest this notion, however.

The idea of balance or equilibrium is confirmed by the many ancient astrological disciplines that give Libra this quality. The Indians, Persians, Greeks and Babylonians all agreed about this. The Greeks called the sign Zugos, meaning Yoke. Unsurprisingly, Libra was associated with Maat, the Egyptian Goddess of Justice; the figure of a woman with scales of balance and the sword of justice still carries a powerful symbolic punch as the representative of the law.

The glyph

The astrological shorthand for Libra does indeed look like the yoke that the Greeks thought the constellation represented. However, it also bears more than a passing resemblance to an Egyptian symbol called the **Akhet**. This sign shows the Sun rising between two hills and the Egyptians called the constellation Ta Akhet, meaning "place of the sunrise." The Akhet also speaks of balance between male and female or the Sun and the Earth, with the space between them being the mediator or balancing factor.

Qualities

Libra was an important sign for Romans since they believed that Italy fell under its jurisdiction, partly because Rome was founded on October 4 when the Sun is in this part of the Zodiac. Latterly, it is agreed that the country belongs to Leo.

Libra belongs to the element of air, and has a gentle temperament, peaceful, affectionate, orderly, and elegant but also changeable and prone to mood swings when the balance is disturbed. Because Libra appears at a mellow time of year when there is a lull in activity after the harvest is gathered in, it is possibly more relaxed and dispassionate than other Zodiac signs. Not surprisingly, Libra is the sign of the diplomat, a person who can see both sides of a story and make an impartial judgement. This quality fits with the fact that Libra is the only inanimate object in the Zodiac.

Scorpio

Polarity:	Negative, female
Quality:	Fixed
Ruling planet:	Mars/Pluto
Element:	Water
Body parts:	Reproductive organs
Color:	Deep red
Gemstone:	Opal
Metal:	Steel or iron
Flowers:	Rhododendron, geranium
Trees:	Blackthorn and other bushy trees
Herbs and spices:	Witch-hazel, aloes, catmint
Food:	Strong-tasting foods
Animals:	Crustaceans, insects
Countries:	Morocco, the Transvaal, Algeria, Norway
Cities:	Fez, Liverpool, Hull, New Orleans, Milwaukee

THE SCORPION

Of all the astrological shapes that are superimposed over their constellations, the stars that group together for the sign of Scorpio really do resemble a scorpion and so it comes as no surprise that ancient astrologers were in complete agreement that this was what the stars represented. Antares, the **red** star that is included in the shape, was known as the Heart of the Scorpion, dedicated to the God, Mars, because of its fiery color.

THE GLYPH

The modern shorthand symbol for Scorpio has a very different appearance from ones that are seen in medieval manuscripts. Then, it looked far more like an actual scorpion. Egyptians use the symbol of an upright serpent to represent the sign (both are poisonous creatures). The modern sigil— which looks like an M with a curved, arrow-headed uplift continuing on from the last upright—could be the severed tail of a scorpion or the male sexual parts. The arrow at the end of the "tail" also looks like the tail of a **dragon**.

QUALITIES

Scorpio appears midway through the fall, a time of decay but also a time of fermentation, when **Samhuin** or **Halloween** is on the horizon. Scorpio rules over this festival, dedicated to the dead. Ancient Egyptians believed that their God, **Osiris**, was sent to the Otherworld while Scorpio was in the Heavens. However, because Scorpio rules over the reproductive organs, the idea of rebirth is never far behind; a child conceived during the reign of the Scorpion is generally born into the sign of Leo. A strong sex drive is an attribute of this sign.

Many astrologers say that Scorpio people may have to face more adversity in their lives than other signs; however, this would assume that they are karmically prepared for this and are more than able to cope. The sting in the tail of the scorpion implies quick wittedness and a sharp intelligence as well as a sharp tongue. Traits also include a deep, passionate nature and a magnetic, shrewd, creative, and intense personality. This intensity is due in part to the influence of Pluto, although prior to the discovery of this planet, Mars was assigned to the Scorpion.

Sagittarius

Polarity:	Positive, male
Quality:	Mutable
Ruling planet:	Jupiter
Element:	Fire
Body part:	Thighs and hips
Color:	Dark blue, purple
Gemstone:	Topaz
Metal:	Tin
Flowers:	Carnations and pinks
Trees:	Lime, oak, birch, mulberry
Herbs and spices:	Aniseed, balsam, sage
Food:	Grapefruit, bulb vegetables, dried grapes
Animals:	Horses, also any animals what are hunted
Countries:	South Africa, Spain, Australia, Hungary
Cities:	Budapest, Toledo, Stuttgart, Cologne, Sheffield, Washington DC

THE CENTAUR/BOWMAN

All ancient astrologers are agreed that the constellation called Sagittarius is conceptually personified by hunting. In India, the bow alone represented the sign. The **centaur** himself appears in the Persian Zodiac, drawing back the bow. In Rome, it was the Goddess of the Hunt, Diana, who wielded the bow and **arrow**.

The centaur itself is half-human; the other half symbolizes a leaning toward a bestial side. This duality can also be interpreted as the spiritual side of man (depicted by the arrow that is just about to be released into the Heavens) being "weighed down" or somehow impeded by the physical world.

THE GLYPH

The sigil for Sagittarius is one of the most obvious in the Zodiac. It shows the arrow, symbolic of spiritual transcendence. Significantly, there is a bar at the base of the arrow, which carries all the connotations of the **cross**; the four elements and the material world. This points, again, toward the duality within the sign, a struggle to balance the world of matter with the world of spirit. Sagittarius is hunting for more than mere game, and symbolizes the notion of a spiritual quest, too.

QUALITIES

Sagittarius comes into the sky at winter, a time when there is a natural pause in the circle of the seasons, a time for hunting. Therefore, the qualities assigned to Sagittarius include a certain nomadic nature and a love of wide-open spaces. The fire that rules the sign has passed from the dangerous explosion belonging to Aries and the steady flame belonging to Leo, and appear in Sagittarius as the flame of spiritual enlightenment, the same flame that appears over the heads of certain saints and other enlightened characters. Sagittarians may spend their lives attempting to unify the material with the spiritual. A very practical sign, Sagittarius is elevated, by the torso of the **horse,** to be able to see the bigger picture and the wider horizon beyond the **trees.** The four hooves, standing squarely on the Earth, echo the four directions of the cross at the base of the arrow; above all else, the Sagittarian aims high while having his feet firmly on the ground.

Capricorn

Polarity:	Negative, female
Quality:	Cardinal
Ruling planet:	Saturn
Element:	Earth
Body part:	Knees, joints and bones
Color:	Black, dark gray, brown
Gemstone:	Turquoise, amethyst
Metal:	Lead
Flowers:	Ivy, medlar, heartsease, hemlock
Trees:	Yes, elm, pine
Herbs and spices:	Knapweed, comfrey, hemp
Food:	Potato, spinach, barley, beet, malt
Animals:	Goat and other cloven-hoofed animals
Countries:	India, Mexico, Afghanistan
Cities:	Oxford (UK), Mexico City, Delhi

THE GOAT

The Capricorn constellation, so the ancients agreed, was definitely a goat; however, it generally appeared as a goat/fish hybrid. For the Persians it was called the Sea Goat, Vahik; for the Babylonians it was the Goat-Fish; for the Greeks it was called the Goat-Horned One. Mahara, meaning Sea Monster, was the Sanskrit name. The only exception was Romans, who saw interpretation of the Goddess, Vesta, in the constellation. Modern images of Capricorn often tend to lose the sea-monster aspect, but older interpretations show it with four **legs** and the tail of a **fish,** or an entire rear end comprised of a **serpent**-like tail.

THE GLYPH

The Capricorn sigil is an unusual squiggle, which could be a sketch of the horns of the goat. However, the glyph appears in various forms. The sign is a combination of straight lines and curves that point to the dual nature of the Capricorn, the material side on the earth and the spiritual side in the water. There was an old saying that time ended with Capricorn. Again, this was because of the time of year that the constellation loomed over the horizon, and its intimate association with **Saturn,** also known as **Chronos,** the God of Time.

QUALITIES

Capricorn comes into the sky at the time of the winter solstice, the "**gateway** of the Gods." In the Far East, this time heralds the New Year. Saturn, the ruler of the sign, denotes patience, perseverance, and industry. The hybrid nature of the symbol points toward an inherent duality. On the one hand is the sure-footed mountain goat, closely in touch with its earth element and aspiring to the heights, worldly and intellectual. On the other is the aspect of the sign that relates to water; unconscious and psychic powers, depth, intuition. Capricorn is hard working and ambitious but with a mystical aspect to its nature. The Saturnine aspect of the sign is reflected in the dignity and self-discipline common to those born under it, who can be withdrawn and contemplative.

It is the quest for people born under this sign to reconcile the two very distinct aspects of their nature; the worldly with the spiritual, the ambitious with the contemplative.

Aquarius

Polarity:	Positive, male
Quality:	Fixed
Ruling planet:	Saturn/Uranus
Element:	Air
Body part:	Circulation, the ankles
Color:	Turquoise
Gemstone:	Aquamarine
Metal:	Aluminum
Flowers:	Orchid
Trees:	Fruit trees
Herbs and spices:	Those that have a sharp or unusual flavour
Food:	Any foods that preserve well; dried fruits, preserves, pickles
Animals:	Large birds that can fly for a long time; the Condor
Countries:	Sweden, Russia
Cities:	Salzburg, Moscow, Leningrad, Hamburg

THE WATER CARRIER

The Greeks and Persians called the constellation the Water Pot. However, for the Babylonians this star cluster was a Goddess and to the Romans, it was Juno.

For the Akkadians, the sign was called "Ku ur Ku" meaning "Seat of the Flowing Waters," or alternatively Rammanu, God of the Storm. The sign is often depicted as a human figure pouring water from some kind of a vessel. This figure can be of either gender. In the Tarot, the Aquarius archetype appears in two possible places; as the card called Temperance, featuring a winged woman circulating water by pouring it between two jugs, or as the Star, which features a young girl, naked, pouring water from two jugs onto the earth. These dual streams of water echo back to the Egyptian concept of the sign, depicting a God who also pours the same two streams of water.

THE GLYPH

The sigil for Aquarius is self-explanatory. It shows wavy lines, representing water. The **zig-zag** shape of the lines, though, portrays the idea of water as an active principle, a life-force akin to electricity. The girl in the portrayal of Aquarius seen in the Tarot card called The Star, actually stands in the water she is pouring, again indicating it as something more than just a liquid. The two streams of water in the sigil point to this same notion, of water as one of the elements but with another quality. Homeopathy relies on the power of water to be able to dilute and yet strengthen the essence of the remedy; this magical power may provide a clue about the meaning of the two lines.

QUALITIES

Before the discovery of Uranus, Saturn, the planet that confers gravity and a certain weight, ruled Aquarius. Uranus, however, adds another element to the Aquarian psyche, that of innovation and a reputation for eccentricity. For example, Aquarius is the sign typified by the Mad Professor archetype. The Aquarian, ruled by air but with a mystical attachment to water, has little regard for material objects and is more concerned with the mind and the spirit, primarily concerned with quenching the thirst of the soul before that of the body. This makes for a certain emotional detachment. The air element makes the sign intuitive and given to leaps of deductive reasoning.

THE AGE OF AQUARIUS

Much has been written about the Age of Aquarius, but what exactly does this mean? The "ages" of the Zodiac work backwards, i.e. the age that we are now leaving is the age of Pisces, which actually comes after Aquarius in the Zodiacal wheel.

The exact date of our entering this New Age is difficult to determine although each age lasts for 2160 years. Some pinpoint the transition to 1962, others say it will start in 2377. It is interesting to note that the preceding age, which for many was associated with Christianity, was the age of Pisces, whose symbol was the fish. This is still a symbol of the faith 2000 years after Christ stepped on this Earth.

The Aquarian Age is said to be the dawning of a time of change. These changes will include freedom in all senses of the word, humanitarianism, and a raising of consciousness and awareness.

The glyph for Aquarius carries within it a clue about at least one of the things that will be a planetary concern with the coming of the New Age—the element of water.

Pisces

Polarity:	Negative, female
Quality:	Mutable
Ruling planet:	Jupiter, Neptune
Element:	Water
Body part:	Feet and immune system
Color:	Sea-green
Gemstone:	Moonstone or bloodstone
Metal:	Platinum or tin
Flowers:	Water lily
Trees:	Willow, alder, trees that like to grow near water
Herbs and spices:	Lime, succory, mosses
Food:	Cucumber, pumpkin, melon, lettuce, turnip
Animals:	Otters, beavers, and other water-loving mammals; fish
Countries:	Portugal; deserts in general
Cities:	Jerusalem, Warsaw, Seville, Bournemouth, Santiago de Compostela

THE FISH

The Greeks and the Persians both called this constellation "Fish." For the Babylonians it was Two Tails. They divided the star cluster into two separate shapes, Simmah, the **swallow**, and Anunitum, the Goddess. The symbol for Pisces is traditionally the two fishes, swimming in opposite directions, their mouths nevertheless joined by a cord. This cord is faint within the actual constellation, but still visible. The Babylonians called it Riksu, the Arabians Al Risha. This cord is a vital part of the sign and has been given esoteric significance.

The glyph

The sigil for the fish comes from Egyptian sources and has hardly changed since this time, unlike glyphs belonging to other constellations. The original Egyptian sign showed the two opposing curves, but they were separate; the connecting line was added in the fourteenth or fifteenth century, making the sign into its current H shape.

Qualities

Although some modern interpretations of Pisces omit the cord, the fact that the fish are joined rather than being separate is very significant, a good demonstration of how a seemingly simple line within a symbol can mean so much. The duality of the fish is well known although it can signify different things, such as the soul that desires the stimulus of the material world, and the spirit that wants to leave these things behind. However, one cannot survive without the other. Pisces carries with this spirit/soul significance in seventeenth-century alchemical writings.

Because of their association with water, fish are symbols of the Goddess, the feminine aspect, and some say that the fishes swimming in opposite directions indicate the supposed female trait of not being able to make a decision, or of a trait belonging to both sexes, of being pulled in opposite directions.

Because the fish symbol is closely aligned to the Christian faith, the Pisces symbol is sometimes found in churches where no other astrological symbolism is displayed. Christ was born at the start of the Age of Pisces. Pisces people are said to be dreamy, impractical, deep thinkers and interested in psychic matters.

The sign comes into the sky just before the Vernal Equinox, just before spring; it is the "last" sign of the Zodiac, and as such represents the idea of rebirth. It is appropriate that fish come from that great **womb** of rebirth, the sea.

Zoso and the four symbols

A very good example of a modern sequence of symbols that perhaps gives an indication of how other magical emblematic amalgams are formed.

Although the symbol was never intended to have a name, it is commonly called the Zoso because the first of the four symbols appears to spell this word. It was chosen by the guitarist Jimmy Page of Led Zeppelin. The band decided that they should use symbols instead of words for the cover of their fourth album (which, ironically, is usually referred to as Led Zep 4).

Page, renowned for his interest in occult matters in general and Crowleyana in particular, has never spoken publicly about the component elements of his own symbol, but it is believed to have originated in an old alchemical grimoire dating back to the sixteenth century. The sigil itself points to the link between the planet **Saturn** and Page's **Zodiac** sign, **Capricorn**. The "Z" is a commonly used symbol for the planet, and the "oso" stands for the element of **mercury**, also associated with Saturn.

The symbols of the other band members are the **triquetra** (chosen by John Paul Jones, bass and keyboards). Drummer John Bonham chose the **Tripod of Life** or Borromean Rings, and singer Robert Plant chose a **feather** enclosed within a circle. The feather bears a similarity to the feather of justice used by the Goddess of Truth, **Ma'at**, to balance against the souls of men, and is also likely to signify transcendence. The **circle** stands for completion and wholeness.

Part Two
A WORLD OF HIDDEN SECRETS

SYMBOLS IN THE ELEMENTS, THE LANDSCAPE, AND THE NATURAL WORLD

It doesn't require a great amount of imagination to suppose that the very first "symbols" that our ancestors noticed—and tried to analyze—were the natural features that surrounded them. Long before man had thought about conveying his own ideas by scoring marks in the sand or scratching them onto rocks, he would have looked to the landscape and the **elements** to help him orient his place in the Universe. This might sound mundane, but open your front door and see what's out there; it might be a **mountain** or a tower block, **trees**, or walls. Maybe it's a body of **water**, or a river … Whatever it is, we make these features into symbols, representative images of our realm of experience. These features become as much a part of our internal landscape as they are a part of our external landscape. The great leap occurs when we realize that our own individual interpretation of reality, whatever form it takes, is a part of the collective consciousness.

The most easily shared experience of symbols in the natural world happens when we look to the **skies,** since this is the common ground of humanity, visible to everyone and full of features whose regularity gives us a way of measuring time. It's no surprise that the **Sun**, with its reliable and regular appearance and disappearances, and its glorious illuminatory powers, is the ultimate symbol of the Godhead, in whatever form it takes. These days, most parts of the **planet** that we inhabit suffer from light pollution, but nevertheless the allure of the skies—particularly the night skies—is compelling.

It was tricky at first, in thinking about this section, to decide what constitutes a symbol within the landscape. After all, what constitutes "natural"? Effectively every **medicine wheel**, **temple**, or giant figure carved into the **Earth** could be a member of this category. Every scarred war-torn zone or area of dense population tells the story of man's interaction with the environment.

It's vital to understand that humankind is not separate from the Universe we inhabit. We are a part of the changes that are happening on Earth. The Gaia hypothesis, named after the Greek Goddess of the Earth and proposed by James Lovelock, puts forward the idea that every single living thing on the planet affects the nature of its environment to make it a suitable platform for life. It's worth repeating that man is an inherent part of this platform, although our perspective tends to be limited. It's no coincidence that Lovelock's theory of complete cohesion coincided with the first ever photograph of the Earth, taken by an unmanned spacecraft in late 1967. Although the impact of this iconic picture may have been diluted due to familiarity since it was first published, its influence has been profound. As Stuart Brand said at the time, "… it's so graphic, this little blue, white, green and brown jewel-like icon amongst a quite featureless black vacuum … This is all we've got and we've got to make it work."

We like to superimpose our own ideas onto the natural landscape, defining our own place in it by controlling it somehow, discovering or inventing patterns, and making order out of chaos. In the end, in this part of the book we decided to concentrate purely on the raw, natural world—the world that belonged to our ancient ancestors—in order to understand the way they thought about the world of which they found themselves a part, and to understand the origins of some of our creation myths.

Here, we are looking at the elements in terms of man's imaginative experience of them rather than the elements considered as fundamental atomic building blocks. The basic four elements that man first defined have a visceral significance, corresponding to our emotions and states of being; they determine the characteristics of a whole variety of

different things, including the **four** "humors" of the natural world (hot, cold, moist, and dry), the signs of the **Zodiac**, **colors,** and— for **alchemists** and others—the four aspects of man. **Fire** equates to the **spirit**, **water** is the **soul**, **air** is the mind, and **earth** is the body. Once again, we see a melding together of the microcosm and the macrocosm. The **Platonic solids** encompass the full range of elements within their geometric shapes. The difference between male/active/thinking and female/passive/intuition is defined by the elements, too; male is perceived as fire and air, and female as earth and water.

Often in the West the fifth element— aether (or ether)—is ignored. Aether is the essential unifying principle and a reminder that the Universe is constructed from a unified diversity. The elements, naturally, are represented in all the features that make up our planet. The tricky thing, of course, is that the form of the elements changes, so we also need to be able to convey this idea. Whereas Heaven seems to be about a correct balance of all the elements working in harmony, Hell is a corresponding imbalance. Popularly it is an (imaginary) place of excess fire, but it is symbolized equally by the savage **winds** that blow across a desert environment, carrying with them—for example—all the pestilential demons of the Assyrian pantheon, such as Pazuzu and Lilitu. Tellingly, when there is an imbalance of the elements on the Earth we call it a "natural disaster."

The basic geometric shapes that are a code for the elements form a fundamental part of understanding symbols, as explained in "**First Signs**." These simple shapes combine and juxtapose with one another to make profound statements or to inspire philosophical concepts that largely strive towards integration and harmony between opposing forces. Squaring the **circle**, for example, is not only a symbolic way of combining spirit with matter, but also a way of joining the created Universe with the greater cosmos. This device is a fundamental principle of sacred and secular geometry. The upward-pointing **triangle**—symbolizing fire—converges with the downward-pointing triangle to make the **six**-pointed **star**, again a symbol that unifies the earth with the **Heavens**. This is reflected in the alchemical principle "as above, so below" that is repeated all over the world, and which is included in the Lord's Prayer; "… thy will be done, on Earth as it is in Heaven." This idea enables some of us to trust that everything is as it should be, and that there is some greater intelligence out there in the darkness beyond. This idea is discernible throughout most of the world's faith systems, reflecting our constant need to bounce back and forth between macrocosm and microcosm. Man's

Medieval astronomer trying to discover the secrets behind the milky way.

relationship to the elements and to the landscape reveals his timeless need to communicate with this higher intelligence.

In this section, each of the elements is grouped together with the aspects of the landscape it represents; water – female – **caves**, fire – male – **mountains**, and so on.

An Elementary Elemental Overview

Chinese Theory of the Five Elements

The most ancient piece of Chinese philosophy is believed to be the *Hong Fan*, dating back to the second millennium BC. The *Hong Fan* outlines the correspondences of the five elements.

In addition, each of the elements rules a **direction** and a **season**, so they have jurisdiction over **time** and **space**.

- **Water** is the nadir, winter, and the northern direction, appearing at the bottom of the map.
- **Fire** is the zenith, summer, and the south.
- Wood is spring, and the east.
- Metal is fall, and the west.
- **Earth**, the central point from which all the others emanate, represents all seasons and directions.

Element	Water	Fire	Wood	Metal	Earth
Number	1	2	3	4	5
Taste	salt	bitter	acid	pungent	sweet
Human character	serious	methodical	learned	friendly	holy
Sky sign	rain	yang	hot	cold	wind
Vegetable	yellow millet	bean	wheat	oil-seed	white millet
Animal	pig	hen	sheep	dog	ox
Musical note	*yu*	*chu*	*chih*	*shang*	*kung*
Bodily organ	kidneys	lungs	spleen	liver	heart
Color	black	red	green	white	yellow
Body element	blood	breath	bones	nails	muscles
Emotion	anger	pleasure	joy	sorrow	love

THE MASONIC SYSTEM OF ELEMENTS

In **Freemasonry**, the elements are used as a way of describing the symbolic journey of the initiate.

ELEMENT	HUMAN ADJUNCT	QUALITY	LEVEL
Fire	Spirit	Ardor and enthusiasm	Initiation
Water	Soul	Sensitivity and emotion	Religion
Air	Mind	Intellectual power	Philosophy
Earth	Body	Materialism	Physical life

THE ELEMENTS AND THE SIGNS OF THE ZODIAC

- Fire—Aries, Leo, Sagittarius
- Water—Cancer, Scorpio, Pisces
- Air—Gemini, Libra, Aquarius
- Earth—Taurus, Virgo, Capricorn

Christian concept of the World Soul.

Landscape and the Elements

Earth

"It suddenly struck me that the tiny pea, pretty and blue, was the Earth. I put up my thumb and shut one eye, and my thumb blotted out the planet Earth. I didn't feel like a giant. I felt very, very small."

Neil Armstrong

Perhaps the archetypal image of the **Earth** is as the Earth Mother, personified as the Goddess Gaia. The Ancient Greek historian Herodotus pointed out that all known names for the Earth are female. A few examples of this include: Shekinah, in the Kabbalistic tradition, becomes Shakti, the female "cosmic energy" of the Hindu philosophies, as well as Kali Ma, "the dark mother;" Erda, who belongs to the Nordic myths; and Gaia, Terra, Europa, and many others. If Earth is the Mother, then the Heavens are the Father, reminding us again of the tenet "as above, so below."

A recurrent theme in creation myths is of a mound of earth rising up from the primordial waters. But the Earth itself symbolizes a **womb**, pregnant with **water**, **minerals**, and the seeds of plant life. As life springs forth from the Earth it also returns back to the Earth when the material part comes to the end of its life, becoming part of the cycle of death and rebirth as the rotting matter provides sustenance for the next generation.

The Cave

The most fitting symbolic form within the landscape of this great Earth Mother is the cave. Whereas **mountains** reach towards the **sky** and belong to the **elements** of **air** and **fire**, the cave itself signifies the **womb**, the magical place of gestation. It parallels the **Athanor** in **alchemy**, where **spirit** takes form, is transformed into matter, and eventually makes its exit into a new world through the vaginal opening or *vesica piscis*, symbolized by the cave **mouth**. When, in the *Tales of the Arabian Nights* Ali Baba unlocks the concealed door of the cave by shouting "Open Sesame!," the relevance of the command is because the sesame seed pod that bursts open symbolizes all the wealth of the Earth, as well as having a sexual meaning.

Caves and caverns are the natural places for the energy of the Earth to be harnessed. As such they were, and are, powerful places for magical and religious **rites** and **ceremonies**. The "Hellfire Caves" at High Wycombe, England, the ancestral seat of the Dashwood family, are a good example of a subterranean locus for occult practices.

Caves can be a place of refuge, but can also become a prison. Whereas mountains are highly visible, the cave is its polar opposite: secret, hidden, hard to find. Yet despite these opposing qualities, caves and mountains have a natural symbiosis because they exist together in the same location; cave complexes are often found inside mountains.

Caves share a further quality with mountains; that of being at the center of the earth, as symbolized by the **Omphalos**. As Gods resided on the loftiest summits of the mountain, Gods were also often born inside caves; **Zeus**, for example, was born in a cave on Mount Ida in Crete. When this particular cave was excavated it was full of offerings and tributes to its God. Lao Tzu, the father of Taoist philosophy, was born in a cave, as was the pre-Christian **Sun** God, Mithras. Mithraic worship often took place underground in the secrecy of caves and caverns. The stable in which Mithras' successor, Jesus, was born was actually cut out from a rock face, yet another example of a God figure being born in a cave. American Indians believe that caves were the gestation places for the embryos of mankind.

Caves are among early man's first sacred places, and such sacred caves appear all over the world, in myth and legend as well as in reality. Aladdin's cave, for example, contained the magic lamp that yielded the **Djinn** that changed Aladdin's fortunes, and so is a symbol of the cave as a repository of valuable secrets. The caves at Lascaux in the Perigord region of France also hold valuable secrets and rich treasures of a different kind. Dating back to the Paleolithic era, the paintings inside these caves show man's preoccupations at this time. The walls are covered with pic-

tures of **horses**, **cattle**, an extinct animal called the auroch, felines, **birds**, and **fish**. The four schoolboys who accidentally discovered the caves whilst looking for a **dog** must have been astounded to realize that the **colors** and pigments of the paintings were almost as vibrant as when they were painted, 17,000 years ago. They were preserved in this way because no natural light existed inside the cave. There's also evidence of ritual worship in the Lascaux caves.

Caves that are hard to find have additional significance as places of secret rites and ritual. In addition, the most elusive of caves are good hiding places; the Dead Sea Scrolls, for example, were discovered in a cave high up a cliff face.

Caves are a natural choice for performing rites and ceremonies since they afford privacy, so knowledge of their location can be kept a secret between initiates. The cave is the forerunner of the **temple**, and conversely many holy temples and shrines found on mountains could be said to be man-made cave symbols. The rock temples of India (such as the Ajanta caves) bear out this symbolism, the temples actually carved into the rock faces themselves, replicating the idea of the cave.

Pyramids are man-made mountain/cave complexes, the grand external structure hiding the burial place within. That they were sites of elaborate burial rites, motivated by the expectation of an afterlife, is a perfect example of the cave as a place of rebirth. These rites and rituals were not the exclusive domain of the Egyptians; evidence of one of the oldest ritual burials in western Europe, dating back 30,000 years, was discovered in the Paviland Caves in South Wales. The corpse of a 21-year-old man covered in **red**

ochre was found; the ochre had also stained the decorative items about his person, including rinds, rods of ivory, and seashells. It's likely that the red ochre used would have been a symbol of **blood** and therefore of life. Additionally, the skull of a mammoth had been buried with this young man, who is believed to have been a tribal chieftain or other important member of society.

The burial mounds, tumuli, and barrows found spread across the world in varying forms similarly represent the idea of the cave; like the Paviland Man, after death people were concealed in these burial "caves" to await rebirth from within this womb-like symbol.

Spiritually, the combination of the mountain and the cave tells us that knowledge and understanding come not only from the external world, but also from the internal world. Plato, the Ancient Greek philosopher, described the condition of man and his limited view of the world in terms of our living in an underground cavern, one shaft of light coming from behind us casting our **shadows** on the wall ahead. We need to realize our limitations, and to understand that the shadows flickering on the wall of the cave are not the actual world, but simply an illusion, or—in Buddhist terms—the "veil of Maya."

WATER

"… the person you love is 70% water …"

As well as this, 70% or more of the surface of the **planet** is water, too.

The nature of water is that it is defined by the shapes of the solid objects that surround it, but that it has no shape of its own. Even when frozen into ice, this "solid" water depends on its environment for the form it takes, even down to the gravity that dictates the shape of icicles. In *The Sacred and the Profane*, Mircea Eliade observes that form "manifests itself above the waters, by detaching itself from the waters." Water, therefore, symbolizes a mass of possibilities, and it's not surprising that most creation stories share a common theme of the **Earth** arising from a primordial, whirling, watery **ocean** from which all other life was created. Part of the story of our own evolution was when amphibious creatures came out of this water and spent their whole lives on dry land. Similarly, the story of a great deluge is universal, whether as an accident of nature or as an act of God. For many religions, this flood constituted a symbolic "washing away of sins" on a grand scale. Recent images from flooded cities, such as New Orleans, are a sober reminder of the devastation that can be wreaked by water's huge, formless mass.

The movements of the **Moon** and the planets dictate the rising and falling of our earthly tides, further underpinning the connection between all the elements.

Individual life gestates in the watery environment of the **womb**. Here we start to make the connection between water and the feminine element, as the continually changing form of the Moon whose visible shape, like water, is also defined by something else; the light of the constant **Sun**.

Baptism, a religious ceremony sometimes involving a complete immersion in water, symbolizes a rebirth and regeneration, underlining the idea that water gave birth to all life. Another vital aspect of water is its ability to reflect; Native American people call a still pool of water, aptly and lyrically, a "sky **mirror**." Water therefore gave man the first means of seeing himself as others saw him, and reinforced the reflective links to the **Moon**.

Like everything else in the world, water is affected by gravity. Water flows downwards, from the highest place until it meets the **sea**, and the river itself is a symbol of the linear aspect of time. This flowing water carries with it the spirit of the **mountains** from which it springs, providing an essential resource. Most of the world's major cities have developed along the courses of rivers, and we find time and time again that both the rivers and the cities are held to be sacred in some way.

The oceans are so deep that, despite all of our exploration, there are still life forms that remain undetected. The oceans also contain surprising aspects, like the deep hot water vents whose apparently poisonous environment can support all sorts of creatures, be they **animal** or vegetable.

Because the deep waters of the sea and lakes symbolize unknown realms, we often find that fairy tales and myths use these watery depths as places where otherworldly spirits dwell. Foggy, misty places—somewhere between the world of the living and the dead—are liminal environments and places of the **spirits**, where the worlds meld one into the other. The Elysian Fields, the place in Greek myth where the souls of dead heroes repose, may be derived from an Egyptian word meaning "field of reeds." Homer describes the **asphodel** and **poplar** that grow there, both water-loving plants.

THE GANGES

The Ganges is one of the world's most holy and sacred rivers, mythologized as the place where the Goddess Ganga, wife of Shiva and daughter of the **Mountain** God, Himalaya, came down to Earth. This happened because a king, Bhagiratha, wanted to save his ancestors; they had been turned to ashes when they accidentally disturbed a holy man as he meditated. Ganga agreed to come to Earth to flow over their ashes and release their souls so that they could ascend to Heaven. To prevent the crashing waters of the Goddess from causing any destruction on Earth, Shiva generously caught the river in his **hair**.

The scale of the Ganga Ma, or Mother Ganges, also has a bearing on its profound importance to Hindus. 2507 kilometers long, the Ganges has its source 4200 meters up in the Himalayas and descends from there, eventually meeting the sea at the Bay of Bengal. The Ganges is the personification of the great Goddess Spirit, Shakti, and so to drink the waters and to bathe in this river are sacred actions. The river is not so much a sacred place as a sacred entity or spirit. One of the most holy places along the river is

Varanasi. The combination of the sacred river and the sacred city are known as a "Mokshadvara," or "portal to liberation," where the **veil** between the worlds is at its thinnest; Varanasi is a liminal, threshold place. To die in Varanasi is considered a privilege, and thousands of pilgrims travel there to scatter the ashes of their loved ones into the Ganges. The stone landing and steps called *ghats* provide space for these pilgrims. Bathing in the river is even believed to cleanse the soul of previous karmic burdens; these are carried away into the sea, just like the ashes and blessings in the form of **flowers** and floating **candles**.

STYX

This is the river in Greek mythology that forms the borderline between **Earth** and the Underworld, or Hades. The river itself is a sort of no-man's land, belonging at once to both places and neither. Here, the water marks the transitional point between two worlds, a symbolism often shared by water **birds** that can effectively move in three elements; **air, earth**, and **water** (such birds are often seen to be messengers between the Gods and man, as well as the living and the dead). A ferryman, Charon, conducts **souls** safely from one side of the Styx to the other. It's still a custom in Greece for coins to be put into the mouth of a corpse, as payment to Charon for the journey.

A magical and mystical place, the Styx's other name is Alpha, the first letter of the Greek **alphabet**, and the one that gives birth to all the others that follow (continuing the imagery of the river as the Great Mother).

The Gods swore their most important oaths on the river. The Styx carried yet another important symbol within its swirling waters; like a **spiral**, it coils around Hades **nine** times. As a river of birth and death, a single drop of the waters of the Styx was fatally poisonous; in spite of this, Achilles' mother, Thetis, dipped her son Achilles in the river to give him superhuman powers since the waters also had the ability to make someone immortal or invulnerable. The only part that missed the dousing was the **heel** that she grasped. An Achilles' heel, therefore, refers to a weak spot.

There are several other rivers in the Underworld of Greek mythology, notable the Lethe, the river of oblivion. **Souls** traveling to the Underworld were encouraged to drink the waters of this river so that they would forget everything that had happened during their lives, and would have no memory of it once they were reborn. However, part of the **Eleusinian Mysteries** told of another river, Mnemosyne, whose waters had the power to make the drinker remember everything about their previous incarnation to carry over into the life to come; it's likely one of the major secrets revealed in the Mysteries was the advice to refuse to drink the waters of the Lethe, and to drink the waters of Mnemosyne instead.

THE OCEAN

Our ancestors envisaged the oceans of the world as a great **serpent** that coiled around the planet. The **cosmic egg**, symbolizing the **Earth** as an egg encircled by the serpent, is a representation of this idea. This partially explains the plethora of ideas about the serpent symbol itself. The vastness of the seas is still a reminder of the formless mass that existed before the earth was "born."

Like deserts, the ocean is a place to be traversed rather than inhabited. It serves as a boundary between the habitable places of the planet, and some of our most epic stories and myths concern the adventures that befall sea voyagers; an example is Homer's *Odyssey*, in which Odysseus attempts to return from Troy across the Mediterranean. More recently, Ellen Macarthur's heroic solo voyage around the world gripped the imagination of people all over the world, since Ellen visibly pitted herself against the elements, a supreme symbol of human potential and the spirit of endurance, serving as an inspirational reminder of what's possible.

Inasmuch as the height of the **mountains** represents the spatial direction of "above," the depths of the oceans are measured as "below." We speak of land as being so many meters "above sea level," this measure serving as a benchmark from which we gauge "high" or "low." The center of the Earth can only be accessed via the sea, and it is telling that this central, fiery core is the place we associate with Hell, a place of sinister and barely known monsters. Knowing this, we can understand why the Christian personification of the Devil borrows the forked **trident** that previously belonged to the Gods of the Sea, **Poseidon** (**Neptune** to the Romans) and Vishnu, who move unfettered in those infernal depths. In the movie *The Forbidden Planet* the most terrifying and invincible creatures of all are the "Monsters of the Id" that come from the depths of man's subconscious, another symbol that has been applied to the fathomless oceans.

AIR

"Imagination is the air of the mind"

Philip James Bailey

Air and **fire** are paired together as masculine elements, in opposition to the feminine **water** and **earth**. Considered the primary element, air is both the life force and the **spirit**, essential to all living creatures; air is also essential to the creation of fire. The Arabic and Hebrew word for air, *ruh*, simultaneously means "spirit" and "**breath**." Geometrically, air is symbolized by an **arc** or **circle,** with a **dot** in the center, in exactly the same way as the symbol for the Sun. Sometimes air is symbolized by a **feather** because of its lightness and because it belongs to **birds**, creatures that move in the element of air itself.

Breathing difficulties are sometimes used as a symbol of a more profound inability to assimilate the overarching spirit of the Universe; this symbol has been used in films to convey the idea of a fundamental dissociation with society in general. "Correct" breathing, or *pranayama*, is one of the fundamental principles of Yogic practice, since air is the very stuff of life, energy, and spirit. Alchemists, too, believed that air contained the vitality of the sunshine, a sort of astral **gold** to match the terrestrial gold they were attempting to create from base elements. St. Martin hit upon this idea when he called air "a palpable symbol of invisible life." Air was considered to be the "**Soul** of the World" by the Greeks and Romans (who called it *anima* *mundi*), as well as by the Hindus, whose word *atmen,* meaning "breath," is also used to describe air, which can be seen as a collective breath. When the final breath leaves the body, then this breath becomes an inseparable part of the *atmen.*

If breath itself symbolizes a very personal relationship to air, then **wind** is a universal experience of it.

WIND

Wind can only be detected by the effect it has on other things, such as the light breeze that creates ripples on **water**, or the powerful gale-force winds that can bend or even break **trees**. Although the Ancient Assyrians believed that pestilential demons rode on the winds that blew over the scorching deserts, bringing disease and disaster in their wake, our ancestors also depicted the wind as a masculine God. The Ancient Greeks—who had an **eight**-sided tower in Athens dedicated to the winds—believed that there were **five** such deities, each one ruling over a different direction under the auspices of an overall King of the Winds. The north wind was called Boreas, which gave its name to the unknown countries lying to the north of Britain called *Hyperborea* (the land beyond the north wind). The south wind was Auster, which gives us the word Australia; the east wind was Eureus, and the westerly wind, Zephyr. In addition, the king of all the winds was Aeolus, whose name inspires that of the Aeolian harp, a stringed instrument that is played by the wind alone. King David is recorded as having a similar instrument, called a kinnor, which he hung above his bed where it could catch the wind.

In the tenth century AD, Dunstan of Canterbury was accused of sorcery when the wind played the strings of his instrument. The Druids had the reputation of being able to control the elements; **cloud**-bursting powers were attributed to them, as was the power of control over the wind. The Druid's wind, legendarily, blew away the would-be Gaelic invaders from the shores of Ireland. This wind was recognizable as a magical force because it blew only up to the level of the top of the sails, like a child playing with a sailboat in the bath.

The Book of Psalms and the Qu'ran both say that the winds carry messages from God, and in this the winds equate to angelic beings. The nature and intensity of the wind was considered an effective guide to the moods of God—his pleasure or displeasure—so that a destructive wind was viewed as the direct outcome of a wrathful God. In the New Testament, the Holy Spirit was also compared to a "strong driving wind." Although winds can presage or symbolize change and renewal, the Doldrums—a part of the Atlantic Ocean that experiences irregular winds, and frequent prolonged periods of calm—have come to symbolize periods of inaction or depression.

Tornado

In Frank L. Baum's *The Wizard of Oz*, the tornado, or whirlwind, picks up poor Dorothy from the plains of Kansas and deposits her, randomly, in another land entirely. The tornado, because of its organized, **spiral** shape, is a symbol of a higher power directing events in the lives of mortals. The supernatural power of the whirlwind is not necessarily benevolent or malevolent, often being represented as indifferent.

FIRE

"Just as a candle cannot burn without fire, men cannot live without a spiritual life"

The Buddha

Fire, more than any other of the four basic elements, has the power to create and the power to destroy. Symbolically, fire is represented by the upright **triangle**, the most basic manmade representation of which is, of course, the **pyramid**, whose name comes from the Greek word for fire. In the natural world, the most obvious form is of the Holy **Mountain**, the mound of earth that rose up out of the primal **waters**. More of this later.

Fire is symbolic, too, of the **spirit**, and of life itself. We speak of the "spark of life" as though it were a form of fire. Eternal flames, used in **temples** and **churches** of all denominations, as well the Olympic torch, symbolize eternal life. In the Acts of the Apostles the Holy Spirit is described as coming down among Christ's disciples in the form of "tongues like flames of fire." The **phoenix**, immolating itself in flame, is also born again from the same fire.

As a purifying force, fire is the preferred method of disposal of bodies in many religions. The flames and **smoke** not only carry the spirit towards the Heavens, but cleanse the **body**, like that of the phoenix, by destruction. For the same reason, fires were used as a form of sacrifice and were a perfect way to make an offering to the Gods. The resultant ashes—the residue left after the flames have done their work—are themselves rich in symbolic meaning. They signify man's return to the dust from which his material body is made. As *vibhuti*, the ashes made from **cow** dung burned in the sacred fire (or *homa*), they are used to smear *tilaka* (sacred symbols of Godly allegiance) onto the foreheads and bodies of Hindu ascetics to show that they have renounced the attractions of the material world in favor of the spiritual. The purifying nature of fire was used as a sort of magical charm by the Celts during the time of Beltane—the "Beltane Fires"—on May 1. On this day, the cattle were driven between two huge bonfires in the hope that this would protect them from disease. Later, the Great Fire of London not only destroyed much of the city, but at the same time purged it of the horrors of the plague.

We may be baptized in water, but we also speak of a "baptism of fire." This implies a difficult ordeal of initiation that happens speedily and effectively, leading to enlightenment after purification. In Sanskrit, the words for "pure" and "fire" are the same.

There's a Fulani saying about fire and water that neatly encompasses their relationship one to another. "Fire comes from Heaven, because it goes up. Water comes from Earth, because it comes down as rain." Whereas water can be as still and clear as a **mirror**, the nature of fire lies in its constant movement, never stopping for a moment until it runs out of fuel.

Fire is also closely linked to passion and sexual energy. When man first discovered how to make fire, he achieved this using an up-and-down rubbing whose friction made the first spark. The sexual symbolism of this practice is obvious. Flames made in this way are seen as either demonic or divine, and there's a primitive belief that fire is somehow gestated inside the genitals of a sorceress. The erect phallus, too, is a symbol of fire.

THE MAGIC MOUNTAIN

The symbolic significance of high places

In mountains, the male element of **fire** meets the female element of the **Earth** Mother.

Ask any keen mountaineer why he chooses to step so far out of his comfort zone as to even endanger his life and the archetypal answer—coined by Everest pioneer George Mallory—is "because it's there."

But there has to be a more profound reason to explain why someone would voluntarily endure scorching **sun**, searing **wind**, freezing ice and snow, avalanches, rockfall, and potential death in order to reach the top of a mountain.

Mountains and their symbolism are rooted very deep within the human psyche, and it may well be that our latter-day mountaineers would find it difficult to put into words the exact nature of their fascination. In the same way that the Fulani say that the ascent of flames means that they belongs to the Heavens, similarly, the ascending shape of the mountain draws parallels between it and the nature of fire.

And yet, with a little contemplation, it's easy to understand this ancient intrigue, to see why every country has its holy mountain, and to comprehend why so many myths and legends are associated with them; some of these stories concern "real" mountains (**Mount Sinai**), and some are about mythological mountains (**Mount Meru**).

Mountains are the place where Heaven and Earth meet, and also where man meets his Gods or receives messages from them. Sacrifices are carried out on mountain tops in the belief that these high places are closest to the Gods and Goddesses which are being propitiated (on high peaks in the Andes traces of human sacrifice have even been found). If fire is used for these sacrifices, making a bonfire on the top of the mountain means that the offering is even closer to the Gods.

Mountains are symbolic of transcendence, and are a physical manifestation of man's desire to elevate his **body,** mind, and **spirit**. The top of a mountain is a place of exposure, but also of refuge, since the high vantage point means that everything below can be seen clearly. When viewed from above, the peak of the mountain looks like the center of the world, symbolic not only of the **World Axis** but also of the **Omphalos** (the **navel** of the world). Mountains are symbols of the unknown, of uncharted territory, in both a physical and a spiritual sense.

Mountains, or the "eternal hills," appear to transcend the passage of time, retaining their identity as landmarks for thousands of years in spite of the many changes going on all around them. Because of this, they have come to symbolize solidity, fortitude, eternity, and stillness; in the Bible we read "I look up unto the hills, from whence cometh my strength."

Any fabricated structure that emulates these fundamental mountainous qualities—

great height, pyramidal shape, aspiration, and transcendence—are in themselves mountain symbols. These man-made mountain "emulators" include sacred buildings such as the **Pyramids** and **ziggurats**, the **stupa** and the **pagoda**, and also more primitive constructions such as the tump and the cairn. Even the **altar** in a **church** or other place of worship is a man-made symbol of a mountain; altar means "high place."

Chomolungma

Originally India's most important deity, Chomolungma is a Tibetan name, meaning "Goddess Mother of the Universe." Her name in Nepal is "Sagarmatha" meaning "Goddess of the **Sky**." The mountain located on the border between China and Nepal that carries her name and her spirit stands 8850 meters high and is the highest mountain in the world.

This descriptive and evocative Tibetan name was replaced in 1865 with the mundane name, Mount Everest, after the predecessor of the then British Surveyor General of India (Sir George Everest). Allegedly, no local name could be found for the most significant mountain on Earth.

The Goddess of Chomolungma is said to take vengeance on people for invading her home. For the people who live in the area, this mountain was never meant to be climbed; it was the abode of Gods and **spirits**, and not a place for man. When Everest was first climbed in 1953, it was an event equal in symbolic significance to the **Moon** landings, since—like the Moon—Everest symbolized a step into the unknown. Although well over 3000 climbers have made an ascent of the

peak, over 200 people are known to have died on it.

Chomolungma is one of **five** Goddess sisters, all associated with mountains. It's considered to be a Goddess of wealth; nowadays, with the booming tourist trade in the area created by the increasing number of people who wish to climb—or just to see—this holy mountain, the Great Mother has indeed provided wealth for her people.

Mount Kailash

Paired together with the holy lake Mansarova, Kailash is a sacred mountain for both Hindus and Buddhists, and is situated in Tibet. The word *Kailash* means "Treasure of the Snow Mountain." The shape of the mountain is archetypal; a huge **pyramid,** its pointed summit way up in the **Heavens** at 6600 meters high.

Mount Kailash is accorded even further sacred status when viewed from the south. The vertical and horizontal rock and ice strata form the symbol of the **swastika**, a representation of the **Sun** and one of the oldest and most common symbols in the world.

Kailash is thought to be the place where many Gods congregate, and accordingly it's a popular place of pilgrimage. Buddhists believe that if you walk around Kailash just once, then this action will atone for the sins of an entire lifetime. A tenfold circumnavigation will stop you entering Hell for 500 years' worth of reincarnations. If the pilgrim can manage to walk around the mountain one **hundred** times, then he will achieve Buddha-like status. This would have to be a very determined pilgrim, since Kailash is famously inaccessible.

Unlike a holy mountain such as Kangchenjunga—the world's third highest mountain—which climbers are permitted to ascend bar the final few feet to the summit, no ascents at all are allowed on Kailash. Mount Kailash is often associated with another symbolic but mythical mountain that has also seen no ascents: **Mount Meru**.

Mount Meru

The most sacred and holy mountain in Hindu mythology, the description of the fabled Mount Meru (also know as Sumeru) is incredibly evocative and fantastical. So high that the **Sun** is said to travel around it, Meru exists in a rarefied ideal atmosphere where all is perfect and transcendent. It has its base in Hell and its summit in the Heavens, and is encircled by **seven** rings of golden mountains with seven circular **oceans** separating them. The slopes of Meru are covered in glittering **gemstones** and exotic **trees** abundant with ripe **fruit**. The whole edifice rises out of a huge ocean, and on the summit is a **golden** palace, home to both Indra—the king of all the Hindu Gods—and to Shiva.

Meru is surrounded by four continents, the southernmost of which, Jambudyipa, corresponds to the **Earth**. Further away, and somewhere to the north of Jambudyipa, is a magical land called Shambhala, the gateway between the physical and spiritual realms, where enlightened souls make their home before they finally achieve Buddhahood.

For centuries, the idealized land of Shambhala has been sought by explorers who have confused it with a real, earthly place, missing the finer subtleties of the symbolism of both it and Mount Meru as places of aspiration that are symbolic of the soul. Images of Meru are often used in **mandalas** or as a part of meditative practices.

Mount Olympus

It's said that to spend a night on Mount Olympus will result either in madness or in communion with the Gods; it's likely that one may be a result of the other. Homer described Olympus as a place which never has storms and which is swathed in cloudless "aether" or "pure upper air."

Mount Olympus is the highest mountain in Greece and is 2917 meters high. Because its base is at sea level, the vertical elevation of this peak is particularly impressive. It's likely that Mount Olympus started out as an idealized mountain like Mount Meru, since ancient legends refer to the mountain but give no specific location for it, and several mountains were named Olympus.

Mount Olympus is home to the major deities of the **Greek pantheon**. In fact, there's a legend that holds that the Gods actually built Mount Olympus for their own use. According to tradition, these Gods and Goddesses, not at all worried about the old saying about living in glass houses, lived in crystal palaces on the mountain. Originally home to the Mother of the Gods, Gaia Olympia, Olympus is said to be the throne of Zeus, the king of the Gods, and his wife Hera; his sisters Demeter and Hestia, and his brothers Poseidon and Hades; and Zeus' children, Aphrodite, Apollo, Ares, Artemis, Athena, Hephaestus, and Hermes.

Mount Sinai

Situated on the Sinai Peninsula in Egypt, Mount Sinai is the place where, according to the Bible, Moses received the **Ten** Commandments from God. Mount Sinai itself is actually a collection of peaks. Sinai means "The Mount of God," which may have given Moses a clue about where to receive the wisdom of the Supreme Being in the first place, since the mountain had this name prior to his momentous adventures there. The actual peak that features in the biblical episode is also called Mount Musa or the Mountain of Moses, and at 2285 meters is not the highest in the area; this distinction belongs to Mount Catherine (2673 meters). However, Mount Musa is also the place where Buraq, Mohammed's **horse**, ascended to Heaven. Thus, Musa gains further credence as a place of holy and sacred significance.

The KunLun range

The KunLun range in China is vast in extent, stretching for 3,000 kilometers. The highest peak—aptly named in view of the spiritual symbolism of these mountains—is called the Goddess and stands at 7167 meters.

The mountains themselves are believed by Taoists to be paradise itself. Indeed, these Taoists would retreat into the mountains to attain enlightenment and to leave the material world behind. The Taoist deities are called *Sien*, which literally means "Mountain People."

It's believed that the Jade Palace of Huang Di, a fabled emperor and the founder of Chinese culture, is in the KunLun Range. There's also a legendary magical fairyland here, called the Xuangpu.

Kaf

Kaf is an imaginary mountain from the realms of Muslim mythology. Despite the fact that it does not exist in the "real" world, it is nevertheless a powerful symbol of an idealized state and a symbol of attainable perfection. Kaf is seen as the mother of all other mountains, real or imaginary. It is situated at the ends of the Universe, where the visible and invisible worlds meet.

An early belief about the planet Earth that was also entertained by Muslims was that the planet was a flat disc. Kaf was separate from the Earth and existed beyond a vast plain of darkness that would take four months to traverse. However, once there, this magical mountain would be well worth the arduous journey. Kaf was said to be made of a sparkling **emerald** that was so bright that the light from it tinted the **sky**.

Many of Kaf's aspects reflect the symbolism attached to all mountains. For example, there's a version of a story which says that Kaf stands on a rock, called the Post, which is at the center of the Universe, and that Kaf and this base rock provide the stability which keeps the rest of the Earth safe from earthquakes and tremors. This is symbolic of the mountain as the **World Axis** and also as the **Omphalos**, the center of all things.

Kaf features in many tales, including in the *1001 Nights*. In the stories of the traveler, Bulukiya, an angel tells him; "Know, O Bulukiya, that this is the mountain Kaf, which encompasseth the World ..."

Later on, we learn about some of the glories that lie beyond Kaf itself which are symbolic of the "unknown territory" of the mountain symbol:

"Behind this mountain is a range of mountains five hundred years' journey long ... And behind the mountain Kaf are **forty** worlds, each one of the bigness of this world forty times told, some of **gold** and some of **silver** and some of **carnelian** ..."

The most famous story about Kaf is told in a book called *The Conference of the Birds*, a book written by Sufi poet Farid Ud Din Attar that is full of rich symbolism. This story features the simurgh, a **bird** who has existed since the beginning of time and who is the personification of God. A flock of birds decide to take the arduous journey to Kaf, where the simurgh lives. One by one the birds find excuses to drop out of the pilgrimage until **thirty** birds, led by the **hoopoe,** eventually complete the journey, only to discover that they themselves, collectively, are their own divinity; simurgh means "**thirty** birds."

VOLCANO

Like any natural phenomenon (including animals) that has a perceptible destructive power, volcanoes are revered as much as they are feared, and they are often given the status of a deity to attempt to appease them. The unpredictable nature of the active volcano makes it particularly "alive" and spirited, and, although volcanoes share much of the symbolism of the **mountain**, the crater in the center that vomits forth its bubbling rivers of **fire** and molten lava lends it a further dimension: that of a Goddess who regenerates the souls of the dead in her magical **cauldron**. **Pele**, the Polynesian/Hawaiian Fire Goddess, is still worshipped at the Kilauea volcano in Hawaii, where latter-day thrill-seeking tourists scale the flanks of her home and show their appreciation by hurling cheap bottles of whisky into the crater below. One of the most iconic volcanoes in the world is Mount Fuji.

Mount Fuji

A sacred symbol in Japan and an essential element of Japanese culture and tradition, myths and legends about Mount Fuji—called the Peak of the **White Lotus**—are numerous. This is no surprise, since Fuji has existed for half a million years

Mount Fuji Yama (to give it its full name), also known as the "Never Dying Mountain" is so revered that it's a symbol for its country, Japan. Like other mountains around the world, Fuji Yama is believed to be the abode of many Gods, including the Supreme Being, Kunitokotachi, and as such is the symbolic guardian of the country. Its perfect triangular shape pierces the sky at 3776 meters.

The name *Fuji* comes from the Aino Goddess of **Fire,** Fuchi. It's said that Mount Fuji is the home of another powerful Goddess, Sengen, who will cast from her slopes any pilgrim who is not pure of mind. Despite this potential danger, every year from July through to the end of August, thousands of pilgrims come to climb Mount Fuji after they have undergone a ritual purification. Part of this rite includes scattering salt, rice wine, and **water** into the crater itself, arguably a more elegant offering than that made to the Hawaiian Pele. Despite its original dedication to the Fire Goddess, women and girls were not permitted to undertake this pilgrimage until 1872 and the coming

Meiji Era, otherwise called the Period of Enlightened Rule.

Incidentally, since mountainous terrain comprises about 80 per cent of Japan's land mass, it's not surprising that a whole system of beliefs and religious and spiritual practices has been built up around the idea of mountains as holy and sacred places. This system is called *Sanganku Shinko*, meaning "mountain creed." Shinto—the indigenous faith of Japan—holds that every aspect of the land held its own **spirit,** called Kami. The affairs of human beings and these spirits were inextricably linked, and Kami activity was particularly strong in mountainous areas. As beneficent creatures, it was believed that the Kami came down from the mountains to help with the agriculture in the plains during the growing season, then returned home when the crops were harvested. This equates to the universal notion that mountains are weather-makers. Huge stone boulders are situated at the base of many Japanese mountains, including Fuji, where rituals are carried out to welcome the Kami or to wave it goodbye.

The spiritual appeal of mountains in Japan also gave rise to a group of religious ascetics called Yamabushi. The Yamabushi are a cross between hermits, magicians, and priests, and they are familiar with herbal lore, healing practices, and charm making. They retreated into the mountains to gain enlightenment and to heighten their spiritual awareness.

THE SKY

The Heavens and the features in them form a universal symbolic language, since they are the one consistent aspect of the natural world that can be shared by many people at the same time. It could be said that this shared experience is akin to **music**. Indeed, all the planets and stars do resonate, each playing its own "note" that resounds, collectively, as the Music of the Spheres.

Primarily, the Heavens—"up there"—are seen to be the abode of an all-encompassing superpower. This divine spirit very generously guarantees the fertility of the **Earth** by raining down upon it, providing heat and light via the clockwork regularity of the **Sun**, illuminating the darkness with the **stars, planets,** and the **Moon,** and communicating messages by means of various signs and symbols in the sky, including **cloud** patterns and **rainbows** by day, and **shooting stars** and **comets** by night. The Chinese ideogram for Heaven—*tien*—stands for all that is above the (human) **head.** The Immortals lived in a realm so transcendent and so high above that mortals could only dream of its glories, although mythologies from all over the world are replete with stories of the Kingdom of Heaven. For Viking warriors, Valhalla—the hall of slain warriors—was a place of continual feasting and merriment, and the ultimately desirable destination after life on Earth. For Christians, Heaven is often viewed as a paradisiacal place full of **angels** with harps, all shining brightness and beauteous song.

The idea that there are "steps" to Heaven is shared by many cultures. There are different "spheres" or "realms" of Heaven, generally

seven or **nine,** which signify the stages of spiritual progress or transcendence necessary to progress to the highest echelons of this rarefied atmosphere. These stages of Heaven are also reflected in religious buildings, such as the nine-stepped **pyramids** of the Mexicans. The Aztecs felt that there were **thirteen** different Heavens, lyrically characterized as distinct places. Here they are, starting with the "Heaven" that is closest to the Earth:

1. Land of the Stars
2. Land of the Tzitzimime (frightening skeleton-like entities that will be unleashed on the Earth when the Sun eventually dies)
3. Land of the 400 Guardians of the Heavens
4. Land of the Birds (birds are a fundamental symbol of transcendent souls)
5. Land of the Fiery Serpents (shooting stars and comets)
6. Land of the Four Winds
7. Land of Dust
8. Land of the Gods.

The next **five** Heavens are the homes of the Gods. The **thirteenth** and highest Heaven is the home of the great Mother and Father, the Heaven where babies come from and whence the spirits of stillborn babies return.

In terms of a graphic symbol for the sky, it's frequently represented as an **arch** or vault shape, visible, for example, in the domed roofs often found in sacred buildings. In the creation symbol of the **cosmic egg,** this dome shape is the top half of the egg, and the lower half is the Earth. This original link between Heaven and Earth, that was subsequently broken, is a common theme in creation myths and it seems as though man has struggled to reconnect with his heavenly origins ever since. For Ancient Egyptians, the relationship between Heaven and Earth was symbolized by the Goddess Nut, her body forming the **arch** of the **sky** with her husband, Geb, representing the Earth beneath. For the Egyptians, the fructifying Heaven belonged most definitely to the female principle. This was the Goddess that gave birth to the mighty Sun God, Ra.

The preconditions for "entry" into Heaven vary according to faith, although there is a very practical school of thought that says Heaven—and indeed Hell—is what we make of them ourselves.

THE SUN

Although the **Sun** is generally perceived to be the masculine element that balances the feminine **Moon,** there are nevertheless several Sun Goddesses as well as Sun Gods. For many, though, the glory of the Sun makes it the absolute physical manifestation of the Godhead—or Supreme Being—and therefore beyond mere sex. The Sun also equates to the **Eye** of God, as depicted, for example, in the sun-like rays of the **All Seeing Eye** of the Masonic tradition. Some tribal peoples see the Sun as the "good," right eye of this Divine Being, whereas the Moon is the "bad," left eye.

To our ancestors, when the Sun tipped over the edge of the **sky** on the western horizon it disappeared into the Land of the Dead. They believed, therefore, that as well as being the bringer of life, the Sun could also take life away—Godlike powers indeed. The Aztecs called this "disappeared" aspect of the Sun the "**black Sun.**" As such, the Sun

De fole x luna Dpalogus pzimus

The Sun and the Moon

becomes a malevolent force. Generally, however, the heat and light of the Sun are seen worldwide to be celestial gifts conferred to our **planet** and all the life to which it plays host.

The Sun is personified, symbolically, in many differing ways, including the petals of **flowers** (particularly the **sunflower**), and the unruly mane and golden color of the astrological sign it rules, **Leo** the **Lion**. The **eagle**, called the "lion of the skies," is used as a symbol to represent the glory of the Sun in the form of a **bird**. For the Druids, the **stag** represents the Sun. In **alchemy**, **gold** is the metal of the Sun.

THE MOON

Because the Moon is illuminated at night by the light of the **Sun**, it inevitably carries with it all the positive—and negative—traits of the female. Looking at the bigger picture, though, without the light of the Sun, none of the **planets** in our solar system would be illuminated, and life on **Earth** would not exist, at least in the way we know it. Earth, then,

shares some kind of sisterhood with the Moon in that they are both reliant on the Sun for their illumination.

The Moon is visible primarily at night, and night time is associated with **death**. It made sense for our ancestors to believe that the souls of the dead must exist in the lunar atmosphere, an ancient belief that caused some consternation at the time of the first Moon landings.

Whereas the light of the Sun represents intuition and deductive reasoning, the Moon—because it is a **mirror** to the Sun—signifies the accumulation of knowledge based on a more inductive and painstaking way of learning. The **owl**, a nocturnal **bird** that shares the same symbolic space as the Moon, is therefore the bird of knowledge. The **color** of the Moon means that it is connected with the metal **silver**.

In human beings, the female menstrual cycle copies the cycle of the Moon. Traditionally, women menstruate at the time of the new Moon, and ovulate when it is full. However, artificial lighting and manmade environments mean that these cycles do not always coincide. The word "menstruation" comes from the Greek word, *mene*, meaning Moon. This word also means "month," although we have a solar system for measuring the months as well as the lunar one.

THE MILKY WAY

The *Via Lactia*, the *Darb al Labana*, the *Melkweg*, *la Voie Lactée*; not every culture describes our own galaxy in milky terms, but the majority do. The number of **stars** it contains is, quite literally, astronomical, estimated at somewhere between 200 billion and 400 billion.

This is our "home" galaxy, and what we can see of it—when we are lucky enough to have a night **sky** unpolluted by artificial light sources from Earth—is the edge-on portion of a sparkling, **spiral**-shaped cascading river of **stars**. What an inheritance! It's not surprising that this vast body of stars has inspired man's imagination for millennia and has given rise to many lyrical stories. For all North American Indians, it's the pathway that illuminates the way to the next world. The Finns, Lapps, and Estonians are among those who see it as a road for the **birds** on their back-and-forth journey carrying messages from the Gods to humankind. (In a satisfying twist, scientists have recently discovered that migratory birds are indeed likely to orient themselves by the Milky Way.)

Others, such as the Samoyed tribes, believe it to be the **spine** of the **sky**. Another poetic image of the provenance of the Milky Way, which exists in the mythology of the Ancient Greeks and Egyptians, describes it as the milk spilled from the udders of the celestial **cow**—Hera for the Greeks, and Hathor or **Isis** for the Egyptians. In the Hindu stories of the *Bhagavata Purana*, all the stars in the sky are compared to a huge celestial **dolphin** swimming through the Heavens; the Milky Way is the belly of the dolphin, and its Sanskrit name translates as the "Ganges of the sky."

For the Spanish, it's called the *Camino de Santiago*, since pilgrims on the road to Santiago de Compostela in north-western Spain used it as a guide. In a beautiful example of the tenet "as above, so below," the actual pilgrims' way itself was at one time called "the Milky Way."

THE POLE STAR

In the northern hemisphere, the Pole Star is the fixed center of the skies, the hub of the great wheel of the Heavens and effectively the astral representation of the **Axis Mundi.** The constancy of the Pole Star has made it a welcome sight for sailors, nomads, and other travelers and navigators for millennia, a symbol of safety and security in an unknown terrestrial environment. But how does one go about identifying it?

There's a very distinctive constellation called the Plough in the UK, the Big Dipper in the US (and Ursa Major to astronomers); these two vernacular names, symbolically, tell us a lot about the two cultures. Whatever you want to call it, it's a series of **seven stars** that form a large ladle shape. If you imagine a line joining the **two** stars at the front of the bowl of the ladle, and then continue the line for a distance of approximately **five** times the length of the space between the two stars, you'll reach the Pole Star.

In mythological terms, the Pole Star is frequently placed at the center of the celestial Universe, right over the center of the corresponding terrestrial center. For the Asiatic peoples of central India, Asia Minor, and Central Asia, the Pole Star firmly pinpoints the position of the highest peak of the symbolic world mountain. **Altars** in the holy buildings of these people are similarly oriented towards the north. The Pole Star is seen as the ultimate throne of God in his Heaven, and the Samoyeds call it the "nail of Heaven." Some Native Americans see it as a hole in the sky, one of three holes that connect the three worlds. For Muslims, the **Ka'aba** (the holiest of holies in Mecca) is in line with the Pole Star, connecting the Earth to the Heavens.

THE PLANETS

Since antiquity, we've believed that the planets of our solar system exert an inexorable influence over the affairs of the **Earth** in general, and of man in particular. Planets are differentiated from the stars in that they move in an orbit around a **star**; the origin of the word for planet is the Greek, *planaomai*, meaning "wanderer."

Traditionally, there were **seven** planets, which tallied conveniently with the number of days in the week and the visible **colors** of the **rainbow**, the **seven magical metals**, the seven Heavens, the seven stages in the Great Work of **alchemy**, the Seven Deadly Sins, and so on. Of course, each of the planets is also named for its God. Perhaps the most visible

sign of this planetary influence is found in the **Zodiac**. In the **Kabbalah**, the planets are referred to as spheres, and they also come under the influence of **angels**.

The planets also rule over the metals, and the days of the week whose names they bear.

Day	Planet	Metal
Monday	Moon (Moon day)	Silver
Tuesday	Mars (*Mardi* in French)	Iron
Wednesday	Mercury (Wotan's day)	Mercury
Thursday	Jupiter (Jupiter or Thor's day)	Tin
Friday	Venus (Freya's day)	Copper
Saturday	Saturn	Lead
Sunday	Sun	Gold

Kabbalistic Table of Planetary Correspondences

Planet	Angel	Universal function	Spatial bearing	Operation of the spirit
Sun	Michael	Brings light to the world	Zenith	Will
Moon	Gabriel	Strengthens hope, sends dreams	Nadir	Imagination
Mercury	Raphael	Civilizing influence	Center	Emotion and intuition
Venus	Amael	Love	West	Love and fellowship
Mars	Samael	Destruction	South	Action and destruction
Jupiter	Zachariel	Organization	East	Judgment and command
Saturn	Oriphiel	Supervision	North	Patience and perseverance

We also owe the construction of the musical scale to the influence of the planets. Legend has it that music was invented by the **Muses**, who simply listened to the sound made by each of the seven planets as it sang, spinning in its celestial orbit. The harmonic frequencies made by the planets were believed to keep the cosmos in existence.

THE CONSTELLATIONS

Given that we view the **skies** as the domain of the Gods, then the fact that the constellations themselves form the shapes of these deities, as well as fantastic stellar **animal**s, isn't at all surprising. The most famous of these is the "circle of animals" that makes up the **Zodiac**, which is examined in detail in Section One.

The stars appear to be immortal, and by imprinting our own myths and legends into the skies, we immortalize them too. There are hundreds, if not thousands, of these stories and there is insufficient space here to analyze all of these celestial symbols. One of the most easily recognizable constellations is that belonging to Orion, the great and handsome Hunter, whose loyal **dog** appears as the constellation Sirius. Orion was the lover of Eos, the Goddess of the Dawn, and his position in the **sky** is so prominent that it was once used to track the course of the year.

The legend of Orion appears in one of the oldest pieces of Greek literature, in the tales of Hesiod that date back to the eighth century BC. Orion was the son of the sea God, **Poseidon**, and Euryale, the human daughter of the king of Crete. This divine male/human female relationship occurs time and time again in all the world's mythologies and sym-

bolizes the union of Heaven and Earth, or the union of opposites. Like his father, Orion could walk on **water.** He also liked a drink or two, and after walking across to the island of Chios he celebrated by drinking so much **wine** that he attacked Merope, the daughter of the island's king, Oenopion. Oenopion was justifiably enraged, so he blinded Orion, who then groped his way to the island of Lemnos. Here, Hephaestus, the blacksmith God who was one of the **twelve Olympians**, advised him to travel as far east as possible so that the **Sun** God, Helios, might heal him. After his sight was restored, Orion—possibly a stubborn character—decided to return to Chios to exact his revenge upon the king who had blinded him in the first place, but the wise Oenopion hid himself. Orion then traveled to Crete, where his hunting prowess made him a fine partner for Artemis; his bloodthirsty enthusiasm was such that he threatened to kill every beast on Earth. Gaia, the Earth Mother, was alarmed at this threat and sent a small but deadly creature—the **scorpion**—to deal with him. Orion was so handsome, however, that the Goddesses asked Zeus to place him among the stars, so making him possibly the world's first pin-up. Zeus added the scorpion to the Heavens—the constellation **Scorpio**—as a warning of what happened to Orion.

SHOOTING STARS

A shooting star is simply a small piece of space debris of any size between a grain of sand and a boulder, whose trajectory is rendered visible as it burns up when it comes into contact with the **Earth**'s atmosphere. The beauty of such an apparently banal event—which touches the most matter-of-fact observer with a sense of wonder and privilege that they looked at the right bit of the **sky** at the right time—continues to inspire poetry, lyrics, legends, and myths. Whoever sees a shooting star will hopefully have the quick wittedness to wish upon such a **star**, even if the likelihood of actually catching it and putting it in your pocket is remote. Our ancestors believed that these stars carried direct messages from the divine realms, or were otherwise the souls of falling **angels** or other celestial beings, an idea used beautifully in Neil Gaiman's film, *Stardust*, in which the star itself is personified as a beautiful and feisty girl who finds herself alarmed to be stranded on **Earth**.

COMET

The origin of this word is the Greek, *cometes*, which means "**hair** of the **head**." It's believed that Aristotle first used the word to describe these "stars with hair," whose fuzzy haloes or tails do indeed look like tresses of light. The same comets reappear periodically in our skies; notably, a depiction of Halley's Comet appears on the Bayeaux Tapestry that dates back to 1066. This, however, is a relatively recent record compared with the Babylonian tablets that listed its appearance as far back as 164 BC. It is visible in the sky every 75–76 years; the last time it was a feature of our night skies was in 1986, and the next time it's due will be in 2061. As befits such a potent symbol, the appearance of a comet is believed to coincide with momentous events that affect the **Earth** as a whole. The tsunami of December 2004, for example, has been attributed to a comet called Maccholz 2; as ever with these sorts of theoretical warnings, any "interpretation" is usually possible only after the event.

Bright **stars**, comets, and other unusual cosmic phenomena presaged the births not only of Christ, but of other portentous souls, including the Buddha and the Hindu God, Agni, who shares with Christ a mother who was, paradoxically, a virgin. As we've seen from the consistent records of Halley's Comet, pinpointing such a notable celestial event should be relatively easy. However, though astronomers and astrologers have labored long and hard to try to find a celestial event that coincides with the birth of Christ in Bethlehem, there is nothing so far that suggests that this famous star was ever anything other than a symbol in the first place.

CLOUDS

The changeable nature of clouds, made of billions of particles of **water**, makes them an excellent symbol of ambiguity. Their undefined state, as full of potential as a **seed**, led the Sufis to identify the unknowable nature of the cloud with that of Allah prior to his physical manifestation. The constantly changing shapes of clouds meant that they were used for divination, notably by the Celts, whose practice of the exotically named *neladoracht* was extensive.

The imagery of the cloud is sometimes used in the same way as the **veil**, as something that obscures from view anything that is too glorious for us to look upon, at least all in one go. To have your **head** in the clouds implies a dreamy, impractical nature, necessarily separated from the cares of the world by being oblivious to them. Saints and sages are often to be found floating up toward the Heavens, using clouds as a sort of celestial vehicle. In Greek mythology, the clouds were the daughters of **Ocean**.

THUNDERBOLTS

It makes sense to imagine that the sound of thunder in the Heavens is attributable to the Gods raging around in the **sky**, angered by something and preparing for vengeance. It is for this reason that the key thunder Gods are depicted grasping the distinctive triple-headed **trident** shape of the thunderbolt, which looks like a sheaf of barbed **arrows**, a symbol of their power and dominion over one of the most dangerous phenomena observed in the Heavens. Sometimes the thunderbolt is symbolized, pictorially, by a tool such as a hammer or an axe, like Thor's magical hammer **Mjolnir**, or as **Labrys**, the double-headed axe belonging to **Zeus**, or the **Vajra** that belongs to the Hindu God, Indra. Taranis, the Celtic God whose name means "thunder," is identified not only by his ferocious expression but also by the rather phallic-looking thunderbolt scepter he carries in one hand as well as a large **wheel** in the other. The African God, Faro, carries his thunderbolts in the form of whips that also represent lightning.

The double-edge of both the Labrys and the Vajra indicates the dual aspect of the thunderbolt symbol. Not only does it destroy but it also creates, since it represents the transformative powers of the Heavens over the Earth. The thunderbolt might be dangerous, but it is accompanied by replenishing rain. Additionally, any person or place struck by a thunderbolt is instantly rendered holy. **Animals** struck down by a thunderbolt were considered sacrosanct, the chosen ones of the Gods. Siberian tribal peoples raised such creatures up on platforms as a way of offering them back to their destroyers.

The **Vajra** represents another aspect of the thunderbolt, that of the divine inspiration that makes a metaphorical rather than a physical strike; it therefore represents the power of the word and the mind.

LIGHTNING

The lightning bolt shape—again a symbol of the Gods' dominion over the elements—is a distinctive **zigzag**, similar to that of the *sig rune* that was appropriated as the logo of Hitler's SS. The shape of this rune not only looks like the letter "S" but harks back to the Norse deities whose powerful imagery inspired many of the symbols of the Nazi regime. Unsurprisingly, lightning is a phallic symbol, often represented as a jagged **scepter**. Mithras, the God who preceded Christ, was also born of a virgin. A supernatural lightning flash impregnated his mother; here it signifies the spark of life, the quickening of the **soul**. Perhaps Mithras' mother was struck by a sort of divine "coup de foudre," which in French means both love at first sight as well as a "bolt of lightning."

Rainbows

Our ancestors, wherever they were in the world, saw the rainbow as a bridge between Heaven and Earth, and the idea that it is unlucky to point at a rainbow stems from the fact that it is impolite, somehow threatening, to point at a person lest the wrath of the Gods be invoked. Another primitive idea was that the rainbow can somehow suck people up into the **clouds**. The Incas, who believed that it was the multi-colored feathered crown of Illapa, the God of rain and thunder, shared this fear of the rainbow. They did not even dare look at the rainbow and would cover their **mouths** with their **hands** when one appeared.

Among the celestial beings that used the rainbow as a bridge is the Buddha, who returned to the Earth via a **seven**-colored stairway. For the Australian Aborigines, the rainbow appears in the form of the multi-colored **serpent** that created the Earth and was the mother of all human beings. This serpent analogy is also found in China, where one of the **Eight Immortals** is transformed into a rainbow that is coiled like a sleeping serpent.

The seven **colors** of the rainbow carry a deep significance for followers of Islam, who see these hues as all the qualities of the Divine Being made visible in the material world. Similarly, in India these seven colors belong to each of the Seven Heavens. The rainbow that appeared towards the end of Noah's journey in the **Ark** symbolizes the reunion of God and humankind. In the Bible, God says to Noah: "… I set my bow in the clouds, and it shall be a token of the covenant between me and Earth" (Genesis 9: 12–13).

In Norse mythology, the rainbow appears as Brisingamen, the exotically beautiful necklace of the Goddess **Freya**, and was a bridge, called Bifrost, between the Heavens and the Earth. Similarly, Ishtar had a necklace of rainbows, and in Greek myth **Iris** wore a cape made of rainbows, since she was the rainbow Goddess.

Natural places of worship

Human beings have always animated the natural world—its rocks, stones, lakes and pools, valleys, and hills—with **spirits** that are a manifestation of a divine life force. Sometimes these "sacred" spaces would have been part of the hunting territory, places blessed by the Gods as a site of a successful hunt, or places where, perhaps, magical herbs (that might help the shaman access the realms of the Gods) might be found. The most potent and universal of these holy sites is **the sacred grove**.

The sacred grove

Although we will look at individual **trees** as symbols in Section 4, as a living feature of the landscape the forest has always constituted a truly magical natural shrine, the tree being an immediate object of worship. In the first century AD, Seneca observed:

"If you come upon a grove of old trees that have lifted up their crowns above the common height and shut out the light of the sky by the darkness of their interlacing boughs, you feel that there is a spirit in the place, so lofty is the wood, so lone the spot, so wondrous the thick unbroken shade."

Modern tree huggers follow a long line of peoples of all faiths and nationalities who revere the tree. Woods and forests were, along with the **cave**, among man's first specific places of worship. If you've ever spent time in a forest or stumbled upon a natural grove of trees, you'll understand why. As Virgil said, it seems as though the Gods favor "… wild trees, unsown by human hand." Such a place shares some of the features of the cave. The lofty canopy of a grove of trees has a similarly potent silence and stillness, punctuated by the occasional breeze or the calling of **birds**, perhaps the sudden movement of an animal. There is a natural sanctity about such places that is utterly universal, which later builders of **temples** and cathedrals must have tried to emulate; these buildings are comprised of columns that simulate tree trunks, have high, domed ceilings that are like the forest canopy, and lend a sense of **space** to those within them. Just like a forest grove, the light in the temple is dim. In a church the subdued light filtering through the stained-glass windows imitates the sunshine gleaming softly through dappled leaves of the grove.

In the *Journal of the Bombay Natural History Society*, researchers Gadgil and Vartak point out that:

"… sacred groves and sacred trees belong to a variety of cultural practices which helped [Indian] society to maintain an ecologically steady state with wild living resources."

Perhaps the best-known tree and forest worshippers are the Druids. Indeed their very name comes from the old Celtic roots for words meaning both "tree" and "truth," with the addition of "vision"; therefore the Druid is effectively described as "those who know the tree/truth." For Druids, all trees were sacred but the **oak** was the most important of all. The groves of the Druids were called Nemeton, a place distinctly different from a "normal" forest, frequently fenced off within a square enclosure surrounded by a ditch. The presiding deity was the Goddess Nemetona.

Sacred groves existed all over Europe. In the Caucasus mountains, for example, each community had its grove in the same way that a village might have a **church**. Some groves were particularly sanctified because of their great age, and the trees within them were never to be cut down. In Scandinavia, every single tree in the grove at Old Uppsala was sacred. It's also likely that the concept of the **Christmas tree** had its origins of the sacred groves of the Germanic tribes.

Tragically, many of the sacred groves were destroyed by adherents of the incoming Christian religion, who were anxious to show allegiance to their one, jealous, masculine God in the face of the multiple deities of the old order in which the Great Mother was prominent. Groves suffered because they were dedicated to Goddesses. The Emperor Theodosius, in the fifth century AD, was particularly zealous in this respect, issuing an edict that all sacred groves—some of them thousands of years old—should be chopped down unless they could be proven to be in some way compatible with Christianity. This is why churchyards often have a **yew** in them.

The land would have been holy specifically because this tree of death and rebirth was present in the first place. The spirit of this mysterious and magical tree must have penetrated even the sensibilities of these timber-hungry Christians in order to have survived until the present day. Some of the trees are now thousands of years old.

Other groves famously dedicated to the Goddess include the famous site of Diana Nemorensis, "Diana of the Wood," which inspired Sir James Fraser's book, *The Golden Bough*. Situated near the small town of Ariccia, the lake beside the grove was called "Diana's Mirror." In his seminal work, Fraser describes a particular tree at the center of the grove that was heavily guarded; no timber was to be taken from it except by the occasional runaway slave who had the good fortune to reach it unharmed. The slave would then have the chance to fight for his freedom.

The sacred grove of Dodona was the site of the most ancient Hellenistic oracle. Likewise the figurehead of the *Argo*, the ship sailed by Jason in Greek myth, had oracular powers since she had been cut from timber from Dodona. It seems that this particular sacred grove was a veritable treasure trove of predictive tools. Not only could the future be forecast by the sound of the **wind** rustling through the leaves of the trees, but the priestesses there had the skills to understand the language of the **birds**. People traveled from far and wide to consult the "**doves**," which was also the name of these priestesses.

There are believed to be somewhere in the region of 14,000 sacred groves in India, which have not had to survive the ravages of any invading religious group. Although these groves may not be protected, they continue to be used, dedicated to diverse deities, and honored by the local communities. In Japan, the Shinto **Torii** that marks the boundary between sacred and profane space is as likely to appear before a naturally holy place, such as a **pine** forest, as much as any manmade **temple**.

TIME, SPACE, AND THE SEASONS

The number **4** is not only prominent in the number of elements, it also refers to the number of the **seasons**. The seasons apply not only to the cycle of the year, but also to the life of man, and the symbols for the seasons of nature serve a dual purpose. In terms of the time periods within a day, spring is morning, summer is noon, fall is the evening and winter is the night. Such analogies recur in art, literature, and film, and are so commonly understood as to be almost unnoticeable.

- Spring—Popular depictions of spring include the gamboling **lamb**, seasonal **flowers** and plants (such as young shoots and buds, and flowering shrubs). Spring is the time of rebirth and renewal, fresh hope, and new beginnings. The archetypal color for spring is the pale **green** of these young shoots. **Hermes** is among the Gods of Spring
- Summer—Sometimes depicted as a **fire-**spitting dragon, perhaps a sheaf of corn, seasonal flowers, or as the **Sun** symbol.

Stronger, brighter colors apply; **red, orange, yellow**. The Sun gods—Apollo and Ra, for example—belong to this season

- Fall—A time of harvest, fall is represented by the basket or **cornucopia** brimming with **fruit** or vegetables. Grapes or **vine** leaves represent Dionysus, God of Autumn. The color **brown** is added to the oranges and yellows of summer
- Winter—A bare, leafless tree, snowflakes or a blazing fire are all symbols of winter. Its colors are **black**, **silver**, and **gray**.

DAWN

The joyful, optimistic start to a new day, the Greeks personified the dawn as Eos, who, regular as clockwork, opens the gates of Heaven every morning with her rosy **fingers** for the **Sun** God, Helios, to ride through. Dawn symbolizes the triumph of light over dark and, consequently, of good over evil. We say that "the darkest hour comes before dawn," meaning that things are often at their most difficult when the end is in sight.

DAY

The day represents a regular and routine pattern of events. The **Sun** rises in the east, and sets in the west, making the world bright and highly visible, and marking the span of a day, which is devoted to worldly matters, work, play, and social interaction. The Bible tells of the creation of the world, which took place over a **six**-day period, with the seventh

set aside for rest. This seventh day of rest, no matter on which day of the week it falls, is common to all cultures, representing time out from everyday concerns, providing a time of reflection, meditation and, for many, worship. Since God, as a superpower, would have no need for rest, this seventh day also represents the time when God decided he could leave his creation to its own devices and allow mankind to get on with its own life. These **seven** days also represent the seven Heavens through which man is supposed to pass before he attains enlightenment.

TWILIGHT

In the same way that a threshold or doorway signifies a transitional point from one kind of space to another (for example, between the sacred and the profane) twilight represents a liminal area in temporal terms. It's the time when the two distinctly different worlds of night and day converge, the bright **white** of the day meeting the black of the night to make a fuzzy **gray** area, similar to the place where **water** and land meld together to make a marshy, indeterminate, and "in-between" area. Twilight is associated with the western quarter, where the **Sun** sinks down before it "dies." It's the time when non-human spirits and entities can be glimpsed; **fairies**, pixies, **elves**, and spirits both benevolent and malevolent all belong to the twilight.

THE ELEMENT ENCYCLOPEDIA OF SECRET SIGNS AND SYMBOLS

Night

The Greeks personified night as a mother Goddess, Nyx, who was the mother of the **sky** as well as the daughter of Chaos. Nyx governed all things noctural: sleep, dreams, death, night-loving **animals**, and occult matters. She is depicted being drawn across the dark sky by **four** black **horses**, and followed by the **Fates** and the **Furies**. This may be the Greek representation of night, but it's shared by other cultures, too; the Mayans used the same hieroglyphic symbol to describe the concepts of night, death, and darkness. Latterly, the night has become synonymous with matters belonging to the subconscious, and we speak of a difficult time as being a "dark night of the **soul**."

Why is it that a two-week period is known as a "fortnight" rather than a "fortday"? We owe this term to the Welsh/Celtic word for a week, *wythnos*, which translates as "eight nights." According to Caesar, the Celts and the Gauls reckoned time in terms of nights, not days, probably because the night has a feeling of completion and ending about it, whereas the day belongs to beginnings. Night wipes clean the slate of the day, and symbolizes a time in which anything can happen.

The directions

Looking at the four cardinal directions—**north**, **south**, **east**, and **west**—we can see the logic that associates them respectively with **winter**, **summer**, **spring**, and **fall**, as well as night, day, dawn, and twilight. There are two other important directions, though: "above" and "below," which equate to Heaven and Earth.

The directions themselves, though, have their own symbols. Particularly lyrical are the images that come from the Druid tradition, using four of their sacred **animals**. Many Druid ceremonies involve opening the ceremonial circle to the elements and the directions, their spirits being honored and respected in the hope that they will bless the proceedings.

In Druidic tradition, the north is personified as the "great starry **bear** of the **Heavens**," the south is the "great **stag** in the heat of the chase," the east is the "hawk of the dawn," and the west is the "**salmon** of wisdom."

Feng Shui and the directions

Feng Shui seeks to create harmony within the Universe by correctly aligning any human influences to those of the greater cosmos. An understanding of the **elements** and **directions** is essential to this art, and there are some interesting correspondences within Feng Shui. The Chinese actually invented the first compass as an object of divination, developed from the shaman's baton that was used not only as a drumstick but was spun on the drum as a means of fortune-telling. If the "drumstick" was made from magnetic **lodestone**, then the directions could be properly ascertained. Latter-day versions of the Feng Shui compass are used for the same reasons, to ensure the correct alignment of new buildings and structures.

- North—Masculine, the second son, the planet Mercury, water, midwinter, midnight, danger, madness, flowing motion, red, ear, Moon, lakes, pig
- South—Feminine, the second daughter, the planet Mars, fire, lightning, female soldiers, the eye, the Sun, midday, drought, bitterness, pheasant, snail, tortoise
- East—Masculine, the first son, the planet Jupiter, wood thunder, spring morning, galloping horse, flying dragon, young men, beans, bamboo shoots, excitement and stimulation, movement and roads
- West—Feminine, the youngest daughter, the planet Venus, metal, the sea, evening, enchantress, mouth and tongue, serenity and joy, reflections, death, sea, mid fall

In Feng Shui, the central point of all the directions is the Earth.

Part Three

FAUNA

THE SECRET SYMBOLS
OF THE ANIMAL REALMS

This section not only encompasses real animals, insects and birds, but also takes a look at some of the more fantastical creatures that occupy a significant space in our collective psyche (although it's always advisable to keep an open mind about the existence of supposedly imaginary creatures; there are enough sightings, for example, of Sasquatch and various Big Cats for all but the most hardened of realists to dismiss their existence out of hand).

It's fascinating to see how we continue to anthropomorphize our animals, and also how we still feel the need to invent hybrid creatures sharing aspects of two or more animals, and how these creatures appear in different times and in disparate places. The winged horse, for example, appears as Pegasus in Greek myth,

as Buraq, who carried Mohammed from Earth to Heaven, as the Chollima of East Asia, or, in the *Harry Potter* books of J.K. Rowling, as the Thestral, the sinister steed visible only to those that have had direct experience of death.

The attributes of all our animals, real or otherwise, give us an incredibly rich and diverse catalog of symbols. Sometimes, the reasons behind these symbolic meanings are due to historical misconceptions about the habits of certain creatures, and probably date back to a time when we were less well informed than we are now. These curiosities—such as the beaver being a symbol of chastity because of the notion that it would rather eat its own testicles than be captured— give us a delightful insight into the minds of our ancestors.

Animal Magic: The Mystique of Birds and Beasts

Given the way we worship our domestic pets, it is hardly surprising to find that our ancestors deified animals too. This is nothing new; the Greek historian Herodotus (*c.*484–425 BC) reported that an Egyptian would rather let his house and possessions burn, so long as he could save his **cat** from the conflagration. Indeed, for Egyptians the cat was so sacred that bereft owners shaved off their eyebrows as a sign of mourning when their animals died. Archaeologists have found numerous mummified animals, suggesting that they were accorded the same funeral rites as human beings.

Animal symbols feature on some of the earliest magical art known to mankind, inscribed on the walls of the Paleolithic caves in places such as Lascaux in France, for example. Native people all over the world have their own tribal symbols, or totems, with which they share physical and spiritual qualities. Totemistic belief holds that a certain animal is the ancestor of the clan, and the people are named accordingly; some of the illustrations in this section show some of these ancient tribal symbols.

Sacred animals were either never eaten, or were eaten only as part of an important ritual sacrifice, when the whole community shared the meal, believing that they absorbed the spirit of the sacred creature. Until such a time as the animal was ready to be sacrificed, killing it was taboo. In India, the **cow** was so much more useful for its **milk** than its meat that every part of the animal is connected to a deity, and the animals still wander about freely even in heavily-congested cities. Even the most ardent Western meat eater will usually balk at the thought of cooking and eating a dog, a horse, or a cat.

Throughout history, every culture in every country in the world has given its Gods the features and attributes of animals and birds, and these are far too numerous to list here. The Egyptian God **Anubis** has the head of a jackal; the Hindu God **Ganesh**, remover of obstacles, has the head of an **elephant**. Pan, the Greek Nature God, has the antlers and legs of a **deer** or a **goat**. This kind of animal symbolism is not restricted to pagan beliefs, however. The **Four Evangelists** of the Christian faith are depicted, too, as animals, and the Holy Spirit is symbolized by a **dove**.

The perceived qualities of animals make them pretty much universal in their symbolic meanings, at least for the animals that are common everywhere in the world. The desired virtues of a warrior, according to an ancient Arabian saying, are the courage of the **bear** and the **lion**, the cool and stubborn strength of a **wolf**, the vengefulness of the **camel**, the keen sight of the **crow**, the chastity of the **magpie**, the vigilance of the **owl**, and the cunning of the **fox**.

Our ancestors glorified animals even further by placing them in the Heavens, the abode of the Gods. Here, the circle of animals in the **Zodiac** reflects aspects of man's nature that are closely linked to these starry creatures, emphasizing the important part that animals have to play as synonyms for both spiritual and physical cosmic powers. Other constellations are named after the animal shapes our ancestors saw in the stars; in fact, the **Heavens** have far more animals in them than they have human figures, outnumbering even the deities that appear in human form.

Further, at the time of death, animals have a significant part to play as psychopomps, creatures that guide the **soul** through the labyrinthine realms of the Underworld into the world beyond. The dog is particularly significant in this role, and it seems that the dog is man's best friend not only in this world, but also in the next.

ANT

Despite its apparent insignificance, the ant was one of the teachers of the wisest of kings, Solomon, and is a sacred creature in Islam.

Given the habits of the ant, it is no surprise that this tiny creature is primarily a symbol of industry. Because it often carries seeds and grains, in Ancient Greece the ant was sacred to the Goddess of the Harvest, **Demeter**. However, the industry of the ant seems to be concerned with one thing, the storage of material goods. Therefore, despite all its hard work, the ant is a symbol of materialism to Buddhists.

The teamwork of ants is notorious and many tiny ants together can shift loads far heavier than they are. The ant is a good example of the "sum of the parts being greater than the whole," and for Hindus this represents the idea of the Godhead.

For the Bambara people of Africa the ant is a fertility symbol. The anthill itself, representing the female sexual parts, has magical powers that can help infertile women, and if necessary the women of the tribe will sit on an anthill to help them conceive.

APE

See **Monkey**.

BADGER

A nocturnal animal, the badger is a slow-moving creature of habit, and some badger tracks and sets are hundreds of years old. The badger in the Kenneth Grahame book *The Wind in the Willows* is a domesticated creature that loves his cave-like house, and in real life the badger will use his vicious claws, when necessary, to guard his precious home. Because he is nocturnal, the badger shares an affinity with the **Moon**, hidden secrets, and occult knowledge; therefore, he is a symbol of good-natured cunning.

In the UK, place names with "brock" in them are a clue that badgers make their homes in the vicinity. Brock is an old English word for badger.

In Japan, the animal is affectionately called "old badger" and has much the same meaning as the **fox** in the West. The badger is a symbol of good luck and well-being and appears at the **doorway** of restaurants as an emblem of prosperity.

Bat

For fans of horror movies, the bat has become an animal to be feared; it not only becomes entangled in long **hair**, but the **vampire** bat is a satanic agent that sucks the **soul** from the body along with its life**blood**. However, there is more to the bat than purely negative symbolism.

In China, the ideogram for good luck, "fu," sounds the same as the word for "bat" and so the animal is a lucky charm. To see **five** bats at once represents the Five Happinesses: health, wealth, longevity, a virtuous life, and a good death. Like the Taoist **Immortals**, bats live in **caves** and so they, too, are symbolic of longevity and immortality. Some bat caves in the East have remained unchanged for thousands of years; the bats that live there are revered as sacred animals.

The nocturnal nature of the bat has given it some negative associations. It is symbolic of the night devouring the day; the bat is said to swallow the light because it wakes at dusk, the time between day and night. Native Indian tribes in Brazil say that a bat swallowing the **Sun** will herald the end of the world, and the Mayans believed that the bat was a harbinger of death. Christian belief, too, regards the bat with suspicion because it is seen as an incarnation of Satan.

However, the nocturnal nature of the bat makes it, like the **owl**, a creature that has access to hidden knowledge and secret information, able to detect things in the hours of darkness that are not accessible to diurnal creatures. Before echolocation was recognized and understood, the bat's ability to find its way about was a source of great intrigue, adding to the mystique of the animal.

Because female bats are the only flying creatures that suckle their young, it is considered a good mother.

Bear

For the Celts, "bear" was synonymous with "warrior." The name of the greatest Celtic king, Arthur, shares the same root as the name for bear—"artos," meaning "bear-like." This warrior-bear attribute was not restricted to the male; in the kingdom of the Gauls, there was a ferocious warrior-queen called Artio. The Greek Goddess of the Hunt, Artemis, also shares the bear's name.

The bear is an earthy creature, and in northern European pre-Christian society, it represented worldly power and authority, the equivalent of the **lion** in other societies.

The bear is associated with the **Moon**. As the Moon disappears for a time, so does the bear, when he hibernates during the winter months. Diana/Artemis, the Goddess of the Hunt (who also has close links to the Moon), is often depicted with a bear, and can shape-shift into the form of a bear. The **constellations** Ursa Major and Ursa Minor—the Great Bear and the Little Bear—are the stellar incarnation of this Goddess. These constellations are always visible in the northern hemisphere, and so are effective markers for the seasons.

The bear is not only a powerful creature with great strength, but it is instinctive and intuitive, too, both lunar qualities that command respect. Ancient Siberian tribes said that the earth was the "**ear**" of the bear.

The Finno-Ugric people were among those that had a bear-cult, believing that the bear carried the spirits of the tribal ancestors, and there were graveyards for bears until relatively recently. The people laid out the **bones** of the bears very carefully, so that the animal could return from the dead. The power of the bear is borne out by the fact that the actual word for the animal was seldom used, replaced with other terms such as "the brown one" or "bruin," "the old fellow" or "honey eater." This is because the power inherent in **names** was such that to utter the name of the animal was equivalent to invoking its spirit. Bears were considered mediators between man and God.

Shamans absorbed the spiritual and material energy of the bear by wearing bearskins, while warriors went off to do battle wearing bearskins or carrying parts of the bear, such as its claws or **teeth**, as magical **amulets**. The bearskin hats of the Guards at Buckingham Palace, still worn today, are a remnant of these more primitive times.

There's a European legend about an early saint, Corbinian, who is said to have tamed a bear and even got him to carry his baggage over the mountains; it is an analogy for the Christian Church taming the "savages" of Europe.

Native Americans have a specific kind of witchdoctor called a Bear Doctor, able to take on the form of a grizzly to vanquish the tribal enemies.

BEAVER

Typically, the beaver is a symbol of industry, renowned for its building skills and often used as a logo for these reasons. We say that a busy person works like a beaver.

However, there are other aspects to the animal. It has God-like status for some Native American tribes, and its **bones** were taken special care of, kept in a secret place for a year and then buried with due ceremony to bring good fortune to the hunt. Because the beaver carries with it a strong sense of home, family and domesticity, for Native Americans it has all the instinctive qualities of the female.

There is a curious legend about a beaver hunted for the valuable medicine allegedly contained in its **testicles**. Rather than be captured, the beaver bit off his own testicles and threw them in front of the hunter, thus rendering himself valueless to the predator who was, nevertheless, free to take the object he desired. This peculiar anecdote gave early Christians the imagery they needed to make the beaver a symbol of chastity and purity, willing to cast off all impurities in the face of a Devil who then departed, thwarted.

BEE

In the ancient world, the bee was a very important insect indeed, because the **honey** it produced was not only one of the few naturally sweet substances that was available at the time but is also a good preservative. The importance of the bee is reflected in its appearance on coins from Ephesus dating back to the fifth century BC, and in Minoan symbolism where the Goddess appears as half woman, half bee. In Egypt, the bee was the symbol of the Lower Kingdom.

The bee itself is symbolic of industry and mutual cooperation; however, there is also a spiritual side to this insect. One of the symbols of Aphrodite was a golden honeycomb, and it was believed that the souls of her priestesses inhabited the bodies of bees. These priestesses were called Melissae, a word that has the same root as that of honey and bees. Male counterparts equating to drones, called Essenes, accompanied the Melissae. Essenes were eunuchs.

Because bees produce wax, they are frequently linked to places of Christian worship such as abbeys, since the monks and nuns used the wax to make candles for the church.

Bees are symbolic of order and of immortality. They are also a symbol of the supremacy of the female; a queen bee needs only to mate once in order to be able to spend the rest of her life producing **eggs**. The unfortunate drone whose task it is to impregnate the queen splits in half once the task is accomplished. The rest of the bees in the hive, called worker bees, are female. The drones, unable to feed themselves, rely on the worker bees to feed them, but once the queen is fertilized the efficient worker bees simply stop feeding the drones until they starve to death, at which point they are dragged to the entrance to the hive and unceremoniously kicked out. The worker bees also decide between themselves when the time is right to create another queen, and are agents of the destiny of their unborn monarch since all that separates the regal bee from her proletariat sisters is a substance called Royal Jelly

If a bee has to defend herself, then the sting will be ripped from her body and she will die.

Thus bees are symbolic of great heroism and sacrifice, unlike the **wasp** that can sting time and time again.

As with many winged creatures, the bee is able to communicate in ways alien to human beings. The bee performs an elaborate **dance** to indicate the whereabouts of a particularly rich crop of flowers. Bees are believed to have magical powers to foresee the future, and are considered by many to be deities in their own right. It is perhaps for this reason it has been customary, for hundreds of years, for the beekeeper to tell the bees all the news of the household, particularly of births or deaths; a swarm of bees was regarded as carrying the **soul** of the deceased away with it.

Because bees feed on the nectar of flowers, and therefore fundamentally on sunlight, they are agents of transmutation, making something from nothing. Bees are mystical creatures that not only understand some of our most ancient and powerful symbols but create them, too. They construct their honeycomb from thousands of perfectly symmetrical hexagons, and in turn, this structure contains the many secrets of the **Flower of Life** and of the six-pointed star or **hexagram**.

BEETLE

See **Scarab** or **Ladybird**.

BISON

See **Buffalo**.

Boar

The symbolic tradition of the boar is thousands of years old, dating from a time when the animal was more prevalent in the world than it is currently. The wild boar, whose legacy was a wealth of symbolism and mythology, was extinct in the UK by the seventeenth century.

Like a hermit, the boar tends to lead an isolated existence, living alone in **forests** or woods. Therefore, the boar is symbolic of a solitary spiritual quest. In the Celtic pantheon, the boar is a symbol of power, the raw power that can be channeled in any direction under the power of the will. The battle standards of the Gauls were painted with the effigy of the boar, and their coins were engraved with it. Boar symbols were carved onto stones, to signify the ferocious nature of the warriors in any given area. In Scotland and Ireland there are ancient **monoliths** called boar stones; the precise reason for their presence is open to debate. It is possible that they mark the sites of a boar hunt or the slaying of a boar. In some of the stones, though, images of a comb and a **mirror** appear alongside the animal. This is because the boar was associated with the Celtic Goddess Arduinna, who also lived among the trees; the Forest of the Ardennes was named for her.

Because it roots around in the undergrowth for food, the boar belongs to the **Earth** element. In Hindu mythology, Vishnu takes the form of a boar to raise the earth up to the level of the waters and so make the planet habitable. In Persia, the name for boar—"boraz"—was added to someone's given name as recognition of bravery.

The boar, then, is symbolic of protection and ferocity, spiritual solitude and courage. Where the boar appears as a heraldic emblem, it represents these qualities.

Bobcat

See **Lynx**.

Buffalo

The marshy **wetlands** that the buffalo inhabits are universally acknowledged to be "transitional" places, territory that sits somewhere between the seen and unseen worlds. Therefore, the buffalo carries with it a significant amount of symbolism as a creature that has two hooves in the material world of man, and the other two in the spirit world of the Gods and the ancestors. It makes sense, then, that the Tibetan Spirit of **Death** has a buffalo's head and that the Hindu God of Death, Yama, sometimes takes on the form of the buffalo. The Montignard tribes of Vietnam carried the idea further, believing that the buffalo was the spiritual equivalent of a man. When they sacrificed the buffalo, therefore, they did this with a very deep respect for the animal, since once it was released from its earthly constraints, it would be able to intercede between the tribe and its Gods.

The **white** buffalo comes with huge significance attached to it for Native Americans, due no doubt because the appearance of such an animal is an incredibly rare occurrence; odds of one in a million have been quoted. To them, the appearance of such an animal is on a par with the reappearance of Christ. The place where a white buffalo is born is liable to become a focus of pilgrimage. People come to give gifts to the animal because of its sacred significance as a harbinger of peace, plenty, and good fortune.

There is a Sioux myth about how the white buffalo came to be so important. A buffalo, disguised as a woman wearing white skins, appeared to two men, one of whom treated her with respect, while the other was cruel and disparaging. The buffalo/woman turned the latter into a heap of **bones**, but to the other she gave the gift of **music** and taught certain rituals. The birth of a white buffalo calf is regarded as the reincarnation of this White Buffalo Woman, who comes as a sign of reassurance when the world is experiencing troubled times.

BULL

The sacred stature of the bull dates back to at least 3000 BC, when early Hebrews carved the effigy of a God, called El, who appeared in the shape of a bull, at the end of their ritual **staffs**.

The bull is the archetype of brute masculinity, fecundity, tyranny, and ferocity. In Greece it was sacred not only to **Poseidon** but to **Dionysus**. **Zeus**, the King of the Gods, took on the form of a bull to seduce the mortal Europa. Tricked into thinking that she had tamed the creature and gained its trust when it knelt before her, the moment she climbed onto its back it carried her away, a symbol of passion and lust.

The bull also has its part to play in the story of Hercules and his monumental labors. A bull that is wreaking havoc on Crete tests Hercules' huge strength. He strangles the

bull into submission, and it is shipped away to Athens.

Bull sacrifice is such an ancient rite that any definitive origins are uncertain, and although in the Ellora Caves there is a painting of the Goddess **Kali** slaying a bull, its ritual slaughter is far older than the purported age of the painting (c.AD 500–1000) suggests. To ancient man, the bull was such a supremely powerful animal that being splashed in its **blood** conferred immortality. In Rome, a bull cult introduced from Asia Minor in the second century BC inspired a ritual called the *taurobolium*. The initiate stood in a trench, immediately below a board with holes pierced in it. A bull, standing on top of the trench, had its throat slit, and the hot blood gushed down through the slats, drenching the devotee. This gory ritual was the reenactment of a Mithraic legend about the bull's blood as the origins of all life, and so rejuvenated the body and **soul**.

A remnant of the earlier bull sacrifice still takes place today, in the Spanish bullfights that have become synonymous with the country and its people. This particular ritual is a throwback to the same Mithraic legend as the *taurobolium*. This legend says the bull was the first creature on Earth. Mithras killed the bull and all other living things sprang from the blood that was spilled on the ground. Many of the oldest bullrings in Spain are on the sites of former Mithraic temples or at least are very close to them. Spain is not the only country to have bullrings; they also exist in South America and France.

The Celts shared these same beliefs about the bull and had their own ritual sacrifice of the creature. In this instance, though, the purpose of the ceremony was shamanistic in intent. The tribal "seer" ate the bull's flesh and drank its blood in the hopes that the act would induce dreams of prophecy, specifically aimed at choosing candidates for kingship.

The bull is immortalized in the night sky, being one of the symbols of the astrological **Zodiac** in the form of the constellation **Taurus**.

BUTTERFLY

Unlike the **bee** that goes from flower to flower with a great sense of purpose and intention, the butterfly seems to flutter about quite aimlessly, no great ambition lurking behind its beauty.

In view of the fact that the Greek word for butterfly, *psyche*, is the same as that for **soul**, it is interesting to note that winged creatures are universally thought to be able to communicate with other worlds and higher powers. There was a belief that human souls incarnated into butterflies between lifetimes. The connection between the spirit and the butterfly reaches across the world—from the Celts, who believed that the butterfly was a human soul in search of a mother to the Aztecs, who believed that the last breath exhaled by a dying person took the form of a butterfly.

The lifecycle of the butterfly is highly visible at every stage, from grub to caterpillar, then pupae, and on to the chrysalis that hatches open to reveal the butterfly. This procedure has caused the butterfly to become a symbol of transmutation and metamorphosis. Because of the period of gestation inside the chrysalis, which is like a tiny tomb, it is also an emblem of death and resurrection.

In Japan, the butterfly is the archetypal symbol of femininity and vanity, although two butterflies together are symbolic of love and **marriage**.

Some Native Americans—particularly the Blackfoot—believe that the butterfly brings dreams. They have a stylized butterfly symbol, which looks a bit like a **Maltese Cross**, which they embroider onto babies' cribs and clothes in order that they might sleep well and have sweet dreams. If a Blackfoot Indian paints a butterfly onto the wall of a tribal lodge, it is an indicator that any other patterns painted or drawn there were not simply the work of a man alone, but were inspired by the Great Spirit, for whom the painter acted merely as a conduit.

CALF

When Moses received the Ten Commandments from God on **Mount Sinai**, he was gone for longer than expected. Growing restive, the Israelites asked Moses' brother Aaron to make a God for them to worship. Ever inventive, Aaron gathered all the **gold** trinkets and pieces of **jewelry** that the crowd of Israelites could muster between them. Then he melted the metal down and constructed a statue of a Golden Calf that was accorded due worship and prayers. In the meantime, an angry God told Moses what was happening: the Israelites were worshipping false idols and therefore he was going to exterminate the lot of them. Moses interceded to spare the lives of the Israelites, and destroyed the statue.

This story gains further clarity when we know that for the Egyptians, the calf was the child of the great Goddess **Isis**, and was one of the forms taken by her son, Horus. They worshipped a golden calf called "The Horus of Gold" and the Israelites also carried a great regard for this "false God," willing to give up their wealth to construct his effigy. It would have made sense to Aaron to provide his people with the object they desired, as a focus for their worship.

As a symbol of innocence and a creature popularly used in ritual sacrifice, the calf came to be associated with Christ. The "fatted calf" was a calf that was kept especially well fed so that its meat would be particularly tasty. This privileged calf was slaughtered only on very special occasions, for example in the Bible story when the prodigal son returns to the bosom of his family.

The Vedic tales of India refer to the **Sun** as "the golden calf."

CAMEL

The camel has a disdainful expression that some might see as a sign of a bad temper. Despite its truculent demeanor and stubborn reputation, the camel is invaluable to man, the only creature that can carry him across a desert. A symbol of sobriety and temperance and commonly known as "the ship of the desert," the camel can survive for long periods without drinking and has been used by man for thousands of years to help him travel to otherwise inaccessible places.

The camel has become a pictorial metaphor for the Middle East, and its image appears on all sorts of products that come from the area.

Since the camel protects man on his perilous journey across parched land, the allu-sion of it as a guardian is implied in the Persian Holy Scriptures. In the Avesta, winged camels watch over the Earthly paradise.

St. John the Baptist, among other ascetics, chose another aspect of the camel as inspiration for his unworldly lifestyle. The creature's austerity meant that the coarse material made from its **hair** provided a suitable cloth for robes.

CAT

Even the most common household moggie has a mystique about it and the potential for the supernatural powers that man has ascribed to cats for thousands of years

Typically, in Western civilizations, the cat (particularly if it is **black**) belongs to the witch; it is her familiar, her companion and her alter ego. As such, the cat shares magical secrets and arcane knowledge which, of course, she cannot explain to mere mortals, since they don't speak her language. There is an unspoken communication between the witch and her grimalkin that transcends any language used by other creatures.

In the Saga of Eric the Red there is a very complete description of a witch or prophetess that was a mistress of rune-craft, the art of reading the **runes**. Part of the description of her costume includes a hood "lined with white cat skin" and "cat-skin mittens."

The Ancient Egyptians regarded the cat so highly that they revered it as a deity. Bast was the cat goddess, and mortal cats whose fur was of **three** different **colors**, or who had **eyes** of different shades, were honored in particular for their Bast-like appearance; it is not just the black cat that holds power. Bast is often depicted with a knife in her paw, having beheaded Apophis, the enemy of the **Sun**.

Egyptian priests believed that cats carried the magnetic forces of nature and so close proximity to the creatures enabled them to access these powers. If a cat died a natural **death** in the home, the Egyptians would shave their eyebrows as a sign of mourning.

Artemis/Diana, the Goddess of the Hunt, was associated with the cat, also notorious for its hunting skills.

When it sleeps, the cat curls itself into a **circle** with its **head** touching its tail, making a shape that is very similar to the **ouroboros**. Like this ancient mythical creature, the cat is a symbol of immortality.

However, the cat does not have such an honorable reputation everywhere, for example in the Buddhist tradition. Because it was absent at the physical death and spiritual liberation of the Buddha, it is viewed with suspicion as a base, earthly creature, lacking respect, which really should have been present at such an auspicious occasion. The only other creature that was not there was the **serpent**. The link between the cat and the serpent comes in the **Kabbalah**, too, and also in Christianity; in pictures where the cat appears at the feet of Christ it carries the same negative imagery as the snake.

Although black cats are the archetypal good-luck symbol in the West, in Islam the opposite is true. Cats are regarded favorably unless they are black, in which case they are viewed with great suspicion since **djinn** can transform themselves into black cats. Additionally, the magical powers of the cat are ambivalent, used either for or against

man; this refers to the indifference with which a cat treats its prey.

In the Western tradition of cat lore, the animal has **nine** lives, whereas its Eastern cousin has to manage with only **seven**.

A Persian belief about the cat echoes the idea of the witch with her familiar. Some people are born with a *hemzad*, a spirit that accompanies the person throughout his or her life and takes the form of a cat. That its **blood** is particularly powerful for writing charms further underlines the universally "magical" nature of the cat. In Africa, too, the clairvoyant powers of the animal are renowned, and so medicine bags made of cat skin are imbued with supernatural powers.

Caterpillar

The Latin name for the caterpillar is the same as that for evil spirits, so for the Romans the caterpillar was a creature of bad omen. Not only that, but the caterpillar crawls along the ground. Close proximity to the **earth** is universally considered the sign of a base creature.

However, the caterpillar also symbolizes knowledge and potential; the caterpillar in *Alice in Wonderland*, for example, dispenses wisdom to Alice and represents her inner self. This caterpillar sits on a toadstool that looks very much like the fly agaric—an hallucinogenic plant—and also smokes a hookah; Lewis Carroll has given this particular caterpillar parallels with a shaman.

For Hindus the caterpillar symbolizes the transmigration of the **soul** as it moves from the stage of earth-bound caterpillar to **butterfly**, itself universally acknowledged as the embodiment of the spirit.

Chameleon

To say that someone has chameleon-like tendencies means that they can change to fit their surroundings, somehow hiding their true selves in the process, a mysterious, unknowable person. Yet its very changeability is what defines the chameleon and makes it unique. Despite this, for early Christians its ability to change its **color** equated the chameleon with the Devil, able to change himself in order to deceive people and remain undetected.

However, the chameleon has more than one aspect to its symbolic significance. To the pygmy tribes of the Congo, the chameleon is the Creator of Mankind. Because the chameleon can climb up to the top of the very highest **trees**, it can communicate directly with the **Sun** God. In legend, it was responsible for all the animals that populate the planet. Because of its climbing habit, the chameleon is associated with the **Sky** Gods and the element of **air**.

The chameleon is believed to attract thunder and rain, again thanks to its proximity to the sky. A spell giving the shaman or magician power over the weather involved a sacrificial burning of the chameleon on a **fire** made of **oak** wood, itself one of the timbers that attracted the wrath of the storm-gods.

Cicada

The first literary mention of the cicada is in the Iliad, reputedly written in the seventh or eighth century BC, where Homer calls them "sage chiefs exempt from war." This is likely to refer to the peaceful and melodious sound that they make.

The sound of cicadas chirruping in the warm evening **air** is very beautiful, and it is not surprising that the insect has musical links, some of which explain the provenance of the cicada. There is an Italian myth that the cicada was created by the Gods after the **death** of a mortal woman who was an exceptional singer, since when she died the entire world seemed empty and bereft without her **music**.

Socrates tells a story that cicadas were once human beings that lost interest in everything but music when the Muses introduced it to mankind. These people even forgot to eat and drink, and started to waste away. The Muses rewarded them for this devotion and saved their lives by transforming them into cicadas. The chirruping of the insects is said to be the sound of them reporting every evening to the Muses about what has happened in the world of Men during the day.

Like other winged creatures, cicadas represent disembodied **souls**, and there is yet another Greek myth about this aspect of the insect. The Goddess of the Dawn, Eos, loved a mortal, Tithonus. Although Eos managed to gain immortality for her lover, she forgot to ask Zeus for eternal youth for him, and Tithonus' voice got higher with each passing year until he eventually shriveled into the form of a cicada.

The cicada is thus a symbol of immortality. In China it represents the spirit as it disengages itself from the body at the moment of death, and so a carving of the insect was placed on the **mouth** of the dying person to hasten the process. For the same reason the cicada is depicted on funerary items.

However, because the insect seems to respond to the calls of the farmers in the paddy fields, it is a fortunate omen, an emblem of wishes and dreams that come true.

COUGAR

See **Jaguar**.

COW

Because of its **milk** that is a staple food for many human beings, the cow is arguably one of the most useful animals in the world. It was one of the first animals domesticated by humans, and its symbolic importance is rich. It is emblematic of fertility, abundance, wealth, the universal Mother, and of rebirth. The cow is also a gentle and compliant creature.

It is not surprising that the cow is universally thought of as a mother figure. In Egypt the cow was personified as Ahet, the mother of the **Sun** itself. To make themselves fertile Egyptian women wore **amulets** of the Goddess Hathor, with the head of a cow, in her guise as the Creator. In Europe, too, the cow was the mother-ancestor of all living things, called Audumla, the milch-cow. In Greek myth, one of the names for the great Cow was Europa, which means "full **Moon**." The **stars** were said to be the children of Europa.

Curiously, the cow was also considered a psychopomp, a creature able to conduct the souls of the dead to the Underworld. Once, there was a custom whereby the cow was brought to the sickroom, and in what must have been a distressing and rather frightening ritual, the dying person was encouraged to grasp the tail of the cow as he breathed a last **breath**. The psychopomp aspect of the cow is still celebrated in the Nepali festival called the Gai Jatra or cow festival. In a boisterous celebration, every family that has lost a member during the course of the year has to take part in a procession, leading a cow, or, if no animal is available, then a child dressed in a cow costume is considered to be a fair substitute. The cow is believed to guide the **soul** on its final journey, including a voyage through the **Milky Way**, the constellations of stars said to be the milk splashed by the great Cow that was the Mother of the Universe.

The cow as a sacred animal is a fundamental part of Hindu iconography. In India the cow is so revered, and treated so gently, that it often causes a traffic hazard as it ambles along busy city roads. There are several reasons for the sacred status given to the creature. Not only does the Hindu faith have respect for all animals (vegetarianism is a tenet of the faith), but the God Krishna was a cowherd for a time, and one of his names is Bala Gopala, "the child who protects the cows." Hindu deities rule over each and every part of the cow. During times of famine, the cow is far more useful as a creature that can produce limitless amounts of milk, than as a dead beast that would provide meat for a limited period only.

COYOTE

The Coyote shares many of the characteristics of the **Fox**; it is the trickster God, the miracle-worker, the shape-shifter, and as such plays an important part in Native American belief. Because coyotes can be heard howling at night, they are often associated with the **Moon**. The coyote is one of the sacred animals that can open the door to the other world and it acts as a messenger between this world and the next. The coyote is sometimes held responsible for all the evils of the world, and in the countries where it makes its home it is generally a symbol of bad luck.

CRAB

When **Isis** tried to reconstruct the body of her murdered husband **Osiris**, there was one part missing. The Nile crab, named the Oxyrhynchid, had devoured his penis. So in Egypt the crab was a cursed creature. Elsewhere, the crab is closely associated with the **Moon**; their growth is affected by the lunar cycles and it is possible that their appearance at the edge of the sea as the tides turned would have promulgated the link.

The crab appears as the zodiacal sign of **Cancer**, looming over the horizon at the time of the summer solstice and another reminder of the turning of the tides of the seasons as the sun starts its descending path. The crab also appears in the **Tarot**, as part of the symbols on the eighteenth card that is named the Moon. The lobster features on this card too; like the Moon, both creatures sometimes move forwards, and sometimes move backwards.

CRICKET

See **Grasshopper**.

CROCODILE

A dangerous creature with a strange and frightening appearance, wherever the crocodile appears in the world it has a rich set of meanings attached to it.

The creature that is feared is also often revered as a way of appeasing its collective spirit. The Egyptians even honored the crocodile with its own city, Crocodilopolis, where sacred, tamed crocodiles lived, treated like kings and decked in **gold** and jewels. These Egyptians deified the crocodile as a god called Sobek, who had the body of a man and the head of the crocodile. Sobek keenly observed the ritual of the weighing of the **souls** after **death**, waiting for the ones that could not explain their actions, at which point he would eat them.

Because the crocodile can stay still for so long before striking very quickly, for some, such as the Chinese and the Cambodians, the crocodile symbolizes lightning. In Cambodia the word for the deity that governs the **earth** and **water** has the same name as that of the crocodile—Nak.

In many myths, the crocodile is one of the sacred creatures that helped create the planet. Because the animal is equally at home in water and on land, it makes sense that it would have been present when the earth was "born" from the **sea**, a legend that resonates in creation myths all over the world.

The crocodile, in its guise as the devourer, is synonymous with birth, which cannot happen without death. The significance of this aspect of the croc is enacted by the adolescent boys of Liberia as part of a rite of passage. Prior to the ritual circumcision that marks their entry into manhood, the boys are sent out into the **forest** to fend for themselves. This time in the forest can be as long as four years, during which time the boy is said to have died and been eaten by Poro, the spirit of the Great Crocodile. After a period of "gestation," Poro spits the boy out, minus his **foreskin**.

The image of the crocodile as a dishonest trickster is expressed perfectly in the notion of "crocodile tears," the hypocritical tears that the crocodile is said to shed for its victims.

DEER

In the Celtic pantheon, the deer is thought of as an otherworldly creature, belonging to the world of the **fairies** and having magical powers. Considered one of the oldest known creatures, its home in the darkness of the **forest** means that it can be party to hidden secrets. Flidass, the Celtic Goddess of Wild Things, had a chariot drawn by deer.

There are some elements of deer symbolism that are universal, namely its meekness, gentleness, and swiftness. Despite the masculine energy of the **stag**, it is a feminine animal, associated with the Goddess in her aspect as a hunter. The antlers of the deer hold significance, too, emblematic of the **tree of life** and of fertility and vitality.

That the deer appears prominently in Paleolithic **cave** paintings is a reminder of the amount of time that it has been considered a significant animal. Shaman connected to the spirit of the deer by wearing their antlers and skins. They believed that the deer could communicate with the Gods. For this reason, also, the deer was regarded as a psychopomp, one of the sacred creatures that acted as a guide

for the **soul** on its journey to the Afterlife. The Scythians reflected this idea by using the deer motif on funerary equipment, hoping that this would help speed the soul to its final destination.

In Buddhism, the deer is a reminder of the teachings of the Buddha, since he began his calling in a deer park. In Hindu stories, the Goddess of Learning, **Saraswati**, takes on the form of the deer, and followers of the Goddess hope that sitting on deerskin mats will help them absorb her knowledge.

DOG

One of the traditional pet names for the dog, Fido, comes from the same Latin root as the word "fidelity," and the trust and faith that a dog and its owner invest in one another is a defining feature of their relationship. For thousands of years man and dog have been close companions, living together, working together, and forming a close bond of mutual understanding. Every society has its dog mythology, its deities and its symbols. The dog is often the companion of a God, too, in addition to being a psychopomp, guiding the **souls** of the dead to the next world. On a more earthly level the animal can be a guide dog or a guard dog, directing and protecting, one of the greatest allies known to humankind; man's best friend, indeed.

The dog's keen sense of smell takes on almost supernatural connotations, a skill denied humans and something that cannot be seen or detected by us. This is part of the reason why the dog acts as mediator between the seen and unseen worlds, seemingly gifted the powers of second sight and psychic abilities. The Egyptians were very keen that their corpses would smell as sweet as possible so as not to offend the sensitive nose of the **jackal**-headed God **Anubis**, who shepherded these souls through to their next dwelling place.

Supernatural dogs include the Hounds of Annwyn who, in Norse mythology, hunted alongside Odin. The greatest Celtic hero, Cuchulain, means "Hound of Culann," an echo of the dog's importance as a hunter. The highest possible compliment to pay a hunter was to compare him to his dog. In Teutonic mythology the dog Garn stands at the gates of Niflheim, the land of the dead, in the same way that Cerberus, the three-headed "Hound of Hell" guarded the gates of Hades, and he appears in a more up-to-date form as Fluffy, the monstrous dog that watches over the Chamber of Secrets in the *Harry Potter* book by J.K. Rowling.

Shamans, who wore robes made of dog skin to help them access its otherworldly powers, assumed the magical nature of the dog. The Ancient Mexicans sacrificed the dog whose master had died, and laid the body on top of the grave so that the creature could walk with his master one last time through the **nine** rivers of the Afterworld until they reached the end of their journey.

While some witches have **cats** as familiars, others have their dogs, in honor of the Goddesses of Death and their hounds. **Hecate**, the Goddess of the Underworld and the Queen of Witches, had her dogs; like the Devil, she haunted **crossroads**, her pack of hounds at her feet. Latterly Sirius Black, Harry Potter's shape-shifting godfather, keeps a close eye on his charge by changing into a great black dog. Sirius, of course, is named after the Dog Star.

It is a telling sign among humans that often the animals with the greatest cultural and symbolic significance are the ones that it is considered wrong to eat. The majority of the world sees the eating of dog flesh as a great taboo. However, although many people revere the dog in this way, it is also seen as an unclean animal by followers of Islam. Mohammed decreed that any utensil that a dog had eaten from should be washed thoroughly **seven** times before it was once more fit for human use.

The **yellow** dog is a symbol of the **Sun**. In Persian mythology Ahura Mazda has a yellow dog that drives away evil spirits in the same way that the sun drives away the night and the darkness.

In **alchemy**, the symbol of the **wolf** devouring the dog is an analogy for the purification of **gold** by antimony, the penultimate stage of the "great work" of transformation. In this instance, the close relationship between these two creatures indicates the need for self-sacrifice to achieve a desired aim.

Dolphin

The dolphin has become ubiquitous as a symbol of the so-called New Age, due in part to its benevolently smiling appearance, its intelligence, its ability to communicate verbally with others of its kind, and the fact that it's a mammal that is comfortable in an environment normally reserved for fishes.

The name comes from the Greek *delphinos*, meaning "**womb**." The name of the Delphic Oracle where the priestesses gave their prophecies holds the same root; the **temple** was dedicated to Apollo, who arrived at Delphi in the shape of a dolphin.

For thousands of years the dolphin has been considered a helpful friend to humankind. It also acts as a psychopomp or guide to the other world. This is a fitting role for the dolphin given its ability to exist in a dimension alien to humans and because it has been seen to save those who might otherwise have drowned. In Greek art, the dolphin is often depicted on vases and in friezes, carrying the souls of the dead on its back to the Isles of the Blest. Dolphins like to speed through the **water**, accompanying ships, and so they are vanguards of the Gods of the Sea, such as **Poseidon/Neptune**, who could protect humans, if he chose, from the ravages of the oceans.

The dolphin is symbolic of metamorphosis. There is a Greek legend about some pirates who, after capturing Dionysus and tying him up, fell overboard and turned into dolphins.

The tendency of the dolphin to help those in trouble at sea has also become the subject of fable. Arian, a beautiful youth and poet dived into the sea to save himself from sailors who were threatening to kill him. Dolphins saved him from drowning by lifting him out of the sea, and he rode to safety on their backs.

In its role as the saver of souls, the dolphin is compared to Christ and also to the Roman **Sun** God Mithras, whose worship was superceded by that of the new God of Christianity.

Donkey

To call someone a "silly ass" is a derogatory term which implies that the ass is unintelligent; it is fair to say that the donkey does have a reputation of being obstinately stupid and, fair or not, this overarching quality forms a significant part of its symbolic meaning. Stupidity is a dangerous characteristic and this may well be why the donkey's reputation is that of a dangerous, almost demonic creature.

The ass is also a symbol of lewdness, carnality, and the lower sexual urges. There is a Greek myth in which Apollo turns the **ears** of King Midas into those of an ass because he eschewed the formal temple **music** in favor of Pan's pipes, inferring that the King would rather enjoy sensual pleasures than take a more enlightened delight in the harmony of the spirit and the higher mind. Asses were sacrificed to Apollo at his temple in **Delphi**.

The donkey has long been seen as the poor man's **horse** and so it symbolizes poverty and humility; Christ rode on the back of an ass when he entered Jerusalem, and his parents Mary and Joseph traveled in the same way. It is the she-ass in particular that is a symbol of humility, fully aware of the reasons to debase itself in the eyes of a perfect God.

However, not all the symbolism associated with the ass is negative. The ass also symbolizes kindness, patience, fortitude, and courage.

ERMINE

This is a type of stoat that lives in snowy places. Although its fur is pure **white**, a **black** tip at the end of its tail mars its otherwise perfect environmental camouflage, making the animal an easy target. Because of its beautiful color and thick softness, the ermine's pelt was highly sought after, its rarity and expense making the fur a status symbol for royalty, nobility, and certain members of the clergy who were the only people wealthy enough to be able to afford to buy it.

The ermine itself symbolizes purity. There was a notion in the Middle Ages that if it fell into muddy water, for example, and its coat became sullied, it would become rigid with shock and eventually die. So the ermine came to be an emblem of moral as well as physical purity. Those fortunate enough to own its fur were lent these impeccable credentials by association.

FERRET

See **Weasel**.

FIREFLY

In China, the firefly is the kindly helper of poor students and academics, assisting them to see their **books** as they struggle to read in the dark. As well as providing physical light, the firefly provides spiritual illumination and enlightenment, too.

Like other winged creatures, the firefly is regarded by many as a disembodied **soul**. Its ghostly appearance reinforces this idea. However, because it brings light to dark places, the firefly is not simply considered to carry the soul of an ordinary person but rather the spirit of a great hero.

FISH

Inevitably, the fish is the most prominent symbol of the element of **water**. From hereon in the symbolic meaning of the fish cascades into all sorts of other areas.

The fish lives in the depths that are synonymous with the Underworld, and it has access to secret places that are forbidden to humankind. Water is closely linked to the **womb**, and the idea of birth and rebirth, and so the fish takes on this meaning too, and because they quite literally have access to hidden depths, the fish is party to secret and sacred information—the Vedas, which are said to contain all arcane knowledge, were delivered by a fish acting as the avatar of Vishnu. Similarly for the Celts, the **salmon** was a fish associated with wisdom and hidden knowledge. Christ chose from fishermen for his disciples, and early Christians, who had to keep their religion a secret, identified one another by a piscine symbol called the **Ichthys**.

The fish has links with the female element, too. Not only is the sacred symbol known as the **Vesica Piscis** fishlike in its shape but the female sexual parts give off a fishy scent, further promoting the links between the eternal feminine and the element of water and the sea. In Syria, the Goddess Qedeshet is generally depicted with a fish.

Fish can lay vast numbers of **eggs** and therefore are symbolic of fertility and life. In the East, a pair of fish is used as a lucky charm in wedding ceremonies. In China, the fish is paired with the **crane** as a symbol of longevity.

There is an astrological sign that features two fish swimming in opposite directions—**Pisces**—and in Buddhism, a pair of golden fish is one of the **Eight Auspicious Symbols**.

FLY

Although any creature with wings is symbolic of the **soul** or spirit, few people would choose to be associated with the fly. Flies are associated with dirt, decay, rotting matter, and filth. That they symbolize death and rebirth is positive, but any benefit to be had by regeneration is overshadowed by the fact that they lay their **eggs** in putrefying material, such as corpses. Consequently they spread toxins via their feet and proboscis.

It is because of this habit that the fly is associated with pernicious influences, with demons, and with disease and plague. Flies are symbols of supernatural powers, but generally these powers are perceived to be malevolent. The arch demon Beelzebub has many names, including the Lord of the Flies. However, as is the case with many pre-Christian deities, it is worth bearing in mind that in the sense that the fly is the conductor of a soul, then Beelzebub's name actually meant Lord of the Souls and that he originally had a more benevolent nature as a psychopomp, one of those that guided souls into the other world.

In Egypt, flies appeared in various materials as amulets. In this case it is believed that they served two functions: to imbue the wearer with similar fertility, and to protect from real flies.

FOUR DIGNITIES

For Buddhists, the Four Dignities are those animals whose characteristics act as a reminder of four important aspects of the Buddha nature as well as the four major compass points.

These animals and their meanings, then, are as follows:

1. **Dragon**: Communication and compassion; rules the West, the **sea**, and the element of **Water**.
2. **Tiger**: Confidence, awareness, modesty, and kindness; rules the South, the element of **Air**, and **forests**.
3. Snow **Lion**: Cheerfulness and certainty, youthfulness and delight; rules the East, the mountains, and the element of **Earth**.
4. **Garuda**: Direct action, wisdom, and fearlessness; rules the North and the element of **Fire**.

FOUR SACRED CREATURES

Also called the Four Spiritually Endowed Creatures, in China these are the **tortoise**, the **phoenix**, the **dragon**, and the Ky-Lin, a unicorn-like creature. All are particularly auspicious good-luck symbols that are worn as **amulets**.

Fox

Wiliness, slyness and cunning, craftiness, trickery and guile, and yet wisdom too: these are all the qualities that are generally accepted throughout the world as belonging to the fox. An intelligent animal, Reynard, the famous fox that appears in fairy tales, has human characteristics and often converses with men and women in their own language.

The first recorded instance of hunting the fox with hounds is from the sixteenth century, but the tradition is supposed to be much older. Although the animal was hunted for its beautiful pelt, the actual chase often turned into an escapade that resulted in a slaughter so bloody that the fur itself was rendered completely useless. The reason for the persecution of this creature, beyond mere straightforward culling, remains a mystery, although it may stem from early Christian belief that made the fox synonymous with that most cunning of tricksters, the Devil.

Despite its reputation as a sly old fellow, in many tales the fox also has a role to play in helping humankind. In Japan, the fox is a particularly good influence. It is both a symbol of fertility and sacred to Inari, the God of Plenty. Inari often takes on the form of the fox, and shopkeepers, housekeepers, and businessmen of the Shinto faith keep a little shrine in their homes dedicated to this fox God, so that he will watch over their affairs.

Because foxes live in holes and tunnels in the ground, they are attached to the **earth** element and accordingly are the totem animals of several earth deities. The fox is also the symbol of the seducer or, most dangerously, the seductress; the "foxy lady" is aptly described.

The fox is the totem animal of Dionysus, whose seductively foxy priestesses wore fox skins.

Frog

In fairy tales, all it takes for an ugly frog to transform into a handsome prince is a single **kiss** from a beautiful princess. In this story, the frog is a symbol of transformation. The frog is a transformational creature in real life, too, and because the life cycle of this amphibious creature is carried out in so visible a manner—from mating to spawn to tadpole to fully-grown frog—it is a reminder of resurrection and the cycle of life, of birth, **death**, and rebirth. Egyptian mummies were wrapped with **amulets** depicting the image of the frog as a charm to help the person's soul to be reborn.

Because they appear as the weather is starting to get warmer, frogs are emblematic of spring and new beginnings.

The frog's links with **water** are obvious, and it often appears on rain charms. In Ancient China, the frog's image appeared on the drums that were played to summon thunder, the herald of much-needed rain. In Egypt, the frog symbolized fertility (because of its enthusiastic mating habits and abundant spawn) and so they were sacred to Hekit, the Midwife of the Gods.

"Frog" has become the English-speakers' nickname for the French, who notoriously eat frogs' legs as a delicacy. Indeed, before the French ruling classes adopted the **Fleur de Lys** as their emblem, the frog was France's national symbol.

GAZELLE/ANTELOPE

Possibly the most striking and beautiful feature of the antelope is its **eyes**, and one of the highest compliments that can be paid to almost any Eastern woman is to tell her that she has the eyes of a gazelle.

As well as being beautiful, the large eyes of the gazelle are sharp, too, able to detect movement as far as four miles away. This acute vision makes the creature sacred to the Goddess of Wisdom, **Athena/Minerva**, who shares the sharp eyes and perception of the animal. This ocular faculty was also noted by the Egyptians, who attributed the powers of prophecy to the gazelle. The annual flooding of the Nile was a critical time for them, and they believed that the gazelle gave warning of it by sneezing.

Another quality of the gazelle that has informed its symbolic meaning is its ability to run very fast. Speeds of up to seventy miles per hour have been recorded just 15 seconds after a standing start, and the animal can sustain speeds of 30–45 mph with no problem. This is why, in the Rig Veda, the gazelle carries the wind on its back.

For Native Americans, the swiftness, the vision, and the peaceable nature of the animal made it sacred, its **bones** kept safely for a year before being disposed of in a ritual that called on the spirit of the antelope to assist in the hunt. The animal was accorded with magical powers as a teacher of humankind, and is one of the spirit animals that the skilled shaman can transform into.

GOAT

Horny in all senses of the word, the goat is arguably most infamous as a symbol of lust and procreation, a reputation gained in no small part from the influence of the so-called **Goat of Mendes** (sometimes called **Baphomet**) in Ancient Egypt. This powerful deity was worshipped in a way that involved slaves copulating with goats in a ritual intended to honor the procreative power of nature. This Egyptian God was identified by the Greeks as Pan, the God of Nature, who sometimes wore goatskins. Later, for Christians who were keen to demonize any trace of the old pagan religions, the goat became the personification of the Devil.

Romans, too, saw the goat as a symbol of lasciviousness and fertility. Barren women were advised to have sexual congress with goats or, alternatively, to have their backs whipped with the skin of a sacrificed goat, cut into strips. This ritual was believed to purify the women and may even have inspired the name of the festival during which it was performed—"**Lupercalia**"—possibly from *luere per caprum*, meaning "to purify by means of the goat."

The abundant shaggy **hair** of the goat as well as its **horns**, contribute to its perceived sexual virility. It was said that one male goat could service one hundred and fifty females, and the goat/human hybrid the **Satyr** was believed to be the outcome of such degenerative carnality, a salutary lesson of what could happen if humans surrendered to their baser desires.

In some places, the goat is a symbol of **fire**, and in particular the fire associated with **lightning**. This imagery occurs in the Vedic tales from India where Agni, the Lord of Fire, is seen riding a goat. Similar symbolism is found in China and in Tibet, the creature seen as a messenger that conveys the blessings of the Gods in their Heavens to human beings on Earth. The Ancient Greeks, too, have the she-goat as a symbol of lightning. For them, the goat was immortalized in the constellation **Amalthea**, emblematic of the goat that suckled **Zeus** on the sacred mountain, Mount Ida. If the constellation was visible then storms and rain should be expected, and once more language provides a clue about the reasoning of ancient man; "aegis" is the word shared by both goatskin and stormy weather.

Finally, what of the scapegoat? The first mention of it occurs in the Old Testament. A ritual involved two goats. One was set free and the other sacrificed. The liberated goat, however, was laden with the sins of the people and sent out into the desert to perish, its death often hastened by its being pushed over a cliff; the name of this cliff, Azazel—"the goat that departs"—was also the name of a **demon**. The concept of the scapegoat exists today as a term for someone who takes on the blame for the wrongdoings of others, and has sometimes led to the goat symbolizing an unrepentant sinner.

GRASSHOPPER

The grasshopper, or cricket, is considered to be a symbol of good luck in China and likewise in Mediterranean countries, especially if it is seen in the house.

For the Greeks it was sacred to Apollo, but otherwise the grasshopper is seen as a symbol of death and resurrection since it lays its **eggs** in the **earth**, with the newly hatched creature appearing out of the soil.

HARE

Because the hare is a nocturnal creature, she carries all the symbolism of the **Moon**; light in the darkness, concealed wisdom, arcane information, intuition, and the Goddess. The Moon is symbolic of rebirth and resurrection, because of its visible phases, and the hare shares these qualities, too. Significantly, in some parts of the world the shape of the hare is visible in the face of the Moon, further reinforcing the mystical connection between the two.

The hare is renowned for its fertility, and it is in this guise that it is simplified as the **Easter** Bunny. The Springtime Goddess, Eostre, governed the cycles of fertility and so her symbol was the **egg**; hence the **chocolate** eggs given to children at Easter, a remnant of a pagan tradition that has never been satisfactorily explained away by its Christian adoptees.

The fact that an animal is not eaten is generally a sign that it has sacred status, and certain Muslim sects refuse to eat the flesh of the hare because they believe that it is the reincarnation of Ali, the Prophet's son-in-law, who intercedes between True Believers and

Allah. Pre-Christian Celtic people similarly regarded the hare as being too sacred to consider eating; they were kept as pets.

Some Native American tribes that have adopted Christianity link the hare with Jesus Christ, since the previous savior of these people was a Great Spirit Hare called Menebuch that had Christ-like qualities. Menebuch came down from the Heavens to educate humankind in all his ways, and to protect them from monsters and evil spirits.

Three hares joined at the **ears** and running in a **circle** in the form of a **triskele**, is a mysterious ancient symbol that seems to have transcended cultural boundaries and geographical borders. At the center of the circle, the ears of the hares form an equilateral **triangle**. This motif appears in Buddhist caves 2500 years old; in Muslim artwork and designs; in synagogues and in several places of Christian worship throughout Europe. There is no definitive interpretation of the symbol although it may represent the attributes of the **Triple Goddess**, an age-old concept that transcends religious dogma. The hare, because it is a lunar creature, belongs to the Goddess.

Hedgehog

In many places, the hedgehog, like the **porcupine**, was believed to be the inventor of **fire** and so is associated with the **Sun**; the shape of the spines accounts for this. The most distinctive characteristic of this creature, these same prickly spines makes the hedgehog a symbol of bad-tempered wrath, because they are quickly raised up if the animal feels itself to be under threat.

In myth, the hedgehog used their spines to roll about in lush fruits such as **figs** and plums, which it then took home to consume in private. Therefore the hedgehog became a symbol of greed and gluttony.

Hind

An old name for the doe, the hind is essentially a female symbol, gentle and shy, a mother and yet a virgin. There are several Goddesses that have an association with this lovely forest animal, notably **Hera**, the Greek Goddess of Love and Marriage, **Diana/Artemis**, the Goddess of the Hunt, and the Celtic Goddess of the Woodland, Flidass.

Genghis Khan was said to be offspring of a hind and a blue **wolf**, symbolism that is almost alchemic in its nature: the herbivore mating with the carnivore, the marriage of spirit and matter. The hind is also the form taken by the **Valkyries**, who carry spirits of dead warriors into the Afterworld.

The Ceryneian Hind in Greek mythology is the origin of the Golden Hind. This animal had antlers of **gold** and hooves of brass, could run like the wind, and was sacred to Artemis, the Goddess of the Hunt who, like the hind, was chaste. Capturing this animal was one of the labors of Hercules.

For the Celts, the hunt for the hind was a metaphor that implied the search for wisdom.

HIPPOPOTAMUS

The hippo has had a very bad press when it comes to its symbolic significance.

It was generally believed that the creature preferred to mate with its own mother, while the Egyptians gave one of their evil deities, Typhon, the head of a hippopotamus. Generally, the animal is felt to be a cowardly and irreligious character.

HORSE

For millennia the horse has enjoyed a spiritual, symbolic, and mythical significance that arguably surpasses that of any other living creature. Accordingly, its symbolic significance is massive and varied. That the horse has long enjoyed a vital link with humankind as a hunting companion, a beast of burden, as a means of travel, and as an agricultural asset is demonstrated by its image being seen in Paleolithic cave drawings, such as at Lascaux, dating back approximately 30,000 years. The symbolism of the horse is inextricably linked to the story of man; such is the close association between the equine and human species.

The horse belongs to the **Sun** and the element of **fire**. Horses proudly draw the chariot of the Sun God. At the same time, the horse also belongs to the **Moon** and the element of **water**, since it carries on its back the God of the Oceans, too. It was believed that where a horse stamped, a spring appeared, and so the animal becomes a life-giver. In Greece there is a sacred well, called Hippocrene (the Horse's Well), which is shaped like a **horseshoe** and is dedicated to the **Muses**. Pegasus, the Winged Horse, was held to have created this particular sacred well.

The horse symbolizes life and **death**, darkness and light, good and evil, depending on the context in which it is seen. As well as being a bringer of life, it is also a psychopomp, a creature that guides dead **souls** on the journey to the next life. As well as having spiritual significance, like the **dog** with which it shares many characteristics, the horse is valuable in purely practical terms, too. It represents power and wealth, since having a horse—or many horses—confers superiority on the owner, not only in terms of monetary value but in the distances he is able to cover and the speeds at which he can travel. This leads to another aspect of the horse—it is a symbol of freedom. Despite the fact that it can be trained the horse is not inferior to man but is his equal.

The color of a horse, too, carries great significance. Where a **white** horse appears, it is a symbol of the virginal, the spiritual, and the godly. The Buddha, for example, chose to ride a white horse. The Virgin Queen, Elizabeth I, is depicted on a white palfrey. The **black** horse, conversely, often symbolizes death and the dark forces. A golden horse is emblematic of the Sun and the solar deities.

Horses were used by warriors and so are linked with **Mars**, the God of War, and with all the associated male attributes: virility, sexuality, and strength. **Wotan/Odin**'s horse, Sleipnir, had supernatural powers, possessing eight legs as well as being able to gallop over water as though it were solid land. However, the horse is also closely associated with the feminine and medieval texts draw parallels between the woman and the horse, speaking, for example, of the necessity to keep both on a firm rein. A mare generally leads herds of horses, and Horse Goddesses include Epona, the mother-Goddess of the ancient Britons, and **Rhiannon**. The sacred status of horses meant that the sacrifice of such a creature was a rare and profound event, and even today, there is repugnance among many people at the thought of eating horseflesh; not eating an animal is a sure sign that it is regarded as sacred.

Hyena

The hyena, the predatory hunter who seems to laugh as it hunts down and kills its quarry, is emblematic of cruelty and heartlessness and is often considered to have few if any redeeming qualities. However, its prodigious sense of smell has accorded it divinatory powers, and its ability to crack tough **bones** with its immensely strong jaws means that for Africans who live in close proximity to it the hyena is emblematic of understanding and learning.

A carrion eater that exists purely on the earthly plane, the hyena carries none of the symbolism of the **vulture**, which also eats waste, but is considered divine because it operates in the element of **air**. It is impossible for the hyena to transcend either the coarseness of its surroundings or the degrading acts it has to commit in order to survive.

Despite all this, the hyena is considered to have magical powers, and is considered something of a magician. Allegedly, it could hypnotize any animal by walking around it three times, it could imitate the human voice so accurately that it could cause people to leave their homes, and it was believed to have a jewel in its **eye** that enabled it to see into the future. Witches and wizards were able to change into hyenas, it was believed, in order to travel to their unholy sabbats.

Jackal

One of the first images that springs to mind when we think of the jackal is the Egyptian jackal-headed God, **Anubis**. Wild **dogs** were considered to carry the spirit of this God. Jackals are swift runners, able to cover long distances in a short space of time, and are renowned for their aggression.

Jackals have an unearthly howl, often heard in the dead of night, its favored hunting time. Because jackals are scavenging animals that feed on corpses, and because they were known to frequent graveyards, the jackal is associated with the dead. Anubis looked after the deceased, supervising the funeral rites, the mummification process and the journey to the other world; here we see the symbolism of the wild dog as psychopomp and as a messenger between the worlds.

To Buddhists, the jackal symbolizes someone whose fate it is to be rooted in evil, unable to understand the tenets of the faith.

In Hinduism, jackals accompany the Goddess **Kali**, in her guise as the destroyer.

JAGUAR/PANTHER

For purposes of simplicity, this entry refers to both creatures as the jaguar. They carry much the same meaning since they are color variations of the same species.

To Native Americans, the name of the jaguar is synonymous with a creature that "kills with one blow," while the word "panther" comes from the Greek *panthera*, meaning "all beast," showing just how important our ancestors considered this animal to be.

The Mayans believed that, since the dawn of time, **four** jaguars guarded the entrance to their valuable maize fields. Since these people followed a lunar calendar, the jaguar, a nocturnal creature, connected to their Goddess of the **Moon**, who is sometimes depicted with the claws of this great cat. Its association with the night and therefore occult knowledge gave the jaguar the gift of second sight and prophecy, which explains why it sometimes appears depicted with four **eyes**, two for normal sight and two for supernatural vision. The jaguar was one of the major deities of the Mayans, appearing on their calendars, and venerated in the form of the Jaguar Priests who officiated at only the most important and sacred rites and rituals. The Incas, too, revered this big cat and built temples in its honor.

While the jaws of the jaguar were emblematic of the gates of Heaven, it was also considered to be the Lord of the Underworld, no doubt because of his ability to kill swiftly and surely, and was therefore one of the many creatures with the sacred responsibility of guiding soul to the world beyond. In the same way that the **lion** and the **eagle** are juxtaposed in many cultures, the jaguar was similarly aligned with this bird, which was called the "jaguar of the skies." Gods and kings wore the skins and **feathers** of sacred animals as status symbols, and the Aztec Emperor sat on a throne of eagle-feathers and jaguar skin. The animal carries the same powers of creation and destruction as the fire that, legend says, it brought to humankind.

When there was a solar or lunar eclipse, it was thought that the planets were swallowed by a gigantic cosmic jaguar, which would similarly devour humankind at the end of the world. Thus, the jaguar was a powerful creature to be both worshipped and feared.

LADYBIRD

A member of the beetle family, the **red** and **white** polka dots make the ladybird a great favorite among children and it is mentioned in numerous poems and nursery rhymes.

The ladybird has always been dedicated to the Goddess, and after the pagan religions were superceded by Christianity it was said to be named for the Virgin Mary. Wherever the ladybird appears it's a symbol of good luck (in Turkey they are known as "lucky bugs"), of prosperity and of fertility, since it is a prolific insect. If a ladybird crawls across a girl's **hand**, folk belief says that she will be married within the year.

The ladybird is also a symbol of protection. In the Middle Ages, so the story goes, aphids and other pests were ruining crops. In desperation, the farmers prayed to the Virgin for help. Soon afterwards, thousands of ladybirds appeared and decimated the aphids; therefore, the ladybird is a reminder of the power that can be found in little things, and the notion that the whole is more than the sum of the parts.

The ladybird is well able to protect itself from larger predators because it gives off a scent that is repellant to would-be attackers. Therefore this little insect is symbolic of self-reliance.

The number of spots on the back of the ladybird is significant, too, and are said to be a marker of the time it will take for something good to happen—six hours or six days, for example.

LAMB

It might seem odd that the adult version of the lamb—the sheep—carries quite negative symbolism, as a creature that blindly runs with the flock, unable to think as an individual. The term "sheep" is generally used pejoratively.

However, the lamb is a much more positive symbol. It stands for innocence and purity, the spiritual, the compliant, and gentleness. Further, the lamb is a symbol of spring, of new hope, and of triumph over adversity. The first lamb of the season, as the most potent personification of these qualities, was usually sacrificed to the Gods.

The sacrificial nature of the lamb carries resonance through the Christian, Jewish, and Muslim faiths. Hence, the symbolism of the Christ as the Lamb of God, sacrificed for all mankind but resurrected by a beneficent God.

There is a specific symbol, the Paschal Lamb, which perfectly embodies this notion; the lamb appears with a **halo** and a banner, symbolizing both sanctity and victory.

The lamb is also a symbol of peace, and where it appears with the **dove**, this aspect is compounded. Sometimes the lamb and the **lion** appear together, a universal symbol of concord and harmony and the balancing of opposites.

LEOPARD

The skins and other body parts of sacred animals were believed to carry the spirit and energy of the creature that could be conferred upon the owner or the wearer. The more powerful the animal, the more powerful was its pelt. When Ancient Egyptian priests wore leopard skins during funeral rites, they did so to show that the God Set, who was the destroyer and enemy of mankind, had been vanquished and so held no threat to the **soul** of the departed. The leopard, as the great destroyer, was closely aligned to the God.

As a symbol of bloodthirstiness, cunning, and power the leopard has no equal. These qualities were shared by many warrior castes that aligned themselves with the leopard. Bacchus, too, was depicted with this animal, which to early Christians was generally perceived to be a particularly evil and destructive creature, associated with the Devil himself.

The conversion from sinner to saint—as in the case of Mary Magdalene—is symbolized as the leopard that changes its spots for a coat of uniform color.

LION

One of the most powerful animals and appropriately laden with rich symbolic meaning, the lion is synonymous with the **Sun**, and as such is best personified as **Leo**, the **Zodiac** sign that has the great golden **star** as its ruler. The lion even looks like the Sun, with its tawny coat and shaggy golden mane.

The lion is the totem animal of kings and emperors, of Apollo, of Mithras, of Christ, of Krishna, of the Buddha. Its counterpart, the **Eagle**, is called the Lion of the Skies.

Christ is known as the Lion of Judah, and Mohammed's son-in-law, Ali, who acted as mediator between the Prophet and the people, was called the Lion of Allah. Krishna is known as the "Lion among Wild Creatures" and the Buddha is the "Lion of the Shakyas."

The Egyptian image of two lions facing away from each other represents the two horizons, as the creatures watch over the birth and death of the Sun. In a logical progression, this came to represent the concept of "today" and "tomorrow," past and future. Here, the lions observe time and space.

The lion, with its shaggy **halo** of a mane, might seem to be the ultimate personification of male energy. However, there are female deities who share the attributes of the lion, and the lioness is a ferociously protective mother. Hathor, the Egyptian Goddess, has the **head** of a lion when she appears in the aspect of Destroyer. Cybele, the Phrygian Earth Mother, rides in a chariot pulled by lions, and the lion, as well as the **bee**, was sacred to her.

In Hindu iconography, too, the lion has a part to play as a manifestation of feminine power. Shardula, the lioness, represents the power of the spoken word, universally acknowledged as the essence of Creation.

Because of its great strength and because of the ferocity with which a she-lion will protect her cubs, it is no surprise that the lion has a protective influence. Accordingly, **amulets** and charms featuring lions were once very popular. Different gemstones represented different aspects of protection; a lion carved onto **garnet** protected the traveler, for example, whereas a lion on **jasper** guarded against fevers.

There is a negative side, however, to the great power of the lion. It is no accident that the collective noun for a group of lions is a Pride, and the sin of pride is said to be the negative aspect of the Zodiac sign of Leo. Further, power can lead to corruption unless there is an awareness of moral and ethical values. The male lion can also be a symbol of laziness, and it is a well-known fact that the lioness is the one who does the majority of the hunting and cub-care.

Although it is an effective killer, the lion is not a confrontational creature and generally prefers a peaceful life. When they hunt, they hunt together, symbolic not only of fellowship but strength and safety in numbers.

In Japan, the lion has its own feast day, January 1. On this day the Lion Dance performed, with three or more dancers representing the animal. The first wears a fearsome lion **mask** and the rest comprise its body. The entire lion then wends its colorful way through the streets, driving out evil spirits and bringing prosperity for the rest of the year.

Lizard

Lizards are attracted to the heat of the **Sun**, closely linked to its light, and synonymous with the **soul** that seeks knowledge and enlightenment. Christian symbolism regards the stillness of the lizard, basking in the warmth of the sun, as the equivalent of religious contemplative ecstasy. Egyptian **hieroglyphs** provide further evidence of the lizard as a benevolent creature, where its symbol means "plentiful." In other parts of Africa, the lizard is a messenger between man and God, and one of the key messages given by the creature, rather unusually, was that there was no life to be expected after **death**.

Because the lizard, like the **snake**, sloughs off its dead skin, both creatures symbolize rebirth and regeneration. Therefore, the lizard was the favored animal of shamans because it apparently has power of life over death—it was believed that the lizard could walk in both the seen and unseen worlds, the worlds of the living and the dead.

The importance of the lizard to the Inca people is demonstrated by its dramatic appearance carved into the Pampas Colorado of Peru as part of the famous **Nazca Lines**. This small creature appears as the largest single symbol, 590 feet (180 meters) long, and properly visible only from above, from the viewpoint of the Gods. Because the lizard seems to be difficult to kill and has a tough scaly armor-like skin, warriors wore this skin as a protective **talisman**.

Locust

Although insects are comparatively small creatures, when they mass together as a group they can achieve a lot in a short space of time, whether creative or destructive.

The locust is a good case in point. Several times the Bible mentions a "plague" of locusts that descend in a cloud to consume precious crops and harvests, making short shrift of an entire year's worth of work. In this sense, the locust may be used as a symbol of invading forces. The symbol of a cloud of locusts still creates a frisson of fear as a precursor to an apocalyptic event.

Lynx

A nocturnal animal that lives a solitary and private existence, the lynx symbolizes hidden mysteries, occult knowledge, and clairvoyance. One of its perceived characteristics is its keen sight, and at one time people believed the animal could actually see through **tree** trunks, walls, and even **mountains**. This is a good example of how an animal can take on symbolic characteristics that have nothing to do with the truth and everything to do with appearances—the lynx does not have extraordinary eyesight at all. Despite this, the animal came to symbolize clear-sightedness in both a literal and metaphorical sense.

The lynx used to be far more prevalent in the British Isles than it is today, and it shares the root of its name with that of the great British God of Light, **Lugh**. The harp was a significant musical instrument for many people including the Celts, and if it had strings made from lynx-gut, it made **music** that was considered particularly divine and sacred, carrying the magical properties of the animal in its melodies.

One of the more curious beliefs about the lynx was that its urine hardened into precious stones. The lynx, however, buried this gem in the ground so that no one could find it. Therefore, Pliny the Elder and others who subscribed to this strange theory argued that the habit contributed to the lynx's reputation for greed.

MANTIS

The Praying Mantis is so-called not because it is a particularly spiritual insect, but because of its shape and stance. The female of the species has a sinister reputation for eating her husband so it is not surprising that she is a symbol of trickery and deception. Nevertheless, in certain parts of Africa it represents the Creator.

Adding to its trickster reputation, the insect sometimes feigns indifference, sitting for long periods in its distinctive praying position before making a lightning strike. The Japanese name for the creature, Kamakiri, represents this tendency very well, since it means "sickle cut." The fighting skill of the mantis is renowned—there is an Oriental martial art called Praying Mantis, said to have taken its inspiration from the fighting prowess of the animal—and the insect can kill much larger creatures than itself, hence its use as a symbol of power on Samurai swords, buckles, and other artifacts.

MOLE

Once, the mole was regarded as a magical animal with the power to see into the future, effectively because it moves in a dimension that is alien to man, living in the bowels of the **earth** in a state of blindness but nevertheless able to access hidden information. This is a quality that it shares with other creatures that operate under cover of darkness such as the **owl**. Elizabethans believed that if they ate the **heart** of a mole then they would acquire its divinatory powers, provided they were able to stomach the results; in order to have the desired effect the heart had to be wrenched out of the animal and eaten while it was still pulsating.

In a thirteenth-century bestiary the mole appears as an emblem of the earth element, and as a symbol of healing, the mole was the attribute of the Greek God Asclepius, and also of the Indian God Rudra. The secrets that the mole has access to in its underground domain include knowledge of the mysteries of death; once mastered, it made sense that the mole would be able to heal the sick and even bring the dead back to life.

It is possible that the underground network of tunnels constructed by this creature influenced and inspired ancient **mazes** and **labyrinths**.

MONKEY

Many animals simply symbolize aspects of their own personality. The monkey is mischievous and agile, and has a wily intelligence. It is also a good mimic, although it is not always certain that the animal understands precisely what it is imitating; in this sense the monkey is a symbol of randomness. A recurrent theme of the monkey is as an emblem of chaotic, unguided, unconscious action. In Christian symbolism, the monkey has a rather unfavorable aspect, representing the idea of man degraded by sin, and therefore reverting to a lower life form.

In the Ramayana, it is a monkey called Hanuman who helps Vishnu rescue his bride from a **demon**, and is deified as a reward. The monkey is a sexually active, fertile creature, and in India women are known to strip off their clothes and hug the effigy of Hanuman in the belief that this will help them to conceive.

In Ancient Egypt, apes were held in such high esteem that they were accorded burial rites of a similar status to those of human beings. This may be because the monkey shares so many of our characteristics. Monkeys also have a propensity for anger, and the Egyptians, recognizing this, used the hieroglyphic symbol of the monkey to mean "angry."

In the Mayan calendar, too, the monkey held prominence, regarded as hard working, a gifted orator, and talented at artistic pursuits in general. To call someone a monkey was considered to be a great compliment. In Japan, however, it is unlucky to use the word "monkey" in a wedding ceremony because of a curious superstition that to do so might cause the bride to run away. However, monkey dolls are given to children to protect them since all monkeys—even stuffed toy ones—can drive away evil spirits. The monkey appears in the **Chinese Zodiac**, too, and people born under its sign are said to be intelligent, agile, decisive, and entertaining.

Moose

A sacred animal for Native Americans, the moose is closely linked with the **raven**, considered a gift from this God-like **bird**. The animal is symbolic of male energy in that it is a good and persistent hunter; conversely it is also a female symbol, partly because of its unpredictable nature.

The moose is often happy standing neck-high in **water**, where it grazes on aquatic plants such as water **lilies**, and this link with water and the **earth** further underlines its feminine traits. Another characteristic of the moose is its solitary nature. It does not travel in herds, preferring to live singly. The calf is weaned at six months and its mother drives it away prior to the birth of a new baby. Therefore, the moose is symbolic of detachment and independence.

Moth

A nocturnal creature, the moth is considered the **butterfly** of the night although it carries rather more sinister symbolism than its frivolous sister.

One of the archetypal images of the moth is of it dancing around a flame. This nocturnal creature craves light so much that it will immolate itself in pursuit of it. There is a dichotomy about this image. On the one hand, it symbolizes the sublimation of the ego as **death** makes the **soul** a part of the collective unconscious. On the other, it is an emblem of stupidity, vanity, and hubris.

The markings on the **wings** of certain moths carry a symbolism all their own. For example, the image of the deaths head on the back of the moth of the same name speaks for itself, and to find this moth presages bad luck.

Like the butterfly, the moth symbolizes the disembodied soul. However, the moth is also seen as a destructive force since, unlike the butterfly, it can do damage and is sometimes seen as a pest. Although the clothes-eating moth is something of a rarity, moths in general have suffered a bad reputation and the tendency is even mentioned in the Bible:

So man wastes away like something rotten, like a garment eaten by moths.

[Job 13:28]

MOUSE

The mouse, such a small, seemingly insignificant creature, is one of the forms taken by the great God **Apollo**. There is a dichotomy with this symbolism, representing the idea of the God in both his aspects—as destroyer and as protector. Apollo, like the mouse, destroys by spreading plague, whereas in his guise as the Harvest God it falls to Apollo to save the crop from the attentions of the little creature.

In Europe, the mouse was symbolic of the soul leaving the body, an idea shared by other tiny creatures. It was believed that the soul/mouse escaped through the **mouth** as the dying person breathed their last **breath**. This supposition was so well founded that it even has witness reports.

In Christian iconography, the mouse is a bad influence because it allegedly gnawed at the foot of the **cross**, symbolically undermining the major icon of the faith.

The mouse also appears with the great elephant-headed Indian God **Ganesh**. Curiously,

the huge Ganesh is described as "riding" this tiny animal. The physical improbability of such an arrangement does not matter, however, since this is a symbol of Ganesh's humility.

OCTOPUS

The octopus, living in deep waters, has two main angles to its representative meaning. Because it lives in the depths and because of its sea-monster appearance, it is linked with the spirits of the Underworld and with the Devil. However, where it is used as a motif in Cretan art, it carries a similar symbolism to that of the **spiral** and the **spider**'s web, themselves both emblematic of the creation of the Universe.

OTTER

In common with other animals that move in the element of **water**, and in particular of animals that can appear and then disappear below the surface of the rivers and streams which they inhabit, otters are symbols of the **Moon** and therefore of feminine magical powers. It is interesting to note that Hermione Granger, heroine of the *Harry Potter* books, has a personal protective **totem** animal in the shape of an otter, which is perhaps a more discreet emblem of mystical wisdom than, for example, the **owl**. Since lunar creatures are regarded as having access to hidden information and secret knowledge, it makes sense that otter skin has a powerful magic symbolism embedded into it. Therefore it is used in rites of initiation by some Native American tribes.

This skin is used to make medicine bags, in which the tribespeople secrete their most sacred **stones** and **shells**. They believe that the otter has a God-given immortality and so the skin is used during the ritual enactment of death and resurrection.

The watery habitat of the otter represents for many, including the Celts, the places where the dividing line between the worlds is at its most hazy, and therefore the otter acts as a psychopomp, conducting souls to the Afterlife. The intimate knowledge that the otter has of his intricate domain of waterways and underground tunnels means that the animal can similarly find its way through the circuitous route to the next world.

Ox

The ox stands for patience, strength, and hard-working amiability. As a beast of burden, the ox is an invaluable asset to mankind especially in his agricultural efforts. Only valuable animals were deemed to be worthy of sacrifice to the Gods, and it is a mark of the esteem in which the ox was held by the Ancient Greeks that sometimes one hundred oxen—a hecatomb—would be offered up as sacrifice. Odysseus' crew, when they were starving, slaughtered and ate the sacred oxen on one of the islands they arrived at, defying the orders of their captain. All of them died except for Odysseus.

It is not just in India that the **cow** is considered a holy animal. The ox is sacred in many parts of North Africa, too, and the plowing of the first furrows of the season is an act of magical significance, accompanied by much ceremony.

As a religious symbol, the ox is the emblem of St. Luke the Evangelist, because in his testament Luke writes of the passion of Christ: because the ox is an animal of sacrifice, there are parallels with the animal and with Jesus.

Pig

Calling someone a pig is a pejorative term, implying that the person is dirty, greedy, and generally uncouth. Unfortunately for the animal itself, these insulting qualities are almost universally considered to be true.

The pig is regarded as ignorant, gluttonous, and selfish, an animal that wallows in its own filth (notwithstanding the fact that the animal is actually extremely clean and scrupulous), one of the animals considered "unclean" by both Hebrews and Muslims and which is forbidden as food to followers of these faiths. To throw "**pearls** before swine" is to offer something to someone who is unable to appreciate it.

In Tibetan Buddhism, the pig represents worldly desire in all its forms—lust, material possessions, food. It sits at the center of the **Wheel** of Dharma as a symbol of things that tie us to the cycle of materialism, holding us back from spiritual enlightenment.

However, there's another side to the coin. All animals that were considered holy or sacred were also forbidden to be eaten, and the pig, too, despite its negative connotations, held sacred status, linked to the Mother Goddess in lots of different faith systems. The sow is a prolific mother, giving birth to many piglets. The fecundity of this creature means that she is associated with **Demeter/Ceres**, the Earth Goddess and mother of the harvest.

To Hindus, as Varahi, she is the **boar**-faced Goddess who protects holy buildings. Durga, also, takes on the form of the pig as Vajrabarahi. The Egyptian Goddess of the Night, Nut, was depicted on **amulets** as a sow being suckled by her piglets. The Celtic Mother Goddess, Ceridwen, was called the Old White Sow, and both the deity and the pig were associated with the **Moon**. Only the Gods were considered worthy to eat the meat of the pig.

In China, the pig is one of the auspicious animal signs of the Chinese Zodiac, where it symbolizes hard work, love of family, and a caring nature. However, it seems that pigs might fly before they manage to shake off some of their more unfortunate associations.

PORCUPINE

The fearsome, spiky appearance of the porcupine makes it a perfect symbol of fighting power, able to attack from both near and far (although it cannot, as people once thought, actually shoot its barbs at people). As such, it was adopted as a device in **heraldry**, used most notably by the Duke of Orleans who founded the Order of the Porcupine in 1397. The Knights attached to this Order recognized one another by the porcupine emblem engraved on their **rings** and pendants.

For Native Americans, the porcupine was a sacred creature, said to have brought **fire** to humankind. It was associated with the solar power. It's likely that this was down to the spiky, flame-like appearance of its quills, sacred items in themselves, often used to decorate clothing and **headgear**.

In Nigeria, the porcupine is believed to be able to carry messages between Man and God and so is used by shamans in divinatory practices.

PORPOISE

See **Dolphin**.

RABBIT

Incredibly fecund, the rabbit is a symbol not only of fertility, but also of sexuality and lust, personified by the "bunny girl." "Bun" is an old English word and refers to the distinctive circular shape of the animal's tail. Although the rabbit didn't make its appearance in the British Isles until the twelfth century, its prolific breeding habits meant that it was soon prevalent everywhere and it adopted a little of the same symbolic meaning as the **hare**, minus the mystery accorded the hare as the more elusive nocturnal creature.

Because of its fecundity and gregarious nature, the rabbit is a symbol of love and peace for some Native Americans. There is a courtship ritual called the Rabbit Dance.

The rabbit's **foot** is still seen by some as a particularly potent good-luck charm. While having its foot severed is presumably not very lucky for the rabbit itself, as a totem object the foot is believed to bless its owner with the same fertility and swift-footedness as the animal. The efficacy of the piece of rabbit worn as a charm did not escape the Lakota warriors, who believed that an armband of its skin would enable them to run as fast as the rabbit itself.

Rat

For some superstitious people in Britain, especially those that have links to the **sea**, it is taboo to call the rat by its name, so it's called the "longtail" instead. This is because rats traditionally leave a sinking ship, and this ancient idea runs so deep that rats are still viewed as harbingers of doom. This points towards the power of the rat, since to mention a **name** is to call on the power of its owner.

In the West, much of the symbolism of the rat carries negative connotations. To call someone a "rat" means that they are immoral, despicable, dishonest, and greedy. Rats are considered unclean, scavenging animals, associated with bubonic plague and other diseases.

However, the rat is also a resilient creature and its intelligence and ability to survive almost anything is universally acknowledged. Even these seemingly positive traits are given a negative twist, however, described as "cunning." The intelligence of the creature is seen to be purely self-serving and somehow immoral.

In the Hindu belief system, in contrast, the rat is the creature of foresight and prudence. In addition, in China the rat is one of the rulers of the years of the **Zodiac**, where it symbolizes imagination, creativity, adaptability, and ambition.

Salmon

One of the most sacred creatures of the Celts, the salmon is a symbol of wisdom and esoteric knowledge. In fact, in this culture, the salmon is arguably the epitome of the **fish** symbol in general. To eat the flesh of the salmon was once akin to a shamanistic act, a means of attaining its wisdom as well as its reputed powers of second sight. Celtic folklore teems with anecdotes about the powers conferred by this sacred fish, which is generally depicted living in holy wells and itself eating magical food, such as hazelnuts and rowan-berries.

Finn, one of the most celebrated heroes in Celtic myth, was accredited with immense wisdom and far-sightedness, qualities he attained just by having an accidental taste of some salmon. He was cooking the fish for his master when some of the hot cooking oil splashed onto his **thumb**, which he licked.

The salmon is synonymous with the idea of rebirth and of reincarnation since it traditionally returns to its breeding ground, leaping upwards against the current of the **river** to do so.

Despite the coming of Christianity, the salmon kept its prominent place as a sacred symbol; the use of the fish as an emblem of Christ no doubt helped.

Scarab

The scarab is one of the most important symbols in Ancient Egyptian belief, but why? What relevance, if any, does it have today? Modern Egyptians still believe that dried and powdered scarabs will help them to become fertile. However, it is as the sacred animal belonging of the God of the Rising **Sun**, Khepera, that the scarab is important.

The Ancient Egyptians observed that the scarab beetle rolled its own ball of dung along the ground in the same way that the Khepera rolled the Sun across the sky. They also believed that the scarab hatched itself from this dung ball, symbolizing **death** and rebirth. As a God, the scarab was depicted with the **wings**, **legs** and tail of a **falcon**.

The scarab was placed on top of the **heart** when a corpse was mummified. This was so that the heart, symbolizing the conscience, would not be able to speak because the scarab was in the way. Therefore, the soul could say nothing that might otherwise hinder its access to the Afterlife. Such was the power of the scarab that its image appears everywhere in Ancient Egyptian art and artifacts, on seals and **amulets** and on pieces of jewelry.

The prominence of the scarab for the Egyptians, however, seems to be a very recent trend when we realize that the beetle has been an important symbol since the Paleolithic period, between 10,000 and 20,000 years ago.

SCORPION

Because the scorpion is so dangerous—it has enough venom to kill a man—in the countries where it lives its name is often not mentioned in case the scorpion is somehow "invoked."

Instead it is referred to euphemistically. Whenever this happens we know that an animal is particularly potent.

The scorpion is constantly prepared to attack, the sting in its tail always unsheathed. As such, the insect is the embodiment of brute aggression. This aggression is further promulgated by the fact that the female scorpion will only ever give birth once; her progeny have the grisly habit of destroying their mother by digging their way out of her belly.

The scorpion was a **hieroglyph** in Ancient Egypt and was sacred to the Goddess Selket, who had either the body of a scorpion and the head of a woman, or (more usually) the body of a woman with a scorpion sitting on her head. The power of this Goddess resided in her ability to wield the power of the scorpion against her enemies; however, she could also use this power as protection from scorpions, too. Selket also had power over **snakes** and other poisonous reptiles, protecting pregnant women in particular.

In Hindu belief, the scorpion is a reminder of the constant nearness of death, and is regarded as a "threshold" creature that can open the **doorway** to the next world. Similarly, in the Epic of Gilgamesh, the "Scorpion People" guard the gate to the Underworld.

SEAL

The word "seal" had Anglo-Saxon origins, from *seolb* meaning "to drag," referring to the creature's clumsy movements when on land. In the **sea**, however, the seal is quick and graceful, and uncannily human looking. This is possibly why there's a long tradition of humans turning into seals and back again. In Greek legends the changeling was often a young girl who needed to transform herself in order to escape the pursuit of an amorous God. It would be a quick, clever, and conclusive escape to be able to change into a creature that lived in another dimension to that of the pursuer.

These stories have lead to the seal becoming a symbol of virginity, not for the reason of higher motives such as morality or virtue, but because of fear of the kind of sacrifice involved. **Poseidon**, the Sea God, made the shepherd Proteus the God of the Seals, with the power to shape-shift into any form he chose. Psychologists, therefore, combine both these myths to view the seal as a symbol of the sort of repression that can take many forms.

In the British Isles, the **selkie** epitomizes this hybrid creature, equally at home in the sea and on land, and there are countless tales of sailors seeing **mermaids**, which, on closer inspection, seemed to have transformed themselves into seals …

SERPENT

Lying on its belly close to the **earth**, limbless, hairless and cold-blooded, the snake represents the opposite end of the scale to the loftier spiritual heights to which Man aspires. The snake, or serpent, is arguably one of the most prominent animal symbols, and carries with it diverse and contradictory meanings.

Some of those contradictory messages include the serpent as a symbol of evil but also of healing powers; of cunning and also of wisdom; as a life form that is so base that it

must be capable of reaching the greatest of spiritual heights. The serpent is considered, unsurprisingly, to be a phallic symbol, yet is also one of the oldest emblems of female power, seen, for example, held in the hands of the priestesses on Knossos as a symbol of their wisdom and power. This image brings to mind the latter-day snake handlers of certain charismatic churches in the United States, who believe that so long as they have faith then the snake will not bite them.

The dichotomy of the serpent symbol is embodied in the story of Adam and Eve. Demonized as an evil influence (the Devil himself) that persuades Eve to offer the forbidden fruit of knowledge to Adam, this fruit nevertheless contains knowledge and in eating it, the pair open their eyes to a wider world. As a phallic symbol, the snake also makes Adam and Eve aware of their own sexuality, and the first thing they do after this realization is to cover their genitalia with **fig** leaves. Medieval Christian illustrations of the serpent twining up the **tree** often depict it with the face of a woman, as though to compound the role of the female as evil temptress, causing the man to stray from the straight and narrow path of ascetic virtue. This association of the snake with feminine qualities, however, is not unique.

The serpent is a symbol of regeneration, reincarnation and of healing powers.

The physical characteristics of the creature that give it this reputation include shedding its **skin** and continuing to pulsate after it appears to be dead. The snake is also a very long-lived animal. The snake in this guise is seen twining up the healing rod of **Asclepius**, and of Hygeia, the Greek Goddess of health. In addition, the **caduceus**, which is almost universally accepted as the primary symbol of the healing arts, has two serpents coiling up it, forming a figure-of-eight (an **infinity symbol**) as they epitomize opposing forces in union, striving for the top of the staff. In ancient times, this symbol was the attribute of kings and gods who were seen to have power over **death**, and to the snake were attributed powers of prophecy and the interpretation of dreams. Indian women who desired children honored a similar symbol set up in the grounds of **temples**.

The **hair** of the Goddess Medusa, which was made of snakes, was originally a sign of her immortality, wisdom, and sacredness. It was only when the dominant power shifted from maternal to paternal that she became an object of dread—the Gorgon.

Where the snake is seen with the **eagle**, the bird represents the powers of good triumphing over the powers of evil. In India, the mythical eagle-like **Garuda** was also called Nagantaka, "he who kills serpents." The serpent Nagini, which is the familiar of the arch-villain Voldemort in the *Harry Potter* books, borrows its name from the ancient Indian serpent deity and epitomizes perfectly the idea of the serpent as a symbol of evil and of regeneration.

Evidence of the god-like status of the snake to the Native Americans, too, is evident in structures such as the 4,000-year-old **Serpent Mound** in Ohio. To Native Americans the snake was a dangerous creature, which deserved respect at the same time as suspicion. In fact, such was the reputation of the snake for telling lies and weaving deceit that the forked **tongue** of the creature was adopted as a description fitted to untrustworthy people, namely, the white man.

The **ouroboros**, the ancient circular emblem of a serpent continually swallowing its own tail, epitomizes the symbol that stands for eternity and continual renewal.

Snail

Because the snail disappears and reappears into and out of its shell, it is a lunar emblem, symbolic of seasonal renewal. Snails generally come out when the ground is moist, so they were logically believed to be bringers of **rain**.

Since the snail carries its "house" with it, it is a symbol of self-sufficiency. The **spiral** shape of the snail's shell has significant meaning, since the spiral itself is a sacred shape, the **Golden Mean**. The Mayans took the snail shell as their inspiration to create a glyph for the concept of **zero**; thus, a humble little creature is immortalized in the symbolic rendering of a discovery that, quite literally, changed the world.

The trail of the snail resembles the secretions of not only the **vagina** but also looks like **semen**. Some Africans believed that the snail contained a reservoir of semen. Thus the snail is also a symbol of fertility. In Christian iconography the snail is used as a symbol for a wicked and lazy person, and its slime is considered a sign of lewdness.

SPIDER

Although many people seem to have a particularly irrational fear of spiders, the arachnid family is a curious and interesting one, and the creatures themselves certainly deserve more than the usual horrified reaction.

The motif of the spider as creator/creatrix is repeated all over the world. In many creation myths, it is the spider that weaves the fabric of the universe. However, the seeming fragility of the cobweb led to suppositions that what the spider made was, in fact, no more than the illusory **veil** of "reality" that the Vedic scriptures call Maya. The idea of spinning and weaving is also an attribute of the **Fates**, in both Greek mythology and in the Qu'ran.

Native Americans called the spider the "Thinking Woman," who has the power to both make the world and destroy it if it is not to her satisfaction. In Africa, the spider was supposed to have supplied the materials that created the first man and woman, and also wove the network of the Heavens. Because it could travel in any direction and could fly through the air on its magical thread, the spider was seen as a go-between between Man and the Gods.

Because of this power to move in different dimensions, the spider was used as a means of divination. The African bird-eating spider is particularly skilled in this art, apparently, and symbols are placed at the entrance to its home in such a way that the spider will disturb them as it enters and exits. These disturbances are interpreted as auguries.

Many peoples regard the spider as a disembodied **soul**. Some Vietnamese people believe that the spirit leaves the body during sleep and takes on the form of a spider; therefore, it is very bad luck to kill the creature. It is the spider, too, that weaves the boat that guides the souls of the dead to the Afterlife.

SQUIRREL

It used to be said that a squirrel could travel from the east coast of England westwards to the Irish Sea without once setting foot on ground, so dense were the **forests**. This may be no longer possible, but the symbolism of the squirrel has survived the loss of much of its habitat and it is still seen for many as the epitome of business and industry, and symbolic, too, of the collector (at best) or the hoarder (at worst). This equates the squirrel with selfishness, despite its need to store away food in hidden caches to ensure its winter survival.

In Nordic mythology, the Squirrel lived in the **World Tree** and was sacred to the God of **Fire**. In addition, in Christian legend, the squirrel was apparently so shocked when Adam and Eve ate the **apple** of the **tree** of knowledge that he hid his eyes with his tail, and so was rewarded with an enhanced, super-bushy tail. However, the aforementioned need for the squirrel to secrete its food meant that, like the Devil, he cared too much about material possessions, and so was associated with evil.

STAG

The **horns** of the stag lend it an especial significance as a magical and sacred animal, and as a masculine symbol; most horned animals carry this association, and because of these antlers, the stag is emblematic of fertility and male sexuality. Like the **goat**, it gives rise to the word "horny," meaning sexually charged. Not only are **amulets** representing the **phallus** often carved from stags' horn, but also in some branches of Chinese medicine, ground up horn is used as an **aphrodisiac**. These same horns, because of their shape and the fact that they regularly drop off and then re-grow, are also emblematic of the **World Tree,** therefore making the animal itself synonymous with the idea of rebirth, and therefore of the **Sun**. It is no accident that the Hopi Indians cut their image of the Sun God from a piece of deerskin.

The Pre-Christian pagan God Pan has the cloven hooves and horned headdress of the stag. Wishing to render the old Gods fearsome to their former worshippers in the hopes that they would turn to the One God of the new religion, the early Christians turned Pan into the Devil, giving him the same characteristics, borrowed from the stag. The Celtic **Horned God** Cernunnos bears a remarkable resemblance to Pan, too. Cernunnos was considered the Ruler of the Beasts and a God of Plenty. And so sacred was the stag to the early Swiss peoples that they were often buried with due ceremony alongside human beings and **horses**.

The behavior of the stag informs its symbolic significance. It is a sensitive animal, able to detect scents in the air from a long way off. Stags are also swift to act and can make a lot of ground in a short space of time. The stag is a courageous fighter, and defends his territory vigorously, determinedly clashing horns with the would-be interloper.

Wherever a **white** stag appears in myths and folktales and in dreams, it signifies the world of spirit. In the Arthurian legends, the appearance of this ethereal creature sends the Knights off on spiritual quests. In China, this stag is the symbol of the God of Immortality, Shou-hsien.

The stag is believed to have healing powers, too, and is sometimes depicted with an **arrow** piercing its side and **herbs** in his mouth. The stag has the reputation of knowing the uses of all the medicinal plants and herbs in the forest so presumably he eats these plants in order to fix his wound. In addition, the stag can apparently kill serpents, and where it is depicted trampling the snake underfoot it symbolizes the victory of good over evil. In this context, and because the stag was hunted to use as a sacrifice, it becomes an emblem of Christ. When this is the case, it appears with a **cross** set between its horns.

TIGER

The very word "tiger" conjures up notions of fierceness, swiftness, and also great beauty. To fight like a tiger is to fight with great savagery.

In China, the tiger, rather than the **lion,** is the King of the Beasts. Like the lion, it

symbolizes nobility, power, ferocity, and authority. There is a theoretical difference between the tamed and untamed tiger; the former is somehow able to direct and control its savage nature, whereas the latter is a much more dangerous proposition, governed by raw animal passion rather than reason. The tiger is also somehow seen as an angry animal; this is partly explained by the legend of the first tiger, said to have been a young boy, whipped many times by his teacher hence the stripes, who was pushed too far, escaped into the **forest** in a furious rage and transformed into the animal.

For any warrior, to eat tiger meat or to wear the skin of the tiger is said to give dominion over the beast. A remnant of this belief is borne out by the image of the old buffer in his pith helmet standing on the head of the tiger skin rug, demonstrating the power of his "superior" male ego in the slaying of the beast. Women were forbidden to eat tiger meat in case it made them wayward or difficult to control.

There are parallels between the **wolf** and the tiger, too, as a symbol of raw sexuality.

Chinese myth has a story very similar to the West's Little Red Riding Hood, which features a tiger in the place of the wolf, and there are stories of a fearsome creature called a were-tiger, a nocturnal monster that is driven to terrible acts by the appearance of the full **Moon**. The tiger is believed to be a shape-shifter, and certain human beings have the power to transform themselves into the beast. In these stories, the tiger lives in a sort of tiger village where all the houses are thatched with human **hair**. As with all magical and powerful animals, the name of the tiger is rarely said, but it is referred to euphemistically, for example as the King of the Mountains.

The savage power of the tiger also makes it a symbol of protection; it would be a very great asset to have this animal on your side especially since they are supposed to be able to consume evil spirits with no adverse effects. Because of this, effigies of tigers were placed on graves. The symbol of the tiger is used, too, as a charm by gamblers since the animal is said to be able to guard money. **Five** tigers, in Chinese myth, guard the Universe from every direction; a **red** tiger in the **South**, a **black** tiger in the **North**, a **blue** tiger in the **East**, a **white** tiger in the **West**, and ruling over all, a **golden** tiger in the center. This golden tiger is also the emblem of the Chinese emperor.

The tiger is a very good mother and will defend her cub to the death. An old wives' tale gives advice about what to do if you have stolen a tiger cub. In order to stop the mother tearing you apart, you must throw a **mirror** in her path, whereupon she will be deceived into thinking that her reflection is actually her cub.

The dichotomy of the tiger symbolism—as a savage creature that also protects—is demonstrated perfectly by its place in Buddhist belief. Along with the **monkey** (symbolizing greed) and the **deer** (symbolizing love-sickness), the tiger, representing anger, is one of the Three Senseless Creatures of Chinese Buddhism. Conversely, in Tibetan Buddhism, the tiger takes its place as one of the **Four Dignities**, where it represents confidence, awareness, kindness, and modesty. Buddhists also see the tiger as a symbol of enlightenment and spiritual illumination.

TOAD

The Chan Chu, or Money Toad, was the companion of one of the eight Taoist **Immortals**, Liu Hai. This little three-legged toad is a symbol of money because he liked to relax in dank, dark places and will only be drawn out by a **gold** coin on a string.

TORTOISE

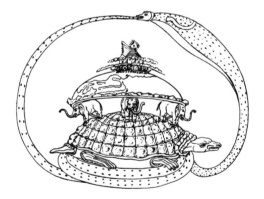

The tortoise may appear to be an innocuous and rather unresponsive slow-moving household pet, but to ancient man it was a living collection of secret and sacred symbols, and as such, it was accorded the same kind of reverence as the greatest Gods.

The **four** sturdy **legs** of the tortoise represent the four elements and the four directions. These legs support the flat underside of the creature, which represents the **Earth**. The dome-shaped shell of the tortoise represents the vault of the Heavens. Thus the tortoise carries the Universe, a task shared by other sacred creatures such as the **whale** and the **dragon**. This is represented in the Hindu **Cosmogram** or map of the Universe, shown here.

The cosmos-supporting tortoise is linked in Hindu iconography to Vishnu, who is said to have emerged from the waters of creation carrying the Earth on his back.

In Mongol tales, a golden tortoise supports the **mountain** at the center of the Universe, which itself symbolizes the **World Axis** or **omphalos**. In Native American belief, too, the **World Tree** grows out of the back of the tortoise.

The longevity of the tortoise makes it a symbol of immortality, and in Japan, it is accorded similar respect to the **crane**, which is also a very long-lived creature. The oldest tortoise on record, called Tui Malila, was at least 188 years of age when she died in 1965. The Mayans honored the tortoise as a lunar animal and give their Moon God a breastplate made of tortoiseshells.

In Greek mythology, the tortoise is associated with the God of the Underworld, no doubt because of its habit of retreating inside its shell. The kingdom of this God was named Tartarus, and holds the same root for the word "tortoise." Its habit of retiring into its shell was viewed by the Hindus as symbolic of meditation—a "turning inward"—so the tortoise is thought to have great spiritual awareness.

In China, legs that are carved to resemble those of the tortoise support imperial tombs, and the tortoise itself is honored as being one of the **Four Sacred Creatures**, along with the **phoenix**, the **dragon**, and the ky-lin, a creature similar to a **unicorn**. In this instance, the tortoise represents the North.

The tortoise was used in several ways for divination; living happily between earth (its base) and heaven (the domed shell top) made the creature the ideal mediator between Man and his Gods. In China, the cracks and fissures on the tortoise's shell were analyzed in order to determine the future course of events.

In **Alchemy**, the tortoise represents the Prima Materia or Massa Confusa, the Confused Mass, the first stage in the transformation of matter to spirit.

Turtle

See **Tortoise**.

Wasp

For many, the wasp is a symbol of bad-tempered irritability because it will sting without provocation. Unlike the **bee**, which is viewed with great affection and for whom the action of stinging results in its own death, the wasp can sting as often as it wishes.

However, in Africa the wasp is considered a sacred creature, able to transmute the profane into something sacred. The wasp is also one of the creatures believed to have introduced **fire** to mankind, so is seen as a helpful and beneficial being.

Weasel

The weasel has a magical reputation, albeit a rather unfortunate one as a shape-shifting creature, once a young woman of dubious reputation until **Hecate**, Queen of the Witches, transformed her. It seems that the weasel is crafty enough to shape-shift into human form again for long enough to marry an unwitting gentleman, but then reverts to her true weasel self once the vows have been said and the register signed on the dotted line.

As well as being associated with Hecate, weasels have a lot in common with other female witches (who were apparently able to transform themselves into weasels). The Ancient Greeks regarded them as harbingers of supernatural evil, so much so that in the event that a weasel should appear in the midst of a gathering then the assembly would hurriedly break up. There was also a curious belief, reported by the Roman naturalist Pliny the Elder, that the weasel "conceives through its **ear** and brings forth its young by way of its **mouth**," which peculiar characteristic made the animal a symbol of speech. There's also a parallel with the Virgin Mary, said to have conceived through her ear when she heard the word of God.

Not everything to do with the weasel is pejorative. It was said to be able to kill the monstrous **serpent**, the **basilisk**, and knew how to use **rue** (the "herb of grace") to restore life. The weasel could intercede between man and God. All these facets of the creature's nature mean that parallels are drawn between it and Christ, who also fought the "serpent" that was the Devil, and interceded with God to spare the souls of mankind.

WHALE

The remarkable story of Jonah and the whale is really a story of initiation, a symbolic **death** and rebirth. The whale in this story was originally referred to as a **fish**, as it was in many old stories. Jonah had been chosen by God as a prophet, but was quite understandably shy of telling the people of Ninevah that judgement would soon be upon them for their wicked ways, so he took to the **sea** to avoid this duty. When a violent storm arose, the sailors decided to throw Jonah into the sea in order to propitiate the Gods. Instantly, the waters calmed, and there appeared a huge "fish" that swallowed Jonah. After three days and nights in the pitch dark innards of this fish, Jonah decided that he had had enough, and that it would be easier to give the prophesy than spend any more time inside the whale. In a fortunate case of either serendipity or divine intervention, Jonah was regurgitated not far from where he needed to be.

Jonah is not the only character to have had the misfortune to spend time inside a whale. This particular form of initiation was the fate of several gods and mythic heroes, from Japan, Vietnam and Polynesia through to Finland.

Jonah described the insides of the whales as *sheol* meaning "the pit," so the gaping jaw of the whale is symbolic of the gates of hell. The stomach of the whale also becomes a symbolic **womb** that gives birth to Jonah. It is signifi-cant, too, that Christ spent the same amount of time inside the tomb before he, too, was reborn; therefore the legend of Jonah's whale was said to prophesy Christ's ordeal.

In Islam, the whale is said to support the Universe. The whale forms the massive base of a tottering pile of objects. On top of the whale stands a **bull**, whose back supports a huge green rock. Standing on the rock is an **angel** that holds up the earth. If the whale starts to wriggle, the balance of the earth can be thrown, which results in **earthquakes**.

Whale hunting is a controversial subject. However, for the Inuit people who have been involved in this practice for thousands of years and so know the animal very well, the whale is the trickster. There is a myth that a beautiful woman lives in a lavishly furnished apartment inside the belly of the whale, and this lovely woman occasionally entertains mariners; a story no doubt invented to comfort a drowning man.

WOLF

The wolf that disguises itself as the grandmother in the tale of Little Red Riding Hood shows the creature as a trickster, with malevolent intentions. However, the disguise isn't very good and the little girl recognizes the wolf by its easily identifiable features—huge **teeth** and massive **eyes**—and so makes good her escape. Here, the wolf is also a sexual predator, another emblem of the animal that has endured since ancient times; the "wolf whistle" is aptly named and the tendencies of the wolf itself are well known. Like the wolf in the fairytale, its true nature is impossible to disguise for long, just like the proverbial "wolf in sheep's clothing."

The wolf also has a reputation of being a loner, hunting not in packs but singly. In Greece, it was associated with the Gods Zeus and Apollo as a symbol of masculine power, energy, and sexuality. The Egyptians, too, worshipped the wolf, at the city of Lycopolis, which was even named for the creature. Here, the wolf also acted as a psychopomp, a creature that guided the **souls** of the dead into the Afterlife. **Anubis**, the greatest of all the conductors of souls, had the head of a wolf or of a wild **dog** or **jackal**. The God of Time, Chronos, has a wolf-like face symbolizing the monster that devours human **time**.

It was a wolf that sucked Romulus and Remus, the legendary founders of Rome. Despite this maternal care, the word *lupa* meant "prostitute" as well as "she-wolf" and the Lupercal Temples were, effectively brothels. Continuing with this theme, there's a saying in France that if a girl is a virgin she is said to *n'a jamais vu le loup*, i.e. to have never seen the wolf; the opposite is true for a girl who has lost her virginity.

The perceived virility of the wolf makes it a potent fertility symbol, and some tribal people call upon the wolf to help them conceive. This idea is symbolized in the folk traditions of the far north-east of Russia, where a wolf made of straw is kept for the year to help the women of the village to conceive easily. The **bezoar**—a hard, stone-like object that comes from the stomach of an animal—is said to be most potent if it comes from the wolf.

The werewolf is arguably the most sinister aspect of this creature. Warlocks were believed to be able to transform into wolves in order to disguise themselves when they traveled to their unholy meetings, and the belief in a wolf/human hybrid is prevalent throughout much of the World.

WORM

The worm is not always the common or garden worm, but is the word sometimes used also for **dragons**, legged **lizards**, and **snakes**. However, it is the former kind of worm that is dealt with here.

To call someone a "worm" means that they are weak, indecisive, and ineffectual. However, the worm itself, as a symbol, carries powerful associations with it, being a creature with connections to both life and **death**: specifically, new life created from the corruption of death. In China, legend says that humankind was created from the worms that fed on the corpse of the first, primordial being. Although it might seem repugnant to us, the task of the worm in breaking down organic matter is an essential job and it seems unfair to despise a creature for such a useful contribution. The worm is a humble creature, literally and figuratively lowly. The worm motif has been used in mythology to show the lowly origins of illustrious people. Cuchulain, the great Celtic hero, for example, was allegedly born from a worm that his mother inadvertently swallowed.

FANTASTICAL ANIMALS

As though all the real animals in this world were not enough, we have invented a vast array of mythical animals, too, which fulfil a symbolic need not provided by the many wonders within the natural world. Some of these fantastic creatures happen to be very convenient for this purpose; for example, hybrid beasts prove a handy sort of symbolic shorthand within **heraldry**, often morphing the qualities and talents of several animals into one zoological curiosity.

Belief in imaginary creatures seems to last for a season, then fades away, to be replaced with the next "fashion." For example, it was once generally held that **dragons** really did exist; uncharted territory is marked on old maps with the legend "here be dragons." Winged, **fire**-breathing, **serpent**-like creatures seem to exist in a similar form all over the world although their names may vary. **Fairies**, too, were regularly spotted, and even photographed in the early part of the last century. Today, it seems that creatures from outer space—and infamous fantastic creatures like the yeti or the Big Cat or the Loch Ness Monster—fill the space that is somehow still not satisfied by all the world has to offer. These newer creatures, too, teasingly allow themselves to be seen but rarely in such a way that they give us incontrovertible evidence of their existence. And why should they? **Ghosts** and similar entities have never gone away, and if we believe the evidence of high street bookshops then it would seem that **angels** and cherubs hover above every corner.

It's interesting to think whether fantastical creatures exist in the past or in the present. If the former, when did they start to become obsolete? If we believe that these creatures truly are mythical, then can they still exist in the present as symbols? The answer to this question has to be a whole-hearted yes. Operating under the premise that if enough people believe in something then it must be true, for the most part these creatures are described here as though they really do exist. Despite their arcane origins, symbolically, these creatures still have a great deal to offer, many of them showing interesting aspects of the workings of the human psyche. It is also worth bearing in mind that illusion exists on many levels and that our own version of reality may be just one of them.

ANGEL

There always seems to have been a belief in the existence of certain (usually invisible) creatures that inhabit a spiritual realm, and which are able to act as mediators between humans and their God or Gods. Indeed, the word "angel" comes from the Greek *angelos*, meaning "messenger." The Hebrew word for such creatures is *malakh*, which effectively translates as "shadow side of God," as well as "messenger." The antiquity of angels is well established, their existence described long before the Old Testament was written, and certainly long before the coming of

Christianity. The first creatures that resemble anything like the angels we know today are from the ancient Akkadian culture, dating back to 2350 BC. It is likely that the angel concept existed even earlier than this, though. Interpretations of these creatures exist the world over, albeit with different names; for example, in India we have Devas, Rakshashas and Rishis; in Africa and Brazil they are called Orishas; in Japan there are Yokai and Oni. In short, there are dozens of interpretations on the theme.

The defining physical characteristic of the angel is its **wings**, themselves symbolic of transcendence from the earthly plane. These wings enable flight, and it is no coincidence that many of the first angel images are feathered **bird**/human hybrid figures.

The history of angelic beings is difficult to pin down. The single most comprehensive and exhaustive writing on the subject is by a somewhat nebulous figure called Pseudo Dionysus the Aeropagite, who listed the groupings of angels that are still commonly accepted today, in a book written in the sixth century AD, called *The Celestial Hierarchy*. Both Pseudo Dionysus and the Bible agree that the multitude of angels is immense, this number being mentioned in the Bible as a mind-boggling "a thousand thousands [angels] ministered unto him, and ten thousand times ten thousand stood before him" (Daniel 7:10). That angels operate in a metaphysical environment closed to humankind is evidenced by the analogy of the many angels that can dance on the head of a pin despite apparently being colossal, multi-winged creatures.

These terrible biblical creatures bear very little resemblance to the high street "angels" that have become almost ubiquitous symbols of the "Mind Body Spirit" movement. The original angels were awe-inspiring creatures that guarded and protected mankind as well as bringing messages from a Divine Being.

The notion that each person has his own guardian angel is, however, an ancient one. This is a comforting idea, especially for children. This is not, however, mentioned as such in the Bible, although it does claim that each one of the faithful is helped by an angel that will protect and guide him throughout his life. It appears that the angel archetype is such a potent symbol that they exist as in our collective consciousness whether or not we believe in any kind of God.

BASILISK

Many supposedly mythological animals have their origins in a perfectly "normal" natural creature. The real-life basilisk is a hooded **lizard** with an inflatable crest on its **head**. However, the basilisk that has occupied a place in the psyche of humankind as a terrifying creature whose glance or breath proves fatal is a hybrid creature, combining elements of **bird** and **snake**. The basilisk, apparently, hatched from a deformed **egg**, which had been deposited on a dung heap by an elderly hen and hatched by a **toad**, all contributory factors to its being a symbol of evil and ungodliness, as befits a serpent hybrid.

The evil basilisk ran amok, alternately smashing up everything in its path or else consuming obstacles with the **fire** it breathed. The Roman writer Pliny the Elder tells the tale of a horseman who thought he had killed the basilisk by plunging a spear into it. However, the creature was so venomous that poison shot back up the spear, killing both **horse** and rider. The successful basilisk slayer needed to get the animal to glance into a **mirror**, at which it would self-destruct, killed by its own reflection.

Curiously, the only natural creature that could face the basilisk without suffering any ill consequences was the **weasel**, provided it had eaten **rue**, the "Herb of Grace," beforehand. In Worcester Cathedral in the UK there is a carving of a basilisk with a weasel at either side. These weasels have foliage in their mouths, and here the basilisk symbolizes Satan defeated by the Old and New Testaments.

Psychologists say that the basilisk represents the unconscious mind that needs to be confronted and understood.

BEHEMOTH

There are conflicting reports as to the origins of the behemoth and what form it takes. It could be a derivative of the Hindu **elephant**-headed deity **Ganesh**, since most pictures of the creature depict it with the head of an elephant and an upright body like that of a man. The word "behemoth" is the plural of a Hebrew word meaning "animal" and accounts from the Bible—where it appears in the Book of Job—describe it thus:

He eateth grass as an ox.
Lo now, his strength is in his loins, and his force in
*   the navel of his belly.*
He moveth his tail like a cedar; the sinews of his
*   thighs are wrapped together.*
His bones are as strong pieces of brass; his bones are
*   like bars of iron.*

Further on we are told:

Behold, he drinketh up a river and hasteth not: he
*   trusteth that he can draw up Jordan into his*
*   mouth.*

By the way, the ox mentioned is not the gentle domesticated beast of burden, but the water ox or **hippopotamus**.

The behemoth, then, is symbolic of the force and strength of the animal nature, combining elements of the most powerful and brutish of creatures. The word is often used to describe something almost unfeasibly large and powerful.

The male behemoth, which lives on land, has a female counterpart, the leviathan, whose dominion is the **sea**. An ancient myth says that at the Day of Judgement these creatures will slay each other in a terrible battle, their bodies served up at a huge banquet, and their skins used by God to create shelter for righteous people. Both creatures are also described as demonic entities.

CENTAUR

A **horse**/man hybrid, the centaur appears as the archer in the astrological sign of **Sagittarius**, and wherever he appears, he is a symbol of lust, the **arrows** signifying ejaculation as well as hunting prowess. Therefore, the centaur represents the animal nature of the male human. Greek myths tell us that the centaur lived wild on the mountaintops, eating raw meat and unable to drink any **wine** at all without getting extremely drunk.

Centaurs are often depicted with sad faces, because they know that the brute force and lust that they represent needs to be balanced with spiritual power. Therefore, the centaur represents the constant struggle in human beings between spirit and matter, intuition and knowledge, conscious and unconscious.

CHIMAERA

A hybrid creature constructed from the body of a **goat** and the tail of a **snake** or **dragon**, the chimaera also has the head of a **lion** and secondary head with a goat-like appearance. It is first mentioned in Homer's Iliad. Generally held to be female, despite having the head of a lion rather than a lioness, her mother was Echidna, a **fire**-breathing monster with three heads (including that of a one-eyed lion) and the hind-quarters of a dragon and the body of a goat. Chimaera's father was equally fearsome, having a hundred snakelike heads each of which breathed fire, and serpents around his thighs. Given these antecedents, it seems as though the chimaera got off lightly; her appearance could have been even stranger.

Chimaera was said to be the mother of the **sphinx**, and sighting her was a very bad omen indeed, presaging storms, shipwrecks, and other natural disasters, **volcanoes** in particular. Chimaera was eventually destroyed by Bellerophon with the help of Pegasus, the flying **horse**. By flying through the air, the fiery breath of the chimaera could not injure Bellerophon.

The provenance of the chimaera symbol is extremely ancient and it is possible that it may represent the spirit or embodiment of volcanic action.

DEMON

The idea of a creature that is the personification of evil forces is ancient. There are incantations designed to repel "demons" that date back as far as the first millennium BC although they are not referred to as such. Essentially, in a world that is comprised of opposing forces, there must be a balance of male/female, black/white, good/bad. It makes sense that we need there to be a shadow side to good forces.

Although the demon, as it is commonly accepted today, is seen to be a malicious and ungodly creature that is the epitome of evil, the word originally meant something rather different. The Greek "daemon" was a divine being with its own energies and powers; each person had such an aspect to their **soul**, which was connected to the Great Spirit and could be responsible for sudden flashes of inspiration or enlightenment; literally, their "genius." This essential spirit helped its human owner to connect with a higher consciousness. Places, too, had their "demons," represented, for example, in the spirits of the elements: the **salamanders**, **sylphs**, **nymphs**, and **undines**. Philip Pullman's *His Dark Materials* trilogy uses the notion of this familiar spirit in a beautiful and memorable way.

Many of the pre-Christian deities of all nations had these creative, demon-like qualities. However, these ancient entities, if not absorbed and re-named as saints, were heavily discredited by the early Church and made into evil entities in the effort to replace the old pagan Gods with the one patriarchal God of the Christian faith. These evil beings, or demons, are described in many different ways and include **fairies**, **pixies**, **elves**,

goblins, and many others. To "demonize" something or someone is to "represent as a demon," i.e. to discredit or contaminate in some way.

Lilith, the first wife of Adam, is commonly described as an "arch demoness." Lilith already existed in a different form as the ancient Goddess **Astarte**, who is connected to **Venus/Aphrodite**, but Lilith's refusal to adopt the missionary position, among other things, meant that she was cast out and replaced with the (seemingly) much more compliant Eve. Thereafter, Lilith was accused of all sorts of diabolic misdemeanors.

There is also the idea that demons are the result either of **angels** mating with ordinary human women or they are angels who have rejected their god-like nature. These evil demons are supposed to be able to take possession of human people in order to carry out their evil plans. Psychologically speaking, the demon has come to symbolize the difficult part of the personality or psyche that a person has to come to terms with in order to achieve balance and peace of mind.

Djinn

Also called Genie, the Djinn are Arabic spirits. Muslims viewed them with the same suspicion that Christians accorded to creatures belonging to the Old Religion, although Djinn are believed to be redeemable if they turn to Allah.

Although the word Djinn does not have the same origins as the word "genie," which comes from the Latin *genius*, they share a similar meaning as the superior part of the **soul**, a sort of familiar, psychic double, or "super-ego." They also represent the part of the soul that is enhanced by enlightenment.

In the story of Aladdin, the magical lamp that he polishes so assiduously represents his soul. The polishing represents enlightenment, brought about by conscious effort, and the genie that emerges is symbolic of Aladdin's enlightened self, possibility, and potential; the three wishes represent discipline and lessons learned as a result of direct experience, and also the necessity to curb desire.

Double-headed eagle

This curious symbol is believed to have originated with the Hittites, a powerful race from Asia Minor. The double-headed **eagle** is popular throughout the world, and like its single-headed brother, often holds a **serpent** in its talons or sometimes a **hare**, a lunar symbol that is therefore the opposite of the solar eagle.

The double head of the eagle effectively doubles its strength and eagle-like qualities. It is also called the Eagle of Lagash. This was the ancient Sumerian city that used it first as their royal crest. The Turks then used the symbol. It represents omniscience, since it can look in two directions at once. As a symbol of absolute power, it appears on several national coats of arms including those of Imperial Austria and Russia. It is also used as a Masonic symbol.

Dragon

Ancient maps, showing uncharted territory, are sometimes enscribed with the legend "Here Be Dragons." The word "dragon" comes from the Greek for "**snake**," a creature with whom it is associated, as well as sometimes being referred to as a "**worm**" from its Germanic name, *wurm*.

For an imaginary creature, the influence of the dragon is far-reaching, existing in similar forms all over the world, an important archetypal emblem. The dragon can be symbolic of power, sovereignty, and spirituality, as well as of a variety of elements. The dragon can be an agent of good, to be encouraged, or an agent of evil, to be destroyed. Dragons have keen eyesight which often makes them guardians of treasure and keepers of secrets of some kind, a trait which gives them great wisdom as well as clairvoyant powers.

In China, the Dragon is the chief of the **Four Divine Creatures**, only one of which, the **tortoise**, is real. The other two are the **unicorn** and the **phoenix**. The dragon represents the spirit of change, an important principle in the Taoist religion. In both China and Japan the dragon symbolized royalty, and appeared on the garments of the Emperor and the Mikado. The very word "dragon" was used instead of Emperor: "the Dragon's Face" meant the face of the Emperor, "the Dragon's Pace" his majestic walk.

The dragon was used as a symbol of power on the shields of Norse warriors, designed both to protect the carrier and to frighten the enemy. In Britain, Uther Pendragon, father of King Arthur, was given a vision of a flaming dragon in the sky as a prophecy that Arthur would become king. This flaming **red** dragon later became the emblem of Wales. Over the border the Englishman George was given sainthood after he effectively killed a marauding dragon that was slowly but surely gobbling up all the young girls for miles around. Here, the dragon represents the Devil, also personified as a dragon in the fight with the Archangel Michael.

In the **Chinese Zodiac**, the dragon is the fifth creature, and equates to **Leo** the **Lion**.

Elf

Similar to the **Pixie**, which is localized in the Cornish peninsula of Great Britain, the elf has a wider range, appearing in folklore that stretches right across northern Europe. Like the pixie, the elf could be a useful ally to humankind and is treated with due respect and consideration. In particular, elves seem to be keen on making boots and other footwear.

Elves discreetly sank into the background with the coming of Christianity, since they belong to the old pagan beliefs. However, their influence in Germanic and Scandinavian myth and legend is pervasive. There are many different kinds of elves; they live in **woods** and on **mountains**, there are elves that prefer watery habitats, and others that favor a domestic setting. In Norse legend, elves live in Alfheimr, which equates with Fairyland.

Like pixies, elves can take a human being away with them for a time, sometimes for several years, although this time always appears as short as the blink of an eye. They can also swap human children for elvish children; these infants, who soon start to develop peculiarly magical characteristics, are called Changelings.

Elves have a malicious side, too. In Germany, the word for "nightmare" is *Albtraum*, and these disturbing dreams are said to be brought by elves. Latterly, J.R.R. Tolkien's trilogy *The Lord of the Rings* has informed our ideas as to the appearance and nature of elves.

Some people believe that ingestion of psychotropic substances that occur naturally in the landscape—such as various kinds of magic **mushrooms**—will induce sightings and/or visions of elves and other nature spirits, since they have dominion over these plants.

Fairy

The term "fairy" tends to be used as a catch-all to encompass all manner of "little people"—**elves**, **pixies**, banshees, and the like—all different aspects of a spirit of nature that is generally held to be invisible to human beings. Fairies have long been cemented into the human psyche and some

people even claim to have seen fairies or otherwise interacted with them, and their symbolic role, accordingly, is important. It has been said that they represent the "paranormal powers of the spirit or the extraordinary capacity of the imagination," and as such can be said to symbolize an escapist aspect of the human mind that transcends the bounds of everyday normality as well as the laws of physics.

For generations, it seems that fairy-folk and human beings have rubbed along, side by side, sharing the same universe. It is possible that these creatures have their origins as the spirits of dead ancestors, which, prior to the coming of Christianity, were believed to take on a different form in order to guard and protect future generations. Features typical of the fairy are its supernatural powers, its ability to render itself invisible to human beings or to shape-shift, its spell-casting powers and its capability of flight. Fairies tend to appear as females but there are exceptions.

Fairies can be benign or malignant, and the natural world is crammed with plants, minerals and the like which can either protect against them or which are their especial domain or property. The **hawthorn**, for example, is a fairy tree and anyone cutting it down or taking parts of it would find it best to ask permission of the fairies first.

The word "fairy" shares roots with the word "fay," which in turn relates to the **Fates** of Greek myth, the personification of destiny. Morgan le Fay, also known as the Fata Morgana in the Arthurian tales, is a fairy, although very different from the tiny sort that little girls see flitting in and out of flowers, as are many of the most powerful fairy creatures throughout mythology. The Shakespearian Queen of the Fairies, Mab, represents the same kind of ambivalence as Morgan le Fay, with a propensity for malice that hints at a strong link between fairies and witches. Both fairies and witches often appear in groups of **three**, another link with the Fates.

In the story of Sleeping Beauty, the fairy that is not invited to the christening shows her dark side by cursing the baby, and is a reminder of the need to propitiate these contrary beings, which do not share the same moral values as human beings.

The time of the fairies is said to be **twilight**, the transitional time between night and day. They can carry away the soul of a person who dies this time and take it back to fairyland. The fairy could be said to symbolize the state of mind between childhood and adulthood, the conscious and the unconscious.

The Fates

The Fates appear in Greek myth as the Moraei, as the Norns in Norse myth, and in Roman stories as the Parcae. These **three** women are the personification of destiny, and are symbolized as weavers, working with the metaphorical thread of life to spin out the destiny of every living being, even, it was said, after **death** on the Earthly plane. Even the Gods were subject to the workings of the Fates and feared them accordingly.

The Greek names of the Fates also reflect this notion of the working of a piece of cloth, the "fabric of life": Clotho, the spinner, spins that thread of life; Lachesis measures the lifespan with her rule or measure; and Atropos—

meaning "unturning" and whose name carries the same root as "atrophy"—decides when the thread should be cut, i.e. when the person should die. Atropos also decided the method of demise. The analogy of the weaver as the one who decides upon the pattern of an individual life is shared by the different manifestations of the **spider** Goddess.

The Fates are generally depicted as heartless, calculating women. There is a wonderful portrayal of them to be seen at Castell Coch, the medieval castle in South Wales that was restored in the nineteenth century by the Marquess of Bute and designed by William Burges.

Father Christmas

Santa Claus, Old St. Nick, St. Nicolas, Sinterklaas, Papa Noel, Kris Kringle: whatever we choose to call him, for children, the concept of Father Christmas all boils down to the same idea; that of a magical, generous character that comes bearings gifts at Christmas time. The idea that good children will be rewarded with gifts while bad children will receive nothing has more than a semblance of the idea of rewards in Heaven for the virtuous and is arguably one of the consequences of the Christianization of a much earlier, pagan figure.

The name and form of this character may have altered over the centuries, and the actual character is an amalgam of different historical and mythological figures. However, it's fair to say that people in the northern hemisphere share a common desire to perk up the winter months with some kind of a celebration, and Santa is a part of this desire.

These days, the popular image of Father Christmas is of a bearded, jovial old gentleman, of portly girth, wearing **red**. Clearly an expert in quantum physics and a past master in time bending, Santa apparently manages to visit every single household where children live, in one very exhausting night, traveling through the skies with a retinue of magical reindeer that have the powers of flight. In fact, his brightly colored garb is a relatively recent introduction, though not, as popularly supposed, wholly invented by the Coca-Cola corporation but certainly popularized by them, inspired by an earlier cartoon that appeared in 1863, by one Thomas Nast whose work appeared in *Harpers Weekly* in the United States. Despite its comparatively recent age, this depiction of Santa as we recognize him today is now ubiquitous; it's an etching showing a smiling old man with **holly** tucked into the brim of his hat, clutching a pipe in one hand with a bundle of toys and gifts under his arm. Prior to Nast's interpretation, Father Christmas's appearance was much more subdued—a taller, slimmer figure dressed in a slubby **brown** or **green** color, as befitting his origins as a pagan spirit of nature.

One of the manifestations of this ancient nature spirit is in the guise of "Old Winter," personified in a Norse ritual whereby an old man went from door to door, fed and watered wherever he went. The idea was to propitiate the spirit of the winter. Santa, too, has food and drink left for him. Similarly, the God **Odin** (who also appears to humans as an old man with a **beard**) had a huge feast at Yule for the slain warriors in Valhalla. Children left their **shoes** stuffed with food for Odin's eight-legged **horse**, Sleipnir; in exchange, Sleipnir refilled these boots with gifts. These customs seem to have merged with the boisterous midwinter **Saturnalia** festival of the Romans. Later, in efforts to Christianize this pagan character, he was linked to St. Nicholas, a fourth-century Christian bishop born in Patara in Turkey who was known for his generosity. Indeed, in some parts of northern Europe, St. Nick still appears in the robes and hat of a bishop.

Santa's reindeer, it seems, are particularly appropriate animals to transport him through time and space. They carry much the same symbolism of the **horse**, able to conduct spirits between the world of the living and the dead. Lapps capture these wild animals in a very canny way. Reindeer are partial to the red and white fly agaric **mushrooms**, which contain psychoactive substances that induce hallucinations of flying. The Lapps scatter the mushrooms where the animals will find them, then simply wait until the reindeer are intoxicated, and lead them away.

The increasing commercialization of Christmas seems to run in tandem with Santa's brightly colored clothes. For example, in parts of India, the symbol of a chubby genie, also dressed in red and white but propelled by a flying carpet rather than by reindeer, heralds the start of a gigantic winter shopping spree.

THE FURIES

Known as the Erinyes ("angry ones") in Greek myth, the three Furies are aptly named since they are the personification of vengeance, and represent an aspect of the **Triple Goddess** as a lawmaker and as the one who metes out punishments.

Their names are Alecto (unceasing), Megaera (grudging) and Tisiphone (the avenger). The heads of the Furies are crowned with **serpents**, like the Gorgon Medusa, and here the serpent is symbolic of the destructive aspect of female power. Furthermore, the **eyes** of the Furies are described as dripping **blood**, and so they present an altogether terrifying sight.

The Furies guard the natural order of things and are quick to punish any transgressor of the natural laws of the Universe; sins such as matricide or patricide were particularly prone to the wrath of the Furies. Additionally, the power of the Furies was such that they were said to be older than the Gods themselves, who were also subject to their rules, as they were the workings of the Fates.

GARUDA

A mythological **bird** belonging to the Hindu pantheon, the Garuda carries the God Vishnu upon its back, being the "vehicle" or steed of the God. Where this description is used, it is generally taken to mean that the God not only rides the creature but also is somehow contained within it, either sharing a part of its **soul** or being able to shape-shift into its form. Garuda is described as a "golden-winged sun bird" and shares aspects of its appearance, as well as symbolic meaning, with the **eagle**, the simurgh and the **phoenix**. The appearance of the Garuda varies. Sometimes it is a bird, sometimes a winged man, and sometimes a hybrid man/bird combination.

Garuda is an ally of man and the enemy of Naga, the **serpent**; the bird is often depicted with the snake in its talons, wrestling it, an image shared by the eagle and symbolic of the struggle between the heaven and the earth (spirit and matter) and also between **fire** and **water**; the hot sun (Garuda) causing the streams and rivers to shrivel up and die.

GENIE

See **Djinn**.

GHOST

The idea that when a material being dies it leaves behind a shadowy imprint that will haunt the places it once inhabited, is one that resonates around the world. The pervasiveness of the idea of the ghost indicates that it plays an important and deep-rooted part in the human psyche. Even the concept of a Heaven or Hell or other Afterlife as a home for the disembodied spirit has not changed the fact that for many people, ghosts actually exist. Ghosts do not have to be human; animals, too, can haunt the places of the living.

Communication with ghosts used to be called necromancy and was considered by superstitious Christians to be one of the Black Arts. Today, this practice is called Spiritualism, and the form of a Spiritualist ritual includes a nod to a Christian God at the beginning and end of the ceremony. This is despite the fact that in Christian belief, the ghosts that still walked the Earth were generally of those people who had not been buried under the auspices of the Church and were therefore to be avoided.

Ghosts can have good or evil intentions. Sometimes, they appear with an essential message that they feel necessary to impart to a living being, possibly as evidence of survival after physical **death**. Ghosts represent the almost universal need for human beings to believe in a form of consciousness that exists after the physical death of the body.

The old festival of Samhuin, renamed as **Halloween**, is said to be the time when the **veil** between the two Worlds is at its thinnest, the time of the ending of the pre-Christian year and the beginning of the new one. This time is traditionally set aside to acknowledge the ghosts of the ancestors.

GNOME

One of the four elemental beings, the Gnome is the spirit of the **Earth**, and is a counterpart of the **undine** (water), the **salamander** (fire), and the **sylph** (air). Gnomes are believed to live in the bowels of the Earth and to have an instinctive and intuitive understanding of the rocks, stones, precious gems and **minerals** secreted there, able to produce fantastically elaborate silverwork, for example, which has magical powers.

The alchemist Paracelsus described gnomes as being "two spans high, and taciturn." Gnomes are said to be fickle, hard to pin down, friendly at one minute and hostile the next, and this awkward reputation extends to most parts of the world. The symbolic meaning of the gnome is of a being, invisible to the naked **eye** and buried deep in the **caves** and tunnels of the subconscious, that comes in dreams, sudden flashes of inspiration or intuition, to reveal something other-

wise hidden, be it a real, physical object or an idea.

Swiss bankers are sometimes described as the Gnomes of Zurich because, like the elemental gnomes, they also guard "treasure," in the form of money, which is kept underground.

Garden gnomes are a popular ornament that originated in Germany in the nineteenth century. They are small, with pointy hats, and often carry spades or other gardening tools. Some believe that this kind of statuary symbolizes the height of bad taste.

GOBLIN

The goblin, like the gnome, is said to inhabit underground areas such as **caves**, tunnels, and mines but unlike the gnome, they can live closer to the surface of the earth, lurking in among **tree** roots and under hedges. They generally have a more sinister aspect than gnomes, being even more prone to malicious behavior, which is particularly directed toward human beings who may have incurred their wrath. In Scandinavia, the word for goblin is *skratti*, which equates to a devil or **demon**.

Hopeful goblins-spotters can find the creatures in various places around the world that bear their name, such as Bryn y Ellyon, "the Hill of the Goblins" in Somerset in the UK, or at the Gap of Goeblin, in France. In Tolkien's *The Lord of the Rings*, goblins equate to the fearsome creatures called Orcs, who live underground and are the epitome of evil brute force.

The Graces

Also referred to as the Three Charities, the Graces represent another, more gentle aspect of the **Triple Goddess** along with the **Furies** and the **Fates**. The three Graces are Aglaia (the youngest of the three whose name means "beauty"), Euphrosyne ("mirth"), and Thalia, the eldest, whose name means "good cheer." They are often depicted in paintings and statuary, three beautiful naked women, one usually with her back to the viewer.

Collectively, the Graces also represent aspects of the Goddess **Aphrodite**, and have dominion over love, beauty, kindness, fertility, creativity, and sensuality. Companions to the **Muses**, the Graces, like them, are believed to inspire artists and artisans to create works of great beauty.

Griffin

The griffin has the body of a **lion** and the head of an **eagle**, sometimes with prominent tufted **ears**. It usually has **wings**, but not always.

The griffin is sometimes confused with the **wyvern**, but has four legs unlike the wyvern with only two. These legs end in eagles' talons, too. As a composite of two particularly powerful creatures, which are themselves rich in symbolic meaning, the griffin is believed to be particularly important, possessing power equal to that of the Gods whom it is often seen guarding. In his play Prometheus Unbound, Aeschylus refers to them as "the sharp-toothed hounds of Zeus that do not bark." The griffin serves as an admirable symbol in **heraldry**, economically representing the attributes of the eagle and the lion in one single animal.

The griffin appears in many civilizations including Greek and Egyptian, and its key feature is to protect precious objects. In Crete, it was considered the guardian of throne rooms, and in central Asia, it guarded the valuable deposits of **gold** and precious gems that could be found there, descending upon anyone who appeared to be a threat and tearing them to pieces with their talons.

In medieval symbolism, the griffin represented knowledge, and later it came to signify the idea of a guardian; the ears represented attentiveness, the lion's body was for courage, the beak stood for tenacity.

The hippogriff, recently brought from mythological obscurity when it starred in the *Harry Potter* series of books by J.K. Rowling, is the product of a liaison between a griffin and a **horse**.

HARPY

In Greek myth, the harpies are monstrous creatures comprised of the bodies of **birds** and the heads of women, with sharp talons, that emit a disgusting smell. The name "harpy" means "snatcher" or "plucker." The harpies eat carrion, and are **three** in number, called "Dark," "Squall," and "Swift Flyer." These names are suggestive of storm clouds, and it is interesting to note that this imagery is carried further by the fact that only Calais and Zetes, the sons of the North Wind, could get rid of the harpies by driving them away. Greedy and malicious, the harpies supplied the Lords of the Underworld with the souls of people who had died before their time.

HOBGOBLIN

Whereas **goblins** dwell outside, in underground places or in gnarly **tree** roots, the hobgoblin likes to stay indoors, literally, by the hob or stove, although the word "hob" can also mean "elf." Originally, hobgoblins were protectors of the home, related to the spirits of the ancestors whose corpses were traditionally buried under the threshold or under the central **fire**, and which guarded the family. Hobgoblins, like other pre-Christian entities, were demonized by the Church in its attempt to turn people away from the old religion in favor of the new one.

IMP

The word "imp" comes from the Greek *emphytos*, meaning to implant or graft, and which came to mean a young bud or a child. The supernatural creature is believed to be the **ghost** of a child, mischievous and often malicious, a sort of junior **demon** and in league with the Devil to plague the lives of human beings. Naughty children are still sometimes referred to as imps, meaning "little devils."

INCUBUS

The incubus is a **demon** that takes the form of an attractive gentleman who seduces sleeping people—most frequently women but sometimes men—and has sexual intercourse with them, in the same way as his female counterpart the **succubus**. This creature sustains itself from the sexual energy released by his hapless partner at the point of orgasm, and repeated visits may even result in the death of the victim.

The provenance of the **incubus** is ancient, first appearing in Mesopotamia as a character called Lilu, the male counterpart of **Lilith**. Both incubi and succubi are not inherently male and female but are able to shift into either form to assuage their prodigious sexual appetites. The female succubi can "steal" sperm from human men, then turn into an incubi and use that same semen to impregnate women.

Sometimes, these demons are able to conceive and give birth to children. The resulting offspring will naturally have supernatural powers as well as being incredibly persuasive.

Both the Shakespearian character Caliban, and Merlin from the Arthurian tales, are examples of such a hybrid, called a Cambion.

KELPIE

Similar to the **Pooka** of Irish myth and the Ceffyl Dwr in Wales, in Scotland the kelpie is a **water** spirit that appears in the form of a **seal** or, more usually, a pure **white horse**. Generally malicious, the kelpie takes delight in luring people onto its back and then plunging into a lake and vanishing, drowning the hapless human. A creature with the same trait appears in Scandinavian stories as a Nix.

The kelpie, it is said, can breed with humans. The resulting offspring is a beautiful fleet-footed creature.

MELUSINE

A **water** spirit akin to a **mermaid** that often appears with a double tail, there are contradictory stories as to the provenance of the Melusine. A medieval fairytale tells of a Count Raimondin who fell in love with a beautiful woman called Melusine, who agreed to marry him provided he promised faithfully that he would leave her alone every Saturday. One day a week she disappeared into her bathroom and spent all day in there; she wasn't simply beautifying herself, but reverting to her true form, described sometimes as having the tail of a **serpent** and sometimes the tail of a **fish**. One day the Count, consumed with jealousy, broke his promise and spied on Melusine as she lay in her bath. She forgave him for breaking his

promise, but Raimondin used this secret as a weapon, calling her a serpent in front of the court during a disagreement. Melusine turned into a **dragon** and flew away, never to return. The lesson of this story is simple: using someone's hidden secret or weakness against them is the worst kind of cowardly betrayal.

The ancient French family of Lusignan are said to have a melusine as a family spirit, who prophesies a **death** by wailing from the ramparts. The melusine appears, too, as a symbol of **alchemy**. Here, she represents harmony and the union of opposites, for example spirit and matter, earth and water, male and female.

MERMAID

Mermaids may be perceived nowadays as creatures that belong only within the realms of mythology and the imagination, but this was not always the case. Until the nineteenth century, there was still a law on the statute books, decreeing that any mermaid found in British waters was the property of the Crown.

Indeed, Christopher Columbus reported seeing mermaids on his voyage to America, although what he actually saw might have been a marine animal called a manatee that, notably, cradles its young in its **arms** in the same way as a human.

The mermaid symbol appears all over the world, and the consistency of her appearance lead many to suppose that they really do exist. With long streaming **hair** and the tail of a **fish**, the mermaid is the epitome of the Goddess figure, naturally associated with the water element and living in the "**womb**" of the **sea**. There are also mermen and a whole population of merpeople hidden in the depths of the sea as well as in freshwater lakes. The very first mermaid stories are from the Assyrian culture and date back to 1000 BC. This first mermaid started her life as the Goddess Atargatis, who loved a mortal man, a shepherd, but who inadvertently killed him. Distraught, she leaped into a lake, meaning to take on the form of a fish; instead, she became a human/fish hybrid, the mermaid.

Unlike the **siren**, whose intention toward man is generally malicious, the mermaid has a kinder attitude to human beings. For sailors, the sight of a mermaid is a warning of stormy weather to come. Mermaids are also supposed to be able to grant wishes, and in Japan, it is supposed that if you can manage to eat the flesh of a mermaid then you will become immortal, like the mermaid herself.

Paradoxically, although the mermaid is a symbol of female sexuality and is an object of desire, the mermaid's tail precludes her having the sexual parts of a normal woman, and so she remains virginal, unobtainable, the object of frustrated dreams and desires and outside of the sphere of physical love; a

Goddess, indeed. There is another side to the mermaid's image that has a generally pejorative meaning. The symbol was used at Ephesus where there is a series of three signs, popularly supposed to be the world's first advertisement. These symbols are engraved onto a paving slab. They are a pointing **finger**, a coin, and a mermaid. Together, these indicated the local brothel, with the mermaid figure denoting the prostitute.

The mermaid is often seen looking at her reflection in a hand-**mirror** as she combs her long tresses; here, she is a symbol of vanity. Mermaids in literature often fall in love with male humans but are thwarted by the inability of the object of their desires to be able to breathe in water, or to exist in the same element. Like the Little Mermaid in the Hans Christian Andersen story, they are prepared to go to great lengths for this love, and in this particular story, the mermaid exchanges her beautiful tail for human **legs**, although each footstep she takes is excruciatingly painful. The other typical attribute of a mermaid is her beautiful voice, and in the story of *The Little Mermaid*, her **tongue** is taken away so that she can neither sing nor explain what has happened to the handsome prince. Most importantly, love, not desire, drives her to exchange her immortality as a mermaid for the **soul** of a human, and in so doing she apparently leaves behind the animal part of herself and becomes a far superior creature.

MINOTAUR

A creature with the body of a man and the head of a **bull**, which King Minos imprisoned in the famous **labyrinth** on the island of Crete.

The story of the Minotaur is as follows. Minos, the King of Crete, had asked the Gods to send a **white** bull as a sign that it was his right to be king, in preference over any of his brothers. White bulls are sacred the world over, and Minos offered to sacrifice such a creature if it appeared, which it duly did. However, this bull was so beautiful that Minos broke his promise, and kept the animal, replacing the sacrifice with a different bull. **Poseidon** was so angry that he made Minos' wife fall in love with the bull, and the resulting offspring was the hideous hybrid creature, the Minotaur, who grew more and more ferocious as he aged.

The monster of Greek legend was propitiated every so often with **seven** boys and seven girls, as an offering from Athens to Crete. The horror ended when Theseus, the son of the Athenian king, volunteered to be sacrificed but managed to slay the Minotaur and find his way out of the **maze** by means of a piece of string given to him by Ariadne.

Psychologists hold that the Minotaur monster represents repression, fed by guilt and evasions, living in the **labyrinth** of the subconscious mind. As well as the ball of twine, Ariadne carried a luminous **crown** that helped to light the passageways, symbolizing the ignorance overcome by enlightenment.

In Hindu and Buddhist iconography, the Minotaur appears as Yama, the God of **Death**, who wears the **mask** of a bull and is master of the labyrinthine network of passages in the Underworld.

THE MUSES

The Muses, of Greek mythology, personify the arts and sciences. Originally, there were only **three** muses, representing the triple aspect of the Goddess Mnemosyne (Memory), an essential skill because without this gift no one would ever be able to remember even the finest poem or song.

During the time of Homer (approximately the eighth century BC), it was common practice for artists to call on the spirit of the appropriate muse before performing. Clio was the muse of history; Euterpe presided over flute playing; Thalia was the comedic muse, juxtaposed by the Melpomene, the muse of tragedy; Terpsichore ruled over lyric, poetry and dance; Erato specialized in love poetry; Polyhymnia was the muse of mimicry, Urania ruled over astronomy; and Calliope conferred the gifts of eloquence and epic poetry.

The word "**music**" shares the same origins, as does "amuse." To "muse" upon something means to consider something. Artists still speak of finding their muse, which symbolizes a source of inspiration that drives the creative force.

NYMPH

In Greek, this word means either "bride" or "doll." Nymphs are spirits or deities that live close to **water**; waterfalls, streams, fountains, lakes, and wells all have their nymphs. Like the water that they are associated with, nymphs are notoriously ambivalent, changeable, and inconsistent. They preside equally over fertility and birth as well as **death** and decay. They are believed to steal children and to haunt the minds of the people who see them, sometimes driving them to madness. Reputedly, nymphs are at their most visible and dangerous during the time of the midday **Sun**, so it is best to avoid the places where they are likely to be at this time.

In Ancient Greece, temples at sacred springs were presided over by priestesses, all unmarried girls, also called "nymphs," and the temples themselves—called "Nymphaeae"— were used specifically for performing wedding ceremonies. Legend has it that these priestesses would give into orgiastic ceremonies at the time of the full **Moon**, hence the term "nymphomania."

PHOENIX

The mythological bird called the phoenix exists under different guises: as the **Garuda** in India, as the Feng Huang in China, as the Ho-oo in Japan, and as the Benu Bird in Egypt. The main characteristic of this great bird, whose symbolic meaning resonates throughout myth, religion, and **alchemy**, is that it is reborn from its own ashes after combusting voluntarily. This unusual habit means different things to different people. To Christians, it is a reminder of the sacrifice made by Christ and his subsequent reward of resurrection and eternal life. For the Dharmic religions, it indicates the triumph of the **soul** over the body, and subsequent reincarnation. For others, the destruction by **fire** signifies the catharsis, or purification, of death.

The phoenix is an astronomical symbol for a cyclic period in China, Egypt, India, and Persia. A new Phoenix period was said to have begun in AD 139. The phoenix is also symbolic of the "dying" of the **Sun** as it goes over the horizon in a welter of flames, and its "resurrection" the next day as it burns back over the horizon. This was the favored imagery of the Egyptians.

The phoenix is said to live primarily on aromatic smoke, not harming anything in order to eat. Therefore it is a popular symbol in Chinese and Indian Buddhist belief systems. In the same way, the bird has become popular in Christian literature and art as a symbol of resurrection and of life after death.

There can only exist one phoenix at a time, and its lifespan is reputedly anywhere between 500 and 1461 years. Its habitat is also debated. Some accounts say that it spends its time in India, but there's also a tale that tells us that the bird's real home is in Paradise. When the time comes for the phoenix to die, he has to fly into the mortal world, taking a journey across the jungles of Burma, across India, and on to Arabia. Here it collects the **herbs** and aromatic **spices** it needs, then it flies on to Phoenicia in Syria, finds a tall **date**

palm tree, and then constructs its funeral pyre. As the next day dawns the bird rises again.

PIXIE

The pixie—or piskie—features prominently in the folklore of the British Isles and it would appear that there is a concentration of the creatures in and around Devon and Cornwall in the south-west of the country. Their typical uniform is of **green** clothes and pointy hat and boots. One of the legends about their origin—that they were followers of the Old Religion doomed by the Christian God to shrink in size until they turned away from the Old Ways—is a reminder of how ancient folk beliefs were pushed into the background with the coming of the new faith.

Pixies have a penchant for mischief making and pranksterish behavior, but are generally more playful than malicious. To be "pixie led" is to get lost, led astray by the pixies; and when things go wrong it is often the pixies that are to blame, acting as a scapegoat for human error. There was an old folk belief that if the householder accepted the pixies as friends and treated them with respect (leaving food and drink for them at night), then they would repay the kindness by undertaking household tasks and chores. The pixie, like **fairies** and other similar creatures, symbolizes a spirit of nature that can exist harmoniously with mankind.

POOKA

In Celtic folklore, the pooka, puca (Irish), or pwca (Welsh) is a changeling creature that can appear as a **goat** or an **eagle**, but which mostly appears as a spirit **horse**; its appearance is usually a warning of death. Like the **kelpie,** the pooka can entice people to climb onto its back, but the resulting journey always results in the demise of the hapless rider. The pooka can speak with a human voice and will sometimes even entice people out of their homes.

This creature is associated with the old pre-Christian celebration of Samhuin, which became **Halloween**. Any crops left in the fields after this time were left in the ground to appease the Pooka.

The horse is one of the creatures viewed as a psychopomp—it can guide the **souls** of dead people on the journey to the Afterlife—and it's likely that the pooka is derived from this horse symbolism.

SALAMANDER

The salamander is one of the four elemental spirits that were first described by the alchemist Paracelsus. It is said to be the living manifestation of **fire** for which flames hold no threat. Conversely, people thought that it was so icy cold that it could also quench flames, and the Ancient Egyptians used the image of the salamander as a **hieroglyph** to describe someone who had died of cold. The religious meaning of the salamander is of a person who can keep their composure, their moral certitude and their peace of mind, while enduring constant attacks.

In **alchemy**, the salamander is one of the symbols for sulfur, which, like the elemental spirit, also feeds on fire.

Satyr

A hybrid creature, the satyr consists of the body of a man with the **legs**, tail, and **horns** of a **goat**. The goat itself is considered to have a lascivious nature and the satyr takes on some of that symbolism. The great Greek Nature God, Pan, was a satyr, possessed of a large and prominent penis as a symbol of the procreative force. However, because the early Christian authorities equated sex with sin, it should come as no surprise that they connected the **satyr** to the Devil. The **Goat of Mendes**, the goat/human figure worshipped by the Ancient Egyptians, is still used as a pictorial representation of Satan. Satyrs attended Bacchus and Dionysus, who gave themselves to a life of wine, women, boys, song, and general debauchery.

Selkie

The selkie appears in folk myths from places where **seals** are prevalent, and so we find it in Iceland, Scotland, and Ireland. It is a shape-shifting creature that can move between seal and human form by putting on and taking off its skin. In one myth, a fisherman steals the selkie's skin while she is sunbathing as a human being. Naked, she is obliged to accept the man's offer of help; subsequently she marries him and bears his children. Many years and several children later, the seal-wife finds the skin, hidden away,

puts it back on, and instantly transforms back into a seal.

Seals can often be mistaken for human beings swimming in the sea, until they disappear beneath the surface, and this is likely to have been the origin of the selkie myths. The story of the seal-wife is an allegorical tale, reminding us that the true nature of any creature cannot remain hidden forever. This carries a similar sentiment to the sad story of the **Melusine**.

Siren

The beautiful appearance and seductive nature of the sirens disguise a monstrous intent. They have the **heads** and **breasts** of lovely and voluptuous women and the bodies and **wings** of **birds**, but it is the loveliness of their faces and the sweetness of their voices that they use, with devastating effect, to lure hapless sailors toward them, so that they can then kill and eat them. Famously, Odysseus had himself strapped to the mast of his ship after plugging the **ears** of his sailors with wax, so that he could hear the song of the sirens and yet be unable to succumb to it. The nature of the siren, essentially, is of an evil that is able to prey upon human weakness. Medieval texts describe them as "stout whores." Sometimes sirens are confused with **mermaids**, but in general mermaids are benevolent creatures whose domain is the most definitely the sea. Sirens are more ambiguous, belonging on sea, land, and air.

The sirens symbolize the dangers of the sea, and death itself. Egyptians believed that they represented dead **souls** that had failed to achieve their destiny and spitefully decided to blight the lives of others, too. As well as epitomizing fatal attraction, sirens were however also depicted as benevolent creatures that could show the way to a better world.

Essentially, the siren stands as a warning against the distractions of desire and of what can happen if man succumbs to physical temptation. The mast that Odysseus made a conscious decision to strap himself to represents the axis of his **soul**, his backbone, and moral fiber.

SPHINX

The sphinx exists in slightly varying forms. It generally has the head of a woman and the body of a **lion**, although the most famous of the sphinxes, the Egyptian ones, do not have **wings**, unlike the Assyrian and Greek versions.

The sphinx, as the epitome of mystery and hidden secrets, has endured for centuries. Her riddle—"what goes on two feet in the morning, on four feet at midday, and on three feet in the evening?"—may have been answered long ago, but mankind is still fascinated by her, and the true significance that lies behind her implacable expression can only be guessed at. She has a reputation as a devourer; the wings given to her by the Greek and Assyrians would suggest that she was of divine origin. Greek legends have the sphinx as an evil monster that ravaged the land of Thebes, asking riddles of anyone who came its way, and devouring those who either answered incorrectly or failed to answer at all.

SUCCUBUS

The **bat**-like **wings**, **horns**, cloven hoofs, and forked tail that are sometimes attributes of the succubus are often overlooked because of her beautiful and alluring appearance. The succubus is a type of **demon** that appears in the form of a beautiful woman that takes great pleasure in seducing men as they sleep, causing them to have sexual intercourse with her. The succubus apparently takes the most delight in abusing monks and other men of the cloth. The sexual energy of the victim nourishes the succubus, although the act exhausts the man so thoroughly that he may even die as a result. **Lilith**, the first wife of Adam, was effectively demonized because she failed to obey her husband, and has been called a succubus.

In the UK, some inns that date back to the sixteenth century still have the effigy of a succubus placed discreetly over the door. This was a secret symbol that the building was also a brothel.

In the Middle East, the interpretation of the succubus is slightly different. Still a beautiful woman in appearance, she wanders the desert, and her mission is to punish adulterers by seducing the guilty man. At the moment of sexual penetration, she slices off his penis with the razorblades secreted inside her **vagina**, and thereafter makes a meal of the unfortunate victim, eating him alive.

Sylph

The sylph is an elemental creature, one of four described by Paracelsus, which belongs to the air. The other three are the **gnome** (earth), **salamander** (fire), and the **undine** (water). Because they are associated with **air**, sylphs are also connected to **breath** and breathing, and are thought to be born on the last breath of a dying person. Therefore, the sylph can also manifest as a **ghost**.

We tend to think of something that is described as "sylph-like" as being wispy and insubstantial, and sylphs are associated with **fairies** and other ethereal beings. However, Paracelsus originally said that the sylph was bigger, stronger and coarser than a human being. The belief in elemental beings was universal, so much so that in the eighth century the Emperor Charlemagne issued an edict that forbad sylphs to appear. His son, Louis the Pious, renewed this edict.

Undine

Undines are very closely related to **nymphs**. According to Paracelsus, the undine is the elemental spirit of **water**. They are beautiful females, mischievous at best and cruel at worst. They are known for their trick of offering to guide lost travelers through dangerous swamps and marshy areas, when the real intention is to lead them astray and cause them to drown. Like **mermaids**, undines are beautiful and coy, and folk-tales tell of their tendency of tempting handsome men to travel with them into the deep waters of the lakes they inhabit. Here, hours pass as quickly as minutes and, predictably, **death** comes swiftly to the young man, his better judgement clouded with lust for the beautiful undine. The undine acts as a reminder of what might happen if we surrender to the powers of seduction.

The other three elemental spirits are the **salamander** (fire), **gnome** (earth), and **sylph** (air).

Unicorn

The unicorn is often depicted in tapestries, where it stands, sparkling **white**, against a backdrop of dark **green** foliage.

This fantastical animal has a double meaning. On the one hand, it is synonymous with purity and chastity, yet on the other, the single horn on its **head** is clearly a phallic symbol. The positioning of the horn, though, in the center of the head and therefore at the symbolic seat of the mind, shows that the horn, in this case, stands for sublimation of the sexual urge. Popular legend says that only a virgin who is pure in mind as well as body can touch the unicorn, and medieval tapestries of the creature with the Virgin Mary were a reminder of the Virgin Birth. However, even this innocuous imagery was prohibited by the Church in the late Middle Ages, regarded as too erotic.

The **lion** and the unicorn often appear as a pair, most notably on heraldic devices. Here, the lion represents the **Sun** to the Unicorn's **Moon**.

VALKYRIE

Valkyries are closely linked to **death**, so their fearsome reputation isn't surprising. In fact, in Norse myth they are the winged creatures—Angels of Death—who watched over the battlefields and snatched up the **souls** of courageous warriors that had been killed in battle, taking care of them and guiding them to the banqueting table of the Gods in Valhalla. The name Valkyrie means "chooser of the slain." More sinisterly, it is also probable that the Valkyries acted as messengers for the Gods, actually leading certain heroes to their deaths and inspiring them to acts of valor for the greater good.

The Valkyrie assumes different forms. Sometimes she appears with the **white feathers** of **swans**, sometimes with **black raven** feathers. In this case, they are also called "Kraken," meaning Crows. As such they have an association with the great Celtic warrior-Goddess, Morrigan, who also appears on battlefields as a crow or raven. Valkyries also appeared in the form of **horses**, and have parallels with the Swedish shape-shifting **witch** called a Volva. Additionally, the Valkyries are said to be either **thirteen** in number, the same as in a coven, or **nine**, which is also the number of **Muses**. This leads to the notion that, like the Muses, the Valkyries could provide transcendental inspiration for the warriors in their care.

VAMPIRE

The concept of an immortal creature, once human, that lives in a tomb and comes out at night to suck the **blood** of living creatures, which then become vampires themselves, is widespread throughout Europe, Russia, and many parts of Asia. The fact that the vampire takes all its nourishment in this way is a reminder of blood's power as a sustaining life-force, and explains why ancient man daubed his dead in **red** ochre, in the hopes that the vitality of the color alone would restore life.

Vampires were once taken very seriously as a threat. In the Middle Ages, a Slav edict placed a heavy fine on any female vampire that was found guilty of taking blood from a man. The classic prophylactics against vampires have remained the same for centuries. These are the Christian **Cross** (since the vampire is the agent of the Devil); the **silver** bullet (the metal encapsulates the essence of moonlight which is necessary to the vampire, and therefore effects a sort of homeopathic poison); **garlic**, a herb of protection that is hated by all demonic creatures; and finally, the wooden stake through the **heart**.

Today, there seem to be fewer blood-sucking vampires around than there used to be. However, the word is used to describe anyone who saps psychic energy from those around them. How to spot a vampire? The key feature is a lack of a reflection, since a reflection is a symbol of the **soul** the vampire doesn't have.

Werewolf

The idea that Gods and Goddesses could shape-shift into the form of **animals** or **birds**, and that shamans could absorb the **spirit** of an animal by wearing skins and **feathers** as part of ritual practice, is ancient. The werewolf is a part of this tradition. However, the reason why a **wolf** in particular should have been chosen to represent the evil side of human nature is worth examining.

The belief in lycanthropy (human/wolf shape-shifting transformation) was an ancient one that existed in Classical times; Virgil wrote about it. He said that the first werewolf was called Moeris, and could perform great magic that included calling up the dead from their tombs. The wolf itself was considered to be a psychopomp, a creature able to conduct the **souls** of the dead into the next world, and there were numerous wolf deities throughout classical civilizations.

As any horror movie aficionado knows, werewolves change into wolves during the time of the full **Moon**. Like **vampires**, they have no reflection, nor do they have a **shadow**. Since both reflection and shadow are symbolic of the soul, in taking on the form of a wolf, the human soul and conscience is left behind, the ferocious nature of the beast taking over entirely.

The belief in werewolves is evidenced by documentation that describes the trials—and punishments—of such creatures, although belief in them was starting to die out by the seventeenth century in Europe. For example, in 1615 a woman was burned alive, accused of lycanthropy. A man, traveling alone late at night, was attacked by a werewolf but managed to chop off its paw. The woman in question was missing a **hand**. Other werewolf trials, carried out under the jurisdiction of the Church, worked with the same kind of logic that was applied to witch trials, often using severe methods of torture until the accused either confessed or died.

Wyvern

The word is derived from a Latin word, *vipera*, meaning "viper" or **serpent**. The wyvern itself is composed of the body parts of several different creatures and its appearance varies from artist to artist. Generally speaking, the wyvern has the head of a **dragon** (and the same **fire**-breathing capabilities) and the tail of a serpent, sometimes with a barbed tip. It has **wings**, and the talons of a **bird** of prey. However, the wyvern differs from other dragon-like creatures in that it has only two **legs**.

French myths say that the wyvern has the **head** and torso of a voluptuous woman, another instance of the female/snake association. This unusual woman has further exotic allure in the **ruby** that is embedded at the point of her **third eye**, said to help her navigate through the Underworld.

Zombie

The zombie is a Voudon term that has become the popular name for a revenant, or one that returns from the dead. Although this could be considered a handy skill, the unfortunate zombie has no **soul**, and will only survive if it has access to a sufficient quantity of meat from normal, soul-containing human bodies.

In this, there is a parallel between the zombie and the **vampire**.

In Haitian myth, a corpse can be reanimated by a powerful sorcerer called a Bokor. The zombie is really nothing but a robot that must do the bidding of the Bokor, since it has no mind of its own; it is simply a ghastly mechanical creature. Although we may think of the zombie as nothing but a handy device for use in horror films, there are several reported eye-witness accounts, with names and dates mentioned, of people seen wandering around several years after their death, a reminder that folklore, no matter how bizarre, carries a powerful symbolic punch.

The European zombie differs from the Haitian one in that it returns to the land of the living for a reason, usually to avenge its own death. This would imply that this type of revenant has a mind and **spirit** of its own.

The term "zombie" has come to mean a person who carries out certain actions automatically, without seeming to apply any conscious thought or decision-making process.

BIRDS: DIVINE COMMUNICATORS

When William Blake, artist, poet, and mystic, wrote the following words:

How do you know
But every bird
That cuts the airy way
Is an immense world of delight
Closed to your senses five?

he encapsulated perfectly the idea that birds, which have been on this planet far longer than humankind and which we see every day as part of the natural landscape, have more to them than meets the **eye**. Their primary symbolic function is as messengers from the spiritual realms, from the Gods. Arguably, the generic symbolism of the bird is one of the most universal of any.

There's no doubt that birds, both "real" and as symbols, have a prominent part to play in the material and spiritual world of humankind. The prehistoric cave paintings at Lascaux, for example, include a prominent scene—called now "Death of the Bird Man"—indicating that there could have been some sort of a bird-cult as far back as Upper Paleolithic times.

In *Jung and his Symbols*, Joseph L. Henderson describes the bird as "the most fitting symbol of transcendence. It represents the peculiar nature of intuition working through a 'medium' … an individual who is capable of obtaining knowledge of distant events … by going into a trancelike state."

In the Qu'ran, the word for "bird" is synonymous with "fate" and in Greek, "bird" and "omen" have the same meaning. Orthomancy, a form of divination that involves watching birds, was common practice all over the world. Birds' flight patterns were observed; the type of bird was considered; their calls and cries were pondered over, and sometimes this divination took the form of an analysis of bird entrails. Ancient Romans wouldn't make any important decisions without first consulting their augurs. Indeed, the Latin word *augury*, which is taken to mean an omen or portent, actually has its root in the meaning of the word "bird" and also gives us "inauguration." Bird augury wasn't exclusive to the Romans but was carried out by Tibetans, Indians, Native Americans, Mexicans, Egyptians, Mayans, and Celts. Sacred places around the world were defined by bird symbols and messages: Mexico City, Rome and the site of the **Omphalos** at **Delphi** were all founded in this way.

The idea, too, that birds somehow revealed the secrets of the **alphabet** to humankind is far reaching. The best-known story is that **Hermes**, the Messenger of the Gods, "invented" the alphabet by watching the flight patterns of birds, **cranes** in particular. Robert Graves in *The White Goddess* tells us that the secret symbols of the alphabet were kept in a crane-skin bag, which makes perfect sense given also that the Alaskans used to use the skins of cranes, **swans** and **eagles** as bags since these skins are the strongest.

It's no surprise, then, that we give our Gods and their emissaries the attributes of birds: **wings**, **feathers**, and the power of flight that signifies physical and spiritual transcendence and the ability to move in a dimension denied to man, at least without mechanical aid. Hermes, as well as having wings on his sandals, acquires wings on the staff that is his symbolic attribute, the **caduceus**. In a beautiful, symbolic circle of completion, the feather or quill was/is a popular means of communicating the written word: the bird communicates in another way.

ALBATROSS

For sailors, this huge sea bird (which can have a wingspan of up to eleven feet) is said to be the reincarnated **soul** of a dead sailor that has come to help make a safe passage for the boat, or perhaps to give a warning of rough weather ahead. Therefore, killing or harming the albatross is the height of bad luck. Coleridge's poem "The Ancient Mariner" reinforced this superstition so successfully that even landlubbers know about it.

In the Pacific islands, the albatross is commonly believed to be a messenger from the Gods, able to sleep on the wing. The bird is revered because of its close connection to the Divine, and on Easter Island one of the statues has the beak of an albatross.

CRANE

There is evidence that the crane has been present on the planet for 10 million years and as well as this, the bird has a long lifespan—up to 50 years—so it is no surprise that, for many, the bird is a symbol of longevity.

The crane is a symbol of communication, too. A legend states that **Mercury/Hermes** invented the **alphabet** by watching the angular shapes of the birds' **wings** in flight. Thereafter the letters were carried in a bag made of crane skin. This idea extends from the Greco-Roman pantheon through to the Bambara in Africa, who believe that the bird was present at the invention of speech.

For Ancient Greeks, the crane was a solar symbol and as such was dedicated to the **Sun God**, Apollo, who disguised himself as the bird whenever he came to visit Earth. Not surprisingly, the exuberant **dance** of the crane was seen as a celebration of life itself and prophesied the coming of spring and the sunshine.

In China and Japan, the crane similarly represents longevity and faithfulness, both traits that are true to the bird. It's also seen as a messenger between the Gods and humans, and is a psychopomp. The **dance** of the crane represents the power of flight and the ultimate arrival of human **souls** in the Land of the Immortals. In addition, the Chinese believed that "heavenly cranes" or "blessed cranes" represented wisdom, and that the birds carried legendary sages on their backs as they flew between the worlds.

DOVE

The dove carries a universal symbolism that is as ubiquitous as the bird itself. The world over, it is associated with the feminine aspect, love, and peace.

Pigeons and doves have carried messages for thousands of years and the notion of this particular bird as a messenger from the Gods is perhaps more pronounced than for others. This is backed up by the story of the dove sent out by Noah to determine how far the **Ark** was from land; the bird returned with a sprig of an **olive** branch, and the juxtaposition of the bird with the olive branch is a sign of redemption, peace, and resolution. Columba—the dove—is the "secret," covert bird symbol of the United States, its soft reasonable femininity counterbalancing the masculine glory of the more visible and overt **eagle**. The dove is also the symbolic bird of Israel.

The dove is a gentle-looking, rounded bird; its call is soft and seductive. It is also often seen snuggled up to its partner, and it may be these characteristics that make it a symbol of the feminine, and of love. It is also a prolifically fertile bird.

The dove is the attribute of the Goddess in any of her aspects; at **Dodona**, the magical oak grove of the Ancient Greeks, the three priestesses were called "doves" and the dove that perched in the sacred oak was said to have oracular powers. In Christian belief, the Virgin Mary—another aspect of the Goddess—often has a dove hovering nearby, as symbol of the Holy Spirit. When Christ is baptized, the Holy Spirit descends on him in the form of a dove.

As well as being a sacred bird in the ancient world, the bird is still venerated today by Muslims. At **Mecca** there are special roosting niches for them, since they are believed to have a direct link to Allah. In Japan, a myth about the dove warning against the presence of enemies makes the bird a good-luck symbol as well as a symbol of war. And in Wales, if a dove is seen anywhere near a colliery then this is an extremely bad omen, a sign of impending disaster. Its presence on one occasion in the nineteenth century resulted in 300 miners refusing to enter the mine.

DUCK

One of the more unlikely symbols of this seemingly innocuous bird is an association with the Devil that was given to it by a thirteenth-century pope, Gregory IX. Gregory took it upon himself to preach a particularly impassioned sermon in which he denounced the bird as the personification of the **demon** Asmodeus, who apparently appeared to his followers in the unlikely guise of a duck and thereafter caused all sorts of unholy goings-on.

Like other migratory birds, the appearance of the duck was an indicator, to ancient man, of the changing of the seasons; therefore, it was believed to have the powers of prophecy. The timing of the birds' laying **eggs**, hatching, etc. forecast the progression of the seasons. Further proof of the clairvoyance of the bird was to be had in its calls. A louder quacking than usual, for example, presaged storms.

The duck is a useful ally, in general a benevolent creature, its links with anything remotely demonic an aberration. Because it is a **water** bird it is linked to **Poseidon/ Neptune**, and in Egypt, where ducks were domesticated 5,000 years ago, it was associated with **Isis** and with the **Sun** God Ra. The duck's take-off, as it skims across the surface of the water and into the **air**, effectively exchanging one element for another, symbolizes the journey of the **soul** into the next world.

As in Egypt, for the Celts the duck was a symbol of the Sun, and ancient archeological finds show the bird depicted with the solar wheel. This symbolism is no doubt due in no small part to the iridescent **rainbow**-like glimmerings of its **feathers**, which are highly sought-after by the Pueblo Indians as sacred and decorative devices.

In the Far East, ducks symbolize happiness and longevity and so are portrayed on wedding stationery, etc.

EAGLE

One of the most important archetypal bird symbols, the prominence of the eagle is a worldwide phenomenon. The eagle is the "King of the Birds" and the "**Lion** of the Skies," and its use as a symbol is clear. It resembles power, authority, nobility, and

truth; it is the ultimate solar symbol. In Greek the name of the eagle shares the same stem as *aigle*, meaning "ray of light."

Notably, the eagle is the symbol of one of the **four evangelists** of the New Testament, St. John. Here, the eagle represents divine inspiration. However, the saying "the enemy of my enemy is my friend" applies here, because the bird is reputedly the natural enemy of **snakes**, and the eagle has been regarded as on the "side" of God ever since the Devil was symbolized as the **serpent** in the Garden of Eden, tempting Adam and Eve away from the straight and narrow path of good towards the twisting and corrupting path of evil. However, the eagle and the snake seen together symbolize the opposing concepts of matter and spirit, Earth and Heaven, instinct and intellect, the mundane and the sublime, and therefore the unity of the cosmos. In Norse mythology, the eagle sits in the great **World Tree**, Yggdrasil, counterbalanced by the serpent that twines about the tree's roots.

The eagle's reputation as a symbol of truth comes from its sharp sightedness; the

eyesight of the eagle is at least four times superior to that of human beings, and combined with its high-flying abilities it means that the bird can see the bigger picture, quite literally. Therefore, it is meant to be able to discern truth from falsehood. Because it flies so high, often appearing to be heading straight for the Sun, people believed that the eagle was the only creature in the world able to gaze directly into the brightness of the Sun without hurting its eyes. Therefore, the bird also symbolizes mental and spiritual enlightenment and the aspiration of a pure **heart**, able to look into the face of God with no fear.

Shamans believe that the eagle communicated their gifts directly from God, the bird acting as intermediary. They believe that the first shaman was conceived after an eagle impregnated a woman, another symbol of the bird as a divine spirit or winged messenger. This has parallels with another winged creature, the **Angel** Gabriel, who told Mary of her impending condition. In both cases, the resulting child is a sort of spiritual hybrid, able to connect God and Man.

The eagle has always been the emblem par excellence of emperors and empires, even prior to its presence on the imperial standard of the Caesars and its latter-day use as the symbol of the United States, where the altogether more humble **dove** balances its grandiose power. The death of an emperor was heralded by the release of eagles into the skies, symbolic of the **soul** ascending to the Heavens. However, more sinisterly, the symbolic power and attributes of the eagle were appropriated by the Nazis to bolster their own image. This is an instance where a powerful symbol can be abused, something that also happened to another ancient solar symbol, the **swastika**, whose implicit benevolent meaning is unfortunately still tainted because of its use by the Nazis.

For Native Americans, the power of the eagle is such that possession of one of its **feathers** is the ultimate accolade, a sacred symbol of the mightiness of the bird and of its special place within the Native American pantheon. The eagle is the "father" of the people, a God, and illicit possession of a feather by anyone who does not have the right to have it is punishable by hefty fines. The eagle feather is not only sacred to Native Americans, but to Hindus, too, where the eagle brought a food called Soma to humankind from the Gods.

For the Aztecs, the eagle was not associated with the lion but with the **jaguar**, and the throne of the Aztec emperor was decorated with eagle feathers and jaguar skin to symbolize his association with these powerful creatures. The eagle "told" the people where Mexico City should be built, duly appearing perched on a cactus growing out of a rock, as decreed by an ancient legend.

The Greeks, too, accorded the eagle with the power to indicate a sacred site, and **Delphi**, the site of the **Omphalos** (the "navel" or the spiritual center of the world) was established at the spot where two eagles, released from the ends of the earth by Zeus, crossed in the sky.

The eagle shares much of the same symbolism as the **phoenix**, i.e. that of the Sun that never dies.

* ** *

GOOSE

If birds in general are symbolic of divine communication, then the goose is also symbolic of a more practical type of message giving. The goose **feather**, strong and durable yet malleable, is the most popularly used feather in the making of the quill pen. In addition, because the downy feathers of the goose are among the softest to be had, their use in mattresses makes the bird synonymous with marital bliss.

The appearance and behavior of the goose was considered a reliable indicator of the weather and of seasonal changes, and because of this it was accorded divinatory powers. The Egyptians depicted the goose in tombs that date back to at least 3000 BC, and the bird was symbolic of the **souls** of pharaohs. Accordingly, when the new pharaoh was crowned, a goose was released at each of the cardinal points to signify the event. As a solar symbol, the goose Seth, Father of **Osiris**, was believed to have laid the Golden **Egg**, an emblem of the **Sun**.

For the Romans, the goose was a powerful symbol of protection and a particular ally of their nation. During the Gaulish invasion of Italy in the third century BC, geese alerted what was left of the almost-defeated Roman army to a surprise attack. From this point onward, there was a turn in the fortunes of the Romans. Thereafter, the bird was honored in an annual procession through the city.

In Greek mythology, the goose is associated with Boreas, the north wind. The Greeks also used the birds to guard houses and as companions for their children. Aphrodite, the Greek Goddess of Love, is often portrayed as riding on a goose, as is Cupid before he grew his own wings.

Both the **swan** and the goose were considered sacred in the pre-Christian British Isles, Julius Caesar being the first to bring attention to this fact when he noted that neither bird was eaten. This was possibly because of both birds' connection to the sun-egg. Although geese are now routinely slaughtered as a delicacy for midwinter feasts, it was originally considered very bad form to kill them, because the killing of the goose equated with the killing of hope for the return of the Sun. In Wales, to see geese at night on a lake was considered very unlucky, since the birds could be witches; in fact the belief that shamans, wizards and witches can shape-shift into geese is prevalent throughout the world.

HOOPOE

Hoopoes are appalling nest-keepers, rarely clearing out any debris. It's also a particularly bad-smelling bird. This could be why it's listed in Hebrew scripture as an "unclean" bird, which is not to be eaten. Despite this, images of the hoopoe feature on the walls of tombs in Crete and Egypt, and the bird has a long association with magic and the supernatural.

As a bird that can communicate between the world of spirit and matter, the hoopoe seems to be second-to-none. According to the Qu'ran, the hoopoe was the bird that told King Solomon about the Queen of Sheba. Moreover, it was the only bird that could tell the King the whereabouts of essential underground springs.

It was commonly believed that the entrails of the hoopoe contained magical properties; as well as helping with vision and memory, they were also held to be an **aphrodisiac**. The bird's innards, dried and worn around the neck, served as a protection against the evil eye. There was a belief among the Arabs that the Hoopoe was a doctor and could cure just about any kind of sickness. Certainly its **blood** and **heart** were used in various folk medicines, and the blood of the hoopoe is said to be a powerful "ink" for writing spells.

The hoopoe is also one of the birds able to forecast the weather, particularly storms, and with good reason. A recent discovery confirms an ancient aspect of its symbolic and superstitious meaning. It seems that the bird is able to detect the minute piezoelectrical charges in the atmosphere can herald either a storm or an earthquake up to ten hours before the event.

The Egyptians used the hoopoe as a symbol of gratitude. This is because they were supposed to take care of their aging parents by preening them and licking their **eyes** if their vision was failing.

HUMMINGBIRD

On the **Nazca Plains** in Peru, artists living centuries ago carved out various shapes and patterns that are indecipherable from the ground, but when viewed from the air, come together in recognizable pictures. Among these images is giant hummingbird that can only be seen when the viewer is about a thousand feet up. Ancient artists painstakingly created this secret symbol, hidden in the landscape, able to be seen properly only by the Gods in their **Heavens** or in a way they could never have envisaged, by modern man centuries later, from the vantage point of an aircraft.

Given its origins in the Americas, it is from this area that the symbolic meaning of the hummingbird comes. In the Andes it is a symbol of death and resurrection. It loses a significant amount of heat at night in order to conserve energy and seems to be dead if it is found at night. In the morning, however, the heat of the sunshine revives it.

One of the more epic myths about the hummingbird concerns a great warrior, Huitzil. His full name was **Huitzilopochitli**, which translates as "the hummingbird from the left." The "left" here refers to the otherworldly realms that run parallel to the known Universe. The warrior's mother conceived him from a ball of brightly colored **feathers**, which fell from the sky.

The relevance of **tobacco** for Native Americans involves the symbolism of the **smoke** that it makes that rises to the Heavens carrying messages to the Gods. Given that birds do the same thing, there are many associations between tobacco and birds, including the hummingbird. In a Cherokee myth, a shaman transforms himself into a hummingbird so that he can find the lost tobacco plant.

Aztec reverence for the hummingbird was profound. Shamans' **cloaks** and **wands** were decorated with the feathers of the bird.

KINGFISHER

The ancient name for the kingfisher is the halcyon, and it carries with it a powerful legend that also explains some of the bird's symbolic significance. The Halcyon Days—an idyllic time of peace and tranquility—refers to the 14-day period just before the end of the Greek winter when the weather is good and the **seas** are calm enough to facilitate the nesting of the legendary bird on the waves, although the real kingfisher does no such thing.

One version of the story that is Alcyone, daughter of the King of the Winds, married Ceyx, son of the morning **star**. They had a perfectly happy marriage until they attracted the wrath of the Gods by comparing themselves to **Zeus** and **Hera**. Thereafter the angry Gods turned the unfortunate couple into birds, and the constant pounding of the seas meant that their nest was smashed to pieces. Zeus took pity on the pair and gave them the aforementioned two-week respite in which they could rear their young.

The kingfisher, as the halcyon bird, symbolizes the marriage of the **sea** and the **sky**, the **earth** and the **air**. It also serves as a warning not to boast of happiness.

LAPWING

Because the nest of the lapwing, at the edge of a body of **water**, is so well disguised, the bird is symbolic of a hidden secret. And although some accounts of Solomon's introduction to the Queen of Sheba have the **hoopoe** as the matchmaker, others give the lapwing this honor.

The name of the lapwing comes from the Old English *Hleapwince*, which means "leap with a waver in it" or "run and wink," which accurately describes the erratic flight of the bird.

Lapwing chicks are able to be up and about very soon after they have hatched, and can run away immediately if there's danger; this precocious behavior gives rise to a phrase, "running about like a lapwing with a shell upon their heads," coined by Ben Johnson, and taken to mean someone who behaves rashly.

The ethereal, sobbing cry of the lapwing means that the bird has sorrowful associations. The Seven Whistlers is an ancient folktale found all over northern Europe. These whistlers give warnings to mankind from the other world. The lapwing or plover is associated with the Seven Whistlers, and there's an old Gaelic name for the bird, the *Guilchaismeachd* or "Wail of Warning." In some parts of Britain, the legend says that the wailing is caused by six of the whistlers in search of the seventh; however, once the seventh whistler is found, the world will end.

There's another legend that says that lapwings were the transmuted souls of Jews who had assisted at the Crucifixion. This gives rise to another folk name for the bird, the "Wandering Jew."

In the Bible, the lapwing is mentioned as an unclean bird, a bird of taboo, which generally means that the bird was considered sacred and should not be eaten.

MAGPIE

The name of this bird not only tells us a lot about its nature, but also points towards the symbolism associated with it. "Mag" means "chatterer," and "pie" comes from "pied," meaning **black** and **white**.

Because the magpie is attracted to bright and shiny objects, it's a symbol not only of a hoarder, but also of a thief. Its clearly defined black and white markings have made it, in Christian belief at least, a symbol of the Devil (because it refused to wear full mourning for the Crucifixion) and elsewhere it is viewed as a trickster, like other members of the highly intelligent corvid family. This ambivalence is reflected in the old counting rhyme about magpies whose verses are alternately positive and negative, like the coloring of the bird itself. The devilish symbolism is exacerbated because the bird can even imitate the human voice, an alarming talent to superstitious minds. In Scotland, it is said that the magpie has a drop of the Devil's **blood** on its **tongue**. Therefore it was important to appease the bird, either by acknowledging it in a greeting ("Good morning, Mr. Magpie") or else doffing the cap or otherwise ingratiating oneself with it.

In Scandinavian territories, it was believed that witches could shape-shift into the form of a magpie, or could shrink down small enough to ride on their backs. This belief is counteracted, though, in Norway where the bird is viewed more favorably. Here, it is given corn to eat at **Christmas**.

The predilection of the magpie for shiny objects means that is linked to **mirrors** and reflections. In Japan a woman would regard her husband's gift of a mirror with some suspicion. This is because of the belief that the mirror could turn into a magpie. This bird then spied on the wife on behalf of her husband. Even today, the backs of some mirrors in China are decorated with the magpie symbol.

In Greece, the magpie was the attribute of the **Wine** God Dionysus. Wine loosens the tongue and causes people to chatter like the bird. This chattering gives us the name Gazette, a journal full of gossipy items, from the Italian for magpie, *gazza*.

OSTRICH

The ostrich is a symbol of avoidance, or ignorance, because of its perceived habit of hiding its head in the sand. Although this characteristic is inaccurate, it is a reminder of just how certain symbolic meanings can be engendered in ignorance rather than in truth. The ostrich, in fact, protects its **eggs** by burying them in sand, and occasionally has need to disguise this place—the nest can contain a collection of up to 30 eggs from different birds—by lying on it. The ostrich is also considered stupid, because it eats sharp objects and stones; in fact these abrasive objects aid digestion.

It is ironic that the two best-known ostrich symbols concern misunderstandings, because as a symbol of truth, the ostrich **feather** is unrivalled. Such a feather is the attribute of the Egyptian Goddess of Truth, Maat, who weighs the ostrich feather against her scales of reckoning. The other side of the scales holds the **heart,** the seat of the conscience. The ostrich feather carries this symbolism because unlike birds of flight whose feathers have one side heavier than the other, the ostrich feather is perfectly symmetrical.

Ostrich eggs are balanced on the tops of the pinnacles of Muslim **temples** in Mali, because the egg is symbolic of the **World Egg**, and carries an inherent reminder of faith and patience because the ostrich's egg has a long gestation period.

There is a story that Barak Baba, the twelfth-century Dervish leader, induced the ostrich to fly. This tale is symbolic of determination, mind over matter, and miracles.

Owl

The Italian word for owl, *strix* or *strega*, also means "witch," and this provides a heavy hint about one aspect of the bird's symbolic meaning. Because the owl is nocturnal, it means that it has access to covert information, occult knowledge, and secrets. It is because of this reason that the little owl is the attribute of the Goddess of Wisdom, **Athena/Minerva**, and also explains its appearance perched on top of a stack of **books** as a symbol of knowledge. The idea that the owl has access to information denied mere mortals is further underlined by the fact the bird can swivel its head an astonishing 270 degrees; quite literally, the bird can see behind itself. Its huge **eyes** add to its wise reputation.

The links with witchcraft and witchery are also because of some of the owl's habits. It lives a solitary existence, only coming together to breed, and usually separating again once the juvenile owls have flown the nest. An efficient hunter, the owl's feathers are particularly adapted so that its flight is silent, and the bird is able to take ten times the amount of small rodents in one night than a **cat**. Its killings are often accompanied by an unearthly screeching, which superstitious country dwellers attributed to supernatural causes. Pliny wrote about certain evil women, "*striges*," who could transform themselves into nocturnal birds of prey to slaughter babies in the dead of night.

The owl is a symbol of the feminine, the **Moon**, and prophecy. The Moon, acting as a mirror of the **Sun**, is itself symbolic of clairvoyant powers, another gift of witches. This gift of second sight, though, generally brings gloomy news, and everywhere the shriek of an owl in the night presages a death. The exception is in Wales, where it signifies loss of virginity.

The owl has other unfortunate symbolism connected with it. Since it chooses derelict buildings in which to make its home, the bird is associated with destruction and decay. However, the Athenians had the owl as the guardian of the Acropolis. In addition, it was held in such esteem as the companion of the Goddess of Wisdom that its image was stamped on coinage, which came to be known as the Owls of Laurium. To "bring owls to Athens" meant the same as the latter-day phrase of "selling ice to the Eskimos."

The owl is also a companion of the infamous witch queen **Hecate**, Goddess of the Underworld. The belief that the owl could come and go between the lands of the living and the dead was not restricted to the Romans and the Britons. The same belief exists for Native Americans, for Africans, in China, in Japan and in India, where the God of Death, Yama, is shown with an owl. The owl is a psychopomp, able to guide the **souls** of the deceased into the Afterlife.

Parrot

Possibly the best-known quality of the parrot is its ability to talk, or more specifically mimic. To learn something "parrot fashion" is to memorize something without necessarily knowing what it means. It is not determined whether the parrot famed as a pet of Julius Caesar that was taught to shriek "Hail Caesar" whenever its master was near, was fully aware of what it was saying.

Parrots are appealing and affectionate and have been kept as domesticated pets for centuries; the Greeks and Romans being among those enamored by the bird. It is frequently regarded as the favored pet of the sailor, especially of the pirate. This is because the birds were taken from their original homes, in South China, as trophies of their voyages by sailors.

Native Americans accord the colored **feathers** of the parrot with the brightness of the **Sun**, and it is a solar symbol because of this. For Brahmins, the parrot is a sacred bird, not to be harmed in any way. It is dedicated to Kama, the God of Love. This is because people in love often unconsciously imitate one another's body language and speech patterns. Consequently, the birds are emblems of marriage in northern India and parrot images are hung in the temples where weddings take place.

There's a traditional series of folktales, originally written in Sanskrit, called "Tales of a Parrot," which is a "chain" of stories similar in style to the Arabian Nights. In this morality tale, the parrot relates 70 stories to stop a woman from taking the wrong path in life.

PARTRIDGE

There are two different suggestions for the origin of the partridge's name; one theory supposes that the name comes from the same Latin root as *perdu*, "the lost one." The other is that the name comes from a Greek word *perdesthai*, meaning an explosive noise and which relates to the noise made by the bird when it leaves its cover. The cry of the partridge is particularly strident, which might lend weight to the latter theory. The partridge's cry is interpreted in China as a love call, despite its discordant sound. This is probably because of the fecundity of the bird, a quality that led to disapproval from the Christian Church. A Latin Bestiary from the eleventh century describes the partridge as being so fertile that even the scent of the male could impregnate the female. This supposedly lewd behavior gave the partridge an evil reputation, despite the fact that it obviously follows the biblical edict to "go forth and multiply." For some reason, the partridge was also regarded as an antidote to poisons.

RAVEN

The raven belongs to the most intelligent of all the birds. To give some idea of its intelligence, if the average IQ for a human being is measured at the 100 mark, then the average IQ of a raven is 138. Its linguistic skills are legendary, and it is possible that the raven can understand as well as imitate human words. It is this intelligence, and the playful nature of the raven, that makes it the ultimate symbol of the trickster.

In some societies, the raven is as important as the **eagle**, and occasionally this **black** bird even surpasses the golden one in terms of its symbolic import. Like the eagle, the raven has few natural predators except for man. Unlike the eagle, ravens will work together for the benefit of the group, and so have come to symbolize the benefits of teamwork. Conversely, in Denmark the term *"Ravn-Mudder"* or Raven Mother is a euphemism for poor parenting skills, and stems from the notion that the bird waits to see the colors of its chick's feathers before starting to feed it.

Even if the raven has never been taught to speak in human languages, its voice carries a surprisingly human inflection and tone. This led to a belief that the bird knew everything, as personified by the ravens that belonged to the Norse God **Odin**. Called Hugin and Munin, from the words for Thought and Memory, the birds flew back to the God at the end of every day where they whispered into his ears all the doings of mankind. Odin—also known as the Raven God—had daughters, **Valkyries**, who appeared as ravens, and similarly, witches are said to be able to shapeshift into the form of ravens, which is how they travel, anonymously, to their meetings.

More sinisterly, the raven is seen as a harbinger of death, as personified in the Morrigan, the great Battle Goddess of Celtic myth who takes on the form of a raven. The raven is a carrion bird and was often to be seen at the sites of battles, making a grim meal of the bloody remains of the defeated army. In addition, the spooky **black** appearance of the bird certainly lends itself to the dark imagery posited by horror stories. In the Mahabharata, the bird is a messenger of **death**, but paradoxically to those of a Western sensibility, this does not necessarily mean that the bird is a symbol of ill omen. However, the idea of the raven as a bird of malice is promulgated by the Bible story that Noah first sends a raven to find land; the raven never returned, and so was seen to be no friend of man. The **dove**, sent out next, returned with the sprig of the **olive** tree and has been a beneficial omen ever since. The ravens sent out by Viking explorers in search of new land seemed to have a better success rate than Noah's bird, however, and in some parts of northern Europe, the bird is seen as a helper of humankind.

The ravens at the Tower of London are a symbol of protection par excellence. Birds have been kept in this spot for over a thousand years, due to an ancient legend that the country would be safe from invaders while ravens remain there. Indeed, this idea is so firmly entrenched in the national psyche that when the raven population at the Tower dwindled during the Second World War, Winston Churchill arranged that ravens be "imported" from Wales to keep the country safe.

Despite its color, the Ancient Greeks had the raven as a solar symbol, and it is dedicated to the Goddess **Athena** and the God **Apollo**.

In Native American belief, the raven is a symbol of the Creator and as such is a powerful protector of humankind. Myths tell that the bird not only made the Universe but also discovered and looked after the first man. The shape-shifting abilities of the bird are mentioned here, too, and as such, the raven is the preferred bird of shamans, who converse with the birds in order to discover what the Gods have in store for mankind.

Rooster

The rooster is part of a large group of former jungle birds from India and Sri Lanka that have been domesticated by man for at least the last four thousand years. The reason for their widespread distribution around the world was due to their use in the 'sport' of cock fighting rather than for their use as providers of **eggs** and meat; these qualities came later.

The rooster would be easy to overlook as a bird of mystic significance. Nevertheless there's a rich history of magical lore surrounding the bird. Its name, the 'cock', says it all, and it's no accident that the name of the bird is the same as a slang word for penis.

The rooster is the ultimate masculine symbol; it signifies the **Sun**, power, pugnacity, and sexual prowess. It appears as the head of the mystical **Abraxas** symbol. These links with the Sun are universal; the frilled **red** comb on the bird's head looks like sunbeams. The rooster's aggressive stance made it a symbol of war for the Greeks and Romans. Aristophanes called it "the chicken of **Ares**," the God of War. Many Christian churches have the rooster on their weathervanes. This is not only because the cock appears with the coming of physical light and therefore spiritual enlightenment, but also because the bird is a poignant symbol within the faith. It crowed once when Christ was born, again when St. Peter denied Christ, and it will crow again as a warning of the Day of Judgement. According to the Qu'ran, conversely, the end of the world will be upon us when the cock stops crowing.

All the solar power and masculine energy of the rooster made it fitting as a sacrifice to the God Apollo. Later, people believed that they could harness this energy by eating the bird, which explains in part why a bowl of chicken soup is said to have such a fortifying effect.

In the East cockerels are bred specifically to live in and around Shinto **temples**. The Rooster also appears as one of the **twelve** signs of the **Chinese Zodiac**, where the attributes of people born under the sign include enthusiasm and a sense of humor.

Because of its association with lust and pride, the cockerel is not a favorable bird in Tibetan Buddhism, and forms one of a trio of 'three poisons' in the Wheel of Life; it stands alongside the **serpent** and the **pig** as a reminder not to become too attached to material things.

Sparrow

Sadly, the sparrow has latterly become a not-so-secret symbol of the decline in the bird population and is held as an example of what can happen as a result of modern farming methods and the use of chemicals. Nevertheless, for thousands of years the sparrow has held a close place in the hearts of people as a symbol of satisfied domesticity, living in close proximity with us, happy to share space, and being so much a part of the natural landscape as to be virtually unnoticeable. The close relationship between humankind and this small, unassuming **brown** bird led to a certain species of it being called the House Sparrow, and it is used in the Bible as an example of something that is cheap and plentiful, described as being sold "two for a farthing" although nevertheless important in the eyes of God. Here, the sparrow is a symbol of the importance of every living thing, no matter how lowly.

The sparrow, because it breeds so prolifically, is sacred to the Greek Goddess of Love, Aphrodite. Sparrow **eggs** were used as an **aphrodisiac**, and Aristotle described the birds as "wanton." Sparrows are also the birds of Cupid.

Stork

When parents think that their children are too young to be told how babies are made, the issue is fudged for a while longer, and the child is often told that a stork brings the infant. The image of the bird flying along carrying the baby in a sling is popularly used on christening cards and other artifacts. This affectation seems to exist across the world, even reaching into the mythology of the Plains Indians. The reason is unclear but it might be because storks will happily live in close proximity to humans. In some parts of Europe cartwheels are affixed to roofs to provide a stable base for the bird's nest, and it is considered a bad omen if this migratory bird does not return to the same spot each year. The reddish pink marks on the eyelids of a newborn child are often called "stork bites."

The stork is famously dutiful towards its parents, so much so that in Rome a Stork Law (Lax Ionia) was passed to ensure that Roman citizens would emulate the bird and take care of their elders.

In Egypt, the stork was associated with the **Ba**, or **soul** of a person, and the Ba was depicted with the body of stork and the head of a human. They believed that the soul could leave the body at night but would return at the same time every morning, a reference to the punctual nesting and migratory habits of the bird. It was for the same reasons that the stork also came to be associated with reincarnation and the transmigration of **souls**.

Swallow

The migratory habits of the swallow are so reliable that they are a universal symbol of the arrival of spring. Because of this they are a welcome sight and most people regard it as a privilege if the bird chooses to live in close proximity to humans. The Chinese even used to date their **equinoxes** to the swallow's arrival and departure. The spring equinox is the traditional time of fertility rites, and resulting pregnancies would sometimes be blamed on the girl's eating a swallow's **egg**. Confucius was allegedly born through this mechanism, which led to his nickname of "The Swallow's Son." There was a great deal of speculation about where the swallow went for the winter months. Aristotle theorized that they hibernated in holes, and an eighteenth-century writer supposed that they traveled as far as the **Moon**.

Legends from as far a-field as Asia, Eastern Europe and the Americas tell of the swallow as a great friend to man, because the bird brought **fire**. This explains the forked tail, which was said to have been burned in the process.

The speedy chatter of the swallow meant that a broth made of the birds would cure a stutterer of this affliction, and another curious recipe cites swallows as an ingredient in a cure for epilepsy. Another cure for epilepsy was to take the swallow stone—a kind of **bezoar**—from the bird, grind it to a powder and take in **water**.

The swallow was associated with the Egyptian Goddess **Isis**, who was said to change into a swallow at night and fly around **Osiris**' coffin, singing mournful songs, until the **Sun** arrived back the next morning.

The one exception to the swallow as a positive symbol comes from Persia. Here, they believed that the bird signified the separation of friends and neighbors, and so represented loneliness, migration, and separation. Despite this, the swallow was still referred to as the Bird of Paradise, and when **Mecca** was besieged by Christian forces, the birds helped save the day by dropping stones onto the heads of the Muslims' enemy.

Swan

The appearance of the swan, an ethereal, otherworldly creature, floating gracefully upon the calm **waters** that resemble the spirit world and the eternal feminine, packs a powerful symbolic punch even without any prior knowledge of the myths and legends surrounding the bird that have aided and abetted its significance. Its pure **white** color, its strength, and its beauty make it a symbol of light, both of the direct light of the **Sun** and the reflected light of the **Moon**.

Despite plenty of evidence to the contrary, the swan is believed to be silent until its moment of **death**, when its song is said to be the first and last sound it utters. Therefore, "swansong" has come to mean the final expression of an artist's work, for example, or a late resurgence before the final demise. Curiously, though, the name "swan" comes from an Anglo-Saxon word *sounder*, which has the same root as "sound" or "sonnet."

Swans are also believed to mate for life and so are emblematic of fidelity and longevity.

In the UK, the swan is under the protection of the crown. This legislation is believed to date back to the twelfth century, and even today only the household of the ruling monarch is allowed to eat the meat of the swan. In Germany, oaths were taken upon a swan.

The swan is the symbol of the poet; druidic bards wore **cloaks** made of swan's **feathers** as a shamanic totem to enable them to contact the spirit of the muse. It was because of this that Ben Johnson refers to Shakespeare as the "sweet swan of Avon." In Ancient Greece, the swan was the attribute of the **Muses** and the symbol of Apollo, the God to whom poetry and song belong. Apollo could shape-shift into the form of a swan, and when he was born, **seven** swans flew around the island of his birth, seven times.

Two swans are frequently depicted as being joined by a chain. This imagery appears all over the world, and although there is conjecture about what this symbol means, it is likely to signify the spiritual and material worlds that the bird symbolizes, because it moves in the elements of **water**, **earth**, and **air**. Sometimes one of the birds appears with a solar wheel, signifying the fourth element of **fire**. Swans pulled the chariot of the Sun. Eros, too, the God of Love, traveled in a chariot drawn by swans in their guise as symbols of fidelity and love.

The otherworldly appearance of the swan has led to its being regarded as one of the shape-shifting birds, and stories from all over the world have the swan transform into a beautiful human girl who will live among humankind until circumstances conspire to return her to her own world once again.

Hindu belief supports this idea of the swan as symbolic of a creature that resides between two worlds. Because it moves in the elements of **water** and **air**, the swan represents both the spiritual and material world. Some myths have the **goose** as the bird that laid the **egg** from which the Universe hatched, but in India, the swan is given this honor: the Hamsa is a mythical water bird that symbolizes the union of spirit and matter, and is symbolized by two swans. The Parama Hamsa represents

A LUNAR BIRD CALENDAR

Inspired by a concept from Robert Graves' *The White Goddess*, this calendar is based around the thirteen moons contained within a year.

From	To	Bird	From	To	Bird
Dec 24	Jan 21	The Pheasant	Jul 9	Aug 5	The Starling
Jan 22	Feb 18	The Duck	Aug 6	Sept 2	The Crane
Feb 19	Mar 18	The Snipe	Sept 3	Sept 30	The Titmouse
Mar 19	Apr 15	The Gull	Oct 1	Oct 29	The Swan
Apr 16	May 13	The Hawk	Oct 30	Nov 25	The Goose
May 14	Jun 10	The Night Crow	Nov 26	Dec 22	The Rook
Jun 11	Jul 8	The Wren			

The entire day of December 23rd belongs exclusively to the eagle.

the Supreme Self, and its name means the Supreme Swan.

It's also worth mentioning the story of the Ugly Duckling, who eventually turns into the beautiful swan. The story is emblematic of the idea of the transformative powers of the bird.

TURKEY

Birds, like animals, naturally carry their strongest symbolic meanings in their place of origin, which in the case of the turkey is in the Americas.

It is a symbol of fertility and motherhood, and because it lives close to the ground and is the avian opposite of the high-flying **eagle**, it's sometimes called the **Earth** Eagle and is representative of the Earth Mother.

To the Toltecs, the turkey was "the jeweled fowl," because of its sparkling **colors**, and was reserved as food only for festivals and ritual occasions. Nothing of the turkey was wasted; after it had been eaten, the **feathers** were used as ornamentation, and the **bones** used to make musical instruments or whistles.

For some tribes, however, most notably the Pueblo, the bird was considered so sacred that it was never eaten but kept for its beautiful feathers alone, which grow back after plucking. Because the bird was felt to be able to communicate with the Gods and could intercede on behalf of human beings, in the Pueblo funeral rites whole turkeys were buried along with the corpse, and occasionally these **bones** are still found. **Prayer sticks** decorated in a specific way with turkey feathers were given to the families of the deceased.

The Mayans used the emblem of the turkey in their codices, where it indicated fertility. The bird was decapitated in rituals designed to ensure that the Gods would favor man with an abundant harvest.

Although the Bald **Eagle** was chosen as the national bird of the United States, Benjamin Franklin was far more enthusiastic that the turkey should have this honor. He suggested that the eagle was a bird of "bad moral character" and that the turkey was the more courageous bird.

VULTURE

An archetypal symbol of death and decay, the vulture frequently stars in cowboy movies where it circles ominously, coasting along on the thermals, an indicator of imminent doom. It is true that vultures are scavenger birds but its supposed talent of being able to predict death is unsubstantiated. The Latin name for the bird, *Cathartidae*, has the same root as the word "catharsis," meaning purification, and much of the symbolism of the vulture follows this idea.

The Egyptians, however, relied on a more wholesome aspect of the vulture's character to inform their own symbolic meaning. A notoriously good mother, the vulture personifies the process of birth and the maternal instinct, and is associated with **Isis**. The Goddess is shown enfolded in the **wings** of a huge vulture, the solar disc behind her. The vulture was so revered that there was also a Vulture Goddess, Nekhbet, who is depicted with the head of the bird. Vultures were called "Pharaoh's Pets" because they were invaluable in keeping the streets clean.

The Greeks believed that the bird was

born of the wind. The bird, for them, symbolized spirit and matter combined in one body. There was also a connection with the God of War, Ares, because the birds appeared at battlegrounds.

Because the bird effectively sustains itself by eating rotting flesh, the vulture was viewed with awe and was accorded the magical powers of a sorcerer. It was regarded as an essential part of the cycle of birth and death and symbolic of the Great Mother.

In Rome, auguries were carried out to determine which of the two brothers, Romulus or Remus, should determine the site of the new city. Romulus was favored by the sighting of **twelve** vultures and therefore was given the casting vote on the whereabouts of the city, and was declared its founder.

Native Americans, too, hold the vulture in high esteem and also see the bird as symbolic of both spirit and matter. A **feather** from the bird, used as a **totem** object, enabled the shaman to "come back to the self" after shape-shifting ceremonies. The bird is a symbol of purification and renewal.

In Africa, the Bambara tribe has a grade of initiates known as "Vultures." The initiate is scorched, and therefore cleansed, by the effects of his initiation, and then has access to the wisdom of the Gods. This process of initiation uses the vulture symbol as one of rebirth, and after the ceremony, the candidate is believed to have transcended physical death and is able to transform dirt, filth, and decay into the equivalent of gold in **alchemy**.

Because of its habits of renewing and recycling, the vulture is favored among Buddhists, and indeed, the fifth Dalai Lama was believed to be able to shape-shift into the form of a **white** vulture. This magical vulture was then able to educate other vultures, especially those that consumed human bodies at the sky burial sites; the birds would also bless these corpses by tapping them **three** times with their beaks. To Buddhists, the vulture's habit of stripping flesh from bones is synonymous with the revelation of truth.

WOODPECKER

Also called the Flicker, the woodpecker is believed to be a magical bird with powers of sorcery and clairvoyance. This may be because its behavior signifies changes in the weather; many of the folk names of the bird throughout Europe reflect this ability, for example *Pic de la Pluie* or Rain Woodpecker in France, and *Ragnfagel*, or rainbird, in Sweden.

The knocking sound made by the woodpecker as it burrows into the **tree** where it makes its home leads to an association with **Odin**, the Norse God of Thunder and also with **Mars**, the Roman God of War. The image of the bird is seen on Roman coinage because the founding twins, Romulus and Remus, were said to have been given solid **food** by woodpeckers, after they had been suckled by a she-**wolf**.

The bird's association with thunder and lightning occurs elsewhere in the world. For example, the Pueblo associate the bird's drumming with the sound of the thunder that is the precursor to rain. Many Native Americans believed that the woodpecker had the skill to be able to avert lightning, and its **feathers** were used in rituals and ceremonies because of this power. Among some tribes, the woodpecker was believed to have brought

fire to humankind.

Sometimes in northern Europe the woodpecker is called the Gertrude Bird. In a story retold by the Brothers Grimm, an old woman, Gertrude, who refuses to feed Christ and St. Peter, is turned into a woodpecker.

Wren

Although the wren is tiny it is known as the King of the Birds and symbolizes the power of humility. Despite its size and modest appearance, the wren is one of the most sacred of all birds and has a large role to play in myths and legends, where it is regarded as a magician, a magical symbol, and an emblem of wise intelligence.

In the Celtic pantheon, the bird is the symbol of the Druid, and its names in Irish, Drui, and in Welsh, Drwy share the same root as the word for Druid. The royal nature of the bird is agreed all over Europe; in Spain, Germany, Italy, Scandinavia, and France the name for the wren is the same as that for "king." (In the Breton language and that of the Pawnee, however, the word for wren is the same as that for "happy.")

One explanation for this symbolism comes in a story where the **eagle** challenges all the birds to see which of them can fly the highest; although the wren is ignored as being too insignificant, the smaller bird wins the race when it secretes itself in the feathered ruff around the throat of the eagle. The wren pops out at the opportune moment when the eagle begins his descent, and wins the race by flying a few inches higher than the bigger bird. Therefore, the strength of the wren is in the might of its intellect and wit, as opposed to mere physical brute force and size.

Because the wren protects its home vigorously, the **feathers** of the wren became a totemic symbol of protection, kept in houses for this purpose. Paradoxically, witches and warlocks were believed to be able to shapeshift into wrens and yet their feathers allegedly protect against these malevolent creatures.

The early Christian Church in Europe tried to enfold into itself the beliefs of the older pagan religions. As part of this, the Church drew parallels between the wren, as a symbol of royalty and humility, and the Virgin Mary, and called the bird "the Lady of Heaven's Hen."

The wren is one of a number of birds that are reputed to have brought **fire** to humankind. This myth also explains the reddish appearance of the bird in flight.

Because of its sacred status, anyone harming a wren should expect dire consequences. Despite this, once a year the rules were lifted, and on St. Stephen's Day, December 26, the Hunting of the Wren took place in parts of the UK, Ireland, and France. The bird was caught, ritually slaughtered, and carried from house to house in a tiny box surrounded by a hoop or bower of **flowers**. The meaning of this curious ritual is unclear. It may have symbolized the death of winter and the coming of spring, since the wren is highly visible during the colder months of the year as it does not migrate; or it may have been because of a legend that the martyr St. Stephen, about to escape from prison, was caught again when the wren inadvertently alerted the prison guard.

Part Four

FLORA

THE CONCEALED WISDOM
OF THE PLANT KINGDOM

Flora may have been a relatively minor **Goddess** of the Greek pantheon, but was elevated in status since she kindly lent her name to all the world's abundant plant life. **Flowers**, plants, and fungi constitute one part of this section, and **trees**, the other.

There are perfectly reasonable scientific explanations about how a **seed**, with the simple addition of the darkness of the soil, **water**, **air**, and sunshine, can transform into something as magnificent as, say, an **oak tree**. However, when those **green** shoots appear above the ground, that's as close a thing to magic as anything you could ever experience. It's not a surprise, therefore, that the seed itself is one of our most significant sacred symbols.

Plants themselves carry all the significance of the **Sun**, since they derive their properties from the power that they accrue from it. The **spiral** spacing of leaves and the shapes of some flowers sometimes conceal the **golden** mean, the depiction of the mystical **spiral** that's the mathematical equation for growth. Plants that have medicinal properties are considered, in the Vedic tradition, to be among the most valuable gifts that were ever given to mankind, and they are treated with the same respect as deities. We owe our knowledge of these useful plants to the intuition and experimentation of our ancestors, who endured poisoning and even death to discover their hidden nature.

THE GARDEN OF LIFE

Throughout the many thousands of years of human evolution, we have been continually surrounded by **trees**, **plants**, **flowers**, and herbs. All the glories of the vegetable world provided an enduringly beautiful backdrop to the early fight for survival, stimulating our senses in diverse ways. As well as appealing to taste, sight, touch, and smell, the sound of plants also gives information; for example, rustling leaves or the snap of a twig might warn of a possible intruder. Plants find ways to survive in even the harshest climates or the most unlikely places. The origins of the word "vegetable" come from the Latin, *vegetare* meaning "to enliven," from *vegetus*, meaning "vigorous" or "active."

When man started to think about his own origins, it isn't surprising that he assumed that a God must have created him, in the same Godlike form, using the very earth that also gave birth to the plants. The name of this first man, Adam, means "clay." It's no coincidence that the idyllic place that was inhabited by this first man was a garden. The plants that surrounded him were his friends and companions, providing food, medicine, materials for his shelters, shade on a hot sunny day, and fuel in a cold winter. Plants also provide fibers that make fabrics; the first piece of **clothing**, after all, was a leaf.

Plants mark the changing of the **seasons**. They die, only to be reborn, appearing in the **spring** like long-lost friends. With the development of agriculture, we learned to harness the energy of plants for our own specific purpose and convenience. The contents of our kitchens today, stuffed with **food** from all over the world, would have been a source of considerable astonishment for our ancestors. Substances that they would never have heard of, from all over the **planet**, are ours, within easy reach. This abundance is thanks to thousands of years of testing and experimentation with plants; eating them raw, cooking them, smoking them, adding them to other substances to see what might happen. Sometimes these experiments had good results, sometimes bad. Even now there are certain mushrooms listed in textbooks as "edibility unknown." It's likely that many people died before the connection was made to poisonous plants.

THE DOCTRINE OF SIGNATURES

Our ancestors were, of necessity, a superstitious people. In searching for the secrets held within plants, it made sense that they applied the Doctrine of Signatures, the belief that something is related to whatever it resembles. After all, they had nothing else to go on. This notion is still influential despite advances in botanical sciences. The **pomegranate** and **tomato**, for example, are fertility symbols because of their abundant **seeds**. The folk names of plants also give us clues about our ancestors' interpretations of them. The

pansy is also called the hearts" ease; the plant is said to cheer the **heart** and takes its name from the shape of its leaves. Another name for **hemlock** is "poison parsley"; it looks like parsley, and is poisonous. This rule does not always apply, though. For example, the **mistletoe** is called "all heal," but the plant is poisonous.

It makes sense that anyone with a comprehensive knowledge of herbs would be accorded due respect; these people could, quite literally, kill or cure. The Breton word for "herb," *louzaouenn*, is also the same as for "medicine." This knowledge of the plant kingdom extended to the herbs and flowers that have an effect on the mind, the plants that contain mind-altering chemicals.

PLANTS AS TOOLS OF TRANSITION

Psychedelic and psychotropic substances act on the mind to give an alternative view of reality, inducing dreams and visions, and providing a gateway to another dimension that is the realm of the Gods. These plants, and their uses, were preciously guarded, a secret held by those that were considered wise enough to analyze these messages: the shaman or sorcerer. Taking such a drug was a rite of passage, a spiritual exploration accompanied by due ceremony to make sure that the initiate arrived safely at the other end of the journey.

Although today we understand these chemical constituents and know how they affect us, the plants that contain them are still given sacred status. The literature and mythos surrounding them is extensive. As well as **ayahuasca**, opium, **cannabis**, peyote buttons, and various magic mushrooms, several more common plant-related substances affect us in similar ways. Alcohol, for example, is the result of fermented plant materials combined with yeast and sugar.

FLOWERS, PLANTS AND FUNGI

Generally speaking, flowers are symbols of love, a fitting association since they are the sexual parts of plants. However, because they fade and die quite quickly, they are also a reminder of the transitory nature of the material world. In Welsh myth, Blodeuwedd, whose name means "blossoms," was a beautiful girl, magically constructed from thousands of flowers. However, she was fickle, like the flowers that were an inherent part of her being, and betrayed her husband.

In exploring the secret symbolism of flowers, there is, it seems, a myth for every single kind of flower on the planet, the imagination of these ancient people being seemingly limitless. The Greeks were particularly prolific in this area. It's almost as though the flowers and the stories work together to offer explanations about all aspects of their "personalities." **Colors**, too, have an important part to play in analyzing flower symbols. The Japanese art of flower arranging, *Ikebana*, uses flowers to write a sort of poetry related to the cosmos, the passing of time, the **seasons**, and **elements**, and there is an extensive flower symbolism completely dedicated to the art. The flower is also used as a symbol of the **soul**; the "Secret of the Golden Flower," in Tantric and Taoist philosophies, is the attainment of spiritual union, an alchemical process that unifies the **spirit**, or essence, with the **breath**, **fire**, and **water**; the "flower" itself is an allegory for the Elixir of Life.

In compiling this entire section, it made sense to group all the plants together (apart from **trees**). After all, some herbs are also flowers, and some flowers have a value in herbal medicine.

ACANTHUS

The acanthus is a thistle-like shrub with long flower spikes, generally preferring warm and dry climates. The large leaf of the acanthus (often up to **twelve** inches long and just as wide) has been stylized and adapted as a symbol, often appearing as a carving at the tops of architectural columns (the Corinthian style). The acanthus, because it is a very resilient plant, is a symbol of immortality. Where it is seen on gravestones, this is its secret meaning.

ACONITE

Also called monk's hood (because of its shape) or wolfsbane (because it has powerful anti-**werewolf** properties), all parts of this plant are poisonous, so much so that even to touch it with bare hands can be fatal. A very pretty **blue** plant that looks a little like a delphinium, its attractive appearance belies its great toxicity.

Aconite was sacred to the great witch queen, **Hecate**, who gave it yet another of its names, *Hecateis herba*. It is one of the sacred herbs said to have been used by witches to help them fly; indeed, if ingesting the plant does not actually kill you, symptoms of aconite poisoning include hallucinations, dizziness, and nervous excitement, all of which may have contributed to the flying sensations experienced by witches.

Not only is aconite said to be able to repel werewolves, but it can change you into one. This is partly explained by a legend. When Hercules was completing one of his labors, he dragged Cerberus, the watchdog of Hades, along with him on his way from the nether regions back to the Earth. The furious **dog** snarled, spat, and frothed at the mouth, and wherever his saliva dropped then up sprang a wolfsbane flower.

Mythology and legend both ancient and modern are full of examples of the aconite being used to murder someone or to help someone commit suicide. Finally, carrying the seed of the aconite will apparently make you invisible.

AMARANTH

Also known as "love lies bleeding" because of its long strings of **red** flower heads, the amaranth is a symbol of immortality. Its name means "unfading" because its flowers are very long-lived. In Greek mythology the flower was sacred to Artemis, who had a disciple called Amarynthus, who was a hunter-priest. In his eponymous village there was a **temple** dedicated to the Goddess, Artemis Amarynthia.

The Aztecs also saw the amaranth as a symbol of immortality. Its flowers were mixed with **honey** to make effigies of the Gods; these effigies were then cut into pieces and shared among the people so that they could ingest the essence of the deity in much the same way that the Holy Communion works today.

The amaranth is believed to have healing powers. In addition, a crown of amaranth flowers is said to bestow supernatural talents on the wearer.

ANEMONE

Anemone comes from the Greek *anemos*, meaning **wind**, an appropriate name for the short-lived nature of this small, fragile flower, which symbolizes the transience of life itself. Ovid said that the flower was both "born of the wind, and carried away by it." The flower is popular in funeral **wreaths** where, again, its symbolic meaning carries a hidden message.

There's a Greek myth, too, which tells the story of the anemone. Aphrodite wept when she mourned the death of her lover Adonis, and as the tears fell on the ground they became anemones. But Aphrodite's sadness didn't last long, and shortly afterwards she took another lover; therefore the flowers also symbolize the ephemeral aspect of love.

Any **red** flower was adopted by the Christians as a symbol of the **blood** of Christ, and red anemones are no exception. In this instance the flowers are also representative of pain and suffering.

ANGELICA

Also called Archangel or the "herb of the angels" because an angel is said to have revealed the healing powers of the plant to a monk. All aspects of this herb carry protective symbolism; as a medicinal herb it is used to treat **stomach** disorders and urinary tract infections, and because of its association with angelic beings, it is scattered around a home to keep out **demons** and other malevolent influences. Native Americans burn angelica during healing rituals and a piece of angelica root can be used as a **talisman** for gamblers. Smoking angelica is believed to produce visions.

ANGEL'S TRUMPET

See **Datura**.

AQUILEGIA

The aquilegia is an unusual, complex-looking and ethereal flower. It is associated with magical powers, and carries hidden secrets within the elaborate folds and ruffles of its petals.

Aquilegia is associated with two **birds** that have opposing characteristics. Initially the flower was called the columbine, after the Latin word for **dove**, *columba*, since its nectar gland is dove-like in shape and because the petals look a little like a **circle** of doves. But Latin monks renamed the flower the aquilegia from the Latin for "**eagle**," *aquila*; this is because the curlicued spurs at the back of the petals look like the talons of the eagle. The eagle, of course, is a flamboyant bird, symbolic of kings, emperors, and power. The dove is the diametric opposite of the eagle, a bird of humble appearance associated with peace and love. The dove is the "secret" symbol of the United States and balances the eagle, which is a more overt sign of this nation. Other names for this flower include the culverwort, from Old English words meaning a "gathering of pigeons."

Sometimes the Columbine is used in religious paintings as a secret symbol for the dove, which in turn represents the Holy Spirit.

The plant has medicinal qualities. It is said to be a powerful antitoxin, and also an **aphrodisiac**. The seeds of the flower are said to cure infertility if they are put under the mattress. This association of the flower with sex meant that it was considered very bad form for a man to give a bouquet containing the flowers since they carried too overt a message.

Because aquilegia has **five** petals, then it is a naturally-occurring **pentagram**, and was believed to warn off evil at the same time as being a flower of witches. The flower is also an example of the **golden mean** occurring in the natural world.

The aquilegia is dedicated to the Norse Goddess, **Freya.**

ASPHODEL

A modest little flower, the asphodel is very ancient and was associated with the underworld in Greek mythology, and a crown of the blossoms was worn by **Persephone**, the Queen of the Dead. The Elysian Fields, the marshy meadows wherein wandered the spirits of the dead, were carpeted in asphodel flowers. The asphodel can be eaten, and its bulb made into a kind of **bread** said to be enjoyed by both the living and the dead.

The asphodel is also a symbol of protection, and is fashioned into **crosses** to strengthen this meaning.

AYAHUASCA

A tall, climbing **forest** plant, ayahuasca is the most important plant in the spiritual life of South America, and is carefully used in sacred rituals so that the shaman or intrepid explorer can reach the depths of his innermost consciousness. The benefits of taking the ayahuasca drug as part of a guided ritual is said to enable the celebrant to witness not only his own birth but also the dawning of creation, receive wisdom from the Ancestors, meet the Great Spirit and also be completely aware of being a part of the All.

The word *ayahuasca* translates as the "**vine** of the **soul**." The bark of the vine is made into an infusion which is then consumed with due ceremony. Popular shared hallucinations as a result of ayahuasca poisoning include witnessing the appearance of God as a great bright **bird**.

BAMBOO

In Japan, the bamboo is one of three lucky trees, along with the **pine** and the **plum**. The roots of the bamboo are incredibly strong and resilient; there's a saying that a bamboo **forest** is the safest place to be in the event of an earthquake, as the roots are strong enough to withstand the moving ground. The bamboo is therefore associated with strength and stability.

The painting of bamboo stems is a spiritual and meditative process for Buddhists and Taoists. The spaces between the **knots** along the straight stem of the plant represent the concept known as "voidness of heart."

The Yek'uana people of Brazil share a name with the bamboo; they call it *uana*, meaning something like "clarinet." They use instruments made from the bamboo to make their sacred and religious **music**. The main ceremony is called the *ua-uana* and the God that is invoked is called Uanaji. Therefore the bamboo, music, people, and God are perceived as sharing the same **soul**.

BARLEY

A useful **food** grain in use since ancient times, barley can also be used to make an alcoholic drink, something the Babylonians had discovered as early as 3000 BC.

In India, the barley is sacred to the God Indra, who is described as "the one who ripens the barley." The plant is abundant in seeds and, in common with other such plants, is symbolic of male potency. As such it is scattered at weddings in order to bring fertility to the bride and groom.

BASIL

Basil leaves are said to contain magical powers, used in both love potions and as a divinatory tool to assess the nature of a marriage or relationship. More practically, the leaves can be used to cure wounds. If a basil leaf is laid on the **hand** of a promiscuous person it will apparently wither. It is the herb of the Haitian Goddess of Love, Erzuli.

The importance of basil is a part of Hindu tradition, too, and is partly explained in myth. The Goddess, Tulasi, was seduced by the God, Vishnu. When she realized what had happened Tulasi was horrified and killed herself. As a result Vishnu declared that she would be a reminder of faithfulness and purity, and would thereafter keep women from becoming widows. The holy basil that sprang from her ashes became a symbol of love, immortality, and protection. The Sanskrit name for this holy basil is *Tulasi*, which means "the incomparable one."

The word "basil" has Greek and Roman origins, meaning "royal" or "king." The herb was believed to be able to counteract the venom of the **Basilisk**, whose name also shared the same origins. Basil can counteract other evil, too, and basil water is supposed to be particularly effective in **exorcism**.

BELLADONNA

This plant is called "beautiful lady" because the court ladies of the Italian Renaissance used it to enlarge their pupils and so render themselves more attractive; however, this name belies the deadly poisonous nature of belladonna, a member of the potato family. Its other name, deadly nightshade, is far more fitting to its toxic nature. Children have been known to die after eating just **two** or **three** berries. Another sinister aspect of the plant is its association with witches, who used deadly nightshade to bring about hallucinatory visions. As with many poisonous plants, however, there are medicinal benefits to be had from the plant, and one of its constituents, atropine, is a **heart** stimulant.

BETEL NUT

The betel nut is the seed of the areca palm that grows all over the warmer climes of the Far East, from India through to the Melanesian Islands. It has been used as both a stimulant and a narcotic for thousands of years, the first recorded use being mentioned in a Chinese manuscript dating back to 1000 BC. The nut is wrapped in a leaf of the betel pepper vine with a piece of shell lime, and the whole concoction is chewed as a stimulant. The areca palm is a sacred plant in India, its leaves and nuts being used to decorate statues of the Gods in Hindu ceremonies.

The betel nut is a symbol of love and **marriage**, and is used in wedding ceremonies and in love potions. This may stem from a legend in which a young man is transformed into an areca palm and his wife into the betel pepper vine. The betel is also used as an **aphrodisiac**.

In some parts of Vietnam, time is measured in the chewing of the betel quid, which takes between **three** to **four** minutes.

BLUEBELL

One of the names of the bluebell genus, *Endymion*, was the name of a beautiful Greek youth. Selene, the **Moon** Goddess, put Endymion into a deep sleep so that she could kiss him secretly every night as he lay, comatose, on a hillside. Because of this deep, dreamless sleep, bluebells were believed to help prevent nightmares.

BROOM

Because the broom shrub has long straight branches with lots of similarly long straight shoots that point in the same direction, it has been used for sweeping for thousands of years, hence the name "**broomstick**."

In Latin, the broom is called *planta genista*, and gives its name to the Plantagenet kings who used it as their emblem.

BUCKWHEAT

A variety of cereal crop that can be milled into a fine flour, buckwheat was brought to Europe by the Crusaders where it was called Saracen wheat. It was later renamed because its seed resembles the beechnut—hence "boc," the Anglo-Saxon word for **beech**.

In Japan, buckwheat noodles—or Soba—are popular, and because buckwheat dough is used by goldsmiths to gather up tiny particles of **gold**, Soba is used as a charm to attract wealth. The noodles are eaten on New Year's Eve to ensure that the coming year will bring good fortune, especially the financial kind.

CAMELLIA

For the Japanese, the camellia is a symbol of friendship, harmony and grace. However, for the Samurai class the flower symbolized death and the fleeting nature of life.

The flower was one of the most sought-after of the nineteenth century, the cause of financial speculation, and very expensive. They therefore became a status symbol that could be enjoyed only by the very wealthy.

The camellia is similar in appearance to the **rose**, but somehow has a more sedate quality for all its elegant sexuality. It is also a symbol of pride and aloofness, as reflected in Alexandre Dumas Jr.'s novel, *La Dame Aux Camellias*, whose heroine carries a bouquet of **white** camellias for 25 days then swaps them for **red** ones, as a signal that she is sexually available.

Chamomile

The chamomile flower takes its root from a Greek word meaning "**apple**," a reference to the distinct apple scent given off by the plant, especially if it is crushed. The Egyptians held chamomile to be sacred to the **Sun** God, Ra, as did the Teutons, who dedicated it in turn to their Sun God, Baldur.

Chamomile has protective qualities, and a wreath of it hung in the home will apparently protect the house from thunder and **lightning**.

Chrysanthemum

The chrysanthemum is the emblem of the Japanese Imperial family. The flower is a solar symbol, and its many layers of orderly petals mean that it is associated with longevity and immortality. There's even an annual festival dedicated to the flower, National Chrysanthemum Day, also called the Festival of Happiness. In China, too, the flower is seen as a symbol of vitality.

The chrysanthemum flowers late into the year, at the end of the summer and into fall; often it is the last flower in the garden, hence its reputation as the flower that brings not only happiness but longevity.

The flower is an ambiguous mix of restraint and exuberance; it is a show-off, whilst retaining a certain orderliness and formality. The name comes from the Greek *chrysos*, meaning "golden," and *anthemum* meaning "flower."

Clover

The clover stands for protection, fertility, and abundance, and if brought into the home serves as a charm to keep away witches. It is worn for the same reason. The clover has **3** distinctly **heart**-shaped leaves, both elements that contribute to its benevolent reputation. The shamrock—the form of clover that is synonymous with all things Irish—was known as the *shamrakh* in Arabic countries and symbolized the **triple aspect** of the Goddess.

The rare **four**-leafed clover is a ubiquitous symbol of good luck, and finding one means that the bearer will be able to see **fairies** and **witches**, and recognize evil spirits. Accordingly, the four-leafed clover can protect from these creatures, too. The four-leafed clover or shamrock carries all the symbolism of the number 4.

Sometimes a **5**-leafed clover might be spotted by those who have particularly sharp eyesight. Because the number 5 combines the feminine **2** with the masculine 3, it symbolizes **marriage** or engagements.

Early Christian proselytizers, such as St. Patrick, used both the shamrock and the clover to demonstrate the three-in-one notion of the Trinity.

COCA

The ancient use of the leaves of the coca plant, which is cultivated primarily in South America, is well known. Mummies dating back to the fifth century AD were buried with a supply of the leaves. When these leaves are chewed, they have a stimulant effect that leaves the mouth feeling numb. The Incas recognized the special qualities of the plant and called it the "food of the Gods," reserving its use for sacred rituals. However, the breakdown of the Inca Empire meant that the restrictions surrounding the plant, as a sacred herb, were relaxed. It's possible that Spanish missionaries exploited the use of the coca plant since chewing the leaves masked hunger and meant the Andean Indians' work output increased. Philip II of Spain decided that the drug was essential to the well-being of the Indians but forbade its use in religious practices. It might be said that this edict signalled the end for the coca plant as a sacred herb. But this would not be the last time that people were exploited because of the drug. The coca plant is now arguably one of the most controversial plants in the world.

The source of this controversy is cocaine, the primary chemical compound of the coca plant. Its usefulness as a medicine is unfortunately belied by its recreational use. Cocaine is highly addictive; not only this, but the value of the drug means that cultivation of the coca plant has profound political and sociological repercussions. It is now US policy to discourage the cultivation of this crop.

COLUMBINE

See **Aquilegia**.

CROCUS

The crocus is perhaps best known for the particular species, *Crocus sativus*, whose stamens give us **saffron**, the bright **yellow** spice that has a color of the same name. Inevitably, the Greeks have a myth that explains the provenance of this color. Krokos was a handsome Greek youth, a mortal boy who was a friend of **Hermes**. Hermes accidentally killed his friend. **Three** drops of **blood** fell on the crocus flower and became the stamens that produce saffron.

The crocus flower itself was sacred in ancient Crete, and was dedicated to the Goddesses **Demeter** and **Persephone**.

DAISY

The scientific name of the daisy is *Bellis perennis*, but it attained its more popular name as a corruption of "day's **eye**," since it opens at sunrise and closes again at sunset. A symbol of innocence and gentleness, there's a Roman myth about the provenance of the flower. A nymph, Bellis, was playing with her friends at the edge of some woods when she drew the unwanted attention of Vetrumnus, the God of the Orchards. To escape his clutches, she changed into a daisy.

In Victorian times, as well as having the association with purity, the flower was a symbol of love; girls would pluck away the petals of the daisy repeating the lines "he loves me, he loves me not" as each petal fell away, and the final petal would give the answer.

The daisy is also a sign of the coming of **spring**, said to have arrived when **nine** of the little flowers could be trodden on.

DANDELION

The dandelion is so-called because the jagged shape of its petals look like the **teeth** of a **lion**; hence, *Dents de Lion*. If this humble little flower was difficult to grow it's likely that it would be highly prized for its beauty; since, however, the dandelion is a common weed, its sensational looks are often taken for granted. In an example of sympathetic magic, because the plant contains a thick milky sap it was believed to be good for the production of sperm.

The dandelion clock, the delicate pompom-shaped seed head of the flower, is associated with old age and the passing of **time**; children count the number of **breaths** needed to blow all the seeds away as a method of telling the time.

DATURA

The datura (also known as angel's trumpet) is a jungle plant with beautiful, bell-shaped flowers. There is a (possibly apocryphal) tale that Victorian and Edwardian ladies, sitting in conservatories full of exotic plants from the far-flung places of the British Empire, would place their teacups underneath the datura plant since the moisture dripping from it caused strange and rather pleasant sensations. These ladies may have been shocked to learn that the effects were produced by the psychotropic chemicals in the plant, which makes the datura sacred for shamans in South America and Mexico, who use it to induce a trance-like state. The seeds are pounded into a paste and washed down with beer.

Datura is highly toxic, having reputedly caused more deaths by poisoning than any other plant; but provided the shaman doesn't take a physical as well as mental trip into the Otherworld, he can enjoy up to three days' worth of auditory and visual hallucinations that apparently include conversing with imaginary beings.

FENNEL

A popular culinary herb, fennel also has magical properties; it is associated with **fire** and sacred to those divinities who ruled over this **element**. Prometheus was said to have carried fire from the **Heavens** to the Earth in a fennel stalk; the pith of the plant is said to be fireproof.

The **thyrsus**, a ritual **staff** made of a large fennel stalk topped with a **pine cone** and **ivy**, was a ritual object used by the followers of Dionysus.

Fennel is a fresh-scented and sharp-tasting herb with reviving qualities, so it is a symbol of rejuvenation.

The use of fennel in any kind of bouquet is a symbol that the recipient is worthy of praise.

Garlic

Garlic has strong antiseptic qualities and is good for warding off disease. As a vegetable symbol of protection, garlic really is second to none. Its most famous use, arguably, is as a **talisman** to ward off **vampires**; the garlic needs to be tied to the bed-head in an attempt to dissuade these demonic creatures.

In the Talmud, it is written that garlic increases the sexual potency of the male, yet during the Greek festivals sacred to **Athena** and **Demeter**, women ate garlic so that sexual abstinence was made easier … something to do with garlic's pungency, perhaps.

Like its relation the **onion**, garlic was believed to ward off snakes, and this could well be because of the efficacy of garlic in treating all kinds of affections. Shepherds in the Carpathian mountains still rub their hands with garlic before milking their ewes; this is a symbolic ritual that has its roots in solid fact, since the antibacterial powers of the garlic can prevent the spread of disease

Garlic used to be carried by brides as a symbol of good luck, although this practice seems to have died out.

In Borneo, garlic is believed to have the power to recover lost **souls**.

Ginseng

Ginseng is one of the plants accorded magical properties partly because of the appearance of its roots, which look like a human being. In the East, particularly in China, ginseng is revered as being the elixir of life and is called *panax ginseng* in recognition of its supposed powers of curing all ills. In Chinese mythology one of the **Eight Immortals** ate a ginseng root that was two feet long, and it is called "godlike." Symbolically, the ginseng plant represents longevity, vitality, vigor, strength, and clarity. Ginseng is also said to be an **aphrodisiac** and to increase both sexual potency and virility.

Gorse

Gorse, or Furze, is the seventeenth letter of the **Celtic Ogham Tree alphabet**, where its name is *Onn*.

Gorse flowers prolifically, even in the winter in some places, so is symbolic of fertility. The bright **yellow** flowers are a cheering sight and represent the **Sun**.

The gorse is an incredibly spiky shrub, and these vicious prickles give the plant protective qualities. Its impenetrable nature means that it can keep out **fairies** and other spirits, malicious or otherwise. This belief was most prevalent in Wales where gorse grows in profusion in wild places, happy in both poor soils and bad weather. Here, country dwellers planted it around their homes and farmsteads, where it provided not only a very effective stock-proof barrier, but kept out **witches** at the same time.

Gorse belongs to the element of **fire**. Not only do the spiny thorns look like flames, but the dry woody stems contain a high concentration of oil, so they catch light quickly and burn well. Cattle were herded through bonfires of gorse before being let out to their summer pasture, ensuring protection for the season.

GOURD

The gourd, in Taoism, is a symbol of good health. One of the **eight Taoist Immortals**, Li Tie Guai, had the gourd as his personal emblem, and because he was able to "escape" from his body, it became symbolic of release from the material world.

Gourds are used as containers for carrying **water**, and as such are emblematic of the body as the container of the **soul**.

GRASS

Often overlooked because it is one of the more prolific plants on the planet, the very mundanity of grass is the factor that elevates its symbolic status. As a litmus, grass is invaluable; dry, **brown**, and dying grass signifies a drought, whereas lush **green** grass is symbolic of healthy land and fertility. The Roman army gave a crown of grass, or *corona graminea*, as the highest of accolades to particularly effective warriors; symbolic of the very land itself, this crown was made of grasses, **flowers**, and weeds pulled from the battlefield. The entire army had to decide whether or not their leader deserved such a high accolade, which was given only after the most desperate of campaigns. Pliny the Elder recorded only **nine** men who had received this honor.

HEMLOCK

The very word "hemlock" conjures up the idea of poison, but curiously, although the hemlock is deadly for humans, it does not harm domesticated animals. The hemlock is symbolic of **death**, pure and simple, and, famously, was consumed by Socrates. After his trial, Socrates was given the death sentence and it was decreed that he must kill himself by drinking hemlock. The great philosopher used his philosophical outlook to great effect and drank the hemlock without fuss, even managing to describe his symptoms as the poison gradually overcame him. The whole episode was described by Plato. To his day, the phrase "to drink hemlock" is synonymous with committing suicide.

Hemlock used to be rubbed onto knives and swords to prepare them to kill the enemy, the poison further enhancing the potency of the blade as an instrument of death. The hemlock plant should not be confused with *Tsuga*, the tree genus of hemlock.

HEMP

Hemp is the name for all the different species of cannabis. *Cannabis sativa* and *Cannabis indica* were species that were smoked in many countries all around the world long before the Conquistadores discovered **tobacco**. Its ubiquity is reflected in its many different names; in India, it is called *bhang* or *ganja* from the Sanskrit words *bhanga* or *ghanjika*: in the Near East it is called *hashish* (incidentally, the origin of the word "assassin") from an Arabic word meaning hemp: in South Africa it is called *dakka*, and the native South American name of marijuana was interpreted by the Conquistadores as "Mary Jane." It's called "weed" just about everywhere.

The usefulness of hemp in making fabric is really overshadowed by its use as a narcotic plant. Its use as a ritual substance is well documented, with evidence dating back as far as Neolithic times. A mummified shaman was found in China in 2003 along with a leather basket containing fragments of seeds and leaves. Shamanistic use of cannabis included burning of the flowers of the plant to induce a trance-like state.

Of late, hemp has been adopted as a sacred herb by the Rastafarian movement and the cannabis leaf symbol is often depicted in the Rasta colors of **red, black**, and **yellow**. It is considered that the use of the herb purifies the **soul**, clears the mind, and promotes peacefulness.

The Mahayana Buddhist tradition sees hemp as a particularly sacred plant because it is associated with the Buddha, who, so they say, lived on one hemp seed per day as he journeyed towards enlightenment.

HENNA

Henna is the name for the dye produced from a small shrub called *Hawsonia inermis* or Jamaican mignonette. This plant likes to grow in hot climates such as India, Egypt, North Africa, and the Middle East.

Henna is made from the ground leaves of the plant and yields a reddish-**orange** dye that has been used by women to decorate and **color** their **hair** and **skin** for thousands of years, its use being both cosmetic and ritual. These decorations are called **mehendi** and the designs carry a rich symbolic tradition all of their own.

Henna symbols painted onto houses, and on **doorways** in particular, are said to protect the home from the evil **eye**. Henna is painted onto the foreheads of cattle and daubed onto tombs to deter evil spirits.

HYACINTH

The scent of the hyacinth is heady and powerful, and the flower itself is said to blossom in the fields inhabited by the Gods. The flowers were once popular in bridal bouquets because of the beauty and the scent.

In Greek mythology, Hyacinth was a beautiful youth who was loved by the God, Apollo. But the God of the West Wind was also enamored of Hyacinth, and when Apollo threw a discus, he blew it off course with the result that it dealt Hyacinth a fatal blow to the head. The flower sprouted up where Hyacinth's **blood** fell on the ground.

Possibly because of the early demise of the beautiful boy who bore the name of the flower, eating hyacinth bulbs was believed to offset the sexual maturity of adolescent males, despite the bulb being poisonous. Up until the eighteenth century, a paste made from hyacinth bulbs was applied to male genitals to stop the **hair** growing.

IRIS

In Greek mythology, Iris was the Goddess of the **Rainbow**. She is a female messenger of the Gods and the equivalent of **Hermes**. Iris wore a rainbow-colored veil that fluttered as she flew, and like Hermes she wore winged sandals. It is Iris who gave her name to the flower, which comes in iridescent rainbow hues of **purple, yellow, blue**, and **white**.

Iris the Goddess is said to guide female **souls** into the next world, and so in Greece iris flowers are put on graves of girls and women as a symbol of thanks to the Goddess for taking care of their spirits.

The Iris used to be called the "sword lily" because of the shape of its leaves, and the Latin name for the flower, *gladiolus*, means "little sword" although the iris and the gladiolus are actually different flowers.

The iris, as well as the **lily**, is one of the flowers that is said to have inspired the **fleur-de-lys**, and like this stylized flower symbol, the iris was an emblem of spiritual belief and worldly authority.

The root of the iris has been used in perfumery for hundreds, if not thousands, of years, and **amulets** made from iris root were said to protect the wearer from malice and magic spells.

In Japan, the iris has power as a purifier and preservative, planted on thatched roofs to protect the home, since it is believed to prevent **fire**. May 5 is the day of the "iris bath" in Japan. The leaves of the *shobu* are steeped in hot **water**, the ritual intended to protect the bather for the year to come. The leaves are also chopped up and added to *sake* as another beneficial blessing.

IVY

Ivy is traditionally seen as the female counterpart to the masculine **holly**, and the two plants are paired together symbolically in **Christmas** and Yuletide songs. Like the **vine**, ivy has tendrils that enable it to climb vigorously, and, like the vine, ivy is associated with **Dionysus**. He is often depicted using the plant to bind the nubile young ladies who would otherwise resist his advances. A **wreath** of ivy used to hang outside shops as a sign that **wine** might be purchased there.

Ivy was believed to be able to both cause and cure drunkenness, and an old cure for a hangover was to drink vinegar in which ivy berries had been boiled. It should be stated here, however, that most parts of the ivy are poisonous and it is not recommended that you try this remedy, no matter how bad your headache.

Houses with ivy growing on them are seen as being protected by the maternal nature of the plant, but the clinginess of the ivy is viewed as a less attractive female characteristic. It is this same binding tendency that makes ivy an ingredient in love charms.

Ivy appears in the **Ogham Tree Alphabet** where it is called *Gort*.

JUNIPER

The juniper berry is what gives the alcoholic spirit, gin, both its name and its delicate flavor. In pre-Christian times the juniper bush was believed to harbor **spirits** so offerings would be made to it to propitiate them. Junipers are symbolic of patience since the berries—which in fact are tiny cones—take **3** years to ripen. Buddhist monks use juniper wood in their sacred temple fires. The wood does not burn very well but gives off an aromatic smoke which is said to aid both meditation and inner visions.

Junipers happily grow in hilly, windswept places so they are symbolic of resilience. There's a legend that the infant Jesus and his parents hid in a juniper bush to escape Herod's soldiers.

Juniper berries are used to aid stomach ailments and are a purgative for worms. The old wife's method of inducing an abortion with a scalding hot bath and a bottle of gin has some truth in it; juniper berries contain a chemical that can cause uterine contractions, and to speak of a girl giving birth "under the savin" (an old word for the juniper) refers to an abortion induced by the plant.

THE LANGUAGE OF FLOWERS

The idea that a posy of flowers could convey a secret meaning, particularly between lovers, was originally an Eastern concept, although the flower as divine messenger is an ancient concept. The Buddha's words manifested as flowers dropping from the sky are an early example. The language of flowers is called floriography, and though this art gives specific meanings to flowers, these meanings do not always tie in with their more generally accepted symbolism.

This idea became popular in Europe (and consequently in America) after Lady Mary Wortley Montagu visited Turkey in 1718. Writing to her friends back home, she described the system she had discovered whereby flowers and other objects were used as a means of communication. This idea, called *hana kotoba*, also existed in Japan. It might seem strange to Westerners to think that the infamous Samurai warriors were particularly fond of this art, but its influence was so powerful that Samurai families often chose specific flowers as their crests, a similar device to the **heraldic** coats of arms.

Objects used to convey secret messages apart from flowers included **fruits** and other **food**, **gemstones** as well as valueless pebbles and even coal. Therefore a Turkish love-letter was not simply a piece of paper or a bunch of flowers, but a parcel or packet containing a very odd assortment of items.

It was flowers, however, that captured people's imagination. By the nineteenth century, the desire to catalogue or collect just about anything and everything spread like an epidemic, and lists of flowers and their meanings appeared in the early part of the century along with several books investigating the idea. Perhaps the most popular book was *Flower Lore, Historical, Legendary, Poetical and Symbolic*, written by a Miss Carruthers who lived in Inverness, and which was published in England in 1879. The book quickly became the standard "dictionary" of flower symbolism on both sides of the Atlantic. The Victorian passion for flowers made such a publication very timely; new territories had been explored and rare exotics were being cultivated in hothouses as status symbols. Real flowers were worn routinely in lapels and in hair as a form of **jewelry**. Floral images adorned stationery, fabrics, and china ornaments.

The language of flowers became more complex. Certain flower arrangements carried meanings that were more than the sum of their parts, and even the way in which flowers were offered was significant. For Victorians, the making of tussy mussies—which were small posies of flowers wrapped up in lace and ribbons—became a popular pastime.

Be that as it may, the lists of flowers and their meanings did vary, and this ambiguity continues today, although some meanings are generic. For example, the **red rose** is universally accepted as symbolizing love. The language of flowers continues to adapt according to how the flowers are used. The **daffodil**, for example, used to mean "unrequited love" but it now means "hope" because it has been used as an emblem for certain charities. The following list has been compiled from several different sources.

ACACIA—Secret love, considered bad luck if given to a woman

ACANTHUS LEAVES—Admiration for the Arts

ACHILLEA—Healing and comfort

ALMOND BLOSSOM—Hope, haste, watchfulness, virginity, and a happy marriage

AMARANTH—Faith, immortality, unfading love

AMARYLLIS—You are sought after, poetry

ANEMONE—Brevity, "go away!"

APPLE BLOSSOM—Preference, better things to come, good fortune

APRICOT BLOSSOM—Timid love

ARBUTUS—Thee only do I love

ARUM—Ardor

ASPARAGUS FERN—Fascination

ASPHODEL—Languor, regret, death

ASTER—Daintiness, a talisman of love

ASTER (China)—Fidelity, variety, I will think of thee

AZALEA—Take care, temperance, passion, chinese symbol of womanhood

BABY'S BREATH—Innocence, purity of heart

BACHELORS BUTTON—Single blessedness, celibacy

BALM—Sympathy

BALSAM—Ardent love

BEECH—Prosperity

BEGONIA—Beware, a fanciful nature

BELLADONNA—Fatal gift to a man

BELLS OF IRELAND—Good luck

BIRCH—Grace, meekness

BITTERSWEET—Truth

BLACK BRYONT/LADY'S SEAL—Be my support

BLUEBELL—Humility

BLUEBELL/BELL FLOWER—Humility, constancy, gratitude

BROOM—Humility, neatness

BUCK BEAN—Calm repose

BUTTERCUP—Childishness, riches

CACTUS—Endurance, my heart burns with love

CALLA LILY—Magnificent beauty

CALYCANTHUS/CAROLINA ALLSPICE/SWEET SHRUB—Benevolence

CAMELLIA—Admiration, Perfection, Good-Luck Gift for a Man, Gratitude

CAMELLIA (Pink)—Longing

CAMELLIA (Red)—You're a flame in my heart

CAMELLIA (White)—You're adorable

CANDYTUFT—Indifference

CANTERBURY BELLS/BELL FLOWER—Gratitude

CARDINAL FLOWER/SCARLET LOBELIA—Distinction

CARNATION (General)—Fascination, admiration

CARNATION (Pink)—I'll never forget you, women's love

CARNATION (Red)—My heart aches for you, admiration

CARNATION (Purple)—Capriciousness

CARNATION (Solid Color)—Yes

CARNATION (Striped)—No, wish I could be with you

CARNATION (White)—Sweet and lovely, innocence, pure love, woman's good-luck gift

CARNATION (Yellow)—You have disappointed me, rejection

CATCHFLY (RED)—Youthful love, I fall victim

CATTAIL—Peace, prosperity

CATTLEYA—Mature charms

CEDAR—I live but for thee, think of me

CELANDINE/PILEWORT/FIGWORT—Future joy

CHAMOMILE/GOLDEN MARGUERITE/ANTHEMIS—Energy in action

CHERRY BLOSSOM (double)—False Hopes

CHERRY BLOSSOM (single)—Education

CHICKWEED—I cling to thee

CHICORY—Frugality

CHRISTMAS ROSE/HELLEBORUS—Relieve my anxiety

CHRYSANTHEMUM (General)—You're a wonderful friend, cheerfulness and abundance

CHRYSANTHEMUM (Red)—I love you

CHRYSANTHEMUM (White)—Truth

CHRYSANTHEMUM (Yellow)—Slighted love

CINQUEFOIL—Beloved child

CLEMATIS—Artifice (ingenuity)

CLOVE—I love you secretly

CLOVER—Fertility

CLOVER (Four-leaf)—Be mine

CLOVER (Red)—Industry

CLOVER (White)—Think of me

COLCHICUM (MEADOW SAFFRON)—My best days fled

COLUMBINE—Folly

COLUMBINE (Purple)—Resolved to win

COLUMBINE (Red)—Anxious

COMPASS FLOWER—Faith

CONVOLVUS MINOR/BINDWEED—Uncertainty, tender affection

CORCHORUS—Impatience of happiness

COREOPSIOS—Always cheerful

CORNFLOWER—Delicacy, refinement

CORONILLA/CROWN VETCH—Success to you

COWSLIP—Rusticity, winning grace, healing, youth, pensiveness

COXCOMB—Foppery, unfading love

CROCUS—Cheerfulness, abuse not, gladness

CYPRESS—Mourning

DAFFODIL—Regard, unrequited love, you're the only one

DAFFODIL (Yellow)—Chivalry

DAHLIA—Dignity and elegance, forever thine, instability

DAISY—Innocence, loyal love, purity, beauty, respect

DAISY (RED)—Beauty unknown to possessor

DAISY (Ox-eye)—Patience

DANDELION—Faithfulness, happiness, love's oracle

DAPHANE CNEORUM/ROSE DAPHANE—I desire to please

DAPHANE ODORA/WINTER
   DAPHANE—I would not have you
   otherwise
DEAD LEAVES—Sadness
DELPHINIUM—Big-hearted, fun
DILL—Lust
DIOSMA—Your simple elegance charms
   me
DOG ROSE—Pleasure and pain
DOGWOOD (FLOWERING)—Am I
   indifferent to you?
DRACAENA/DRAGON'S
   BLOOD/DRAGON LILY—Inner
   power
DRAGON ROOT/GREEN DRAGON—
   Ardor

EDELWEISS/ALPINE CUDWEED—
   Daring, courage, noble purity
EGLANTINE/SWEET-BRIAR/ROSA
   EGLANTARIA—Poetry, I wound to
   heal
ELDER FLOWER—Zeal
ENDINE—Frugality
EPIGAEA,
   REPENS/MAYFLOWER/TRAILING
   ARBUTUS—Budding
EREMURUS—Endurance
EUPATORIUM/HARDY
   AGERATUM—Delay
EUPHORBIA—Persistence
EVERLASTING—Never-ceasing memory

FERN—Magic, fascination, confidence,
   shelter
FERN (Maidenhair)—Secret bond of love,
   discretion
FERN (Royal)—Reverie
FERNS—Fascination
FILBERT—Reconciliation

FIR—Time
FLAX—Domestic Symbol
FLORA'S BELL—Without pretension
FLOWERING REED—Confide in Heaven
FORGET ME NOT—True Love,
   memories, remembrance
FORSYTHIA—Anticipation
FOXGLOVE/FAIRY THIMBLES/DEAD
   MEN'S BELLS—Stateliness, youth
FOXTAIL GRASS—Sporting
FRAXINELLA/CULTIVATED
   DITTANY/GAS PLANT—Fire
FREESIA—Innocence, trust
FUCHSIA (Scarlet)—Confiding love, taste
FURZE—Love for all occasions

GARDENIA—You're lovely, secret love,
   purity, refinement
GARLIC—Courage, strength, get well,
   ward off evil and illness
GENETIAN (Fringed)—Intrinsic worth, I
   look to heaven, fall
GENTIAN (Closed)—Sweet be thy dreams
GERANIUM—True friend, stupidity, folly
GERANIUM (Apple)—Present preference
GERANIUM (Ivy)—Your hand for next
   dance
GERANIUM (Lemon)—Unexpected
   meeting
GERANIUM (Nutmeg)—I expect a
   meeting
GERANIUM (Oak-leaved)—True
   friendship, lady, deign to smile
GERANIUM (Penciled)—Ingenuity
GERANIUM (Rose)—Preference
GERANIUM (Scarlet)—Consolation,
   melancholy
GERANIUM (Silver-leaf)—Recall
GERBERA—Innocence
GINGER—Strength

GLADIOLI—Generosity, I'm sincere, flower of the gladiators

GLOBE AMARANTH—Unfading love

GLOXINIA—Love at first sight

GOLDEN-ROD—Be cautious, encouragement

GOOSEBERRY—Anticipation

GOOSEFOOT—Goodness

GORSE—Endearing affection

GRASS—Homosexual love

GRASS—Submission

GRASS—Usefulness

GUELDER ROSE/SNOWBALL—Winter

HAREBELL/CAMPANULA—Humility, grief

HAWTHORN—Contentment

HEART'S EASR/PURPLE/JOHNNY JUMP UP—You occupy my thoughts

HEATHER (Lavender)—Admiration, solitude

HEATHER (White)—Protection, wishes will come true

HELIOTROPE—Devotion

HENBANE—For males to attract love from females

HEPATICA—Confidence

HIBISCUS—Consumed by love, delicate beauty

HOLLY—Defense, domestic happiness, good wishes

HOLLYHOCK—Fruitfulness

HOLLYHOCK (White)—Female ambition

HONESTY/LUNARIA/DOLLAR PLANT/MONEY PLANT—Sincerity

HONEYFLOWER—Sweet, secret love, generous affection, sweetness of disposition

HONEYSUCKLE—The bond of love

HONEYSUCKLE (Coral)—I love you

HOUSTONIA/BLUET/QUAKER LADIES—Content

HOYA/WAX PLANT—Sculpture

HUCKLEBERRY—Faith, simple pleasures

HYACINTH (General)—Games and sports, rashness, dedicated to Apollo

HYACINTH (Blue)—Constancy

HYACINTH (Purple)—I am sorry, forgive me, sorrow

HYACINTH (Red or Pink)—Play

HYACINTH (White)—Loveliness, I'll pray for you

HYACINTH (Yellow)—Jealousy

HYDRANGEA—Thank you for understanding, frigidity, heartlessness

INDIAN CRESS/NASTURTIUM—Resignation

IPOMACA—I attach myself to you

IRIS—Your friendship means so much to me, faith, hope, wisdom and valor, my compliments

IRIS (Yellow)—Passion

IVY—Wedded love, fidelity, friendship, affection, fidelity

IVY (Sprig of white tendrils)—Anxious to please, affection

JAPONICA—Sincerity, symbol of love

JASMINE—Admirability

JASMINE (Indian)—Attachment

JASMINE (Spanish)—Sensuality

JASMINE (White)—Amiability

JASMINE (Yellow)—Modesty, grace, elegance

JERUSALEM OAK—Your love is reciprocated

JONQUIL—Love me, affection returned, desire, sympathy

KENNEDIA—Intellectual beauty

LADY'S SLIPPER—Win me, capricious
    beauty
LANTANA—Rigor
LARKSPUR—Levity, an open heart,
    lightness, fickleness
LAURISTINUS—Cheerful in adversity
LAVENDER—Love, devotion,
LAVENDER—Distrust
LEMON BLOSSOM—Fidelity in love, I
    promise to be true
LILAC (General)—Beauty, pride
LILAC (Purple)—First emotions of love
LILAC (White)—Youthful innocence
LILY (Calla)—Beauty
LILY (Day)—Coquetry, Chinese emblem
    for mother
LILY (Eucharis)—Maiden charms
LILY (General)—Majesty and honor,
    purity of heart
LILY (Orange)—Hatred, dislike
LILY (Tiger)—Wealth, pride, prosperity
LILY (White)—Virginity, purity, majesty,
    it's heavenly to be with you, youth
LILY (Yellow)—I'm walking on air, false,
    gay, gratitude
LILY OF THE VALLEY—Sweetness, tears
    of the Virgin Mary, happiness, humility
LIME—Conjugal love
LIVERWORT—Confidence
LOTUS—Estranged love, forgetful of the
    past
LOVE IN A MIST—You puzzle me
LOVE-LIES-
    BLEEDING/AMARANTHUS—
    Hopeless, not heartless, desertion
LUCERNE—Life
LUNGWORT—Thou art my life
LUPINE—Imagination

LYCHNIS/CAMPION/MALTESE
    CROSS—Religious enthusiasm

MAGNOLIA—Nobility, perseverance,
MAGNOLIA (Chinese)—Love of nature
MALLOW—Delicate beauty, sweetness
MARIGOLD (Common)—Cruelty, grief,
    jealousy
MARJORAM—Joy, happiness
MARVEL OF PERU/FOUR O'CLOCK—
    Timidity
MEADOW SAFFRON—My best days are
    gone
MEZEREON—Desire to please
MIGNONETTE—Your qualities surpass
    your charms, health
MILK VETCH—Your presence softens my
    pain
MIMOSA—Secret love
MINT—Virtue
MISTLETOE—Kiss me, affection,
    difficulties, sacred plant of India,
MONKSHOOD—Beware, danger is near
MOONWORT/HONESTY—
    Forgetfulness
MORNING GLORY—Affection
MOSS—Maternal love, charity
MOTHERWORT—Secret love
MOUSE-EAR CHICKWEED—
    Simplicity
MUGWORT/WORMWOOD—
    Tranquillity, happiness
MULLEIN—Good nature
MYRTLE—Love, joy, Hebrew emblem of
    marriage
MYRTLE (WAX)—Discipline, instruction

NARCISSUS—Egotism, formality
NASTURTIUM—Conquest, victory in
    battle

NUTS—Stupidity

OAK—Hospitality
OAK LEAVES—Bravery
OLEANDER—Caution
OLIVE BRANCH—Peace
ORANGE BLOSSOM—Innocence, eternal
love, marriage, fruitfulness
ORANGE, MOCK—Deceit
ORCHID—Love, beauty, refinement,
Chinese symbol for many children,
thoughtfulness
ORCHID (CATTLEYA)—Mature charm

PALM LEAVES—Victory and success
PANSY—Merriment, thoughts (you occupy
my thoughts)
PARSLEY—Useful knowledge
PASQUE FLOWER—Unpretentious, you
have no claims
PASSION FLOWER—Faith, religious
fervor
PEACH BLOSSOM—I am your captive
PEAR—Affection
PEONY—Shame, happy marriage,
compassion, bashfulness
PEPPERMINT—Cordiality
PERIWINKLE/VINCA/MYRTLE—
Early recollections, pleasures of
memories, sweet memories
PETUNIA—Your presence soothes me
PHEASANT'S EYE/ADONIS—
Sorrowful memories
PHLOX—Our souls are united,
unanimity
PIMPERNEL/POOR MAN'S
WEATHER GLASS—Change
PINE—Hope, pity
PINK (Mountain)—You are aspiring
PINK—Pure affection

POMEGRANATE FLOWER—Elegance
POPPY (General)—Eternal sleep, oblivion,
imagination
POPPY (Red)—Pleasure
POPPY (White)—Consolation
POPPY (Yellow)—Wealth, success
PRIDE OF CHINA—Dissension
PRIMROSE—I can't live without you
PRIMROSE (Evening)—Inconstancy
PRIMROSE (Red)—Unpatronized merit
PRINCE'S FEATHER—Unfading love
PUSSY WILLOW—Motherhood

QUAKING GRASS—Agitation

RAGGED-ROBIN—Wit
RANUNCULUS—I am dazzled by your
charms
REEDS—Music
RHODODENDRON—Danger, beware, I
am dangerous
RHUBARB—Advice
ROSE (Bridal)—Happiness
ROSE (Burgundy)—Unconscious beauty
ROSE (Christmas)—Relieve my anxiety
ROSE (Coral)—Desire
ROSE (Damask)—Freshness, Persian
ambassador of love
ROSE (Dark crimson)—Mourning
ROSE (Dark pink)—Thankfulness
ROSE (Deep red)—Bashful, shame
ROSE (Dog)—Pleasure and pain
ROSE (Green)—I am from Mars
ROSE (Hibiscus)—Delicate, beauty
ROSE (Lavender)—Enchantment
ROSE (Leaf)—You may hope
ROSE (Musk cluster)—Charming
ROSE (Orange)—Fascination
ROSE (Pale pink)—Grace, joy
ROSE (Peach)—Immortality, modesty

ROSE (Pink)—Perfect happiness, secret love, grace and sweetness, indecision

ROSE (Red)—Love, I love you, respect, beauty

ROSE (Tea)—I'll remember, always

ROSE (Thornless)—Love at first sight, early attachment

ROSE (White and Red together)—Unity, flower emblem of England

ROSE (White)—Innocence, purity, humility, I am worthy of you, secrecy, silence

ROSE (White-dried)—Death is preferable to loss of virtue

ROSE (Yellow)—Joy, jealousy, friendship (one yellow rose with 11 red ones means love and passion)

ROSEBUD—Beauty and youth, a heart innocent of love

ROSEBUD (Moss)—Confessions of love

ROSEBUD (Red)—Pure and lovely

ROSEBUD (White)—Girlhood, heart ignorant of love

ROSEMARY—Remembrance

ROSE-OF-SHARON—Consumed by love

ROSES (Bouquet of full bloom)—Gratitude

ROSES (Garland or crown of)—Beware of virtue, reward of merit, symbol of superior merit

ROSES (Single full bloom)—I truly love you, simplicity.

RUE—Mercy, pity

RUSH/HORSE—TAIL—Docility

SAGE—Domestic virtues, wisdom, great respect, female fidelity

SATIN—FLOWER—Sincerity

SENSITIVE PLANT—Timidity

SHAMROCK—Lightheartedness

SLOE—Difficulty, austerity

SMILAX—Loveliness

SNAPDRAGON—Gracious lady, strength

SNOWBALL—Thoughts of heaven

SNOWDROP—Hope, consolation

SOLIDAGO—Success

SPEARMINT—Warm sentiment

SPIDER FLOWER—Elope with me

STAR OF BETHLEHEM—Atonement, reconciliation

STARWORT—Welcome to a stranger

STEPHANOTIS—Marital Happiness, desire to travel

STOCK—Bonds of affection, promptness, you'll always be beautiful to me

STONECROP—Tranquillity

STRAW (BROKEN)—Broken agreement

STRAW FLOWER—Agreement

SUNFLOWER—Constancy, devotion

SUNFLOWER (DWARF)—Adoration

SUNFLOWER (TALL)—False riches, pride

SWEET PEA—Departure

SWEET WILLIAM—Gallantry

SWEETPEA—Goodbye, departure, blissful pleasure, thank you for a lovely time

SWEET-SULTAN—Felicity, happiness

SWEET-WILLIAM—Grant me one smile, gallantry

SYTINGIA/MOCK ORANGE/LILAC—Memory

TEASEL—Misanthropy

THORNAPPLE—I dreamed of thee

THRIFT (ARMERIA)—Sympathy

TIGER LILY—Wealth and pride

TRAVELER'S JOY—Rest, safety

TRUMPET FLOWER/ANGEL'S TRUMPET/DATURA—Separation

TULIP—Ardent love

TULIP (General)—Perfect lover, fame, flower emblem of Holland

TULIP (Red)—Believe me, declaration of love

TULIP (Variegated)—Beautiful eyes

TULIP (Yellow)—There's sunshine in your smile

TURNIP—Charity

VALERIAN—Accommodating disposition

VENUS FLYTRAP—Caught at last

VENUS' LOOKING GLASS—Flattery

VERBENA—Pray for me, sensibility

VERONICA SPEEDWELL—Fidelity

VERVAIN—Enchantment

VINE—Intoxicating

VIOLET—Modesty, virtue, affection, steadfastness

VIOLET (Blue)—Watchfulness, faithfulness, love

VIOLET (White)—Let's take a chance on happiness

VIRGIN'S BOWER/CLEMATIS—Filial love

VISCARIA—Will you dance with me?

WALL FLOWER—Faithful in adversity, fidelity, lasting beauty

WHITE POPLAR—Time

WILLOW—Forsaken love

WINDFLOWER—Sincerity, symbol of Love

WINTERGREENS—Harmony

WISTERIA—Welcome

WITCH HAZEL—A spell

WOLFBANE/ACONITE/TURK'S CAP/FRIAR'S CAP/BEAR'S FOOT—Misanthropy, chivalry

WOODBINE—Fraternal love

WORMWOOD—Absence, torment of separation

YARROW—Cure for heartache

YUCCA—Yours until death

ZEPHYR FLOWER—Sincerity, symbol of love

ZINNIA (Magenta)—Lasting affection

ZINNIA (Mixed)—Thinking (or in memory) of an absent friend

ZINNIA (Scarlet)—Constancy

ZINNIA (White)—Goodness

ZINNIA (Yellow)—Daily remembrance

LILY

Along with the **rose** and the **lotus**, the lily comprises a sacred trinity of the most important flower symbols in the world.

Not all lilies are **white**, but paleness is synonymous with the flower; we even speak of something as being "lily white." The lily is therefore a symbol of purity, innocence, and virginity. The Angel Gabriel appeared to Mary carrying a lily, and the flower has always been associated with the Virgin. However, both the shape of the lily's petals and its phallic-looking pistils, standing erect from the center of the flower, means that the flower is a symbol of sexuality and reproduction. So the lily effectively contains both male and female reproductive parts; hence when we see depictions of Mary we can recognize the flower as symbolizing virginity, fertility, and motherhood.

The lily is the symbol of the Goddess, in whatever form she may take, and the Babylonian Goddess Lilith—reputedly the first wife of Adam—who was later demonized by the Christian Church, takes her name from the name of the lily or the Lilu (Lotus). The flower is also sacred to **Astarte**, whose name in parts of Europe is Eostre, which gives us the word "**Easter**"; hence the lilies which have become a symbol of this springtime celebration are a secret symbol of a much older association.

If the **Milky Way** is seen as the milk which poured from the **breasts** of the Sky Goddess, then lilies are the drops of **milk** which fell to the ground.

The **fleur-de-lys**, or flower of the lily, is the stylized symbol which sprang from both the lotus and the lily. It is symbolic of the Trinity or of the **Triple Goddess** as well as encompassing all the other associations of the lily; it was used extensively in France, where it became a symbol of royalty and nobility.

The lily—particularly the calla lily—is also a symbol of resurrection, which is why it is used at funerals and sometimes appears on gravestones.

The day lily blooms only for one day, and so is a symbol of a carefree nature.

The lily of the valley has a reputation for attracting **silver**—probably because of the way its white flowers gleam in the darkness of its luscious leaves. It was the flower which grew where witches lived, in dark, often **forested** places, yet was also a symbol of **spring** and new life.

Lotus

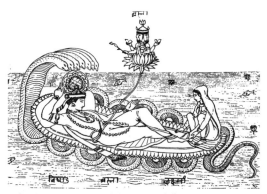

The lotus is arguably one of the most important flower symbols on the planet, along with the **lily** and the **rose**. The lotus can only be grown under hothouse conditions in Western Europe, and for a Westerner to see a lotus growing in the wild for the first time can be an astonishing experience. Both the otherworldly appearance of the flower and its growing circumstances make it obvious that the flower is somehow very special indeed. It's therefore no surprise that the flower is one of the **eight auspicious symbols** in both Chinese and Tibetan Buddhist iconography.

This sensuous and extraordinary flower, with its perfect petals, rises imperiously from muddy swamps, its head above the dirty **water**. The symbolism applied by generations of Egyptian, Indian, and Chinese sages is obvious. First, the flower rises in complete perfection from the murky primal waters of creation. Next, the flower comes from the darkness into the light, woken by the **Sun**; third, the lotus symbolizes the triumph of **spirit** over matter and is a metaphor for the journey to enlightenment.

Because the lotus retreats back into the water during the hours of darkness only to rise again above the surface of the water at dawn, the Egyptians saw it as a symbol of **death** and rebirth.

The tight bud of the flower is a symbol for the Universe. The flower is also an archetypal symbol for the **vulva**, and so is associated with the Goddess.

In all cultures the lotus carries within it a reminder of the **elements**. It has its **seed** within the **earth**; it grows in water; the blossom exists in **air** which also carries its fragrance; and the flower itself is awoken by the Sun, and therefore the element of **fire** which it also resembles, the curious central **circle** surrounded by the rays of petals. In addition, lotus has **8** petals, symbolizing the **four** cardinal directions and the four inter-cardinal directions, as well as the rulers of the eight directions of the Universe, or Ashtadikpalas.

The symbol of the lotus is often partially hidden in **mandalas**, the petals forming a border that is both symbolic and decorative. The Buddha sits in the center of the eight-petaled lotus, detached from the material world with its cycle of **death** and rebirth.

In Hindu iconography, the lotus is seen as the base of the earth from which the holy **mountains** (such as **Kailash** and **Meru**) rise. The stalk of the flower is associated with the

world axis which rises up through this sacred mountain.

The lotus is used as a symbol for each of the **chakras**, the number of petals relating to the role and function of each of these energy centers that are situated along the **spine** and that are said to unfurl like petals with exercise and meditation.

The **colors** of the lotus are also significant.

The sacred lotus is **pink** or **white**, and is a large flower whose petals can reach up to half a meter in diameter. Also known as the Indian or Oriental Lotus, every part of this plant is edible, and the sugared seeds are a treat during various festivals.

The **red** lotus is the ultimate symbol of the Sun and is the emblem of India.

The lotus depicted in stylized form in Egyptian friezes is the **blue** lotus, actually a form of water lily rather than a true lotus. As well as its ethereal color, this lotus contains a psychotropic substance called apomorphine, which no doubt contributes to its status as a sacred flower. The lotus eaters of Greek mythology, immortalized in Tennyson's poem, "Song of the Lotus Eaters," lived in a state of hedonistic bliss brought about by eating the seeds of this blue flower.

Mandrake

Mandrake roots have a very human-looking form, the cause of many odd beliefs about the plant. It was said, for example, to grow where the **semen** of a hanged man dripped onto the ground. When wrenched from its burial place in Mother **Earth**, the mandrake would utter such a terrifying shriek that anyone hearing it would die on the spot. The only way to harvest the root was to get a **dog** to dig it up, causing the unfortunate animal to suffer fatal consequences. In the Harry Potter books, the children that are re-potting mandrake seedlings have to wear protective head-phones.

The Egyptians believed that the mandrake was an **aphrodisiac** and so it also became a love symbol. Since all parts of the plant, if taken in quantity, are poisonous and have nar-cotic affects, as a love philter mandrake needed to be handled with care. As the emblem of the great sorceress, Circe, the plant had particularly powerful magical prop-erties, and was treated with both awe and rev-erence.

Because of the narcotic properties of the mandrake, the Greeks used it to deaden the senses of people during surgical operations. Mandrake may also be related to the herb that the Hebrews used in casting out **demons**. As a vegetable that resembles an **animal**, the mandrake is symbolic of the meeting of two seemingly disparate constituencies. Charms made from mandrake roots were sold at a high price during the middle ages, and were highly prized because of the perceived danger and difficulty of obtaining the roots.

Mistletoe

The sacred **golden** bough of mythology, mistletoe is a mysterious plant, the subject of poem, song, and legend. Its sacred nature is attributable to many factors. It grows only in the **sky**, and never on the ground, so is closer to the Heavens; it is propagated by **birds**, themselves symbolic messengers of the Gods; and its pearlescent berries represent drops of

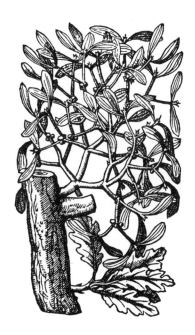

semen, so the mistletoe represents fertility. Mistletoe has healing properties, too, and is often hosted by a sacred tree, the **apple** tree.

A parasitic plant, many people assume that **oak** trees host mistletoe, but in fact, it is much more usual for it to be found growing on old apple trees, among others. Most visible in the winter months when the trees are bare of leaves, bundles of mistletoe look like untidy birds' nests, a scribble in the branches of the tree.

The propagation and growth of the mistle-toe is like that of no other living plant. At one time people believed that it took root where **lightning** struck the tree. In fact, birds play a large part in the life cycle of the mistletoe. The mistle thrush in particular eats the berries that are "planted" when they are excreted. In addition, when the birds scrape their beaks on branches to remove excess seeds, the **seeds** are embedded under the bark where they can take root.

Druids traditionally harvest mistletoe

with a golden **sickle**, a magical tool that represents the **Sun**. It is vital that the plant is not tainted by contact with the ground and care is taken to make sure that it keeps its airy associations intact. It is caught in sheets that are stretched taut around the tree.

As an evergreen, mistletoe symbolizes longevity and immortality, and has become a traditional part of **Christmas** decorations in the home. However, although **holly** and **ivy** have managed to cloak their pre-Christian significance in order to enfold themselves into the mythology of the **Church**, it has been harder for mistletoe to be absorbed in the same way. The plant is an uncomfortable reminder of powerful pre-Christian practices and beliefs, and is banned in many churches. Despite this, mistletoe is sometimes called *lignum sanctae crucis*, since the Church said at one time that the **cross** of Christ had been made of mistletoe wood (an unlikely claim for anyone familiar with the fragile stalks of the plant).

Paradoxically, given that the mistletoe is poisonous, it is also called "all heal." Because of its symbolism, it was used to aid fertility problems, but latterly it has been found to be effective in circulatory and respiratory problems, as well as possessing anti-carcinogenic qualities.

Initially, people hung mistletoe indoors to ward off evil spirits. The tradition of **kissing** under the mistletoe is a remnant of its potency as a fertility symbol, and because of the tiny little "x" (kiss) symbol found on the underside of the berry.

Mistletoe is also a symbol of love. Frigga was the mother of the Norse God Balder, and she extracted promises from all living beings that they would do no harm to her boy.

However, she forgot to include the mistletoe. Balder was killed by a spear made from mistletoe wood. Balder's brightness had been so great that his **death** brought winter to the world, and the tears of his mother became mistletoe berries. When the Gods relented and restored life to Balder, they declared that henceforth mistletoe must only bring love, rather than death, to the world.

MUSHROOM

There's an incident in the Lewis Carroll book, *Alice in Wonderland*, in which Alice seeks advice from a caterpillar that she finds lounging on top of a mushroom, languidly blowing smoke from a hookah. Whatever the intention of the author, this is the epitome of the drug-induced vision, especially since it appears that the mushroom is the highly toxic and highly hallucinatory *Amanita muscaria* (fly agaric). When Alice eats chunks of the mushroom, she appears to grow alternately larger and smaller, another psychedelic phenomenon.

Many mushrooms have "magical" properties, the toxins within them seeming to provide a gateway to another world. Images of **fairies**, **elves**, and **goblins** inevitably have a mushroom or toadstool nearby. In Chinese mythology, mushrooms were one of the sacred foods eaten by the **Immortals**; they induced bodily lightness. Further, the agaric mushroom was said to grow only during times of peace and prudent leadership.

Rock paintings dating back at least 2000 years ago in the Tassili Plateau in southern Algeria depict shamans, apparently dancing around, holding mushrooms in their hands, with mushrooms sprouting from their bodies.

Myrtle

The myrtle is considered to have magical properties. Ownership of a myrtle wood **wand** is said to enable the possessor to communicate with the **spirit** world to which the myrtle is connected. But not only is the myrtle a symbol of **death**, it's also a flower of love, sacred to **Aphrodite**. It is said that when the Goddess came ashore at Paphos, in Greece, she modestly hid her beauty behind the myrtle bush. This is similar to the story of Aphrodite's Roman counterpart, **Venus**, who also hid behind the shrub in order to hide from the satyrs that were chasing her.

Myrtle has **five** petals, an indication that it is the flower of the Goddess.

In Ancient Greece, the myrtle carried sexual connotations; it shares its name with that of the female genitalia. The bud of the flower also resembles the **vesica piscis**. It is perhaps because of these reasons that the myrtle enjoys a reputation as a flower of love and of lovers, and is used in bridal bouquets. However, for a long time this was frowned upon by the **Church** as being bad form, the sexual symbolism of the flower considered bad taste and a relic of pre-Christian pagan times. It is an old tradition that brides should give their bridesmaids a cutting of the myrtle from their own bouquet so that the bridesmaids would find love, too, and so that the love of the bride and her groom would never die.

The combination of the love/death symbolism of the myrtle means that it represents a love that can survive death. Legend has it that whoever suffers the pain of unrequited love or who dies a virgin, might be cheered by the thought that they would have the right to a sprig of myrtle on their graves, and the hope that they might find love in the Afterlife.

Narcissus

The narcissus, or daffodil, is the national flower of Wales. This is possibly because of a mix-up; the **leek** and the daffodil have the same name in Welsh, and the leek was reputedly worn as a sign of recognition by the Welsh during a battle with the Saxons.

The word "narcissus" comes from the same root as "narcolepsy" and "narcotic." The scent of the narcissus is certainly intoxicating, and to eat the highly toxic bulbs can induce a trance-like state.

The enduring legend about this beautiful **yellow** flower is of Narcissus, a handsome young man who was arrogant enough to reject the love of the nymph, Echo. Instead, Narcissus fell in love with his own reflection, seen in a still pool of **water**. He fell into the pool and drowned, and at the edge of the pool there sprang up the flower that bears his name. To call someone "narcissistic" is to accuse them of vanity, a further hidden meaning of the flower.

Another Greek myth firmly cements the narcissus as a flower of the Underworld. **Persephone** is said to have stopped to pick the flower, but as she did so, the ground opened up and swallowed her, throwing her into the realms of the God, **Hades**. This story reflects the fact that the narcissus is among the first to blossom in the spring, as it returns from the hidden depths of the Underworld below.

The daffodil was a popular flower for

funeral wreaths in ancient Egypt. Daffodil bulbs were placed over the **mouth, nose,** and **eyes** of the mummy, symbolizing the deep sleep induced by eating the bulbs.

The wild narcissus has **six** petals, representing the six-pointed **star,** or **hexagram,** with the central trumpet symbolizing the seventh point that embraces the whole.

NETTLE

The stinging nettle originates in Mediterranean areas, and was spread elsewhere by Roman soldiers who planted it wherever they found the climate to be cold. They would warm themselves by rubbing themselves with the stinging leaves, a practice that might seem odd to anyone who has experienced the pain of the nettle sting.

The nettle is symbolic of healing, protection, courage, and also of **exorcism;** it was used to ward off **ghosts,** and in combination with **yarrow** was said to give courage.

Nettles were used in remote healing; the plant was grasped firmly and the name of the patient spoken out loud, the idea being that the pain was taken on by the person carrying out this ritual.

Nettles were the symbol of the God Thor, and like him, were associated with **thunder** and **lightning,** hence its old German name *"Donnernessel."* In deference to this, bunches of nettles would be thrown over the roofs of houses to deflect the **lightning** from the home. A decoction of nettles is said to clear the **blood,** and has been used as an **aphrodisiac.**

Nettles make good strong thread, and nettle fabric was used to make the uniforms of the German army during the First World War when other material was in short supply.

ONION

The onion was considered to be so powerful, both as a symbol and as a useful plant, that there existed a cult in Egypt dedicated to its worship and cultivation. The onion represented eternity, because of its **circle**-within-a-circle structure.

In the Dharmic religions such as Hindu and Buddhism, the fact that the layers of the onion can be peeled away, and that it has no central core, makes it analogous with the ego; eventually, there is no barrier to the **spirit** world and all is One. The first line of the Onion Song by Marvin Gaye reflects this sentiment; "The world is just a great big onion …"

Roman soldiers carried onions, believing that they had the power to ward off diseases. They were a symbol of protection in other ways too. An onion held in the hand, for example, was meant to ward off **snakes;** witches apparently do not like onions, and as well as keeping them in the house to deter malicious spirits, the onion could be worn as a protective charm by those who were unconcerned about their appearance.

ORCHID

The word *orkhis* is Greek for **testicles,** named for the shape of the bulb of the orchid flower. Greek mothers-to-be believed that they could control the sex of their unborn child by eating orchid roots; large for a boy and small for a girl.

Because of this reason and also because of the shape of the flower, which looks like the female genitalia, the orchid scores high as a symbol of sexuality and potency. In China, orchids were used as a charm to ward off barrenness; however, to cut an orchid meant that your children might die.

The beauty of the orchid led to it becoming a symbol of spiritual perfection, and the longevity of its flowers symbolizes undying truth.

PANSY

The pansy has gained a reputation as being a flower of remembrance, in part because its name sounds like the French, *pensées*, meaning "thoughts." The pansy is subject to much anthropomorphism because its petals resemble a little face.

The old English names for the pansy are "love in idleness" or "heartsease," since it was believed that to carry a pansy would reassure the person that they were loved, truly. Hence the pansy represents loving thoughts.

PARSLEY

Parsley has always had association with magical powers, and is seen in some countries as an evil plant despite its usefulness in the kitchen. In Ancient Greece it was the herb which most symbolized **death**, and graves were strewn with it. It was served with meat in order to calm the **spirit** of the slaughtered **animal**.

Parsley can take a long time to germinate,

and it used to be said that it had to visit the Devil **nine** times before the seeds sprouted. If you are brave enough to have parsley in your garden, then it will apparently grow best in a place where the female is more powerful than the male partner. If sowing parsley, the only day on which it can be done that does not throw the immortal **soul** of the gardener into serious risk is **Good Friday**, when Satan has no jurisdiction over the soil.

PASSION FLOWER

At first glance it might seem odd that this climbing jungle exotic, a flamboyant and unusual flower, should have a Latin name comprised of the words for "suffering flower." However, the passion flower was discovered by the Spanish when they invaded the Inca territories in the sixteenth century, and when they came across it they saw it as message of approval from God that it was right to convert the native peoples to Catholicism.

A gothic-looking blossom, the passion flower seems to contain within it certain symbols that the Spanish read as being reminders of Christ's suffering, or Passion. The central part of the flower looks like a **crown** of thorns. The innocence of Christ is reflected in its **white** petals, of which there are **10**, the same as the number of faithful apostles. The styles that emerge from the center of the flower represent the nails used in the crucifixion and the **five** stamens are the wounds endured by Christ.

There are other aspects to the passion flower, though, beyond this strictly Catholic interpretation. Passiflorine, a narcotic substance derived from the plant, induces heavy hypnosis or sleep, and prior to its use as a medicinal plant the passion flower was consumed by shaman who believed that it enabled communion with the unseen world of spirits and Gods.

In modern-day Japan, the flower has become a symbol for male homosexuality.

PEONY

The peony is named after the Greek God of healing and of light, Paeon, which also means a thanksgiving hymn.

Paeon the God used the roots of the flower to heal Hercules' wounds, and so the flower has a long association with healing powers. In addition to Paeon, Ascelepius and Galen also believed in the medical powers of this flower. The roots of the peony resemble the human form, so symbolize man; just like the **mandrake**, the roots scream when pulled from the

ground, and it is fatal to hear this strange cry. The only way to gather up the roots of the peony without personal injury is to trick a **dog** into doing it for you; tie the dog to the roots and then get him to tug them out of the ground as he struggles to reach a piece of meat that you have placed strategically just out of reach.

In addition, the roots have to be gathered by the light of the **Moon**; otherwise a **woodpecker** might happen along and peck out your **eyes**. Anything so difficult to get hold of must necessarily carry great power, and such is the case with the peony root. Epilepsy was one of the many illnesses cured by the plant, and bead **necklaces** made from the peony root were still being worn in the early part of the last century to counteract fits.

The **seeds** of the peony, like the root, were also collected at night; they have a faint phosphorescent glow, which further indicated their magical powers.

Anything that heals also protects, and the woody parts of the peony were used to make charms and **amulet**s.

PERIWINKLE

The pretty, **blue**, innocuous-looking periwinkle flower has long been associated with **death** and witchcraft. It was called the "flower of death" or *fiore di morte* because it was used to make **wreaths** for dead babies, and because those condemned to die wore periwinkle garlands on their way to execution. In some quarters the periwinkle is a symbol of eternal life, so it may well be that the flowers was used in this way as a sign of hope.

It is said to be terribly bad luck to pick a periwinkle that happens to be growing on a grave; this could cause haunting by the **soul** of the deceased.

Another name for the periwinkle is the "sorcerer's violet." The leaves of the flower have hallucinogenic qualities and were likely to have been used in shamanistic practices.

Peyote

One of the holy plants of Mexico, a part of this small, spineless desert plant is consumed as the peyote "button," a small protuberance that is attached to the side of the peyote cactus. The hunt for the cactus itself forms a part of a ritual that has been carried out by the shamans of the area for thousands of years. The psychoactive ingredients in the peyote button include mescaline, and cause vivid hallucinations, allowing the psychic explorer to travel in other dimensions, communicate with **animals**, and experience the world in a heightened state of consciousness. The peyote itself symbolizes a gateway into another world.

The hunt for the peyote, its ingestion, and the hallucinatory process can take several days. Carlos Castaneda records the whole process in great detail in his "Don Juan" books.

Poppy

Because of the narcotic qualities of some of its varieties, the poppy is the flower of sleep and oblivion, a reputation it has had for many centuries. The most common opiates—heroin and morphine—come from the opium poppy, *Papaver somniferum*. Morpheus, the Greek God of sleep, counts these drugs among his attributes, as does **Demeter** in her guise as Goddess both of the **harvest** and of **death**.

The story goes that the God of Sleep made the poppy specifically for Ceres because she could not sleep after she lost her daughter, **Persephone**. Ceres was so tired that she could not get the corn to grow. After the drugs helped her to sleep, all was well again, and it is still counted as good luck to see poppies in a cornfield.

Because of its reputation as a flower that can either cure or kill, there is an ambiguity about the poppy; some see it as a good influence, and some as evil.

Where the poppy head appears in paintings, it often secretly symbolizes fertility, because of its numerous seeds.

Latterly, the poppy has become a symbol of remembrance for those who died during the two world wars. In November, around the time of Remembrance Day, paper poppies are sold to raise funds for bereaved families. The poppy is well suited for this purpose because it grew in profusion in the fields of Flanders. However, the poppy as a symbol of grief for lost warriors is not new; in the *Iliad*, written in the eighth century BC, a description of a dying warrior compares him to a poppy.

The leaves of the poppy are a divinatory tool; when placed beneath the pillow they are said to give the sleeper dreams of the future.

Primrose

The primrose is one of the first flowers of **spring** (its name derives from the Latin, *primus*, meaning first) and so it is a symbol of hope, new beginnings, and fertility. The first primroses brought into the house have special significance, and it is important to pick a nice big bunch, and certainly more than **13** blossoms. Any fewer, and the chickens might not lay so many **eggs** as usual. A single primrose brings disapproval since it foretells a **death**.

The primrose protects against evil spirits and malicious **fairies**, and has healing powers; the Druids knew about these powers, and they knew that the flowers had to be picked by those who were barefoot and sober, otherwise its healing properties might be lost. An infusion of the flowers is said to aid a good nights' sleep.

To Shakespeare, the primrose was a symbol of frivolity. In *Hamlet* he speaks of "… the primrose path of dalliance."

In Christian iconography, the primrose is a flower of mercy and forgiveness and can help to save the **souls** of sinners.

RICE

Rice is the staple food of Asia and indeed of half the world; it is so essential that Asian cultures consider it to be both a gift from the Gods, and the **food** of the Gods themselves. Like its western counterpart, **bread**, rice has spiritual attributes—the qualities of life, light, good luck, abundance, and fertility. It is used in this context in the West as confetti at weddings.

In China, the greeting, "Have you had your rice today?" means "hello" or "how do you do." In Japan, there are hundreds of Inari shrines dotted about the landscape; Inari is the deity known as the "rice bearer." In feudal times, rice was used as currency, and so became synonymous with money.

ROSE

In common with the **lotus** and the **lily**, the rose is one of the most important flower symbols in the world, its influence as a sacred flower pervading all cultures and religious beliefs. The reasons for many of these beliefs is shrouded in mystery, not a surprise given the age of the flower; fossilized roses from 35 million years ago have been found, and **wreaths** of roses have been found in the most ancient tombs. These days, the rose (particularly if it is **red**) is the ultimate flower of love, an ingredient in love potions and philters. As befits the flower of love, the rose is dedicated to **Venus** and **Aphrodite**.

Love is, however, not the only symbolic meaning of the flower. Its beauty springing from the muddy **earth** is a synonym for the triumph of **spirit** over matter, an aspect it shares with the lotus.

Like the lotus, the number of the rose's petals carries meaning. The original wild rose, prior to human cultivation, has **5** petals, an example of a **pentagram** or five-pointed **star** created by the natural world. The rose shares this feature with the five-petaled **apple** blossom (apples are a member of the rose family). The number *5* also balances the female **2** with the male **3**, and so symbolizes **marriage**.

Because of its perfection and beauty, the rose is a symbol of purity. At the same time the flower has undeniably sensuous qualities, in both its luxuriant petals and its scent, equating it with female sexuality. Paradoxically, the rose is at once a symbol of life and of **death**, of heavenly perfection and earthly desire, of fertility and chastity.

The rose is a natural **mandala** or **wheel**, the layers of petals describing a perfectly symmetrical **circle** around its **yellow** center, itself reminiscent of the **Sun**.

The rose is also a symbol of secrecy, perhaps because of the way the petals hide its center, perhaps for some more obscure reason. To speak of something as being *sub rosa*—"under the rose"—means that any information must be kept confidential. Some Masonic lodges and **alchemy** guilds still conduct meetings with a red rose hanging from the ceiling as a reminder of the private nature of the discussions taking place. There are **three** roses on the ceremonial **apron** of the Master Mason, acting as reminders of faith, silence, and secrecy.

The **Rosy Cross** of the Rosicrucians has a rose at its intersection. Here the rose symbolizes the **heart**, life, and secrecy.

In alchemy, the rose carries rich symbolic meaning, too; it is primarily the sign of the union of opposites, (again because the petals indicate $2 + 3 - 5$). Alchemical terminology calls this the "Conjunction." The **colors** of roses are as important within the alchemical tradition as anywhere else and carry the same meanings; the red rose for male energy, passion, love; the **white** rose for female energy, innocence, purity; yellow for compassion and humanity; **pink** for friendship and thankfulness; and **orange** for enthusiasm and optimism. The **black** rose—which does not exist in nature—is symbolic of death, depression, and loss. These colors also have bearing on the phases of the alchemical Great Work.

Roses have long been associated with Mary, mother of Jesus, and rose windows in cathedrals and **churches** are her symbol. In India, the Great Mother was called the Holy Rose.

Rosemary

The name of this herb comes from the Latin, meaning "rose of the **sea**," which refers to its sea-**blue** flowers. There's a legend that these flowers used to be **white** but turned **blue** when the infant Jesus' clothes were laid to dry on a rosemary bush. The plant likes to grow in dry soil and arid places, so is symbolic of fortitude.

Because it is also symbolic of remembrance, rosemary was a popular ingredient in funeral **wreaths**; it is also used as an aid to good memory. The Romans used the scent of rosemary to inspire thoughts and ideas.

This association with remembrance is because the rosemary bush is evergreen, and does not mind poor soil and dry conditions, surviving on into the colder months where less hardy plants would have died.

Rosemary is a useful plant. To avoid **lightning** strikes, evil spirits, and assault, wear a sprig of rosemary. Rinsing hair with rosemary-infused water to make it grow more vigorously may be just an old wives' tale, but nevertheless rosemary is a popular ingredient in modern hair products.

RUE

Sadly for the rue plant, it symbolizes repentance, remorse, and sorrow. The very word "rue" is synonymous with regret. However, it also has protective qualities and Catholic priests use it in bundles to sprinkle holy **water** since they believe it will keep away evil spirits. Rue may have taken on this protective symbolism because it was considered an antidote to many kinds of poison, and particularly effective against the venomous bites of snakes and mad **dogs**. Judges in the assize courts in the eighteenth century carried bunches of rue to ward off any contagious diseases that might be carried by the defendants.

Rue gathered first thing in the morning took on a mystical aspect that was denied the plant when picked at any other time. It was called the "Herb of Grace" and could be used beneficially both in charms and medicine. However, if it was gathered at any other time of the day, it reverted back to "ordinary" rue, useful only in curses.

The **cimaruta**, or "sprig of rue" in Italian, is a particular kind of **amulet** belonging specifically to witches. The cimaruta depicts the plant with various charms amongst its branches.

SAFFRON

The spice saffron is one of the most valuable on the planet because of the difficulty in harvesting it; it is comprised of the tiny stamens of a particular type of **crocus**. Because of its vibrant **yellow** color, it is associated with the **Sun** and also with wisdom, and carries many of the associations of the actual color which is named after it.

The saffron-colored robes of Buddhist monks are a significant part of their identity. Saffron is also made into a paste that is used to mark the followers of certain castes or divisions within Hindu tradition.

SAGE

Unsurprisingly given its name, sage is said to confer wisdom on those who eat it or who drink an infusion of the dried flower as a tisane. It is also a symbol of longevity, protection, and cleansing.

The sage leaf is a divinatory tool, used in the following simple manner. Write down whatever you desire on the leaf and leave it under your pillow for three nights. If you dream of your desire during this time, then your dream will come true.

Bundles of the herb tied up with cotton thread are used as "smudge sticks"; that is, sticks that are used, ritually, to purify a sacred area with their smoke. The smouldering herb has a medicinal scent. This practice originated with Native American tribes but has spread into many other parts of the world.

Spikenard

Spikenard is mentioned in the Song of Solomon in the Bible. It is worthy of mention because of the fragrance of the essential oil that is produced by crushing the roots, releasing an exquisite scent. Part of the valerian family, the plant is well known in the East and prefers high altitudes, such as the **Himalayas**. It has clusters of small **pink** flowers, but it is the scent that gives it its symbolic significance. One of the most costly of all perfumes and worth a year's wages two thousand years ago, it was the fragrance of kings, Gods, and of Heaven.

The plant appears again in the Bible, this time in the New Testament, as the oil that was used by Mary Magdalene to anoint the feet of Christ. Thus, despite its great rarity and fragrance, the plant is also symbolic of humility.

St. John's Wort

Also known as *Hypericum perforatum*, the latter word refers to the tiny little oil glands in the leaves that, when held up to the light, look like little holes; the "hypericum" part comes from the Greek words meaning "above" and "picture." The plant was hung above pictures in order to deter evil influences.

This small, **yellow, 5**-petalled flower blooms close to the day of the feast of St. John the Baptist on June 24. The petals also ooze a **blood-colored** oil when they are squeezed, which lends further credence to the association with the saint, who was martyred on the August 29, in the famous incident in which Salome, the daughter of Herod, asked for the **head** of John the Baptist. This date coincides with the fading of the flower, when the petals are mottled with the brown-red color of the oil contained within it.

For the Celts, the plant was a symbol of the **Summer Solstice**, again because of the time that it blooms and because of its yellow color, emblematic of the **Sun**. This association was so powerful that in the middle ages the name for the plant was *sol terrestis*, which means "terrestrial sun."

Because it is linked not only with the saint who baptized Christ but also with the Sun, St. John's Wort is a powerful symbol of protection. In Greece it was both worn by people and hung over precious objects to avert evil influences. In other parts of the world, it was tied up over **doorways** to keep the home safe.

The oil of the plant is particularly good for treating deep wounds, a discovery made by the Knights Hospitaller of St. John in Jerusalem, whose duty it was to protect pilgrims traveling to the Holy City. The plant is also used to treat depression and melancholy.

Stock

The fragrant stock is a favorite in cottage gardens, and is the subject of a Greek story of love, jealousy, and transformation. **Zeus** was in love with a beautiful nymph, Io, but his wife **Hera** was understandably jealous. Zeus transformed Io into a **white** animal that grazed in pretty fields of scented stocks and **violets** provided by Gaia, the **Earth** Goddess.

The stock is a symbol of everlasting beauty, and of a happy and contented life.

Strawberry

The sacred strawberry is one of the fruits that grew in the Elysian Fields, the resting place of blessed **souls**. There is also strong Christian symbolism associated with the strawberry plant.

The **3** parts of the leaf are emblematic of the Holy Trinity, and the **white** flowers stand for the purity of the Virgin Mary and the innocence of Christ. The **fruit** of the strawberry has neither thorns nor pips and is eaten whole, thereby representing good deeds; the **red** color symbolizes the **blood** of Christ. Where strawberries grow at the **feet** of the Virgin in religious paintings, the plant carries all these different meanings.

The strawberry, in its fruiting stage, is symbolic of fecundity and sensuality, both being aspects of any seeded fruit that are often overlooked by the Christian Church. In the interplay of the sacred and the profane that is an intrinsic part of the allegorical perception of nature, strawberries are symbolic of spiritual development as well as physical sensuality.

There is a legend that mothers whose children have died should not pick strawberries before **Midsummer Day**, because this is the day that the **spirits** of the dead children are taken strawberry picking. The mothers should leave the fruit for their children.

As a symbol of vitality because of its bright red color, there was an old belief that eating plenty of strawberries would ensure a long life. It seems that this old wives' tale, as is often the case, has a basis in truth. Recent research shows that strawberries have anti-carcinogenic properties.

Sunflower/ Heliotrope

As its name signifies, the sunflower has close solar associations, not only because of its appearance, but also because of its habit of turning its head to follow the course of the **Sun** during its journey across the sky. The sunflower has magical powers, too, and adorned the **crowns** of Roman emperors, thereby conferring the ruler with the potent power of the Sun that the flower held within it. The sunflower was later adopted by the Christian **Church** to denote the saints, prophets, and apostles of the faith; as the flower follows the Sun, so the true believer follows God.

The sunflower was sacred to Native Americans; the flowers were used extensively in celebrations and festivities, and the image of the sunflower was carved into **golden** breastplates.

Greek legend had it that a nymph called Clytie and the Sun God, Helios, were in love. But Helios cast aside poor Clytie for another lover. Clytie died of grief and was transformed into the sunflower, destined to live alone and having to follow the course of her former love. Therefore the sunflower, as a symbol, has adopted an aspect of Clytie's personality: the inability to overcome the emotions or to "let go."

The sunflower is a symbol of light, hope, and innocence, and has been adopted fairly recently as a symbol for world peace.

The seed head of the sunflower contains a magical symbol. It shows a perfect example of the **golden spiral** that has been created naturally. This shape is one of the cornerstones of **sacred geometry**.

Tea

There are many different kinds of tea, and lots of different herbal decoctions are called by the name of tea; however, "real" tea, the "cup that cheers," is made from the plant called *Thea sinensis*, a member of the **camellia** family that originated in India.

There is a story telling how, in AD 1510, the Indian prince Bodhidharma arrived in China to spread the teachings of the Buddha. He swore that he would not sleep until his mission was accomplished. This proved to be an ambitious aim, and although he managed several years of non-stop teaching and meditating, the prince eventually fell asleep. When he awoke he was so angry with himself that he cut off his **eyelids**, and where they fell the Buddha caused the first tea plant to grow. Tea leaves have an eyelid shape and the herb contains caffeine, which hinders sleep, so the story aptly explains the origins of both the plant and its qualities. Tea's ability to refresh and revitalize was soon realized and its popularity spread rapidly. Tea first arrived in Europe in the early seventeenth century and soon was so popular and highly valued that it became the subject of a colossal amount of trading. Because it was expensive, it was the provenance of the wealthy, and so tea became a status symbol.

The tea ceremony in Japan is a Zen ritual that aims to remove the ego from the action, and is carried out in accordance with strict guidelines. The English tradition of afternoon tea is not religiously significant but became an essential part of the day after the Duchess of Bedford made it a fashionable habit in the mid nineteenth century.

Thistle

The thistle is the symbolic flower of Scotland, holding this role since pre-Christian times. There's an amusing tale attached to its significance. Apparently, a Viking invader trod on the spiky plant in his bare **feet**, and the ensuing yelp alerted the Scots to the potential attack. The Order of the Thistle, an honor bestowed by the Queen, has as its motto, *nemo me impune lacessit* ("no-one attacks me and gets away with it"), an appropriate motto for an Order named after such a sharp and impenetrable plant.

The spikiness of the thistle gives it a warlike symbolism, and this also makes it an emblem of protection. The power of the thistle breaks curses and malevolent spells.

The thistle has long had a reputation of being able to banish melancholy, perhaps because of its sweet scent, perhaps because of the **wine** with which the thistle flowers were blended to make the required medicine.

Despite all these positive associations, in the Bible the thistle is a symbol of man's fall from grace. When Adam and Eve are cast out from the Garden of Eden, they enter a wilderness wherein grow "thorns and thistles." However, many thistles hold a delicious hidden secret that Adam and Eve might have discovered: the spiny flowers can be cut open to reveal a tasty and nutritious nut.

Thyme

Thyme flowers were once believed to house the souls of the dead. If thyme is seen growing where no other plant will flourish, it is a symbol that a murder has been committed there.

Thyme was brought into any house where there was a corpse, and kept there until the time for the funeral, although it was never used in the flowers which dressed the coffin. The scent of thyme purified the air and kept away any evil spirits.

Thyme was burned in **temples** as an ingredient of **incense**, and is still burned in magical rituals and in spell casting. Specifically, thyme has cleansing powers and is burned to purify the ritual place.

TOBACCO

It's impossible to say precisely when man first started chewing, smoking, or sniffing various dried plants, but it's safe to say that he has done all of these for several thousands of years all over the world. The reasons for this are many; for medicinal purposes, as a stimulant, or as a narcotic, for relaxation, and for ritual purposes. However, no herb used in these ways has gained the worldwide popularity of tobacco.

Originating from the Americas, tobacco was used by Native American shamans long before it was "discovered" by the Conquistadores and other Western colonizers. Drinking tobacco juice was a ritual carried out during training for these medicine men, the juice invoking hallucinations or visions. The juice was squirted into the **eyes** to confer the gift of second sight. Smoking tobacco was considered to be even more profoundly magical an act than drinking it, enabling the smoker to come into direct contact with the **spirit** world, and passing the pipe of tobacco around a **circle** of people signified the unity of the group and the shared

vision. The ceremony began with the ritual pipe, or **calumet**, being offered to the **sky**, then the **earth**; then smoke was puffed towards the **four** cardinal points to acknowledge the **spirits** of the directions and of the **elements**. The **smoke** was blown over people to heal diseases and to confer strength.

The tobacco ceremony was carried out with due solemnity in honor of the sacred properties of the herb; however, when it was introduced to Europe in the sixteenth century, people rapidly became addicted to it. Tobacco "drinking," as smoking was called at the time, became a fashionable pursuit, and by 1610 there were as many as 7000 tobacco shops in London alone.

As with many of the most sacred herbs and plants that were originally designated for use only very occasionally, tobacco is extremely poisonous, and the enormous amount of **deaths** caused by its consumption could arguably be said to be indicative of a general lack of respect for the magical substances given to us by the natural world.

TOMATO

The tomato—because of its **red** color and its succulence—was viewed with great suspicion when it arrived in Europe from the Americas in the sixteenth century. A sensual fruit stuffed full of many seeds, the tomato was called the love **apple** and was believed to be an **aphrodisiac**, and therefore it incurred the disapproval of the **Church** as a lewd fruit.

The tomato as a sexual symbol is also common in Africa, and in Bambara territories couples eat them before making love. Women make offerings of tomatoes to the God Faro.

The biggest tomato fight in the world, La Tomatina, occurs annually in August in the town of Bunyol, near Valencia, in Spain.

VERVAIN

Vervain, or verbena, is one of the herbs that the Romans believed was sacred to **Mars**, God of War, and so they also believed that vervain would repel the enemy. **Crowns** of the herb were worn by envoys sent to other countries, whether they were there for peaceable purposes or otherwise.

Verbena actually means "**altar** plant" because of the use of bundles of twigs that were tied together and used to sweep altars.

Pre-Christian Britons also thought of vervain as a sacred plant, almost as important as the **mistletoe**. It was an essential ingredient in healing, and was also used as both a ritual **food** and in spell casting and enchantments. Methods of use included making a vervain infusion to ward off evil spirits or witches, and placing it in the home to deflect lightning. However, these same witches could also use vervain for their own magical purposes, provided they knew exactly when to pick it; as with other magical herbs, the time at which it was gathered was a crucial factor in ensuring that it would be effective for the intended purpose. The vervain was held in such high esteem by the Celts that it was also known as the Druid's herb.

The herb, if buried in the garden, is said to bring financial prosperity, something else that the plant symbolizes. Juice of the vervain is believed to suppress sexual desire for long periods of time, and is consumed by religious ascetics to make life a little easier. This same juice, if smeared on the body, will enable a person to see into the future.

The symbolism of vervain as a powerful healing plant extends into Christian belief. There's a legend that it grew under the **cross** upon which Christ was crucified, and was used to staunch his wounds.

VINE

In Christian symbolism, the vine, with its far-reaching tendrils, represents the Kingdom of God, and is described as such in the Gospels. Although there are many different types of plant that have vine-like attributes, the vine referred to is the grape vine since, of course, grapes give us **wine**, which is seen as conferring knowledge and immortality. In this sense, the vine and its fruit are inseparable.

The vine grows vigorously and has tendrils that both climb and bind, using available surfaces in order to reach the sunlight whilst using the minimum of energy. In some cultures, including that of the Babylonian, the vine was symbolic of the **Tree of Life** itself. Indeed, the Latin word for vine, *vitis*, came from the same root as that of "vitality." The Sumerian **hieroglyph** for "life" was a vine leaf.

The vine is associated with the Greek God, **Dionysus** (or when in Rome, **Bacchus**). Because vines need to be chopped back in order to grow most vigorously, they are symbolic of renewed vigor after a sacrifice.

The vine appears in the **Ogham Tree alphabet** where it is called *Muin*.

VIOLET

For all its tiny scale and its modesty in growing close to the ground, hiding in among long **grasses** (hence the epithet "shrinking violet"), the flower fairly sparkles out from its hiding place.

The violet was associated with **Aphrodite**, Goddess of Love, although later the modesty and humility of the flower made it a perfect symbol for the Virgin Mary, not least because the little plant is self-pollinating and so a good reminder of the Virgin Birth.

Mohammed called the violet a symbol of the truth of his teachings, since the violet spreads rapidly and flowers twice a year.

The scented violet, *Violet odorata*, has a marvelous perfume and is used in perfumes, love charms, and potions. The violet is also associated with **death** and the spirit world, and is said to grow in the fields where **Persephone** walked before the ground swallowed her up. The **purple** color of the violet is symbolic of death.

WOLFSBANE

See **Aconite**.

WORMWOOD

The Greek word for this herb, *apsinthion*, means "without sweetness" and lends its name to the alcoholic liqueur (absinthe) which is made from it and which can cause a disease called absinthism if too much of it is consumed on a habitual basis. A symptom of this disease is complete paralysis. The drink became so problematic during the nineteenth and early twentieth centuries that it was banned, although it is gaining popularity once more.

Because of its bitterness, the plant symbolizes this quality as well as that of grief or of something that is poisonous to the **soul**. In the Book of Revelation, "Wormwood" is the name given to the **star** related to a devilish figure that, it is predicted, will lay waste to Israel; the star falls from the Heavens and poisons a third of the **water** on Earth. This story is believed to foretell the Last Judgement, symbolized by the poisoning of our waters.

Wormwood was used in magical spells to make the dead rise from their graves, and, rather unexpectedly in view of this, was an ingredient in love philters. The plant is said to confer psychic powers and the gift of second sight

The Latin name for the herb is *Artemisia absinthum*, showing its association with the Goddess, **Artemis**, the huntress and the Great Goddess of the Woods.

YARROW

The yarrow plant takes its Latin name, *Achillea*, from the heroic Achilles who staunched the bleeding of his wounds with yarrow leaves. One part of this tale has its basis in truth, because yarrow does contain **blood**-clotting qualities. This is why it is also called "bloodwort" or "nose-bleed."

Young girls seeking their true loves used yarrow leaves and flowers as divinatory tools. Yarrow stalks are also used in the Chinese divinatory system based on the **elements**, the

I Ching. The yarrow was a sacred plant that symbolized the truth, so its stalks were appropriate for divinatory use; in addition, the stalks grow long and dry well, so make a perfect tool for the job.

Yarrow leaves can avert evil influences from entering any place where they are strewed across the threshold, and could stop witches in their tracks. The plant therefore became a symbol of protection, sometimes tied to cradles to keep the baby safe.

WORLD TREE

It's not difficult to see why the tree is universally revered as a sacred, living being. Trees are not only beautiful but also benevolent, providing food in the form of nuts, **fruits**, and syrups, medicines (aspirin, for example, comes from the bark of the **willow**), and its timber provides material to build houses, ships, and carriages, as well as weapons and tools. Trees, too, provided the material to make gallows, and people were executed by being suspended from their branches.

The tree combines all the elements within it. It has its roots in the **Earth**, which nourishes it; its sap is the **water** element, the "dew of Heaven," as well as being its life **blood**; it has its leaves and branches high up in the **air**. Not only is **fire** produced when its sticks are rubbed together, but the wood provides fuel for that same fire. One of the most important functions of the tree, however, is its processing of carbon dioxide. The destruction of the rain **forests** is akin to a vital organ being removed from a human body. These forests are so great that they even create their own atmosphere, as do the coastal **redwood** forests in northern California. The **Doctrine of Signatures**—the ancient idea that a plant possesses the qualities of the thing that it physically resembles—makes sense in the case of the tree. Denuded of leaves, the branches look like a huge upturned lung, and indeed, trees are the lungs of our planet.

No surprise, then, that our ancestors believed that each tree had its own powerful **spirit**; indeed this idea has never gone away. Bringing an evergreen tree into the home is still an essential part of our Christmas festivities and a continuation of this ancient belief. In pre-Christian Britain, trees were celebrated at the **Beltane** festivals, decorated with ribbons and danced around; this ancient ceremony was banned by the Romans in the fourth century BC, but saw its revival in the form of the **maypole**. Although modern forestry machinery can cut trees at ground level, strip them of their branches and cut them into planks—a "harvester" can do all of this in the space of minutes in the forest, even at night-time—our ancestors believed it necessary to appease the spirit of the living tree in some way before chopping it down. This practice has by no means died out.

The Druids are particularly known for their worship of trees, and they take their name from the same root as the word for "oak," the tree they most revere. But tree worship has been performed all over the world. The **birds** that lived in the trees at Dodona carried messages from the Gods, and the trees themselves were the focus of a particular kind of divination called "phyllomancy," whereby messages were interpreted from the sound of the leaves rustling in the wind. Different people all have their most magical and sacred trees, what might be called their **World Tree**. For the Scandinavians it is the great ash, Yggdrasil, that unifies the cosmos. Siberian people venerate the **birch**, and Germans the **lime**, which they called the *Linden*. The Buddha sat beneath the **Bodhi tree** when he received enlightenment, and the Chinese sage Lao Tzu was born beneath a **plum tree**.

The idea of a World Tree, a giant tree that grows through the cosmos linking the Heavens, the Earth, and the Underworld, is completely universal, constituting a primal image or archetype, having parallels with the **Axis Mundi** and the **Omphalos**. This tree represents not only the idea of something that strives towards the Heavens, but the life-cycle of the tree itself is a reminder of the endless cycle of regeneration; of life, **death**, and rebirth. The **birds** that sit in the tops of the branches of this tree symbolize the souls of unborn beings. The symbolism of the tree is far reaching; it is used to represent the idea of a family; the **Kabbalah** itself is imagined as a tree; and in **alchemy**, the World Tree appears as a naked woman, crowned with sprouting, fruiting branches, **wands** in her **hands**, the **Sun** and **Moon** appearing to her right and left.

The inverted tree with its roots in the air, on the other hand, is a sacred symbol that has largely been forgotten. It is represented physically in the center of **Green Man Maze** in Wales, and symbolizes the idea from the *Upanishads* that the whole Universe is an upside-down tree, its roots in the Heavens and its branches embracing the Earth. The same image appears in Kabbalistic imagery, the **ten** spheres of the **Sephiroth** and their **twenty-two** connecting branches generally represented as a cosmic tree.

ACACIA

The acacia thrives in barren, desert climates, and specimens have endured for thousands of years despite drought and famine. It provides shelter for both **animals** and people from the scorching heat of the **Sun**, and its leaves and **seeds** are edible. These characteristics make it a symbol of protection and resilience. The tree also has vicious thorns that conceal the secrets said to be hidden by the tree. The wood of the acacia is particularly hard and durable, close-grained, of a beautiful **orange** color, impervious to insects, and seemingly incorruptible. This incorruptibility means that the tree signifies purity and its wood is therefore burned only for specific, magical purposes.

The acacia tree was around a long time before the Bible was written, and it is believed that this is what was meant by the **Shittim tree** mentioned in the Old Testament, the timber of which, plated with **gold**, was used to make the **Ark of the Covenant**. One of the trees speculated to have been used to make Christ's **crown** of thorns is the acacia; ancient kings who were sacrificially slaughtered wore these agonizingly painful **crowns**. The **Cross**—sometimes described as a "tree"—upon which Christ was crucified, too, is likely to have been made from strong and durable acacia wood. For the Jewish people, the acacia was so sacred that it would never be used for mundane purposes such as furniture.

One of the foremost symbols in **Freemasonry**, a spring of acacia leaves is laid on the coffin at the funerals of Freemasons in memory of **Hiram Abiff**, builder of King Solomon's Temple. Hiram's story of betrayal echoes that of Christ and is one of the main tenets of **Freemasonry**. Hiram had the sprig of acacia laid on his grave as a sign not only of death and resurrection, but as a reminder that, like the tree, Hiram refused to divulge certain secrets. Its evergreen leaf is a symbol of the immortality of the **soul**, and the acacia, as a symbol of incorruptibility, signifies the purity of Hiram's soul.

The Greek word for "innocence"— *akakia*—is the same as that for the tree. For Freemasons, again, this is particularly apposite since Hiram was also innocent, preferring to die rather than give out the password that could have given his assassins the status of Master Masons. The tree was also the symbol of the Arab Goddess, Al'Uzza, who presides over birth and death, the changing **seasons**, the **planets**, and **stars**.

ALDER

A **water**-loving tree, the alder is often found on the banks of rivers or streams, and in marshes, where it forms a wet woodland called "alder carr." It is the only broad-leafed tree that produces cones, and the fact that the branches can bear leaves, old cones, new buds, and catkins all at once makes it a symbol of fertility and also of the **elements**. Despite its close proximity to water, the timber of the alder does not rot—it was used in the making of clogs—so purity and incorruptibility are added to its symbolic virtues. When it is cut, its sap quickly turns **red** when exposed to the air, and so our ancestors associated this red liquid with **blood** and with **fire**, making the tree especially sacred, associated with health and royalty. In Ireland it was forbidden to cut one down because of superstitions about it

"bleeding." The red sap can be used to make a dye, called "roeim," which may have been used by warriors to give them a fearsome appearance in the same way as the **blue** plant dye, woad, was used by ancient Britons. The flowers of the alder, too, make a **green** dye, and its young shoots give a golden color.

Several other legends are associated with the tree. The Greek God of **time**, Chronos, was associated with the alder. One of his Greek names is Fearinos, and in the **Ogham tree alphabet** the alder appears as *Fearn*. Irish Celtic myth says that the first man was made from this tree, as the first woman was made from the **rowan**.

There's a particular quality of the alder that makes it very handy for making pipe-style type musical instruments. If a twig is cut from the tree, the inner part shrivels up leaving the bark intact. Several of these twigs of different lengths can produce different notes. One of the sacred trees that indicates a gateway into another world, the pigments in its flowers were said to color the clothes of **fairies**. An old belief held that lone alder trees were once witches, who used the pipes made from the tree to whistle for the north wind.

ALMOND TREE

As one of the first trees to flower in the spring, the almond is a natural symbol of hope and new beginnings. Mentioned many times in the Bible, it is synonymous with watchfulness and promise; indeed, its name in Hebrew is *shaked* (pronounced "shaa-ked"), which means vigilant.

The shape of the almond blossom is said to have inspired the **Menorah**, the seven-branched candelabrum which stood on the altar of the Temple in Jerusalem and which is a prominent feature of the Jewish faith today. The Hebrew name for the almond, *luz*, is also the name of a fabled City of Immortals, which can be accessed from the roots of the almond tree.

Eating almond nuts is said to have many benefits. Eating **five** almonds a day is said to ward off drunkenness, and in India almond nuts are considered to be good for the brain. This is despite the fact that some strains of wild almonds contain a deadly poison, prussic acid.

A Greek myth tells us that the almond tree is a symbol of enduring and everlasting love. Phyllis, a beautiful Thracian queen, was married to Demophon, who had to travel back to Athens when his father Theseus died. When Demophon had not returned after a month, Phyllis died of a broken **heart** and turned into an almond tree. When Demophon eventually returned, he was racked with guilt and went to visit the tree; instantly the bare branches were covered in **pink** blossoms and he knew that he was forgiven.

APPLE TREE

The apple tree is a tree of the Underworld, a tree of immortality, and sacred to Apollo. The mythical Isle of Avalon, meaning orchard (from *afal*, the old Welsh word for apple) is the resting place of Celtic kings and heroes, and one of the places where King Arthur is meant to wait until he is needed to rise once more to protect his people. For Celtic people, the apple tree symbolized the World Tree, the axis of the **Universe**. They considered the apple the most magical of fruits, a fruit of immortality and prophecy. At **Samhuin**, or **Halloween**, the time of the apple harvest, the fruit has a large part to play in the rituals and celebrations, including divinatory practices

The apple itself contains a potent magical symbol within. If it is cut across its "equator" (with the stalk at the top), there are **5** pips inside, contained within a five-pointed **star** or **pentagram**. The pentagram, in turn, can be the basis of the **golden spiral**. The spherical shape of the apple symbolizes eternity.

In the biblical story, when Eve persuaded Adam to eat the fruit from the Tree of Knowledge, she also handed him the pentagram hidden inside the fruit (although the Bible never specifically states that this fruit was an apple). Here, the pentagram stands for the spiritual nature of man, and eating it awakens Adam to new possibilities; the flesh combines with the **spirit**, and immediately Adam and Eve cover their genitals, signifying sexual awakening. In Gypsy wedding ceremonies it is customary to cut the apple in the way described above, the bride and groom each eating a half of the fruit.

Magical apples that confer immortality can be plucked from mythological trees all over the world. In Scandinavian stories, apples guarded by the Goddess Idun keep the Gods youthful until the end of the Universe. The Hesperides, in Greek myth, are nymphs that tend a beautiful garden in which grows an apple tree (or trees) whose fruit also confer immortality. These apples are understandably highly sought after, and were given as a wedding gift to the Goddess Hera, by Gaia, the **Earth** Goddess.

In Latin, the word for apple, *malum* also means "evil," and reflects the paradox of the apple as a symbol of both good and evil. Although in the *Tales of the Arabian Nights* the apple of Prince Ahmed cures all ills, in the fairy tale *Snow White and the Seven Dwarves*, the eponymous heroine is poisoned by a shiny **red** apple offered by the witch and falls into the sleep of oblivion.

ASH

Yggdrasil, the "World Tree" of Nordic legends

The ash is one of the more important of all symbolic trees, and it is said to have been the first tree ever created. The plethora of myths and legends about it, which emanate from all corners of the globe, are testimony to its elevated mythological status. Just as the **oak** is the "King of the Forest," the Ash is the "Queen of the Forest," associated with the color and element of **silver**, and other feminine qualities such as **water** and the **Moon**. The Goddess Nemesis, daughter of the **sea** god Oceanus, carried an ash **wand** as a symbol of divine justice. As a counterpoint to this, oaths were taken on spears made of ash wood. The quality of the timber of our symbolic trees provides clues as to their meanings; ash wood is strong, does not split, and because it is hard and close-grained, it polishes well. In the days when wood was used more often than metal for mechanical objects, ash was used to make axles, the hard-polished wood ensuring the smooth turning of the **wheels**. Witches' **broomsticks**, made of ash, helped them to fly quickly through the **air**, as well as providing a powerful link with the Goddess.

Perhaps the most famous ash, and the one that gives the most information as to the symbolic nature not only of the ash but of the tree archetype in general, is Yggdrasil. In northern European mythology, Yggdrasil is the great **World Tree**, whose roots stretch to the very heart of the **Earth** where the Norns dwell. These are creatures that decide the fate of human beings. The extensive roots of this giant tree also reach down to the underground well, Mimir, which is the source of all the secrets of magical powers and mystical revelation. The branches of Yggdrasil stretch right up into the Heavens, sheltering the entire Universe in its branches, a mythic tree that is the one constant feature of a changing world. Here we see the ash as a symbol of stability.

Because the ash was seen to exist in both the worlds of **spirit** and matter, it's a symbol of the union of opposites and therefore of **marriage**. The ash is also a fertility symbol, and **amulet**s of ash wood are said to attract love. Older ash trees sometimes grow or split in such a way that a hole is formed in the trunk; it was customary to pass new-born babies or small children through this hole to ensure their protection or to cure illnesses, showing an aspect of this great tree as the mother-protector and healer. When this ritual was enacted, small tokens of **food** or coins would be pushed into the ground around the roots.

The idea of the ash as a protective tree is obvious given its size and shape. Protective charms were made of the wood, and garters of ash wood were worn to protect against the malevolent powers of witches. The roots of the ash look peculiarly human in shape, similar to those of the **mandrake**, and so were used in healing charms, the root substituted for the person in question. The Ash, or *Nuin*, is the third letter of the **Ogham tree alphabet**.

ASPEN

A member of the poplar family, the aspen does not like to be in the shade of other trees and so often stands alone, preferring damper ground. As its Latin name—*Populus tremula*—suggests, the tree is rarely still because the leaves move at the slightest provocation; because of this the tree has a shimmering appearance, and among its folk names are "shaking" or "quivering" tree. This continuous movement means that the aspen is considered to be particularly good for phyllomancy, divination by the whispering sounds made by leaves in the wind. This constant trembling, legend says, is because the aspen has such acute hearing that it continually reacts to sounds from far and wide, disseminating information to anyone with the skills to understand. The communicative aspects of

the tree mean that it is connected to the God **Mercury**, and placing a leaf under the **tongue** is said to confer the gift of eloquence.

BALCHE

The balche is a tree that was sacred to the Mayans. Its bark was soaked in **honey** and **water**, and poured into a canoe or other similar trough-shaped container to ferment, a process which started almost immediately. The resulting **mead**-like drink is extremely intoxicating and was believed by the Mayans to have magical powers. They used it in rituals, specifically as an aid to problem solving; because they believed that both the tree and the drink had been given to them from the Lord of Creation, then it stood to reason that he would help them work together to solve any issues affecting the tribe as a whole.

BANYAN

The banyan, also known as the vata tree, the bodhi tree or the Asiatic fig, is one of the trees considered to be the **World Tree** by the people who revere it.

This tree is particularly special because the Buddha happened to be sitting underneath one when he was suddenly illumined as to his true nature—the word *bodhi* means "enlightened." Although the particular tree under which he was enlightened is no longer living, a cutting was taken in the second century BC by a Sri Lankan princess, and this tree now grows in Anuradhapura in Sri Lanka, where it is the object of pilgrimage. The banyan can now be found anywhere in the world where Buddhism or Hinduism are practiced, and it is often grown near **temples**; Vishnu, the Hindu God, is often depicted as sitting under a banyan dispensing teachings of philosophy and science to his students. Although it is sacred, it is said to shelter many different kinds of **spirits**, and so it is considered unlucky to sleep under one at night.

The tree grows in quite an unusual way, with its roots reaching down from its branches which then take hold in the ground. This is why the banyan is sometimes called the "walking tree" or the "tree with many **feet**." The structure of the tree, which is a little like a strange organic building that casts a deep shade, makes it a perfect place to meet, and village councils in India (whose national tree symbol it is) still meet under these trees to discuss important matters.

Baobab

This is one of the oldest, largest of all trees, its gigantic, contorted shape a curiously cartoon-like silhouette against the skyline. The tree seems to be an amalgam of **animal**, vegetable, and **mineral**, with a distinct personality of its own. Because of its wrinkly, scored bark, size, and great age, the baobab is sometimes compared to the **elephant**. A creation myth from West Africa says that all the animals were each given their own tree. The **hyena**, appalled to be given the baobab, immediately tipped it upside down, which explains the root-like appearance of the branches.

The baobab shares an important position in the community in places where it is prevalent, such as West Africa and Madagascar. At one time, the people buried their dead in its hollow trunk, no doubt in the hope that this massive, benevolent tree might protect the **soul**. In addition, when a baobab dies, people still commemorate it with a full-scale wake, according this tree a sacred status that is on a par with a human village elder. When the Kariba dam in Zambia was built in the 1960s, the people had to evacuate the spirits from the baobab trees before the trees were submerged by **water**; branches were taken from the trees and attached to baobabs in unaffected areas.

The tree has a spongy, water-saturated bark and a hollow interior that is sometimes used as a reservoir. Every part of the tree is useful, apart from this spongy bark. However, it is as a presence in the landscape that the tree is most important. Highly visible and venerated because of its size and age, the tree itself becomes a sort of **temple**, a place of pilgrimage, and in Australia it has been used to mark sacred burial sites.

Beech

Beech woods are shady, magical places, but the trees are most commonly used in hedging these days (one of the tallest hedges in the world, the Meikleour beech hedge in Scotland, is over 100 feet tall). The tree forms nuts that are packed, **three** at a time, into an outer husk, and although they are edible, they are most commonly used in animal feed. Indeed in medieval times in Europe, pigs were often left to feed in the forest on the "mast"— the collective name for the beech's nuts. The beech, like the **ash**, often plays the role of "queen" to the **oak's** "king."

Like the **birch**, the beech tree is associated with written communication, and thin slices of its bark were used as paper. The name of the beech, *boc* in Anglo-Saxon, shares the same root as "**book**," a concept also found in German and Swedish etymology. It was an old custom to write a spell or magical charm on a sliver of beech wood, then bury it in the ground and wait for the desired item or situation to manifest itself.

BIRCH

The birch, being fast-growing, is often planted with the saplings of slower-growing trees (such as **oak**) in order to shelter them as they develop. Therefore, the tree is seen to have protective qualities. Suitably, given that the birch is often the first visible tree in the forest (hence its nickname, the "pioneer tree"), its name *Beth* is the first letter of the **Ogham tree alphabet**, and as such it represents the start, the beginning, the birth. Accordingly, birch wood was often used for babies' cradles.

The root of the word "birch" is the same as that of "bright," and appropriately its bark, particularly those of the **silver** and the Himalayan birch, is both bright, beautiful, and symbolic of purity. This bark does not rot—lending the tree an aura of indestructibility, and the bark is quite flexible and can be written on; it is sometimes used as a parchment for spells. The *Midewiwin*, or Grand Medicine Society of the Ojibwa Indians, uses birch bark rolls to depict the symbols that serve as a reminder of the secrets of their society, and they become one of the most treasured items of an initiate.

These birch bark rolls have the same sacred significance as the tracing board in **Freemasonry**.

The birch is both male and female, and carries attributes of both; it is the tree of both the **Sun** and the **Moon**. This is partly because the tree carries both male and female **flowers** on the same tree. It is often called the "Lady of the Woods" on account of its slender stem, its graceful, drooping branches, and its delicate leaves. Bunches of small twigs can gather in the branches of the tree; these are known as "witches' brooms."

The birch is a sacred tree not only to the Druids but also to the Siberian peoples, who view it as the epitome of the **World Tree** and of the **Axis Mundi**. The tree is a central part of initiation ceremonies; the shaman climbs the tree to link, symbolically, with the Gods, and the tree is circled **9** times to represent the number of steps to **Heaven**. This ritual circling of the tree is similar to the ancient tradition of dancing around the **maypole**, which used to be carried out using the living tree as the pole.

The sap of the birch tree is sweet and can be used as syrup or made into **wine**, and the inner part of the bark contains a pain-relieving chemical. The birch is also synonymous with corporal punishment, which used to be called "birching."

BLACKTHORN

The blackthorn is a small, gnarly tree, often grown in hedgerows where its vicious thorns make it a good stock-proof barrier. These thorns carry a dual symbolism since they can both attack and defend. The small, bitter fruits of the blackthorn, sloes, are inedible, but commonly used to flavor gin.

One of the folk names of the blackthorn is the "wishing thorn." The branches were once used as divining rods, although negotiating the thorns must have been a tricky business. As "wishing rods," blackthorn branches were made into **wands** for ritual use.

The blackthorn and the **hawthorn** often appear together and are considered "sisters," the blackthorn providing the "dark" counterpart to the "light" of the other tree. Though its blossoms appear very early, often in early April before the leaves are on the tree, the blackthorn is a symbol of fertility. Despite this, it has a dark reputation because the spines often poison anyone they touch. This meant that they can be a dangerous weapon in the wrong hands, used negatively by malicious entities, such as witches. Blackthorn spines were supposed to be used by these malicious women to pierce the **manikins** used in a nasty form of sympathetic magic. In common with other thorn trees, it has been conjectured that the blackthorn tree was used to make Christ's **crown** of thorns.

BODHI TREE

See **Banyan**.

BOSWELLIA SACRA

This is the tree that gives us the aromatic resin called "frankincense," most famously known as one of the gifts, along with **gold** and **myrrh**, which the **Three** Wise Men gave to the infant Christ. The tree is incredibly tough, and can grow in regions where there appears to be no soil at all; it can even grow out of stone by means of a sucker-like protuberance. The tree has therefore become a symbol of resilience.

Frankincense is extracted by slashing the tree to make the sap bleed. This hardened sap is called "tears." Frankincense has been used for thousands of years in religious rituals, and is still used today. The **smoke** is believed to carry the thoughts and prayers of the faithful to the **Heavens**. The aroma itself symbolizes life, hence it was mixed with oils and used to anoint newborn babies. Frankincense is paired with the myrrh that was used to embalm corpses; each substance used at either end of a human life, each effectively a symbol of spiritual transformation.

CASSIA

The cassia, a native of southern China, is an evergreen tree whose bark is used as a spice that tastes similar to cinnamon. The Chinese consider the cassia to be the sacred Tree of Life, the **World Tree** that grows forever in paradise. Whosoever eats the fruit of the cassia will become immortal. The paradise spoken of here is located in a specific area, high up in the **mountain**s of Tibet at the source of the Yellow River.

CATALPA

The catalpa was considered one of the sacred trees of Ancient China, where it occupied the southerly position, associated with the **Sun**. The other three "Trees of the Directions" are the **thuja**, the **acacia**, and the **chestnut**.

CEDAR

In the same way that **oak** groves were sacred in Ancient Greece and throughout Britain, so too were cedar groves sacred in their native locations in the Middle East and North Africa, where similar oracular rites were carried out. The *Epic of Gilgamesh* describes cedar woods as being the dwelling place of the Gods. Long-lived, large, dark-hued, and imposing, the cedar—particularly the stately Cedar of Lebanon—is clearly identifiable, being a symbol of longevity and nobility. The wood of the cedar is tough and durable, making the tree synonymous with the qualities of incorruptibility and purity. Its timber was used in the building of the **Temple in Jerusalem**.

Like all evergreens, the cedar is emblematic of immortality. It is one of the trees which, it is conjectured, was used to make the **Cross** used in Christ's crucifixion; Christ sharing the incorruptibility and purity of the tree. Paradoxically the original **forest** that used to cloak Mount Lebanon has now been reduced to a handful of scattered remnants.

In Roman times, statues of the Gods were carved from cedar wood, its qualities considered suitable for such a sacred purpose; they also used its resin to preserve the heads of the more celebrated of their enemies, an echo of its former use in Egyptian mummification practices. Ancient Egyptians believed that the cedar was a symbol of rebirth, and the fact that its oil is also antiseptic and sweet-smelling made it a particularly good choice as an embalming ingredient. The Assyrians believed that the secret names of the Gods were inscribed on the Cedar tree itself; they also used the sticky **egg**-shaped cones as charms to keep **demons** away. Cedar wood has a particularly fragrant scent, which is used in **incenses**; it is likewise burned by Jewish people to mark the New Year.

CHERRY TREE

The cherry tree has a strong association with Japan, and the image of its profuse **pink** blossoms scattering the pavements is synonymous with springtime in that country. This tree is the *sakura*, or ornamental cherry, which was probably introduced to Japan from China. The progress of the blossoming trees is even tracked by the Japanese meteorological office, the whole nation being involved in the spectacle. As one of the first trees to blossom, it is emblematic of hope and new beginnings, and is the precursor of the **rice harvest** to come. The cherry tree blossoms swiftly—a wise planter will ensure that he has early-, mid-, and late-flowering varieties—and the petals are soon gone, a symbol of the transitory beauty of life itself, and also symbolizing warriors who have fallen in battle.

For the Samurai, the image of crushing the cherry in the hand to reach the hard stone inside was symbolic of the sacrifice of his material flesh and **blood** to reach the inner "stone," his soul and his personality; accordingly, the scabbard of the Samurai's sword is decorated with cherries to represent this search for inner meaning.

In the West, the cherry itself represents hidden fruit, hence the expression "popping the cherry" denoting the loss of virginity. The cherry is a fertility symbol, used in making charms meant to attract a lover. Girls would bore a hole in a cherry stone each night over the **14**-night period of the waxing **Moon**, and all the stones were threaded onto a string. On the night of the full **Moon**, the entire "necklace" was worn around the top of the **thigh**, hoping to attract the desired gentleman.

CHESTNUT

One of the **four** sacred trees in Ancient China, the sweet chestnut signified the westerly direction and the season of fall. Symbolically, it represented foresight; this was because its nuts were collected for later use during the winter.

Elsewhere, the chestnut is symbolic of honesty (it should not be confused with the horse chestnut, which is not a true chestnut at all). The biggest tree in Britain is a chestnut—the Tortworth Chestnut, which in 1766 already measured 50 feet in girth. There is an even bigger one on Mount Etna in Sicily, which was reputed to be able to hold a flock of sheep in its hollow core, in which a house had been built. It was later found to consist of five trees growing together.

CHRISTMAS TREE

Possibly one of the happiest and most delightful of all tree symbols, the **Christmas** tree has come to be associated with the Christian celebration of the birth of Christ, although its origins go back to much earlier pre-Christian times.

The old pagan custom of bringing a living tree indoors in the middle of the dark months of the year and decorating it with **candles** and trinkets was introduced to Britain by Prince Albert, the husband of Queen Victoria. The idea rapidly caught on. Bringing evergreen vegetation in the form of trees, boughs, and branches from the outside to the inside was a magical ritual, a piece of sympathetic magic, meant to encourage the return of **spring** and the growing season.

The timing of the entrance and exit of the tree was critical. Any time before Christmas Eve was too soon for the tree to come inside, and all decorations had to be taken down and the tree removed by Twelfth Night, January 6. This tradition, however, does not seem to signify for the department stores who start to display artificial Christmas trees from September onwards.

The Christmas tree is traditionally an evergreen tree, usually a spruce or a fir, which is cut down from the forest. The tree itself symbolizes immortality and everlasting life, and the lights draped on it are a reminder that during the darkest time of the year, lighter days are just round the corner. The Yule Celebrations in northern Europe were echoed in similar rituals in southern Europe. The Roman God Atys or Attis was a savior God whose life story very much parallels that of Christ. Atys was born on December 25 to a virgin mother, and was sacrificed to save mankind, killed beneath a conifer, remaining for **three** days and nights in his tomb before resurrection. His priests, called *dendrophori* (meaning "tree bearers"), were charged with selecting a conifer from a sacred **grove** that would be brought indoors in memory of the death and resurrection of Atys, who is also linked with **Apollo**, the **Sun** God.

CITRON

The citron (or citrus) tree gives us one of the **Three Blessed Fruits** in Buddhist philosophy. The story goes that the Buddha, sitting in the shade of the tree, picked one of the fruits but found that it was bitter and unpleasant-tasting. He decided to destroy the tree, but changed his mind and spoke to it instead, suggesting that it should make its fruits more pleasant to the taste and more useful. So the tree altered the shape of its fruits, so that they matched the outstretched hand of the Buddha.

As for usefulness, the tree surpassed itself. Bergamot oil is made from it, and the crystallized peel is a delicacy. Because of its many seeds, the fruit is also a fertility symbol. In the Jewish faith, too, the fruit of the citrus tree has sacred status and was brought as an offering to the **Temple**.

CYPRESS

The cypress was regarded, like all other evergreens, as a symbol of eternal life; this is particularly appropriate for the cypress because of the physical longevity of many of its species. Trees have exceeded 500 years in age, and there is one in a Franciscan church near Rimini that is reputed to have been planted by St. Francis of Assisi himself in *c.*1200.

The cypress is associated with funerals in most Mediterranean countries, but is also a positive symbol of incorruptibility and the resurrection of the **soul**. The cypress also smells particularly sweet, a factor that adds to its sacred status; the scent of the cypress wafting over graveyards and cemeteries was believed to purify the **air**.

Because of its symbolic purity and incorruptibility, cypress wood is used to make sacred religious objects, such as the shaku, a **scepter** which is carried by Shinto priests. In Ancient Greece, the cypress was a tree of the Underworld. It was said that the first thing a soul would encounter upon entering the nether regions was a **white** cypress standing by the Fountain of Oblivion, Lethe, whose waters removed all traces of memory prior to the reincarnation of the soul.

DATE PALM

The date palm was the equivalent of the **World Tree** for the Assyrians and Babylonians, its versatile fruit a staple part of the diet thousands of years ago and still important today. The date is eaten on its own, or cooked according to many different recipes and is even made into a sparkling drink. It is also used in cosmetics and as an animal feed, so it is understandable that the tree was considered a sacred gift from God. Cultivation of tree itself stretches back as far as 6000 years ago, and it is an important symbol within Islam, Christianity, and Judaism. It provides not only **food** but also shade and timber.

It was the leaves of the date palm that lined Christ's route into Jerusalem before his crucifixion, and the same leaves are used to make the **palm cross**. The shape of the date palm inspired Egyptian architects, who used a stylized version of the tree for their monumental columns.

Ebony

Ebony wood is intensely dark colored, incredibly dense and hard, and polishes to a high shine. One of the best-known uses for ebony wood is for the **black** keys on a piano keyboard.

The symbolism associated with the ebony tree stems primarily from its color. The King of the Underworld, **Pluto**, had an ebony throne, and so of course the wood was linked to **death** and the Underworld. Because it was also a symbol of strength and protection (on account of its hardness), ebony was once a popular wood for making babies' cradles.

Elder

The elder appears in the **Ogham tree alphabet** as the 15th letter, called *Ruis*. It is a prolific tree, happy to grow in poor soil and dense shade, although it rarely attains the height or girth of which it's capable; an elder with a 2-meter girth is an unusual sight.

One of the most beautiful aspects of the elder is its flowers. Abundant, frothy heads with hundreds of tiny flowerlets reach towards the sky and fill the air with a heady, distinctive, ethereal scent that can be used to flavor sorbets or cordials, or used to make a delicate sparkling **wine**. As well as these more worldly uses, the scent of these flowers, if inhaled deeply, will apparently open up the **doorway** into the realms of the **fairies** and elemental spirits. The berries, too, which appear in the fall, are also used to makes wines and jellies (unless the birds get to them first).

The ancients, particularly the Celts and some Native Americans, believed that the elder held the spirit of the "Elder Mother," a great Mother Goddess or nature spirit that would wreak havoc on anyone chopping down the tree. In England, permission had to gained from "Old Gal" before a tree could be felled. Witches could shape-shift into the form of the elder, and an old superstition says that if an elder tree is "injured" then the tree would not only gush **blood** but would revert back into human shape; the witch would bear the same scars that had been inflicted on the tree.

The association with witches is a powerful one for this tree. Its wood, like that of the elm, was supposed to be used for **broomsticks**, and crowns of elderwood were worn at **Samhuin** to increase chances of otherworldly communication, both audible and visible.

Because the pith of the elder can be removed easily from its surrounding bark, children use the sticks as pea-shooters, and adults use them to blow smouldering embers into flames. This accounts for its Anglo-Saxon names, *ellearn*, meaning "hollow," and *aeld*, meaning fire.

Elm

Sadly, the elm population in both the UK and the US has been decimated by Dutch Elm disease, and this lofty, dignified tree, which used to reach an age of 400 years or more, is now considered lucky if it reaches thirty.

However, the symbolism of the tree is rich, as befits such a beautiful specimen. **Groves** of elms were sacred to the Goddess or the Great Mother, and some believed that the first woman was created by the elm tree. Such a large tree would be seen as a protective force, and the elm was planted in particular in vine-yards to shade the plants and protect the **vines**. As a result it came to be linked with **Bacchus**, the Roman God of **wine**;the vine and the elm were effectively "wedded."

The elm is also connected with **death**, and the wood was used to make coffins at a time when the tree itself was not so rare. The elm has a special affinity with the **elves** that are said to guard burial mounds, so the tree was associated with these places; also, the first elm was meant to have sprung up where Orpheus paused to play his love Eurydice a love song after he rescued her from the Underworld.

The size of the elm meant that they made a good marker in the landscape, so much so that they often had pet names, and were used as meeting places. In the US, the famous Liberty Tree in Boston, Massachusetts, was a colossal elm beneath which the so-called Sons of Liberty met from 1766 onwards. At the time of the American Revolution, an unauthorized meeting was a punishable offence, but it was relatively easy to meet, hidden, beneath the branches of such a tall tree. Soon all **13** colonies each had their Liberty Tree as a place to meet under. The elm itself therefore became synonymous with the ideas of independence and liberty

FIG TREE

There are many varieties of fig tree, and, wherever they appear and in whatever form, they are revered as the **Tree of Life**, symbolic of abundance, plenty, and peacefulness.

The tree under which the Buddha received his enlightenment was a species of fig, appropriately called *Ficus religiosa* in Latin. This tree—also called the **banyan** or the **bodhi tree** (meaning "enlightenment")—is from the same genus, *Ficus*, as those which in Africa the tree house the souls of dead ancestors.

For Muslims the tree is held to have great intelligence, its consciousness only one step away from that of an **animal**. So the fig tree is also associated with knowledge; it's no coincidence that Adam and Eve chose to cover themselves with fig leaves after they had realized that they were naked.

The fig tree's milky sap also contributes to its symbolic meaning. Any tree containing a liquid that looks like **semen** is naturally associated with male fertility. The shape of the fruit of the fig itself, and its many **seeds**, gives further emphasis to the idea of male fertility and sexuality. There is also an obscene **hand** gesture called the "fig," made by sticking the **thumb** through the first and second **fingers** of a closed fist.

The *assathva* is an Indian invocation to the fig tree. The magician sits in the shade of the tree and recites a poem in praise of it; he then circumnavigates the tree in multiples of **seven** circuits. He is meant to do this at least **eighty-four** times before **bathing** and donning new clothes.

FIVE PACIFIC GIANTS

The following **five** species of tree all grow in the north-west of North America on the Pacific coast of both the US and Canada. Apart from the two species of **redwood** discussed below, they are among the tallest and largest of all trees. Their common names, however, are slightly misleading. The western hemlock should not be confused with the **hemlock**, quite a different plant from the one that killed Socrates. The Douglas fir is not a true fir at all, the Lawson's cypress is a false, not a true **cypress**, and the western red cedar has nothing to do—botanically—with the **cedars** of North Africa, the Middle East, and the Indian subcontinent, such as the Cedar of Lebanon and the deodar.

Douglas fir

This huge tree—an introduced specimen is the tallest tree in Britain—is named after the Scottish explorer David Douglas, who died in his 30s after being gored by a **buffalo** in Hawaii that had fallen into a trap that Douglas himself had set. The unusual arrangement of the **seeds** in its cones is explained by a Native American myth which holds that the **three**-ended bracts of the seeds are the tail and two **legs** of a **mouse** which hid from forest **fires** in the cone. The Douglas fir should not be confused with two other giant firs with a similar geographical range: the grand fir and the noble fir, which are true firs from the genus *Abies*.

Lawson's cypress

The several hundred varieties of this tree make it one of the great symbols of suburbia. Bred by nurseries mainly in Britain and Holland, cultivars of the Lawson's cypress can be seen in most gardens in the West, such has been its success. Varieties can be totally different in character from the vast and brooding wild tree, and come in a range of colors from **green** through **blue** to **yellow**, including dwarf varieties that grow no higher than **five** feet.

Sitka spruce

Large specimens of Sitka spruce can be found in the old growth forests of the Pacific northwest, the closest thing in the temperate world to a rain forest. Covered in mosses and tree ferns, these trees grow to an enormous height—the biggest so far discovered is called the "Carmanah Giant" on Vancouver Island, which is 315 feet tall (surprisingly it is less than 400 years old). A similarly massive tree, called Kiidk'yaas, which was sacred to the Haida people, was illegally felled in 1997. Tribal elders believed that this act was a sign that the days of their people were numbered.

It is as a symbol of the unchecked advance of industrial-style agriculture that the Sitka is perhaps best known. Around 100 million saplings a year are planted in the uplands of Britain, forming vast, sterile blankets of uniform forest over much of the north and the west of the country. Ecologists who resent the spread of non-native trees in the country see Sitka spruce as the most culpable tree of all.

Western hemlock

This elegant tree, which can reach a height of 200 feet, has boughs which were used by Native Alaskans—particularly the Tlingit people—to collect herring **eggs** during the spawning season.

Western red cedar

Another enormous tree from the Pacific coast, the western red cedar was particularly sacred to the Native Americans of the region, some of whom called themselves the "people of the red cedar." Its timber was used in the making of **totem poles**, houses, tools, and canoes. The foliage, when crushed, has a distinct scent of **pineapple**.

Hawthorn

The hawthorn, or May tree, is a particularly sacred and holy tree wherever it is found. In the Celtic **Ogham tree alphabet**, it represents the letter H, or *Huath*.

As well as having magical properties, the hawthorn is an incredibly useful tree. When it is cut back to make hedgerows its thorns become sharp, providing an excellent barrier for sheep and other livestock. The berries of the hawthorn provide food for **bird**s and can be made into syrups, preserves, and **wines**. The leaves, too, are nutritious, giving it the nickname of the "**bread** and cheese" tree.

The hawthorn is particularly tolerant of other plants growing close to it and so its presence encourages biodiversity. The hawthorn is a symbol of protection not only because of its thorns. There's an ancient belief that the tree will protect from **fire**, too. Every year a hawthorn "globe" would be woven and brought into the house as insurance against **fire** damage of any kind. The following year the globe would be replaced, the old one being burned and scattered on the fields to ensure a healthy **harvest**.

The **white** flowers of the hawthorn, which blossom in the late spring (hence the name May blossom), have **five** petals, with the matching sepals looking exactly like a **star**. Consequently, as with all members of the **rose** family to which it belongs, the flower is a natural example of the **pentagram**.

The hawthorn is symbolic of fertility and sensuality, underlined by the heady, strong, almost narcotic scent of its flowers that bloom during the time of **Beltane**, when the sap rises in both plant and **animal** life, a natural time for fertility rites and sexual congress.

Although the hawthorn is symbolic of frivolity and mirth, there's a legend which provides a contrasting imagery for tree. Joseph of Arimethea, resting on Wearyall Hill in Glastonbury, leant on his **staff** and in doing so pushed it into the ground. The staff sprouted into a **thorn tree**, and a Christian chapel was built at the site. Traditionally, this magical and holy tree, the "Glastonbury Thorn," blossoms at **Christmas** time and a sprig is sent to the Queen every year. The current tree is a very distant relative of its legendary parent.

Hazel

For the Celts, the hazel was the Tree of Knowledge, the nuts of the tree believed to encapsulate great wisdom. In Druidic lore, it is closely aligned to the **Salmon** of Wisdom, which was believed to have acquired its knowledge from eating magical hazel nuts. Both the Druidic salmon and the hazel nut appear in the fall.

Coll, which means "hazel" in old Irish, was the name of the early Kings of Ireland. *Coll* is also the name given to the hazel in the **Ogham** alphabet. So sacred was the tree that, along with the **apple** tree, it was punishable by death to chop it down or harm it in any way. There is also evidence that hazel branches were buried with the dead in order to confer wisdom in the afterlife.

The hazel favors damp places, and this association with **water** means that the wood makes good dowsing rods, primarily for detecting water in the form of hidden underground wells or springs, but also for finding other things such as mineral seams. These rods were made from coppiced hazel, a forestry practice for which we have evidence from Bronze Age Britain. The combined power of the hazel wood and the perception of the dowser were especially valuable in Cornwall, where they were employed to detect **tin**. However, given the aforementioned penalties for harming the tree, selecting the **wand** or rod from the tree had to be carried out in a specific, ritualistic way, using a sickle. Cutting could take place only at dawn on a Wednesday, since this is the day of **Mercury**, the God that rules the hazel.

Considered to be the tree of witches and also of the Deities who ruled the **sea**, hazel was in these ways further linked with the element of water. In order to gain the protection of these Gods, "wishing caps" of woven hazel twigs were worn by sailors, fisherman, and others who took their living from the seas.

The hazel nut itself was, and still is, a great source of food, the nuts themselves being a symbol of fertility. In parts of Germany, hazel nuts would be handed out by the bride **three** days after the wedding to show that the marriage had been consummated. The nuts were also used in divinatory practices in an attempt to see the future **marriage** partner. Like the **willow**, the hazel is a tree that inspires poetry and song, possibly because of the sound of the wind soughing through its soft leaves.

HOLLY

One of the trees most commonly associated with **Christmas**, like other evergreens, the holly is symbolic of eternal life and immortality; its **red** berries stand for life and vitality, as well as for **blood**. These scarlet berries appear in Christmas songs specifically as the blood of Christ, the redeemer. Both the masculine holly and its female counterpart, **ivy**, are welcomed into churches, unlike the **mistletoe** whose pagan origins are less easy to disguise.

The custom of bringing holly boughs into the home in the depths of winter has its origins in the original pre-Christian idea that its prickly leaves sheltered the **fairy** folk, who were delighted to come indoors at such a cold time of the year.

The Romans also brought holly into the house during the time of the **Saturnalia**, in mid December. Holly trees planted close to the home guarded the house and its occupants from evil influences; the spiny leaves of the "male" tree are a symbol of protection. Holly with smoother leaves has more female attributes.

The name of the holly comes from the Teutonic Goddess Hole, who was the mother of all unborn children and was responsible for naming them. However, so sacred was the holly that it was also named the "holy tree."

The "holly king" is a symbol of a giant man, constructed from holly, who carries a holly club in his hand. The seasonal counterpart to the **oak** king, the holly king is the guardian of the midwinter **solstice**. Holly stands for the letter T in the **Ogham tree alphabet,** and its name is *Tinne*. It is ruled by the element of **fire**.

JUJUBE

A tropical tree native to the Sudan, the jujube proliferates all over Israel and the Middle East, and is arguably one of the most significantly sacred trees in this area. It is also known as the "Christ's thorn jujube" because it's one of the trees that may have provided the **crown** of thorns worn by Christ.

The tree also holds profound meaning for Muslims since Mohammed had a vision when he was resting close to one. Often standing in remote places in the desert, the jujube is symbolic of the point beyond which no person may proceed, and even the **Angel** Gabriel left Mohammed to continue his journey past the jujube on his own. As a tree that survives well in arid conditions, the lone jujube could indeed appear to be standing at the edge of another, unknown world. Consequently, the tree has a practical use as a border marker.

A Muslim story holds that the tree grows in paradise, with each of its leaves bearing the names of as many people who exist on the planet. This heavenly tree is shaken once a year at sunset, after **Ramadan**; the leaves that fall signify those who will die in the coming year. In Israel, it's held that when the jujube is **40** years old, the saints come to sit under it, so anyone cutting down the tree or chopping away branches is destined to be killed by these same saints. Because the tree is further sanctified as being chosen by these saints, it's considered good luck for more ordinary human beings to sit beneath it.

Traditionally, lamps are lit in the branches of the jujube to signify the brightness brought by the Prophet Mohammed. Baby boys are given a jujube twig to hold, in order that they may absorb its symbolic sanctity and strength.

LAUREL

The laurel leaves that are used as a victory **crown** for leaders and great men are actually the leaves of the bay laurel, the plant that also gives us the popular culinary herb. The laurel is sacred to the Greek God **Apollo**, and symbolizes the courage and wisdom necessary for victory. In common with other evergreen plants, laurel also stands for longevity and immortality, further reason why it was used for the victory crown.

Chewing or burning the leaves of the laurel was said to confer the gifts of second sight and prophesy, and were used by the oracular priestesses or Pythonesses in **Delphi** before they gave their prophesies. In China, the plant also symbolizes immortality, and the sacred **hare** which is said to live in the **Moon** uses its leaves to concoct a drug that confers immortality on anyone who is brave enough to take it.

The idea of fame and everlasting life has even lived on in the very name of the laurel itself; the Poet Laureate in Britain is named after the plant.

LIME

In some parts of northern Europe such as Germany and Scandinavia, the lime, or linden tree, has the same powerful symbolism as the **oak** does for the British and the Celts. It should not be confused with the **citrus** tree that yields lime fruits. The lime is deciduous with **heart**-shaped leaves. and can reach great heights if it's growing in good soil (specimens of 40 or more meters are not rare).

The lime is linked to the Norse Goddess **Freya**, and was considered to be her guardian. Because the tree can grow to great size—one in Germany needs over a hundred props to hold it up—it makes a highly visual focal point so was often used as a place of meetings and conferences, in common with other large and distinctive trees. Because the lime is the Tree of Truth, these meetings sometimes took the form of courts designed to uncover the facts of a disputed matter. Despite its great size, the reciprocal protection offered by Freya and her husband Thor, God of Storms, means that it is meant to be impervious to lightning. Like the **baobab**, the lime was given the status of being a member of the village community.

MULBERRY

In China, the mulberry is considered the **World Tree** that connects the Heavens, the **Earth** and the regions below. There was a sacred **grove** of mulberry trees planted outside the eastern gate of the early royal cities, and the tree was associated with this direction because, as the "house" of the Mother of the Suns, the **Sun** rose every day by climbing up the mulberry tree. The wood of the tree was used to make bows that "shot" any evil influences that emanated from the compass points. There is evidence that the mulberry was revered in Islam too, since the tree can be found close to Muslim sanctuaries.

MYRRH

Myrrh is a small, shrubby tree that grows in desert conditions in parts of Africa and in some Arab countries. The resin that hardens after oozing from the "pores" of the bark was used by the Ancient Egyptians in their embalming rituals, and is perhaps best known as one of the three gifts—along with **gold** and **frankincense**—that the **Three** Wise Men brought to the infant Christ. Although we generally think of gold as being the most valuable gift brought to the holy baby, pound for pound myrrh was worth more than gold, and had five times the value of frankincense. Because its scent was used to mask certain aspects of embalming rituals, it's a symbol of purity and cleansing, as well as being valued for its medicinal qualities; these include use as a disinfectant and for healing wounds.

As ever, there is a Greek myth that explains the origins of the tree. Myrrha was the mother of Adonis, the God himself the result of an incestuous union between Myrrha and her father, Theias. When Theias discovered the deception, he was infuriated. **Aphrodite** transformed Myrrha into the tree just as her father shot an **arrow** at her; when the arrow struck, Adonis was born from the tree.

OAK

The "Father of the Forest," the "King of all Trees"; the Oak enjoys this elevated reputation all over the temperate World.

The oak is a tree of great longevity, taking up to **sixty** years before it first bears fruit, and often standing for hundreds of years, an

imposing figure of generational continuity in the surrounding landscape.

The oak is a sacred tree, and as its branches reach right into the **sky** it is able to channel messages from the Gods. The famous oak **grove** at Dodona in Greece was home to the **birds** that carried messages from the Gods via the priestesses there. One particular oak from Dodona was cut down to make the prow of the *Argo*, the ship that carried Jason on his voyages. The beautiful figurehead carved into the prow was able to whisper messages to him, and could forewarn him of any danger he might encounter. There was also a sacred oak grove at Hebron, where Abraham received messages from God.

Before there were **temples** and shrines made by man, the Gods were worshipped under oak trees. The oak is particularly sacred to the Druids, who take their name from the name of the tree, *duir*. The word for "door" is a derivative of the same root; the tree symbolizes a door to another world, the *Siddhe*, the invisible realm of the Celts that runs parallel to the "real" world. Oak, or *Duir*, is the seventh letter of the **Ogham tree alphabet**.

The oak is symbolic of strength (the root of the Latin word for oak, *robur*, is the same as that for "robust"), power, longevity, and protection; it's also a friendly and benevolent tree, proving a useful ally to **animals** and human beings. A practical use of the oak as a great protector is seen in the many oaks that were used to build the ships that repelled the Spanish Armada from the shores of Britain; there are ancient houses still to be seen with beams that came from these ships.

The oak gall is a growth that defends the oak tree from a parasitic **wasp**; these galls take the form of little balls which attach to the branches of the tree. The galls are used in a specific form of divination to see whether a child has been bewitched. Three galls are put into a bowl of **water** under the cradle; if they float, all is well, but if they sink then further measures must be taken to free the child from enchantment.

Because of the great size of the oak, it attracts **lightning**; this gave it the reputation of being somehow able to control the weather and further promulgates its association with the Gods, as the rulers of storms and **lightning**. The fruit of the oak, the **acorn**, provides nourishment and also carries a rich symbolic meaning all of its own. A give-away sign of a witch was that she wore a **necklace** of acorns, since the nut in its cup symbolized the **phallus**, as well as birth and the **womb**.

OLIVE TREE

The gift of the olive, from **Athena** the Goddess of Wisdom to the city of Athens, meant she won the privilege of having the city named for her. The alternative gift that was offered was a spring of water given by **Poseidon**, but the water proved salty and unfit to drink. There's an old spell or charm related to this story. To cure a headache, write the name of Athene on an olive and hold it to your head. This will induce the Goddess to take away the pain.

The olive branch has long been a symbol of peace and of hope. When Noah sent a **dove** from the Ark to see if land was close, the **bird** brought back a sprig of greenery believed to have been from the olive tree. This showed that both land and hope were at hand. To offer someone an olive branch is a universal symbol of peace and the desire for harmony.

Olive oil was of primary importance to any people who seldom ate meat since it has high nutritional value. It is therefore considered to be a sacred plant wherever it grows, and in times past to harm an olive tree was a punishable offence. Because olive trees grow to a great age—olive wood is an antitoxin and has protective powers—they are also symbolic of longevity. In an echo of the **laurel** given to champions, courageous Roman soldiers were given crowns of olive wood symbolizing their invincibility in battle.

The olive tree is the most important of all trees in the Islamic faith, and is a symbol of the Prophet Mohammed. Each of its leaves is said to have one of the names of God written upon it. The olive tree is also a symbol of light, since olive oil is burned in lamps, another practical use whose symbolic meaning attests to the sacred qualities of this tree.

ORANGE TREE

The fruit which is synonymous with its bright, sunshine-like color originates in the Far East, and the name is a corruption of *naranja* (Spanish), which is similar to *narange* (Sanskrit) and *narang* (Persian). There's a legendary story in which Gaia, the Earth Goddess, presents **Hera** and **Zeus** with beautiful, **golden**-colored fruit on their wedding day; these so-called "Golden **Apples** of the Hesperides" are believed to have been **oranges**.

This association of the orange with brides continues even up to the present day, although its origins are different from the Greek myth related above. The Crusaders saw that the Saracens used the orange blossom on their wedding day, not only because of its marvelous smell, but because the prolific tree was seen as a symbol of female fertility (both **flower** and **fruit** appear at the same time on the branches). The custom of brides wearing or carrying orange blossom was brought back to Europe and soon caught on. Oranges are also associated with weddings in China and Vietnam, where newly wed couples are given baskets of the fruit.

Today we largely associate oranges with Israel, Florida, South Africa, and Spain, and the bitter Seville kind are used in making marmalade (oranges were brought to Spain by the Moors in the eleventh century). We now take oranges for granted, but the Moors forbade anyone who was not a follower of Islam to eat the orange or drink its juice, since it was considered to be such an exquisite and heavenly fruit.

Paulownia

To the Ancient Chinese people, the paulownia tree (known as the "**foxglove** tree" in the West on account of its large violet or **purple** flowers) guarded the north gate of the **elements**. As the north is traditionally the abode of the winter and the dead, the tree symbolized regeneration and rebirth. The timber of the tree was used to make the drums that were beaten to follow the course of the **Sun**, as well as the drums that were used in war. The ideogram for the paulownia—*t'ong*—means the same as drumbeat.

In Japan, the paulownia is called the "princess tree." It was once planted to herald the birth of a baby girl, the growth of the tree symbolizing the growth of the child until, when the girl was ready to be married, the tree was chopped down to make her wedding chest. This represented the change from one life to another.

Peach tree

The peach tree is symbolic of immortality. Chinese stories tell of a mythological garden belonging to a beautiful woman called Siwang Mu, the "Royal Lady of the West." In this garden grew the Peach Tree of the Gods, which bloomed every 3000 years, to be followed 3000 years later by the Fruit of Eternal Life.

For some Chinese secret societies, the peach fruit is an emblem of the immortality that can be gained after certain initiatory practices. Since it was believed to confer eternal life, the fruit belonged to the **Eight Immortals** of the Taoist religion, and is also one of the **Three Blessed Fruits** in Buddhism. Indeed, the word for "peach" is also the same as the word for *Tao*.

The tree itself is considered to be the **Tree of Life**. **Wands** made from peach wood were considered to be particularly powerful, as were the *ki-pi*, the calligraphic brushes used in divination to write the ideograms which would foretell the future. Much of the magical power of these brushes came from the peach wood. In both China and Japan the peach tree is said to protect from **lightning**, and figurines carved from its wood were set over doors at New Year to protect the house from this particular threat. The **Shou**, the emblem of immortality that is often found woven into rugs or as wall hangings, is based on the design of a peach stone.

Persea

A form of wild **laurel** that grows in arid regions, this tree was revered by the Ancient Egyptians. The leaves of the tree were used as paper by **Thoth** (the Measurer of Time, the Scribe and Messenger of the Gods, and the recorder of the doings of mankind) and Safekh (Goddess of learning, knowledge, and writing) to write down the names and deeds of the great and good of the nation. Once their names were inscribed, these people had the security of eternal life; the tree therefore symbolizes lasting fame.

Pine

Pine trees are evergreens, which makes them a natural symbol of immortality and longevity. The pine is also a symbol of incorruptibility and fortitude, since it remains untouched by storms and inclement weather.

In Japan, followers of Shinto set two pine trees on either side of the gateway to the home at the time of the New Year Festivities. Shinto is an animistic religion—one of its tenets says that every living thing has a **spirit**—and the pine tree is said to be inhabited by benevolent spirits or "kami." The legendary **Immortals** in the Taoist religions ate the cones, needles and resin of the pine, which made them light enough to be able to fly. The trees are also said to stand at the gates of the City of the Immortals.

The popular **egg** and dart frieze consists of stylized **lotus flowers** and pine cones, and contains hidden sexual symbolism. The flowers represent the **vagina**, and the cones, the **phallus**. The pine also appears in the **Ogham tree alphabet**, where it is called *Ailim*. Although superficially different from the spruce and the fir trees that are traditionally used as **Christmas trees**, pines are part of the same botanical family—the Pinaceae (to which they give their name).

Plum tree

An important tree in the Far East, the plum tree flowers at either end of the year, so is symbolic of spring as well as winter, a sign of hope and new beginnings. Because the blossom appears before the leaves are on the tree, it's also an emblem of purity, this trait implying a sort of virgin birth. Like the **peach** tree, the plum tree is also a symbol of immortality. Lao Tzu, the great poet and philosopher, has the plum tree as his personal emblem since he was apparently born beneath one.

Pomegranate tree

The pomegranate, because of the volume of **seeds** that burst, jewel-like, from inside the fruit when it's cut open, is a powerful symbol of fertility, and therefore it is also considered to be an **aphrodisiac**. Its name means "**apple of many seeds**." Such symbolism meant that it was always present at weddings, although it was not used during sacrificial rituals because it was considered to be an inappropriately seductive fruit.

Aphrodite, naturally, favoured the pomegranate tree. As befits a tree belonging to the Goddess of Love, it's emblematic of passion, sensuality, and sexual love. But older representations of the fruit, that associate it with the forerunner of Aphrodite, the Goddess **Astarte**, show the ancient origins of the pomegranate as a powerful symbolic fruit. The pomegranate tree was also named the Tree of Knowledge. In the Bible, the name of the pomegranate is *rimmon*, meaning "to bear a child"; in Syria the fruit shared the name of the **Sun** God Hadad Rimmon, the deity who also ruled over procreation.

The pomegranate is also linked with **Persephone**, who yielded to sexual temptation; the pomegranate symbol is used as a euphemism for her experience. Persephone was condemned to spend a third of the year in the darkness of the Underworld because she ate the pomegranate fruit during time set aside for fasting. Whoever ate anything during a fasting period was not permitted to return to the human realm; it was only at the intercession of **Zeus** that Persephone could alternate her life between the two realms. During the **Eleusinian mysteries**, the pomegranate was again forbidden because it could distract the **soul** from spiritual matters and draw it down instead to the earthy, fleshy levels.

In Rome, married women wore coronets constructed from pomegranate twigs and in Ancient Egypt corpses of the great and the good were given **necklaces** of the blossoms just before burial, again as a concession to the otherworldly significance of the fruit. In the Buddhist tradition, the pomegranate is one of the **Three Blessed Fruits** and its influence is particularly beneficent, symbolizing fecundity and a prosperous future.

In Christianity the symbolic meaning of pomegranate was as an emblem of compassion, which thereby managed to completely ignore the sensual qualities of the fruit.

ROWAN

The rowan stands for the second letter of the **Ogham tree alphabet**, *Luis*. Because it's at home in mountainous places and is sacred to the Goddess, the rowan is sometimes called the "Lady of the Mountain." It's also called "witchbane" or "witchwood," underlining the belief that rowans act as protectors from witchcraft or malevolent magic. The power of the tree is such that the stake driven through the **heart** of the **vampire** to kill it once and for all was meant to be made of rowan wood.

Although the rowan is a symbol of protection—particularly against witches—it's also said that the trees grow in places where they are needed, primarily where witches make their homes (in Britain, the tree was also known as *witchen* or *wiggin*). Witches themselves favored it as a magical tree, using its wood, berries and leaves in spell-casting and charm-making.

Because the rowan is believed to have magical powers, the wood is among those used for **wand**s and dowsing rods. There's also a charm made of rowan which is particularly efficacious, since it combines the protective powers of the tree with the similar powers of the **Cross**; two twigs are tied together with **red** thread to make a small **amulet**. This was used as a symbol of protection over **doorways** and also over babies' cots to protect the infant from being kidnapped by **fairies** or other mischievous spirits.

The rowan is also symbolic of psychic powers, and is believed to confer the gift of divination. The berries of the tree possess hallucinogenic qualities, and the **wine** or simply the juice made from these berries was favored by the Druids in their shamanic practices. **Grove**s of rowan trees were sacred places where oracular practices were carried out, and which were especially powerful in the presence of **water**.

The berries of the rowan are a bright **blood red** color, so the tree is symbolic of life. They provide a welcome splash of color throughout the fall, and sometimes stay on the tree throughout the winter, as seen from one of its colloquial German names, *Wintersteher*. Irish legends refer to the rowan berries as the "Berries of Immortality" although they are in fact poisonous to children.

Sandalwood tree

The sandalwood tree is in fact a parasitic plant whose suckers attach themselves to other trees in order to survive. The most important part of the sandalwood tree is its heartwood, which is all that remains after termites destroy the rest of the tree; but it is this heartwood which yields the heavenly, ethereal aroma which is so highly prized and which is the defining quality of this plant. Sandalwood oil is accordingly very expensive and is revered by Hindus and Buddhists, as well as by practitioners of aromatherapy. Hindus often put a smear of sandalwood paste on their foreheads as an emblem of the **third eye**, and the scent of sandalwood is said to draw the **soul** closer to the Gods.

Sandalwood oil is a prime ingredient in the **incenses** and perfumes used in holy places such as temples, and the wood itself is used in the construction of those same temples.

Sequoia

The two species of redwood—the giant sequoia (*Sequoiadendron giganteum*) and the coast redwood (*Sequoia sempervirens*)—are the biggest and tallest trees in the world. The largest giant sequoias are even given names, such as "General Grant" and "General Sherman", and they are the biggest of all single living organisms. General Sherman, the outright champion in terms of size, weighs 1500 tons, has a volume of 55,040 cubic feet, and achieves a height in excess of 274 feet. The tallest coastal redwoods, a more graceful tree than the grizzled giant sequoias, have achieved a height of 400 feet. Inevitably, these trees have become symbols of longevity, but not necessarily of survival. The coastal redwood was used extensively for its timber (it is said that San Francisco was built from it) and although the tree is now protected, there is little more than three per cent left of the original 500 miles of forest that spread from Monterey to Oregon.

Although the redwoods have not been adopted by any particular culture as being the epitome of the **World Tree**, they make likely candidates for this sacred status. So tall that their heads are sometimes in the clouds—the upper parts of the coastal redwood are so tall that they cannot draw water from the soil, instead surviving by absorbing the sea fogs that roll in off the Pacific—these trees can be virtually impossible to photograph, and usually all we see of them are their **feet**, with a small human figure dwarfed somewhere in the picture to try to give a sense of the scale. The giant sequoia became known as "Wellingtonia" in Britain, it being seen as a suitable tree to commemorate Britain's most famous soldier, the 1st Duke of Wellington, who had died the previous year. Unimpressed by this attempt to snatch the glory of their own largest tree, the Americans responded by naming it "Washingtonia" after the first president.

Shittim tree

See **Acacia**.

*   *   *

SYCAMORE

Every nation has a particular tree that symbolizes the **World Tree**, and for the Egyptians it was the sycamore. The tree grew in profusion along the banks of the Nile and was called the "Pharoah's **fig**." In common with other World Trees, the **birds** that perched in its branches were considered to be the **souls** of unborn beings. The Gods, too, sat in its branches, and the tree itself was said to be the personification of the great Goddesses, **Isis**, Nut, and Hathor; this latter was called the Lady of the Sycamore. The Egyptians also believed that a sycamore stood at either side of the Eastern Gate of Heaven, through which the **Sun** God **Ra** entered every morning.

Because the World Tree joined the **Earth**, the Heavens, and the Underworld, the sycamore was planted near tombs, where it carried similar regenerative symbolism as the **yew** in the Western tradition. Coffins were made from sycamore, since the Egyptians believed that the use of the timber would enable the corpse to return to the Mother Goddess, Hathor.

TAMARIND

Wherever the tamarind tree occurs naturally—including parts of India, Sri Lanka, and Thailand—it is surrounded with superstition. People believe that it either signals a place of bad **spirits**, or may harbor these evil entities, and therefore needs to be avoided. Even its scent and shade are considered dangerous. The timber of the tree is equally feared, since it contains the essence of these pernicious influences.

The reason for these beliefs is probably due to an acid that the tree secretes during the hours of darkness, making the ground beneath it infertile. The fruits of the tamarind, although bitter, have a cooling effect and form an essential part of spicy Indian cookery. Obviously, people are prepared to take certain risks in order to harvest this ingredient.

THREE BLESSED FRUITS

In Buddhism, the Three Blessed Fruits are the sacred symbols of the Three Great Blessings. The fruits are the **citrus** (happiness), the **peach** (longevity), and the **pomegranate** (fecundity).

THUJA

Like most conifers, the thuja is a symbol of immortality as it remains **green** all year round. Chinese believed that the tree belonged in the East, where, as an immortal symbol, it welcomed the **Sun** every morning. In particular, the thuja belonged to the Immortals, the Deities that ate the resin and seeds of the tree.

VATA TREE

See **Banyan**

WALNUT TREE

In Celtic symbolism, all nut-bearing trees are considered to be sacred since the nut itself holds secret knowledge. The walnut tree is no exception. In Greek myth, **Artemis**, who was gifted with second sight, was transformed into a walnut tree, and so the tree and its **fruit** are associated with the Goddess.

There are stories about the walnut tree harbouring she-devils, too, some of whom would whisper obscenities and lewd suggestions to passers-by. The Church of Santa Maria del Popolo in Rome was constructed from a foul-mouthed tree which used to stand on the site but which was chopped down when its profanities became too unbearable.

Because the walnut prohibits many other plants from growing near it, it has a reputation of being the tree of witches, particularly in Italy. It is also believed that the walnut tree yields a better crop of nuts if it is beaten. This same heavy crop is said to indicate a harsh winter to come.

WILLOW

Because of its shape, perhaps, the willow tree has long been associated with **death** and mourning; one of its varieties—*Salix "Chrysocoma"*—is even called the "weeping willow." Willow branches were believed to ease the passage of the **soul** into the Afterlife, and were placed on the tops of coffins. Graves were lined with willow branches for the same reason. In Ancient Britain, burial places were planted with willow trees to protect the **spirits** of the dead, and the Greek sorceress, Circe, had a riverside cemetery full of willow trees; the corpses of men were put into the topmost branches of the trees where they were eaten by the **birds**. The willow is used in magical rites at **Samhuin** since it helps communication with the spirit world. However, death is not the only meaning of the willow.

The word "willow" comes from an Anglo-Saxon word meaning "pliancy," and willow is the wood of choice in basket making. It's supple and strong, able to make baskets safe enough to hold people underneath a hot-air balloon. Moses was found as a baby floating in a willow basket, hence the tree is a symbol of protection. Witch's **broomsticks** were traditionally bound with willow that was used to tie the broom to the handle; this practice may have been a nod to the **Moon** Goddess, **Hecate**, who rules both the willow and the Moon.

Willow trees are related to the element of **water**. Not only do they like to live by streams and lakes, but the **silvery** color of the leaves, combined with the rippling of its delicate branches, make it even look watery itself. The association with the Moon and water tells us that the tree is also symbolic of feminine powers, conferring gifts of intuition and of clairaudience. The soughing of the wind through its branches makes the tree a good one for the practice of phyllomancy, the art of divination from the sound of leaves in the wind. The Greek poet, Orpheus, carried willow branches as a symbol of the inspiration this sound gave him. Water divining is carried out using willow **wands**; the tree is attracted to water, so will hunt it out with ease.

Willows grow profusely. A twig from a tree that seems to be dead will sprout into new life, even if it is planted upside down. Therefore the tree is a symbol of fertility and, in China, of immortality. Willow seeds were used in a decoction that was meant to be a powerful **aphrodisiac**, possibly because of its rejuvenative powers.

The willow contains a very important chemical constituent, salicylic acid, which is a very effective painkiller. Salicylic acid is the primary ingredient in aspirin, and the meaning behind the willow's folk name of "the witch's painkiller." The willow—or *Saile*—stands for the letter S in the **Ogham tree alphabet**.

YEW

One of the longest-living of all trees, certain yews are in existence today that are said to be up to 9000 years old, although it is difficult prove these claims definitively. The age of a yew tree, aside from any fanciful mythology, can be determined by its girth, and also by the science of dendrochronology, in which the living tree is bored with a special tool and the annual rings are counted.

Because of its great longevity, the yew is a symbol of everlasting life. It grows in an unusual way, too, its new stems growing down the outside of the tree, giving the yew an association with rebirth and regeneration, as the new is born from the old. Adding to this symbolism is its habit of putting in a growth spurt when it is around 500 years old.

So sacred was the yew as a symbol that—to a pre-Christian society—wherever it grew was considered to be sacred ground. It was considered both immoral and illegal to chop down the tree. It is likely that the yew is often seen in churchyards because the **church** itself would have been built on this sacred ground in the presence of the tree, in an effort to align the incoming Christian belief system with pagan traditions. The association of the tree with **death** therefore started to overlay its former meaning. Because the berries of the yew are poisonous, they can effectively carry people into the spirit world.

The hollow center of the yew tree is a symbol not only of the power that lies in empty space, but underlines the significance of this tree as belonging, in part, to a spiritual dimension. Recently, the yew as a symbol of life has been shown in a practical and unexpected way. One of the constituent chemicals of the tree, taxol, has been found to be efficacious in curing **breast** cancer. Yew wood is tough and durable and was used for making shields and spears, and also—using both heartwood and sapwood to gain extra strength—the famous English longbow that helped the English win the Battle of Agincourt in 1415, at which they were completely outnumbered. Hence the yew is also a symbol of the warrior.

Part Five

FLOWERS OF THE UNDERWORLD

THE MYSTICAL CHARISMA OF MINERALS, METALS, AND GEMS

If you pick up an attractive stone or pebble while walking along the beach, the chances are that you are putting something in your pocket that is as old as the **Earth** itself. However, as Confucius said, "better a **diamond** with a flaw than a pebble without," and despite the ancient provenance of both diamond and pebble, it is the sparkling stones, prized primarily for their beauty, which have fascinated us for millennia.

"… So much is true, that gems have fine spirits, as appears by their splendour, and therefore may operate, by consent, on the spirits of men, to strengthen and exhilarate them. As for their particular properties, no credit can be given to them. But it is manifest that light, above all things, rejoices the spirits of men: and, probably, varied light has the same effect, with greater novelty; which may be one cause why precious stones exhilarate."

Francis Bacon, writing in the sixteenth century, describes very well the impact of a gemstone, while observing that there is no empirical foundation for their reputed powers. Despite this, the idea that stones have potencies that are somehow beyond the remit of science is nothing new. Plato, in the fourth century BC, theorized that the **stars** and **planets** transformed decaying vegetable matter into gemstones, which then came under the influences of those planets. This idea has endured. The magical properties of gems and minerals are expounded in *A Treatise on Gems*, written by Rajah Sourindro Mohun Tagore in the nineteenth century AD.

The Ancient Egyptians believed in the mysterious forces encapsulated with gems— mummies were decked in them and numerous stone **amulets** were strategically placed in their tombs for a definite purpose—but it's likely that such beliefs in gems preceded this ancient civilization. The use of crystals in healing, too, is an ancient art and certainly not a recent invention of New Age faddists. The vibrational qualities of gems, for instance, were described in Indian Ayurvedic medicine as well as in Chinese herbal medicine.

Despite this long history, there is as little evidence to suggest that the stones placed on the **chakras** by crystal healers are any more efficacious than the older belief that nephritic **jade** could heal the **spleen** just because the gem and the organ are the same **color**. However, a **Doctrine of Signatures** based on the **color** correspondences of gemstones is a popular technique, and this idea does have an empirical basis, since color has a marked effect on mood.

Many symbols of a mystical or sacred nature are rendered even more awe-inspiring when they are made of gems. The sacred mountain, **Meru**, which is the domain of the Gods in Hindu myth, has a **north** face of **gold**, an **east** face of **silver**, a **south** face made of **cat's eye** and a **western** face—the side of the setting **sun**—fashioned from **ruby**. The Kalpa tree, also from the Hindu tradition, is a **World Tree** archetype constructed entirely of gems, with fruits of rubies, leaves of green **zircon** and **coral**, shoots of **emeralds**, a trunk made of cat's eye, **topaz**, and **diamond**, with roots of **sapphire**.

The Seven Heavens of the Islamic faith are described in terms of gems and metals, as are the twelve foundations of the New Jerusalem. The **breastplate of the High Priest** of the Temple in Jerusalem, too, had **12** gems embedded into it that not only had the powers of prophecy, but also inspired many of our current ideas about gems and their links to the months of the year.

There is another aspect to gemstones and crystals that we should take into account. As Francis Bacon points out, we react instinctively and emotionally to crystals, and this visceral response is too powerful to ignore. In this, the gemstone shares many of the qualities of the **flower** and expresses similar functions, except that the short-lived flower is exchanged for the immortality of the jewel.

Pick up any esoteric gem directory and you will find exhaustive lists of gems and their supposed efficacy. There are hundreds of these correspondences, ranging from the physical (use of **jasper** to unblock the **bladder**,) to the spiritual (**amethyst** for increasing intuitive powers), with a good smattering of the metaphysical (**star sapphire** to unblock the Third **Eye**), the hopeful (topaz to improve wisdom), the superstitious (**agate** to repel the **evil eye**), and the strange (**moldavite** to help integrate UFO activity).

It doesn't matter whether any of these gems "work" in the intended way or not. What's important, in looking at the symbolism inherent in stones, is that there is room for belief in such matters; we love gemstones, and we want to believe that they have magical powers. For many of us, they really do.

ADDER STONE

There are several curious mythological stones, and the adder stone is certainly one of these. It was apparently formed from the collective saliva of a writhing mass of adders, which they would shoot up into the air. The saliva then solidified into the adder stone. An alternative explanation is that the stone comes from the head of a **serpent**. This strange stone seems to occur mainly in the British Isles, although archaeologists have also found them in Egypt. It is associated with pagan ceremonial days, such as the

Summer Solstice or May Day. The stone has several other names, including the Druids' egg, the snake egg, and the magicians' glass. In common with other stones said to have been created from venomous creatures, the adder stone is reputed to have a homoeo-pathic effect, capable of neutralizing toxins and poisons. If you should be offered an adder stone, there are a couple of things to check. It is often glassy in appearance, with a naturally occurring hole running through it. There is also a simple test to prove that it is the real thing. A genuine adder stone is impossible to sink when placed in **water** no matter how much weight is attached to it, and it will float against any current.

AGATE

A variety of quartz known as **chalcedony**, the agate comes in many different colors including **blue** (blue lace agate), and with different patterns and shapes embedded within the stone (such as moss agate and dendritic agate, which has tiny **tree** designs within it). Some agates are constructed of concentric **circles** of differently colored pigments, and when these particular stones are cut and polished to show a **black** or **brown** inner circle surrounded by a band of **white**, they are regarded as a symbol of the **eye** and, like similar **talismans**, are believed to protect the wearer against the **evil eye**.

Followers of Islam also believed that the agate carried protective powers, and that their efficacy was increased if the symbols of Mohammed's grandsons, Hassan and Hussein, were engraved on the stones. Jewish people, too, believed that the stone could somehow protect the wearer from falling or stumbling, and so it was set into **horses'** manes and bridles in order to keep the rider safe. This use of agate as a protective symbol for horses was adapted by European farmers, who copied the idea of using the stones in their animals' bridles in the belief that they would bring a bountiful **harvest**.

Agates are also believed to protect people and buildings from damage by storms and lightning. An agate with a naturally formed hole in it is still nailed above the doorways of some rural dairies so that the **cows' milk** will not be rendered sour by lightning. An added benefit is that this talisman will also stop witches kidnapping the cows and riding them during the night. Such a stone was also carried by sailors in order to keep them safe at sea and to prevent seasickness. In the same way that agate is believed to have a calming effect on tempests, storms, thunder, and **lightning**, it soothes human nature too, and an agate worn by (or in close proximity to) a sleeper will ensure a good nights' sleep and peaceful dreams.

The stone of Sylvester (or stone of St. James) is a banded agate, dark on one side and light on the other. The light side represents the past, and all known events; the dark side symbolizes the future, the unknowable. These stones used to be given as gifts at New Year, symbolizing the past and the future. The different layers of color which are a feature of agates symbolize hidden information about to be revealed.

Agates, it was supposed, had the power to attract divine energies and anyone wearing them would attract the favor of God. Many stones and minerals are believed to have healing powers, and the agate is no exception.

It is mentioned in an Ancient Roman document called the *Materia Medica* that describes the medicinal powers of over 200 stones. Powdered agate mixed with fruit juice was a known cure for insanity, and could also help alleviate kidney disease and boils.

AMANDINUS

The amandinus is a mythical stone of varying **colors** that possesses magical properties. It is said to give the wearer the power to interpret dreams.

ALECTORIUS

The alectorius is a mythical stone that sometimes goes by the less elegant name of the cock stone, because it was believed to have been found inside a **bird**. The stone was **pink**, about the size of a bean, transparent and crystalline; the best kind were said to come from birds that had been castrated (caponed) at the age of three and slaughtered at the age of seven at which time, it was believed, the bird would refuse to eat and drink, a sure sign that the stone was "ripe."

Because the stone was believed to have somehow absorbed the cock's pugnacity, it was the favored charm of wrestlers. When held in the **mouth** it quenched the thirst and invigorated the fighter. There were numerous other reasons for owning the elusive alectorius. For example, it could confer the gift of eloquence on the owner although it would render his wife less talkative and more compliant than before; as well as this, it could make the owner courageous and invincible, alluring and seductive, virile and fertile. If the stone failed to procure these qualities in the owner for some reason, though, all was not lost, since the stone was also believed, most usefully, to render its owner invisible.

AMBER

Amber, like **jet**, becomes electrically charged when rubbed; indeed, the word "electric" comes from the Latin word *electrum*, which means amber. Amber is made from the fossilized resin of **trees**, and although it shares its name with the color most usually associated with it—a deep tawny **yellow**—it also comes in **blue**, **violet**, or even **black**. Amber that is **green** is colored artificially. Before man knew where amber came from, there were many ingenious theories as to its origins. **Lynx** urine, said some; others believed that it was chunks of the rays of the **Sun**, set hard in the **sea** and then washed upon the shore.

The association with the Sun is probably the most powerful symbolic link for amber, and it does indeed look like a trapped sunbeam, especially when the occlusions and faults within the stone catch the light. Many of the uses of the stone reflect this association; amber is said to cheer and revitalize. Amber was also believed to cure all manner of ailments, in particular hay fever, asthma, and other throat and respiratory infections. It could either be taken as a powder or worn as an **amulet**. As a cure for **ear** infections and even deafness it was ground up into a fine dust, then mixed with **honey** and **rose** oil and poured into the ear.

Because amber was once liquid, small insects can sometimes be found embedded in it and this is the most valuable type of amber as well as being the premise of the film *Jurassic Park* (where dinosaurs were bred from DNA taken from these insects). Like jet, amber burns easily, and it was for this reason that in Germany it was called *Bernstein*, meaning "burn stone." The scent given off by burning amber was believed to drive away evil spirits.

AMETHYST

Amethyst is used to describe **lavender/purple** quartz crystals, whose sublime color has lent deep meaning to this particular stone, the importance of which is underlined by its appearance as one of the **twelve** stones set into the **breastplate of the High Priest** of the Temple in Jerusalem.

The **name** itself gives a clue as to its symbolic meaning and supposed efficacy. In Greek, *amethystos* means "non-intoxicating." It was said that the stone, placed under the **tongue** or worn by the drinker, would enable him to consume as much alcohol as desired with no ill-effects, and goblets were made from amethyst for the same reason. One account from 1750 instructs the drinker to wear the stone "bound on the **navel**" to prevent drunkenness.

The Ancient Greeks had a myth that explained why amethyst was a gem of sobriety. **Dionysus**, the God of **wine**, it appears, was aggrieved that his godlike status seemed to be ignored by mortals, so decided to avenge this perceived disrespect and show his power by having his **lions** randomly slaughter the next person to walk by. This happened to be a lovely girl, Amethystos, on her way to worship at the temple of **Artemis**; the unfortunate girl was slaughtered in so horrendously violent a way that Artemis heard her screams, put her out of her misery, and transformed her into a pillar of sparkling transparent **crystal**. In the meantime, Dionysus was deeply ashamed of what he had done and poured wine over the stone as penance; this wine gave the stone its violet color.

Amethyst's reputation as the stone of sobriety may be what still makes it a popular choice for bishops (it is sometimes called the bishops' stone) or it may be the color: the high frequency hues of violet and purple are associated with the spiritual realms. It should be remembered that purple, as a dye, was a costly color to produce and so was reserved for those rich enough or illustrious enough to be able to afford it; yet here was a crystal of that valuable hue, created naturally. No surprise that it was regarded so highly and was seen as a natural symbol of authority.

The Egyptians, too, held the amethyst in high regard, and **heart**-shaped amethysts have been found in the tombs of the Pharaohs, where they would have been placed over the **heart** of the corpse.

The **alchemists** and magicians of the Middle East felt that the amethyst would protect the wearer from evil spells, especially if they were engraved with the **sacred names** of the **Sun** and the **Moon** and combined with **swallows' feathers**. They believed that physical ailments generally sprang from a malaise of the soul, and that the higher vibrational frequencies of the amethyst would help to balance any discrepancies. Therefore the amethyst was powdered and made into elixirs. This is no different from the latter-day belief that the use of the amethyst can harmonize the body, mind, and spirit, helping to bring balance and equilibrium to the wearer.

AMIANTE

The amiante is a mythological, fireproof stone which Pliny the Elder wrote of as being most efficacious in removing or deterring **demons**. The French word for **asbestos** is *amiante*, and so it is entirely possible that this imaginary stone has its origins in reality.

AMMOLITE

An ammolite is generally a fossil that retains a piece of the **nail**, claw, or scale of an **animal**. This substance turns iridescent and the resulting beautiful stone is valued as an **iniskim** by certain American Indian peoples.

AMMONITE

See **snake stone**.

AQUAMARINE

The name *aquamarine* means "water of the sea," and accurately describes this **sea-blue** translucent gemstone. Not surprisingly, the stone is sacred to many of the **sea** deities, and sailors believed that it would bring them a safe passage across the oceans and banish fear during stormy weather. Roman fishermen thought that carrying aquamarines would help them increase their catch. It was also believed to provide an antidote to poison if submerged for a time in **water**.

In the **Kabbalah**, the aquamarine is linked to the **Great Mother**, Binah, because of its associations with the sea and the water element. The aquamarine also has protective qualities.

ASBESTOS

See **Amiante**.

BERYL

See **Emerald**.

BEZOAR

This is the generic term given to "stones" that have been recovered from the insides of animals, held to have talismanic power commensurate with the creature from which they are recovered. One of the most efficacious uses of the bezoar stone also gives us its name. They are believed to dispel poisons, or at least to provide an antidote to them; *pad-zahr*, in Arabic, means "poison removing," and in time this became bezoar. The bezoar was introduced to Europe by Arab physicians during the time of the Great Plague although it was also known to, and used by, the Chinese, the Malays, Peruvian Indians, and Indians.

Bezoar stones were carved and set into knife handles, as a way to protect the knife's owner from poisoning. The bezoar was also believed to confer the gifts of youth and vitality, could prevent asthma, and was used as a treatment for the kidneys and the bladder by being ground into a fine powder and made into an elixir.

BLACK STONE

The reason that **Mecca** is one of the foremost places of pilgrimage in the world today is because it is home to the **black** stone, or **al Hajar ul Aswad**, one of the most holy and sacred items in Islam. The provenance of this stone is unknown, although it is generally believed to be a **meteorite**. Others claim that it was given to Ishmael, the son of Abraham, by the **angel** Gabriel. The story goes that the angel that had failed to prevent the **serpent** from tempting Adam and Eve was trapped inside this stone, a **zircon**, that was turned black by the **kisses** of sinners. At the Day of Judgement the angel, released from this prison, would be able to bear witness to all those who had made the pilgrimage to Mecca. Despite the myths, the only thing certain about the black stone is its great age.

Muslims circling the **Ka'aba seven** times during their ritual pilgrimage will attempt, if they can, to kiss the stone; if this proves impossible they will point at the stone each time they go around it instead. The black stone is regularly anointed with perfumed oil.

The stone is of modest size, measuring approximately 30 cm in diameter. Legend has it that the stone was once pure **white**, but blackened as it absorbed the sins of mankind. The stone itself is now cracked, damage

which may have occurred when it was stolen around AD 930. Others believe it was broken during a siege in AD 638. The stone is held together by a frame of **silver** which is oval in shape; the entire sacred object resembles a large unblinking **eye**.

BLOODSTONE

Also called the **heliotrope**, from the Greek words for "**Sun**" and "to turn," the bloodstone can refer to many reddish stones but generally refers to green **jasper** with **red** markings or flecks. Ancient Egyptians believed that the stone would help with menstrual problems and called it the "blood of **Isis**." Christian statuary often features bloodstone carved into the shape of the head of Christ, artfully making the red speckles appear to be the **blood** pouring from the wounds made by the **crown** of thorns.

Healers and physicians called the stone **lapis sanguinarius**, and it was used primarily to alleviate any blood-related illnesses. It was used to staunch bleeding, to clean the blood, and to clear bloodshot eyes. It aided circulation when dipped in cold water and placed on the body, and it could cure hemorrhoids too.

The bloodstone's connection with the Sun made it the subject of a form of scrying, whereby the stone was placed in a bowl of **water**, where it served as a symbolic representation of a solar eclipse; the passage of the **Moon** across the face of the Sun showed up on the immersed stone.

One of the more curious myths about the bloodstone is that, like its namesake the heliotrope **flower**, it was said to confer invisibility to anyone lucky enough to own it.

This was achieved by the bloodstone dazzling the eyes of the beholder, in which case, it is presumed, they would be able to see nothing at all.

BREASTPLATE OF THE HIGH PRIEST

This extraordinary artifact of the Ancient world has provided the original source for much of the importance of certain gemstones.

The first High Priest of Jerusalem was called Aaron, who lived in 1200 BC. Aaron was the first High Priest to wear the "breastplate of righteousness and prophecy," also known as the *Essen*. The breastplate was connected with the mysterious objects **Urim and Thummim**, which were said to be the powers of judgement and prophecy.

This breastplate had **12** stones, in **gold** mountings, embedded into it in a specific sequence that had been described in the Book of Exodus in the Bible. There has been some speculation as to the identity of some of the stones, as many centuries have elapsed since they were first described, and their names have changed.

Set in four rows of three stones each, the gems are described as follows, from the first row working down:

- Sardius (possible **carnelian**); topaz; carbuncle (possibly **garnet**)
- Emerald; sapphire; diamond
- Ligure (possibly **jacinth**); agate; amethyst
- Beryl; onyx; jasper

Each gem was inscribed with the name of one of the twelve tribes of Israel, and also bears a relationship to the twelve months of the year and the twelve signs of the **Zodiac**. The breastplate itself was tied over the top of the **robe**-like garment of the High Priest.

CARNELIAN

A variety of **chalcedony** which has a specific **orange-red** opacity, the carnelian is among the many gems that used to be referred to as bloodstones, because of its color. Its name is said to come either from the karnel **cherry**, whose color it shares, or from the Latin words for meat, *carne*, or heart, *cor*. The importance of the carnelian is such that it was one of the twelve precious stones set into the **breastplate of the High Priest** of the Temple in Jerusalem.

The carnelian has always been held to be a protective stone, and is sometimes referred to as the "blood of **Isis**," again because of its color. As a carved talismanic object, it was placed at the throat of the mummy in order that the protection of the Goddess would be invoked in the journey through the Underworld. These amulets often had images and symbols—such as the **eye**, the **lion**, and the **hand**—carved into the carnelian. The carnelian which was carved with the symbol of the eye was an efficacious charm against the **evil eye**.

Like other stones of reddish hue, the carnelian was believed to be able to cure diseases of the **blood** and to staunch wounds. Powdered carnelian was taken to neutralize poisons, and carrying the stone about the person was believed to keep the owner in cheerful spirits and to make the person courageous. A more esoteric use of the carnelian is as an aid in astral travel.

The Ancient Greeks believed that the carnelian could satisfy all the heart's desires; this is similar to Muslim beliefs about the carnelian, which they called the **Mecca** stone, since it could make wishes come true. Finally, the symbolism of the carnelian as one of happiness and bonhomie means that, if placed under a sleeper's pillow, it will bring happy dreams.

CAT'S EYE

Any stone which has an occlusion within it that causes light to refract in the same way as in the **eye** of a **cat** can be given this title. The actual name given to the process is called chatoyancy. The true cat's eye, however, is a stone called **chrysoberyl,** which is composed of thin fibres running in the same direction that reflect light in the manner described.

Wherever the symbol of the eye appears in a naturally occurring stone or indeed elsewhere in nature, the object is seen to have protective qualities. The cat's eye stone is no exception. The cat's eye is also used as a charm to counter the effect of spells and sorcery, in particular the malice caused by the **evil eye**. In Arab regions, it was believed that wearing the stone could render the wearer invisible; something to do with the eye of the stone affecting the sight of the viewer, no doubt.

CELONITE

See **Chelidonius.**

CHALCHEDONY

See **Agate.**

CHELIDONIUS

Another of the imaginary stones, the chelidonius is a version of the **bezoar**, believed either to come from the body of a **swallow** (Pliny the Elder's *chelidonius lapillus* or swallow stone) or, alternatively that it was a precious stone made from the **eye** of the **tortoise**, in reality the *chelonia gemma* or **celonite**. This stone was believed to cheer the spirits and dispel melancholy, but presumably not in the case of the animal from which it came.

The chelidonius could cure headaches, fever, and jaundice, and could take away any pain in the eyes. It was important that the swallow stone be taken only from a young swallow, and that it did not touch any other stone or **water**, or fall on the ground. If any of these things happened, then the stone would not work. The chelidonius stones were **red** and **white** in color.

CHRYSOBERYL

See **cat's eye.**

CHRYSOLITE

See **topaz.**

CHURINGA

A sacred artifact of the Australian Aborigines, the churinga (or turinga) is made either of stone or of wood. Owned either collectively as part of the tribal belongings or by individuals, the churinga is a valued and treasured possession, believed to contain a part of the **soul** of the person or the tribe, and so is carefully guarded. Some churingas are large, some small, while some bear sacred inscriptions. Generally they are long and oval shaped. Whatever its appearance, the churinga is to be seen and handled exclusively by male initiates. Each churinga carries its own provenance of legends, songs, chants and rituals. Each aspect of the churinga is revealed to the initiate over a period of several years. Effectively, the churinga is a spiritual map and journal of the life and times of the tribe.

CITRINE

The **yellow** color of the citrine (a type of quartz) not only gives us the origin of its name but means that it has become symbolically associated with the **Sun**, warmth, and vitality. The **stomach** area also shares the same association with the yellow section of the spectrum, for example in the system of energy centers called **chakras**, and so the citrine is believed to be able to cure ailments related to this part of the body.

For the Chinese, the citrine is supposed to bring wealth, and can only be given by a generous person. Possession of the stone brings abundance, prosperity, success, and wisdom. It is referred to as the "stone of success" and as such was worn by emperors who believed that it would increase both intellectual capacity and wisdom. Because the citrine is associated with wisdom and learning, it has become a lucky charm, both for students taking examinations, and for teachers and professors.

COPPER

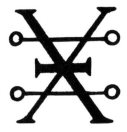

The chemical name for copper—*cuprum*—has the same root as the word for the island of Cyprus, where major deposits of the ore were once found. Cyprus was sacred to the Goddess **Venus**, and so copper was her metal and also the metal associated with the **planet** which bears her name. Copper was one of the **seven magical metals** of the Ancients, and all seven relate to the planets and their associated deities, as well as to the days of the week.

Copper was well known to ancient man and has long been a source of protection against **lightning**, since copper rods act as conductors and will direct the electricity into the ground. As a result, copper was considered protection against other evil influences. In Egypt, mummies had a copper disc, engraved with magical signs and symbols, placed beneath their **head**. This disc was called a *hypocephalus*, and made use of the heat-retaining ability of the metal to keep the corpse warm. **Amulets** made of copper could be easily engraved with invocations or charms, and copper was considered to have healing powers.

Even today the use of copper bracelets as an antidote to the aches and pains of rheumatism is widespread. People believe that this works because the skin absorbs minute copper deposits (turning the skin a tell-tale **green**). However efficacious these copper bracelets may be (and there is plenty of evidence to support the claim that they do actually aid pain relief), there is no definitive evidence as to how they work. Copper is also said to sooth insect stings when laid over the affected area.

CORAL

Coral is made of millions of the tiny **skeletons** of sea creatures called coral polyps. When these creatures die they form the familiar beautiful and strangely shaped coral reefs.

Because it comes from the **sea** and because it generally ranges through the **pink** or **red** end of the color spectrum, coral is associated with the Mother **Goddess**. It has therefore long been regarded as a stone which will protect babies and children, and is given as a gift to infants even today as a nod to this ancient belief. Sometimes coral was given as a teething **ring**, although this practice became less frequent as the stone gained in value. It was held to be a pain-reliever when babies were teething, and so the circular ring doubled up as a protection to the infant as well as giving the child something to chew on.

Plato said that coral changed color to indicate poor health, turning pale if the owner fell ill. The different colors of coral signified their symbolic power, and it seems that the prospective user would have to be very careful. Pink or red corals guarded against the **evil eye** and would send malicious spirits packing; however, **brown** or darker-colored corals were apparently attractive to malevolent spirits and demons. This belief also extended to Eastern regions where it is still considered extremely unfortunate to wear or even possess dull or discolored coral.

In some parts of Italy, coral is called the "witch stone," and is used to keep witches and wizards at a distance. The coral used for this purpose is even more efficacious if carved into the shape of the **cornus**—a **hand** with the **fingers** partially curled over apart from the first **finger** and the little finger, thus making the sign of the devil's **horns**. As with any object that has a link to the Goddess, coral is a fertility symbol. It is tied to **trees** and **vines** to ensure a good **harvest**, and is also worn by women to ensure their own fertility.

DIAMOND

The Greek word for diamond is *adamas*, meaning both "untamable" and "hard." It gives us the word "adamant" or "adamantine," which is also used as a term of reference to describe the brilliance of the stone. The diamond is the hardest of all minerals, and is used as a measure of the toughness of other stones.

One of the stones on the **breastplate of the High Priest** of the Temple in Jerusalem where it was said to shine brilliantly in the presence of truth and innocence, the diamond is not only tough, but extremely beautiful and relatively rare, qualities which make it one of the most costly precious gems. Traditionally it is the stone used in engagement **rings** as a symbol of betrothal, although the notion that an eager suitor should be obliged to spend a month's salary on the ring for his future wife is nothing more than a cynical ruse, invented relatively recently by a leading diamond house to persuade people to spend their money.

The diamond, therefore, became a symbol of love and commitment, although its use in rings was originally as a protective **talisman**. Knights and warriors liked to set diamonds into their sword hilts and shields for this reason. But these diamonds did not sparkle in the way we recognize today; they remained as they had done when they came out of the ground. The diamond is so hard that it will easily score a mark on glass, and during the time of Queen Elizabeth I "scribbling **rings**" were all the rage. These were rings into which a diamond was set with the sharp point facing upwards. The stone was used to scribble messages on windows, usually little love letters or secret messages.

Diamonds come in different shades of subtle colors: **yellow, blue, pink, white, green, orange**, and even **black**. However, the rare diamond which has a **red** flash within it is held by Indians to be symbolic of disaster, and signified a swift **death** for its wearer. Because of the fire which flashes within a well-cut and polished diamond, the stone is associated with thunder and lightning. In India it is even named **Vajra**, meaning **lightning**.

Diamonds are believed to absorb both good and bad energy, and people who use gemstones for healing purposes need to be very careful not to upset the delicate balance of the stone. In Persia, diamonds were viewed as suspicious stones, probably for this reason. Some notorious diamonds—no doubt the object of much envy, greed, and sometimes even bloodshed—have curses attached to them and are believed to be "unlucky" in the hands of their owners.

One of the more notorious of these cursed gems is the Hope Diamond. The stone seems to have left a trail of ruined lives and devastation in its wake. The bad fortune surrounding the stone started when it was stolen from the **forehead** of the statue of the Goddess Sita in India, and some believe that the malice surrounding the stone is because the Goddess subsequently cursed anyone who touched it. The original thief was reputed to have been torn apart by wild **dogs**. The diamond passed through the hands of Marie Antoinette and Louis XVI, both of whom were beheaded. It was eventually purchased by a wealthy banker, Philip Hope, and then inherited by his nephew Thomas, who lost his entire fortune shortly thereafter. Next it was bought by Ambul Hamid, a Sultan of Turkey, who lost his title and was forced to sell the diamond. It was bought by Mrs Edward Maclean, wife of an American newspaper magnate. She lost both her fortune and her only son, who was killed in an accident.

The Koh-i-Noor diamond—whose name means "**mountain** of light"—at one time belonged to Shah Jahan, who built the Taj Mahal for his wife, Mumtaz. It was believed that whosoever owned the diamond would also rule the world. By the time it was presented to Queen Victoria in 1850, it had a reputation of bringing ill luck to any male owner. Queen Victoria took this superstition very seriously and decreed that ladies alone should wear the diamond; since then it has only been set into the crowns of female members of the royalty.

EAGLE STONE

This stone has several names, including the aquileus and the praegnus. It was meant to be found either in the nest of an **eagle**, or embedded in the stomach or neck of the bird. Whatever the case, the stone—if it ever existed—would have been extremely difficult to get hold of, and so numerous magical powers were ascribed to it.

Its main use, however, was as a **talisman** for pregnant women. The stone itself was meant to be hollow and contained a smaller stone inside it (called the calimus) which rattled about when the stone was shaken. It was believed that the stone itself was pregnant, giving it one of the names mentioned above. Hence this stone is an example of sympathetic magic, and if tied to the **thigh** of the mother-to-be during childbirth would help to coax the baby from the **womb** and therefore make the birth an easy one. The timing had to be right, however, for if the stone was left too long it could cause a prolapse.

EMERALD

One of the most precious of all stones, the emerald comes from the **beryl** family. A perfect emerald is difficult to find and is therefore extremely valuable, although even the flawed kinds are costly. Its importance as a beautiful and valuable mineral has been acknowledged since ancient times. One of the most famous emerald mines was in Upper Egypt and belonged to the Queen of Sheba. The mine itself was said to be guarded by evil spirits. These emeralds were accorded magical status, and were said to grow, flourish, or diminish according to the seasons, and to change in intensity with the phases of the **Moon**. This belief—that emeralds "ripened"—was also held by the Peruvians, who reputedly had a Temple of Esmerelda, which contained a massive stone, together with lots of smaller stones which were called her "daughters." This temple has never been discovered.

The significance and value of the emerald is confirmed by its appearance as one of the twelve stones set into the **breastplate of the High Priest** of the Temple in Jerusalem. The emerald was also mentioned as one of the stones which would provide part of the foundations for the New Jerusalem.

Thoth—also known as Hermes Trigmestisus, **Hermes**, or **Mercury**, the God of writing, communication, and knowledge—wrote down the secrets of the Universe on a great emerald tablet, the **Smaragdina Tabula**. The emerald is therefore symbolic of arcane information, and carries with it the wisdom of the Ancients. The emerald was placed at the throats of mummies as they were embalmed, so that the limbs of the corpse would retain their vigor in the next life, since emerald **green** is a color that is symbolic of spring and renewal.

Because it was dedicated to Mercury, the emerald was carried as a **talisman** by travelers to keep them safe on their journey. Emerald talismans were also used to exorcize **demons**. If given as a gift between lovers (for example as an engagement **ring**), the emerald would ensure a long and happy life. However, if either partner should be unfaithful, then the emerald would start to fade in its brilliance, so the stone represents truth.

As a healing stone, the emerald was believed to cure upset **stomach**s and to ease melancholy and a "sad **heart**." Further, it was said to neutralize poisons caused by **scorpions, snakes**, and **wasp** stings, and even calm epilepsy.

FLINT

The word "flint" or "flinty" is used to describe a person or an object that shares the inherent qualities of this mineral: a hard, tough steeliness. Famously, flint can be used to create **fire** when it is struck against a piece of steel, making a spark which is strong enough to set the fire smouldering. This is not the only reason why flint is connected with the element of fire.

Flint was a valuable commodity for Neolithic man, who used it to make tools such as **arrowheads** and hammerheads. When these artifacts were uncovered during the Middle Ages, it was believed that they were the fossilized tongues of **serpents**. They were mounted in **silver** settings and used as a charm to protect cattle from bewitchment by malicious **elves** and **fairies**.

These arrowheads, encased in silver, looked like the physical embodiment of **lightning** flashes, and so their practical use and symbolic meaning gradually changed from useful tools to protective **talismans** that worked by a process of sympathetic magic, guarding homes and byres against damage by storms, lightning, and fire. In other parts of Europe, excavated flint hammerheads were

believed to be a physical manifestation of thunder, since Thor, God of Storms, carried a hammer. And so the connection between flint, fire (in the form of lightning), and storms was firmly cemented in the imagination of medieval man. These arrowheads were considered to have healing properties too, able to cut into and remove **kidney** stones. In Ireland during the Middle Ages, any woman who discovered such an arrowhead was immediately accorded special status because of the magical power of this sacred stone. It would be soaked in **water** and the water given to the sick person to drink as a kind of medicine.

The usefulness of flint as a blade was also well-known by the Ancient Egyptians. They used it to make a special ritual knife used to make the first incision into a **body** as the first step in its embalmment. In certain parts of the world flints and other stones were thrown up out of the ground by the action of the plough, and these stones would be painstakingly removed by **hand**. However, when there were more stones lying on the surface of the ground the next morning, the logical conclusion was that the stones had been breeding overnight.

GARNET

Although the garnet can be transparent, **green, yellow, orange, ultraviolet, brown**, and **black** (although not **blue**), it is the **red** garnet which is the best known. Because it generally has a rich, dark color similar to that of veinous **blood**, the garnet has long been associated with this vital liquid, and is said to be efficacious in treating bleeding wounds, blood disease, and hemorrhages. The garnet was even believed to have been able to staunch bleeding wounds, and so was used as a protective **talisman** by soldiers from the Crusades onwards, being set into sword hilts and shields.

The name "garnet" comes from **pomegranate**; indeed, the jewel does look similar to the sparkling **seed** of this **fruit**, and is similarly associated with the fertility of the **womb**.

As well as being able to heal wounds, garnet is also believed to be able to inflict mortal wounds on the enemy. In 1892, when Indian and British troops were fighting one another in Kashmir, the enterprising Hunza tribesmen used spherical garnets as bullets interspersed with more regular ammunition. These jewels, used as weapons, caused many serious injuries or fatalities to the British forces.

A very tough stone, the garnet is one of the twelve stones which were set into the **breastplate of the High Priest** of the Temple in Jerusalem. Garnets are often carved into cabochon shapes, with a curved underside to maximize the light pouring through the gem, which has extremely high refractivity because of its hardness. A popular way of presenting the stone since ancient times, this way of carving a garnet is called a "carbuncle." Such is the light given off by this carbuncle that the Qu'ran says that it gives light to the Fourth Heaven. There is also a legend that Noah's Ark featured a huge garnet set on a pedestal; this stone gave off such a great amount of light that it illuminated the ship both day and night. The refractive quality of the garnet is one of the features that makes it a symbol of protection, providing light in the darkness and causing enemies to flee.

As a healing stone, the garnet is said to regenerate the body and spirit, and to throw off melancholy, although there are strict instructions as to its usage. As a **heart** stimulant it was particularly effective, but if worn for too long or if the patient did not remain conscious and calm throughout the process, the close proximity of this fiery, blood-red stone could over-stimulate the passions. Similarly, when used to cure melancholia, the side-effects could be insomnia—an indication of just how stimulating was the stone considered to be.

GEMSTONE CORRESPONDENCES

Associations between gemstones and the signs of the **Zodiac**, the **planets**, the months of the year, days of the week, anniversaries and birthdays, **chakras** and more, tend to be something of a moveable feast, varying according to different writers and depending on individual spiritual beliefs. The stones attached to the months and the seasons, for example, differ according to the religion and country of origin of the authority that is consulted. In addition certain stones tend to go in and out of fashion. Adding to the confusion are the changes in the names of stones, as well as alterations to the calendar dates over the centuries that have meant that the traditional stone for one month sometimes spills over into the next.

The following charts give the most popular definitions of these correspondences. The links between planets and their metals are listed toward the end of this section under **seven** magical metals.

Gemstones and the planets

SUN: Amber, diamond, topaz
MOON: Moonstone, pearl
EARTH: Amber, jade, ammonite
MERCURY: Agate, opal, citrine
VENUS: Malachite, rose quartz, emerald
MARS: Hematite, ruby, spinel
JUPITER: Sapphire, lapis lazuli, turquoise
SATURN: Jet, onyx, coral
URANUS: Opal, amethyst
NEPTUNE: Aquamarine, coral, pearl
PLUTO: Diamond, jade, zircon

Gemstones and the Zodiac

ARIES: Diamond, bloodstone
TAURUS: Emerald, lapis lazuli
GEMINI: Agate, citrine
CANCER: Moonstone, pearl
LEO: Peridot, amber
VIRGO: Aquamarine, carnelian
LIBRA: Jacinth, amethyst
SCORPIO: Opal, sapphire
SAGITTARIUS: Turquoise, topaz
CAPRICORN: Onxy, garnet
AQUARIUS: Garnet, aquamarine
PISCES: Amethyst, bloodstone

According to the esotericist and prolific occult author Walter Richard Old ("Sepharial"), 1864–1929, who was the first President of the British Astrological Society, the stones that belong to the birthsigns vary slightly from those listed above. He has the ruby belonging to Cancer, the sardonyx to Leo, the sapphire to Virgo, the opal to Libra, the topaz to Scorpio, and the amethyst to Aquarius.

Gemstones and the months of the year

JANUARY: Garnet
FEBRUARY: Amethyst
MARCH: Heliotrope, jasper
APRIL: Diamond, sapphire
MAY: Agate, emerald
JUNE: Emerald, pearl, agate
JULY: Onyx
AUGUST: Carnelian
SEPTEMBER: Peridot
OCTOBER: Aquamarine, beryl
NOVEMBER: Topaz
DECEMBER: Ruby

Gemstones and the chakras

Starting from the crown chakra and working down, the colors of the chakras have a strong bearing on the gems that are said to represent them. In this chart, the first gem listed is said to close the chakra, and the second one will open it.

7 CROWN CHAKRA or SAHASRARA: Amethyst, diamond
6 THIRD EYE CHAKRA or AJNA: Lapis lazuli, amethyst
5 THROAT CHAKRA or VISHUDDA: Aquamarine, blue topaz
4 HEART CHAKRA or ANAHATA: Emerald, rose quartz
3 NAVAL CHAKRA or MANIPURA: Amber, citrine
2 SACRAL CHAKRA or SVAD-HISTHANA: Jade, ruby
1 ROOT CHAKRA or MULADHARA: Hematite, garnet

Gemstones and the elements

Air: Agate, citrine, lapis lazuli, opal, rose quartz, sapphire, turquoise

Fire: Amber, citrine, fire opal, garnet, heliotrope, ruby, spinel, topaz

Water: Amethyst, aquamarine, coral, lapis lazuli, moonstone, pearl, tourmaline, turquoise

Earth: Amber, ammonite, emerald, jet, magnetite, malachite, jade, onyx

Ether: Amethyst, diamond, opal, pearl, rock crystal, sapphire, tourmaline, zircon

GOLD

Gold, considered to be one of the most precious and beautiful metals of all, is inextricably linked with the **element** of **fire** and with the **Sun**, which it represents both in appearance and in symbolism. In mythology, the passage of the Sun is often described as a golden chariot traversing the **Heavens**. Gold has the benefit of remaining unaffected by tarnishing or corrosion of any sort, and so is an emblem of immortality. Even if it is melted or liquefied by heat, gold retains its color and luster. It is surpassed by platinum in terms of actual monetary value, but retains the upper hand in terms of symbolic meaning because of its color and thousands of years of adoration.

Gold has always had magical powers ascribed to it, the Ancients believing that it was actually made from sunbeams buried underground. Egyptian mummies of the highest castes were encased in gold, denoting the immortality of the **soul**. Gold was one of the **three** gifts brought by the Magi to the infant Christ. And even today, gold is still the most popular metal for use as wedding **rings**, because it is seen to confer a long and happy life to the married couple.

Although gold is a symbol of purity because of its physical incorruptibility, paradoxically, gold has also taken on some extremely negative connotations. The striving for gold can cause corruption in men once greed for the precious metal takes hold; as an object of desire it can bring out the very worst in people. The story of King Midas is a case in point. Midas wished that everything he touched be turned to gold, and once **Dionysus** had granted him this wish, Midas soon realized it was a terrible curse. Unable to eat because his **food** turned to gold, unable to hug his daughter because she turned to gold, too, Midas eventually asked Dionysus to remove the curse, which he did by having the King wash his hands in the Pactolus River, which is now in modern-day Turkey. The myth not only explains the origin of the gold deposits in this river, but effectively proves the later Shakespearian idea that "all that glistens is not gold."

Alchemists used gold to symbolize the soul, and the search for the **philosophers' stone** also signified the conscious efforts made by them to purify the spirit, since the material stone could be created only in tandem with spiritual growth and development.

GZI STONE

In Tibetan Buddhism, this is a carved, etched, or naturally colored **agate** stone, possibly prehistoric in origin. They tend to be found when fields are ploughed up, or near burial sites. There are numerous beliefs about the origins of these stones. Some believe that they are the jewels that the **deities** discard, dropping them to earth when they become damaged or chipped. They could be the droppings of the mythological **garuda** bird, or perhaps the petrified remains of some living creature, a **worm** for example.

Gzi stones generally appear in two forms. One type is cylindrically shaped, made from **black**, **brown**, and **white** agate, with circular "**eye**" symbols. The other is rounded, made from **chalcedony** or **carnelian**, with **spiralling** bands. The most valuable is the **9-**eyed gzi stone; its value is the equivalent of a small farmhouse. The gzi stone is now much copied, although it is not always made in the traditional materials know to our ancestors. They even appear manufactured from china or plastic.

HAG STONES

This is a stone that features a naturally made hole in it, and can be made of any mineral, although in Britain the flint hag stone is the most usual sort to find. Also known as **witch stones**, snake's eggs, **adder stones** or holy stones, there are all manner of beliefs ascribed to these objects. In particular, they were believed to be able to protect **cattle** from witches who would take them out at night and ride them, leaving the farmer to discover the tell-tale signs of filthy, exhausted animals the next morning. The stones would have string or ribbon passed through the holes so that they could be hung above the **doorway**, where they would handily also stop **milk** from curdling; this belief was so strong that farmers in some parts of Europe, whilst milking their cows, would hold a hag stone in such a way that the milk poured through it.

Part of the protective efficacy of this symbolic object is because the stone was formed by the action of **water**, and magic cannot work in running water, so the stone retains the resonance of this ancient idea. Hag stones with multiple holes in them, however, were meant to be powerful tools used in spell-casting by the very witches they were named after; stones with **three** holes were particularly powerful since these evoked the **triple Goddess**.

Even **camels** are protected by hag stones; its symbolism takes on a different aspect in the East, though, since the stone resembles an **eye** and so protects from the **evil eye**. There is further symbolism associated with these curious stones. Looking through the hole is said to enable another world to be viewed: the **fairy** world or the spirit world. Put simply, the solid part of the stone represents the material world, and the hole in the middle, the spirit world, the void, the "no thing." It is for this reason that the **wreath**, the hoop-shaped floral tribute, is often used at **funerals**.

Hematite

As its name would suggest, hematite is associated with **blood,** because of its **iron** content and its **color.** Sometimes it is also referred to as "**bloodstone.**" Although the stone, generally used in **jewelry,** is a shiny gunmetal color, it also contains **red** streaks, and if it is scraped into a fine powder, it yields a pigment called **red** ochre that is the color of dried blood. This ochre was considered to be a sacred substance, associated with life-giving blood and rebirth, and ancient burial sites have been found where the corpse has been daubed in this powder, presumably in some sort of symbolic ritual to ensure life after death. Olmec tombs have been found containing highly polished "**mirrors**" of hematite, always buried with female bodies.

The Romans made hematite sacred to **Mars,** the God of War, and the stone was used by warriors as a protective and strengthening **amulet** during battles. This ancient association was gloriously corroborated when significant deposits of hematite were discovered on the planet Mars in 2001. Hematite is believed to confer courage, strength, and endurance, improve the circulation of the blood, and is a means of staunching bleeding.

Iniskim

For Native Americans—particularly the Blackfoot—an iniskim is a magical stone used for sacred purposes such as divination, or in rituals to ensure good hunting. These iniskim are generally fossilized pieces of stone, often **ammolite**; an ammolite is a fossilized **sea** creature that has retained a piece of its **shell** and so has a colorful, iridescent hue.

The most valuable iniskim are those which have **four** or **five** protrusions that may give the stone the appearance of a tiny **buffalo.** Since the buffalo is such a sacred animal to the Blackfoot people, such a stone is a **totem** of the animal and carries its powers too. Ownership of the stone allows the person to communicate with the **spirit** of the buffalo.

Iron

It may be one of the cheapest and most abundant of all metals, but iron has great relevance in both symbolism and the practical application of magic.

Iron is one of the primary constituents of **blood,** and the metal and the liquid smell similar; therefore, iron has been perceived to be the "blood" or life force of the **Earth** itself. But it is not only the Earth which has high iron content, since early iron that was used by man originated largely from **meteors.** In Tibet, this "sky iron" is used for making the singing bowls, the vibrational frequency of which is believed to attract good spirits, and heal both **body** and **soul.**

Iron had the reputation of being repellant to **witches, ghosts,** and other malevolent entities. Numerous folktales have the supernatural creature being rendered powerless by being struck with iron. When iron appears in the form of the **horseshoe,** its power is increased because the horseshoe is a symbol of the protective **Goddess**, the **crescent moon**, the **chalice**, or the **yoni**.

The **red** color of rusting iron further promotes the idea that iron is a life force. Anything which grows in the earth must therefore by default contain some of this spirit, especially corn, since it was such an important crop. To appease this spirit, people would take a bite at a piece of iron, thereby rendering the spirit harmless. For Australian Aborigines, iron is also considered a magical, sacred material, and is used in rites and ceremonies along with blood; the two are interchangeable.

Iron is associated with the planet **Mars**, not only because of its red color but because of its strength and hardness, and the **fire** needed to alter its shape. The gift of blacksmithing—working with iron—was said to have been given by the Gods themselves.

JACINTH

The jacinth is a yellow form of **zircon** that was held in high esteem by the Crusaders who, along with other travelers, used it as a **talisman** to ensure safety during their journey; it provided protection from both robbers and **lightning**. The jacinth was also used in a magical spell, whereby a loaf of **bread** would be marked with the stone; thereafter the bread would be efficacious in removing spells and enchantments if eaten by the victims of such trickery.

Jacinth is one of the many stones said to change color as a warning or omen. For example, it was believed to turn **red** if stormy weather was in the offing. There is some truth in this, because the stone does tend to turn cloudy if the air is damp, but it resumes its brilliance when the weather is hot and sunny. In this sense, it acts as a natural barometer.

In general, the jacinth is a symbol of all things good, rendering its wearers beloved of both God and man alike. It is said to remove melancholy, cheer people, and promote a good night's sleep. The only downside to the wearing of this stone was that it was said to cause miscarriages.

JADE

There are two kinds of jade: jadeite and nephrite. Although they are quite difficult to identify from each other, jadeite is the harder and the rarer form of this precious stone.

Although we think of jade as being primarily **green**, it also comes in **yellow**, **white**, **pink, mauve**, and **black** forms. The apple-green jade—the rarest form of the stone—was considered to be so special that the Empress of China issued a decree that all carvings of this color belonged exclusively to the Imperial Collection, hence it became known as Imperial Jade.

Jade is associated with midwives, and its proximity to a pregnant woman is said to ensure an easy birth. The origin of this belief possibly comes from the story of the Babylonian **Goddess Ishtar**, and her journey into the Underworld. At each of the **seven** gates of Hades, she had to remove an item of **clothing**, and at the fifth level she took off her jade **girdle**, which was said to help assist with childbirth. In addition, jade is said to ease **stomach** pains, a cure which was used most famously by the Greek physician Galen. Nephritic jade has a color similar to that of the **spleen**, and this may explain its potency as a cure for this part of the body; this association is known as the **Doctrine of Signatures**. Similarly, dark **red** jade—like other red minerals—was said to be efficacious for the flow of the **blood**. In China, a tonic of powdered jade was said to soothe the nerves and act as a general pick-me-up. The color of the jade, again, was very important; the greener the jade, the more successful the treatment, since green is the color of spring and of renewal.

The physical qualities of jade inform its symbolic meaning. Its polish suggests knowledge and education; its smoothness, kindness; its strength means that it is the stone of righteousness; and its rarity stands for purity. China is not the only country where jade is held in high esteem. The Maoris also view the stone as having magical properties. The power of Maori jade as a protective force is enhanced when it is carved into the form of various deities, as in the **Manaia**.

Jasper

Jasper is an opaque stone that is generally reddish **brown** or a dull **green** in color. Because it is relatively easy to carve, it was a popular stone to use as an **amulet**, and the different images engraved on it gave the amulet different powers. It was believed that the stone could somehow understand the meaning of the image depicted on it. For example, an **arrowhead** was meant to bring good fortune, while a **hare** would protect against evil influences. Egyptians used **red** jasper specifically to make amulets of the **tyet** or **Knot** of **Isis**, since the dull dark red color signified the **blood** of the Goddess. This amulet was placed on the neck of the mummy to protect its soul during the journey to the Afterlife.

The famous Greek physician, Galen, carried a jasper amulet engraved with the picture of a man carrying a bunch of herbs, and he believed that the stone helped him in his medical diagnoses. The use of jasper as an amulet extended to the Native Americans too.

Hildegard of Bingen said that a piece of jasper held in the hand of a woman during childbirth could protect the baby and its mother from evil spirits, and jasper was also believed to aid childbirth, probably because of its associations with blood. Jasper also appears on the **breastplate of the High Priest** of the Temple in Jerusalem.

Jet

Jet is in fact **wood** that has rotted and been compressed over millions of years. At the end of this process it turns into a stone that is easily carved and, when polished, takes on a brilliant luster. Jet famously comes from Whitby, a little town on the north-east coast of Yorkshire, although this area is not the only source of the material.

Because of its color, jet has long been associated with **death** and mourning (its presence in burial chambers dating back 10,000 years testifies to this). It became very fashionable when Queen Victoria ordered great quantities of jet **jewelry** that she wore when she was in mourning for her deceased consort, Prince Albert. Victorian Britain was fascinated with death, and soon the demand for jet jewelry achieved staggering proportions. In 1870 the jet industry in Whitby alone employed 1500 people. However, the association of jet with death and funerals became so pronounced that the use of the stone was pretty much exhausted once the trend had passed, and the many other properties of the stone were largely forgotten about.

These properties included the power to repel **serpents** when jet was burned, and the treatment of toothache when an elixir of jet was boiled in **wine** and applied to the **mouth**. When jet is rubbed with a piece of cloth it becomes charged with static electricity (in the same way as other organically created stones, such as **amber**) and can pick up small pieces of tissue or lint; therefore jet was believed to attract good fortune. If the jet is rubbed very briskly, it sometimes gives off smoke, which had the power to drive away the **demons** that were as black as the jet itself. A jet **cross** nailed to a door would keep out evil spirits and jet **talismans** were carried to protect the owner from devilish forces.

LAPIS DRACONIUS

A mythical stone and difficult to acquire, lapis draconius (also known as dragon stone) had to be taken from the head of the equally **imaginary dragon**, although it's likely that unscrupulous traders may have given any genuine stone such provenance, thus increasing its value. Witness accounts of those who claimed to have seen the dragon stone vary. Some said that it was **pyramidal** in shape and colored **black**; others claimed that it was transparent. The stone was only efficacious if it was taken from the head of the dragon while the creature still lived, although it would be hoped that the intrepid dragon-slayer would

have chosen his moment carefully.

Traditionally, the dragon would be persuaded to come out from its **cave** with pleasant **music**, and then knocked out with some kind of opiate that had been used to impregnate the **letters** of magical spells embroidered onto the **cloak** of the slayer. Once acquired, the stone would provide an effective antidote to any poison, and render the owner invincible. Anyone reputed to possess such a stone would be likely to have few enemies, another contributory factor to the existence of the myth.

LAPIS LAZULI

The **golden** specs which are scattered throughout this beautiful **blue** stone like **stars** in a dark **sky** are in fact flecks of **iron** pyrites. The color of lapis is what makes it important, and it is ground into a fine powder in order to make the ultramarine pigment used in painting. The Ancient Egyptians called this stone **sapphire**, but from their descriptions we know that it was lapis lazuli to which they were referring.

Blue is a symbol of purity and chastity, and much of the symbolic meaning of lapis lazuli relates to its color. Although many of the stones examined in this section of the encyclopedia are symbolic of fertility and may somehow aid childbirth, the lapis is an exception in that it was used to cause miscarriage, and so was called the "stop stone." An **amulet** of lapis lazuli was used for this purpose.

The lapis lazuli was sacred to the Egyptian Goddess of Truth, Maat. Since truth is about seeing things correctly, the stone was believed to be particularly potent in treating the **eyes**. A paste of ground lapis, **milk**, and mud from the Nile was used to create an ointment. In a nod to its association with the eye, there is also a New Age belief that the stone can help to open the **third eye**.

LAPIS PHILOSOPHORUM

See **Philosophers' stone**.

LAPIS SANGUINARIUS

See **Bloodstone**.

LEAD

A weighty metal, it is no surprise that lead symbolizes heaviness and an oppresive burden. It is the attribute of **Saturn**, and both the planet and the God (who is often depicted as a grim-looking hunched old man carrying a **scythe**) share these somewhat morose qualities, from which the word "saturnine" is coined.

In **alchemy**, lead is described as the "base metal" which will hopefully be transmuted into **gold**. In order to do this, alchemists made great efforts to free themselves from the limitations of the material world as symbolized by this heavy metal.

LODESTONE

Lodestone refers to a type of **magnetite**, although the stones have a slightly different crystalline structure one from another. Magnetite is relatively common but the lodestone is rare; in addition the lodestone needs to be electrically charged—by **lightning** for example—before it acquires the magnetic properties that have made it such an important mineral. The compass was invented because lodestone existed; if this discovery had not been made, then the course of world history would have been very different.

The potential of the powers of the lodestone, which is attracted to the **Earth**'s magnetic field, was first spotted by the Chinese who adapted it to make the world's first compass. From about AD 100 onward, there are references to a "south pointer," most likely to have been a lodestone "spoon," whose curved base would have allowed the stone to spin freely within an indented hollow.

Although exploited initially by the Chinese, the lodestone was also familiar to the Ancient Greeks. Pliny the Elder writes of a herdsman, Magnes, whose **iron** hobnailed boots and the iron tip of his **staff** attracted pieces of lodestone. Many ancient people believed that stones had **souls**, and the ability of the lodestone to attract things to it and to cause things to move must have seemed magical indeed, as though the stone had a mind of its own. Accordingly, the stone was given **water** to drink and iron filings to eat. Ancient Egyptians gave the stone the name of Haroeri, meaning "Grandson of the Earth Goddess."

Although it was lightning which gave the lodestone its power, it also attracted lightning, so it was not to be carried or worn during a **storm**. Because the lodestone attracts things to it, it was associated with both attraction and retention; shopkeepers believed that it encouraged customers, for example, and prostitutes used it to attract clients. It was also held as a symbol of love and the attraction of opposites.

The **temple** of Konark, on the coast of the Bay of Bengal in India, is reputed to have had such a huge and powerful lodestone mounted on the top of its **Sun** Temple that it caused shipwrecks because the vessels were both drawn towards the stone and because their compasses were affected by it. Rumor has it that the stone was removed by Muslim voyagers, with the result that the temple eventually fell down.

MAGNETITE

See **Lodestone**.

MALACHITE

A beautiful stone with ripples of **blue-green** markings, malachite contains **copper**, which gives it its color. It was found in King Solomon's copper mines near Eilat, and was prized by the Ancient Greeks and Romans who made **amulet**s and **talisman**s from it.

Some malachite has markings which are similar to the **feather**s of the **peacock's** tail, complete with the "**eyes**"; this stone is called peacock malachite and is sacred to the Goddess **Juno** because of her associations with the bird. This variety of the stone was made into amulets that were believed to provide protection against the **evil eye**, because of the eye symbol which formed an inherent part of its design. The charm was given further protective powers since it was carved in the shape of a **triangle**. Furthermore, malachite amulets were given to children to help promote teething and protect them from witchcraft. Malachite is also said to aid a good night's sleep, and so was attached to the cradles and beds of babies and infants. As a healing stone, malachite was believed to counteract feelings of faintness and, if powdered and taken in **milk**, would ease the pain of a heart attack.

MERCURY

Mercury—or **quicksilver**—is one of the three elements which alchemists believe are essential to all life. The other two are **salt** and **sulphur**. Mercury is seen as symbolic of the **soul**. In India, **alchemy** is called *rasavatam*, which means "way of mercury." Alchemists also believed that the qualities of mercury meant that it could be transformed into any metal, and so it was a vital ingredient in the transmutation of base matter into **gold**, the ultimate aim of many who practiced their art.

Mercury is a **metal**, a **planet**, and a God. Here we are dealing with the mineral aspect of mercury, although it's sometimes hard to separate these three in terms of their symbolism. Mercury is one of only **four** metals which is liquid at room temperature; its name "quicksilver"—suggesting something that is difficult to handle, whimsical, and swift moving (indeed mercurial)—fittingly describes the metal in this state.

Mercury is not harmful when it is in insoluble form; however, as soon as it's in soluble form—as in methyl mercury—it becomes extremely toxic. Lighthouse lanterns float in a circular vat of mercury, and the vapors used to make some lighthouse keepers go mad, although the cause was undiscovered for many years. Similarly, the phrase "mad as a hatter" derives from the insanity suffered by milliners as a result of the use of mercury nitrate as a solution that helped the felt fabric to matt together and so strengthen the material. Symptoms of mercury poisoning include hallucinations, tremors, and dementia.

Moonstone

The moonstone is aptly named. Its opalescent, milky semi-opacity really does have a moonlight-like quality. Some stones have a **white** spot inside them that reacts in a similar way to the occlusions in **cat's eye**-type stones, in that it appears to move inside the stone. This was at one time believed to be a trapped moonbeam, and the stone used to be called the "astrion," since it was believed to contain light from the **stars**, which it could collect if it was held up to the night **sky**.

The links between the **Moon** and the moonstone are further strengthened by the belief that the stone shares the same waxing and waning pattern as its celestial counterpart. The moonstone was also believed to help focus the mind and the intentions. If held in the **mouth**, they were said to inspire the person into knowing which endeavors would be best undertaken, and which not. Effectively, the moonstone is believed to help the owner to tap into the intuition and psychic powers which have long been considered a quality of the Moon.

The moonstone was used as a **talisman** by travelers, who believed that it would afford them protection. It was also used as a charm by those seeking love, and who hoped that they would find what they were looking for by wearing the moonstone on the night of a full Moon.

Olivine

See **Peridot**.

Onyx

Onyx is mentioned as one of the twelve jewels featured in the **breastplate of the High Priest** of the Temple in Jerusalem.

The actual word *onyx* means "claw" or "nail" in Greek, and the story goes that the mischievous Cupid cut **Venus'** nails one day while she was sleeping on the beach. Cupid left the **fingernail** shards scattered around the sand dunes, but the **Fates**, wanting to make sure that no scrap of the Goddess would be wasted, turned the fingernails into onyx stones.

Onyx comes in a wide range of colors, sometimes striated, sometimes plain. The reddish colored onyxes are called **sardonyx**, which was useful in Roman times for the carving of seals, since the wax never stuck to the stone. Sardonyx could also ward off charms and curses, keeping its owner happy and healthy. Onyx is often heavily patterned, and the stones that resemble an **eye** are used as an amulet of protection against the **evil eye**.

Onyx was used in magical rituals to conjure up **demons**, and it may well be this property that meant that the stone should never be worn at night lest the wearer suffer from nightmares. In Arabic, the word for onyx is *el jaza*, meaning "sadness"; the stone has the reputation of draining energy and causing melancholy. It's also considered to be an unlucky stone, and again this could be because of its association with demonic beings.

Remaining on the theme of bad luck, both Indians and Ancient Egyptians thought that wearing onyx may cause passions to wane, and lovers to part. However, onyx had a reputation for healing powers, too. Hildegard of Bingen recommended that onyx be "soaked" in **wine** for up to thirty days; the resulting elixir would be used to touch the eyes in order to clear eyesight.

Opal

The iridescence of the opal is caused by the large amount of **water** retained by the silica from which the stone is made, sometimes constituting as much as ten per cent of its mass. This water content causes the opal to have a higher degree of sensitivity than any other gemstone, a quality which informs not only its physical characteristics but its symbolic meaning too.

Because of its ethereal beauty, the opal has always been a favored gem; its changing **colors** have also given the stone a distinct personal identity, as though it has a **soul** of its own. Changes in temperature can affect the opal; a sudden move from a hot room to a cold environment can even cause the stone to crack.

The reputation of the opal as being unlucky seems to be a belief held only by Western people. Sir Walter Scott's book *Anne of Geierstein* may have contributed to this reputation. In the story, Anne is a baroness who wears a precious gem in her **hair** that is not actually ever named as an opal in the book but that carries its qualities. This stone acts as a perfect litmus for the Baroness's moods, flashing **red** when she is angry and sparkling when she is happy. The story becomes more sinister. Holy **water** is splashed onto the stone, which shatters; Anne faints, and is found turned to dust like the stone.

Another reason might be because the opal is said to glow brighter around a person who is just about to die. Because the stone reacts to temperature, this may well be true rather than just a superstition, since the fever of a sick person could affect the brilliance of the stone.

The opal's unfortunate reputation is not, however, found anywhere else in the world. Its name comes from the Sanskrit *upala*, which simply means "precious stone." In Greece and Rome, it was called the *paederos*, meaning "precious child," and also *opthalmus*, meaning "**eye**." Because the opal was associated with vision, this was extended to mean psychic vision and second sight.

The opal as the symbol of the **eye** meant that it was also a symbol of protection. There's a story that an enormous opal was set into the crown belonging to the Holy Roman

Emperors in order to watch over them. The opal was also believed for some reason to render the wearer invisible, and although its effectiveness in this direction seems never to have been proven conclusively, the stone became a symbol of thieves for whom invisibility was an undoubted asset. This belief about the opal would also have contributed to its reputation in some parts of the world of being unlucky.

Many opals originate in Australia, and when they were first discovered there Queen Victoria was understandably delighted, ordering a large amount of opal jewelry and restoring the gem to favor for a time, despite its reputation in the West.

The Aborigines believed that the opal contained a **fire** within, and one of their dreamtime legends tells the story of how fire was discovered by a **pelican**. This bird, called Muda, had been sent by the people to explore the Northern Territory. He discovered a plain full of colored stones, obviously opals, and as he pecked at one with his beak, sparks shot forth and so **fire** was discovered. As a result, the opal also represents fire.

Pearl

The origin of the pearl, as an irritating piece of grit which manages to get inside the **shell** of a mollusk, is completely belied by its symbolism, the mythology surrounding it, and above all its beauty.

The name of the pearl derives from the Latin, *pilula*, meaning a ball. It shares the same origin as the word "pill." If the **diamond** is the epitome of the masculine gemstone, then the pearl is equally prominent as a feminine symbol; its softness, its rarity, its gentle luster, and its origins in the **sea** ensure this is the case.

Pearls are sensitive objects, both physically and in a symbolic sense. They like an even temperature since their high **water** content makes them liable to cracking or even breaking. In the same way, pearls are responsive to changes in body temperature and to chemicals such as perfumes or hairsprays, and so a dull pearl is said to signify illness in its owner.

The most valuable pearls are those that have formed naturally, and—as with other gems—people have lost their lives trying to attain that elusive large, perfect pearl. But pearls can also be cultivated by the simple insertion of a piece of mother-of-pearl into the host mollusk. These pearls are gathered after three to four years.

The pearl, because of its whiteness and perfection, is a symbol of purity, and is dedicated to the **Moon** Goddess in all her forms. As with other organically based gems, there was originally some confusion as to how pearls were actually made. One theory—posited by Pliny the Elder—was that pearls were the result of dew drops falling into the mollusk shell, which had then somehow solidified. The **color** and luster were explained as **rainbows** which had fallen on this dew. Another more sinister belief was held by the pearl fishermen of Borneo. They would set aside every ninth pearl. These pearls were placed all together in a bottle with two grains of **rice** for each pearl. The bottle was stoppered with the **finger** of a dead man and the whole placed in a **tree** in the belief that more pearls would be "born" as a result.

In China it was believed that both raindrops and pearl are made of **dragons**' spit. Both fall to **Earth** when dragons are fighting in the Heavens. Because water and **fire** are diametrically opposed and pearls are associated with water, then pearls are considered an effective charm against damage by fire and **lightning**. The pearl and the Moon are closely associated, and because the Moon rules over lovers, pearl, ground into a fine powder, was used to make an **aphrodisiac** potion.

PERIDOT

Like other **green**-colored stones, the peridot was referred to as an **emerald** in ancient times, although it is actually a type of **olivine**. The name is believed to have originated either in the French word *peritot*, which means "unclear," or from the Arabic, *faridat*, meaning "gem." To add to the confusion, in Greek, *peridona* means "to give richness."

A stone that answers the description of the peridot appeared on the **breastplate of the High Priest** of the Temple in Jerusalem, a mark of the esteem in which it was considered. Both the Ancient Egyptians and the Romans treasured the peridot, and it was often used as an **amulet**, with effigies and inscriptions carved on it. For example, a peridot featuring the image of a **vulture** would ensure that **demons** would give the wearer a wide berth. A peridot amulet with a torch depicted on it was believed to attract wealth to its owner.

A necklace of peridots was said to dispel melancholy and make the wearer cheerful and optimistic. Wearing the beautiful green peridot was said to preserve the owner from jealousy; this is probably an instance of sympathetic magic, since green is traditionally the color of envy. As an amulet set in **gold**, the peridot prevented nightmares and gave the wearer a good nights' sleep.

During the Middle Ages the peridot was thought to ease **liver** problems and aching muscles; latterly, practitioners of gemstone healing believe that the stone has properties conducive to helping the wearer find solutions to problems. The peridot is sacred to the Hawaiian Goddess of volcanoes, Pele.

PIROPHOLOS

One of the mythical stones, anyone wanting to get hold of a piropholos would need to have a strong stomach because it had to be recovered from the **heart** of a man who had been killed by poison. The stone is bright **red**, is impervious to **fire**, and will guard the owner from **thunder**, **lightning**, and **storms**. Its principal value, though, is that it is believed to protect the owner from a sudden death, although unfortunately can do nothing to avert a lingering illness.

QUICKSILVER

See **Mercury**.

ROCK CRYSTAL

Crystallos is the Ancient Greek word for ice, and accurately describes this completely transparent, clear stone. Because of its appearance and name, rock crystals were believed to be icy cold, and Roman ladies of fashion would carry chunks of it, imported from Asia Minor, in order to keep cool during hot weather. Rock crystal ground into a fine powder was believed to be a cure for dysentery, and could help calm fevers when placed on hot skin, another nod to its icy nature. Necklaces of rock crystal were believed to help nursing mothers keep up a good flow of **milk**.

Although some **crystal balls** are made of polished glass, the finest and most costly ones are made from clear quartz crystal, and the largest one in the world, measuring over 30 cm in diameter, was made of clear rock crystal from a stone found in Burma. Since the stone's clarity symbolizes the "clear vision" or clairvoyance needed to be able to see future events before they unfold, the stone is said by some to allow a sort of psychic time-travel. Quartz is also connected with a more practical aspect of **time**, too, and is used in watches, clocks, and other timepieces. When charged with electricity, quartz crystals will vibrate very regularly and it is this vibration that causes the clock mechanism to move.

For Australian Aboriginal medicine men, the rock crystal carried such magical significance that they believed they owed their powers to a piece of the stone that had been embedded into their bodies in a painful and bloody procedure. These stones, called "**ultunda** stones," were one of the factors that made the medicine man different from other tribal members, and accorded him his special status.

Native Americans considered the clear quartz crystal to be a good hunting **amulet**, and thought that the stone was a living entity that needed to be treated well; accordingly, the stone would be "fed" with the **blood** of the kill.

As any child knows, a magnifying glass can be used to focus rays of sunlight so that the resulting heat can set **fire** to things. Rock crystal was used for this purpose, too, and Roman soldiers used the same method to cauterize their wounds, which must have been a painful and painstaking process.

RUBY

The word "ruby" is synonymous with **red**; indeed, it comes from the Latin word *rubens*, which has the same meaning. A powerful and valuable precious gem, in India the ruby is called *ratnaraj*, meaning the "Lord of Precious Stones." Hindus call their most precious and valuable rubies "Brahmins," and these particular stones had to be protected from contact with inferior rubies in case of contamination. Further evidence of the stone as a symbol of royalty can be found in the title of the former kings of Burma, who were known as the "Lords of the Rubies."

The ruby is one of the hardest stones, second only to the **diamond**. During the time of Pliny the Elder, rubies—like other red stones—were categorized as one of the *carbunculii*, a grouping that also included **garnets** and **spinels**.

The color of the ruby plays a major part in its symbolic meaning. They are the **color** of vitality, the life-giving forces and passion, and were considered to be so powerful that, if thrown into water, they would make the water boil. The light from the ruby was also said to shine through any cloth wrapped around it, and so it was impossible to hide. This idea of precious stones generating light rather than just reflecting or refracting it occurs time and time again in the writings of the Ancients, and a ruby was said to have been set on the roof of the Temple of the **Holy Grail** so that the Grail knights could be guided towards it in the dark. This leant the ruby spiritual significance in addition to its worldly value. In Hindu legends, the ruby lights up the underworld, Kantha. There's an old legend that the ruby starts out as a clear stone but ripens in the ground during the course of hundreds, if not thousands, of years.

The ruby was a symbol of protection, and if a landowner touched all 4 corners of his estate with a ruby then the land would be protected from **lightning** and **storms**, and **harvests** would be prolific. Similarly, wearing a ruby in such a way that it touched the **skin** would protect the wearer from ill health, particularly if the stone was placed on the left side of the body since the color of the ruby meant that it was instantly connected to the **heart** and the circulatory system.

Although the ruby is a symbol of passion, it also represents conscious control of the emotions. It was believed to restrain lust and to clear the mind. Like other red stones, it could staunch the flow of **blood** and this led to the belief that to own a ruby would make a warrior impervious to injury by weapons made of steel, including the gun. To be particularly effective the ruby had to be embedded beneath the skin.

The **spinel** is sometimes mistaken for a ruby, and they are sometimes even referred to as rubies. For example, the "Great Balas Ruby" that forms a part of the British Imperial state crown is actually a spinel.

SALT

The **sea** is full of salt, and so there is an inextricable link between the mineral, salt, and the **element** of **water**. However, salt is frequently produced by allowing sea water to evaporate on the ground, and so salt is also associated with the **Earth**; witness the popular saying "salt of the earth," meaning that a person is good, grounded, and honest.

The cuboid structure of salt is further reason for it to be a symbol of the earth element, as well as making it an emblem of protection. Salt has a practical use as a preservative of meat, fish, and other foodstuffs; it has therefore taken on the same symbolic significance—as seen in **rites** and **rituals**—to sanctify and protect holy or magical places. It is used for this reason from cathedral services to the **Magic Circle**. It is possible that this practice is a residue from a time when **blood** from sacrificial animals was used for this purpose, the blood being sprinkled with salt to soak it up.

The use of salt as a means of preserving foodstuffs was invaluable to our ancestors, especially to those making long voyages by sea when fresh meat would be virtually impossible to procure. Salt is also able to bring out flavors in any food to which it is added, and was considered to be so valuable a commodity that it was used as currency to pay people for their work; hence the word "salary" from the Latin, *salarium*.

Because salt is valuable in so many ways, spilling it is considered to be a bad omen. This is still counteracted by superstitious people, who make a **cross** in the salt then throw some of the salt over their left shoulder, supposedly into the **eye** of the Devil.

Alchemists hold that salt—which represents the human body—is one of the three vital natural ingredients, called the **three alchemical principles**, and that it forms a trinity with **sulphur** and **mercury**.

SAPPHIRE

The sapphire is made from carborudum, the same extremely hard material that goes to form the **ruby**.

Although the word "sapphire" is synonymous with **blue**, sapphires themselves can also be **yellow**, **pink**, **orange**, **violet** or even multi-colored. However, the most sought-after and valuable types of sapphire come in the traditional rich blue color.

Because all blue stones used to be known as sapphires, it is sometimes difficult to separate out the mythology that belongs to the sapphire as we know it today. Its blue color gives the sapphire a connection with the **sky**, the Gods, the world of spirit, and it was a favored stone of ecclesiastical ornament because of this symbolism. Added to this is the origin of the word "sapphire" as the biblical *sappur*, which was the name given to the material from which the throne of the Gods was made; presumably it refers to the blue of the Heavens. Blue is also connected with purity and chastity, and the sapphire carries

this symbolism too. Buddhists believe that the close proximity of the stone will promote prayer and meditation. For Hindus, the sapphire is associated with good health, happiness, and wealth.

As is the case with many of the rarer and more valuable stones, sapphires are thought to be efficacious in medical use. A paste made from finely ground sapphires was meant to cure ulcers and boils when applied to the **skin**. It was also believed to be an efficacious antidote to poison, as well as being able to clarify the thoughts and aid a good night's sleep. Along with other blue-colored stones, the sapphire was believed to be able to cure **eye** troubles.

The sapphire is a very beautiful stone; this may be why it was believed to cheer the soul and dispel melancholy. It also enjoyed a more esoteric use, as a **talisman**. Those seeking advice from the Delphic oracle were advised to wear a sapphire amulet, and witches used the stone as a kind of fixative for spells.

There is a particular kind of sapphire known as a "**star** sapphire," which carries with it a very exclusive kind of power. If viewed at a certain angle, a star can be seen trapped within the confines of the stone. The rays of this star are believed to personify the **three** qualities of faith, hope, and destiny, imprisoned within the matrix of the stone, which has been sent to observe the actions of the owner and to confer good fortune on their endeavors.

SARDONYX

See **Onyx**.

SERPENTINE

As a striking instance of the **Doctrine of Signatures**—in which the appearance of an object provides a clue as to its use and its meaning—serpentine not only looks like the snakeskin that gives it its name, but is also believed to provide a cure against snakebites if its use as a talismanic prophylactic against these creatures fails to provide a first line of defense.

Since the **snake** is an animal that is closely connected to the **Earth**, then serpentine, too, is believed to hold "earthing" qualities. As a cure for rheumatism, sufferers were advised to hold pieces of the stone in their hands while sitting in the light of the **Sun**.

SEVEN MAGICAL METALS

The first **seven planets** first recognized by our ancestors continue to have a huge influence on mankind. Other aspects of these links are explored elsewhere, but metals were among the many items that were mystically linked to these planets.

Each of these planets has its own metal. These seven magical metals are **silver** (the **Moon**), **mercury** (**Mercury**, the planet), **copper** (**Venus**), **gold** (the **Sun**), **Iron** (**Mars**), **tin** (**Jupiter**), and **lead** (**Saturn**).

In the Dharmic religions, sacred artifacts (such as singing bowls and temple statuary) are made using a mixture of all seven metals.

SILVER

As **gold** is to the **Sun**, **silver** is to the **Moon**. It is the archetypal female metal, imbued with connections to the Goddess in all her forms. The link is plain to see because the Moon appears silver. The superstition of turning a silver coin in the pocket at the sight of a new Moon is a throwback to this ancient connection.

In the same way that the Moon is a cosmic **mirror** illuminated by the light of the Sun, the mirror is a sheet of glass with a fine layer of silver applied to one side. Silver goblets were filled with water and used for scrying; **water** is also inextricably linked with silver and the Moon. Because evil spirits such as **vampires** have no reflection, silver gained a reputation for being able to repel and even destroy them; hence the use of silver bullets as the ultimate weapon against these **blood**-sucking **demons**.

As a precious metal, silver has been used for making coins since 700 BC, when it was used in the form of electrum. The term "sterling," referring to the monetary currency of the UK, comes from sterling silver; one Troy pound of this was the source of the original "pound sterling."

Like the Moon, silver is associated with psychic powers and intuition, so the clairvoyant or **crystal ball** reader traditionally requests the client to "cross my palm with silver," not purely as a payment, but to help the psychic powers flow.

SNAKE STONE

The snake stone is reputedly a heavy, rough, **black**, spherical stone that is extracted from the head of a **serpent**, although it is likely that this stone is actually a substance called **tabasheer**. Indian snake charmers were particularly adept at removing the stones from the heads of the snakes in their charge and could sell them on at a high price.

Snakes are venomous; therefore, in an instance of sympathetic magic, the stone was used for removing poison. The snake stone would seem to cling to the bite before falling off when it was completely saturated with poison, whereupon another stone would be brought into use. The stones were "cleaned" by soaking them in **milk**; when the milk clotted and went **green**, the stones were considered detoxified and ready for use again.

ST. HILDA'S STONES

When Whitby Abbey in Yorkshire was being built in the seventh century AD, legend has it that the local people beseeched its directress, St. Hilda, to rid them of a plague of **snakes** that was infesting the area. The obliging saint turned the snakes to stone, whereupon they tumbled from the tops of the cliffs. The resulting stones—to Ancient man—were clearly made from coiled snakes. These snake stones are in fact **ammonites**, the fossil of a mollusk with a **spiral** shell, but because of the legend of St. Hilda the fossils took on a powerful talismanic value. Canny sailors would sometimes carve snakes' heads into the ammonites to give them added value, both monetary and symbolic.

STONE OF DESTINY

A seemingly exotic name for a heavy block of sandstone (it weighs 152 kg) with an inscription of a **Latin Cross**, the provenance and the age of the Stone of Destiny is what accords it sacred status. There are several different stories concerning the stone. One is that it was the pillowstone of Jacob, and had once been kept in the Temple at Jerusalem. Another theory is that the stone belonged to the early Gaulish settlers, who brought it with them to Scotland. A third legend says that it was a portable altar used by St. Columba.

Whatever the truth, ownership of the stone has been a contentious issue over the centuries, so great is its reputation. It was kept at the now-ruined Abbey of Scone in Perthshire, and was used during the coronations of the kings of Scotland and the kings of England. When Edward I of England defeated Scotland in the thirteenth century, the stone was apparently taken away from its Scottish home and installed in Westminster Abbey as a symbol of Scotland's defeat and the new sovereignty of England. There are, however, rumors that the original stone was hidden by the canny Scots and the English conquerors took a replica. The stone, real or not, was placed on a bracket beneath the seat of the Coronation Chair in the abbey, and every subsequent monarch has been crowned while sitting on the stone.

In 1996 the Stone of Destiny was returned to Scotland and the journey of this simple block of sandstone made national headlines, so powerful was its symbolic meaning. The stone is kept behind armored glass at Edinburgh Castle, but when the occasion arises, it will be transported back to Westminster Abbey for future coronations.

SULPHUR

Along with **salt** and **mercury**, sulphur forms the "holy trinity" of substances that are the three vital minerals of nature in **alchemy**. Indeed, sulphur is an essential ingredient in all living cells. Alchemists believe that sulphur represents the vitality or life-force of man.

A bright **yellow** chemical, it's likely that sulphur obtained its name from the Arabic word for yellow, *sufra*. Sulphur is sometimes referred to as "brimstone," particularly in the Bible, where the "fire and brimstone" of Hell unfortunately awaits non-believers and sinners.

Although sulphur itself has no odor, it's highly flammable, and when it is burning it releases the particularly noxious-smelling fumes of sulphur dioxide, which smell like rotting eggs. Sulphur used to be burned in sick rooms, in the belief that the smell would purify the air by carrying away any contaminants. Sulphur is often to be found in naturally occurring springs, the give-away being the scent of the gas. Despite its horrible smell, people flock to these springs since these waters are believed to have a beneficial effect on the health. It used to be the practice to give children doses of sulphur and molasses every year as a tonic, although this practice has now died out.

SWALLOW STONE

See **Chelidonius**.

TABASHEER

The tabasheer, strictly speaking, is not really a stone. It is the sappy secretion of a kind of bamboo, whose native name in Malaysia and Indonesia means "rough bamboo." The fluid thickens until a **white** solid remains, which looks a little like a piece of a **sea shell**. This material is tabasheer.

As a **talisman** for warriors, the tabasheer was bound to the **skin** so tightly that the stones sometimes became embedded into the body. It was believed that this made soldiers impervious to injuries from steel. When Genghis Khan encountered eight such warriors in Japan, all of whom had tabasheer "implants" and whom it seemed impossible to kill, he had the enterprising idea of having his men abandon the use of steel blades, so the eight warriors were successfully bludgeoned to death with wooden clubs instead.

Another use for tabasheer is in traditional Chinese herbal medicine. It is ground into a fine powder, and used to allay fevers, **liver** infections, and **stomach** problems.

THE NINE GEMS

A traditional Indian belief gives every one of the nine planets its own precious gem. These *navaratna* are as follows:

1. Moon – Pearl
2. Sun – Ruby
3. Jupiter – Topaz or yellow sapphire
4. Venus – Diamond
5. Mercury – Emerald
6. Mars – Red coral
7. Saturn – Blue sapphire
8. Rahu – Hessonite garnet
9. Ketu – Cat's eye.

These two final planets, Rahu and Ketu, correspond to the northern and southern parts of the **Moon** in Western astronomy. These, effectively, are the parts of the Moon that feature in eclipses, so they are also called the "eclipse planets."

TIN

One of the **seven magical metals**, tin is associated with the **planet Jupiter**. In **alchemy**, both tin and the planet share the same symbol.

Tin does not corrode, and is classically mixed with **copper** to create the alloy, **bronze**. Tin has been used in this way since at least 3500 BC. The earliest tin mines were those in Cornwall and Devon in England. In fact, the British Isles were so famous for their tin production that the islands were referred to by the Greeks as the *Kassiterides*, meaning the "tin-producing" lands. Tin and the tin mines came to be associated with the **fairy** folk or little people that also proliferated in the area, especially those that were believed to live in the underground tunnels that contained the metal.

TOPAZ

Although the topaz can be an amazing **blue** color, or even **pink** or **red**, it is best known as a **golden yellow** gemstone. The topaz itself is symbolic of something which is hard to find, and it is this quality that gives it its name.

All golden yellow transparent stones used to be called "**chrysolite**" in Ancient Greek, which means "golden stone." The most beautiful chrysolites were to be found, so legend has it, on a place called **Serpent** Island. Whether this place was real or imaginary was at the time open to conjecture, and Pliny the Elder named this island Topazos, after the Greek word for conjecture—*topazein*. We now know that the island in question is the place the Crusaders called the Isle of St. John and which the Egyptians called *Zebirget*. The stone was dedicated to the **Sun** God, Ra, since its **color** and sparkle were reminiscent of the rays of the Sun. The inhabitants of this island were given an exclusive license to collect the precious golden stones, which were reputedly visible only in the dark.

The physical qualities of stones often inform their symbolic meaning. Because topaz cools down rapidly after being immersed in hot **water**, it is believed to have the power of calming frayed tempers and high passions, and of cooling fevers. The stone would be touched to the **skin** of plague victims in an attempt to cure their ulcers and blisters. The coolness of the stone was also acknowledged by the Indian sages. One of the more peculiar and inexplicable notions concerning the topaz, however, was the idea that it emitted a milky fluid which could be used to prevent rabies.

Hildegard of Bingen set great store by the ability of the topaz to correct dim vision. This was achieved by soaking the stone in **wine** for three days and three nights, after which the resulting liquid would be applied to the eyeball.

Tourmaline

Tourmaline comes in a veritable **rainbow** of colors. It wends its way through the spectrum, starting with a transparent crystal, and then on to the palest **pink,** through to peach, **yellow, blue, green, brown, red**, and all the shades in between. An Egyptian legend held that the stone absorbed the colors from a **rainbow** on its way through the depths of the earth to the surface, and the stone was sacred to the **Sun** God, Ra. Because of its many hues the stone has a vast array of different names, too. Some tourmalines show colors layered through their core like a stick of rock, and the outer color of this tube-shaped crystal may be a completely different color to those on the inside. Tourmalines like this frequently have pale pink or yellow in the center, graduating to dark green on the outside. These are called "watermelon tourmalines."

The tourmaline has electrical and magnetic properties that make it a useful stone in technical applications. Pliny the Elder wrote of a stone that he called *lychnis*, meaning "lamp," which when heated (either by the **Sun** or by applying friction) could attract straws and other fibrous material. The Ancient Greeks used the tourmaline to help kindle their lamps, while Dutch colonists in Africa—one of the places where the stone can be found—used tourmaline crystals to draw ash from their meerschaum pipes. If the stone is electrically charged and then allowed to cool down, it will have a positive charge at one and a negative charge at the other. This has made the stone symbolic of harmony and balance between opposing energies.

Tourmalines form in a natural **wand** shape and so are used in rituals, since they provide a pointing stick constructed by the natural world. The many colors of tourmaline are believed to give it protective qualities.

Turquoise

The very finest turquoise stones come from Iran, and so it is no coincidence that the name means "Turkish stone" (Iran used to be part of the Ottoman Empire). One of the qualities symbolized by the turquoise is that of sensitivity. This is because the stone can be affected by changes in the body temperature of the wearer, or by the chemicals in perfumes and sprays. If the owner of a turquoise dies, it is said that the stone will turn pale and colorless until it is given to a new owner, when it will in time regain its former beauty. In the same way, the stone would become pale if its owner was sick and so was considered to be an effective litmus of the health of its owner.

For the Aztecs, the turquoise was considered to be so sacred that no single person was allowed to own one; they all belonged to the Gods, and to the Gods alone. The stone was used to decorate the iconic **death masks** of these people.

When the Mayan empire was effectively destroyed by Cortez, the sacred nature of the turquoise was passed on to the Pueblo people. This "stone of the Gods" is also held in high esteem by Native American people. Although its use is now widespread and has become so popular that it has become a symbol of the people themselves, it was originally the preserve of the medicine man and the shaman, who were closest to the Gods and so had some jurisdiction over the stone.

Turquoise was one of the stones believed to afford protection from the **evil eye**, and also prevented falls and stumbles; it became the favored talisman of horsemen, and was woven into the manes of their **horse**s as a protective charm. Turquoise was also believed to counteract the affects of poison from **snake** or **scorpion** stings.

The turquoise seems to be a particularly useful and happy stone for its owner; it is said to make friends of enemies, and is symbolic of generosity and affection. However, the stone is meant only to confer luck where it is given, not bought.

ULTUNDA STONE

This is the name given to the magical stones said to be embedded into the bodies of Australian Aboriginal medicine men; these stones are reputedly the source of their magical powers. The Ultunda stones are not something that the medicine man is born with, but can be transferred from person to person provided they are initiated. The process of embedding sounds painful. The stones are inserted into the **skin** or hammered into the **skull**. Whether or not these stones actually exist or not is a mystery guarded carefully by the medicine men. The stones themselves are symbolic of occult knowledge or secret information.

WITCH STONE

See **Hag stone**.

ZIRCON

See **Jacinth**.

Part Six
SACRED GEOMETRY AND PLACES OF PILGRIMAGE

WHAT IS SACRED GEOMETRY?

Geometry means, quite literally, "measurement of the **Earth**," a term coined by the Ancient Greeks. Man needs to have boundaries and a system for defining **space**, and geometry fulfills this need. Geometry becomes sacred when it pleases the **Gods**, and in order to accomplish this, a structure has to be designed and built with the conscious aim of creating a harmonious resonance with the natural—that is, divinely created—world. Geometric reasoning provides not only a framework for the solid, material plane, but enables us to measure the movement of the **stars** and the planets, helping us to understand our own place in the **cosmos**.

The notion of sacred geometry was not restricted to the Ancient Greeks. The elaborate patterns and shapes of Islamic architecture were also influenced by the idea that

certain measurements are an inherent part of a divine plan. Gothic and Renaissance architecture follow its tenets too. The influence of sacred geometry extends from the **Pyramids** to latter-day buildings, both secular and sacred. Modern building technologies mean that fluid, organic shapes can now be incorporated into large structures, such as Gaudi's Sagrada Familia in Barcelona, Jorn Utzon's Sydney Opera House, and Norman Foster's 30 St. Mary Axe (widely known as "the Gherkin") in London.

But what of these proportions, and how do they differ from "normal" systems of measurement? The key word is "harmony." This short introductory piece can't claim to be an exhaustive treatise on sacred geometry, but outlines some of the basic principles.

There are certain proportions that the Ancient Greeks designated as sacred. Spatial proportions are only one aspect of these measurements; the principles of sacred geometry underpin the harmonics and frequencies of **music** and **color**, as well as natural forms.

Numbers, like **letters**, are sacred symbols in themselves, so man already had the basic tools needed to gauge these divine quantities. For our ancestors, numbers and letters were intrinsically connected and certain symbols encompassed both; phi, for example, was also called the golden mean, the golden section, the golden ratio, and the divine proportion.

GOLDEN SECTION

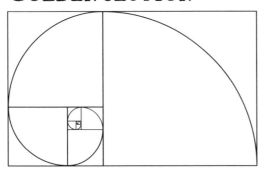

Whatever you want to call it, of all of the many secret signs and sacred symbols this is perhaps one of the most exciting, occurring in the natural world in the most unexpected of places. If you clench your **hand**, tucking the index **finger** into the base of your **thumb** and wrapping the thumb in tight, you create the golden section. The **spiral** shapes of **shells** and ammonite fossils, and the **seed** heads of **sunflowers** all obey its mathematical rules. Stylized patterns of unfurling fronds of the **tree** fern in Maori art are another example. The series of numbers called **Fibonacci sequence** (see Section 7, **Numbers**) provides a sort of instruction manual for the construction of this never-ending spiral shape.

Technically, the golden section is described as any point on a line that divides that line in such a way that the smaller part is

in the same proportion to the greater part, as the greater part is to the whole. The divine proportion exists in every line of the **pentagram**, and this may help explain why this five-pointed star is such a satisfying and intriguing symbol.

PLATONIC SOLIDS

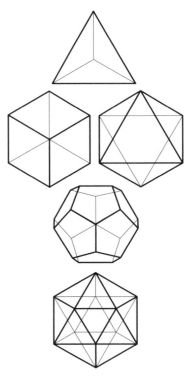

Despite being named after the Greek philosopher and mathematician Plato, there is plenty of evidence that these shapes—said to encompass the 4 classic elements of **earth, air, fire, water**, together with the elusive 5th element—had been discovered at least a thousand years before his time. In fact, the first three shapes were identified by Pythagoras.

Plato described his discovery in 360 BC. Because they are related to the elements, the Platonic solids are said to encompass everything within the known Universe.

These shapes are regular polyhedrons. That's to say, they are multi-sided, three-dimensional figures whose points or corners all touch the sides of an **orb**. There are literally millions of irregular polyhedrons, but only five regular ones. Each of the elements is represented by the solid object to which it relates.

Earth is the twelve-edged **cube** or hexahedron, fitting as a symbol for the solidity of the Earth as a planet as well as a concept. **Fire** is a six-edged tetrahedron, its **pyramid** shape appropriately flame-like. Air is a twelve-edged octahedron. Water is a thirty-edged isocahedron.

The fifth element—ether or aether—was identified as such by Aristotle, although it was commonly accepted in the East much earlier. Although Aristotle did not identify the element with the fifth Platonic solid, the thirty-edged dodecahedron, Plato had commented that God used the shape to arrange all the constellations in Heaven.

One of the enduring images of the five Platonic solids is the model proposed by Johannes Kepler, a German astronomer working in the early seventeenth century. At this time, there were **five** known **planets**, and Kepler sought to establish a relationship between these planets and the shapes of the solids. Although this original idea was abandoned, Kepler's experimentation did result in the discovery that planetary orbits are not circular.

The Platonic Solids may not at first appear to be particularly secret or sacred. However, their discovery was of profound importance in our understanding of how the Universe works, and the beauty of their regular geo-metric forms is a great influence on sacred geometry and architecture.

PLACES OF PILGRIMAGE

Inevitably, the buildings that most noticeably follow the principles of sacred geometry tend to be places of worship or tombs, but this isn't always the case, as we'll see when we look, for example, at the **hogan** and the **yurt**. Sometimes natural features of the landscape are encompassed as an inherent part of a building, like the **church** that originally dominated Glastonbury Tor. The use of high places to site **temples** or other places of worship gives an added value to the man-made structure, not only by making it more prominent in the landscape, but because of the shared symbolism of the **altar**, the holy building and the **mountain** itself, that all signify man's attempt to reach the divine.

Some of the places included here are very well known; some of them are rather obscure. Some of them are grand, some of them are humble and probably not the sort of places that you would usually associate with a "pilgrimage." However, all of these generic or specific structures have been chosen because they were designed with the conscious use of sacred geometry, man's attempt to please God by creating a little piece of Heaven on **Earth**. This single intention effectively renders them holy. The form of this celestial reflection might change, but the meaning stays the same. Like all symbolic disciplines, sacred geometry continues to grow and evolve, just like the **spiral** pattern defined by the **golden mean**.

Some entire cities are revered as places that follow the heavenly archetype, such as Varanesi, Jerusalem, and Mecca.

BOROBUDUR

This Buddhist temple in central Java built in the eighth century AD is a remarkable example of sacred geometry in that its form, structure, and intention resemble a conceptual map of the Universe. This temple is imposing from a distance and even more astonishing close-up because of the sheer level of detail in the ornamentation and the subtleties of the construction.

Like other Buddhist structures, the Borobudur follows the form of the **mandala** (which is itself a diagram of the cosmos) with each of the faces of the **square** base facing the cardinal directions head on. **Seven** square terraces surmount the platform at the base—each being successively smaller than the last—so that the building assumes a stepped shape. On the last of the square platforms are three raised circular levels each set with circular **stupas** numbering 72 in total, and the whole is surmounted by a single, central stupa that appears to skewer

the rest of the building into the ground. Each of the 72 stupas contains a statue of the Buddha, although it can only be seen with some difficulty through the latticework. This filigree stonework serves to illuminate the closeness of the worlds of spirit and matter.

Each square side of the temple has a stone staircase leading to the circular levels, symbolizing the Earth (the square levels) meeting the Heavens (the circular layers).

When viewed from above, the building forms a perfect mandala structure. Even when painted on a flat surface, the mandala provides a compelling aid to meditation; the temple at Borobudur is a living representation of this cosmic map, and pilgrims, moving about the sacred structure, are reminded that their physical lives run parallel to the spiritual tenets of their faith.

CHARTRES CATHEDRAL

One of the most impressive and mysterious of all the cathedrals in France, Chartres is in the Gothic style and was built in the twelfth and thirteenth centuries. However, its site is much more ancient—the ground underneath Chartres is an ancient pre-Christian pagan mound, with a grotto, called the "Pregnant Virgin." A Roman temple replaced the Druid temple that was built on the earlier site. Chartres remains an important focus for the specific worship of Mary.

If the human body and the cosmos reflect one another, then Chartres is a part of this reflection. The geometry of the building is a **cross**-shaped **mandala**, representing the **nine** gates of the human body.

Legend, myth, and mystery stick fast to Chartres. Relatively unchanged since it was completed in the early thirteenth century, there are suggestions that the Knights Templar brought the lost languages, such as the Language of the **Birds**, and the treasures of Solomon, and secreted them inside the cathedral. It is even rumored that the **Ark of the Covenant** itself is hidden in the crypt of Chartres. Notably, there are no burial places within the cathedral. Many of these secrets could arguably be held to be an inherent part of the actual material and construction of Chartres, since the early masons were party to the arcanum of sacred geometry and construction methods that inspired the fraternity of Freemasons in the first place. These secrets exist in many dimensions, and include the use of **sound**, shape, and **color**, as well as material form.

As there are nine "gates" to Chartres, nine knights were legendarily involved in its design. These were the knights who excavated Solomon's temple in the eleventh century and who returned with its secrets in the first place. In an uncanny echo of the "Pregnant Virgin" grotto that the cathedral stands on, Chartres boasts possession of a **veil**, the Sancta Camisia, said to be the one actually worn by Mary when she gave birth to Christ. This veil, given by Charlemagne in 876, was initially housed in an earlier, wooden church that stood on the site, which was destroyed by fire. The *Sancta Camisia* was thankfully saved, and the main body of Chartres, as it stands today, was completed in just 26 years, between 1194 and 1220.

Of the many unique features of Chartres, two of the most talked about are the **rose** window and the **labyrinth**, also called the "Road to Jerusalem." Situated on the floor of the nave and effectively functioning as a barrier to the sacred space at the altar, if the western wall of the cathedral were folded down to the labyrinth, the rose window would match its space exactly.

There is one path to the center of the labyrinth, and the center itself is a **6**-petaled flower that could conceal a **Star of David**, the two convergent **triangles** that say "as above, so below." Pilgrims in modern times are more likely to walk the **11** circuits that measure exactly **666** feet to the center, but formerly the journey was taken on the knees, symbolic of the journey to the Holy Land.

CHURCH

It's impossible to describe every single kind of church, but they all possess certain shared features that have symbolic significance.

Early Christians met simply and often secretively at one another's houses to share a meal and discuss issues of the faith. These spiritual pioneers knew that they faced persecution if they were discovered, so they recognized each other by the symbol of the **fish**, often scratched hastily in the dust on the ground. When Christianity was wholeheartedly embraced by the Roman Empire in the third century AD, however, the design of the basilica—a Roman public meeting hall—was adopted for religious use by most of Western Europe. The word *basileus* means "king," and this religious building therefore honored the King of Heaven.

Oriented to the compass points, a Christian church—from above—looks like the **Cross** of Christ, a clever piece of design by Christian architects and commensurate with other holy buildings that represent one of the major symbols of their faith in three-dimensional form. It's easy to imagine that the architects of these sacred buildings must have wanted their God to recognize them as he viewed the Earth from above.

The long end of this cross—the nave, so-called after the Latin word for ship and implying that the church is a "ship of souls" —effectively symbolizes a spiritual journey or pilgrimage to the focal point of worship, the **altar**, which is always situated at the "short" end of the cross at the eastern end of the church, the place of the rising **Sun**. This journey from west to east also represents the journey from the material world to the spiritual, and from ignorance to illumination. The font, symbolic of the beginnings of life, is always situated at the western end of the church since this is, symbolically, the entrance to the church in both a physical and spiritual sense. It is the western side of the church, with the main entrance, that is the public face of the building.

At the front of the nave is the pulpit, where the officiating holy person reads from the Scriptures. The lectern that holds the Bible is often decorated with an **eagle** whose **wings** support the book. The eagle is the symbol of St. John the Evangelist.

The "arms" of the cross form the transept, and contain side chapels and places for monks, nuns, and pilgrims. The intersection of the long and short arms of the cross is marked by the spire. This tall tower not only dominates the landscape as a visual reminder of the church, but equates to the **Axis Mundi**.

Church design and the use of symbols became more and more elaborate as the wealth and mystique of the Church increased. The northern end of the transept carried all the pagan connotations of this direction as a place of cold, dank evil, and usually contains representations of scenes from the Old Testament. Many people still regard the northern entrance of the Church as the "devil's door." The southern transept, by contrast, represents the opposing qualities of goodness, sunshine, and warmth, and often contains scenes from the New Testament.

The paintings, sculptures, and stained glass windows within churches often served to remind those who could not afford a Bible, or who could not read, of scenes from the scriptures.

Churches also contain an area called the sanctuary, whose original meaning is "holy place." This was where the Blessed Sacrament was kept. It used to be the custom that criminals who managed to get to the sanctuary without apprehension were effectively shielded from the law, and so the word gained an alternative meaning as a "safe place."

DELPHI

This was the holiest place in Ancient Greece, defined as such when **Zeus** released two **eagles** from the ends of the Earth. Delphi, on the southern slopes of the **holy mountain**, Parnassus, was where they met.

As the **navel** of the Earth, this sacred spot was marked by the **Omphalos** stone, a conical artifact carved with a criss-cross pattern whose actual meaning is uncertain but which may represent the crossing of **birds** in the air. The Omphalos was the heart of the chamber of the Delphic oracle, from where the priestess—Pythia, the Python—uttered her oblique pronouncements, never about future events, but about current concerns. Apparently, clouds of scented vapors emanated from this cave. We'll never know whether these were natural gasses rising up from the ground or whether the priestess inhaled sacred and hallucinatory **herbs** to enhance her capacity for clairvoyancy. Such was the reputation of the Delphic oracle that foreign monarchs traveled huge distances to consult her. An eternal flame burned inside the *hestia*, or hearth, of the oracle.

Etymology can provide valuable clues about all sorts of things including sacred places. "Delphi" comes from the same root as the word for **womb**, and so it's likely that there was an earlier site there dedicated to the Earth Goddess, Gaia. The Delphic shrine to **Apollo** was believed to be where the powers of Heaven and Earth met. Apollo's temple increased in size and became more elaborate over the years and is still a sacred place of pilgrimage.

All that remains of the once-extensive complex are impressive ruins, although the temple was once full of statues, inscriptions, and valuable treasures that were brought in honor of the oracle. Many of these treasures were looted by Nero, and the temple was eventually closed down in AD 390 by Emperor Theodosius as being un-Christian.

Dogon Granary

For the Dogon people who live near Timbuktu in Mali, grain itself is such a precious and sacred substance that the granaries it's stored in are repositories for other valuables, too, and the building itself carries a host of symbolic meanings. Grain and other crops flourish despite the infertile and inhospitable climate.

Distinct structures with smooth, curved walls made from baked mud, the interior and exterior architecture of the household granary reflects the creation myths of the people. The indigenous faith of the Dogon is animistic; that is, they believe that every single object carries with it a spirit. The door and the lock of the granary itself tell the story of the Nommo, the Dogon ancestors that came from the **sky**. The carvings of these ancestor spirits protect the granary and its contents.

The granary itself is divided into **8** partitions, representing the eight internal organs of the body and the original eight seeds that, legend has it, the Nommo ancestors originally gave to the people. The granary itself represents the "belly of the world," an eternally fertile female figure.

The Dogon themselves have a long history of astronomical observations, and traditionally identified the moon of Sirius, called Sirius B, many thousands of years before there were telescopes powerful enough to detect it. Curiously, the Dogon describe the Universe as "infinite, but measurable."

Glastonbury Tor

The myths surrounding Glastonbury Tor are made even more mysterious because there are so few precise facts known about it. Not only do these myths populate the tor with Druids, Wiccans, **fairies**, and other spirits, but King

Arthur is also meant to be buried there, as well as the Celtic Gods of the Underworld. It seems that the possibilities of this magical place are as colorful, entrancing, and exotic as the imaginations of the pilgrims that go there.

What *is* known, however, is that this imposing conical hill (which is what *tor* means) forms an awe-inspiring silhouette against the **sky**. Viewed from above, the mound resembles a **vulva**, so has become a natural icon of feminine forces. The land surrounding the tor was once watery fenland, and so the tor itself would have been an island, a good, easily defended vantage point for the Celts who lived there. Adding to the myth, the area was referred to as Ynys yr Afalon, leading one to suppose that this must have been the Avalon of legend, the "Isle of **Apples**."

One of the more intriguing aspects of this hill is the **spiral** path that twists its way around from the bottom to the top of the tor. This path forms **7** terraces. There are several explanations for these terraces. Overlooking the mystique of the place for the moment, theories have suggested that they may have had an agricultural use for growing crops, that they were made by grazing animals, or that they were defensive ramparts.

However, the most obvious explanation—given the position and appearance of the tor, and that it was an obvious place of pilgrimage—is that spiral path served the same purpose as the steps or paths associated with other natural or man-made sacred places that also have seven levels of ascent. People still climb the spiral path of the tor, not only as a physical journey but also as a spiritual one. The seven levels correspond to the seven planets known to ancient man, and with whom the Deities were inextricably linked; it's for the same reason, for example, why the **Ziggurat** also has seven levels. In some parts of Wales, it's still the custom to walk to the top of the nearest high place around the time of the **Lughnasad** festival at the beginning of August.

The existing tower on the top of the tor serves as a bitter punctuation to this sacred landscape. Once there was a fifth-century fort in the same position; this was replaced by a medieval church, St. Michaels, which remained there until 1275 when it was destroyed by an earthquake (on September 11, the same day of the year that the Twin Towers were destroyed in New York). The church that was rebuilt some 80 years later lasted until the Dissolution of the Monasteries; after that tower was used as a place of execution, and the last Abbot of Glastonbury Abbey was hanged there. All that remains of the tower today is a haunting, roofless ruin.

GLASTONBURY ZODIAC

There are few places in the British Isles—or arguably, anywhere else in the World—that has the mystical charisma of Glastonbury. This is a place steeped in legend, reputedly the focus of the Arthurian tales, and believed by many to be a place where the seen and unseen worlds meet. John Dee, the renowned magician, seer, and astrologer to Queen Elizabeth I, was fascinated by the place, and he is reputed to have been the first person to propose that a representation of the celestial **Zodiac** occupies the sacred land in and around the town.

Several hundred years later, a woman called Katharine Maltwood elaborated on the idea. Born in 1878, Katharine was an artist and scholar, whose marriage to a wealthy advertising manager, John Maltwood, enabled her to devote her life to art, sculpture, and most of all to her overriding interest in antiquarian matters. In particular, she was intrigued by the story of the purported visit of Joseph of Arimathea to Glastonbury, and by the Arthurian tales. While living in Somerset she made the discovery that would make her famous among future generations of seekers after the esoteric and the marvelous.

In 1929, Katharine claimed that the outlines of the characters of the astrological **Zodiac** were traceable in various earthworks in a ten-mile radius around Glastonbury town, publishing these discoveries in her book, *The High History of the Holy Grail*. Using large-scale Ordnance Survey maps, the shape of **Leo** the **Lion** was the first that she noticed. Such was her fascination with the quest that in the 1930s she commissioned aerial photographs—at what must have been very great expense for that time—to be taken of the entire area. Her discoveries caused a sensation that was to be overshadowed by the outbreak of the Second World War.

Today the idea of the Glastonbury Zodiac is treated as fact by some, but others see it purely as a flight of fancy, the product of a vivid imagination and people's desire to associate an even greater meaning and mystery to a place that is already crammed full of the amazing and the fantastical.

GREEN MAN MAZE

There can be few finer examples of a magical symbol hidden in the landscape than the **Green Man** Maze at Penpont House near Brecon in Wales. Although the term "Green Man" was not coined until the late 1930s, the name perfectly epitomizes the notion of a spirit of nature, living in among the leaves from which he is made. The maze is hidden in a wild and magical part of the countryside, and what's even more surprising is that it was constructed as recently as 2000 as a celebration not only of the Millennium but also of the 40th birthday of the landowner, who, with his wife and family, also helped build the maze. That the Green Man can only be viewed in full from above—the viewpoint of the Gods—makes it even more intriguing.

The maze was designed by David Eveleigh, specifically in accordance with the principles of sacred geometry. He used dowsing methods to align the Green Man with the points on the horizon of the **Solstice Sun**; the design incorporates the ancient **Sun wheel** symbol, as well as a **pentagram** overlaid on an **Elven star** to give the proportions and structure that form the basis of the design. At the very center of the maze is the root of an upturned **tree**, a symbol that had significance not only for the Celts but is also mentioned in the *Upanishads*.

HINDU TEMPLES

Like all other holy buildings, the core of the Hindu temple is a **womb**-like inner sanctum, or *vimana*, that houses the effigy of the deity to whom the temple is dedicated. There's usually a space around this chamber to allow worshippers to circumnavigate the shrine—always in a clockwise direction—following the path of the **Sun**.

Directly above the *vimana* is the main tower, or *shikhara*. From the outside, this appears as a highly decorated and colorful stepped construction, representing the ascent to **Heaven**, a symbol of the holy mountain, *Mount Meru*. The series of steps are designed using the same motifs, sometimes portraying stories of the deities. These repetitive, graduated patterns represent the notion of **death** and rebirth, the **soul** gradually reaching the top of the tower and achieving ultimate union with the collective conscious, or Brahman.

Hindu temples are split into two categories; the Nagara of northern India, and the Dravida of the south. The main variation is that the Nagara tower is more dome-shaped in comparison with the pointed towers of the Dravidian style.

The most noticeable difference between most Western places of worship and the Hindu temple does not lie in the sacred intention of the building, but in the way people use them. A Hindu temple is liable to be a bustling, busy place at any time of the day or night, full of people milling about who have come to make *puja*, or worship. Puja offerings might include fragrant *malas*, or garlands of **flowers**, ghee, **rice**, **fruit**, and **incense**. All these things are purchased outside the doors, where there's a jumble of shoes belonging to worshippers. To be anything other than barefoot inside a temple is an act of profanity and disrespect.

The *gopura* or gateway tower marks the main entrance to the temple. Like the Shinto **Torii**, these gopura demarcate the transitional point between secular and sacred space.

HOGAN

This is the traditional dwelling of the Navajo people of the south-western US. Constructed of timber and earth, the hogan seeks to replicate the home that the **coyote** and **beaver** Gods made for the first man and woman.

These people did not operate with the Western demarcation between secular and sacred space, and the hogan itself is a replica of the cosmos, as straightforward an example of sacred architecture as we are likely to find.

The doorway of this circular, single-roomed house faces east, welcoming the morning **Sun** and receiving the blessings of its rays. This eastern entrance is also favored by certain tunnel-nesting **birds**, and by wild **bees**. The hogan has a central hearth. The southern half of the room represents the male element, while the north half belongs to the female. This male–female union is also symbolized in the physical construction of the hogan. The first stage in its building sees a forked, female log placed toward the north, with a straight male log pointing towards the south, resting in the cleft. These logs demonstrate a strong union between the husband and wife, and make an obvious fertility symbol, as well as providing a solid foundation for their home. A third forked log is placed towards the west, balancing the entrance. The rest of the building is constructed from stacked logs and other materials. **Gemstones** are secreted among the logs, and the whole might be covered in mud or earth against the elements.

Like any sacred building, the hogan is consecrated before use. This involves chanting from an ancient song called "The Blessingway" that describes the making of the original hogan. A clockwise pilgrimage around the building honors the path of the Sun.

MECCA

For Muslims, Mecca symbolizes the actual point on **Earth** where the **vertical axis** of Heaven (and space), and the **horizontal axis** of human existence (and time) intersect.

One of the most famous of all holy cities, a pilgrimage, or *hajj*, to Mecca at least once during their lifetime is an essential part of the spiritual life of any Muslim. This journey is so significant that it forms the fifth of the **five** symbolic Pillars of Wisdom, the foundations of the faith. The main focal point of this journey is the Great Mosque, which was built to surround the **Ka'aba** that stands in the center. This a large **cube**-shaped building, built by the prophet Abraham after his wife Hagar found water in the desert at the Well of Zamzam. This well, revealed by an **angel**, saved their son Ishmael from dying of thirst, and inspired Abraham to build the Ka'aba in the first place. Muslims hold that the Ka'aba mirrors a heavenly house, and that it sits on the site of the first house built by the first man, Adam. It is expressly forbidden for people of other faiths to enter Mecca; the first Western woman to do so was Lady Evelyn Cobbold, who wholeheartedly embraced the faith and performed the Hajj in 1933 when she was 66. The explorer and scholar Sir Richard Burton had entered the Ka'aba itself in the nineteenth century; aware that the penalty of his discovery would be death, he resorted to subterfuge, disguising himself as a Sufi to gain access.

The origins of the word *Ka'aba* are the same as for "cube," and the dimensions of this granite building are imposing; it is nearly 14 meters high, with sides of 11 meters and nearly 13 meters. The **four** corners of the

Ka'aba point roughly to the four points of the compass, and the building is the focal point for prayer. Wherever they may be in the world, the devout pray towards the Ka'aba, and have special compasses to help align themselves correctly. In the eastern corner of the building is the sacred "**black stone**," generally accepted to be the remnant of a **meteorite** and possibly the original reason for the sanctity of the place. Prior to the coming of Mohammed, this stone was the focal point for worship of the Goddess, Al'Lut. The Goddess had **7** Priestesses, and pilgrims circled the holy stone—which resembled the vulva—seven times in honor of the seven known **planets** of the Ancient world.

The Ka'aba is entirely covered in a **black** silk cloth, which features a band of **gold** embroidery illuminating texts from the Qu'ran. The **doorway** into the building is two meters above the marble base, and is accessed by a wooden staircase on wheels. Cleaners are permitted into the building twice a year, when it is swept with simple brooms, washed with water from the ever-flowing Zamzam, and then sprinkled with rosewater. Few have entered the Ka'aba, but inside there's a marble floor, gilded **silver** panels and more texts from the Qu'ran.

Aspects of the Ka'aba and the Grand Mosque in Mecca are designed so that pilgrims can re-enact some of the key scenes in the story of Hagar. For example, an elevated walkway at the top of the tiered building is where the faithful run back and forth seven times to symbolize her desperate attempts to find water. Pilgrims also travel to the small town of Mina, where they throw stones at **three** pillars representing Satan.

MEDICINE WHEELS

We examine the use of the medicine wheel as a graphic device that is a **mandala**-like focus for meditation in Section One. The original medicine wheel, however, is constructed as a living part of the landscape although, like the **stone circles** that are in many ways their larger European counterpart, the reasons lying behind their design and construction remain something of a mystery.

The largest of these stone wheels, sometimes called the American **Stonehenge**, is the Bighorn Medicine Wheel at Medicine Mountain. Situated at an elevation of 9640 feet, it's an impressive sight, and the plain it lies on is a sacred place in its own right; for hundreds of years ceremonies marking rites of passage were held there by diverse peoples, including the Cheyenne, Arapaho, and Shoshone.

Made from half-buried rocks laid out in the shape of a giant wagon wheel, it has 28 spokes emanating from a hollow-centered central cairn that is about three feet tall. Each spoke is 36 feet long, and the whole is 245 feet in circumference. Surrounding this central wheel are six smaller cairns, each with an open side, giving it a C-shaped appearance from above. Like Stonehenge, certain points on the wheel align to the **Sun**, the **Moon** and the planets; specifically, the central cairn and another one on the outside of the rim perform exactly the same function as the heel stone of Stonehenge on the day of the summer **solstice**. It is likely that each of the 28 spokes represents the days of the lunar cycle. Other lines in the medicine wheel describe earthly demarcations for celestial bodies, including Sirius, Rigel (a star within the Orion constellation), and Aldebaran. The age of the Bighorn Medicine

Wheel is indeterminate. The wheel shares the meaning of the **circle** as a symbol of eternity with no beginning or end, showing the endlessness of the passing of **time**.

Menhir

A large, upright standing stone, our ancestors obviously spent a great deal of time and effort to find and quarry the stones, shape their tapered tops, drag them into position, and make them stand upright. But why? Unless they are part of a group of stones, such as a stone circle, there is no consensus of opinion as to what menhirs actually signified.

The word *menhir* comes from two Breton words, meaning "long stone." They are most often seen in Western Europe but appear as far afield as Asia and Africa, too. Theories about their function—or symbolic meaning—include, in no particular order:

1. Territorial markers
2. Part of a calendrical system
3. Sites of sacrifice

Until recently, we were not even absolutely sure as to their age. It was believed that they belonged to the Bronze Age (*c.*3000 BC) but recent evidence suggests that they may be much older.

Any tall, narrow object can serve the function of marking time by means of the **shadow**, popularly represented as the gnomon that stands firmly in the center of the sundial. It's possible that the menhir may have served this function as well as being a symbol of fertility; there's an obvious phallic nature to these mighty stones.

As with many ancient artefacts, the early Christians had a deep-rooted suspicion of menhirs, and many of them were toppled. Others were explained away as being put there by demonic forces; the Rudston monolith in Yorkshire is one such example. Standing at 26 feet high, the stone weighs at least 80 tons and is believed to be as deep as it is high. The stone stands right next to the tiny village church and local legend says that the Devil threw the stone at the church but narrowly missed it because of his poor marksmanship; a conflicting tale says that God threw it, punishing some people who were desecrating the churchyard.

Rudston itself means "cross stone" (*rud stan*), and the stone was apparently "Christianized" at one point with the addition of a **Cross** perched on its top.

Nazca Lines

The Pampa Colarada desert near Nazca, high up on a plateau between the Andes and the Pacific Ocean, is one of the driest places in the world. Scattered over a vast area of 200 square miles are more than a hundred massive **animal** shapes. These shapes are so huge that they are fully visible only by the Gods, or via a means of transport that the people who created them two thousand years ago could never have dreamed of: a helicopter or airplane.

It has rarely rained in the Nazca valley during the last 10,000 years, and the shapes that were created by arduously scraping away the topsoil—in much the same way that the similar shapes were made in Britain and elsewhere—are protected from vehicles or footprints. Some of the lines are more than five miles long, requiring an amazing feat of concentration by their constructors to get the form right without ever being able to see the final result. Their work was also carried out achieved in dusty, arid conditions. The shapes include geometric patterns, as well as human figures, a **serpent**, **flowers**, a **lizard**, a **spider**, and several varieties of **bird**, including the great warrior God **Huitzilopochtli** in the form of a **hummingbird**.

No one knows specifically why these drawings were made. Theories include their use as some sort of calendrical system, or even as landmarks for visiting UFOs. Arguably, the most logical suggestion is that the shapes were made to communicate with the Gods, to please them as they looked down to Earth.

NEWGRANGE

Situated in the north east of Ireland, Newgrange is a huge construction dating back at least 5,000 years. As a sacred space, it emulates the idea of the **cave** as a secret place of ritual, the **womb** of the **Earth**, a place of death and rebirth.

From the outside, Newgrange is an imposing sight. It comprises a mound of earth surrounded by a stone wall, encircled by numerous standing stones and almost a hundred roughly worked stones laid end to end. The edifice is 11 meters high and almost ninety meters across. Mounds like this were later thought to be the homes of the numinous beings that inhabited the place: earth spirits, **fairies**, and creatures from the Otherworld.

In front of the entrance to Newgrange is a large stone, beautifully engraved with **spiral** motifs. These shapes would have been chipped into the stone with **flint** tools, and the precision achieved is remarkable. The spiral symbol is associated with the passage of time and the cycle of the **soul** through death to rebirth, often depicted as a **labyrinth**. There is nothing labyrinthine, however, about the innermost part of Newgrange. A long, narrow passageway ends in the main room, a vaulted space with three flat-roofed chambers. Seen as though in an X-Ray from above, the passageway and the three chambers form a **cross** shape. The main "hall" has a roof that's been constructed artfully by stacking stepped stones so that it resembles the basic shape of a **bee** skep.

One of Newgrange's secrets was discovered as recently as 1972. In the roof over the entranceway is a hole that allows a shaft of light to fall onto the triple spiral pattern more than eighteen meters away inside the chamber. This happens just once a year, at the winter **solstice**. Other megalithic monuments are believed to have an astronomical connection, but this feature of the roof at Newgrange plainly proves the point.

Archaeologists have found bone fragments contemporary to the era in which Newgrange was built, suggesting that it was also a burial chamber. The use of the spiral motif and the way the chamber lights up all indicate that the architects of Newgrange connected the cycle of time and the passage of the **Sun** with the journey of the soul.

OBELISK

An obelisk is a tall, tapering, needle-like pillar, with a **square** base and a **pyramid** on top. The name comes from a Greek word, *obeliscos*, meaning pointed pillar. We tend to associate these structures with Ancient Egypt, but they also existed in Rome, Assyria, and Ethiopia.

The conventions surrounding the building of obelisks demanded that they should be eight to ten times as tall as they were wide at the base; for example, the obelisk called "Cleopatra's Needle" on the bank of the River Thames in London is 92 feet long and 15 feet in diameter.

Obelisks symbolize the rays of the **Sun**, which get broader as they reach **Earth**, hence the tapering shape of the structure. The sides are generally engraved with inscriptions to the Sun God Ra, to whom they were dedicated. In Ancient Egypt, the obelisk attained cult status as a symbol of this God, and were generally set in pairs, one slightly larger than the other.

The obelisk is a phallic symbol, emblematic of the Earth God Geb, as he reached up to the **sky** Goddess Nut. It is also a symbol of the **World Tree** or **Axis Mundi**. There are thirty or so obelisks standing around the world, with the greatest concentration being in Rome, which boasts eight Egyptian and five Ancient Roman obelisks. These previously pagan symbols were exorcized and crowned with a **Cross** in order to make them acceptable to Roman Catholic sensibilities.

The Egyptian Government gave obelisks to Great Britain, France, and America. Transporting these giant stone pillars caused something of a headache.

PAGODA

The pagoda has its origins in another piece of sacred architecture, the **stupa**, and like the stupa, the pagoda also came from India, spreading throughout the world as Buddhism gained influence.

Originally intended to house saintly relics or religious texts, the pagoda is rich in symbolic meaning, although the actual elements of their construction vary. A particular feature of pagodas in China is their "underground palace." In China an underground burial system is the norm—as opposed to in India, where over-ground methods are employed—and since the pagoda's main purpose was as a reliquary, the underground palace encompassed the Chinese method of burial within an Indian Buddhist structure.

This underground palace has the exotic name of the "**dragon** cave" or "dragon palace." The space is circular or hexagonal in shape, and although it may contain many rare treasures, the most important item is a stone container, highly decorated with precious **jewels** and **gold**, that contains relics of the

Buddha or other saints. The entire "cave" is highly decorated with friezes and statues, and, because daylight cannot penetrate, the painted decorations stay bright and vibrant-looking.

On top of the underground chamber is the base of the pagoda's distinctive storied tower. Early pagodas had low, plain bases; later example, their designers wanting them to look grander, have much larger bases, and some have a decorative pedestal on top of the base. The base and the pedestal are square, reflecting the element of earth and the four directions, as well as providing a physically solid foundation for the pagoda. Pagodas are built in many different materials: stone, wood, brick, even **metal**.

As for the actual tower that comprises the most identifiable part of the pagoda, this can be either hollow or solid. The shape of it may vary too; the symbolism of the tower is the most important aspect. The tower represents the **Axis Mundi**, the conceptual pole that connects the **Heavens** to the **Earth**. It also symbolizes man's desire for elevation and enlightenment. The tower has several storeys, each capped with a roof whose edges flick upwards to repel evil spirits.

At the very top of the pagoda is the steeple. A vital part of the building, this represents the "country of the Buddha" and so also represents whichever country the pagoda happens to be in. Like the stupa, this steeple often bears the symbols of the **Sun** and the **Moon**, and is surmounted with a shape resembling either a **flame** or a **lotus** bud, both being symbols of enlightenment.

The obvious hazard of such a tall building with metalwork on the roof is, of course, **lightning** strikes. Pagodas are an open target and many of the Japanese wooden pagodas were razed to the ground. This element of danger, however, only serves to charge the building with even more heavenly energy and power.

PANTHEON

The Pantheon, tucked away in relative obscurity between other buildings in modern Rome, is possibly one of the most remarkable achievements of Western civilization in terms both of **sacred geometry** and architecture. It is an especially awe-inspiring piece of design when we consider that it was built almost two thousand years ago.

Literally meaning the "temple to All Gods" in Ancient Greek, the Pantheon was conceived around AD 50, at a time when the old **deities** had not been usurped by Christianity. It was intended as part of Augustus Caesar's plan to rebuild the city in his own image and was erected in honor of the Gods and Goddesses that had assisted in his rise to power. The temple was not completed, however, until the following century by the

Emperor Hadrian.

The features of the Pantheon which give clues to its having been constructed following the principles of sacred geometry are the **rectangular** porch with a **triangular** pediment sitting squarely on top, the **circular** shape of the main temple area, the domed roof representing the Vault of Heaven, the proportions of the building, and the symbols inlaid into the floor. These are among the basic units of measurement that **Pythagoras** calculated as being part of the harmony of the cosmos and, as such, were believed to have been devised by the Creator. This celestial harmony is reflected in the Pantheon. The measurements of the building are also calculated according to Pythagoras' rules of sacred geometry. The main temple is 44 meters in diameter and 44 meters from floor to ceiling.

The dome of the Pantheon is a particularly magnificent piece of engineering. The internal volume of the main temple is 1520 square meters and has no reinforcing support. It was only 1500 years later that the size of its dome was exceeded, marginally, by that of the Church of Santa Maria del Fiore in Florence. Because it is a symbol of the Vault of Heaven, the dome was a particularly popular piece of design for sacred buildings, and cities vied with one another in a sort of architectural one-upmanship to find new ways of building bigger and better ones.

The dome of the Pantheon is open to the skies, and this opening is called the *oculus*, or "great eye," symbolic of the **Sun**, and is nine meters wide. The ceiling has graduated ribs that are not only a structural feature designed to lighten the load, but also represent the major planetary Gods of Rome: **Mars**, **Venus**,

Mercury, **Jupiter**, and **Saturn**.

The Pantheon was built using heavy materials for the foundation and base, and uses gradually lighter types of stone as the building gets higher. The floor of the building contains marble from all over the Roman Empire and is comprised of a particular kind of mosaic called *opus sectile*, which uses large slices of stone. This elaborate mosaic forms a **squared circle**, yet another feature of sacred geometry, and a magical symbol in itself.

Part of the design of the Pantheon—in its original conception as a temple to honor all Gods—was the installation of apses, or niches, which contained the shrines of these deities. However, with the coming of Christianity the Pantheon was adapted to the new faith, the shrines were removed, and the building was renamed the Church of Santa Maria Rotunda. These apses now contain the tombs of Italian kings, as well as that of the Renaissance artist Raphael.

PYRAMID

At its most basic, the upward-pointing **triangle** represents the **fire** that is the meaning of the word "pyramid" in Greek. The pyramid itself is an incredibly strong construction, both symbolically and practically, with the solid base of the **square** supporting the **four** triangles that meet at the peak or axis of the pyramid. The shape is as impregnable and daunting as it looks.

The Pyramids themselves have become a symbol of Egypt, and together with the **Sphinx**, capture the essence of that country more completely than any modern advertising logo could ever do.

There have been countless books written about the Pyramids and the symbolism of the shape is not to be confused with any claims of "pyramidology." Essentially, the pyramid represents the axis **mountain** of the world. This mountain is said to have risen from the waters of creation and represents existence itself. Furthermore, the **cavern**-like aspect of the Pyramids, in which the bodies of the Pharaohs were interred with elaborate rites, represents the natural **cave** to which early man was attracted, not only as a **womb**-like place of refuge but also as a place where religious rites could take place in secrecy. The sloped shape of the exterior of the Pyramids is echoed in their internal passages, which also slope steeply; these angles help the **souls** of the interred Pharaohs ascend to Heaven.

We still have a primal belief that the closer man is to the **sky**, the nearer he is to **Heaven** and to the Creator. The shape of a pyramid provides a way for man to achieve this goal. Stepped pyramids culminate in a flat platform where the world of spirit meets the world of matter, the construction acting as a reminder of the convergence of the material and the ethereal. The Ancient Egyptians further demonstrated this idea by another symbol, an inverted pyramid balanced on top of an upright one, also known as the "creation sign"; the upper symbol represents inspiration pouring down from the Heavens (the **chalice**-shape as a sign for water is an obvious clue), whereas the base pyramid shows aspiration, a striving for the perfection of Heaven. This symbol itself represents the same concept as the **Star of David**: "as above, so below."

ROSSLYN CHAPEL

This small chapel, also called the Collegiate College of St. Matthew, is set in the sleepy rural hamlet of Roslin some **seven** miles south of Edinburgh. It is the subject of intense scrutiny, attracting worldwide curiosity as a result of Dan Brown's blockbusting novel and the ensuing film of *The Da Vinci Code*. In the book, Brown posits that the **Holy Grail** itself was hidden in the chapel, and that the bloodline of a child born to Christ and Mary Magdalene can be traced directly back to the building.

The crazed excitement and conspiracy theories surrounding Rosslyn mean that fact has become increasingly hard to separate from fiction. Unsubstantiated rumors of the esoteric articles secreted in the chapel include the **Ark of the Covenant**, the original **Stone of Destiny**, and even the **Holy Grail** itself. The mystical charisma of Rosslyn is so powerful, however, that it needs no media frenzy to exacerbate its importance.

The chapel was commissioned by Sir William Sinclair (or St. Clair) in 1446. It seems as though the chapel was the start of a much larger Catholic church, and, like other grand ecclesiastical buildings, was seen as a way for Sir William to accumulate future credits in Heaven to atone for his transgressions on **Earth**. It is also rumored that Sinclair's interest in arcana was because he was none other than Christian Rosenkreuz, founder of the Rosicrucian Order.

This small chapel is smothered in elaborate and accomplished stone carvings. These include **angels** and **demons**, **roses**, **stars**, **elephants**, **pyramids**, **serpents**, plants that were not available in Britain at the time the chapel was built, and many depictions of the **Green Man**. There are other carvings that retain their secrets despite centuries of investigation and conjecture, along with dozens of **Masons'** marks as testimony to the anonymous craftsmen that worked on the building.

The 213 stone cubes that seem to represent Chladni Patterns—the shapes made when fine powder laid on a taut surface is subjected to certain frequencies—is explained in Section 8. Among the other features of the chapel, the "Apprentice Pillar" is particularly notable. While the Master Mason was abroad, investigating designs for the pillar, the legend goes that his apprentice dreamed that he himself had carved it. His vision was of such power that he set to work. Upon his return, the Master Mason was so jealous of the ornate pillar that he killed the hapless apprentice with a blow to the **head**; both characters, and the grieving mother of the apprentice, have been immortalized in stone. This myth seems to have originated in the eighteenth century, and bears some resemblance to the story of **Hiram Abiff** that lies at the heart of **Freemasonry**.

At the base of the pillar are eight **dragons**, from whose **mouths** emerge **vine** tendrils that **spiral** up the pillar. This is said to be a representation of the **World Tree**. At the top of the pillar is a Latin inscription that translates as:

"**Wine** is strong, a king is stronger, women are stronger still, but truth conquers all."

There is a plethora of **Green Man** carvings in the chapel—110 in all—peering out stonily from all directions. The Green Man is an ancient idea of a spirit of nature, found in a similar form all over the world. It is an unusually pagan image to appear so prominently in a Christian place of worship. These carvings appear youthful when they appear in the eastern side of the chapel, gradually ageing as they move west with the course of the **Sun** and the passage of time.

Despite generations of research, it seems that the mysteries of Rosslyn will remain unsolved. Perhaps the biggest conundrum is the juxtaposition of so many seemingly pagan images in the context of a Christian place of worship; perhaps the designers of Rosslyn were wise enough to realize that integration is the surest path to wisdom and understanding. Today, however, the trustees of Rosslyn have a less esoteric problem to solve—how to cater for the recent and dramatic increase in visitors, from 30,000 a year in 2000 to 120,000 in 2006. All these people, crammed into what has been described as a "stone storybook," in a room measuring just 69 by 35 feet.

SERPENT MOUND

Some natural features of the landscape represent mythological creatures or suggest the shapes of **animals** or **birds**; others are manmade, and the efforts taken to construct such monuments are a reminder to us of just how important certain images were to the people who designed them

One of these manmade structures is the **Serpent** Mound in the north-eastern US. (The symbolism of the serpent is examined elsewhere in this book.) The mound was built some 2000 years ago by Native Americans, either the Hopewell or Adena people. The

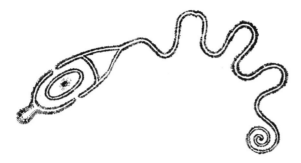

earthwork is built of **yellow** clay and stones, and takes the form of a 382-meter-long snake, its tail end curled into a **spiral**, and with what appears to be an **egg** in its mouth.

Although it's impossible to say precisely why the mound was constructed, the primal importance of the serpent as a magical symbol is well documented. It was one of the most important animal symbols not only for Native Americans but for the Celts, Hindus, Assyrians, and others. It has been argued that this serpent represented a particular deity; because the serpent was a symbol of the powers of the **Earth** it would make sense to construct it in such a way that the deities up in the **Heavens** would be able to see it. The creature lies at the edge of a promontory and burnt stones in the center of the "egg" suggest that **fires** were once lit there. This fire would have been visible for miles around and possibly signified that the snake—the numen of the place—was "awake" and protecting her people. The egg is a symbol of fertility and rebirth, and the spiral at the other end of the tail suggests the coiled power of the energy of the Earth.

St. Peter's Basilica

The largest building of religious significance in the world—it can accommodate 60,000 people—and effectively the "mother church" of the Roman Catholic faith, St. Peter's Basilica in the Vatican City, Rome, was built in the honor of the One God. It is, however, a reminder of symbolism's overarching universality that the Basilica shares several features with a pre-Christian building in the same city that was built in honor of many Gods and Goddesses, the **Pantheon**.

St. Peter's Basilica is reputed to have been built on the site of St. Peter's grave after he was martyred (his crucifixion being carried out, on his own request, on an **inverted cross**). Excavations in the 1930s did reveal a small shrine located directly underneath the main altar. Whatever the truth, the building is associated with the spirit of St. Peter. It's a characteristic of sacred places that they have a numen, or presiding deity or spirit, whatever form that entity might take.

The basilica's shared use of universal architectural symbolism can also be seen when it is viewed from above. Whatever the aims of the various architects, there are remarkable similarities with other sacred buildings belonging to faiths other than Roman Catholicism. The **circle** of the Dome sits within the confines of the **square** structure below, symbolizing the union of spirit and matter.

Inside the Basilica, too, are symbolic reminders of the sacredness of the place; great works of art and statues honoring the worthies of the Catholic Church, such as Queen Christina of Sweden who sacrificed her throne in order to convert to Catholicism.

There is also a statue of St. Peter, his stone foot deeply eroded by the **kisses** of millions of pilgrims over the centuries. Whereas in the Pantheon the niches that once contained the statues of the deities now house the tombs of Italian kings, in the basilica there are 39 such niches containing the statues of some of the Saints.

St. Peter's Basilica is replete with works of rich symbolic meaning; for example, a piece by Bernini in honor of Pope Alexander VII shows a **winged skeleton**, lifting a fold of **red** marble drapery. He holds an **hourglass,** a reminder that time is short and **death** inevitable. The praying Pope is flanked by four statues, representing Justice, Prudence, Charity, and Truth. The latter also symbolizes religion, and in a visual pun, she is shown standing on a globe, with England directly underfoot. The thorn that pierces the **foot** of Truth symbolizes the trouble that the English gave the Roman Catholic Church.

Stone circles

Why would our ancestors want to quarry gargantuan pieces of rock, at a time when the only tools available would have been stone, **fire** and **water**, and then somehow drag these colossally heavy and cumbersome slabs several hundred miles to erect them as part of a stone circle?

Although the use and intention of stone circles remains obscure despite centuries of conjecture, their sheer scale and the difficulties of construction suggest that these mysterious structures were among man's earliest attempts to please their Gods. Standing stones and circles remain the subject of much speculation. Some believe that they were sacrificial sites of Druidic worship. Other suggestions include their use as burial places, temples, meeting places, or sites of Goddess worship. The early Christian Church damaged many circles—as recently as 1560, a **twelve**-stone circle on the sacred island of Iona was demolished. When structures are so ancient that their original use has long been forgotten, it's inevitable that myths spring up to explain their provenance. The Merry Maidens circle in Cornwall, for instance, is said to be young girls turned to stone as punishment for dancing on the Sabbath.

Whatever their original use, it seems certain that many of these circles, scattered across north-western Europe, act as a calendrical system. Their stones are aligned carefully to mark specific astronomical events, the phases of the **Moon** and the position of the **Sun** at the moment of the **solstices**.

Stonehenge

The most impressive single **stone circle** of all is arguably Stonehenge in Wiltshire, England. The scale of Stonehenge is vast; when it first comes into view its impact, set against the gently rolling backdrop of Salisbury Plain, is breathtaking. Constructed between 3000 and 2100 BC, the standing stones of this megalithic monument were quarried from the bluestone that is found only in the Preseli mountains in Wales, some 385 kilometers away.

Stonehenge is an evocative place and remains a primary focus for neo-pagan groups, especially at the time of the summer **solstice** when the "heel" stone of the circle aligns with the rising **Sun** cresting over the horizon. Pagan worship at Stonehenge resumed again after hundreds of years in 1905, performed by the Ancient Order of Druids that was founded in the nineteenth century. For years the site of peaceful pagan worship and a month-long rock festival, in 1985 the infamous incident known as the "Battle of the Beanfield" occurred. New Age travelers converging on the site at the time of the solstice for the free festival were prevented from doing so by the police, some of whom were dressed in riot gear. The incident resulted in smashed cars and caravans, and a great deal of violence towards the travelers.

Access to Stonehenge, especially at the time of the solstice, is now carefully controlled. The stones, however, stand as a powerful symbol of the freedom to choose not only one's Gods, but also the way in which they are to be worshipped.

STUPA

If there's an archetypal example of sacred architecture in Buddhism, then the stupa—or chorten—is it. These beautifully elaborate constructions are as encrusted with as many symbolic meanings as they are studded with **jewels**, and the perfection of their shape and form is said to represent the very mind of the Buddha himself.

Originally, the stupa, which in Sanskrit means "heap," was just that; a simple earth mound that covered the relics of the Buddha, whose cremated ashes were divided into **eight** parts. The urn and embers made up the number of the original **ten** stupas. The

Emperor Ashoka subsequently opened up these original stupas, redistributing their contents among the thousands of others that he had built on his conversion to Buddhism in the third century BC. As the buildings themselves grew more elaborate and the symbolism gained in complexity, they became far removed from their origins as mounds of earth, becoming symbols of the veneration of the Buddha rather than simple funerary monuments.

Nothing is left to chance in the construction of a stupa, with every single element and aspect being carefully planned. Although it's not possible for every stupa to contain the actual relics of the Buddha, there is generally soil from the eight places where his ashes were buried, as well as relics of other Buddhist saints, religious texts, and statues of the Buddha and other deities.

Here are some of the elements of the Stupa, with their symbolic significance explained in depth. First, the base of the stupa; this is always **square**, and aligned to the **four** cardinal directions. Its solid base represents the **earth** element and also the four corners of the Earth. The four gates at the base are often protected by deities. **13** steps lead to the spire that rests on the top of the dome. The first **10** steps symbolize the ten steps to enlightenment, and the final **3** stand for the three levels of super-consciousness.

The next essential element of the stupa is the hemispherical dome that sits on top of the square. This represents the **World Egg**, as well as the Vault of the **Heavens**. It also looks like the rising **Sun** or a pregnant belly; indeed, it's referred to as the "**womb**," a female symbol to balance the male form of the square. Not only is the dome a womb; it's also a tomb, so the hemisphere is a reminder of the cycle of **death** and rebirth.

On top of the dome is the conical spire. This spire represents the **Axis Mundi** as the element of **fire**—the upright **triangle** at the pinnacle provides this clue. As flames reach for the sky, so the spire represents energy rising upward. The parasols along the length of the spire are symbols of protection, but their number, which varies, also has significance. The parasol is also one of the **Ashtamangala**, or Eight Auspicious Objects of Buddhism. Next is the symbol of the crescent **Moon**, symbolic of the element of **air**. The crescent Moon is an ancient feminine symbol, since the menstrual cycle is marked by the phases of its waxing and waning. Then there's the **circle**, symbol of wholeness, completion, without end or beginning. The circle in this instance signifies **space**, and also the **Sun**. Together, the symbols of the Sun and the Moon represent Absolute Truth and Relative Truth.

At the very summit of the stupa is a jewel-like shape. This carries the same symbolism—the flame of enlightenment—as the flame that is sometimes seen coming from the top of the head of the Buddha. It also equates to the Sahasrara **chakra** of pure bliss.

In its entirety the stupa represents the physical form of the Buddha. The base is his **legs**, the dome his torso. At the place where his **eyes** would be is a second **cube**-shaped structure, or *harmika*, which is placed between the dome and the spire, and which is sometimes decorated with the **wisdom eyes of Buddha** symbol. Inside the stupa, the relics of the Buddha, which are placed inside the "womb" of the dome, symbolize the germ of new life.

Pilgrims walk around the stupa in a clockwise direction. This represents the path of the Sun and effectively "winds up" the energy of the construction, which **spirals** upwards to the Heavens in the same direction as the Sun. Both its interior and exterior are highly decorated, often with precious minerals and metals. Finally, when viewed from above, the stupa appears as a **mandala**.

Although they have their origins in the East, there are now stupas in many other countries of the world. Although there are stupas small enough to sit on a tabletop, the largest one in the world is the Phra Pathom Chedi in Thailand, in the town of Nakhon Pathom, which is 127 meters high.

SYNAGOGUE

The word "synagogue" means "assembly," and its décor adapts to the circumstances and surroundings of the country and environment in which it is situated.

Prior to the synagogue, hereditary priests, known as *kohens*, officiated in the rites, and the worshippers stayed outside the main body of the **temple**, making their burnt offerings to God. The rabbis who subsequently officiated at the synagogues were part of a democratic movement; a marked difference between the temple and the synagogue is that, whereas God was believed to reside in the temple, the synagogue is an unconsecrated building. The emphasis of the synagogue is on education, and the study of the Talmud (the Jewish laws and legends) is given priority. Despite this secular angle, however, the synagogue retains its status as a sacred building.

The main focal point in any synagogue is the **ark**, a box which contains the scrolls of the Torah, the first **five** books of the Bible that God gave to Moses. Although the ark may be highly decorated, it is distinctly not an object of veneration, and is only important inasmuch as it contains the Word of God. The ark is set into a wall that faces the direction of the original Temple in Jerusalem. This symbolizes the fact that although the physical Temple no longer exists, the idea of it remains close, a reminder of the sense of exile. Prayers are often directed towards the coming of the Messiah, which is believed to coincide with the rebuilding of the Temple for the third time.

God is not portrayed figuratively anywhere in the synagogue, a feature shared by Islamic places of worship. Unlike Christian churches, which have highly decorated windows and paintings depicting scenes from the Gospels, the designs and patterns in the synagogue are more abstract and indeterminate.

TEMPLE MOUNT

One of the holiest cities in the world, Jerusalem is a place of pilgrimage to Jews, Muslims, and Christians, as well as tourists from all faiths and nationalities. For Jews, it is the most holy site; for Muslims, it ranks as their third most holy place after **Mecca** and Medina. Because the Church of the Holy Sepulchre is built on the spot where Christ is said to have been buried, Jerusalem is the holiest place for Christians, as can be seen from the series of Crusades that took place in the Middle Ages in an attempt to secure it for Christendom. All these sometimes conflict-ing faiths are in close proximity to one another, with the result that this holiest of cities has also been the site of some particularly unholy conflict.

King David made Jerusalem the capital city of Israel in around 1000 BC. His son, Solomon—reputedly one of the wisest men in the world—was instrumental in the building of the famous Temple that was to provide a permanent home for the **Ark of the Covenant**, as well as providing a focus for worship. This Temple was to prove highly influential for centuries to come, inspiring many features of Masonic temples.

The room in which the Ark was kept was called the "Holy of Holies," a sacred place or *Adyton* which could be entered only by the High Priest on one single day of the year, Yom Kippur. Many treasures were taken from the Temple, however, when Nebuchadnezzar II deported the Jews before destroying the building in the sixth century BC. Cyrus II of Persia liberated the people in 538 BC, and the Temple was rebuilt, albeit in a more modest form than previously. King Herod decided to restore the Temple to its full glory during the first century AD, although the Romans destroyed it not long afterwards. It is said that the construction of the third temple will coincide with the coming of the Messiah.

The name "Temple Mount" was given because the site of the original Temple was believed to be on Mount Moriah, where Abraham had been prepared to sacrifice his son Isaac. In the Talmud it is stated that the world itself was created from the Foundation Stone on the Temple Mount.

Although the Temple is no longer there, the whole site is full of places with sacred significance.

The Western Wall

The Western Wall is all that remains of the First Temple in Jerusalem, and it is this area that is also called the "Wailing Wall." Jewish people come here to lament the loss of the Temple, and also to pray; little slips of paper carrying prayers can be seen stuffed into every available nook and cranny of the wall.

The Court of the Priests

In common with sacred symbolism the world over, the very center of the Court of the Priests contained an **altar**; this represented the world mountain or the mountain of the gods, and therefore the **Axis Mundi**.

The Dome of the Rock

In Islam, the Jewish Dome of the Rock is called the "Noble Sanctuary." In the center of this building—whose golden-domed roof is the main focal point of the city—is the Foundation Stone of the World, said to be the place where Heaven and Earth meet. This is believed to be the same stone on which Abraham attempted to sacrifice his son, and where Mohammed ascended to Heaven on his magical **horse**, Buraq, to receive the Islamic prayers from God. The **Ark of the Covenant** had been placed upon this rock during the time of the First Temple, and the rock was used for **blood** sacrifices during Yom Kippur during the time of the Second Temple. Because the rock was in the Holy of Holies, only the High Priest was allowed access to it.

The Well of the Souls

Directly beneath the Foundation Stone is the Well of the Souls, a small natural **cave** whose southern walls are strengthened to support steps. This is the place where Mohammed is said to have ascended to Heaven, and it's reputed that the Last Judgement will take place here. Again, we see the symbolism of the cave as the **womb** of the **Earth**, and as a place not only of death but of rebirth.

TRULLI

Trulli are fairytale-like little houses found in southern Italy, particularly in the town of Alberobello in Puglia. These tiny dwelling places are made of **white** stone with a distinctive conical roof, and were originally built to avoid the punitive taxes that were applied to permanent dwellings; because Trulli were dry stone buildings, they could be collapsed hastily if necessary.

The symbols displayed on their conical roofs are the most interesting aspect of the Trulli. These symbols include **alchemical** signs, magical symbols, symbols to deter the **evil eye**, and symbols of the **planets** and Gods. At the top of each pointed roof is another symbol, called the *pinnacoli*, or pinnacle. This feature is probably a throwback to the ancient worship of the **Sun** God, and the fact that most Trulli face east would corroborate this idea. The symbols on each Trulli are the personal expression of the owners and are a wonderful example of the expression of spirituality within a domestic environment.

Yurts and tipis

As the simplest magical symbols often encapsulate the most concentrated meanings, so our most basic dwelling places can often say just as much as the largest or most imposing **cathedrals** or **temples**.

The yurt is the portable dwelling belonging originally to the nomad peoples of Central Asia, although the popularity of the structure has extended way beyond this area. The yurt is circular, its walls built from a trelliswork of sticks that concertina together so that they can be transported. Traditionally, the "walls" are made from felt or other fabrics. The dome-shaped roof, or *shangrak*, is also made from wooden lattice and although the rest of the yurt will be replaced over the years, the *shangrak* is something of an heirloom, passed down from generation to generation.

The roof has a central hole that enables **smoke** to escape from the centrally positioned hearth. The smoke from the **fire**, ascending through this hole, is symbolic of the **Axis Mundi**. The smoke carries the prayers and wishes of the yurt-dwellers—as well as offerings of food—directly to the Gods.

The **tipi** is a similarly portable, circular construction that imitated the greater cosmos, although the ground space is more **egg**-shaped than circular. *3* poles, tied together, make a tripod; these three foundation posts represents man, woman, and the Great Spirit. Next, a number of poles are woven together and supported by the junction of the foundation poles. The number of poles depends on the circumference of the tipi. Finally, the whole is covered with a semicircular piece of cloth, made in such a way that smoke flaps can be positioned, using two separate poles, according to the direction of the wind to allow smoke to escape from the central hearth. This central pillar of smoke has the same symbolic meaning as that of the yurt.

Ziggurat

Ziggurats are **pyramid**-like models of the cosmos that originated in the late third to first century BC in Mesopotamia.

Strict attention was needed to ensure that the **four** corners of the ziggurat were exactly aligned to the cardinal directions. A main staircase ran from the base to a small shrine at the summit of the structure. As with any tall building, the aim was to replicate the idea of the holy mountain; indeed, the word *ziggurat* has the same root as the Babylonian word for "mountain peak." There was a ziggurat at Larsa, now in modern-day Iraq, whose name translated as "The House of the Link between Heaven and Earth." Numerous creation myths tell of a primeval mound that existed before the separation of the **Earth** and the **sky**, and it's likely that the designers of ziggurats and similar constructions, like the Pyramids, wanted to replicate this.

Ziggurats generally had three, five, or seven terraces, each narrowing proportionately. In the case of seven such terraces, the number corresponded to the first seven planets and their deities, and each level was painted according to the colors associated with these planets and Gods. The first level, for **Saturn**, was **black**; the second, for **Jupiter,** was **white**; the third was **red** for **Mercury**; **blue** for **Venus**; **yellow** for **Mars**;

and **silver** for the **Moon**. The seventh and uppermost level represented the **Sun** and was painted **gold**.

Not only could man ascend to the Gods by climbing the ziggurat, but the Gods could also descend from the Heavens by the reverse route, emulating certain occasions in mythology when this has happened; for example, when Moses received the **Ten** Commandments from God at the top of **Mount Sinai**, or when the Gods on Mount Olympus spoke to the people below in thunder and lightning.

The ziggurat also shares symbolic meaning with the **Axis Mundi** and the **Omphalos** as the center of the world. Climbing to the top of the building marked the completion of a spiritual journey, and the physical levels of the pilgrimage corresponded to spiritual levels of cleansing and enlightenment.

Part Seven

NUMBERS

THE BAIT THAT ATTRACTS THE MYSTERIOUS

On a superficial level, numbers are simply handy implements for counting things. However, underpinning the idea of the number as a basic tally device is a profound system of philosophy and symbolism that resonates through the entire world, operating in remarkably similar ways throughout most cultures and belief systems.

This notion, that numbers represent not only physical quantities but also the inherent qualities, laws, and powers of the Universe, is very ancient. It is described and explained in various ways, and is reflected in the mystery traditions, including those of the Pythagoreans, Babylonians, and Hindus as well as in the **Kabbalah**. The form of the number, its conceptual nature, and its symbolic meanings carry sacred and mystical significance, a hidden code that can be cracked to reveal the secret construction of the Universe and man's place within it.

As any mathematician or accountant knows, numbers need to be handled with care. They are the ultimate precision tools that demand complete understanding in order to be wielded accurately. What numbers can do as mathematical instruments is an inherent part of their nature and of their secret symbolic significance.

Is the Universe actually ruled by numbers? Were they discovered, or invented? If we did not know about numbers, would the **Sun** still rise in the **East** and set in the **West**, would the **seasons** still run in the same way without the measurements we have accorded them, and would the **Moon** still swell and diminish with the same regularity? Of course they would. None of these things would change. However, numbers give us the means to make sense of the cosmos and to help explain our own place in it as a small part of a much larger whole. For example, take the second as a measurement of time. There are **sixty** seconds in a minute, sixty minutes in an hour, **twenty-four** hours in a day (and twenty-four is **six** times **four**). The Sumerians created this sexagesimal measuring system some four thousand years ago and, of course, it remains in use. The whole package is neat and integrated, however much of a construct it may have been in the first place.

WHO "INVENTED" NUMBERS?

This is not an in-depth study of the technical origins of numbers, but a brief explanation to help set them in context. Whereas there is a great deal of mythology about the provenance of **letters**, which the Gods are said to have gifted to mankind, it seems that the provenance of numbers is less exotic and man alone is happy to claim the credit for them, despite their mystical significance.

There's debate as to whether numbers came from India or China. Whatever the truth of their origins, it is certain that numbers came before letters. Someone, somewhere, at some point, realized that the number of animals in front of him could be married to the number of **fingers** on the **hands**, and so the digital adventure began. It probably started in one of the more fertile, agrarian parts of the world, where excess produce would need to be counted so that it could be bartered or protected against theft. After all, if you don't know how many **sheep** or bags of grain you have, you don't know how much they are worth.

When a child learns about numbers, he uses exactly the same system, counting the fingers of the hands and then progressing to the **toes** too. Thereafter, he uses visible tokens of some sort to extend the range of available numbers. The Greeks and Romans did exactly the same thing, using small pebbles, called *calculi*, from a word that originally meant "limestone."

This simple tally system gave rise to a method that is still in use today. Roman numerals were adapted from an earlier Etruscan method that began as a set of lines drawn to represent the fingers. It's believed that this system derived from Italian shepherds making notches in a piece of wood in order to keep count of their sheep. One line for 1, two lines for 2, three lines for 3 and four lines for 4 were succeeded by the V for 5 which effectively could be drawn on the hand, the line going down the **thumb** to the wrist and back up to the little finger. The X for 10 could be these two V shapes placed end-to-end.

Because this method of counting is called a Base 10 numerical system, every tenth V (or X) had an extra stroke added to it. C, standing for *centum*, "hundred," was used as the symbol for 100 and gives us the "cent" still in use today. At this time, zero did not exist as a symbol, although the Romans defined it as *nulla*, meaning "nothing." This absence of a **zero** symbol proved a serious setback to the notation of Roman numerals, and so the Hindu/Arabic system (which is believed to have been developed as early as 400 BC) gained popularity until it became the most widely used system of written numbers on the planet today.

NUMEROLOGY

Numbers are the Universal language offered by the Deity to humans as confirmation of the Truth.

[St. Augustine of Hippo, 354—430]

Numerology is the term used for the belief in the mystical, esoteric relationship between numbers and living things, physical objects, ideas, and concepts. Known to be one of the most ancient symbolic sciences, Plato called it "the highest level of knowledge." The Greeks, Romans, Indians, Chinese, and Kabbalists considered numerology to be an essential part of the construction of the Universe. In Africa, the Fulani people accorded numbers with such powers that the amounts of things closely associated with a person—such as his age in years, number of children, heads of **cattle**, etc.—was never mentioned, since to do so was to squander a little of that power.

Modern skeptics might consign latter-day numerology to the same rubbish bin as fortune telling, but numerology should not be dismissed so lightly. Many Hindu families will not **name** a child unless the numerology of its name forms a harmonious relationship with that of its date of birth, for example.

Pythagoras said that "Numbers rule all things," and agreed with the ancient Chinese belief that numerology somehow held the key to our understanding of the harmony between the worlds of spirit and matter, Man and God, microcosm and macrocosm. The **I Ching** hints at this correlation. Pythagoras further posited that mathematics, **music**, architecture, and **color** all resonated together in a harmonious balance that numbers could help explain and define.

Numerology does not remove numbers from their practical role as defined by mathematics, but enhances their status as arbiters of a greater truth.

Many of the ancient truths associated with numbers, which go back as far as the Chaldeans, were not recognized by the early Christian Church, who viewed this ancient art with the same distrust that was applied to **astrology** and other forms of "magic," and considered it to be ungodly or somehow devilish. Therefore, over time, the Church systematically undermined many of the concepts of numerology and so its mysteries were largely lost, although a little of the secret language of numbers has been reconstructed.

Though there are different types of numerology there is consensus about the meanings of certain numbers. Here is a brief guide to the generally accepted ideas about the first eleven numbers. Zero, that mysterious "no number," whose discovery is possibly one of the most important in human history, is included.

0. The nothing, and yet the "everything."
1. The Oneness of all, the individual.
2. Duality, balance, separation.
3. The spirit, communication, wisdom.
4. The Earth, solidity, understanding, order.
5. Harmony, justice, protection, love.
6. Marriage, union of male and female, balance of opposites.
7. Spirituality, the occult, intelligence.
8. Eternity and infinity, justice.
9. The limited and the limitless, experience and virtue, completion.
10. Death and rebirth. Perfection.

YANTRA

The Hindu philosophy of numerology is called Yantra, and uses an individual's date of birth in combination with their names to discover aspects of someone's personality as well as their destiny, favorable omens and conditions, and any traits or aspects to be aware of. The meanings of the numbers from one to nine in this system accurately convey the idea of the changing of the seasons as well as man's progress on the planet, and are as follows:

1. Seed
2. Germination
3. Sprouting
4. Testing or trials
5. Growth
6. Budding
7. Blossom
8. Fruit
9. Harvest

The zero is represented as the **bindhu**, or dot, such as the one that marks the position of the **third eye** in the middle of the forehead.

To find the number of the "life path" in Yantra, the numbers of a person's date of birth are added together. For example, a birth date of August 7, 1963 works out as $8 + 7 + 1 + 9 + 6 + 3 = 34$, which reduces to the single number of $3 + 4 = 7$.

RELATIONSHIP BETWEEN LETTERS AND NUMBERS

There is some debate as to how the relationship between letters and numbers should be interpreted in order to work out the numerical value of a word or name. Different disciplines accord slightly different numerical values to the letters of the alphabet, but generally, the following table is applied:

1	2	3	4	5	6	7	8	9
A	B	C	D	E	F	G	H	I
J	K	L	M	N	O	P	Q	R
S	T	U	V	W	X	Y	Z	

Again, compound numbers are reduced to a single digit.

PYTHAGORAS

It seems essential, here, to say a little about Pythagoras, whose beliefs about the qualities of numbers have had such a profound and far-reaching effect. This Greek polymath, born sometime between 590 and 580 BC, is called not only the Father of Philosophy (a term he coined that means "one who seeks knowledge"), but also the Father of Numerology (although numerology was around a long time before he discovered it). It's true to say that his ideas, observations, and teachings certainly influence many of the existing notions about numerology as well as the esoteric and mystical science of numbers.

Pythagoras has become almost a God-like figure and stories told about him confirm this superhuman status. The Oracle at **Delphi** told his parents that their unborn son would make a huge difference to humankind, and some believed that he was actually a God that had taken human form in order to teach.

Pythagoras traveled extensively and was initiated into most of the mystery traditions, including the **Eleusinian**, the Chaldean, Egyptian, and Babylonian. He was familiar with the inner workings of the **Kabbalah**. He also spent a great deal of time in India studying the Hindu systems of **astrology**, mathematics, and, of course, numerology.

Back in Europe, he established a school at Cremona where he gathered a few devout students around him, and began to promulgate the ideas for which he is still famous, thousands of years later. Accounts of his death vary. However, Pythagoras was an outspoken, controversial figure whose views were not always popular, and his end may well have been violent.

Pythagoras taught that the knowledge of music, geometry, and astrology was essential to understanding God, Man, and Nature, since all were interconnected. The **planets**, he said, were as alive and as conscious as human beings and possessed the **souls** of great divinities. He taught the concept of transmigration, which effectively amounts to reincarnation. Pythagoras introduced the world to the system of symmetrical geometric shapes, the **Platonic Solids**, consisting of the tetrahedron (with four equilateral sides), the **cube** (comprised of six squares), the octahedron (with eight equilateral **triangles** as sides), the icosahedron (with twenty equilateral triangles as faces), and the dodecahedron, which is comprised of twelve equilateral pentagons. These shapes represent the physical forms of the sacred numbers from which they are made.

Pythagoras also said that numbers had souls, too. In Pythagorean numerological theory, numbers have characters and personalities as well as magical powers. The secrets locked within numbers are as infinite as the numbers themselves. These mysteries continue to evolve, an ever-circling **spiral** of possibilities.

THE FIBONACCI SEQUENCE

Speaking of spirals, the Fibonacci sequence is a mathematical sequence of numbers that perfectly explains certain spatial relationships that occur in the natural world, and so is a key tool in **Sacred Geometry**. It might sound complex, but although the sequence has had a profound effect on the way we explain the Universe, it is simple to work out. Each number is the sum of the two previous numbers. Starting with zero, then:

$$0 + 1 - 1$$
$$1 + 1 - 2$$
$$2 + 1 - 3$$
$$3 + 2 - 5$$
$$5 + 3 - 8$$
$$8 + 5 - 13$$
$$13 + 8 - 21$$
$$21 + 13 - 34$$

And so on into infinity. Numbers that belong to the sequence have a magic all their own and are relatively easy to work out.

What follows is an investigation into the qualities of certain numbers. Obviously, although every single number has significance, it's true to say that the first series of single digits, because they are the "building blocks" of all other numbers, are the most important, symbolically.

Zero

It's hard to know where to put zero. Should it go at the beginning or the end of this section? A magical **circle**, indeed, it encompasses everything and yet stands for nothing. The invention or discovery of zero has had profound implications on man's development; it was the last "number" to be recognized as such.

Conceptually, zero is the symbol that stands for "no thing." In Buddhism and Taoism, it represents the Void, which existed before Creation, and in India, the word for the concept of zero was *Sunya*, the Sanskrit word for void or vacuum. In Islamic belief, zero represents the essence of divinity, and Pythagoras said that the zero indicated perfect form. However, if zero is placed after a number, then this number is increased tenfold, giving the infinite and limitless possibilities of such a simple symbol as defined by the **Kabbalah**.

The representation of zero as a blank space appears in India in the fourth century BC, and the Egyptians, similarly, used a gap to represent the concept. The Babylonians used a pair of slanted lines to represent the zero. The Mayans were using the zero at least a thousand years before anything similar was seen in Europe. In Mayan calendars and codices, the zero is represented by the humble **snail-shell**, whose spiral form inspired the symbol. The first known use of this shell symbol was around 36 BC. The Romans used the word *nulla*, meaning "nothing," and by around AD 720, this had been abbreviated to the letter N.

There has been fierce debate as to whether zero can really be a number at all; this question so vexed the philosophical Ancient Greeks that it caused intense arguments about existence itself and the nature of nothing. Must nothing also be something? How *could* nothing be something?

Zero in the form we know it today, as the oval shape so similar to the Cosmic **Egg**, was first used in the Indian numerological system and appears in a Jain text dated AD 458. This circular shape is an entirely appropriate symbol for the zero concept, which, like a seed, represents potential and possibility.

The Indian and Greek concepts of zero were amalgamated by a Persian mathematician and scholar called Al Khawarizim, and the zero as we know it today comes from this source.

In the **Tarot**, the zero is the number of the **Fool**, the card of enthusiasm, innocence, and guilelessness fatalism.

The first nine numbers

One

The **straight line** is one of the simplest basic symbols. A human being, standing upright, is the perfect representation of the number 1. *Homo sapiens* is the only creature on **earth** that stands naturally erect on two **feet**, and the number 1 demonstrates this graphically as well as being a symbolic reminder that man is unique in the **animal** kingdom; truly, one of a kind. One is the number of confidence, and of the One God, but it is also the number of the "one-ness" of the many. It is the number of the mythological first man, Adam. It is the

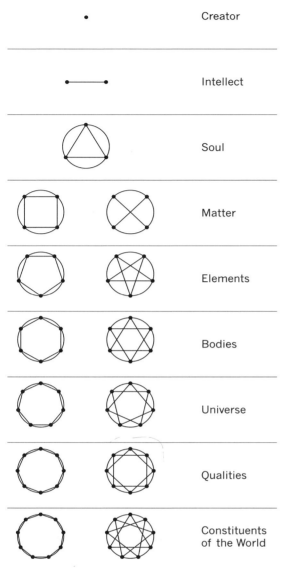

	Creator
	Intellect
	Soul
	Matter
	Elements
	Bodies
	Universe
	Qualities
	Constituents of the World

Number symbolism in Islamic Mysticism.

World Tree and the **Axis Mundi**. Turn this line on its side, and it becomes the horizon.

One is generally the number of the individual and the leader. It's often seen as a male, "yang" number, a solar number. This means that the number 1 is also the number of the autocrat and the dictator as well as that of the divine.

One stands alone, at ease with its individuality, symbolizing the ego and the self.

Followers of the Greek philosopher Plato described 1 as "the summit of the many."

Strictly speaking, the Pythagoreans did not regard 1 or 2 as numbers at all. There was a school of thought that associated 1 with the **Monad**, i.e. the "noble number, Sire of Gods and Men," the whole which is made of many parts. To this school of philosophers, 1 represented the mind, the intellect and hermaphrodism, since the 1 was both male and female. One is seen as being full of potential, effectively giving birth to all other numbers.

In the Yantric number system of the Hindus, One, or *ekah*, stands for the universality of spirit, called the Para Brahman. This energy is beyond the laws of time and space. Despite the multitude of deities in the Hindu system, the One stands for the unifying spirit that binds them all into the same energy.

The phrase "odd one out" implies the eccentric, the maverick and the one who stands on the fringes of society as a matter of course. It's the number of the only child, the number of the person who will question the rules of a society built to operate around the needs of the many rather than of the individual. One is about "out of the box" thinking and lateral solutions.

In the **Tarot**, 1 is the number of the **Magician**, the secretive loner who has the powers to amaze and confound us.

Two

The vertical line of the number 1 is joined by another, and so makes the form of the Roman numeral II.

The Arabic symbol for 2 does a very interesting thing if you hold it up to a **mirror**; it forms the shape of a **heart**, the universal symbol for love and, specifically, two people in love. This is purely coincidental, but is, nevertheless, a pleasing little trick.

Despite the notion of two being somehow better than one, two is also the number of division, and is expressed perfectly in the Bible:

And God made two great lights; the greater light to rule the day, and the lesser light to rule the night: he made the stars also. And God set them in the firmament of heaven to give light upon the Earth, and to rule over day and night, and to divide the light from the darkness.

[Genesis 1:16—18]

The Pythagoreans saw 2, or the Duad, as a symbol of opposition and also of audacity, because it had had the cheek to separate itself from the first number. As they revered the 1, or Monad, the 2 was despised as a symbol of polarity. If 1 represents the Heavens, then 2 is the depths of the **seas**, which reflected the Heavens and therefore 2 was capable of illusion and became associated with Maya, the Great Void. The magi carried **mirrors** with them as a reminder of this illusion, since mirrors reflect, another quality of the 2.

The number 2 gives us the positive and negative aspects of all things; indeed, without the number 2, positive and negative themselves would not exist. Day and night, light and dark, good and bad, male and female, attraction and repulsion, life and death, these are all encompassed by the number 2. Two is the number of balance, but is also the number of conflict and schizophrenia. It is the number of the first woman, Eve.

In the Yantric system, the number 2, Dwau, similarly symbolizes the two paths of opposites, encapsulated as the Vama Marga (left **hand**), which is materialistic and literal and straightforward and the Dakshina Marga (right hand), which is subtle, spiritual, and oblique.

In the **Tarot**, 2 is the number of the **High Priestess**, underlining the female, "yin" nature of the number that is sacred to all female deities.

THREE

As the man and the woman have the potential to create a third, so one and two make three; a neat twist. Now, the third vertical line joins the other two giving us the Roman numeral for three and the potential to make a **triangle** and a **circle**, if the points of the triangle are joined up with three **arcs**.

It's because the number 3 gives us this potential circle—and a new dimension—that it becomes the first true magical number. There are countless examples of groups of three: the Holy Trinity of Father, Son, and Holy Ghost; the **Triple Jewel** of Buddhism in which Buddhists take refuge—Buddha, Dharma (ultimate truth) and Sangha (virtue)—and also faith, hope, and charity.

Then there's Brahma, Vishnu, and Shiva in the Hindu pantheon, who represent the Trinity that is God; in Ancient Babylonia there was Anu, Bael, and Ea (Heaven, Earth, and the Abyss, or Hell); there's the Three Wise Men who visited Christ; the three **Fates**; and the three parts of time, Past, Present, and Future.

There's a satisfaction about things that happen in threes, a feeling of "third time lucky" and the completion of a cycle. Fairy stories often use this device: Goldilocks and the Three Bears, or the three wishes that are often granted by a benevolent super-being such as the **genie** that pops out of Aladdin's lamp. Under Muslim law, a man can divorce his wife simply by saying "I divorce thee," but this phrase has to be repeated the magical three times in order for it to be meaningful.

The Pythagoreans considered that the number 3 was the first true number. The Triad represents the first "equilibrium of unities" and it was for this reason that the God Apollo used a **tripod** from which to give oracles. Three was seen as the number of wisdom, understanding, and knowledge.

In the Tantric system, three is called Trayah, and again, there are several important threefold concepts. There are three sources of Karma and three types of Karma; there are three vanities that can bind the person to the **wheel** of rebirth. In the Ayurvedic system there are three qualities (*doshas*) pertaining to human beings, who have the following in various proportions: Vata (wind), Pitta (bile), and Kapha (phlegm).

In the **Tarot**, 3 is the number of the **Empress**, the embodiment of the female principle that symbolically links the Heavens with Earth and who carries within her the triple aspect of the Goddess as virgin, mother, and crone.

Four

Now a new shape can be made which had no way of existing previously. As the third point of the number 3 gave us the **triangle**, a fourth point gives us the potential not only for the **square** but also for the **cross**. The circle of the Earth can now be divided, and where the lines of latitude and longitude meet, a cross is formed.

Four is a masculine number and gives us, among countless other things, the number of the cardinal directions, North, South, East, and West; the **four evangelists**, Matthew, Mark, Luke, and John; the four **elements** of **earth**, **air**, **fire**, and **water**, and so on. In the Sufi tradition, there are four gates through which man has to pass on his way to enlightenment.

Four has wholeness about it, an organized and orderly number that likes to make sense of things. There's something about the square that is protective and stable, which holds things, box-like, within the embrace of its confines. The sober square so often provides the framework for the exuberant, circular **mandala**.

In **alchemy**, there are four key ingredients that go towards the making of the **Philosopher's Stone**; these are sulfur, **mercury**, **salt**, and azoth. In the **Tarot**, 4 is the number of the **Emperor**, the archetypal male figure, the father, the King, the patriarch, who likes to create order and harmony in the Universe that is enfolded within the number itself, which holds a hidden secret: if the numbers within 4 are added together—1 + 2 + 3 + 4—the whole adds up to **10**, which implies the start of a new cycle, a rebirth or reincarnation. These ten numbers form the Holy Name, or **Tetragrammaton**.

In Pythagorean philosophy, the 4 or Tetrad was considered to be the root of all things, the perfect, intellectual number. They believed that 4 symbolized God and this theory was explained in a secret and sacred discourse that described the concept of God as "the Number of Numbers" because of the reasons described above.

Pythagoreans also held that there were four parts to the **soul**: mind, opinion, science, and sense. These tally with the four qualities that Jung said were inherent in man: sensation, intuition, thinking, and feeling.

In the Yantric system of Hindu numerology, the 4, or Chatvarah, represents the four paths to God and the Self, which are wisdom, devotion, meditation, and action.

FIVE

Now things start to get even more exciting. The dots that add up to 5, if placed symmetrically, give the potential for a five-pointed star (**pentagram**) or for a five-sided shape (pentagon). The 5, like the 3, is constructed from adding an odd number (3) to an even one (2), thus blending male with female. The pentagram itself is a mystical symbol that also holds within it all the qualities of the 5.

Five is a number of balance, its central dot acts as a pivot for the two on either side. It's also the numerical symbol of a human being, which forms the five-pointed star shape when legs and arms are outstretched, as in Leonardo's famous drawing of Vitruvian Man.

In the Western world there are four elements, but in the East there's a fifth, or **quintessence**, that binds them all together, called ether. Alchemists indicate this with a five-petaled **rose** in the center of a **cross**, redolent of the Rose Cross Lamen.

The Pythagoreans held that the pentagram—or Pentad—was a sacred symbol of health, vitality, and light. The holy number **10** is divided equally into two parts by the Pentad, which also symbolizes the triumph of spirit over matter.

In Japanese Buddhism, there are five directions, the existing cardinal point plus the center. And in the Mayan civilization, five was the symbol of perfection, possibly related to the five digits on a **hand**. In Islam, five is a "lucky" number and it occurs time and time again. There are five hours of prayer, for example, and five senses, and five keys to the mysteries of the Qu'ran.

Pancha is the name of the number 5 in the Yantric system, and it stands for the five functions of the Divine, namely creation, preservation, destruction, obscuration, and liberation. There are also five layers or bodies of Man: physical, vital, astral, wisdom, and bliss.

In the **Tarot**, 5 is the number of the **Hierophant** or the Pope, who represents the face of God on Earth.

SIX

Six was described by Pythagoras as a "perfect number" because 1 + 2 + 3 − 6; also, 1 x 2 x 3 − 6. God created the world in six days. The Hexad was called the Form of Forms and the Maker of the Soul because the harmony of its arrangement was said to symbolize the harmony inherent within the soul. Because of the equally balanced **triangles**, the two groups of three that comprise the number 6, it is the symbol of **marriage**. Six is dedicated to **Venus** as the Goddess of Love but seems to have no connection with the spiritual nature of love or with the Creator. However, the number 6 gives us the tools we need to make that most powerful of magical signs, the **Star of David**, which is the embodiment of the phrase "as above, so below."

Because six can be split into two groups of **three**, it's seen as the number that can go either way, and is as likely to be evil as much as it is good. It's this precarious balance that crops up time and time again in examining the symbolism of the number. The symbol for 6 itself has ambivalence; flip it the other way up and it becomes a 9. Six is the number of the marriage of opposites, an image and its reflection making up the whole.

In China, 6 is an extremely auspicious number, and the number of heaven. The **I Ching** is based upon two sets of three diagrams that combine to make a **hexagram**; the 64 hexagrams of the I Ching contain a sort of predictive dictionary of the human condition by describing various elemental combinations.

In Tantra, the number 6 is called Shat. There are several sets of important sixes: six noble virtues, six revealed views of the Universe, six lower **chakras**, and six higher ones. In the **Tarot**, 6 is the number of the card called the **Lover**, and shows a young man at a **crossroads** trying to decide between two girls of equal merit, although Cupid hovers in the background, bow and arrow at the ready, about to make the decision for him. The image demonstrates perfectly the dilemma that belongs to the number 6.

The witch's curse—or hex—is so-called because six represented the number of copu-lation, the union of the **Triple Goddess** with her mate. The word itself was the original derivation of the word "hag."

The Egyptian hieroglyph for six shows male and female genitalia, underlining the sexual connotations of this number. For them, 3 was the number of the Goddess and 6 meant her union with God. The fairy-tale command "Open, Sesame" is actually a Sufi love charm and "sesame" has been corrupted from *seshemu*, the Egyptian word for inter-course. The symbolic "**cave**" that needs to be opened is the female genitalia or **yoni**.

Early Christian authorities deemed 6 as the number of sin because of its association with physical love.

SEVEN

The number 7 is very busy; it seems to be everywhere. The Sumerian and Babylonians identified the seven days in a week, and the number of the traditional **planets** that give us much of our mythology is seven. There are seven deadly sins, which are balanced by seven cardinal virtues. There are seven Orders of **Angels**, seven colors in the **rainbow** and seven pure notes in the diatonic scale. Seven gives a pivotal point to the inde-cision of the number 6, rendering it satisfy-ingly complete and whole.

Very early on, it seems, this number was given special status as a number of complete-ness and perfection. For the Ancient Egyptians, 7 was the number of eternal life. Legend has it that the prophet Mohammed, when in Jerusalem, ascended into the seven **Heavens** and came into contact with the Divine, and so the **Dome of the Rock** mosque was separated into seven sections to honor this experience. Pilgrims make seven circumnavigations of **Mecca**.

The Pythagoreans called 7 the Septad, and said that it was "worthy of veneration." It was both the number of religion (because of the seven celestial spirits related to the seven planets) and the number of life. In the Septad, the 3, comprising the mind, spirit, and **soul**, meet the Tetrad, or 4, which is the number of the world. Therefore, the resulting 7 represents the mystic number of Man as symbolized by the three-dimensional shape of the cube: six sides, with the seventh element the space inside. The sides of the **cube** represent the directions (the cardinal points plus above and below) with man at the center.

The phase of the **Moon** lasts for 28 days, which is 4 x 7. Happily, $1 + 2 + 3 + 4 + 5 + 6 + 7 - 28$.

God created the world in six days, reserving the seventh to rest; therefore the seventh day is a holy day or holiday. This relaxation time also connects God with man, proving that even a deity needs a break now and then.

In Tibetan Buddhism, the soul rests in an intermediate stage after death for a period of 49 days; that is, 7 x 7. In Japan, souls are believed to rest on the roofs of their homes for the same period of time. The Sufis, too, hold the number 7 in great reverence, and this is exemplified in Farid al-Din Attar's *The Conference of the Birds*, in which the seven stages towards enlightenment are symbolized as seven valleys that the birds have to travel through before they can find their leader.

In the Hindu Yantric system of numbers, Sapta represents the seven **chakras** or energy vortices that correspond to the seven notes of Indian classical **music**. There are seven higher planes of consciousness (the seven Heavens), opposed by seven lower planes of consciousness (hells).

There are seven alchemical operations: calcination, dissolution, separation, conjunction, fermentation, distillation, and coagulation. In the **Tarot**, the number 7 card is the **Chariot**. The card depicts a young man, a king, in a chariot driven by two **horses**; this young man knows where he is going and is full of determination.

Eight

In general, eight is seen to be a good number, a symbol of cosmic harmony and balance. The inter-cardinal points balance the **four** cardinal directions.

For Pythagoreans, the 8 or Ogdoad was called the "little holy number" and considered sacred for several reasons. The **cube** has eight corners; also, in the Pythagorean numerical system eight is an "evenly even" number, and the only such number under 10. This is to say that the eight is divided into 2 x 4, and further, into 4 x 2. The **serpents** that twist up the staff of the **caduceus** make **figure-of-eight** shapes.

There are eight trigrams in the **I Ching** that go to make up the 64 hexagrams, itself constructed of 8 x 8. An important part of the Buddhist doctrine is the Eight Auspicious Items, or **Ashtamangala**. In the Yantric system, 8, or Ashta, is also an auspicious number. Ashtanga yoga comprises eight aspects, said to lead the practitioner to the Divine.

In Hindu belief, each of the eight directions of the Earth is ruled over by a God. These eight divinities are related in turn to the eight petals of the **lotus** that resides, symbolically, inside the **skull**, a reminder of the microcosm and the macrocosm. Additionally, there are said to be eight qualities that belong to God; these are innocence, purity, self-knowledge and omniscience, freedom from impurities, benevolence, omnipotence, and bliss.

The figure 8 itself forms a symbol called the **lemniscate**, which is the scientific sign for infinity as well as having the same meaning at a more philosophical level, where it stands for the cycle of birth, life, death, and rebirth in the same way that the eighth day—following the six days of work and the seventh day of rest—denotes the day of renewal and invigoration.

In the **Tarot**, 8 is the number for **Justice**, again reflecting the universal idea that 8 is the number of balance. It is the first card of the second set of the major Arcana, reinforcing the idea of 8 as a symbol of renewal.

NINE

As it is **3** x 3, the number 9 has magic status and is a sacred number. For Hindus, it is the number of Lord Brahma, the Creator. It is also the numerological sum of Ba'hai, and so is seen as a symbol of perfection and unity, which explains the use of the nine-pointed star in this faith.

The Pythagoreans recognized the 3 x 3 as the Ennead, which is the first square of an odd number. However, because it falls one short of the perfect **10**, it was classified as an unfortunate number, sometimes even seen as evil because it is the inversion of the number **6**. However, it was also considered limitless since there was nothing beyond it but infinity as represented by the 10, the perfect Decad.

The **Eleusinian mysteries** described the nine spheres through which human consciousness must pass on the journey of its rebirth into a new body. Apollonius of Tyana recognized the sacred status of the number 9, and set aside the ninth hour for silent meditation and hymns. The Ancient Romans held feasts of purification for newborn baby boys when they were nine days old, and buried their corpses nine days after the actual death.

In the Tantric system, 9 is called Nava. There are nine virtues of Dharma, the rules of living according to divine law. There is also a great festival called the Durga Puja, in honor of the Goddess; this takes place over nine nights with the tenth night being the culmination of the celebrations. The Nava Ratnas are the nine gemstones that are considered particularly precious; these are the **pearl**, the **ruby**, **cat's eye**, **beryl**, **diamond**, red **coral**, yellow **sapphire**, the **emerald,** and the blue sapphire. The use of all nine of these stones makes for a very powerful **talisman** or **amulet**.

Because it is the last single-digit number, there is a sense of completion and wholeness about the number 9. It is for this reason that nine represents achievement and culmination of a task. In addition, nine is the zenith of achievement for a single-figure number. Because human embryos need nine months of gestation, nine is the number of Man. Man also has nine physical apertures, symbolizing nine channels of communication with the world. There are nine known planets in our Solar System. In the Tarot, 9 is the card of the **Hermit.**

It's interesting to note that 666—also described as the number of the Beast—adds up to 18 using numerology, and 1 + 8 is 9. No great evil there, but a simple matter of fact.

TEN AND BEYOND

TEN

The first number that requires more than one digit, 10 is the foundation stone of the digital age, and despite any high-tech connotations, is the number of choice simply because of the number of **fingers** and **thumbs** on the **hands**. This simple fact has also given us the decimal counting system. Happily, the number 10 is infinitely malleable and versatile.

Pythagoras believed that 10 was the most sacred and greatest of all numbers, and the Tetraktys (a shorthand version of the name of God) was devised from it based on the premise that 1 + 2 + 3 + 4 − 10. The Decad was a holy number, the first number to need a second part. Pythagoreans took oaths on this sacred number. Pythagoras further described it as the "nature of number" and said that it symbolized the world and heaven, since the latter has to encompass the former. The Ancient Greek philosophers decided that there were ten orders of the Heavenly Bodies.

Ten is a satisfying number, and 10 of anything seems like a complete set; for example, the Ten Commandments. In the **Kabbalah**, there are ten **Sephiroth**, emanations from the mind of God that represents the Universe and its workings. Ten, in this instance, symbolizes the unity of Creation and the synthesis of all things.

In Hinduism, the tenth state, or Avastha, is the point at which self-consciousness (one of the three imperfections) is shed, and unity with the Divine is attained. There are 10 rules of good conduct (Yamas) in the same way that there are Ten Commandments in the Bible.

The Mayans, however, regarded the number 10 as unfortunate, since it belonged to the God of Death (Thoh). However, in Africa 10 is a lucky number and a symbol of fertility, since it's comprised of 6 and 4, both fortunate numbers in themselves.

In the **Tarot**, the number 10 is the number of the **Wheel of Fortune**.

ELEVEN

Eleven is considered to be the number of woman, since the female has 11 apertures in her body. The unborn child receives 11 divine powers via these holes. Numerologists consider that 11 is a "master number" that should not be reduced down into a single digit.

However, some traditions are suspicious about 11. If 10 is the number of completion and wholeness, then there is an idea that 11 must be the number of excess and extravagance (an idea perfectly defined in the movie *This is Spinal Tap*, where the amplifier goes up to number 11). Coincidentally, Apollo 11 was the first manned spacecraft to land on the **Moon**. The Eleventh Hour has a sense of urgency about it. Since the clock runs to 12, then this is that last hour in which something can be done. The First World War ended on the eleventh hour of the eleventh day of the eleventh month, of course.

The black magician Aleister Crowley was especially fond of the number 11, since it carries occult significance. The "**K**" that he added to the word "magic" enjoys special status because it is also the eleventh letter of the alphabet.

The eleventh card of the **Tarot** is either **Justice**, or **Strength**. This card stands at the mid-point of the numbered series of cards.

Twelve

There are 12 calendar months in a year, 12 signs of the **Zodiac** that guard those months, 12 Apostles, 12 Tribes of Israel, 12 Knights of the Round Table. As there are 12 months in the year, so the hours of the day are also split into two sections of 12. There were 12 Imperial symbols in China, these being the **Sun**, the **Moon**, a **constellation** of three stars, and a **mountain**, all of which represented the features of the Universe. A pair of **dragons** represented yang (male) energy, and a pheasant represented female yin energy. The rest of the symbols were millet (prosperity), waterweed (purity), a pair of bronze cups (strength and cleverness), and flames (intellectual prowess). The axe symbolized the Imperial power and authority to punish, and the final symbol was the **fu** (the power to judge).

In more recent years, the European Union decided to put 12 stars on their flag. This is nothing to do with the number of member states, but an acknowledgement of something that Ancient Man was aware of; that 12 is a number of perfection. This is because 12 is the result of the number **4** (four **elements**, four cardinal points, four corners of the Earth) being multiplied by the number **3** (three levels of the Universe, three aspects of any God); i.e., the multiplication of the number of the Earth with the number of the Heavens. In Africa, this 3 x 4 equation is expressed in the form of a myth in which each of the four points of the compass was whirled round three times; this resulted in the sound of creation, which resulted in the formation of the **Cosmic Egg**.

In the **Tarot**, the number 12 is the number of the **Hanged Man**; suspended from a rope by his foot, this unfortunate soul has the time to contemplate his place in the larger Universe.

Thirteen

Are you a triskaidekaphobe? If so, it means that you're one of the thousands (or possibly even millions) of people who believe the number 13 to be unlucky. And some of you may even be among those who refuse to leave the house if the thirteenth day of the month happens to coincide with a Friday. Sometimes the number 13 is excluded from door numbers, or the thirteenth floor will be skipped over and effectively labeled as 14, so deep-rooted is this superstition.

Thirteen has long been regarded by many as an unlucky or inauspicious number. The **Kabbalah**, for example, says that there are 13 spirits of evil. It's still considered unlucky to have 13 people sitting down to dine because it is a reminder of the Last Supper, where Christ was betrayed by one the of the 12 disciples who were eating with him, Judas Iscariot.

However, it's not all black for the number 13. Despite the year being divided up into 12 calendar months, there are actually 13 lunar months, i.e. 13 sets of 28 days in a year. Therefore the Mayans regarded 13 as an auspicious number. There is also said to be a secret, hidden, thirteenth sign of the **Zodiac**, Arachne, the **spider** whose web binds the network of the Heavens. In Classical Antiquity, the thirteenth member of a group was considered to be the leader, the exalted one. **Zeus** sits at the head of the **12 Olympian deities**, for example, in the same way that Christ sat among his disciples or King Arthur with his twelve knights at the Round Table. A coven consists of 12 members plus a leader. In addition, a baker's dozen is one more than 12, so 13 effectively represents good value for money. This stems from medieval England when **bread** was a scarce commodity and punishment was harsh for bakers who short-changed their customers. Therefore they would give away a free loaf with every 12 sold to make sure that no mistakes were made.

The Apollo 13 **Moon** landing was beset by bad luck, and an explosion could have resulted in a disaster. However, no-one died and the crew returned to Earth safely, so it could be said that the number 13 was lucky for them.

The number 13 is shown in several places on the United States' currency bills, and in this instance there is no hidden sinister meaning; simply, there were 13 states that joined the original Union.

In the **Tarot**, 13 is the number of **Death**. This represents initiation and facing fears. Presumably, these fears might include that of the number 13.

FOURTEEN

The phase of the **Moon** is split into two sets of 14; one where the Moon is waxing, or growing larger, and one where the Moon is waning.

In **Freemasonry**, the significance of the number 14 has not gone unnoticed, and due attention is paid to the fact that the body of **Osiris** was reputed to have been cut into 14 pieces by his murderer, his jealous brother Typhon, and the pieces scattered to the four winds. **Isis**, Osiris' wife, found the pieces and gave them a more fitting burial. Thus, the number 14 came to be associated with **death** and resurrection.

A part of the process of resurrection or reincarnation must necessarily be a lack of memory, the idea being that it might not be very constructive for the returning soul to be able to remember what went before. Therefore, 14 is the number of forgetfulness. The Ancient Greeks believed that a soul about to be reborn drank the **waters** of Lethe, which was a river in Hades. Drinking this water caused the soul to forget everything in preparation for its return to an earthly body.

The fourteenth letter of the Hebrew alphabet is called Nun, and in the **Kabbalah**, this represents the idea of the spirit or **soul** dressed in the material body. In the **Tarot**, this is equivalent to the card called Temperance; Temperance mixes liquid from a **blue** jug with that of a **red** jug. This mixture gives **violet**, the color of temperance and the color of the spiritual and the material combined. As chance would have it, temperance is also the card of reincarnation; the character carefully pours the violet liquid, the **spirit**, from one vessel to the other.

In China, 14 is considered one of the unluckiest numbers. It's pronounced as "one four" but these words, in Chinese, mean the same as "want to die," hence this unfortunate coincidence reflects back onto the number itself.

FIFTEEN

Fifteen is the product of two sacred numbers: 3 x 5. The Sumerian Goddess **Ishtar** was attended by 15 priests and her city, Ninevah, had 15 gates. Because Ishtar was the Goddess of both war and physical love, her number sometimes has negative connotations although the understanding of the number holds the key to greater spiritual comprehension.

In the **Tarot**, 15 is the number of the Devil, since 1 + 5 gives us the ambivalent number 6, which apparently does not know right from wrong.

However, it's not all bad news for 15. Because each **Moon** effectively waxes for 15 days, there are 15 steps to freedom and personal enlightenment in the **Passover** Seder or meal. Seder means "order" or "arrangement."

To Kabbalists, 15 is the number of energy points that run down the center of the body.

SIXTEEN

Sixteen may be sweet, but as the square of the number 4, it's also powerful, encapsulating four times the strength of the Tetrad. Therefore, the number represents the attainment of physical, earthly power. The sixteenth card of the **Tarot** is the **Tower**, which

carries a reminder of the consequences of the arrogance that sometimes accompanies material gain.

SEVENTEEN

Seventeen is an almost universally important number. With few exceptions, it's generally seen to be beneficial, redolent of spirituality and immortality, rebirth and transformation.

Why, though? In understanding the significance of certain numbers, their component elements can provide clues as to their meaning and significance. Seventeen is comprised of 1 + 7 giving the number 8; 1 is the number of the One God, and 7 is the number of completeness and perfection. Eight is the number of cosmic balance and harmony, and these qualities are compounded by the reappearance of the number 8, which is added to 9 to make 17: 9 is also full of rich spiritual significance.

This 8 + 9 is also the number of consonants in the Greek alphabet, broken down into eight semi-vowels or semi-consonants, and nine mute consonants.

In Islam, particularly amongst Sufis, it's believed that the sacred name of God is comprised of 17 letters, which will be given to the 17 people who rise from the dead and spell out this name. It's for this reason that 17 words are used in the call to prayer, along with 17 liturgical gestures used in the daily prayers. The number reappears time and again in Islamic tradition and folklore; for example, 17 pieces of advice are whispered into the **ears** of kings during their coronation. In addition, the Sufi alchemist Gabir Ibn Hayyan says that the shape of all things in the

Universe is 17, although precisely what this means is well hidden within the usual protective cloak of mystery that wraps up all alchemical arcana.

In the Bible, the Flood is reputed to have started on the seventeenth day of the second month and finished on the seventeenth day of the seventh month. It's perhaps for this reason that Greeks still believe that the seventeenth of any month is an auspicious day for cutting wood to build a boat or ship.

In the **Tarot**, 17 is the number of the **Star**, an auspicious card of the major Arcana that expresses the notions of rebirth, change and transformation, in accordance with the beliefs about the number 17 in general. The card shows the figure of a naked woman pouring water from two jugs into a stream; behind her are eight stars, one large one and seven smaller, representing the 1 + 7 of 17 and also of the number 8. This eight-star symbolism also occurs in **alchemy**, where the seven stars revolving around the eighth larger star represent the seven stages of the alchemical process that go toward making the "whole," symbolized by the eighth star.

There are exceptions to the universal esteem in which 17 is held, however. For the Egyptians, it was considered unlucky, since **Osiris** was slain on the seventeenth day of the month. In Rome, the Roman numeral for the number—XVII—is an "anagram" of VIXI, meaning "I have lived," the implication being that the person is alive no longer.

In Japan, the Haiku poem is comprised of 17 syllables.

EIGHTEEN

Eighteen is the number of the **Moon**, in not only the **Tarot** but elsewhere. The Moon itself is a symbol of intuition, mystery, and femininity.

There are elements of the eighteenth Tarot card that are quite disturbing. The Moon drips **blood**, and these drips are caught by a ravening **wolf** and a **dog**. A **crab** or **scorpion** climbs up from the nether regions to join in the feast. These images point to the number 18 as a symbol of the material trying to destroy the spiritual.

However, it's not all doom and gloom for 18. It is, of course, the product of 2 x 9, meaning that the good qualities of the 9 are doubled in intensity. The Sufis say that 18 is a sacred number and so they give gifts in multiples of 18. There's also a Hebrew prayer called "Shemone Esre" which means "eighteen," and lists 18 blessings. This is because, in the system of applying numerological values to letters (**Gematria**) the word for "life," has a value of 18.

In Norse mythology, too, the number 18 has special significance. The God **Odin** was said to have pinpointed 18 wisdoms, which correspond to the 18 consonants in the Elder Futhark runic system that the God is also said to have discovered.

NINETEEN

Numerologically, 1 + 9 – 10, which in turn is related to 1, so 19 has much of the same symbolism, by default, as these two previous figures. This is reflected in the Islamic notion that 19 is the numerological value of the word

Wahid, which also means "One," and is one of the names of God. Similarly, it is the number of letters in the Arabic phrase, "In the name of God, most Gracious and Merciful."

Nineteen has special powers. It's a prime number, divisible only by itself and 1. Moreover, because it is made up of the first single number and the last single number, there is a feeling of completion about it, a beginning and an end. In the **Kabbalah**, 19 is the number of spiritual activity.

The Jewish calendar is based around the number 19, because there's a 19-year cycle of the **Moon** in relation to the **Sun**. A full Moon will occur on roughly the same date every 19 years. The Babylonians, too, were aware of this 19-year cycle.

In the **Tarot**, 19 is the number of the Sun, again referring to its close association with the number 1, also a masculine, solar number. All the goodness associated with the Sun— happiness, honor, success, courage—are also qualities that belong, symbolically, to the number 19.

Twenty

Man can count up to ten by numbering the digits on both of his **hands**, and he can count to 20 by including the **toes**. Therefore, 20 is the number of man in many civilizations, including the Mayan. There was an ancient measurement of land based on the space needed to grow enough maize to keep one person alive. This space was 400 square feet (20 squared). The Mayan year was 400 days long, which also corresponded to this measurement, all based on the number of fingers and toes.

In the **Tarot**, the sense of completion about the number 20 is symbolized in the meaning of its card, namely, **Judgement.** The Judgement card stands for awakening, realization, a call to action, and the realization of purpose in life, as pictured by three naked figures, one of which is rising from a grave. These figures are roused to action by the trumpeting angel that floats above them.

In the **Kabbalah**, 20 is the number of fundamental wisdom, the wisdom that belongs to man as an innate part of his psyche.

Twenty-one

Looking at the component parts of 21, we see that $2 + 1 = 3$, which in itself is a magical number, being the first number that broadens our perspective with a new dimension. Add to this the fact that 21 is 3 x 7 (or 7 x 3), with seven being one of the most sacred numbers, and we start to understand something of the significance of this number.

It is no coincidence that the age of majority in many countries around the world was traditionally held to be 21, when, figuratively speaking, the person reaching this birthday was given the "**key** to the door," symbolizing the responsibility of adulthood as well as an initiatory "unlocking." In the Old Testament, 21 is the number of perfection, and is the number of the attributes of wisdom. Solomon, renowned for his own sagacity, wrote of it thus:

I preferred her before scepters and thrones, and esteemed riches nothing in comparison of her … neither compared I unto her any precious stone, because all gold in respect of her is as a little sand, and silver shall be counted as clay before her.

[The Wisdom of Solomon, 7:9]

In the **Tarot**, 21 is the number of the World, and the last card of the major Arcana. The card shows an androgynously female figure, standing within a **vesica piscis** of **laurel** leaves. The elements are represented by the images of an **ox**, an **angel**, a **lion**, and an **eagle** (respectively, **earth**, **air**, **fire**, and **water**), as are the cardinal points. The whole makes a victorious, triumphant picture.

In the **Kabbalah**, 21 represents the path of conciliation and the blessings of God.

Twenty-two

There are 22 letters in the Hebrew alphabet, and 22 cards in the Major Arcana of the **Tarot**; this is not a coincidence. In the **Kabbalah**, these 22 letters are believed to give expression to the Universe, and the Tarot cards also reflect the qualities of the Universe. This notion—that everything in the world is somehow encompassed in the number 22—is also reflected in the beliefs of the Bambara and the Dogon people, who believe that not only is 22 a symbol for the span of time from the creation to ultimate perfection and completion, but that all mystical information is embraced by the symbolism contained in the first 22 numbers. Twenty-two is also the number of books in the Avesta, the sacred scripts of the Zoroastrians.

Twenty-three

Known as the Royal **Star** of the **Lion**, in purely numerological terms 23 is an auspicious number, announcing help from higher places or people, success, and fame. However, with 23, all is not quite so simple and much of the mysticism surrounding this number comes from a relatively recent source, Discordianism, more of which in a moment.

If 22 is somehow able to encompass the whole of the Universe, then what of the numbers that come after it? As its immediate successor, logically, 23 must herald the beginning of a completely new world, a world not ruled by the same harmonious laws as the preceding 22. In addition, 23 comprises 2 (female) plus 3 (spiritual energy), combining to make 5, the number of harmony and balance, reflected nicely by the 23 chromosomes that are each contributed by the male and female during conception.

Discordianism is a modern, "prankster" spiritual movement, which started in 1958, and one of its central tenets is called the "23 Enigma," a belief that everything in the Universe and all events are somehow connected to the number 23. The Goddess who presides over the Discordians is called Eris, the Greek Goddess of Strife and Discord, who is also known as the Queen of the Night.

This belief has had far-reaching effects, and it's fair to say that the Discordians influenced writers such as Robert Shea and Robert Anton Wilson, who write about the 23 Enigma and the Rules of 5s $(2 + 3 = 5)$ in their *Illuminatus* trilogy. There are even two movies about the phenomenon. The most recent is *The Number 23*, starring Jim Carrey, in which his character is so much in the thrall to the number that he believes is controlling his life that he gradually descends into madness. The other movie is also called *23*, further enhancing the conspiracy theories surrounding the number with its plot—computer hackers stumble upon secret societies that all share a link to the number *23*.

TWENTY-FOUR

In the Bible, the Book of Revelation says that there are 24 elders sitting around the Throne of God. As 12 is the number of the harmonic balance between time and space and the cycle of the Universe, so 24 represents the balance between man and God, and the worlds of matter and spirit.

In the **Kabbalah**, 24 is the Path of Imaginative Intelligence.

TWENTY-FIVE

In numerology, 25 is a "good" number, signifying wisdom and strength gained via experience rather than theory. The circumstances during which the wisdom is gained may not always be the happiest, but the outcome, nevertheless, is positive.

This notion is corroborated in the Kabbalistic symbolism of 25, which is seen as the Path of Trial.

Because 2 + 5 − 7, all the symbolism of the number 7 applies to 25 too.

THIRTY-THREE

Because 33 was the age at which Christ died, this number stands for the Christ-Consciousness, which in itself means nurturing, responsibility, higher levels of awareness, and spirituality. It's also the number of the educator and the healer.

In the Sagrada Familia Church in Barcelona there is a **magic square** called the Subirach Square, named for its inventor. The magic sum of this square is 33.

The 33rd degree in **Freemasonry** is generally held to be the highest degree, although some Masonic orders have further degrees above this one. In this context, 33 represents illumination and freedom from superstition or the received opinion of organized religion.

THIRTY-SIX

In both Tantric and Buddhist philosophies, 36 is the most sacred of all numbers. This is because it's considered to be the number of Heaven. Thirty-six doubled (36 x 2 − 72) is the number of Earth, and 3 x 36 (108) is the number of humankind. Buddhist and Hindu **rosaries** have 108 beads.

One of the more mystical aspects of Judaism says that there are 36 "Tzadikim Nistarim," or saintly people, on the Earth at any one time. According to the Talmud, if any one of these people were not present, then the world itself would end. These people are unknown to one another, and although they possess magical powers, they are not themselves aware of their special role, which is to justify mankind in the eyes of God.

Apparently, when the time comes these chosen ones will know exactly what to do. As it is also believed that these 36 special people are too humble to ever believe that they could be one of the Tzadikim Nistarim, 36 has come to represent humility.

FORTY

Forty, it is generally agreed among most religions and belief systems, is the number of symbolic **death**, initiation, trial and testing, preparation, and waiting. Both Moses and Mohammed received their "call" from God at this age, as did the Buddha, the very epitome of the idea that "life begins at forty." In addition, Muslims believe that the Qu'ran should be read every 40 days.

It's said to be unwise to attempt to study the **Kabbalah** before the prospective student has reached 40.

Knowing about the symbolic meaning of this number means that we have a deeper understanding of the 40 days and nights that Christ spent in the desert being tempted by the Devil, and the 40 years during which the Children of Israel wandered in the wilderness. Other examples of the number 40 that reveal a period of trial or tribulation are the 40 days of the deluge, the 40 days that Moses spent on Mount Sinai, and the 40 days of denial or **fasting** during Lent.

The Ancient Egyptians also fasted for 40 days, in memory of the 40 days between the death of **Osiris** and his reappearance. This is the same number of days between the crucifixion of Christ and his ascension to Heaven, too. For the Babylonians, 40 days was the length of time between the disappearance and reappearance of the Pleiades, a time of floods, storms, and other dangers.

In Africa, where the deceased person is over 105 years old, the funeral lasts for 40 days. In other cultures, the period of time after which it might be safely assumed that the **soul** has left the body is 40 days, after which the mourning customs are relaxed. For example, an Altaic widow was free to remarry after this period. Among some Native American tribes, a second burial is customary, and this takes place 40 days after the first interment. In Islam, a memorial is held 40 days after a death.

The period of isolation for suspected plague victims during the middle ages was set at 40 days, thus giving us the word "quarantine."

FORTY-TWO

Douglas Adams immortalized this number as being the secret of "life, the Universe, and everything," in *The Hitchhiker's Guide to the Galaxy*.

FORTY-NINE

The product of 7 x 7, for Tibetan Buddhists, 49 is the number of days that it takes for the dead **soul** to be reborn into another body.

FIFTY

Do you know why the Olympics are held every four years? It's because the original Ancient Greek games were held at Olympia every 49 or 50 moons or "lunations."

The number 50 signifies a new beginning, coming as it does directly after the 7 x 7 cycle, which adds up to 49.

The Goddess **Kali** has 50 **skulls** in her necklace. Each skull represents a letter of the **alphabet**.

FIFTY-SIX

This is the number of the minor Arcana cards in the **Tarot** system.

SIXTY

The Babylonians had the same symbol for 60 as they did for one, and it's for this reason that 60 remains a crucial number not only in symbolism but also in practical applications today. For example, there are 60 seconds in a minute and 60 minutes in an hour. Six times sixty gives us the number of degrees in a circle (360).

In Judaism, 60 represents transformational power, and there's a rule in the Torah called the Law of Nullification, which sets down a 1:60 ratio. This means, for example, that if a fragment of non-Kosher food finds its way into the cooking-pot, then its effect is rendered obsolete provided the contents of the rest of the pot are 60 times greater than the errant ingredient.

Sixty is represented by the letter Samech, which itself is symbolized by a **circle**, and

conceptually carries with it the idea of an all-inclusive state and the transcendental light of God. In addition, it's said that **fire** comprises only one sixtieth of Hell, and that a sixtieth part of **Manna** is **honey**, in the same way that a dream is one-sixtieth part of prophecy.

In Ancient Egypt, 60 represented longevity.

SIXTY-FOUR

The number of hexagrams in the **I Ching**.

SEVENTY

Seventy, according to the Bible, is the span of years accorded to man's life on earth. St. Augustine encapsulated 70 as the fulfilment of an evolutionary cycle, which tallies with the Biblical statement. Numerologically speaking, 70 represents enlightenment.

EIGHTY

In Buddhism, the Buddha is recognized by 32 primary characteristics and 80 secondary characteristics. These indicators include slightly upturned **fingers** and **toes**, unwrinkled **skin**, a long and beautiful face, and **hair** that never goes **gray**.

ONE HUNDRED

The ancient Babylonians worked to a base of 60, whereby anything x 60 was increased exponentially. We work in a base of 10 (the decimal system), so any given number will be increased likewise. One hundred is, of course, is 10 x 10; though when we use the phrase "a hundred times better than/nicer than …" it can just mean "a lot" or "many times" more rather than the actual number. Therefore 100 is symbolic of exaggeration. One hundred is also a beautifully rounded number, a satisfying number, and is a number of perfection.

ONE HUNDRED AND EIGHT

This is a sacred or perfect number in Hinduism and Buddhism and the other Dharmic faiths, and as such crops up in various places. *Malas*, or **rosaries**, always have 108 beads that assist in the repetition of a mantra, as do the *juzu* or prayer bracelets of Zen priests. Hindu deities are reputed to each have 108 names. One hundred and eight is the number of sins in Tibetan Buddhism, as well as the number of earthly temptations in the Japanese Shinto religion, where temple **bells** are rung 108 times to welcome in the New Year and say goodbye to the old, and also to remind the citizens to beware of these transgressions. Similarly, the Angelus bells of the Catholic Church are tolled 108 times.

Further, 108 is the product of 12 x 9; this represents the nine planets and the twelve months of the year. It is also a product of 4 x 27, symbolic of the four quarters of the **Moon**

in the 27 "lunar mansions." There is even more significance to these figures. Pranayama yoga, the yoga of breath control, calculates that the human being needs to take 21,600 breaths in a 24-hour period; therefore, the 12-hour "daylight" number of breaths is 10,800.

The sacred significance of this number has also extended its influence to Oriental martial arts where, for example, one of the major disciplines associated with Karate, the Suparinpei, translates as "one hundred and eight"; and there are 108 pressure points of the body in the South Indian and Chinese schools of martial arts.

There are 108 sacred **stars** in Taoist and Chinese **astrology**, and Siva's cosmic dance consists of 108 poses.

666 … THE NUMBER OF THE BEAST?

Do you suffer from hexakosioihexekontahexaphobia? If so, you fear the number 666: the so-called Number of the Beast. If you do, you are not alone; this series of three sixes strikes fear into the hearts of many who encounter it, even causing some people to protect themselves with the sign of the **cross**, although they may not be entirely sure of the reason why.

This number first occurs, other than as a natural phenomenon, in the First Book of Kings in the Old Testament, and refers to the amount of wealth that came to King Solomon, possibly because of his partnership with the Queen of Sheba. However, much of the superstition associated with this number stems from a chapter in the New Testament Book of Revelation, here quoted from the King James version:

Here is wisdom. Let him that hath understanding count the number of the beast; for it is the number of a man; and his number is Six Hundred Threescore and Six.

[Revelation, 13:18]

Since then, there have been many theories about to whom, or what, this description refers. For Christians, it has come to represent a catch-all idea of an Antichrist, a title conferred at different times to various enemies of the Christian religion, including the Emperors Nero and Domitian, Genghis Khan, Napoleon, and Hitler. Even the Roman Catholic Church and various popes have been identified as this Beast.

Latter-day notions about the meaning of the number result in speculation that it might provide some kind of code whereby the Devil will brand people in order that they will be able to buy or sell. Credit cards, barcodes, social security numbers and microchip technology have all come under the scrutiny of conspiracy theorists, with varying levels of incredulity and paranoia.

It's also interesting to note that the atom of the chemical element carbon, which forms the basis of all life on Earth, is comprised of 6 neutrons, 6 protons, and 6 electrons.

People who like to play around with the idea of being a dangerous, satanic type have adopted the number. These include the self-styled Great Beast, Aleister Crowley, who made 666 a part of his personal **sigil** and spent some time experimenting with various interpretations of this nickname, eventually translating it into Greek as "Therion," since

in this language the **Gematria**, or numerical value of "Great Beast" adds up to 666. Some latter-day musicians, usually those of a heavy/death metal persuasion, share this fascination. The satanic connotations of 666 are ambivalent in the **Kabbalah**, however, where it is not only the number of the solar **demon** Sorath, the opposite of the Archangel Michael, but it is also regarded as a sacred number that depicts the entire Universe.

But the devilish associations of 666 don't give us the true picture of this mysterious symbolic number. It is the number belonging to Hakathriel, also known as the Angel of the Diadem. And in **Sacred Geometry**, it is called the **magic square** of the **Sun**. This particular magic square is constructed in such a way that the first 36 numbers add up to 111 on horizontal, vertical or diagonal planes. The entire square adds up to 666, and the number's significance predates the Bible.

The architects of **Chartres Cathedral** may have known about the earlier significance of this number, since the **labyrinth** there measures exactly 666 feet long.

Numerologically speaking, 666 adds up to the number 18, which breaks down to 9; given that 9 is known to be the number of man, perhaps this simple explanation is what lies behind the biblical quote; 666 refers to the material part of man—the "beast"—rather than his spiritual aspect.

Finally, in China, the number, when spoken aloud, sounds like the phrase "Things going smoothly." This has made it one of the luckiest numbers in Chinese culture and so it is used on banners and good-luck cards.

MAGIC SQUARES

❖

The tradition of the magic square is ancient, going back at least as far as 2800 BC. There is a legend from China about people trying to appease the God of a flooding river. The God sent the people a turtle that had a magic number painted on its back, which mystically enabled the people to control the torrents.

Magic squares can be made of either **numbers** or **letters**. In the case of the former the numerals are set in a square grid pattern, each column or row of which adds up to the same number. This number is called the Magic Constant, and has significance in itself; the square format enhances the vibrational power of the series of numbers and also of the magic constant contained within it. The magic square somehow entraps all the potency of the number or letter within it.

The most basic magic square comprises nine squares in three rows of three. Magic squares are believed to have great potency depending on its magic constant, and they are used as charms and talismans, and in the casting of spells. The magic square is created according to the intention of the ritual, and is afterwards then burned, crushed, torn up or otherwise destroyed, so "releasing" the magic into the world.

Magic squares can become very elaborate, as in the series called the **Kameas**, which were originally created by the sixteenth-century occultist philosopher Cornelius Agrippa. This particular series describe the magic constant number of the Sun, the Moon, and five planets. Kameas are designed for **sigils** to be drawn over them or incorporated into them.

Significant or magical names can be used as well as numbers; there's a satisfying palindromic kind of fun to be had in creating them. One of the most famous is the Sator Square, which features in a number of magical treatises including the Key of Solomon.

There's a magic square at the Sagrada Familia Church in Barcelona whose magic constant is 33, the age of Christ at his crucifixion.

1	14	14	4
11	7	6	9
8	10	10	5
13	2	3	15

ONE THOUSAND

A thousand is symbolic of "many," and the phrase is used in this way, rather than as an accurate enumeration of an amount. It was said that the first man, Adam, should have lived for a thousand years but was punished for his transgressions by having his life expectancy curtailed.

Millenarianism is the name given to belief in a thousand-year cycle often adopted by religious or spiritual groups; for example Christians believe that Christ will reign for a thousand years after the Second Coming, although the Catholic Church were quick to condemn this putative thousand-year period as purely symbolic. Hitler portrayed what he perceived as the glory of his Nazi regime by saying that it would last for a thousand years; in fact it was a hundredth of this time.

TEN THOUSAND

In Ancient Egypt, the hieroglyphic symbol for 1 is a vertical line, like a **finger**. The symbol for 10,000 is, therefore, a huge finger. Symbolically, 10,000 represents a number so large as to be virtually uncountable. In Chinese culture the **swastika** is the sign for 10,000; both the number and the sign represent the entire number of beings and manifestations in the Universe, and therefore stands for everything in the known world—all objects, essences, and concepts. The **scorpion** is also used as another symbol for the number 10,000, since the words sound similar.

Ten thousand is a symbol of plenty and of fruitfulness. It's also a symbol of power and invincibility, as defined by the 10,000 men who comprised the guard of the Persian King and who were called The Immortals, and also by the 10,000 men who belonged to the Grand Old Duke of York in the nursery rhyme.

Part Eight

SACRED SOUNDS, SECRET SIGNS

THE INTRIGUE OF RESONANCE, LETTERS AND LANGUAGE

This book is, for the most part, comprised of the most important and versatile secret symbols you'll ever see; the letters of the **alphabet**. Even as your eyes are scanning this page, you are instantly translating the meaning of these curious squiggles that effectively contain all the secrets of the Universe. Although the symbols bear no relationship to **sounds**, nevertheless we hear the sounds that they represent. We hear these sounds, and grasp their complex ideas thousands of times a minute. This section looks at how these signs, sounds, and ideas converge, and also how other signs are used to keep certain information clandestine.

SOUND

Everything in the Universe has its own frequency, its own vibration. The human **ear** cannot hear some of these frequencies, but they exist nevertheless. A simple example is the **dog** whistle that is heard by dogs but

seldom by their human owners. Some frequencies are so powerful that they can destroy physical objects; again, a good example is the soprano whose top note is so pure that it can shatter glass. In the Bible story, the walls of Jericho were destroyed not by physical force as such, but by the power of sound. Certain very low frequencies can destroy matter by scrambling molecules. Sound can cause avalanches. There's a wonderful scene in the film *The Man Who Would be King* where the two protagonists, searching for a lost city, cross miles and miles of snowy wastes to find themselves cut off by an impassable ravine. The way behind is no longer traversable. Reminiscing about their lives, they laugh helplessly at their hopeless predicament, and this loud laughter causes an avalanche of snow that bridges the gap of the ravine, enabling the travelers to continue their journey.

Each **planet** emits its own frequency, as does the **Earth** itself. The natural harmonic of our home planet is said to be F sharp, an idea that was agreed by ancient peoples including the Egyptians (the Great Pyramid "plays" this note) and the Chinese, who called it Hu; interestingly, Native Americans tune their flutes to this note.

Does all this mean that our most secret and sacred symbols are inspired by something that cannot be seen, but only heard? Sounds can only be interpreted by us as written squiggles, and like the wind, we can only gauge this phenomenon by its effect on something else. Arguably, the most important symbol in the world is something that cannot be touched or seen.

Tarot expert Jean-Claude Flornoy, in a fascinating essay entitled *The Language of the Birds*, tells how he stumbled on an audible secret, hinted at in a visual clue:

At the Romanesque-Byzantine abbey built by Eleanor d'Aquitaine at Souillac, the capital [top] of the eighth ambulatory pillar depicts doves putting their beaks into an owl's ear. This is Athena's owl of course, and represents access to knowledge … During one of my visits to Souillac I calmly pursued my labyrinth while paying special attention to the different images sculpted on the capitals in the choir. Coming to the eighth pillar and not understanding the image, I put my back against it and closed my eyes, creating as much stillness as I could, and waited. I was not disappointed. After some minutes of meditative idling, my ears were ripped apart by a terrible noise. Emerging from my torpor with a powerful shock and opening my eyes, I found that I was alone except for a tourist who was standing at the entrance in the process of putting a postcard into an envelope!

It was this infinitesimal sound which had, from sixty meters away, blown my head away …

I understood that this was the sound's second harmonic, audible only from that specific spot. That is why the birds unstop the owl's ears and offer you access to what the ancients call the "third ear."

Ancient megalithic structures, such as **New Grange** in Ireland, and Wayland's Smithy in England, seem to have been constructed in order to exploit this effect. Indian Mogul palaces were designed so that guards could clap at certain points, knowing that the resultant loud echoes would act as an intruder alert system. The Whispering Gallery at St. Paul's Cathedral in London is constructed in such a way that a whisper can be heard in the part of the gallery that is directly opposite the person whispering.

WORDS

Many faiths seem to be in agreement with one thing at least: the notion that the primal resonance of a word, or sound, gave birth to the Universe. Understandably, the source of this primal sound is held to be divine. In the Bible it's described like this:

In the beginning was the Word, and the Word was with God, and the Word was God.

[John 1:1—3]

*   *   *

In the Qu'ran is written:

Words of Truth that have the power to express the Truth are like flourishing trees whose roots, or branches, or direct meanings are established deep in the earth of the heart, and whose branches, or subtle meanings, reach high into the sky of mystical knowledge.

The power of a word is such that it is considered to be the very seed of creation. The old saying "sticks and stones my break my bones but words can never hurt me" does not take into account the potency of a curse; whether or not its power lies in superstition does not make its consequences any less real. Similarly, a blessing carries with it wishes that are a powerful force for good.

For the Greeks, *logos*—"word"—meant not only the spoken word or phrase, but it was also inextricably linked to the intellectual faculties and ideas. The gift of eloquence belonged to the Gods, or gave God-like status to those who had mastery of it. A politician without the skill of oratory will never be a powerful leader. The Druids, for whom the oral tradition lasted long after the "invention" of the written word, had all sorts of charms and rituals guaranteed to confer eloquence: a cinquefoil leaf under the tongue, for example. Learning by repetition was considered the purest way of gaining information; the transference of words from one person to the next was to retain the purest intention of the words, unsullied by the "middle man" of **writing**.

LETTERS AND WRITING

The journey from primal sound to a deliberate word to written symbol is a mysterious one. In the same way that children learn to draw before they can write, early man's first "writing" was symbolic, a pictorial representation of ideas. The history of writing is well-documented elsewhere, but the sacred and momentous nature of the **alphabet** is indicated by the universality of stories of its divine invention: Thoth for the Ancient Egyptians, **Hermes/Mercury** in the Greco-Roman tradition, **Odin** in the Norse myths, and Ogma of the Celtic pantheon. In the Hindu religion, **Sarasvati** is not only the Goddess of Speech but is also called Lipidevi, the Goddess of the Alphabet. **Letters**, along with **numbers**, are the most potent secret signs and sacred symbols of any; their secrets so ingrained into our consciousnesses that we tend to take them for granted.

The letters of any alphabet carry great power; they are not just letters, but calendars, calculators, symbols, and concepts of divinity. It is worth remembering that, not so very long ago, reading and writing were arts reserved for the powerful and priestly castes, because with these gifts came the power of knowledge. These people had the power to transcribe the very Word of God. The first printed texts were religious ones. Once man could read and write—and could therefore decide which ideas he preferred— in certain ways, the power of the secular and religious authorities were considerably weakened.

The **Hebrew** language is said to contain secrets that only God might know. These secrets are dangerous, because they have the power to perform miracles such as raising the dead. The Torah compares the vowels of the alphabet with the living **soul** of a human being and says that the consonants, in contrast, belong to the world. Significantly, the vowel symbols are circular in shape, whereas the consonants are **square**. The vowels are seen to be spiritual in their nature, possibly because they are formed freely, without needing to connect the **tongue** or the **teeth**. Therefore, the constructed consonants symbolize the world of matter. It's also said that God gave Adam 32 letters, but that some 10 of them were lost, resulting in the 22-letter alphabet we have today.

Although writing is a fantastic tool, in some ways it "kills" ideas by giving them a permanent form. Ideas change; revolutionary theories become everyday fact. As with any of the signs and symbols in this book, it is as well to be aware of this when investigating the hidden meanings behind the alphabets themselves.

ABRACADABRA

```
A B R A C A D A B R A
  A B R A C A D A B R
    A B R A C A D A B
      A B R A C A D A
        A B R A C A D
          A B R A C A
            A B R A C
              A B R A
                A B R
                  A B
                    A
```

This ancient word may well have been inspired by the Aramaic "Avra Kedabra"—"I create as I speak"—or words to that effect. However, there are other theories about the origins of this word. In no particular order, then:

1. It was derived from the name of **Abraxas**.
2. It was derived from the Hebrew phrase "Abreq Ad Habra," meaning "Hurl your thunderbolt unto death" or "Strike dead with thy lightning" (in this case, its efficacy as a charm to ward away illness would make sense).
3. It could be from the Aramaic "Abhadda Kedabhra," meaning "Disappear as this word," which accurately reflects exactly what happens in the charm (because as the word diminishes and finally disappears, so would any malevolent energy).
4. The first letters of the word could be derived from the initials of Hebrew words for Father (Ab), Son (Ben), and Holy Spirit (Ruach Acadsch).

Chances are that this is such a powerful symbol because all of these theories make sense, so it would have universal appeal.

Although most accounts say that the charm was in use until the Middle Ages, there's curious proof of its efficacy in a small thirteenth-century church in a remote valley in Wales in the UK. St. Michael and All Angels Church at Cascob on the edge of the Radnor **Forest** has an Abracadabra charm engraved on a tablet on one of its walls. In the seventeenth century a local girl, Elizabeth Lloyd, was apparently possessed of evil **demons,** and this symbol was used to drive them away, along with the **astrological**

symbols that are carved below. There's even a possibility that this tablet was made by the alchemist Sir John Dee, who was astrologer to Queen Elizabeth I, and lived nearby.

ALPHA AND OMEGA

These are the names of the first and last letters of the Greek alphabet. Alphabets in general are believed to hold within them all the secrets of the Universe, so the Alpha and Omega encompass these secrets within a circular whole, a beginning and end, a completion. The Book of Revelation contains the following:

"I am Alpha and Omega, the beginning and the ending," saith the Lord, "which is and which was, and which is to come, the Almighty."

[Revelation 1:8]

These letters are often seen in association with other Christian symbols, inscribed on **altars** and **crosses**, for example.

AUM

The Aum, or Om, is a living symbol and exists, in varying forms and names, in Hinduism, Buddhism, Taoism, and Sikhism. Sometimes it translates as "So be it" and in this, it is similar to the Hebrew "Amen" or the "Awen" of modern Druidry. The Aum is the symbol of The Word, the sound that was present at the Creation of the Universe. This concept is expressed in the yoga sutras of Patanjali, which state, "God's voice is Aum." The Aum is used at the beginning and the end of prayer and is a chant which, when used consciously, helps the chanter to become a part of the All. The notion of such a primal sound is universal.

In the same way that there are three parts to the symbol that contribute to the whole, the Aum symbolizes the three Gods: Vishnu, Shiva, and Brahma. In yoga, the sound is used as a meditation on the breath and the nature of the Universe, and involves all parts of the lungs as it is chanted.

Hindu Aum

Tibetan Aum

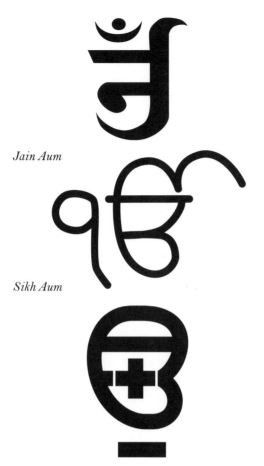

Jain Aum

Sikh Aum

Upkar

This last symbol, the Upkar, shows how the Sikh "Ek Onkar" symbol has been slightly altered to encompass a sign that has universal meaning as one of healing and protection. Here, the symbol is also the logo for the northern Indian hospital that shares its name. It means "the welfare of all" and combines the symbol of the **Red Cross** (physical and medical welfare) with the spiritual aspect of the Aum.

BISMILLAH

There are different variations of this beautiful symbol, which hides within its curlicues and flourishes the sacred name of God. Bismillah, in Arabic, means, literally, "In the Name of Allah," and it is the first word in the Qu'ran.

Islamic law forbids representations of animals or people, so the calligraphic form has been developed to a high art, as in the Bismillah symbol. "Bismillah" is spoken as a sign of respect before prayer, before meals, and before important undertakings.

BLAZES, TRAILS AND TRAVELERS' SIGNS

Blazes are symbols that mark trails or tracks. Sometimes the blazes are, as the name would suggest, overt and easily understood; sometimes necessity dictates that the signs are covertly hidden within the landscape so that only the initiate will be able to follow the track.

The former kind of blaze tends to be visually arresting and transcends boundaries of nationality or culture, often used, for example, in tourist destinations. In **forests** these route indicator signs will usually be at **eye**-level, perhaps painted onto a **tree**. Of course, it's important that this type of sign can withstand the elements. So there's nothing particularly secret about this kind of everyday signage.

The other kind—the covert kind—is different. Often used by hunters, these signs might emulate methods used by Native Americans. One of the most basic of these signs is a small nick of bark taken from a **tree,** which marks the trail. The size of these axe blazes vary according to the skill of the

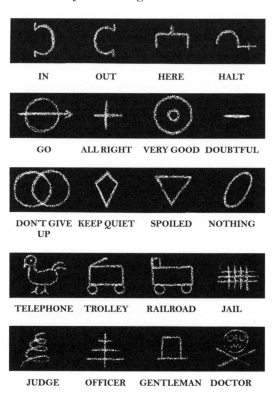

| IN | OUT | HERE | HALT |

| GO | ALL RIGHT | VERY GOOD | DOUBTFUL |

| DON'T GIVE UP | KEEP QUIET | SPOILED | NOTHING |

| TELEPHONE | TROLLEY | RAILROAD | JAIL |

| JUDGE | OFFICER | GENTLEMAN | DOCTOR |

| DOG | WOMAN | WEALTH | KIND-HEARTED WOMAN |

| CAMPING HERE | BE GOOD | IF SICK WILL HELP | SAFE CAMP |

| WELL-GUARDED HOUSE | AFRAID | TELL PITIFUL STORY |

| DANGER | BE PREPARED TO DEFEND YOURSELF | MAN WITH GUN | BAD DOG |

| UNRELIABLE MAN | UNSAFE PLACE | YOU WILL BE BEATEN |

maker. The idea is to make them as small as possible yet noticeable to anyone knowing what to look for.

In areas where there are no trees and a trail still needs to be made, inventive use is made of the natural environment. A popular device is to snap a twig on a bush and leave the broken part dangling, connected by a slim thread of bark. This indicates the trail. If the twig is broken off, the torn end of the twig might indicate the direction to be followed. If the trail is to cover an area of open grassland, a clump might be twisted into a **knot**; significantly, sometimes more than one knot might be used. Otherwise, stones might be stacked on top of each other or next to each other in a particular way.

SMOKE SIGNALS

A highly effective although highly visible sign, smoke signals can nevertheless carry secrets, and are primarily used by Plains Indians. Making a smoke signal seems to be the dream of every child but it takes time to create the fire needed to make a decent amount of smoke. Here's how to make your own smoke signals.

First, make a very hot and clear **fire** from as much dry material as you can muster. When the fire is burning well, cover it with damper, **green** material. Rotten wood is good, too. Then, **three** or **four** people each need to take a corner of a blanket, using it to cover and uncover the fire, releasing smoke at intervals pre-arranged with the people you are communicating with.

Although a funnel of steady smoke will indicate where a camp is, other signals are possible: a steady sequence of double puffs is the equivalent of an SOS.

Throughout history, there have been times when people have needed to cover their tracks or otherwise hide the route they were taking. Romany and nomadic travelers of any sort have each used their own systems of signs and signals to communicate with each other over distances, telling of routes or passing on news. Latterly, the cheap availability of mobile phones has meant that traveling people have no problem in meeting up with one another. This wasn't always the case, and not so very long ago it was necessary to have a set of secret signs and symbols, which would enable communication whilst on the road.

Patrin, or patteran, is the name given to the indicators made by Romany people along their chosen routes. Coming from a Romany word meaning leaf, a patrin could be a drawn sign or a sign constructed discreetly from natural objects found in the landscape; a bundle of twigs, a **feather**, or a snapped twig.

Hobo signs

During times of extreme economic depression, it has often been necessary for people to leave their homes and take to the roads in terms of employment in order to survive. Times were particularly desperate during the Depression in the United States in the early part of the twentieth century. Although many saw these destitute people as vagrants, most hobos were desperate for any work they could get; indeed, a hobo differentiated himself from a tramp, who was seen to be unwilling to work. Despite poverty (or maybe because of it) there was a strong bond between fellow travelers and this bond resulted in a series of symbols that could be interpreted by those following, and which could provide hints and tips gained from the experience of those who had gone before.

Although it is hard to date such symbols precisely, it seems that they started from the 1880s and had died out by the Second World War. The signs were drawn on fence posts, on the sides of the railroad, on paths; in short, anywhere where those on the lookout would notice them. They were usually written in chalk or coal or marked with anything that was readily available.

Chai

Often seen these days on souvenirs and artwork from Israel, the Chai is the secret symbol that consists of the Hebrew letters Het and Yod. Together these letters spell "chai," which means "living" and refers not only to God but also to the Jewish people.

The Jewish system of numerology, the **Gematria**, shows that these letters add up to **eighteen**, which is considered to be a favorable number. Therefore the Chai symbol is also a lucky charm.

Da'wah

Literally meaning "summons" or "call," the Da'wah is a secret method of incantation, a "call" to a whole mystical tradition, in a similar way that the **Hebrew alphabet** is far more than a simple series of letters.

Using the Arabic alphabet, each letter has finely tuned associations with the names of God, **numbers**, the **elements**, perfumes, **planets**, **spirits** and **angels**. Each letter also has its own nature.

To master the Da'wah the adept must follow a strict moral code and diet. Once the esoteric mysteries of the Da'wah are mastered, they confer a God-like power over the Universe.

Gematria

The Gematria is a system of numerology where letters and **numbers** are linked and although this method is used elsewhere, Gematria applies specifically to the Hebrew language, and is explained in many mystical Jewish writings.

Although there are 22 letters in the **Hebrew alphabet**, 27 numerals are needed to express each number up to 999 (one through nine, 10 through 90, and 100 through 900). The mystical Hebrew numeric system notes that the missing final five letters of the numeral system match exactly with the alphabet's five word-final alternate forms.

Here is the Hebrew Gematria chart showing the numeric values of each letter:

Aleph	A	1
Beth	B	2
Gimal	C/G	3
Daleth	D	4
Heh	E/H	5
Vav	St/V	6
Zayin	Z	7
Cheth	E/Ch	8
Teth	Th/T	9
Yod	I	10
Caph	K	20
Lamed	L	30
Mem	M	40
Nun	N	50
Samech	Ch/S	60
Ayin	O	70
Peh	P	80
Tzadi	Q/Tz	90
Qoph	R/Rh/Q	100
Resh	S/R	200
Shin	T/Sh	300
Tav	Y/U/Th	400

Some interesting correspondences can arise; in *Math for Mystics*, Renna Shesso points out that the numerical values for "**lion**," "**cheetah**" and "**tiger**" all reduce down to 5. Other words that have the same numerical value share the same qualities, and can be used to reveal still other aspects of the Divine.

GREATEST NAME

The Greatest Name generally refers to the most holy and secret name of God, the name that carries the entire essence of divine power. This idea is common throughout many faiths. This name usually encompasses the notion of "light" or "glory." In the Bahai faith the symbol of the Greatest Name is a calligraphic rendering of the phrase "Glory of Glories," or "Ya Baha'ul-Abha."

INVOCATION

At the heart of many magical practices, whether they belong to a conformist religious belief or more pagan tradition is the idea that calling a name can invoke the spirit or entity that is connected to that name.

An invocation can take the form of a supplication, or a command. Most faiths have a standardized form of invocation—the Lord's Prayer, for example, in Christianity. However, sometimes the invocation of a spirit is an invitation for it to take up residence for a time in a physical host, i.e. possession. This form of invocation or "inviting in" is sometimes the desired outcome of Voudon ceremonies where the **spirit**, or "loa," is summoned into the body via a series of ecstatic rituals that involve chanting, **dancing**, and drumming.

In the case of spirit invocation, these entities need to be "bound" or otherwise constrained by means of magical **seals** or symbols.

'K' in magick

Sometimes, magic is spelled with a "k" as in "magickal." This final "k" was a conceit introduced by Aleister Crowley at the beginning of the twentieth century, in order to differentiate stage magic and conjuring tricks of a purely mechanical nature with the intentional ritual magic of a supernatural nature that can allegedly cause changes and alter the course of events.

For Crowley, the fact that the "k" is the eleventh letter of the alphabet gave it even more magic(k)al significance. According to the laws of **gematria**, where each letter has its corresponding number, **eleven** is the number that corresponds to the realm of the **Kabbalah** concerning the forces of evil that have to be conquered before the magic(k)al practitioner can truly call himself an adept.

People who are aware of the provenance of this conceit may choose to use it or not, depending whether they wish to align themselves with the teachings of Crowley or any of the mystical orders that he was affiliated to.

Kalachakra Seal

This is a beautiful, elaborate, and evocatively meaningful symbol, a major device within Tibetan Buddhism. It can be seen in monasteries and other holy places and in itself is emblematic of the arcane and occult knowledge into which relatively few lamas are initiated. The meaning of the Kalachakra exists on many levels.

The seal is comprised of a calligraphic rendering of letters, using a script called Lantsa or Ranjana. This secret and sacred script was

developed from Sanskrit and is used only for religious scripts, texts, **mandalas**, and **mantras**. Many holy documents written in the Ranjana script were destroyed when China invaded Tibet.

The Kalachakra Seal, which is also called The Tenfold Powerful One, contains many elements. Hidden within its curlicues are the **seven** syllables of the Holy Mantra called the Kalachakra. The mantra is "Ham Ksa Ma La Va Ra Ya."

The remaining **three** elements that give the symbol its tenfold nature are the **crescent moon**, the disc of the full **Moon** or the **Sun**, and the flame of **fire**.

But what does the Kalachakra actually mean?

Both the symbol and the sound of the letters that comprise it are inextricably linked. It is also often drawn in **color**, as the colors are important symbols in themselves. The syllables are written one on top of the other, and interlock together. The whole stands on a stylized lotus (symbolic of the heart), with the character for "emptiness" and "bliss" set to the left and right, respectively, of the Kalachakra symbol. The framework of the Kalachakra is important, too, and represents a mandala made of flames. This is called the Circle of Wisdom.

If we examine each aspect of the Kalachakra, then, here's what we find.

First, many symbols have an element that is not drawn or shown in any way, but is implied. Here, it's the letter A, which is emblematic of **space**.

Next, the syllables, including the colors that they might appear as:

- Ham (**blue**): indicative of formless realms; the vacuum; the spiritual world; bliss; enlightened wisdom; the Gods
- Ksha (**green**): represents the world of form and desire; the material world. This syllable means the body, the mind, and the power of speech
- Ma (multi-colored): a reminder of the **Holy Mountain**, Mount Meru. It relates to the **spinal column** of the body, which, like the Mountain, ascends towards the Heavens
- La (**yellow**): the grounding **earth** element
- Va (**white**): the element of **water**
- Ra (**red**): the element of **fire**
- Ya (**black**): the element of **air**

Collectively, the elements within the Kalachakra represent the spiritual and material life of Man; the elements; the **Wheel of Time**; the emptiness of the void, and the pregnant seed of creation. It has inspired the calculations of calendars and astrologers.

KAMEA

A particular kind of **magic square** that is intended to incorporate a **sigil**. The whole is used as a charm or **talisman** or as a tool in casting a spell. The kamea is a Kabbalistic invention.

MAGICAL NAME

This is a name given to a newly initiated member into a magical group or cult. A "magical" name is necessarily that which belongs to a magical society, but adherents of many religions will change their name or add a new name to their existing one. Catholics and Muslims, for example, follow this practice, symbolic of belonging and acceptance by the religious community as well as a rebirth into the chosen faith.

MANI STONE

In Tibetan Buddhism, a Mani stone is a stone, pebble or rock inscribed with a **mantra**, or prayer. The stones are to be found everywhere and serve as devotional offerings. Mani stones appear singly or stacked up in large piles. The most common mantra to be found painted or carved onto the stones is **Om Mani Padme Hum**, the same mantra which is found on the long pieces of paper inside **prayer wheels**.

Mantra

This is a sacred phrase or series of sounds that, when repeated over and over, is believed to effect a corresponding spiritual vibration. The mantra has similarities to a prayer except that it tends to be specific to the Dharmic faiths. Whoever chants a mantra becomes unified with the greater cosmos. "**Aum**," "**Om Mani Padme Hum**," and "Nam Myoho Renge Kyo" are all examples of mantras. The visual symbol for the mantra is the **Yantra**.

The mantra does not work if it is translated. It's important that the syllables of the original phrase are pronounced correctly. Like a magical spell, the correct mantra, it is believed, can accomplish anything provided the person chanting it is in the correct frame of mind, mentally and spiritually prepared. The power of certain mantras means that they are taught only with great care to those who are worthy of using them.

Music

The devil's chord

Music is truly divine, and legends from all over the world and from all faiths agree that it was invented by the Gods.

Pythagoras, like the Chinese before him, knew that music carries the harmony of the cosmos, encompassing the vibrational values of **numbers**, **shapes**, and **sounds**. He called this theory the "Music of the Spheres," a universal symphony of interconnectedness. If sound is the most common unifying factor, then music is the sublime aspect of this connection. The same mathematical rules that underscore **sacred geometry** also apply to the measurements that rule the harmonic or discordant vibrations of strings played together.

Music can reflect our mood, or can alter it. In myth, music can bring enchanted sleep as well as rousing soldiers to battle. It has much in common with perfume; it is invisible and yet all pervasive and can be experienced by many people at the same time. Like the scented **smoke** given off by **incense**, music plays an important part in sacred and magical rituals, a unifying factor in orthodox religious ceremonies as well as in pagan ones.

In the same way that certain music heralds a change of scene, mood or action in a film, sometimes music needs to symbolize the presence of evil. The Devil's Chord, or "Diabolus in Musica," consisting of a dissonant and spooky sounding interval such as an augmented fourth, is so evocative of menace that it was allegedly banned from Church music in the Middle Ages. An example of what this sinister chord sounds like? Try the opening bars of Jimi Hendrix's "Purple Haze."

Rosslyn Chapel in Scotland, site of much mystical conjecture, recently added a new discovery to its trove of secrets. There is a series of carved stone cubes in the Chapel, each with a particular pattern etched onto it. The patterns equate to Chladni patterns. If sand, **salt** or some other fine powder is poured onto a taut surface (such as the skin of a drum) which is then subjected to a tonal frequency, the vibrations cause the powder to make symmetrical patterns, including the diamonds, rhomboids, flowers and other designs that appear on the stone cubes.

The discovery was made after twenty years of research by Thomas Mitchell, whose son, Stuart, has written a piece of music called "The Rosslyn Motet" that is based on the notes encoded in these stones.

NAME

A **rose**, by any other name, as Shakespeare pointed out, may smell as sweet; but would it really still be a rose?

A name carries the essence of the power and spirit of its owner, hence in many faiths the true Name of God is a great mystery, shrouded in oblique references and rarely spoken aloud. In the Jewish faith, only the High Priest pronounces the Name of God. The belief is that the power of the name of God is such that the whole world will be struck dumb if it were shouted out loud, hence the vital necessity to keep it a secret. In Islam, too, there are 99 names of God plus one more, unknown name, the **Greatest Name**. God and the Name of God are identical, and to know all these names enables a person to enter Heaven.

The Ancient Egyptians felt that the name was a living thing, an inextricable part of the person it described. Often, when people become affiliated to a religion, they are given another name as part of their initiation, a sign of their rebirth, a new identity conferred by allegiance to the faith.

The power of the name is also the reason why, in the *Harry Potter* books by J.K. Rowling, the name of the arch villain Voldemort is rarely said, replaced instead with "you know who." In the **fairy** tale, knowledge of the name of the gnome Rumplestiltskin will buy power over him. It's an old superstition that a child without a name is somehow without a **soul**, and is therefore at risk of exposure to evil influences.

In the Celtic lands, the name of a person and their job, occupation or function was the same. This tradition lives on today, particularly in parts of Wales where the person is described by both name and occupation; Dai the Post, for example.

NOTARIKON

A kind of acronym, this is a method, in Hebrew, of using the letters of a word as the initials for a phrase. This "hidden" phrase generally gives a different way of interpreting the word. Sacred words or the secret names of God were given this treatment, which was a way of hiding their true meaning. These codes are often embedded into sacred texts, hence the importance of preserving the original written form.

A simple example of a Notarikon is the word Amen, which is constructed from the initial letters of the phrase "the Lord and Faithful King."

OM MANI PADME HUM

This is the most important and profound **mantra** in Tibetan Buddhism, and the words are engraved onto **mani stones** as well as written on the scrolls of paper contained within **prayer wheels**. The phrase means, "**Aum**, to the Jewel in the Lotus, hum."

These six seemingly simple syllables have a deeper meaning that lies at the very heart of the faith. The resonance is affected not only by the physical components of the mantra but also by the intent of the acolyte. Buddhists believe that not only does the chanter add to his own enlightenment in the process of repeating this magical phrase, but that the consciousness of humanity is raised at the same time.

PONTOS RISCADOS

This is a special **sigil**, used to invoke the Gods (or Orishas) peculiar to the specific magical practices of Brazil. It seems that supernatural beings respond well to such symbols, since they are similar to the magical sigils used by such illustrious luminaries as Aleister Crowley and John Dee. Each entity has its own particular sigil, which is drawn on the ground in special colored chalks as part of an invocation.

SATOR WORD SQUARE

```
S A T O R
A R E P O
T E N E T
O P E R A
R O T A S
```

This word square is an ingenious palindromic construction, and can be read in any direction: forward, backward, top to bottom, and bottom to top. The oldest example of it that has been discovered so far is in the ruins of Herculanaeum, an ancient Roman city that was destroyed in the volcanic eruption that also decimated Pompeii in the first century AD. Thereafter, it crops up in all sorts of places: in the cathedral in Siena, in a small chapel near Rennes-le-Chateau in France, in Malta, Syria, and the UK. It appears on the front cover of the infamous magical tome *The Book of the Sacred Magic of Abra Melin the Sage*, which is considered to be the ultimate guide to the **Kabbalah**.

Both the meaning and the provenance of the SATOR square are a mystery. Effectively a literary labyrinth that does not yield its secrets easily, it has been claimed as a Christian conceit because the letters can be rearranged in the form of a cross to read thus:

```
P
A
T
E
R
PATERNOSTER
O
S
T
E
R
```

The left-over pairs of A and O can be taken to mean **Alpha and Omega**, the first and last letters of the Greek alphabet.

The literal translation of the square is:

- SATOR: sower, planter
- AREPO: could be a proper name
- TENET: to hold
- OPERA: work, effort
- ROTAS: wheels

Therefore, "Sator, the sower, holds the wheels by his work," or "The sower, Arepo, holds the wheels with effort."

This meaning can be interpreted in several ways, its relevance squeezed into the preferred ideology. The implications of some kind of analogy to sowing and harvesting, **death** and rebirth cannot be ignored. Scholars have puzzled in particular over the word Arepo, since it appears nowhere else; it would not be beyond the bounds of possibility that the inventor of this word square put it there because it "fitted" and simply gave it a meaning later. However, it is close to a Celtic word meaning "plow," which aligns nicely with the agricultural references.

Many people believe that the SATOR square is imbued with magical protective properties, the net of elegantly placed words having a depth of meaning that transcends the literal. Dutch settlers in Pennsylvania used it as an **invocation** to protect their cattle.

SEALS

Magical seals are used in **invocations**, to bind or otherwise harness the power of an entity or **spirit**. A seal is a sort of signature for the spirit and the understanding of it by the conjuror is akin to knowledge of a **name**.

There are dozens and dozens of such symbols, many of them listed in grimoires such as the Lesser Key of Solomon or *Lemegton Clavicula Salomonis* that was compiled in the seventeenth century from much earlier sources. Curious and decorative, these seals are used in ritual magic, often in conjunction with **amulets**.

SIGIL

Although a sigil is the name applied to a signet or seal that belongs to a fraternity order, as a magical symbol it is less straightforward.

THE ELEMENT ENCYCLOPEDIA OF SECRET SIGNS AND SYMBOLS

A sigil is a symbol that belongs in particular to the Western tradition of magic. The word itself has its origins in a Latin word, *sigilum*, meaning "seal," and it is a personalized glyph or emblem that carries a specific meaning or intent. The **Monad** of Dr John Dee, for example, is a sigil.

There is a Hebrew word, *segulah*, which may or may not be related to the sigil, but which describes very well what a sigil actually is. *Segulah* means "a word, action, or item of spiritual effect." This has similar meaning to that of "**talisman**." Sigils generally appear in a drawn or written form although it is possible for them to be rendered in **sound** or as a solid three-dimensional object.

The sigil itself sometimes looks simple, sometimes more elaborate, but in either case its design and creation will have a complex series of meanings attached to it. Sigils are frequently made up of lots of different elements; the Norse **Binding Rune** is an example of a particular kind of sigil. Astrological signs and their corresponding **planets** also have their sigils.

The magicians of medieval times used sigils to call up **angels**, **demons**, and other diverse spirits. Each of these entities had its own sigil that represented its "essence," a sort of spiritual autograph or signature, so the sigil was a powerful tool in the right hands—or the wrong ones. Pages and pages of these signatures appear in grimoires and other magical texts, notably in the Lesser Key of Solomon. This anonymously written seventeenth-century work contains a handy at-a-glance guide to the personal sigils of the 72 Demons of Hell; for the adept, this would be the equivalent of a telephone directory to dial up entities from another dimension.

Command of the sigil, combined with correct attention to ritual detail, gives the conjurer power over the being that he is calling upon.

Self-professed adepts Aleister Crowley and Austin Osman Spare famously used sigils in their personal quests of mystical exploration, but the use of sigils is not a thing of the past. Latter-day practitioners of magic also employ them, and the method of doing so is strikingly simple given their purported efficacy. See *Sigil Magic*, page 524.

STONEMASONS' MARKS

Sometimes small and puzzling marks can be spotted on the sides of old buildings and stone structures. These are stonemasons' marks. In the same way that a painter marks a canvas, a stonemason "signs" his work by means of such a symbol.

Stonemasonry is one of the earliest trades, and any ancient stone building is testimony to the skills of these artisans, whose names might largely be forgotten but whose legacy remains. The **Pyramids**, the **Parthenon**, the **Pantheon**, Ziggurats, **temples**, **churches**, and **cathedrals**—all were built by stonemasons.

Despite the difficulty of leaving a signature on a building, the stonemason did not

SIGIL MAGIC

❖

The object of the exercise is to cast a spell that attracts the object of your desire, a sort of tool for cosmic ordering. The sigil provides the focus for this spell.

1. Decide what the desired object actually is. Precision is vital. For example, it's not enough to simply ask for money: what if the fortune comes as a result of the death of a loved one, for example?

2. Write down a sentence that expresses the outcome that you want.

3. Now reduce the sentence so that no letter is repeated.

4. Here's the fun part. Reduce the letters down further into shapes. It doesn't matter if some of the letters are upside down, and upper or lower case is of no significance either. For example, the letter P also contains within it an I, lower-case L, a C, an F and a lower-case D (if you flip it upside down).

5. Once you have accounted for all the letters, arrange them in a design that pleases you. If you can draw it in one single stroke and contain it in a circle, so much the better.

6. Next you need to write your sigil on a piece of paper or parchment, with as much due ceremony as you choose to muster.

7. The final part of this kind of sigil magic requires the symbol to be "charged." This can be done by using the symbol as a focus for meditation, and then burning it or otherwise forgetting all about it.

The sigil illustrated on page 522 is the result of the following desire: "*The Element Encyclopedia of Secret Signs and Symbols* helps people understand one another and makes the world a better place."

This lengthy sentence reduces down to the letters THELMNCYOPDIAFSR-GUKWB

These letters can be rendered down in lots of different ways but the final sigil can be drawn in one continuous movement and wrapped in a circle.

remain entirely anonymous. He often carved a personal symbol into his work, a secret sign that acted not only as an autograph but also as a form of quality assurance. These marks were generally quite angular; sometimes **runes** or runic shapes were used since straight lines are generally easier to scratch into stone then more rounded forms.

In the Middle Ages, most craftspeople had their own guild. These guilds had their own systems of organization that included a certain amount of ritual and ceremony. Each separate guild of stonemasons had a "mother mark" and the individual mason used this as the basis for his own personal signature, which he had to swear not to change.

TEMURAH

Like **Gematria** and **Notarikon**, Temurah is a way of rearranging the letters of certain words and sentences in the Bible to give an alternative, mystical meaning. **Atbash**, for example, is a Temurah cipher.

TETRAGRAMMATON

Words carry a great power, and to speak a word out loud "enables" the word. **Names** in particular carry the most power, and there is no more potent name than the Tetragrammaton.

This magical name is sometimes drawn in the form of the earlier Pythagorean **Tetraktys**, a sign that represents the Universe.

Quite literally, Tetragrammaton means "four-letter word" in Greek (although it

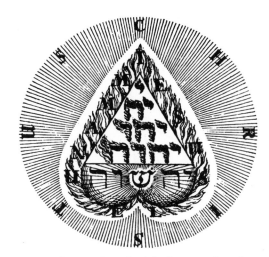

mustn't be confused with the popular slang meaning "expletive") and refers to the secret name of the God of the Israelites, written in Hebrew. This name is so holy and powerful that it can never be spoken, apart from just once a year at Yom Kippur by the High Priest within the **Holy of Holies**. To avoid using this name it is referred to as "The Name" or "Elohim" or "Adonai."

The letters of the name are yodh hev vav hev, and God is said to have explained to Moses that the name means "I Shall Be" or "I Am." These letters are pronounced "ee ah ou eh" (hence Jahweh), and will often be seen as a part of magical **amulets** or **talismans**.

The actual Name of God is said to be **72** letters long and was written on a long slip of paper secreted inside the High Priest's jeweled **breastplate**. When the Name was invoked, the **jewels** would light up in a certain sequence, thereby allowing the priest to communicate directly with God.

WATERMARK

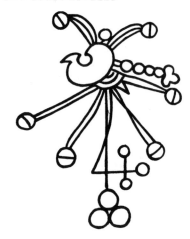

Sometimes, certain terminology is so familiar that we seldom stop to think of its origins. Foolscap paper is a case in point. This commonly used size of paper, known less exotically as A4, is so-called because of the symbol of a fool's cap that used to be embedded into the paper in the form of a watermark, and its use can be traced back to 1479.

As a way of hiding a symbol there can be few better ways than the watermark. It is likely that the method of making watermarks was the result of a happy accident. Methods of making paper by hand have altered very little over the centuries; a thin layer of wet pulp is spread over a sieve and left to dry, when the resulting sheet of paper can be peeled from the mesh. If a piece of wire is placed on top of the sieve before the pulp is spread over it, then the image of the wire shows up when the paper is held up to the light because the paper is very slightly thinner at that point. This method is believed to have been discovered by the papermakers of Fabiano and Bologna in late thirteenth-century Italy.

Papermakers quickly realized that their paper could be protected (from theft, for example) by the use of such a mark, which could also be used as a sign of quality assurance and as an identity for the maker. At the same time, the watermark might be used to convey a secret message of some kind. Henry VIII of England, for example, commissioned a watermark for his own supply of paper that showed the image of a hog wearing a miter, to show his contempt of the Pope.

Although it is almost impossible to prove the mystical use of certain watermarks, it seems as though certain symbols speak for themselves. These include the paper branded with Rosicrucian symbols that was used by Francis Bacon in letters and in editions of his books that were published privately. Specifically, his book *The Advancement of Learning* shows his Rosicrucian sympathies in the watermark which includes the initials C.R., standing for the legendary founder of the Order, Christian Rosenkreutz.

Papermaking skills were brought to Europe from the East by the Knights Templar and other crusaders returning from the Holy Land, although, as we have seen, the discovery of making watermarks was an accident that happened in Europe. The Cathars— a sect deemed by the Church to be heretical because of their dualist beliefs—were persecuted to the point that they were forced to flee their homeland in France, and were scattered around Europe where they had to make a living in any way they could; papermaking was one of these skills. They allegedly identified one another and kept track of their supporters by means of a watermark used on their "Lombardy Paper." The meanings of these marks are difficult to analyze but their distinctly mystical-looking nature would seem to support this theory.

Secret scripts and ciphers

As soon as the majority of us were able to convey information to one another by means of reading and writing, we began to invent different sorts of alphabets so that we could still keep some things a secret. It seems that the desire to keep certain information concealed comes naturally to us; even children invent certain changes to their speech or writing that are designed to hide their true meaning.

Necessarily, these secret alphabets and ciphers were often invented by closed societies, such as the **Freemasons**, or practitioners of magic who wanted to keep information within their own **circle** of trust. Many of these secret alphabets are mere substitution ciphers, that is, they replace the existing letters of an alphabet with different symbols whilst retaining the underlying rules of grammatical construction. Others, such as the **Enochian script**, are true languages in their own right.

Secret scripts, codes, and ciphers are not only the province of sorcerers and magicians. Codes are essential tools during times of war to keep information safe from the enemy. For example, Navajo was used as a code during the American assault on the Pacific during the Second World War. The complexity and rarity of the language, which was never written and was spoken only by the Navajo tribes and perhaps some thirty others at the time, meant that the Japanese never cracked it. The author Beatrix Potter kept her wry observations about the society and politics of her time to herself, since she invented a code that she used to write her journals from the ages of fifteen through to thirty. These codes were so complex that they were only deciphered some twenty years after her death.

It's worth bearing in mind that our "normal" alphabets are replete with arcane secrets that go way beyond them being mere visual symbols of sounds.

Adamical alphabet

See **Enochian script**.

Aiq Bkr alphabet

This is a substitution, or **Temurah** cipher, based on the letters of the Hebrew alphabet. The **22** letters of the alphabet are put into a grid of **nine squares**, meaning that each square will have two characters and some will have three. The letters can be substituted for any in the same square; a simple cipher, but comprehensible only to those that know what to look for. Aiq Bekar is also called the "**Kabbalah** of Nine Chambers."

Alchemical alphabet

Secrecy was a fundamental part of any alchemical operation, and the substances and processes of this ancient art were deliberately veiled by sequences of symbols and pictures designed to convey information without using words. Several different alchemical alphabets appeared in the sixteenth century, simple substitution ciphers based on Roman lettering.

Alphabet of arrows

This alphabet is a substitution cipher based on the letters of a mystical alphabet that actually appears to have a proper grammar and syntax all of its own—Edward Kelley and John Dee's **Enochian** language. The alphabet of arrows appears in a work by Aleister Crowley (see **alphabet of daggers**).

Alphabet of daggers

A substitution cipher using the letters of the Roman alphabet as a base, this script has little dagger symbols that combine to spooky

effect. It first appears in Aleister Crowley's work *The Vision and the Voice*, in which Crowley takes a visionary journey into the realms, or "aethyrs," inhabited by the **angels** of John Dee and Edward Kelley. The **alphabet of arrows** follows the same pattern but is a substitution cipher for the **Enochian** alphabet, and is found in the same book.

Alphabet of Honorius

See **Witches alphabet**.

Angelical script

The angelical script shown here is a simple substitution cipher, created by Cornelius Agrippa in the sixteenth century. However, the **Enochian script**—which is a "proper" grammatical language—is also sometimes called "angelical writing."

Atbash cipher— Zgyzhs xrksvi

The unpronounceable words in the heading shows "Atbash cipher" written as it would be in its own code. Atbash is a substitution cipher, simple enough to understand but confusing to look at. Imagine the Roman alphabet written normally, left to right, on one line. Then write the alphabet again underneath, this time starting at the right and placing the

A beneath the Z. Atbash was originally based on the **Hebrew alphabet**. One of its uses was to confound any casual enquiries into the inner workings of the **Kabbalah**.

BIND RUNE

See **Runic alphabet**.

CELESTIAL SCRIPT

Among the alphabets that Cornelius Agrippa wrote about, the celestial script is one influenced by the **Hebrew alphabet**. This script was used to communicate with angelic beings, a use which some students of the occult still practice today. The letters are also used in making charms and **amulets**.

COFFIN TEXTS

Coffin texts were the magical symbols and spells written by Egyptians on the coffins of the deceased, their primary function to ensure the survival of the **soul** in the Afterlife.

However, the advent of coffin texts marked a profound social change. Their predecessors, the **pyramid texts**, essentially fulfilled the same purpose as the coffin texts but were the exclusive domain of royalty. The appearance of the coffin texts meant that almost anyone could have the benefit of the magical commands that carried such power. The consequences, for a society who believed so fundamentally and profoundly in an afterlife, meant that the prospect of a non-exclusive Heaven now existed, even if the offer was still only open to those who could afford it.

As well as spells of protection (which might show **serpents** and other dangerous creatures being stabbed in the back) and charms for a "blessed existence" after **death**, the coffin texts consisted of maps and descriptions of the Land of the Dead, a sort of guidebook to the Afterlife. Perhaps the most famous of the coffin texts was the Book of the Two Ways, which describes the complete journey between the two worlds.

DAVIDIAN ALPHABET

This Arabic script is first mentioned in a book written in AD 855 by an Arabic scholar of magical lore. The title of this book translates as the awe-inspiring *Book of the Frenzied Devotee to Learn about the Ancient Scripts*.

Also called Dambudi, the Davidian script is named for King David of Israel whose son, Solomon, was renowned for his wisdom. Even now, thousands of years after his death, Solomon is held in reverential awe by Arabs, and many others, as the greatest magician who ever lived.

The alphabet is imbued, by association, with Solomon's powers. Said to be the Father of **Freemasonry**, Solomon's polymath skills included the ability to understand the language of **birds**. Stylistically, the alphabet is derived from **Hebrew** letters. The letters of the Davidian script are believed to be so infused with occult meaning that they are the very embodiment of mystical power. The Arabs that used it referred to it simply as *rihani*, meaning "magic."

ENOCHIAN SCRIPT

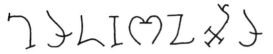

Many magical scripts used in grimoires and other manuscripts as a way of ensuring the secrecy of their contents, are actually no more than a cipher, using different symbols to represent the letters of an existing alphabet. Even where Roman and **Hebrew** letters are used in such a "magical" alphabet, the underlying language is still usually English or Hebrew. However, there are a few exceptions, and the Enochian tongue is one of these.

In the sixteenth century Dr. John Dee (a renowned mystic who was the astrologer to Queen Elizabeth I) and Edward Kelley claimed that **angels** imparted both the script and language to them. Dee was an extremely well read and learned scholar, conversant with languages and with a passionate interest in the angelic realms. He was also an extensive diarist, and in his journal, he mentions the angels that God sent to communicate directly with his prophets. Dee was inspired to try to find his own angels since knowledge of their language would be the most powerful tool that any magician could have in his kit. He set about this extraordinary task with the help of Edward Kelley, an alchemist and clairvoyant medium or "seer." Kelley saw the letters in a vision while scrying with a **crystal ball**. Apparently, when Kelley complained that he could not see the letters properly, the angels caused them to appear on a piece of paper, where they were easy for Kelley to trace before they faded away.

Dee himself didn't refer to the script as "Enochian." He called it "**Angelical**" or "The Celestial Speech," or sometimes "**Adamical**," since the angels told him that the language had been taught by God to Adam, who used it to communicate with both God and the angels. It had also been the language used to name all things. The epithet "Enochian" came about because Dee believed that the great biblical patriarch Enoch had been the last person to understand the language.

This arcane tongue had apparently been lost when Adam was banished from the Garden of Eden, a myth that carries a powerful symbolic punch—if mankind can no longer communicate with a divine creative spirit then he is lost indeed, truly cast out. Adam's vague memory of the language is said to have resulted in an early form of Hebrew. During this time, Enoch was the only person who could fully understand the language, but the book he wrote describing it was lost in the Great Flood. This notion, that a divine language existed prior to the Deluge, was a popular one at the time of Dee and Kelley.

There are **21** alphabetical characters in this arcane language and, in common with other angelic scripts, it is written from right to left, although the letters demonstrated above are used as a left-to-right cipher.

Ian Fleming, the author of the James Bond books, suggested that Enochian script be used to flush out evidence of a Nazi conspiracy within Britain during the Second World War, but the plan never came to fruition.

There could be a strong argument in favor of teaching the Enochian script in schools today, though, since exponents of Enochian magic claim to be able to use it to summon angels and to work with them. There is a downside, though: both the spoken and written language was used extensively by

Aleister Crowley's Golden Dawn organization until they deemed it too dangerous. It was therefore abandoned.

GREEK ALPHABET

In common with the **Hebrew alphabet**, the Greek alphabet is commonly used in magical ritual, although since this classical language isn't taught as frequently as it once was, where it appears in latter-day grimoires it is more likely to be used as a simple substitution cipher rather than as a fully-functioning language system.

Here are the correspondences of the letters of the Greek alphabet with numbers and conceptual meanings.

Greek Character	Letter	Sound	Meaning	Numerical Value	Organ of the Human Body
Α	Alpha	A	cattle	1	head
Β	Beta	B	demon	2	neck
Γ	Gamma	C	divinity	3	shoulders
Δ	Delta	D	fourfold	4	breast
Ε	Epsilon	E	ether	5	diaphragm
Ζ	Zeta	Z	sacrifice	6	belly
Η	Eta	E	joy	7	genitals
Θ	Theta	Th	crystal sphere	8	thighs
Ι	Iota	I	destiny	10	knees
Κ	Kappa	K	illness	20	shins
Λ	Lambda	L	growth	30	ankles
Μ	Mu	M	trees	40	feet
Ν	Nu	N	hag	50	feet
Ξ	Xi	X	fifteen stars	60	ankles
Ο	Omicron	O	sun	70	shins
Π	Pi	P	solar halo	80	knees
Ρ	Rho	R	fruitfulness	100	thighs
Σ	Sigma	S	psychopomp	200	genitals
Τ	Tau	T	human being	300	belly
Υ	Ypsilon	Y	flow	400	diaphragm
Φ	Phi	F	phallus	500	breast
Χ	Chi	Ch	property	600	shoulders
Ψ	Psi	Ps	heavenly light	700	neck
Ω	Omega	O	abundance	800	head

Whereas the Hebrew alphabet is believed to have been gifted to humankind by God via Moses, the provenance of the Greek language is subject to several different legends. Perhaps the most colorful is that the God of Communication, **Hermes**, invented it after he was inspired by the shapes of the wings of a flock of **cranes** in flight. In *The White Goddess*, Robert Graves tells us that the letters of this alphabet were kept in crane-skin bags, in homage to the bird. Another story says that the three **Fates** invented the five vowels and the letters B and T. Palamedes, whose other inventions included counting and currency, invented the next **eleven** letters, while the rest were added by Epicharmus of Sicily, and Simonides.

The Greek alphabet has been extremely influential and is the origin of most European alphabets. It is also the oldest alphabet that has been in continuous use; the Ionic form still in use today was standardized 400 years before the birth of Christ.

Each Greek letter has embedded into it a sound, a meaning, a number, and a corresponding organ of the human body. The esoteric correspondences of the letters of the Greek alphabet mean that it is an effective tool in ritual and in divinatory practices in much the same way as the **runes**. **Gematria**, the art of interpreting the numerical correspondences of the letters, shares the same root as the word "geometry," therefore it's not surprising that so many Greek letters are used in the mathematical formulae that are also an essential part of **sacred geometry**. Like the Hebrew alphabet, the Greek alphabet is believed to hold within it all the secrets of the Universe.

Hebrew alphabet

The **Kabbalah** calls the Hebrew alphabet the "letters of the **angels**." Its sacred provenance is explained in the legend that Moses received it on the top of **Mount Sinai** in an instance of direct communication with God. In common with other lettering systems such as the **Greek**, **Runic**, and **Ogham** alphabets, each Hebrew letter has specific concepts embedded into it, both mundane and esoteric. Each letter also relates to a **number**, giving rise to yet another mystery tradition called the **Gematria**. There is an even more profound aspect to the Hebrew alphabet, though; it is an inseparable part of the cohesive philosophical system of the Kabbalah. The lettering system of the Hebrew alphabet contributes to the encoding of this profound mystery tradition, itself a deeply rooted component of magical custom with tendrils that extend, web-like, throughout diverse esoteric disciplines.

Because of the dual meanings attached to the **twenty-two** Hebrew letters, it means that they act as a useful everyday tool of communication while having another facet for the initiate. Thus, each letter has secrets hidden within it. These secrets are related not only to the allegorical aspects of the Kabbalah and of the **Tarot** system (the Major Arcana of which relates to the letters of the alphabet) but also includes the **planets**, the **seasons** and **elements**, the days of the week, the stages in the life of man, and his concerns. Additionally, the Hebrew alphabet notably gives the means for the spelling and pronunciation of the **Names** of God.

From all this we can gather that Hebrew was "invented" with mystical intent, each letter representing far more than the sum of its parts. Hebrew reads from right to left, and knowing this makes the letters look a little more accessible for the neophyte. If the meaning of the letters is known then the shapes start to suggest these meanings; for example, the second letter, Beth, means "house," and the letter clearly resembles a picture of a house. However, "house" carries with it other concepts, such as the ideas of "home," "mother," and "domesticity."

Because the Hebrew alphabet carries with it a resonance born of almost three thousand years of mystical use, it is frequently used in magical texts and grimoires, a handy device for concealing occult knowledge. However, sometimes the authors of these texts are not quite as erudite as they might appear to be, and often Hebrew isn't used as a language but only as a series of symbols, the English language transcribed into Hebrew characters.

Here is the Hebrew alphabet with its corresponding meanings and numbers.

✳ ✴ ✳

Hebrew Character	Name	Sound	Mundane Meaning	Esoteric Meaning	Numerical Value
א	Aleph	A	cattle	father	1
ב	Beth	B	house	mother	2
ג	Gimel	G/C	camel	nature	3
ד	Daleth	D	door	authority	4
ה	He	H/E	window	religion	5
ו	Vau	V/St	nail	liberty	6
ז	Zain	Z	weapon	ownership	7
ח	Cheth	Ch	fence	distribution	8
ט	Teth	Th/T	serpent	prudence	9
י	Vod	I	hand	order	10
כ	Kaph	K	palm of hand	force	11
ל	Lamed	L	ox-goad	sacrifice	12
מ	Mem	M	water	death	13
נ	Nun	N	fish	reversibility	14
ס	Samekh	S/Ch	support	universality	15
ע	Ayin	O	eye	balance	16
פ	Peh	P	mouth	immortality	17
צ	Tzadi	Tz/Q	fish hook	shadow	18
ק	Qoph	Q	back of head	light	19
ר	Resh	R	head	recognition	20
ש	Shin	Sh	tooth	sacred fire	21
ת	Tau	T	cross	synthesis	22

✳ ✴ ✳

HIEROGLYPHS

The **pyramid texts** are considered to be one of the earliest examples of symbols used with magical intent, employed to inscribe spells that would guide the **soul** of the deceased into the Afterlife. Hieroglyphs are still widely used in magical scripts at least five thousand years later.

The word comes from the Greek, meaning "sacred carvings" and the symbols were called the "Speech of the Gods" by the Egyptians. Hieroglyphs consist of pictorial motifs which were used initially for magical purposes, as described above, hence the name.

Mastery of hieroglyphic writing was a complex matter since there were 900 pictorial symbols, and in general it was only the priestly castes that had the skills to access their mysteries. There was a script reserved for common, more secular use called demotic. This was a simplified form of the hieratic scripts used exclusively by the priests. In AD 391 the Roman Emperor Theodosius closed all non-Christian **temples**, providing the final nail in the sarcophagus for hieroglyphs, whose use had dwindled rapidly even before this time.

The Rosetta Stone, discovered by Napoleon's troops in 1799, served as an invaluable aid to the translation of both hieroglyphic and demotic writing since the same text appeared on the stone in both forms and with a version in **Greek**, which provided the key to translating the first two.

Many hieroglyphs work according to the principle whereby the sound of the word is symbolized by a picture; for example, both "I" and "**eye**" could be represented by a picture of an eye. This appears to be relatively simple since it's the kind of code that's seen in children's puzzle books. However, start to compound these pictograms to create longer words and then add in the cultural context of the symbol and the obstacles to the full comprehension of hieroglyphics start to become apparent.

Many of the symbols used in Part 1 of this encyclopedia were originally hieroglyphics whose use as part of an ancient language has expanded into a universal meaning; the **ankh**, for example, is globally accepted as a symbol of eternal life and of protection. This meaning transcends the barriers of spoken language and culture.

The commonly used hieroglyphic alphabet is based on the values given the hieroglyphs by Sir E.A. Wallis Budge, the renowned Egyptologist. The symbols can be used as a cipher, and appear on magical **talismans** and **amulets**.

ILLUMINATI CIPHER

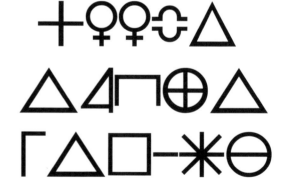

The Illuminati are notoriously well known for a supposedly secret society, despite the fact that an atmosphere of mystery clings to the very name, and there is still speculation about many aspects of the organization. The Society, founded by Adam Weishaupt in Bavaria in 1776, is arguably the subject of more controversy and hysteria than any other closed organization. However, an understanding of the social, religious, and political climate at the time of its founding, and Weishaupt's reasoning behind the tenets of his order, might serve to clarify some of the known facts about the Illuminati.

Weishaupt was a former Jesuit and a professor of law at Ingoldstadt University. He has been called a **Kabbalistic** magician, an ungodly atheist, a fascist and an anarchist. Thomas Jefferson, however, called him an "enthusiastic philanthropist." Weishaupt founded the Illuminati from within existing Masonic orders, so effectively it was a society within a society. New and progressive ideas were spreading through Europe at the time, and Weishaupt hoped that the Illuminati would foster an environment for debate and discussion, and chose the name to reflect this ideal of enlightened individuals determined to make the world a better place.

Membership of the society grew slowly, due in no small part to the rigorous study that was demanded of its adherents. However, the idea was that members would rise to positions of power well versed in philosophy and the new progressive ideas, and would therefore be able to influence the creation of an idealized society, and by 1784 the order had extended its influence throughout most of central Europe.

Necessarily, secret scripts and ciphers had a large part to play within the organization, given the Illuminati's known opposition to the religious and political ideals of the time. Members had secret names: Weishaupt was known as Spartacus, for example, and other nicknames included Cato, Hermes Trismegistus, Menelaus and Agrippa. They even had their own calendar system, based on an ancient Persian system. Initiates were instructed in a relatively simple substitution cipher, and had to correspond with their teachers in this cipher until such a time as a more elaborate code was taught to the initiates. It is this more complex code that is illustrated on page 534.

In 1785 the Bavarian government banned secret organizations, specifically naming the Illuminati. Weishaupt fled, and instructed the existing lodges to go underground; many members were incarcerated by the authorities. The Illuminati's current-day fame owes its existence to two factors: firstly that the Bavarian government published some of the papers it had seized from the Society in 1786; and second, the outbreak of the French Revolution in 1789 and the suggestion that the Illuminati might have had something to do with the troubled political climate of the time.

KAMA SUTRA CIPHER

The encryption code is an ancient device, and one of the first recorded instances appears in the Kama Sutra, which was written in the fourth century BC. As well as the well-known records of sexual positions, the Kama Sutra lists 64 useful skills for women; the housewifely arts, such as cooking and dressing, are listed alongside more unusual talents, including chess, conjuring, carpentry, and perfume making. Also listed is something called "Mlechitta Vikalpa," the art of secret writing, designed so that ladies could conceal their liaisons.

The Kama Sutra cipher is personal to the user, substituting letters of the same alphabet for one another, so is easy to devise but almost impossible to decipher without the key.

KNIGHTS TEMPLAR ALPHABET

The Knights Templar, whose original mission was to protect pilgrims traveling to the Holy Land, soon amassed terrific wealth. They invented an alphabet based on the segments of the **Templar Cross**, and used this secret code in their letters of credit.

MALACHIM ALPHABET

A **22**-character alphabet inspired by Greek and Hebrew letters, the Malachim alphabet is mentioned by Cornelius Agrippa in his *Book of Occult Philosophy*. Malachim is a Hebrew word meaning "**angels**" or "regal" and although not much else is known about it, the alphabet is used among some high degrees of **Freemasonry**.

MASONIC ALPHABET

See **Rosicrucian alphabet**.

OGHAM TREE ALPHABET

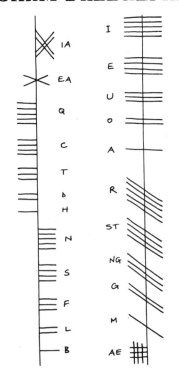

The clue that the Ogham **Tree** alphabet is a set of sacred symbols is in its name. It is named after the Irish Celtic God Ogma, the deity of learning and poetry who was said to have invented the alphabet itself. Ogham actually means "language."

The alphabet has 25 characters that are all associated with **trees** and shrubs, hence the alternative name, the Tree alphabet. These "letters" are broken down into sets of **five**, and the whole is grouped together as a "**grove**." This is symbolic not only of a collection of trees but also of the sum of knowledge contained in each tree, each smaller part making a greater whole—it is no coincidence that the Celtic words for "knowledge" and "wood" sound the same.

The trees represented by the Ogham symbols vary slightly, but the generally accepted order is as follows:

Tree	Name	Letter
Birch	Beth	B
Rowan	Luis	L
Alder	Fearn	F
Willow	Saille	S
Ash	Nuin	N
Hawthorn	Huath	H
Oak	Duir	D
Holly	Tinne	T
Hazel	Coll	C
Apple	Quert	Q
Vine	Muin	M
Ivy	Gort	G
Reed	Ngetal	Ng
Blackthorn	Straif	St/Z
Elder	Ruis	R
Elm	Ailm	A
Gorse	On	O
Heather	Ur	U
White Poplar/Aspen	Eadha	E
Yew	Ioh	I
Aspen	Ea/Koad	Ea
Spindle, Gooseberry	Oi	Oi
Honeysuckle, Beech	Ui	Ui
Guelder Rose	Io/Pe	Ia
Pine, Witch Hazel	Ao/Xi	Ae

There seems to be no definite evidence as to the actual origins of the alphabet. Some believed it was based on the **runes**, and the letters do look similar, although this may be simply because straight lines are easier to engrave onto wood. Several examples of Ogham inscriptions can be found in the British Isles, and all date between the fourth and seventh centuries AD although it's likely that the alphabet is from an earlier date. The only surviving records of it are left on enduring stone, since leather or bark would have decayed over the centuries. There are also some stones showing the Ogham symbols next to Latin letters. These stones were generally used to define ownership and boundaries of land. The inscriptions are read by starting in the bottom left-hand corner, working up, then across the top to the next vertical line of writing.

Sometimes the Ogham script is referred to as the Beth-Luis-Nuin alphabet, in the same way that we use A-B-C. Looking at the chart, it would be easy to suppose that the most obvious name would be Beth-Luis-Fearn; however, the Beth-Luis-Nuin is a throwback to an earlier sequence of trees/letters.

Although the individual Ogham symbols are simple, they represent a more complex whole. As well as having a tree associated with each letter, there was a **hand** signal, a **spirit**, and a concept also embedded into it.

Like the runes, the Ogham letters are also used as a tool of divination.

Robert Graves extrapolated the idea of the Tree Alphabet to make a tree calendar. Because the Druids gauged their months according to the phases of the **Moon** there are 13 months in this particular system of measuring time.

Passing the River

One of the magical scripts based on the **Hebrew** language and known in Latin as *Transitus Fluvii*, this script is among those described by Cornelius Agrippa in his sixteenth-century work on occult philosophy.

The name may refer to the passage of the Jewish people across the Euphrates River when they returned from Babylon to rebuild the **Temple at Jerusalem.** Like **Hebrew**, the alphabet has **22** characters.

Pictish swirl script

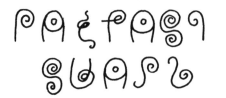

Another simple substitution cipher based on the 26-letter Roman alphabet, some sources claim that this script is part of some "forgotten" Pictish writing system, but this is unlikely to be the case. It is more likely that Pictish swirl script is a recent invention inspired by the **spiral** patterns seen on ancient Celtic stonework, for example at **Newgrange**. The script is given more weight and importance by being linked, spuriously, with an ancient culture. However, Pictish swirl script is used by latter-day practitioners of Wicca in spell-casting and is a good example of a secret alphabet.

Pigpen Cipher

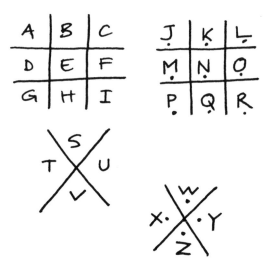

Also called the Masonic or Freemason's cipher, the peculiarly named pigpen cipher is so-called because letters are laid out in a grid pattern that resembles a pigpen. The letters are exchanged for the symbol defined by the part of the pen they sit in. The code was devised by Freemasons in the seventeenth century to keep their accounts and correspondence private.

To the uninitiated, the cipher looks rather like a simple graphic design. A good example of it can be seen on the gravestone of one

Thomas Brierley, which also contains other Masonic symbols. Although the stone has been damaged in the years since Thomas was buried in 1785, the script appears to read "Holiness of the Lord."

PYRAMID TEXTS

The Ancient Egyptians were obsessed with the idea of an Afterlife, a concern that informed many rites and rituals. Uppermost in the minds of these people was the idea that the **soul** should be protected in its journey to the Afterlife. As well as the mummy being swathed in an arsenal of charms, **amulets** and other prophylactic devices, the **pyramids** in which the pharaohs were interred were encrusted with magical spells too, all designed to protect the soul on its epic voyage and to appease the gods and other creatures it might meet along the way. Many of the passages in the pyramid texts describe the glories to be enjoyed by the pharaoh in the Afterlife.

Among the spells and charms is a curiosity called the Cannibal Hymn that seems to have been designed to warn the very Gods themselves about the powers of the pharaoh; this song tells of the pharaoh devouring the deities.

Although the pyramid texts have proved difficult to date with complete accuracy, it is possible that they go back to 3000 BC. This makes them the oldest magical and sacred texts in the world.

ROSE CROSS CIPHER

See **Rosicrucian alphabet**.

ROSICRUCIAN ALPHABET

Also known as the **Masonic alphabet** or the **Rose Cross cipher**, this is a straightforward replacement code. The symbols represent the **26** letters of the Roman alphabet. The alphabet is used by both Masonic and Rosicrucian societies in order to keep certain information a secret to the uninitiated.

The Rosicrucian alphabet is based, like the **Aiq Bekar**, on a grid system of nine squares, divided up as follows:

ABC	DEF	GHI
JKL	MNO	PQR
STU	VWX	YZ

Each letter is represented by the part of the grid in which it is contained. This is straightforward enough with the first letter in the grid, for example, A. The second letter is denoted by the same part of the grid except with the addition of a dot. The third letter is given two dots. Thus the letter A would be drawn as:

And B drawn as:

Royal Arch cipher

One of the cipher alphabets based on a grid system, the Royal Arch cipher is possibly the best known of these types of codes. Its name refers to one of the degrees within Freemasonry. It is based on a grid of nine squares with two letters in each square, with the remaining eight letters occupying the spaces in an X-shaped figure.

Runic alphabet

Also known as the Futhork (or Futhark) alphabet for the same reasons that the sequence of letters on a keyboard is sometimes called Qwerty (i.e. because the order of the first few letters spells the word), the divinatory properties of the runic alphabet have been explored extensively, although the letters were used for secular as well as spiritual purposes. The oldest script symbols of the ancient Germans, runes were used in Britain, Scandinavia, and Germany before the Latin alphabet superceded them. Unfortunately, the early Christian Church destroyed many runic inscriptions, although there are still fine examples of markings on ancient artifacts, standing stones, etc.

The word "rune" comes from an Old English or Norse word meaning "mystery," "secret," or "whisper." There's also a Finnish word, *runo*, meaning "song." The runes themselves were considered to be of divine origin, in common with other alphabets.

The Scandinavian epic poems, the Eddas, describe how the God **Odin** brought the runes to mankind after a strange ritual whereby he hung from the great **ash tree**, Yggdrasil, for **nine** days until he saw the runic symbols reflected in the **water** below. This story has parallels with the tale of Edward Kelley's discovery of the **Enochian script** by scrying with a **crystal ball**. Such was the power of the runes that it was said that they could bring the dead to life. Therefore it's likely that knowledge of the runes was an esoteric matter initially restricted to an elite few, in common with other alphabets, the knowledge of which was great power. Ancient texts, in which runes are given magical powers, confirm this theory. The supernatural powers of Odin himself, which included the ability to fly, shape-shift, bring the dead back to life, and to see into the future, were all a result of his ability to understand the runes.

The shape of the runes is very distinctive. They are constructed of upright parts called staves, and diagonal lines. Notably, runes have no horizontal lines. This is because they were initially scored onto wood, and horizontal lines are more difficult to cut into the grain. Later, the symbols would be engraved onto rock and stone. Tacitus, the Roman historian, wrote a book in AD 98 called Germania about the lands and customs of the German people, and in it, he mentions the tradition of augury or divination by "lot," which happens to be another meaning of the word "rune." It would appear likely that Tacitus is describing runes when he speaks of small pieces of wood, generally cut from fruit trees, which were scored with distinguishing marks and tossed onto a **white** cloth. The pieces were then analyzed to decide the will of the Gods, although, it has to be said, the available information as to just how the runes were used as a tool of augury is sketchy.

There are several different runic systems but the one which is seen most often is the oldest version, known as Elder Futhark. The alphabet consists of 24 symbols, each of which encapsulates a small universe of meaning. Every rune carries not only a **sound** and a **shape** and a **name** of its own, but also has both a mundane and a mystical meaning (which enables the alphabet to be understood on many levels) and is connected not only to a God or spirit but also to an idea or concept.

Adding to the layers of complexity in understanding the Runic code is the fact that each individual rune can translate into a word or phrase that would have carried significant conceptual meaning to the people who invented them. For example, whereas "a," "b," and "c" are nothing but symbols that indicate a sound, the first three letters of the runic alphabet—"faro," "gurus," and "purses"—are complete words in themselves, meaning "cattle," "aurochs," and "giant" respectively. In order to understand the runes, the skilled reader needs to step back in time and intuit the concerns of the people that invented them; top of the list of priorities would be basic survival, **food** supply, and protection from enemies and the elements. On top of this,

each rune also has a complete story associated with it.

The material used for making the runes had significance, too. Ancient man believed that everything on the Earth was alive and animated with a spirit, and so the stone, wood, or leather on which the runic symbol was engraved would itself have contributed to the sacred status of the object. The runes were used for spell-casting, to bring healing and fertility, and to influence the tides and the weather. They were used to curse and to remove curses, to protect, to assist in both birth and **death**.

Runes are arranged in groups, called *aett*, plural *aettir*. The Elder Futhark consists of three *aettir* of eight runes.

Here is the list of correspondences and meanings for the characters of the runic alphabet. The first group of 24 runes is the Elder Futhark, arguably the most used runic system.

*   *   *

	RUNE NAME	TREE	ELEMENT	DEITY	MEANING
First Aett					
ᚠ	Feoh	elder	fire/earth	Freya	cattle; moveable wealth
ᚢ	Ur	birch	earth	Thor	auroch; the power of wild cattle
ᚦ	Thorn	oak	fire	Thor	a giant; attack and defense
ᚬ	As	ash	air	Odin	Yggdrasil; the primal sound, Aum
ᚱ	Rad	oak	air	Ing	a vehicle; a journey; action
ᚲ	Ken	pine	fire	Heimdall	fire, a torch, a beacon
ᚷ	Gyfu	ash/elm	air	Gefn	sacred mark, a gift to the Gods
ᚹ	Wyn	ash	earth	Odin	joy; harmony with the flow of events
Second Aett					
ᚺ	Hagal	ash/yew	ice	Urd	ice or hail; transformation
ᚾ	Nyd	beech/rowan	fire	Skuld	necessity
ᛁ	Is	alder	ice	Verdandi	icicle
ᛡ	Jera	oak	earth	Freya	the cycle of time, fruition
ᛇ	Eoh	yew/poplar	all	Ullr	yew tree; regeneration, longevity
ᛈ	Peorth	beech	water	Frigg	womb; fate or destiny
ᛉ	Elhaz	yew	air	Heimdall	defense; the splayed hand
ᛋ	Sigel	juniper	air	Balder	sun; triumph over the darkness
Third Aett					
ᛏ	Tyr	oak	air	Tyr	sky; justice
ᛒ	Beorc	birch	earth	Nerthus	regeneration; the breasts of the Earth Goddess
ᛗ	Ehwas	oak/ash	earth	Freya	an intuitive bond (as with horse and rider)
ᛘ	Manu	holly	air	Heimdall/ Odin/ Frigg	humankind, humanity
ᛚ	Lagu	osier	water	Njord	the womb, the sea, the balance of opposites
ᛜ	Ing	apple	water/earth	Ing	potential; male energy
ᛟ	Odal	hawthorn	earth	Odin	land, property
ᛞ	Dag	spruce	fire/air	Heimdall	balance; night/day, black/white etc

The next set of runes, the fourth *aett*, is called "the *aett* of the Gods," and is sacred to the Norse deities called the Aesir. This particular set of five (not eight) runes was developed in Britain.

So far, we have 29 runes. Around AD 800, the Northumbrian Anglo-Saxons added four

further runes: Cweorth, Calc, Stan, and Gar. These form the first four runes of the final group, which is sometimes referred to as the fifth *aett*.

The final five runes have known meanings, but are rarely used.

RUNE	NAME	TREE	ELEMENT	DEITY	MEANING
ᛘ	Ac	oak	fire	Thor	oak tree, the acorn and future potential
ᚩ	Os	ash	air	Odin	mouth, speech; the primal sound of existence
ᛄ	Yr	yew	all	Odin/ Frigg	yew tree, bow
ᛡ	Ior	ivy	water	Njord	Jormungand, the World Serpent
ᛠ	Ear	yew	earth	Hela	dust, death, the grave; an end and a beginning

RUNE	NAME	TREE	ELEMENT	DEITY	MEANING
ᛢ	Cweorth	bay/beech	fire	Loge	funeral pyre; a ritual bonfire
ᛣ	Calc	maple	earth	Norns	grail, cup; something that is full, and yet empty
ᛥ	Stan	witch hazel	earth	Nerthus	sacred stone
ᚸ	Gar	ash/spindle	all	Odin	spear of Odin
ᛝ	Wolfs-angel	yew	earth	Vidar	wolf-hook; used to capture wolves; hence to bind
ᛉ	Ziu	oak	air/fire	Tyr	thunderbolt, justice
ᛟ	Erda	elder/birch	earth	Erda	Mother Earth, protection, enclosure
ᛈ	Ul	buckthorn	air	Waldh	turning point
ᛋ	Sol	juniper	fire	Sol	the sun

Bind rune

The bind rune is constructed for specific magical or ritual purposes. It is a combination of two or more runes that together make a **sigil** or symbol that is more than the sum of its parts. The Skulds Net, or **Web of Wyrd**, is a bind rune.

Sig rune

The Sig or Sigel rune is also called the **Sun** rune and represents a sunbeam. However, when it is tipped slightly it resembles either the letter S or a lightning bolt shape. As such, it was doubled up and used in Nazi insignia and its meaning changed to "Victory" from the German *Sieg*.

SKULDS NET

See **Web of Wyrd**.

THEBAN SCRIPT

See **Witches alphabet**.

TREE ALPHABET

See **Ogham Tree alphabet**.

WEB OF WYRD

A **Bind rune** comprised of three upright staves, with two sets of **three diagonal** lines criss-crossing to form an orderly trellis, the Web of Wyrd holds within it every single rune symbol and, therefore, all possibilities for the past, the present, and the future.

The Web of Wyrd is a reminder of the laws of cause and effect, or karma. It tells us that all actions, however small, affect each other and that everything is connected. The Web predates the coming of Christianity in the West, and is related to an era when time was thought of as cyclical rather than linear.

Although it is a commonly held misconception that "wyrd" means the same as "weird," meaning strange, it doesn't. Wyrd carries the same root as the word for "worth," or "to become." Latterly, certain scientific theories have been expounded which seem to prove the interconnectedness of every single thing in the Universe. James Lovelock's Gaia Hypothesis is a notable example, showing that this Norse concept, which is so ancient as to be impossible to date, is as valid today as it was several thousand years ago.

WITCH'S ALPHABET

The **Theban script** or **alphabet of Honorius** is also called the witches alphabet because of its popularity in Books of Shadows, where it's used to encode magical spells. The alphabet is first mentioned by Johannes Trithemius in his *Polygraphia*, published in the early part of the sixteenth century. Cornelius Agrippa, a student of Trithemius, also describes it in his *Three Books of Occult Philosophy* published in Antwerp in 1531. The Honorius in the alternate title is Honorius of Thebes, who wrote a learned tome on magic called *The Sworn Book of Honorius*.

Trithemius was an interesting character. Made a Benedictine abbot at the age of 21 in 1483, he also had a reputation of being a magician, a reputation borne out by his book *Steganographia*. This remarkable work was about black magic and the use of spirits as a means of long-distance communication. The book itself was written in code, and the works of Trithemius formed the cornerstone of the Golden Dawn society almost five hundred years later.

It's possible that the witches alphabet started out as a Latin cipher used by early tenth-century alchemists to keep their discoveries secret. The **26** letters of the alphabet are substitute symbols for the Latin alphabet and so anyone conversant in the script—most likely to be another witch or wizard—would be likely to be able to translate it with no problems, thus rendering questionable its efficacy in disguising certain spells or charms.

WRITING OF THE MAGI

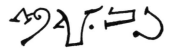

Said to have been invented by Paracelsus in the sixteenth century. Paracelsus was an alchemist and occultist who, like Cornelius Agrippa, was an acolyte of the influential Trithemius (see **Witch's alphabet**). The script was used by its inventor to inscribe or engrave the names of angelic beings on **amulets**, which were used for healing or protection. Not much is known for certain about how Paracelsus invented this script but it is likely that it was inspired by other occult alphabets of the time.

Part Nine
THE BODY AS A SACRED MAP

In an attempt to comprehend the deeper mysteries of the Universe, ancient man understandably started with the most accessible and easily definable thing that he knew—himself. This means that the human body, with its **head** in the **stars** and its **feet** on the ground, is the most universal of all sacred symbols. Our ancestors believed that man held all the secrets of the Universe within his physical body, both inside and out.

The first book of the Bible contains a short statement encapsulating a profound idea that has obsessed us for thousands of years: "So God created man in His own image" (Genesis 1:27). Philosophers, theologians, poets, artists, and mystics have all tried to explain this idea in their various ways.

In the thirteenth century the philosopher Albertus Magnus said that not only was man the image of God, or *imago dei*, but that he was also the image of the Universe, or *imago mundi*, and the Theosophist Helena Blavatsky wrote in the early twentieth century, "Man is a little world—a microcosm inside a great Universe."

Additionally, in what is arguably the most profound act of mutual adoration ever witnessed, man created God in the image of himself. Ancient man believed that deities ruled over each part of the human body, and this meant each part was suffused with godly qualities and mythologies. For example, we have the **All Seeing Eye** of God or the **Eye of Horus**, the feet of the Buddha or of Vishnu, and the **phallus** of Priapus. The Ancient Greek **Pythagoras** believed that to disfigure the body in any way was a sacrilegious act against the dwelling place of the Gods.

The magic resonating in **numbers** also plays a part in defining the nature of man, according to the Pythagoreans. The number **five** is universally accepted as the number of man because it is the number of the most important extremities of the human body: the head, **hands**, and feet. The feet are synonymous with the elements of **earth** and **water**, the hands with **air** and **fire**, and the head is ether, the fifth element that rules over all the others.

Our latter-day ideas about the human body do not differ very much from these ancient beliefs. Like Pythagoras, we sanctify the body by calling it a "temple" and we give powers to certain bodily parts that have ostensibly nothing to do with their fundamental mechanical roles. These associations prevail despite all our advancements in the study of human biology and physiology. The **heart**, for example, is the symbolic seat of all emotions in general and of love in particular; to be "gutsy" is to be brave and forthright; if someone vents their **spleen** they voice their irritation over something; and if we say that a person's head rules his heart then we mean that the intellect prevails over the emotions.

Our practical ways of using our bodies have dictated the ways in which we make sense of the greater universe and how we relate to it. For example, our **ten** fingers govern the way we count and provide a name for the digital way of measurement that works in base 10. Because a man generally fights with a weapon in his right hand and defends himself on the left side with a shield, the right side of the body has come to be associated with attack and the left with defense. Accordingly, the right side is the masculine side, linked to the **Sun**, **fire**, and light; the left side belongs to the feminine, the **Moon**, **water**, and darkness.

The physical and spiritual aspects of man are inextricably linked to the greater Universe, too. The physical body provides an encasement for the spirit for as long as the material body survives. Put another way, the physical body is effectively the clothing for the spirit, and each aspect of the material body reflects the **soul**, the **breath** of life, preserved within it.

The Greeks visualized the actual Earth as a giant human being twisted into a ball, with Delphi as the **Omphalos** or navel of the world. Early philosophers stated that all things represented the body, if not in actual form then certainly in essence. The natural world is full of analogies to the human body.

Mountains equate to the nourishing **breasts** of the Mother Goddess, and **caves** become her womb or bowels; **trees** and certain rocks become phallic symbols.

Effectively, man's body is a sort of measuring stick for the Universe.

Centuries after the Greeks, Leonardo da Vinci demonstrated this idea in a drawing called The Vitruvian Man. Vitruvius was a very influential Roman architect of the first century BC. Because of the philosophical belief that the science of mathematics provided the underlying foundation for everything, the idealized proportions for buildings that had been defined by Vitruvius inspired Leonardo's drawing. His famous sketch shows the figure of a man, set inside a **circle** and a **square**, with the **navel** set at the exact center of the image.

These perfect proportions occur in architecture, art, **music**, and harmonics. Somehow, we instinctively recognize the "divine proportion" and the harmony created wherever it is applied. The drawing is perceived as the ultimate rendering of the body, its measurements a symbol of both the divine intention and nature of God.

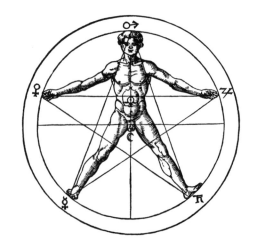

The Kabbalistic **Tree of Life** is often superimposed over a human figure, the proportions of the tree aligning perfectly to the parts of the body that represent the esoteric principles of this arcane magical system.

The idea of the body as a blueprint for the larger Universe is found in astrology, too. Here each one of the **Zodiac** signs rules over a different body part. The first sign, **Aries**, has jurisdiction over the head and from here the authority of the signs flows downwards through the body to the last sign, **Pisces**, which rules over the feet.

ADAM'S APPLE

The Adam's apple is actually a protruding piece of thyroid cartilage that develops at puberty, but only in the male. It is so-called because it is said to symbolize the piece of the **apple** of knowledge that got stuck in Adam's throat after Eve, encouraged by the **serpent**, coaxed him into eating the fruit.

The Adam's apple can be a bit of a pain in the **neck** for transsexuals, cross-dressers, and female impersonators, since it can be the one giveaway sign that the apparently well-dressed lady is in fact a gentleman. The offending lump can, however, be removed by surgery.

ANKLE

Because, in Greco-Roman myth, **wings** sprouted from the ankles of **Hermes/Mercury**, this part of the body came to be associated with transcendence. However, the ankle is also a sexual symbol; for the

Chinese, the shapeliness of a woman's ankle is commensurate with her skill in lovemaking. As a discreet sexual symbol, the ankle is often tattooed as a way of drawing attention to it.

ARM

Arms convey the idea of strength and protection. They also stand for safety and justice, as in "the strong arm of the law."

Some deities have more than the usual two arms. Brahma, for example, is depicted with four arms to show his omnipotence. Shiva, too, shows innumerable arms as a symbol of his action, energy, and accomplishment. This idea—that the arms signify activity—was shared by the Egyptians, and they used the arm to convey this concept in their **hieroglyphs**.

In the Celtic legend of St. Mela, the priest-king Nuada had his arm hacked off in battle. Because he could no longer rule, Nuada was usurped by Bres, whose reign turned out to be a disaster. Bres was summarily forced to surrender his power, and Nuada was welcomed back to the throne after an artificial arm was fashioned for him out of **silver**. This arm, obviously, could not be used, but its restoration effectively symbolized the parallel restoration of Nuada's leadership and authority.

For the Bambara of Africa, the forearm in particular is believed to be symbolic of the communication between God and man. It is this part of the arm that enables **food** to be put into the **mouth**, because of the pivotal action of the elbow (itself a symbol of the divine nature). Therefore the forearm also represents the distance between man and God, the cubit. This measurement happens to be 22 fingerbreadths; this corresponds to the Bambara's belief that there are 22 categories of created beings, and **twenty-two** is also the number of the Universe. Is it a coincidence that 22, in the **Tarot**, is the number of cards in the Major Arcana? We can only guess at the nature of this link.

Raising the arms to the **sky** implies a passive state of acceptance and is often used as a spiritual gesture, opening up the entire body to heavenly influences, removing the ability to exert the will via the arms and the hands. In a similar gesture, prisoners raise their arms to show that they cannot access weapons. This is not a purely practical gesture of submission but is also a symbol of spiritual or physical defenselessness and of surrender.

AUFU

See **Five Bodies of the Egyptians**.

AURA

The psychic energy-field that surrounds the physical body and that is also said to emanate from some inanimate objects. We use the term "aura" to describe the feeling given off by someone; we might say, for instance, that someone has a pleasant aura. The aura itself is invisible to most people but some psychics claim to be able to see it, describing it as a sort of colorful luminous mist. Those gifted enough to be able to see the aura and its **colors** say that it can be used as a diagnostic tool to analyze illnesses, character traits, or moods.

BEARD

Symbolic of masculinity, strength, and wisdom. Usually a beard belongs to an older man, and because it is assumed that with age comes experience, wisdom is seen as part of the equation too. A popular image of God is of an "old man with a beard." The longer the beard, the wiser the owner was considered to be. Philosophers, heroes, and kings, as well as many masculine deities from all cultures, are generally depicted with full beards, and in Ancient Egypt certain queens were depicted with beards too, both to show their authority and to make them the equals of men. Imitation beards were the attribute of Gods and pharaohs, and took the form of long, slender, plaited, and ornamented braids that were attached to straps that ran around the **ears**.

So powerful was the link with the beard and a sense of authority and experience that in Irish myth the hero Cuchulain was forced to conjure up a false beard for himself, made from **grass**, because otherwise he looked too young and the Irish warriors would have refused to do battle with him.

For Jewish people the beard was a sign of the dignity and wisdom brought by age and was accorded due respect, kempt and perfumed at all times. **Kissing** the beard was a sign of reverence. In the same way that unruly hair is sometimes seen as a sign of disrespect for authority or even of madness, a disheveled beard carried the same connotations.

To have your beard cut off by your enemy was, for many, the ultimate insult, and the victim would hide away in shame until the beard had grown again. However, sometimes beards were shaven off by their owners as a sign of mourning.

Blood

Blood and its **color** are inextricably linked, one the symbol of the other, the **red** standing for life, energy, vitality, and the element of **fire** and (by association) the **Sun**: all the attributes of blood too.

For early man, the link between the color and the life-giving properties of blood were so powerful that some burial rituals included the corpse being daubed in red powders and unguents, an example of sympathetic magic in the hope that the red color would be enough to restore the **soul** to life. An example of this can be found in the ritual burial of a young tribal chieftain at the Paviland Caves in South Wales.

Blood is symbolic of the idea of kinship, and to speak of a "blood line" refers to generations of the same family. The term "**blue blood**" as a description of the aristocracy came about because the veins of the nobility showed through their pale **skin** because they were unused to manual labor or exposure to the elements.

Then there's a tradition of the symbolic mixing of blood to show allegiance. This sign of kinship is incredibly ancient and the ritual is still sometimes carried out at Romany weddings; a swift cut into the **hand** or the **arm** of the participants and the mingling of the blood is all it takes to swear eternal loyalty.

Menstrual blood, since it comes from that most sacred of places, the **womb**, is accorded with particular magical power and is symbolic of feminine energy and the **Moon**. This particular blood was used in rites and ceremonies since it was believed to have the most potently charged magic of any kind of blood. Tantric practices say that a man can become spiritually empowered if he drinks menstrual blood. This is symbolic of him accepting female power in addition to his own male energy. Blood is used as ink in magical rites, to imbue certain words and names with vitality.

Ritual spilling of blood, in the form of sacrifice, was believed to propitiate the Gods, and where blood is deliberately spilled on the **Earth**—as in some of the ancient **harvest** rituals—it is believed to bring fertility. Similarly, we speak of the spilling of blood during a war as being a sacrifice to the greater good, a noble and courageous act.

One of the major symbolic elements of the Christian mass is the sharing of the blood of Christ. The red wine held in the chalice is believed by some Catholics to change into the actual blood of Christ by the act of transubstantiation; for Protestants, it is enough that the wine is symbolic of the holy blood.

To be hot blooded describes someone who is fiery and passionate, apt to act first and think later.

Bone

As well as giving structure to the body, bones survive for a long time after death, and so are imbued with magical properties. Symbolically, bones carry the essence of the creature that they were once a part of, and there's a curious but relatively common belief that somehow or other an intact set of bones can be remade into a live body. This idea is seen in **fairy** tales, myths, and traditions from all over the world, such as in the Lapp belief that the bones of a **bear**, if carefully preserved, will come back to life and the animal will allow itself to be hunted once again. Bear "burial" places have been found where the bones of the bear have been carefully reconstructed. These sites also show evidence of respectful funerary rites. In a similar practice, the Plains Indians would bury the bones of the **buffalo** with due care and attention so that the animal would be able to come back to life.

The bones of small animals were used by shamans in divinatory rites. Over two thousand years ago, in China, bones were heated up and the resulting cracks interpreted as indicating a prediction. Bones as predictive devices were used in other ways, too; for example they were thrown upon the ground in the act of "casting the bones," a term of reference still in use for other divinatory methods, such as **rune** stones.

The human body contains one bone that has particular relevance as a sacred symbol, and its name gives it away. In Latin, *sacrum* means "sacred," and the bone of the same name is the large, curved, and heavy one that sits at the base of the **spine**. This particular bone was sacred for the Greeks, too, who called it the *hieros osteon. Hieros* means not only "sacred," but "temple." *Osteon* means "bone." Therefore this sacred bone acts as a temple to other sacred parts of the anatomy, namely the reproductive parts. In Ancient Egypt the bone was sacred to **Osiris** and as the "seed" bone was the key to resurrection, since it protected the **semen**.

Because of its size, the bone is one of the very last in the body to rot, along with the **skull**. For this reason—its longevity—the bone was used as a vessel during religious and magical rites and rituals.

Because bones are such an important part of the body and because they are believed to hold the essence of their owner, the bones of saints are considered holy relics, imbued with magical powers, and kept locked away in churches. They were believed to be so holy that devils and **demons** would keep well away, and if the bones were dipped into **wine** or **water**, the resulting liquid would be infused with mysterious powers including the ability to cure various ailments.

BOWELS

The care with which the intestines were removed from the body by the Ancient Egyptian embalmers is a mark of the significance of this organ, which they believed had magical powers. The bowels were preserved in a special vessel, a canopic jar called a Quebehseneuf, with a lid in the shape of a **falcon**'s head. The three other internal organs that were removed, each kept in its own canopic jar, were the **liver, lungs** and **stomach**. The bowels and organs had to be protected from **demons** and other entities, and the jars were believed to give this protection.

BREAST

Clearly, the breast is the symbol of motherhood, the female principle, comfort, nourishment, and abundance. It is also a symbol of beauty and of fertility. The breast is the first point of contact for the newborn baby as he suckles his first food, **milk**, hence the primal nature of the breast as a symbol. The Egyptians believed that the **stars** of the **Milky Way** were milk spilling from the breasts of the **Moon** Goddess, who was the source of all the other stars, too. The right breast is said to represent the **Sun**, and the left, the Moon.

In Hebrew, the word for "breast" is the same as for "girl" and also "liquid measure." This indicates the idea of the breast as a symbol of restriction, since any measurement must necessarily be finite.

To return to the bosom is to be enfolded in safety like a child, and dying is sometimes referred to as returning to the "bosom of the Earth."

The breast is a potent sexual symbol, as the fashion for breast augmentation would indicate. There is an idea that the bigger the breast the more sexy the owner. Stereotypical sex symbols generally show prominent breasts and in less liberal times than those that we currently enjoy in the West, pin-ups who showed rather a lot of cleavage were banned.

Mountains are seen to be symbols of breasts. Hence, many mountains have female names, for example Annapurna in India, whose name means "Great Breast Full of Nourishment," or Mount Olympus in Greece, named after the Goddess Gaia Olympia, also known as the Deep Breasted One.

There are Goddess depictions that appear to show supernumerary breasts. These may be a symbol of the ultra maternal nature of the Goddess, however, these "breasts," as in the statue of Artemis at Ephesus, may also represent bulls' **testicles** as symbols of male virility.

BREATH

Invisible yet essential, breath represents the idea of the **soul** or **spirit** and the animating life-force. In the biblical story, God brings Adam to life by breathing into his nostrils, therefore sharing his breath, and in Taoist belief there were said to be **nine** original "breaths" that entwined together to create physical space and therefore the prerequisite for everything that exists in the Universe. In Hindu belief, similarly, the factor that unifies everything is seen as breath, or *atman*. Like the soul, the breath is believed to be immortal and imperishable, but when the breath is taken away the physical body will perish. Yogis believe that control of the breath, or pranayama, is the key to health and also to enlightenment, an idea that is also held by Chinese mystics.

The act of taking in breath is, quite literally, equated with inspiration, when an idea comes to the willing recipient as though from divine sources. Expiration—breathing out— is equated with the idea of **death**.

The breath is also equated with sound, the two being inextricably linked in the act of Creation. For the Druids, the breath carried magical properties, and breathing or blowing onto something often constitutes a part of magical practice in mystical traditions all over the world. In Persia, **amulets** had magical power blown onto them by the sorcerer, the final and most vital part of the spell.

CAUL

This is an extra piece of **skin**, a thin membrane that sometimes covers a baby's head when it is born. Not every baby is born with a caul, which gives added protection to the face of the baby. Because of this the membrane itself is regarded as a powerful sacred object with immense powers of protection and was considered, like the **placenta**, to be an ineffable part of the owner. The caul is symbolic of a **cloak** or cape but has extra significance since it is a physical part of the newborn baby, and therefore takes on sacred status.

The caul would protect its original owner for as long as he or she lived, but was only considered to be lucky, however, if it was kept intact. If sold, the luck would pass on to the new owner. Because of the protective properties of the caul they were in high demand among sailors and fishermen, who regularly had to pit their lives against stormy seas and rough winds and generally needed all the supernatural help they could get. The importance of the caul is signified by their monetary value. In 1813 *The Times* newspaper advertised a caul for sale for twelve guineas, a huge amount of money at the time considering that the daily wage for an agricultural laborer was approximately 18 pennies per day.

CHAKRAS

Symbols can sometimes be used to represent things not visible to the naked **eye**. Although some would regard chakras as a concept rather than as a reality, there are others who believe in their actual existence, and there is

plenty of evidence to support this in thousands of years of esoteric Eastern beliefs.

Chakra is a Sanskrit word, meaning "**wheel**" or "**circle**," and refers in this instance to a series of subtle energy centers that rise up along the length of the **spine**. The chakras are said to spin, and are envisaged as **lotus** flowers (another name for them is the "lotus centers"). Each chakra/lotus is a different **color** and has a different number of **petals** according to each particular chakra's meaning and function, in relation not only to the body, but to the mind and spirit too. Meditation and yoga are believed to help balance the chakras, which in turn promotes good health. Any depiction of the chakras contains the symbol of the great **serpent** Kundalini curled three and a half times at the base of the spine, which relates to the primal creative energy that rises up through healthy chakras when a person is ready to be awakened to such an experience.

Starting at the base of the **spine**, the first chakra is called Muladhara and is symbolized as a **red** lotus flower with a **yellow square** in the center of its four petals—the square is of course a symbol of stability as befits a chakra that is ruled by the **earth** element. The Muladhara chakra is related to all the basic instincts of survival and is located at the pelvic floor area.

The second chakra, Swadhisthana, is located in the groin. It controls emotions, sexuality, and creativity and its lotus flower symbol is **orange**, has **six** petals, and relates to the element of **water**.

Next is the **navel** or solar plexus chakra, Manipura, symbolized by a **yellow** lotus bearing **ten** petals. It is related to the higher emotions and digestion and is ruled by the element of **fire**.

The fourth chakra is called Anahata, and affects the **lungs** and the **heart**. It is ruled by the element of **air** and is represented by a **green** lotus flower with **twelve** petals.

After Anahata comes Vishuddha, the **throat** chakra, related to communication and growth. This chakra is situated near the thyroid gland and its lotus flower is sky **blue** with sixteen petals.

The penultimate chakra is Ajna, and is situated at the **third eye** in the forehead. Its lotus flower is **violet** and has **two** petals. Associated with the pineal gland, which is sensitive to light, Ajna is related to enlightenment and intuition.

Finally, at the top of the head is Sahasrara, the **crown** Chakra, embodied as the symbol of the **thousand**-petaled lotus. Sahasrara sits above the head and outside the physical body.

CLITORIS

Effectively the clitoris is the female equivalent of the penis, reacting to stimulus in the same way by becoming engorged with **blood** and super sensitive. It is interesting to note that the clitoris is perceived as representing the male element in the woman, in the same way that the **foreskin** represents the female element in the man.

The controversial operation of female circumcision—sometimes called female genital mutilation—is something that has been carried out for centuries, particularly in Africa and in Egypt. The reasons for it have remained unchanged. The operation ranges from the relatively simple removal of the hood of the clitoris to the removal of all external genitalia.

There are numerous reasons reported for this operation. The removal of the clitoris means that the sexual desire of the female will be decreased, and the procedure is thought to promote chastity, as is the stitching up of the vaginal opening. In societies where clitoral circumcision is traditional, then it is considered the "correct" thing to do, and sometimes hygiene is given as the reason. The removal of the clitoris is also performed as a rite of passage, carried out at puberty. Some believe that the sexual satisfaction of the male is increased if the female is circumcised.

For cultures where clitoral circumcision is not the norm, the practice is viewed as symbolic of the subjugation of women, who, it is presumed, are treated as second-class citizens by having the capability for sexual arousal removed.

Ear

Before it was common for people to be able to read and write, the way to receive information was aurally. Therefore, the ear is symbolic of knowledge and also of memory.

However, the shape of the ear as well as its function gives clues about other aspects of its symbolic significance. It is shaped like a **spiral** or a whirled **shell**, a shape not dissimilar to that of the vulva; therefore, the ear is also a symbol of birth. In a Hindu story, Karma, the son of the **Sun** God Surya, was born from the ear of his mother. This analogy is carried a step further in depictions of the Virgin Mary receiving the message of the Holy Spirit, in the form of a **dove**, through her ear. This idea—that she could receive the Spirit in the same way that she could hear a sound—also promulgates the idea of the Virgin Birth.

In China, large ears and long earlobes are associated with both longevity and wisdom; the philosopher and founder of Taoism, Lao Tzu was nicknamed "long ears." The Buddha is also depicted with extended earlobes as a sign of his wisdom and royalty. Ears with pointed tops generally belong to the God Pan, and also to **fauns**, **satyrs**, **pixies** and similar otherworldly creatures.

In the symbolism of Ancient Egypt, the ear is associated with the cycle of life, with the right ear receiving the "air of life" and the left, the "air of death."

Piercing the ears is an ancient practice that is still carried out all over the world, and these piercings have often been used to carry a secret code. For example, the Bible speaks of a pierced ear as being a sign of servitude or subjugation. However, wealthy Romans would pierce their ears so that their earrings could provide one more indicator of their wealth. Sailors pierced both their ears in the belief that this would give them better eyesight. And even today, the Bektashi dervishes of the Sufi faith pierce one ear to show their celibate status.

There are records of an ancient Irish druidic charm that concerns the ears. "Briamon Smethraige" is said to be a spell in which the druid rubbed the ear of the person in question and so caused his "death." This is likely to have been a symbolic **death** rather than a physical one, and the rubbing of the ears a symbolic action that was the equivalent of sending someone to Coventry, i.e. stopping them communicating with anyone.

Eye

The symbolism of the eye occurs in so many places and in so many different forms that its pervasiveness symbolizes the **All Seeing Eye** itself. The eye is closely associated with the idea of light and of the spirit, and is often called the "**mirror** of the **soul**." When a person dies one of the first things that is done is that the eyes are closed, a timeless gesture that signifies the departure of the essence of life. Generally, the right eye is considered to be the eye of the **Sun**, the left, that of the **Moon**.

The eye represents the "god within," for example as the "**third eye**" whose position is designated by the small dot called the **bindhu** above and between the actual eyes. The Buddha is always depicted with this third eye. Here, the eye signifies the higher self, the part of man's consciousness that is ego-free and can guide and direct him. Whereas the eyes are organs of outward vision, this "eye of wisdom" directs its view internally as the "eye of dharma" or the "eye of the **heart**."

As an occult symbol, the unlidded eye has its origins as the symbol of the Egyptian Goddess of Truth, Maat, whose name was synonymous with the verb "to see"; therefore the concepts of truth and vision were closely aligned. The same eye symbol appears as the **Eye of Horus**, or **Udjat**. This stylized eye, with a brow above and featuring a curlique underneath, represents the omnipresent vision of the Sun God Horus, and is a prominent symbol within the Western magical tradition where it represents, among other things, secret or occult wisdom. This eye was painted on the sides of Egyptian funerary caskets in the hope that it would enable the corpse to see its way through the journey to the Afterlife. In Celtic magical lore, too, the eye equated with the Sun, and the **planet** and the eye shared the same name, Sul.

The All Seeing Eye, the eye within a **triangle** with rays emanating from the lower lid, is used not only in **Freemasonry** (where it stands for the "Great Architect of the Universe," for external vision, and also for inner vision and spiritual watchfulness) but in Christian symbolism too.

The eye symbol is used as a charm, painted on the sides of humble fishing boats, in order to protect the boat from the **evil eye** and to somehow confer this inanimate object with the power of sight of its own, a notion which follows exactly the same reasoning behind the practice of the Egyptians painting eyes on the coffins of their dead. Belief in the evil eye is ancient, referred to in Babylonian texts dating back to 3,000 years before Christ. This is the idea that some people can curse an object (or a person) simply by the act of looking, as though the eye itself can direct a malevolent thought. It is a mark of the profound belief in the concept of the evil eye that there are so very many charms said to protect against it.

FINGERNAILS

Fingernails are a highly visible symbol of the occupation, and therefore the status, of their owner. The fingernails of manual laborers and servants would necessarily need to be kept short; conversely, the nails of the wealthy could be allowed to grow and as such were once a symbol of royalty, aristocracy, and the financially well off. In China, elaborate nail guards were worn. These were made of precious **metals** and were studded with jewels. The custom of decorating or painting the nails is ancient and originates in the Orient, where henna was used to dye the nails. These days, long fingernails are not restricted to the elite classes since anyone of a mind to have long, highly decorated nails can simply glue them on as a fashion statement.

Along with **hair**, fingernails are one of the bodily substances considered to be a particularly powerful ingredient in casting spells against the owner, therefore they are disposed of with care lest they fall into the wrong **hands**. There is also a form of divination using the fingernails. Onimancy is carried out by observing the fingernails, polished with olive oil, of a male or female virgin, and divining the meaning behind any lines or marks upon them.

The Greek word *onyx* means "fingernail." The story goes that, while Aphrodite was sleeping, Cupid cut her fingernails with one of his arrows. The nails fell on the sand where the **Fates** decided to turn them into the precious stones so that no part of the Goddess would be lost.

FINGERPRINTS

The patterns of whorls on the tips of the fingers are said to be completely unique to the individual, with no two people sharing the same pattern. As such, the fingerprint represents the idea of individual personality, and the notion of the "fingerprint" has come to mean any unique and ineffable indicator.

FIVE BODIES OF THE EGYPTIANS

The Ancient Egyptians believed that there were **five** aspects to the body, and they gave each of these parts its own name.

The physical body was called the Aufu. Next, the Ka was the double, the equivalent in Western ideology of the astral body. Like its Western counterpart, the Ka was able to travel separately from the physical body, and could explore the more subtle planes of conscious existence. The Ka, too, was considered to be the part that conferred vitality to all the other bodies, a part of the divine creative energy. When Egyptians died, it was said that they had "passed their Ka." Funerary priests were referred to as "servants of the Ka."

The Haidit was the **shadow**, the equivalent of the unconscious mind. The Haidit was also capable of astral travel.

Perhaps the most intriguing of the five bodies was the Khu. The Khu would be "awakened" once the person was able to distinguish between conscious and unconscious thought processes. The awakening of the Khu could be achieved by meditation, through the ritual use of **mantras** or other magical spells, and through certain physical movements similar to yogic *asanas* or postures.

The Sahu was the "spiritual body" and considered to be the highest of the five. Once the person was aware of the Sahu then he or she would have the ability to perceive the Gods and would undergo spiritual transformation. A person that was known to have complete awareness of the Sahu would be likely to belong to the priestly castes, or would be a magician.

FOOT

Footprint of the Buddha

The foot is a symbol of strength, stability, and resolve (after all, we need them to support the rest of our body), and of our connection with the **earth**—again, the reasons for this are obvious. When we say that someone has his feet firmly upon the ground, we mean that the person is down-to-earth, sensible, and practical.

The feet have always been used as a way to measure something; the old imperial measurement of a "foot" was based on its average length, 12 inches. Pacing out any distance helps us to measure something, and in the same way that we might work out the dimensions of more prosaic things, both Buddha and Vishnu measured out the Universe: the Buddha by taking **seven** steps in each direction and Vishnu by taking just **three** strides, across Earth and the Heavens.

In China, the foot was seen as a symbolic measurement not just of **space** but also of **time**. The sign of a footprint indicates "I was here and continue to be here," and pilgrims take ritual journeys to follow in the footsteps of those they revere—to make the same journey, to see the same sights, to feel the same sensations. To walk any distance for such a purpose is a meditative process, and the pace of walking on foot—at just under **four** miles an hour—is said to enable man to recognize his true place in the world.

Bare feet is a sign of humility, and to walk upon holy or sacred ground with no footwear is an age-old ritual whose significance is as powerful today as it was thousands of years ago. Conversely, to walk in bare feet is also to walk in power, since the feet can directly absorb the energy of the Earth. Latter-day Druids and witches generally carry out their ceremonies with bare feet in order to tap into this power. Natural footprint-shapes on rocks are believed to be the footprints of certain holy people who have left an indelible mark. It's considered that the bare feet can pick up vibrations from the Earth and from the holy people who have set foot in the same places.

In India, shoes are removed not only in **temples** and ashrams, but in the home too. This is because it is believed that footwear can pick up negative influences from the outside world. Removing the shoes is also a sign of respect for the cleanliness, both physical and spiritual, of the place one is entering. Shoes are also removed on entering a mosque, and Moses approached the Burning Bush barefoot.

The Footprint of the Buddha—or Buddhapada—is a popular symbol for Buddhists, showing the soles of the Buddha's feet imprinted with other items of symbolic importance, such as the **eight** auspicious objects. The Buddha Footprint is used as a symbol to indicate the places he visited during his life on Earth.

In the yogic tradition, it is considered the height of rudeness to point the soles of the feet in the direction of the guru or even at his image.

To wash someone's feet is a symbol of humility, since the feet come into contact with the ground. Conversely, having one's feet washed is a sign of purification; again, the symbolism is obvious.

In China, the practice of foot binding was popular for a thousand years. At the age of six or even earlier, girls' feet were wrapped tightly in bandages so that the **bones** would break. The muscles atrophied, and the feet stayed tiny; a three-inch foot was considered perfection, and was called the "gold lotus." No one is entirely sure how this custom started. It may have been in an attempt to emulate a concubine who danced in silk-wrapped feet. Bound feet became a symbol of wealth and power, since only the rich could afford to keep a woman who was unable to walk. The custom died out after it was banned in 1911 by the government of the Republic of China.

One of the signs of a demonic being, or a being that is less than human, is that it will have extraordinary feet—cloven hooves in images of the Devil, for example, or the reputed **six toes** of the witch.

FORESKIN

The process of removing the foreskin, called circumcision, could be considered to be an act of mutilation, although evidence of it goes back to the Stone Age. However, for many, this operation is considered to be correct practice and in the best interests of the man or boy concerned.

There are various explanations for circumcision. Aside from any particular religious or spiritual ideas, it is believed that the removal of the foreskin is a hygienic practice, and may prevent sexually transmitted diseases and genital cancers. Evidence for these claims is not, however, conclusive. To apply a more symbolic meaning rather than a practical reason, then, for some the cutting away of the foreskin is statement of detachment from the sexual and material self and signifies a cutting away of God's bond with matter, in the same way that a baby's **umbilical cord** is cut. There is also a sacrificial element to circumcision: to propitiate the Gods with the removal of a part of the body which is, after all, essential to the survival and continuation of the human species.

Circumcision may be best known as a Jewish practice, but it is also carried out by other people, such as the Dogon and the Bambara in Africa. These tribes believe that the foreskin embodies the material form of the female **soul** in the man, and this anomaly is rectified by its removal, thereby restoring full masculinity to the man. And so circumcision is a symbol of initiation into manhood. The foreskins are transformed into "sun lizards."

In the Jewish faith, the foreskin is removed as a sign of God's covenant with the people of Israel. It is obligatory, according to religious law, for all Jewish males to be circumcised, unless it could put his life at risk. Carried out on the eighth day after birth, January 1 is known as the Feast of the Circumcision in the Roman Catholic religious calendar since this is the day on which Christ would have had the procedure.

As a holy relic, the foreskin of Christ is a potent symbol. Remarkably, as many as 18 "Holy Prepuces" appeared around Europe in the Middle Ages.

HAIDIT

See **Five Bodies of the Egyptians**.

HAIR

Hair, the **crown** of the head, has always been believed to hold an essence or life-force that is inextricably attached to, and a part of, its owner, even when the owner is separated from the hair. Therefore a strand of hair is an essential ingredient in magical spells to gain power over someone. This ancient belief actually has solid roots; a small clump of hair can tell an analyst which vitamins and minerals the person needs, and hair can be used to test for DNA. It is still considered bad luck and potentially dangerous to let hair fall into the wrong **hands** and some people—in particular the Vietnamese—are very wary about the disposal of hair for these reasons.

Hair is symbolic of energy, power, and sensuality. It's also an important part of human identity and personality. Removing the hair can effectively remove these attributes. The power held in the hair has been accepted since time immemorial. To lose hair is, for many, psychologically distressing; it's as though a part of the personality disappears along with the locks. In the Old Testament, the mighty warrior Samson is betrayed by Delilah when she persuades him to reveal the secret of his great strength—his long hair—and she cuts it off when he is asleep, allowing him to be captured by his enemies. Samson's strength returned when his hair grew back to its former length.

Locks of hair are kept as a direct link with its owner, and in Victorian times elaborate **jewelry** containing the locks of the departed became fashionable as a part of the general interest in all things relating to death.

To have unruly hair is to indicate a separation from conventional society, a sign of someone who flouts the rules, whose ideas are different from the norm and whose long hair is a symbol of freedom from the constraints of society. This is not a recent symptom of societal changes (such as the long-haired hippies of the flower power era), but predates the time when people wore flowers in their hair in the 1960s and 70s. Traditionally, witches and wizards had unruly and disheveled hair and lived apart from their neighbors, as did the hermit, whose long **robe** and tangled hair are an archetypal uniform. The "mad professor" who teeters between genius and insanity is given away by his hair, which stands on end. His concerns are so great that he has no time to attend to his tresses.

In Greek and Hindu mythology, the Gods and Goddesses who have the wildest, most disheveled hair are the ones who are the most dangerous or who have demonic qualities. Medusa, for example, whose head was a mass of writing snakes is a fine example of a continual bad hair day.

What we do with our hair signifies a great deal but varies in different cultures. The Romans would let their hair grow as a sign of sorrow, whereas the Greeks would cut it.

In China, the same notion of tousled hair belonging to someone who is separated from society is reflected in the uncombed hair of those who are in mourning.

Cutting the hair carries great symbolic connotations. The first time the hair of a child it cut is a rite of passage not only for the child but also for its parents. Some societies believe that it is unlucky to cut hair before the child is at least a year old, since to do so is to deprive the child of some of its life-force, therefore leaving it vulnerable and unprotected.

Our hair is a symbol of our individuality, and to make someone cut or shave his hair is to wield power over that person. If a man joins the army or is imprisoned, the taming of his hair is one of the first things to take place. Here, the cutting of the hair implies uniformity and discipline. Similarly, in Roman times one of the signs of slavery was short hair. Gaul remained independent so its people retained their flowing locks and were known as the Gallia Commata ("Hairy Gauls"). A ritual shaving of the hair indicates purity and a fresh start, and it's an almost unconscious ritual to cut one's hair at life-changing moments.

Sikhs do not cut their hair. The hair is seen as a sacred symbol of strength, and keeping it long and uncut is a sign that the Sikh has accepted this gift from God, but is free from vanity about it since his hair is kept covered up by his **turban**. In this case, hair includes all bodily hair, and the rule applies to both men and women.

Because long, flowing hair is a sign of virility, power, and the material world, a shorn or shaven head is a sign of worldly renunciation. Religious ascetics often follow the tradition of shaving the hair. The tonsure of the monk or priest is a sign of spiritual devotion. This ritual shaving is not restricted to men; some nuns and particularly orthodox Jewish women shave their heads as a symbol of the rejection of worldly and sensual matters. St. Paul recommended that women cover their hair when inside churches since spirits were meant to be attracted to loose, uncovered hair. In Bavaria in the eighth century the wanton connotations of loose flowing hair were carried to an extreme degree, and "lewd loosening of the hair" carried such seductive temptation that it was considered on a par with adultery. Women who attended church for the first time after childbirth, for the ritual known as "churching," had to cover their hair with a **veil**.

Hairstyles can tell us a lot about people, particularly in traditional societies. In India, to wear the hair in two plaits is the sign of an unmarried woman. Conversely, in Russia, a single plait was a sign of virginity, whereas a pair of braids was the hairstyle of the wife.

And then there are the dreadlocks traditional to Rastafarians. This style of tight braiding was adopted just before the Second World War to identify with the style of hair worn in Ethiopia. The lionine look of dreadlocks also paid homage to the Emperor Haile Selassie, the "**Lion** of Judah." Dreadlocks in the West originated among a small number of people in Jamaica but spread throughout the world as reggae music gained popularity.

HAND

Word origins frequently give clues as to the nature of objects and ideas. The Latin word for hand is *manus*, which carries the same root as the word, among others, "manifestation"; a clear indication that to be "manifest" is to be held in the hand or created by the hand.

The hand is possibly one of the most accessible and expressive parts of the human body. We shake hands as a sign of greeting; we can use our hands to make signs and symbols, to gesticulate and to communicate. Literally, we can "talk with our hands" and the hands as instruments of language are used throughout the world. We can use our hands to communicate with someone even though we may not speak the same tongue; the universality of hand gestures transcends nationality and cultural background.

In the **Kabbalah**, the left hand of God signifies justice, and his right hand, mercy. Blessings and benedictions are given with the right hand. To give someone your hand is to imply trust, for example when we speak of giving someone's hand in marriage. When we meet someone we shake each other's right hand; this is a sign of friendship and trust and also shows that neither person is wielding a sword.

This right-left symbolism of the hand occurs several times. The right hand is associated with cleanliness and the left, with dirt, and in some countries to offer something with the left hand is seen as an insult.

Hands, as an extension of the will and of the intention, carry a great power. In the practice of "laying on of hands," they are used as agents of healing energies.

Hand gestures

The silent eloquence of **hand** gestures and signals can speak volumes. The "V for Victory" sign, **palm** forward, index and middle fingers extended, is recognized all over the world, and the pejorative version of the same sign, palm turned around, is also universally understood. There's an apocryphal story about the origins of this particular signal. During the Hundred Years War, the bow and arrow were the major offensive weapons. The English were famous for their skill in handling the longbow, and if they were captured, the French chopped off the index and middle **fingers** that were used to pull back the bowstring. Therefore, the gesture, as a signal of taunting defiance, was born.

The meanings of certain hand gestures can alter according to where in the world they are made. A good case in point is the *mano fico* or "sign of the **fig**," made by thrusting the **thumb** between the middle and index fingers of the curled hands. The "fico" may have been a good-luck charm for both the Ancient Romans and for latter-day Brazilians, but elsewhere in the world the gesture is not only insulting but also threatening. The *mano cornuta*, or "**horned** hand," also has a dual meaning. The index and little fingers are straight, whilst the thumb curls around the other two fingers. This signal is also called the "**goat's** horns" and while it may be an ancient sign used to ward off the **evil eye** by emulating the horns of the devil, others see it as a mark of allegiance with evil forces. If the sign is made behind someone's head, surreptitiously, then this indicates that the person's partner is cheating on them; it refers to the horns of the goat, an animal that has a particularly lascivious reputation.

The Japanese **beckoning cat** or Maneki Neko uses a welcoming gesture that is recognizable everywhere, whether made by feline or human. The palm is at shoulder height and facing outwards. There's another beckoning sign that uses the index finger, curling repeatedly in a hook-like gesture as though to reel something in. This gesture asks the person to come close.

The sign of benediction or blessing is universal, too. Here, the index and middle fingers are extended whilst the others curl into the palm. This signal is first registered in use by the Romans, who used it as a sign to gain attention or to indicate that the user was going to speak, a more elaborate version of the "hand up" signal used by schoolchildren who want to answer a question in the classroom. This ancient hand gesture is used to bless holy **water**, **wine**, **bread**, or other items; its use transcends religious boundaries and is used by the Pope as well as those of a more pagan persuasion, such as druids and Wiccans.

The clenched fist is a symbol of power, of unity. It's a sign of victory and defiance, and power is held closely in the hand.

The crossed fingers signal is a universal sign of hope or of good luck, generally used when some wish is expressed aloud. The signal has one of two meanings. First, the **cross** is a protective gesture that averts the evil eye. Second, any bad luck is "trapped" in the cross shape. However, if someone tells a lie, he might surreptitiously make this gesture, making sure that it cannot be seen, to avert any bad luck involved in the telling of the lie.

The "thumbs up" signal has come to mean approval, whereas the "thumbs down" sign means the opposite. Although the gestures are regularly used by makers of epic gladiatorial movies to signify decisions over the life or death of a gladiator, their origins are indeterminate, and may actually date back to a time when the thumb print was used to seal documents.

Mudras

This Sanskrit word is derived from the verb *mud*, meaning "to please," with the inference being that the Gods are the ones that are being pleased. It also means "seal," "sign," or "mark." Mudras are **hand** signals, but with a more sacred nature than the secular gestures described above. They have spiritual meanings not only because of their intention, but because each part of the hand and the fingers is dedicated to a deity. Mudras are used in yoga and **dance** as well as in religious pictures and statuary. Images of the Buddha, for example, generally show his hands in the silently eloquent gestures that are rich in meaning.

When used in yogic practices, Mudras not only help to focus the mind on abstract ideas and the intention behind the pose or *asana*,

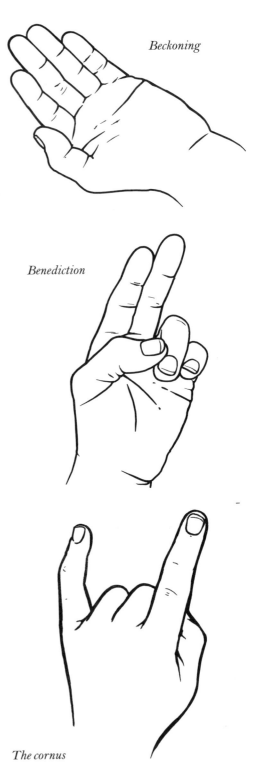

Beckoning

Benediction

The cornus

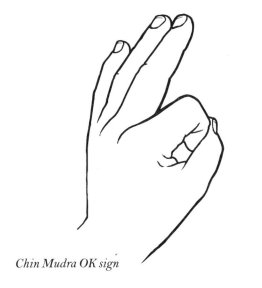

Chin Mudra OK sign

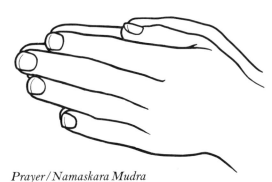

Prayer / Namaskara Mudra

Mano Fico

but experts say that the movements themselves have a direct connection to the nervous system and can help with **breath** control, etc.

Each of the fingers itself carries several different symbolic meanings. They are dedicated to each of the **five elements**: the thumb is space, the index finger is **air**, the third finger represents **fire**, the fourth **water**, and the little finger **earth**.

Some universally accepted gestures have their origins in these sacred signs. For example, the Chin Mudra is effectively the same as the "OK" sign, symbolic of approval, or "all is well." Here, the tips of the index finger and the thumb close in a **circle**. The other three fingers are straight. Because in Hindu belief the **thumb** represents the universal spirit and the index finger represents the individual spirit, the circle made when the fingers touch is symbolic of the self that meets the universe, making a **circle** of completion or wholeness.

Another mudra that is known universally is the Anjali Mudra or the Namaskara Mudra. Again, Westerners will recognize this as the gesture of prayer, both hands together at chest level. The touching palms represent the connection of spirit and matter. The gesture also seals and contains energy. Often accompanied by a bow, the word *namaskara*, or *namaste*, means "I bow to you."

HEAD

The head and the **heart** operate in tandem as the logical and the emotional aspects of the body as a sacred map. The head is symbolic of the intellect, the mind, wisdom, reasoned thought, and of a ruling power or the "top" of something—for example, the Head of State. Because of its spherical shape the head is also likened to the Universe. To bow the head before someone is to submit to them; to nod the head indicates assent (at least in the West).

The head and the face are the most easily identifiable parts of the body, and so were considered to be a great trophy in more war-like times. The head, removed from the body, means instant annihilation. For a warrior to return with the actual head of his enemy meant that he also somehow acquired the potency of that enemy; the head was a status symbol of war and would sometimes be preserved in oil so that there would be no doubt as to both the identity of its owner and the certainty that he was dead. In the same way, the head of an animal is considered to be the most valuable trophy of the hunter, a gross display of man's dominion over the animal kingdom, and the more savage the animal the more kudos is accorded its killer.

However, in myth, not all decapitated heads were rendered lifeless. This is in accord with the ancient notion that the head contains the real seat of the **soul**, the essence of the person and of life itself. It follows, then, that these disembodied heads carried great wisdom and therefore could act as oracles. In the Celtic tale of Bran the Blessed, Bran is decapitated but his head continues to be able to talk lucidly, and tells his people that he needs to be buried at the White Hill in London; so long as the head remains there then Britain will be protected from invasion. The White Hill is now called Tower Hill. The Norse God **Odin** is said to have derived much of his wisdom from the oracular head of an earlier deity called Mimir.

To sever the head from the body was to separate the physical from the spiritual, and the ritual of touching a sword to either shoulder during the ceremony of knighthood is a reminder of this idea.

The Hindu Goddess **Kali** is easily identifiable by her **necklace** of severed heads, which are said to be the source of her wisdom. They also represent the **letters** of the **alphabet** and comprise the "beads" of her sacred **rosary** or "japamala."

HEART

Physically, the heart is responsible for keeping the **blood** flowing around the body at a regular pace. Symbolically, it has come to represent so much more than this simple pump-like action. In the same way that the **head** represents the wisdom born of knowledge and learning, the heart contains the wisdom of feeling and empathy. The heart is symbolic of compassion, love, and charity.

The heart symbolizes the very center of the being, both physical and spiritual, and has been twinned with the **soul** since time immemorial—even before the Egyptian "heart-soul" was weighed by Maat, the Goddess of Truth. As the last organ left in the mummy, the ideal heart was meant to be as light as a **feather**—Maat wore the **ostrich** feather that has equally-balanced fronds as a symbol of justice. The heart should not be weighed down by misdeeds or untruths.

In many religions the heart symbolizes God. In the Hindu faith it is called the Brahmapura or House of Brahma. In Christianity it is the Kingdom of God. In China it is the Home of the Spirit. The notion of the heart being at the center of the body and the seat of the divine is extrapolated out into the world, too, where in the Jewish tradition we find that the Holy of Holies is the heart of the **temple** of Jerusalem, which itself is the heart of the world in Judaism.

This idea of the heart containing the "home" of God is symbolized by the **Kabbalistic** image of the inverted heart that contains the letters of the **tetragrammaton**, the secret **name** of God.

In Islam, the heart is symbolic of the inner life of a person, of meditation and contemplation. Called the Qalb, in the Sufi Islamic sect the heart represents not only God's mercy but is believed also to contain the essence of God, controlling the physical organs of the body as well as the thought processes.

If we look at the shape of the heart, it's rather like an inverted **triangle**, and indeed, this is a simplified heart symbol. The heart is also sometimes represented as a **chalice** or, in Ancient Egyptian hieroglyphs, as a vase; in all these instances we see the heart as a receptacle. The heart shape is also similar to the shape of the female pubic mound or the **yoni**; the cuneiform symbol for woman is heart shaped and is likely to be based on the same body part.

To put your heart and soul into something is to invest a project with as much energy and commitment as can be mustered. When we make a vow and we put our **hand** on our heart, this shows our sincerity to keep the promise.

The heart is believed to be the first part of the body to be created while the fetus is in the **womb**, and also the first organ to die. The heart of Joan of Arc was believed to have survived the flames that killed her when she was burned at the stake, a symbol of her truthfulness and a sign that she was indeed chosen by God.

The heart became associated with love relatively recently, in the Middle Ages, and today the stylized heart symbol is synonymous with both the word "love" and the concept, and is most prevalent around the time of **St. Valentine's Day** on February 14.

The "sacred heart" is popular in Catholic iconography. In this symbol Christ is portrayed with a flaming heart that is encircled with a crown of thorns and surmounted by the **cross**. In this particular instance the heart refers to the manner of his **death**, with the **fire** indicating the fire of eternal love.

Heel

Achilles, a hero of the Trojan Wars in Greek myth, was seemingly invulnerable and unconquerable because his mother, Thetis, had dipped him into the river **Styx**, the boundary between this world and the Underworld. However, Thetis overlooked one thing; because she held her son by the heel it remained untouched by the magical waters of the river and although it was Achilles' only weak spot, it meant that when the Trojan prince Paris shot him in the heel with a poisoned arrow, it was enough to kill this great hero. This is a powerful myth and has meant that the phrase "Achilles Heel" stands for a vulnerable place or a weakness.

Incidentally, the plant achillea, also known as the **Yarrow**, is so-called because Achilles is said to have known about its healing properties, using it to staunch the bleeding of his warriors' wounds.

The Semang, a tribe belonging to the Malay Peninsula, believe that the **soul** exits the body through the heel.

HYMEN

The Greek word for "**veil**." In the secret symbolism of the sacred body the hymen refers to the membrane that stretches across the vulva before it is pierced, traditionally, the first time that the female has penetrative sex, with the result that her virginity, or maidenhead, is no more. This physical veil is rent, symbolically, at the wedding when the bride lifts the veil that is part of her bridal attire. The cutting of the cake, too, by the newly-weds is also a symbol of this physical act.

In the Greek Pantheon, Hymenaeus was the God of Weddings. He was also a deity of both youth and song, and gives his name to the "hymn," which actually started out as a specific wedding song rather than the generalized religious song that it has come to mean today.

INTESTINES

See **Bowels**.

KA

See **Five Bodies of the Egyptians**.

KHU

See **Five Bodies of the Egyptians**.

KIDNEY

The kidney is considered by some, including the Jewish people, to be the base of the feelings, and an organ that carries power and passion. It was also considered to be the core of hidden desire and sexual drive, operating in tandem with the **heart** as the organ that held intimate thoughts.

KNEE

Kneeling is a sign of subjugation, of deference, and of humility, and the knee itself is a symbol of power and strength since the joint supports almost the entire weight of the body. To "bring to the knees" is therefore symbolic of taking away power.

LEG

As the pillars that support the rest of the body, the legs are symbols of strength and stability. Further, because they enable us to get from place to place, effectively removing barriers, they are symbols of communication and of locomotion. When we say that something "has legs" we mean that it is full of potential, and will endure.

The symbol for both the Isle of Man and Sicily, the **triskelion** of **three** conjoined **legs** (also called a Trie Cassyn) is of ancient origin. The symbol appears on fifth-century BC coins from Asia Minor, and appears in connection with the Isle of Man from the thirteenth century onwards. It also appears some three hundred years earlier on coins, minted in honour of the Nordic King Analuf, who governed both the Isle of Man and Dublin. Like other **triskele** forms, these three Manx legs are a solar symbol and, significantly, must always appear to be "running" in a clockwise direction since the reverse is considered a malevolent symbol.

LIVER

The Roman physician Galen said that the liver was the home of passions; there is agreement about this symbolism in many societies. The liver is regarded as the seat of anger in the Talmud and the word "bile" or "gall" (a substance secreted by the liver) has come to mean bitterness or spite. The liver is connected with courage and strong feelings in the Arab countries, and in Chinese medicine the liver is similarly seen as generating strength.

This connection between the liver and strength stems from the fact that the liver is able to regenerate its damaged tissues. In Greek myth, Prometheus was punished by the Gods for showing human beings how to make **fire** by being tied to a rock where an **eagle** pecks out his liver, which grows back overnight so that the torture can be repeated over and over again.

In an example of sympathetic magic that demonstrates a symbolic transference of the strength imbued into the liver symbol, in Cambodia unfortunate wayfarers were captured and their galls removed; a liquor would be made from these galls which was used both to fortify generals and to anoint the heads of the **elephants** that were used in battles.

The liver has been used as a divinatory tool; the *haruspex* or "inspector of entrails" in Ancient Rome was trained to deduce what the future held by examining the entrails of animals and in particular the livers of **sheep**. In Babylonia, hepatoscopy relied on the **blood** produced by the liver to carry out the practice, with each part of the organ being associated with a particular deity. There are still clay models of these livers, complete with demarcations, in existence today. One of the most famous is the Piacenza Liver, from northern Italy. This bronze sculpture of a liver assigns a deity to the various regions of the district that are symbolized on the model itself.

MOUTH

The mouth speaks, eats, and breathes, three fundamentally important aspects of it as an essential bodily organ. But the mouth is also a **cave**-like structure similar to the **vagina**, and because of this similarity the mouth is often given sexual connotations, too, and there are vulva/mouth synonyms to be found all over the world. The most frightening is the notion of the "vagina dentate," where the vagina has teeth just like a mouth and so could bite off the penis. Like a mouth, the vagina has lips (labia).

As the cave is a source of hidden secrets, so is the mouth. In this case the secrets come in the form of words. Words carry a great power, and the mouth shares in this power as the "home" of the sacred sounds and syllables it produces. Because of the magical powers of **sounds** and speech, gagging the mouth as an initiatory rite symbolizes secrecy, that which must not be spoken of.

The mouth can be depicted either as a gentle pair of lips which can **kiss** and whisper secrets and sweet nothings, or conversely as a greedy, gaping maw, which can devour and destroy anything that enters it.

In Ancient Egypt, a ceremony called the Opening of the Mouth was carried out on all corpses before burial. The priest opened the mouth with two implements, one a hook, the other a small golden object shaped like a **finger**. This ceremony was carried out so that the dead person would be able to speak the truth in front of the deities who would question him in the next world.

NAVEL

Leonardo's picture of the perfectly proportioned Vitruvian Man shows the navel as being in the exact center of the picture, and indeed the navel—as the **omphalos**—represents not only the center of the human body but also the center of the Universe. These navel symbols are to be found in various places all around the world, usually in the form of large stones with a domed top, with one of the most famous being at Delphi, center of the worship of Apollo. In India the navel takes the form of the **lingam**. The navel is the point of contact between the mother and the unborn child and so has sacred significance as the place where spirit and matter meet.

In yogic practice the navel corresponds to the very center of transformational energy and is a point of concentration and meditation, hence the phrase "navel gazing" to mean someone who is lost in thought.

NIPPLE

The nipple has conflicting symbolism; it is an erogenous zone and a sign of sexual arousal but also of motherhood. In some countries the sight of an erect nipple under clothes is considered to be offensive, and in Japan special plasters are stuck over them so that they don't show.

Piercing the nipples, among some tribes, was a sign of strength and virility. In Central America nipples were pierced as a rite of passage, from puberty to manhood. Piercing the nipples as a fashion statement is nothing new: there was a trend for it in the late nineteenth century, and chains would sometimes be stretched between the nipples.

NOSE

The nose is a symbol of intuition; to be able to "sniff something out" or to speak of something that "smells wrong" indicates use of the predictive faculties. Additionally, scents and perfumes are extremely evocative and carry information that can be analyzed only by the nose. This information goes beyond the bounds of language and straight to the part of the brain that stores memories—the oldest and most primitive part.

The nose is also the organ that takes in oxygen and then expels it, and because breathing is a sacred spiritual act, the nose is similarly seen as imbued with spiritual properties.

Several tribes that rely on hunting for survival, including the Yakut in Siberia and the Tungus in the Altai regions, believe that the nose or snout of an animal contains its spirit, because the nose is the instrument of the breath and breath and spirit are closely associated. Therefore the snout would be set aside as a **totem**, used as a charm to protect homes and possession.

In Japan, to have a long nose is considered to be a sign of pride and arrogance. To be "nosy" is to have a curiosity beyond the bounds of politeness and so in this instance the nose is a symbol of prying or meddling.

PALM

Among the lines and wrinkles of the palms of the hands is a whole system of secret signs and symbols, and someone trained in their mysteries can apparently interpret the temperament of the owner from them. Palmists also claim that they can divine the future from these lines and symbols.

It is difficult to be entirely certain of the history of palmistry, but it is true to say that it is an ancient art that probably originated with the prehistoric Aryan people of Mongolia. In accordance with the original notion that each body part contains an aspect of the greater Universe within it, each of the fleshy mounds of the palm correlates to one of the **seven** traditional planets, the **Sun**, **Moon**, **Mercury**, **Venus**, **Mars**, **Jupiter**, and **Saturn**. Each of the **fingers**, too, belongs to a planet; the index finger belongs to Jupiter, the middle finger to Saturn, the fourth to the Sun, and the little finger to Mercury.

The symbols discerned in the wrinkles of the palms are named according to the shapes they represent. These include **stars**, **crosses**, **triangles**, **squares**, **circles**, and **arrows**. Their meanings vary according to where on the palms they are found. The lines around the base of the palm and the wrist are called bracelets. The lines on the palms, too, have a variety of different meanings that are all self-explanatory: the line of the **heart** governs the love life and emotions, the line of the **head**, the intellect. The line of life indicates the life expectancy of the subject. Other lines refer to health, fate, levels of sensuality, intuition, etc.

PHALLUS

The phallus is a symbol of male energy and creativity, and as an extrapolation of the idea of man as being made in the image of God, it's also the symbol of the life-giving principles of the male deity. The phallus is a symbol of resurrection and new life, given the different states of the penis being "asleep" or "awake."

The phallus is symbolized in many forms, most of them obvious although not necessarily erotic. The phallus is essential to life. **Trees**, towers, **standing stones**—all have their phallic connotations as symbols of strength, support, and also as the foundation of life and the Universe, and the phallus is sometimes referred to as the **tree of life**. The **omphalos** also has phallic connotations although strictly speaking this is a symbol of the **navel** as the center of the world.

The phallus as a symbol is as old as mankind itself, and the oldest known representation of it is a stone object, found in southwest Germany, dating back 28,000 years.

In Hindu temples, the phallus is depicted as the upright **lingam** that stands in the shallow bowl that represents the **yoni**, the two sacred symbols working in tandem as the male and female energies.

In Ancient Rome, jewelry representing the phallus was believed to give protection against the **evil eye**. And in Greece, the God Priapus is depicted with an oversized phallus as a mark of his power and virility, giving us the word "priapic."

Philtrum

This is the grooved space between the top of the lip and the base of the **nose**, and was considered by the Greeks to be a potent erogenous zone, hence its name, which means "to **kiss**." Some believe the indentation was made by the **finger** of God when he created man.

Putting the finger to the lips indicates silence. In Jewish folklore, it is said that an **angel** visits each child in the **womb** and teaches it everything there it is to know. However, just as it emerges into the world the same angel touches the baby's philtrum, causing it to forget all this information, which it will then spend its lifetime trying to relearn. Hence the philtrum represents the retention of divine or occult knowledge.

Placenta

Although for many the placenta may be considered as nothing more than clinical waste, for others it has garnered sacred symbolic significance because it provides nourishment and protection to the unborn child. The placenta is a symbol of the life, the spirit, and the physical manifestation of the human being.

The placenta—since it is "born" along with the child—is accorded respect in many parts of the world and is treated with due ceremony. The Maori people, for example, bury the placenta as they would a human body; indeed, there is a shared word for placenta and land, *whenua*. The **funeral** rites given to the afterbirth indicates the link shared between the newborn child and its unformed "twin," and the land. The burial of the placenta effectively ties the child to the land. In Africa and among some Native American tribes, the placenta is given a full burial for similar reasons.

The belief that the placenta and its owner are inextricably linked is a common one. In south-east Asia the word for placenta is the same as that for "jacket," since the placenta is seen as the first piece of clothing that the child possesses. It is believed that after death the **soul** searches for the place where its placenta is buried so that they can be as one again.

In an example of sympathetic magic, Filipino mothers will bury the placenta along with **books** in the belief that this symbolic act will make for an intelligent child.

Animals, after giving birth, regularly eat the placenta, since it is stuffed full of vitamins and minerals and is a great source of nourishment for the new mother.

Sahu

See **Five Bodies of the Egyptians**.

Saliva

Saliva is an agent of destruction and also an agent of creation. For example, there is a biblical anecdote about Christ restoring the sight of a blind man by rubbing his eyelids with saliva. The precursor to this story is possibly a recipe from Ninevah, in which **milk** and saliva from a "temple harlot" are mixed together to cure blindness. Along with mothers' milk and menstrual **blood**, saliva was one of the three sacred liquids, rendered magical because they contained the essence of female power.

Spitting, though, can either be a curse or a protection, depending on how it is used. To spit over the **shoulder** was to spit in the **eye** of the Devil, and could therefore offset bad luck. Spitting in someone's face is an undeniable sign of aggression and a huge insult. Similarly, to spit on a grave is the ultimate symbol of disrespect to the dead person.

SEMEN

Semen is symbolic of the **seed** of potential, not just of new life but also of new ideas and innovations. The Roman physician Galen said that semen actually originated in the brain, and this notion was generally accepted until the Middle Ages.

Because semen contains the very essence of male power and of life itself, it is a potent ingredient in some magical spells. Aleister Crowley, for example, was fond of using his ejaculatory fluid to "charge" certain aspects of his magic(k)al endeavors. Even today, certain practitioners of folk magic will harvest semen—perhaps storing it in the freezer until needed—in the hopes that it will imbue a spell or charm with virile potency.

SHADOW

The dark shape cast in the presence of bright light, the shadow has come to represent so much more than a simple physical phenomenon. Psychologists since Carl Jung have used the word to refer to the unconscious mind, the "dark side," the aspect of a personality that might be difficult or disagreeable to deal with but which, nevertheless, is an inherent part of the psyche.

The shadow comes and goes, a fleeting thing. It is an insubstantial, ghostly presence, not quite real. For followers of the Dharmic religions the shadow is a symbol of the illusory nature of the world in which we live. Plato, the Greek philosopher, amplified this idea with his theory about the **Cave** of Shadows. In this famous allegory, he described what he perceived to be mankind's lot; he is imprisoned in a cave and chained up so that he can look in only one direction; a **fire** burns behind and above and the prisoner watches only shadows dancing on the walls, shadows of objects he cannot see.

In many parts of the world, the shadow equates to the **soul**. Traditionally, creatures that do not have a soul have no reflection and no shadow. The lack of a shadow is the sign of a person that has sold his soul to the Devil. **Vampires** have neither reflections nor shadows. In the Taoist faith, however, the lack of a shadow does not imply that evil is afoot, but rather the opposite: the **Immortals** traditionally cast no shadows, being so transcendent as to be barely physical. They also stood directly beneath the **Sun** as the source of power and light that would have cast the shadow. In this sense, the lack of a shadow is symbolic of peace and harmony since the person is placed firmly in the center of his own Universe.

The shadow is symbolic of influence, too, as in someone who is said to cast a long shadow.

In witchcraft, the Book of Shadows is the name given to the book of spells and rituals pertaining to the craft.

SHOULDER

Symbolic of strength, power, and effort. If a person has broad shoulders then they are able the take a lot of responsibility, both physically and mentally. To put the shoulder to the **wheel** means that all a person's strength is concentrated on whatever the task requires.

SKIN

As the outside layer of the body and its largest single organ, the skin is symbolic of protection. We use the terms "thick skinned" or "thin skinned" to mean someone who is either completely insensitive or over sensitive.

For a shaman, wearing the skin or pelt of an **animal** will help him absorb the power of the animal itself. It also implies dominance over the animal that had to be hunted in order to get the skin in the first place. Skins of sacred animals are often made into bags to contain certain magical items.

In humans, in less enlightened times than now, differences in skin color resulted in gross misunderstandings and prejudice. Fair skin was regarded as a symbol of wealth since the owner was presumed not to have to subject himself to manual labor; conversely, a dark skin carried the opposite meaning.

SKULL

The skull is possibly the most important **bone** in the human body, instantly recognizable for what it is (unlike most other bones), and was believed to contain the life-force of both the body and the spirit. If the skull is severed from the body then this results in instant death, hence the power held within the skull or **head**.

The skull, typically, is a symbol of **death**. It also symbolizes the vanity of worldly things and the transitory nature of time. In the Christian religion the skull was meditated upon as a reminder of the closeness of death, and therefore God's Judgement. Skulls often appear on older gravestones or in tombs.

There's an ancient tradition of talking skulls that possessed oracular powers. The skull of Orpheus, for example, kept on the Greek island of Lesbos, was reputed to have these talents.

The head or the skull was also an important trophy of war, and some warriors would use the skull of an enemy that they had slaughtered as a drinking vessel, a grisly but effective demonstration of supremacy.

In Mexico, during the festival called the Day of the Dead, for example, the skull takes on a festive appearance, and colorful models of skeletons and skulls made of candy serve as a reminder of the nearness of death and the necessity to celebrate life.

In **alchemy**, the skull, with the grave and the **raven**, is a secret symbol of a stage of work called "mortification," which is itself symbolic of a dying to the world, a throwing off of earthly things and eventually a return to the **earth**. Similarly, in **Freemasonry**, the skull represents a cycle of initiation, a symbolic death preceding a new life.

SOUL

Mind, body, and soul: the essential trinity that describes what we are. The soul, though, is a difficult thing to quantify; does it exist outside the physical body, and if so, in what form? The belief in a "**ghost**" that leaves the body at the moment of its physical death is a concept that transcends religious and cultural belief and is closely linked with the **breath** as the essence of life. The Latin word *animus*, the Greek *anemos*, and the Sanskrit *aniti* all mean "**breath**" or "**air**," and refer to the soul, literally, as an animating factor. The Celts, too, called the soul the *anamon*, which is closely linked to the word for harmony, and also to the Mother Goddess, Ana.

That the soul is immortal is also a deeply routed idea, but there are many different beliefs about it. The soul can somehow be recycled (reincarnation), or else becomes part of a collective "oneness" that is a part of the Godhead. Some believe that there is a heaven or a hell that the soul is sent to, depending on its actions during its earthly existence. Others believe that the disembodied soul can somehow haunt the places that it has known while locked into the corporeal body, occupying a sort of parallel universe. Some cultures explain these different aspects of the soul by assuming that each person has several different sorts of spirit; a good example is the Buryat belief. The Buryats are an ethnic Mongolian people who believe that one soul goes to heaven or hell, one remains on earth as a mischievous spirit, and a third reincarnates in another body.

Birds and winged creatures such as **moths** or **butterflies** are believed to contain the soul of a dead person, the **wings** here symbolizing the idea of transcendence.

Throughout history people have tried to identify the seat of the soul within the body. Once, people believed that it was lodged in the **heart**. The seventeenth-century philosopher René Descartes placed it squarely in the pineal gland, the small gland in the brain that, among other functions, produces melatonin. In yogic practice and metaphysical belief the pineal gland is associated with the **third eye**, a mysterious inner eye that can somehow be awakened, resulting in telepathic communication.

That the soul can somehow be bought or sold is an idea that is so old that it is impossible to determine where it first came from. Catholic missionaries used to amass collections of souls that had been "saved." If the soul is sold to the Devil, on the other hand, the person loses his **shadow** and his reflection, both aspects that are linked to the concept of the soul or spirit. To be described as having no soul means that the person is less than human, bereft of passion, emotions, or a conscience.

SPINAL COLUMN

The backbone of the human body, the spinal column is symbolic of the **World Axis** and also of the **World Tree**. In Tantric belief systems, the column of energy that rises up the spinal column through the **chakras**, symbolized by the great **serpent** Kundalini, carries the same symbolism as the **staff of Asclepius**.

The spinal column symbolizes strength, hard work, and moral fiber. The spine also represents the **ladder** that ascends to the Heavens and back down again.

Spleen

The spleen can be symbolic either of good humor, cheerfulness, and laughter, or, conversely, it can stand for irritability and melancholia. However, the overriding symbolism of the spleen is that of changeability.

Stomach

To talk about the guts of something, a machine, for example, is to discuss its innermost workings, the most important part of it. In the symbolism of the body the stomach and the guts are one and the same. To say that we "can't stomach something" means that something is intolerable, and "butterflies in the stomach" refers to a fluttery nervous feeling. In Ghana, twin **crocodiles** joined at the stomach is an **adinkra** symbol for the belief in democracy. The gut or stomach is also associated with the solar plexus **chakra**.

The guts are strongly associated with instincts. To feel something in the gut is to feel something with the intuitive faculty, when the logical mind is overridden by the instinctive, base, animal side of human nature.

Sweat

At the most practical level, sweat is symbolic of hard work. But on a spiritual level, sweat is imbued with the spirit of its owner and so is considered to be a magical substance, and can be used in spells as an energy charge.

The saunas of northern Europe may have health benefits, but they were originally used as a way to enrich the spirit by ritual purification. The sweat lodge rituals of Native American tribes, too, are carried out as part of a greater ceremony that involves **fasting** and chanting. Heated rocks in the center of the lodge (which is crammed with as many naked or scantily-clad people as space will allow) have cold **water** poured over them, generating a considerable amount of steam. The sweat is considered to be an offering to the **Sun** God.

Teeth

A good set of teeth is a sign of youth and health, an attractive attribute, and also a status symbol, which many people spend a lot of money to acquire. Conversely, to lose one's teeth is a sign of old age and decrepitude.

Symbolically, it's said that a smile that shows the teeth originates in the baring of the teeth to warn off a potential enemy. Certainly, to show the teeth in such a way that the lips are curled back is a threatening gesture.

When the **milk** teeth of children fall out in order to make way for the permanent teeth, these little teeth are "bought" by the **fairies** in order to assuage the child for the loss. The actual milk tooth itself carried something of the essence of the child and is a potent magical object, which should be hidden lest it fall into the wrong **hands**. The power of the tooth, which carries the energy of the creature it originally belonged to, is reflected in the teeth that are worn as decoration by warriors. To be "armed to the teeth" means to carry as many weapons as is humanly possible.

The wisdom tooth holds sacred significance. The Irish Druids would perform a spell designed to bring about poetic inspiration by putting the **thumb** on the wisdom tooth, biting down hard, and then dedicating a song or poem to the Gods. This ritual is called the Teinm Laegda in Old Irish, and although the correct translation of the term is the source of heated debate, nevertheless, here we see the tooth as a source of wisdom and inspiration.

Long teeth, too, are regarded as a sign of wisdom, because older people have longer teeth (due to their gums receding), and it is commonly supposed that with age comes wisdom.

TESTICLES

To have "balls," one of the many slang words for testicles, means to be courageous, strong, audacious, and upfront. The testicles are a symbol of potential generations to come since they contain **semen**. The Latin word *testis* means "little witness" and an oath or "testament" (a word that shares the same root) would be sworn on the testicles as acknowledgement of their vital role, i.e., swearing on the lives of one's (future) children and grandchildren.

The Greek for testicle is *orkhis* means testicle, and **orchid** flowers are so-named

because their shape is similar to that of the organ.

THIGH

The thigh is a symbol of sturdiness and strength, but as well as this literal interpretation of meaning there are several instances where the thigh is seen as some sort of secondary **womb** or generative organ. For example, in Islamic tales, Fatima, the daughter of the Prophet, is said to have given birth to her sons from her thigh, and this belief has given Fatima the epithet of the "Muslim Virgin Mary." The Greek God **Dionysus**, too, was said to have been born from the thigh of his father, **Zeus**.

In the Bible, the thigh is used as a euphemism for the **testicles**; this usage goes back to Hebrew times. There are several passages in the Old Testament book of Genesis that speak of swearing an oath by putting the hand "under the thigh"; it's likely that this interpretation was used since the top of the thigh is close to the testicles, a word which comes from the same source as "testament."

THUMB

The opposable thumb is one of the crucial body parts that separate man from the rest of the animal kingdom in that it enables us to grasp objects. The thumb is considered to be masculine, and a phallic symbol, and also equates to God; in yogic practice the thumb is associated with the male element of **fire**.

The thumbs-up symbol, meaning agreement or approval, dates back to the Middle

Ages, where two parties reaching an agreement would squeeze their thumbs together; hence the gesture came to be a sign of harmony. Movies about ancient Rome that use the thumbs up/thumbs down gesture to save or end the life of the gladiator, however, are likely to have using the gesture spuriously; there is no evidence to show that this signal was used for such a purpose.

The "rule of thumb" refers to a vague measurement, an estimate. The thumb is roughly an inch long so is a useful tool for guestimation purposes.

Tongue

The tongue is an essential tool in the creation of **sounds** and coherent words, and so it is often seen as a synonym for language. To speak of the "native tongue" is to refer to a person's first language, in the same way that, biblically, the magical ability of "speaking in tongues" meant the ability to speak in such a way that people of different nationalities would supposedly hear the same words and yet understand the meaning.

Anyone accused of speaking with a forked tongue is accused of being a liar or deceiver. The term refers to the forked tongue of the **serpent** in the Garden of Eden who persuaded Eve to "corrupt" Adam by coaxing him to eat the **apple** of wisdom. Similarly, in Africa the Bambara say that liars have "striped" tongues since in its purest form the tongue is said to be "of one color"—a single unadulterated "color" being symbolic of the truth.

Symbolically, to cut out the tongues of enemies renders them powerless, since speech is such a vital aspect of humanity.

In the West, to stick out your tongue at someone is considered to be rude and insulting. This is likely to be because the extended tongue has sexual connotations and resembles the **phallus**. Depictions of the Devil often show him with a fleshy, protruding tongue, and the gargoyles who scare away evil spirits from their stony vantage points of the sides of **churches** and cathedrals stick out their tongues, rendering themselves even more frightening and insulting to any happenchance little **demons**.

The sexual implications of the tongue as a phallic symbol gives potency to the many deities who are depicted with protruding tongues, such as Kali; her extremely long, outstretched tongue symbolizes creative energy.

In some parts of India, Tibet, and China, however, to stick out the tongue is seen as a sign of greeting.

Umbilical cord

The umbilical cord is the lifeline between the mother and the unborn child and therefore holds a particular significance as a symbol of dependence. The image of the tiny, vulnerable astronaut, bobbing around in the vastness of space, connected to life only by the pipeline that connects to his mother ship, is a poignant symbol of both the fragility and strength of the umbilical cord. In this instance the astronaut is provided with oxygen from the mother ship, but effectively the symbolism is the same.

When we speak of someone as being symbolically attached by an umbilical cord, we mean that there's an unhealthy link, a reliance on an external agent that should perhaps be severed

The severing of the umbilical cord is not only a practical act but also carries symbolic significance, as the material body is finally released from the spirit world. The umbilical cord will drop away naturally from the baby after **seven** days, and certain African tribes consider that the child is not completely born until this happens. The cord itself is considered to be a particularly potent magical charm, given that it has been a source of sustenance, life, and energy from the greatest protector a child will ever know, its mother. The cord is carried as a **totem** in a small bag around the child's neck.

This use of the cord as an **amulet** is not restricted to African tribes, and in other places around the world the cord is preserved so that it can be buried, when the time comes, with the rest of the earthly remains of its original owner, since it is seen as an essential part of the body. In Japan, the umbilical cord is kept intact as a symbol of the bond between mother and child.

In some parts of the UK it is considered bad form for the cord to touch the ground at any point, while in Hungary, the umbilical cord was kept safe since witches were said to be able to use it to suck **milk** from **cows** at a great distance. In the same country the child is sometimes fed its own dried and powdered umbilical cord in order to make it strong and healthy.

Hopi Indians regard the umbilical cord as housing the **soul**, and it is kept during childhood in case the child should die, in which instance the cord is used as an escape route for the soul, which can then be reborn.

When a woman is found to be pregnant, in many societies she ceases to wear **knots** of any kind, since, in the tradition of sympa-thetic magic, the knots may somehow cause the umbilical cord itself to become knotted and affect the birth of the baby.

Vagina

There is mystery and ambiguity surrounding the vagina symbol. The word itself comes from the Latin for "sheath" or "scabbard." It represents a gateway or a **cave**, and the Bambara see it as a place of hidden knowledge and secret treasures. The vagina gives birth to the child, and yet appears to swallow the penis, a fact which has caused it to be a symbol of both fear and desire among men. The "vagina dentate" is the most terrifying representation of all vagina symbols, the toothed vagina that could potentially bite off the penis. This frightening extra feature belongs to the legendary **succubus** of the Middle East.

The vagina is symbolically represented by the **vesica piscis**, the sacred gateway through which spirit joins the world of matter, and in essence by the **yoni**, the Hindu representation of it as the bowl or receptacle from whence springs the male **lingam** or **phallus**.

Womb

As the sacred place where new life is gestated, and therefore the ultimate symbol of the Mother, the womb carries powerful symbolic meaning and there are many different representations of it.

The womb is a natural place of safety and security, of dependence, and it is seen as deep, silent, and nurturing. It's a place of contemplation, of spiritual and physical growth, and of potential.

Because the entrance to the womb is **cave**-like, then the cave in the natural world is also a symbol of the womb, the Earth Mother, and the place where hidden mysteries are kept. Extrapolating further, the **temple** is the manmade symbol of the womb; no surprise that the Sanskrit word for "temple" is the same as that for "womb."

The Egyptian **Ankh**, the **tau cross** with the **circle** on top, could be construed as a womb symbol; it is not only the same shape but also carries connotations of the cycle of life and rebirth. Both the **labyrinth** and the **spiral**, too, can be interpreted as secret signs of the womb.

YONI

Although the yoni is effectively a symbol of the **vagina**, there's a subtle difference in the inference. Vagina comes from a Latin word meaning "sheath," i.e. the receptacle for the penis, whereas yoni is a Sanskrit word meaning "divine passage" or "sacred temple." The child was considered as being born from a yoni of **stars**, the passage of stars that are effectively the constellations that are in the **sky** at the time of birth. In Hindu temples, the **lingam/yoni** is an important symbol of the harmonic balance between the male and female energies.

Part Ten

RITES AND RITUALS, CUSTOMS AND OBSERVANCES

We use certain rites, rituals, customs, and observances to mark key moments in our lives. These tend to split into three categories. First, there are the key events in our own lives, such as being named or getting married. Then there are commemorative events in the history of a people. Finally, there are the events that punctuate the seasons. Many of our customs reflect this universal desire to mark the passage of time and the turning of the **wheel of the year**. The many different ways in which we like to bring light into the darkness of midwinter is a good example of this, such as **Christmas** for Christians (although this festival has become so popular that it has extended way beyond any boundaries of faith) or the **Diwali** festival of Indian culture. It's interesting to see how aspects of these seasonal festivals change as the religion varies, although the fundamental reason behind them remains largely unaltered.

BIRTHDAY

Any anniversary acts as a marker in the **circle** of the year, and the birthday is the most personalized example of this, seen as a time either of celebration, or reflection, or both. However, the celebration of the day of one's birth is by no means universal, and nor does everyone delight in acknowledging their own aging process.

The actual day of a birthday is believed to have a bearing on the characteristics and prospects of a person, because of the **astrological sign** and numerology associated with it. The phrase "Many Happy Returns," refers to the return of the **Sun** into the planetary house it occupied on the original day of birth.

Certain ages are marked with some sort of rite of passage, although some of these "special" birthdays tend to be a moveable feast and can vary in different places. For example, in the West the **twenty-first** birthday used to signify the "age of majority" or adulthood; this has since been changed to **eighteen**. In many Asian countries, the fourteenth birthday is the day on which the child symbolically becomes an adult. This logically ties in with puberty.

In the West, people optimistically suppose that "life begins at **forty**," whereas in Japan the fortieth birthday is called *shoro*, meaning "the beginning of old age," since this was the age that Confucius ceased his traveling. However, the Japanese forty-year-old need not be filled with gloom for long; he can look forward to his sixty-first birthday, called *kanreki*, marking the completion of a sixty-year cycle. Therefore the lucky 61-year-old Japanese birthday boy or girl wears a **red** kimono and matching **hat** and is "new born" on this day.

In many countries, a significant feature of a birthday is a party and a cake, with the same number of **candles** as the years of the birthday. Traditionally, these candles are blown out in exchange for wishes. In China, noodles rather than cake are an important part of the shared celebration, since they symbolize longevity.

There are, of course, a variety of different **gemstones**, or birthstones, that are attached to each of the birth signs. We explore these in Part 5.

CHRISTMAS

To understand the true meaning of the festival we now call Christmas we need to delve back into the mists of antiquity.

Once, December 25 was the day on which people celebrated the **birthday** of the Phrygian **Sun** God, Attis. He was venerated far and wide, and was said to have been born in the country that is now Turkey. However, Attis was superceded by another God, with an uncannily familiar life story. This new God was born on the same day as Attis, in impoverished circumstances, to a virgin mother. He died, and was subsequently resurrected. The tenets of his faith included the notion of a brotherhood of man and the promise of eternal life in return for adherence to a pure moral code. This faith proved very popular among Roman soldiers, who spread the word even further into Europe during the course of their campaigns.

So, this new God must have been Christ? Wrong. It was Mithras.

There's still at least one temple to Mithras left in Britain, just south of Hadrian's Wall in Northumberland. In Mithraism, December 25 was called *Dies Natali Invicti Solis*, "The Birthday of the Unconquered Sun." It seems as though the need to inject a little brightness and cheer into the darkest time of the year, when the **wheel** of time carries us through the winter solstice, is symbolically more important than any of the divine beings that have successively blown out their birthday cake candles at this time. The Birthday of the Unconquered Sun is really the aptest description for what has come to be known as Christmas.

Despite meaning "Christ's Mass," this holiday is celebrated all over the world whether people are Christian or not. December 25 is for most the zenith of the festivities, although the change from the Julian to the Gregorian calendar has resulted in a 14-day anomaly, and for some January 6 is the "true" Christmas.

Prior to Christianity the Anglo-Saxons called this generic midwinter festival *geol*, the precursor to Yule, a name still used by those who might wish to distance themselves, or the festival, from any Christian connotations. Some of the customs of *geol* still prevail, most notably of the Yule Log. Although its appearance these days is more likely to be a log-shaped cake covered in plastic **holly** and lopsided robins, the original was more imposing. It was a gargantuan chunk of a **tree**, which had to be found rather than chopped down. This tree was then dragged to the largest fireplace in the area where it burned for the duration of the festivities, a symbol of light and heat in the darkness and a welcome reminder of the Sun. The Yule **candle** signified the same thing. Like the log, the bumper size of the candle was important because it needed to burn for a long time. Christian churches adopted this tradition, too, using giant candles that towered over the congregation as a symbol of spiritual illumination. Today, the largesse of this mammoth torch has shrunk down into the advent candle, marked into 24 neat segments that burn politely from December 1 onward.

As well as emulating earlier Anglo-Saxon traditions, Christmas revelries owe a great debt to the Roman festival of the **Saturnalia**. This was the time that **Saturn**, the God of **Time**, was loosened from his shackles, gifts were exchanged, and the world turned upside down as servants and masters swapped places, a quaint custom adopted as the Lords of Misrule. Saturn effectively reappears again in the starring role of **Father Christmas**, benevolent dispenser of gifts to all and sundry but to children in particular. He pops up again at New Year as Old Father Time, looking old, care-worn and surprisingly skinny despite the excess of mince pies and sherry, dressed in sackcloth and carrying a sickle.

The enthusiasm for Christmas celebrations waned from the period of the Reformation, due in no small part to the puritanical church authorities frowning on their excesses as being "papist." Christmas was actually banned in England in 1647, and though there were areas of defiance, the celebrations dwindled. Hard to imagine now, but by the early nineteenth century there was a very real possibility that the festivities might be forgotten entirely. However, they were revived by Charles Dickens, whose story *A Christmas Carol* is still considered by many to be the very epitome of the Christmas message; a concentration on goodwill to all men, a time for families, and generosity of spirit.

Despite a general (although sometimes uneasy) tolerance towards the liberal sprinkling of pagan practices that encrust what's loosely accepted as the birthday of Jesus, many churches have managed to overlay the heathen symbolism of the festival with Christian values, no mean feat considering they hijacked the heathen celebrations in the first place. The practice of bringing greenery into the house is a good example. The **holly tree** not only provides a home to nature spirits, but its prickly leaves are also phallic symbols of fertility. However, holly also symbolizes the crown of thorns worn by Christ at his crucifixion; the **red** berries, his **blood**. A cup made of **ivy** is said to prevent drunkenness, hence its association with **Bacchus**, an influential deity during the gluttony and largesse of the Saturnalia, but these links seem largely to be overlooked by the Church. **Mistletoe**, however, with its overt sexual symbolism (the berries look like **semen** and of course it's traditional to **kiss** underneath hanging sprigs of the plant) has pagan roots so powerful that it still manages to resist Christianization, and so is still banned in many churches. The **Christmas Tree** itself originated in mainland Europe, a way of venerating the spirit of the **World Tree** by bringing it into the home and decorating it. Although German enclaves in the UK already had their decorated trees, when Prince Albert, consort of Queen Victoria, brought one into the Royal household then the custom really took off. Purist Christians excuse the tree by turning it into a symbol of the **cross**, or "tree," that Christ died upon.

Sharing food is an important focus of the Christmas celebrations. What's on offer for dinner alters according to the dictates of fashion and availability, but meat tends to figure prominently on the menu. The early mince pie contained meat, unlike today's mixture of vine fruits and spices, and they were shaped like the manger that Christ was laid in, sometimes with a pastry baby on the top. The traditional cannonball-shaped Christmas pudding, however, is a relatively recent tradition, adapted in the seventeenth century from a thick plum porridge. The pudding, traditionally, should be made from **thirteen** ingredients, one for each of the apostles and one for Jesus. The practice of putting charms and trinkets into the Christmas pudding might be dying out, but the charms that people tried not to break their teeth on used to have a specific symbolism of their own. These traditional bibelots included a boot, a **bell**, the thimble, a **ring**, a **wishbone**, button and **horseshoe**, as well as the **silver** sixpence. The boot signified travel, the thimble a happy but single life, and the ring, **marriage**.

DANCE

Dance, a form of wordless communication that carries with it a great degree of freedom and spontaneity, was at one time a very important aspect of any kind of ritual worship. To dance is a joyous act, celebrating the spirit of life, a union of body and **soul** and an expression of freedom of the spirit. Dancing in a repetitive rhythmic way enables the dancer to forget the self, to become as one with the rhythm and the music; like a shamanistic ritual, dance can send the dancer into a state of trance or ecstasy. Although many places of formal Christian worship might not appear to have an awful lot to do with dancing, Christ was called the Lord of the Dance and said to his disciples "To the Universe belongs the dancer." This "Lord of the Dance" epithet has parallels with the Hindu God Shiva, in his incarnation as Nataraja, the Cosmic Dancer, whose dance, or *tandava*, encompassed the whole of creation including the primordial sound, **aum**. The Tantric Buddhist deity, Buddha Amoghasiddhi, is also called the "Lord of the Dance."

Indian dance forms, used as part of the yogic discipline which seeks to unify body, mind, and soul with the harmony of the Universe, is rich in elaborate symbols; every hand gesture or **mudra**, foot position or expression of the **eyes** is deeply meaningful. Human beings carry within them a rhythm, which the Tantric tradition calls the *nada* or "sound of power"; this is the human heartbeat.

Dancing may appear to be a form of complete abandonment, but the truth is that there needs to be a healthy dose of discipline and practice before the movements can appear to be effortless, as anyone who has even tried to learn a simple dance such as the waltz will testify. Dancing is akin to playing the body in the same way as a musical instrument.

Ritual dancing, intended to make the participants "get out of it" in order to allow spirit possession, has a great part to play in Voudon ceremonies. The Whirling Dervishes of the Sufi tradition perform a sort of dance called Sema, although the word actually means "hearing," making a connection between the shapes of the dance and the universal sound, **aum**, and does not always involve the distinctive whirling.

Death

Although people may never again aspire to the immensely elaborate funeral preparations of the Ancient Egyptians, whose obsession with the idea of the Afterlife informed much of their culture, the disposal of the body of a dead person is, nevertheless, an important rite of passage. Arguably, any funeral preparations and rituals are carried out as much to comfort the living than as a guaranteed assurance of any great certainty about anything that might follow.

Ultimately, the body is the symbol of the person that remains behind after the spark of life has left it. As such, the ritual of its disposal is an important part of human life, a sign of respect for the body, effectively the **grail** that contains our spirit. These rituals tell us a lot about the philosophies of the people that take part in them.

Death itself is an inevitable part of life, an ending and a completion but, symbolically, a marker of change and, therefore, a new beginning. Death is the ultimate initiation, the supreme mystery and it's no wonder that we continue to be fascinated with it.

Thinking about what must follow the physical death of the body has preoccupied us since the dawn of time, a longing for something "else" that caused Paleolithic people to daub their corpses in **red** ochre in the fervent hopes that the **color** alone, the same as the life-giving **blood**, would somehow restore life or bring back the **soul**. Famously, the Egyptians buried their dead with everything they might need in the next life; who can say that they were deluded? People who subscribe to the idea of former lives often seem to have enjoyed an episode as an Ancient Egyptian. Egyptian corpses were honored in an elaborate ritual that preserved all of the organs as though they might come in useful later on, and these mummies were fairly smothered with **talismans**, **amulets**, and magical devices intended to ease the journey into the Afterlife or otherwise propitiate the Gods that they would meet on the journey.

Opinions about what happens after death differ widely. Cultural and religious ideals don't give any answers either, since the tenets of any single faith can exist on different levels according to the sensibilities of the individual. A fundamentalist Christian, for example, might believe in a Heaven that belongs to a virtuous soul and is "up there," and a Hell belonging to the lower regions that an "evil" one will be dispatched to. However, such a simplistic idea leads to profound metaphysical problems as to the nature of good and evil in a faith system in which a fundamentally benevolent deity is believed to have created everything in the first place. It's also interesting to note that reincarnation of some sort was the generally accepted belief in most countries of the world prior to the coming of Christianity, whose idea of a punishment/reward system could be used as a political tool.

But what of the rites that accompany death? The way that bodies are disposed of often has an underlying practical nature that has as much to do with topography and climate as any deeper meaning. Burial, possibly one of the most popular forms, dates back 200,000 years and remains of burial mounds appear all over the world. Cremation, or disposal by flames, is the preferred method in India and Japan. Some burial methods prefer to preserve the corpse for as long as possible, using elaborate and highly secure coffins, whereas others, such as those of orthodox Jews and Muslims, prefer that the process of decomposition happens as quickly as possible, the body being wrapped in a simple shroud. In common with the Ancient Egyptians, some bodies are buried alongside possessions that the owner enjoyed in real life, and as archaeological finds these objects have given us a great deal of insight into the lifestyles and interests of our ancestors.

However, what future archaeologists might make of such eccentric burials as that of Mad Jack Fuller, buried in a 25-foot high **pyramid** in the grounds of the village church in Brightling, Sussex, is anybody's guess. Jack is allegedly clothed in full evening dress, seated at a table with a roast chicken and a bottle of claret, the floor around him covered in shards of broken glass to stop evil spirits stealing his dinner.

The positioning of Jack's corpse might be unconventional, but most Christian burials see the corpse flat on its back, arms crossed over the chest, oriented east–west to emulate the layout of a church. Muslims are buried with the face turned towards Mecca, and in some ancient cultures warriors were buried upright, presumably to show their readiness to do battle, even in death. Suicides were sometimes buried upside down, as a continuance of punishment; perhaps losing the mortal soul was not considered pain enough. A further punishment for society's deceased miscreants was to be buried in unconsecrated ground, itself symbolic of being outside conventional society that somehow made the soul vulnerable, since the body was laid to rest outside the safe confines of Church-approved earth. The corpses of souls that might be prone to restive activity in the Afterlife were buried at **crossroads**, to confuse them.

Arguably one of the most exotic and dramatic ways of disposing of a body is in the ritual of the **sky** burial. Believed to have been practiced initially by the Zoroastrians and once common in Tibet, here the corpse is left to the elements, often on high places such as specially constructed buildings called Towers of Silence. Sometimes, the corpse is carefully dismembered and thrown to the **vultures**, considered **birds** of rebirth. The body here is considered to be simply an empty vessel, nothing to do with the soul that has departed. The custom of the sky burial is itself dying, though, because of the vast expense of the ritual.

One of the universal rituals that follow a funeral, no matter what faith or culture, is for the living to enjoy some sort of feast afterwards. This is not only a celebration of life, but harks back to the ancient practice of sin-eating. This is where the transgressions of the departed person are "eaten" by the guests at the funeral, thereby allowing the soul to rise, unencumbered, to Heaven. In fact, as recently as the nineteenth century there were still "professional" sin-eaters in the UK, likely to be an impoverished and starving person, who would eat the bread and ale passed to him over the corpse, and accept a coin. These actions symbolically transferred the sins of the dead person to the sin-eater.

The idea of death in general, rather than of human death in particular, is celebrated in different ways around the world. The old Celtic festival of Samhuin, which falls at the end on October when the new **Moon** is closest to **Earth** and therefore the **veil** between the worlds is perceived to be at its thinnest, is these days more popularly celebrated as **Halloween**, and tallies with Walpurgisnacht in northern Europe. The Mexican Day of the Dead, held at the same time of the year, is perhaps one of the more colorful expressions of death, with gaudy skeletons cavorting in the streets, death-head candies, **music**, and dancing, and a great deal of revelry.

DIWALI

It is an inherent part of the human psyche to want to bring light into the darkness, and the Diwali festival does just this for Hindus, Sikhs and Jains. The name means "festival of lights" and it celebrates the victory of good (light) over evil (dark).

Diwali is one of the major festivals in the Indian calendar, of equal significance to **Christmas**. Like Christmas, it is celebrated not only as a spiritual festival but as a secular one, too. For many, Diwali marks the beginning of the New Year. As well as bringing external light into the dark streets by means of **candles**, lanterns, colored decorations, and lots of glitter, a major part of the Diwali festival acknowledges the inner light, or *atman*, the essential part of each human being which, once awakened, is the source of unconditional love and unity with the All.

The time that Diwali takes place differs slightly from year to year depending on the position of the new **Moon**, but it is generally at the end of October or the beginning of November. Its form varies in different areas but the overarching sentiment is the same. Like Christmas, it is a time for families and friends to come together, sharing meals and exchanging sweets and gifts. The money spent during Diwali makes a significant contribution to the Indian economy in the same way that Christmas does in the West. Sweets are a major part of the Diwali festival, and most families continue to make and consume the delicacies that have become traditional to them.

There are several myths featuring deities from the Hindu pantheon that explain the origins of Diwali. The epic poem the Ramayana describes how Rama returned to his home city with his wife and brother after slaying the evil **demon** king Ravana, again a simile for the triumph of good over evil/light over dark. As the victorious party went along their way, people brought lights and lamps to illuminate their path. Southern India celebrates Diwali a day earlier than people in the north, since the hero traditionally traveled from the bottom of India to the top. In another story, Krishna's wife, Satyabhama, killed the demon Narakasura. The demon asked that his death be celebrated with lots of colorful lights.

Diwali takes place over five days, with specific rituals belonging to each of these days. The first day is Dhan-trayodashi. This means "wealth" and "thirteenth day." It falls on the thirteenth day after the full Moon, and is dedicated to Lakshmi, the Goddess of Abundance. This is a propitious day for shopping and is generally the day that people buy their Diwali gifts.

The second day, Naraka Chaturdas, commemorates the day on which the demon Narakasura was slain. For southern Indians, this is the main day of Diwali, and it starts early, when the **stars** are still in the **sky**, with a ritual, cleansing bath followed by a special ritual offering, to **Krishna**. The children light firecrackers, and families and friends gather together to share elaborate meals. Like **Halloween**, because there is no Moon, special offerings are made to the spirits of the dead.

The third day is Diwali, when there is no Moon to compete with the brilliant lights of the festival. The fourth day is Govardhan Puja. A mountain of decorated **food** symbolizes the Govardhan Mountain that Krishna lifted to defeat Indra, the God of Rain and Thunder. Husbands give presents to their wives on this day. Bhayitika is the final day of the festival, and is a special day for brothers and sisters, who make great efforts to spend time together.

Easter

Although Easter is one of the most significant festivals in the Christian calendar, more often than not the religious side is overlooked in favor of a more secular celebration. Moreover, some of the symbols of Easter are distinctly at odds with one another. How does a **chocolate** bunny, for example, have anything to do with the resurrection of Christ? The fact is that the Easter celebrations are an interesting amalgamation of the old pagan celebration of spring and fertility, the **Passover**, and the **death** and subsequent resurrection of Christ.

Most countries in the world that follow Christian traditions use a word for Easter that is based on the same word as for the **Passover**, Pesach, from the Paschal **Lamb** that was sacrificed at this time; only in Britain, Germany, and in some of the Slavic territories this is not the case. It's possible the Last Supper that Christ shared with his disciples was in fact a Passover meal. The Paschal Lamb, with its **halo** and banner, is also symbolic of Jesus Christ, who like the lamb was sacrificed to the greater good. Lambs, of course, are first seen gamboling around the fields in the spring, so no symbolic anomalies there.

The timing of Easter varies from year to year. Easter Sunday, the main focus of the event that celebrates the crucifixion and resurrection of Christ, falls on the first Sunday after the full **Moon** following the vernal equinox on March 21. And so Easter can either be "late" or "early," and the date can vary anytime between March 22 and April 25.

Eostre, or Ostara, was a pagan Goddess of Spring and fertility, celebrated around the time of the spring equinox. Because rebirth is

THE ELEMENT ENCYCLOPEDIA OF SECRET SIGNS AND SYMBOLS

a recurrent motif in many pagan religions, the death and resurrection of Christ slotted nicely into an already-existing theme. Eostre is the root of the word estrogen, the female hormone, and the **egg**, as a powerful symbol of potential new life, is celebrated at Easter in the **chocolate** eggs given to children. In Russia, the egg takes the form of *pysanka*, delicately painted hard-boiled hen's eggs.

The Easter celebrations take place over three days, the first of which is Good Friday. Preceding Easter is Lent, a **forty**-day period of abstinence and **fasting**. After such abstinence, chocolate eggs are a welcome reward.

Good Friday commemorates the day that Christ was crucified. This is a holiday; blacksmiths in particular do not work because one of the sons of their patron God, Vulcan, forged the nails that were used to pin Christ to the **cross**. In churches, special services take place at 3 p.m., traditionally the time that Christ died. Because the sacrament is never given on Good Friday, the service doesn't take the form of a Mass.

On Holy Saturday, again, the sacrament is forbidden until after sunset. **Altars** are quite bare, and often draped in **black**. After sunset, the Easter or Paschal Vigil takes place. A bonfire is lit outside some Catholic churches as a symbol of the "light of Christ." Mass is said and the sacrament is given.

On Easter Sunday, the celebrations are much more joyful, the somber tone of the previous two days not appropriate given that this is the day that Christ rose from the grave. This is the day that families and friends gather for a meal. In a throwback to the earlier pre-Christian celebrations children hunt the eggs that have been hidden for them by the Easter Bunny, which is the disguise

taken on by the **hare**, an ancient fertility symbol.

The hot cross buns eaten in bulk at Easter are often thought to be symbolic of the crucifixion; in fact, they are far older. The bun represents the shape of the **Moon**; the cross divides it up into its four quarters. This is also the same as the ancient **Sun Wheel** symbol. Other traditional Easter fare includes the simnel cake. This is a fruit cake with eleven round marzipan balls on top. These represent the eleven loyal disciples

ELEUSINIAN MYSTERIES

Rites and rituals carry different layers of significance for the different people that take part in them. For some, the sacred implements, songs and gestures have a purely symbolic role to play. For others, sanctified items carry unearthly supernatural powers. Arguably for most people, any idea of symbolism, magic or a deeper meaning is lost in an unthinking sense of duty, tradition, and an obligation to take part.

The Eleusinian mysteries operated on all these levels. Arguably the most important of all the mystery traditions of antiquity, there were two parts to the Mysteries; the Lesser Mysteries were celebrated annually at a town called Agrae, and the Greater every five years at Eleusis. It is a mark of their significance that they continued from 1500 BC until the fourth century AD. Aspects of the Mysteries carried immense power, including visions, communion with the Gods, and promises of power and glory in the Afterlife, so it's no surprise that these secrets were guarded jealously.

The secrets of all mystery traditions are rarely written down, but are passed on orally. This means that there can be no account that can be absolutely certain. Added to the problem is that initiates, at the start of the ceremony, swore on their own lives that they would not speak of the Mysteries to anyone not initiated. We know, for example, that a part of the ceremony revealed the contents of a casket and a covered basket. But what they contained is unknown; historians have speculated on an **egg**, sacred **seeds**, and a **golden serpent**.

At the heart of the Eleusinian mysteries was the story of **Demeter**, the Greek Goddess of Agriculture and fertility and her daughter **Persephone**. Persephone was picking **flowers** one day when she was spotted by Hades, God of the Underworld. Liking the look of her, he caused the ground beneath her feet to open, and she fell through the hole into his subterranean realm. Demeter, distraught at the loss of her girl, abandoned everything to go and search for her daughter. The Corn Goddess carried two torches, symbolic of the tools she needed to find Persephone: intuition and reason. In the meantime, a terrible drought affected crops and livelihoods because Demeter's attention was elsewhere.

With the help of Zeus, Demeter found Persephone not far away from Eleusis, and in her gratitude she taught the people there the secrets of agriculture. However, during her time in the Underworld, Persephone had eaten a **pomegranate** given to her by Hades. Like the **apple** given by Eve to Adam, this fruit represents sexual awakening, a rite of passage; because she ate it, her penance was to spend four months of the year in the Underworld with its God. The consequence of this was eight months of good weather when the land was fertile, and four months of drought when Demeter mourned her daughter.

This makes sense given the climate in this part of Greece two and a half thousand years ago. The arid drought, when plants withered and died, was followed by refreshing rains and the prodigious appearance of new shoots. Plants seemed to spring up overnight. This related to Persephone's reunion with Demeter, and it was this that the Eleusinian mysteries celebrated effectively, death and rebirth.

The Lesser Mysteries

Dedicated to Persephone, these took place annually in the spring, possibly at the time of the equinox. Their purpose, described by Thomas Taylor in his *Eleusininan and Bacchic Mysteries*, sounds remarkably progressive and appropriate for our own spiritual quest, thousands of years later:

The Lesser Mysteries were designed by the ancient theologists, their founder, to signify occultly the condition of the unpurified soul invested with an earthly body, and enveloped in a material and physical nature.

In other words, Persephone symbolizes the **soul**, or psyche, of man, that belongs in the higher worlds of the spirit, the corporeal being described by Plato as the "sepulcher" of the soul.

The Underworld that Persephone falls into symbolizes the lower, material world; her acceptance of the pomegranate the soul's choice to be limited by earthly things. At the heart of the secrets was the tenet that a man would be no better in death than he had been in life if he did not take advantage of his time on earth to rise above ignorance; if not, he could be doomed to an eternity of endlessly repeating mistakes. His **soul** would sleep in Hades in the same way that he had slept (remained unaware) during his earthly life. The challenge was for the living spirit to overcome its dead, animal personality and body.

Another of the tenets of the Lesser Mysteries was the evil of suicide; the consequences were so awful that they could not be spoken of.

After initiation the candidate was given the title of "Mystes," meaning one that had clouded vision, or who viewed the world through a veil. It is the source of the word "mystic" and implies that the person had reached a **veil** that could be torn aside when the time was right. The clarity when this final obstacle was removed would come with initiation into the Greater Mysteries.

The Greater Mysteries

These took place at the opposite end of the year, toward the end of summer, and were dedicated to Demeter. Again, Thomas Taylor describes their doctrines:

The Greater ... obscurely intimated, by mystic and splendid visions, the felicity of the soul both here and hereafter when purified from the defilement of a material nature, and constantly elevated to the realities of intellectual (spiritual) vision.

The Greater Mysteries taught its acolytes the secrets of spiritual regeneration, and the way to liberate their higher spiritual natures from the bonds of ignorance ad unawareness. The means of lifting the "veil of unreality" had a key part to play in this quest, and there is a distinct element of shamanism about the practices undertaken to help realize these truths. Sacred objects were carried into the Temple or Eleusinion; initiates bathed in the **sea**, a physical cleansing that symbolized a deeper symbolic purification. A sacrifice, an all-night feast, and a procession to the Eleusinion followed.

At Eleusis, everyone fasted in acknowledgement of Demeter's **fasting** while she searched for her Persephone. The fast was broken by the taking of a herbal drink called *kykeon*.

This drink has been the subject of much debate. Its ingredients included **barley**, a grain that can be affected by a fungus called ergot, which has psychoactive properties. These properties would have been especially potent after fasting and may have contributed to the "lifting of the veil of ignorance" which was to take place in the part of the hall called the Telestrion, where only initiates could enter; discussion of anything that was seen or heard in this great hall was punishable by death. Visions of God and the Afterlife could well have been triggered by psychoactive ingredients, often used in sacred rites and ceremonies since they were discovered, agents used to reveal an alternative way of viewing the Universe.

The finale of the celebration of the Greater Mysteries was a huge party, the sacrifice of a **bull**, and a feast. This all took place in the Rharian Field, said to be where the first ever grain had grown.

The Eleusinian mysteries and their pagan significance gradually dwindled away with the coming of the Christian religion. Unlike many of the old customs and traditions that could be absorbed into the new faith, the very nature of the Eleusinian mysteries was secret; therefore, there was nothing to absorb. At the end of the fourth century AD the old sacred sites were finally desecrated by the intolerant new order, keen to appease their one jealous God.

EXCOMMUNICATION

Effectively meaning to be taken away from a community, this expression refers specifically to a rite of Catholicism in which a member is removed from the Church. To be excommunicated is a very serious matter indeed, and is a rare thing. There are **ten** misdemeanors that mean instant excommunication. These are apostasy (renunciation of the belief), heresy (any practice that runs counter to the doctrine of the Church), schism (causing a separation within the Church), desecration of the Eucharist (the consecrated **bread** and **wine** of the sacrament), trying to absolve someone of adultery, ordination of a bishop without the permission of the pope, procurement of an abortion, and finally, being an accomplice in any of these preceding nine sins.

The basis of excommunication is "anathema." Put simply, this is a curse of the Church, denouncing a person or doctrine. The word is translated in several different ways but is generally held to mean "cursed." Anathema preceded excommunication as a practice and is an even stricter form of it.

Excommunication still happens from time to time, although as a practice it had its heyday in the Middle Ages, when it was used as a weapon to discredit persons of rank, particularly within the government, who fell out of favor with the Church. At this time, the shame of excommunication was emphasized by a very public ceremony, the person in question symbolically banned from the Church by **bell, book**, and **candle**.

Prior to a more sanguine reinterpretation of the rules in 1983, there were two levels of excommunication. The first degree, "*vitandus*," meant that the person was to be avoided completely by other members of the faith. The second, lesser degree was "*tolerates*," or tolerated, and as the name suggests this was where Catholics were still allowed contact with the excommunicant, and were able to do business with them and maintain social connections. Subsequently, however, the Church has embraced a more progressive attitude, hoping to embrace the excommunicant once more within the bosom of the Church.

Famous excommunicants include Fidel Castro, in 1962, for communism; Napoleon Bonaparte; the English king Henry II, who had the Archbishop of Canterbury, Thomas à Becket, assassinated; Henry VIII; Martin Luther; Cervantes; Robert the Bruce; and a whole group of noblemen who tried to protect the Cathars, who were believed by the Church to be a heretical group.

Fasting

The Bible, the Qu'ran, the Upanishads, and the Mahabharata all advocate fasting, and indeed, most faiths embrace the ritual as part of a spiritual discipline. This is possibly due, in no small part, to the fact that not eating can induce hallucinations and a feeling of light-headedness akin to religious ecstasy. Fasting, too, is a shamanic practice, undertaken to help initiates communicate with the spirit realms. Some people claim that fasting is as good for the body as it is for the spirit and advocate an annual "detox" that may have perceived spiritual benefits. It may be that our ancestors also felt that giving the body a rest from heavy foods was beneficial.

The strictures regarding what does and does not constitute a fast are, to pardon the pun, something of a moveable feast. For example, some Roman Catholics might say that fasting involves refusing everything except **water**; others will see it as abstinence from meat, or they might eat just one solid meal per day. Eating fish rather than meat on Fridays is a fast. There's a very rigorous form of fasting peculiar to the Catholic Church, called a Black Fast. This entails eating just one small meal a day and abstaining from all animal products, including dairy. However, this severe form of fasting could also be used by less scrupulous people as a spell to curse enemies. One Mabel Brigge was even executed in 1538 for "performing" a Black Fast against Henry VIII and the Duke of Norfolk, which signals the power of such a seemingly simple action that can have devastating consequences; refusing to eat.

For some Jews, fasting is very strict and means having nothing at all pass the lips, even cleaning the teeth or taking medication is prohibited (except where this might endanger life). The major fast in the Jewish calendar is during Yom Kippur and also Tisha B'Av, the commemoration of the day two thousand years ago when the Temple of Jerusalem was destroyed and the Jews were cast from their homeland.

For Hindus, fasting tends to be specific to the deity that is worshipped, and in Buddhism, monks and nuns generally abstain from eating after their midday meal; this they consider an aid to meditation.

For Muslims, the month of **Ramadan** and its observances include fasting from sunrise to sunset. In the Christian calendar, the period of fasting is during the forty days of Lent, preceding **Easter**, a reminder of the time that Christ fasted during his time in the desert. These days, the Lent fast is more likely to be about giving up one particular kind of food, such as **chocolate**. It might also mean abstinence from cigarettes or alcohol, or maybe sexual activity.

Fasting can also be used as a form of protest, threatening the life of the person who refuses food, often for political reasons.

Halloween

Halloween is the abbreviated term for All Hallows Eve, the day before All Saints Day. This was the Church's attempt to associate their own saints with the time of the pagan spirits. Today it is personified by the image of the witch, abroad at night on her **broomstick** with her **black cat** perched alongside. Witches can also make boats from undamaged eggshell halves, apparently, and so are sometimes seen abroad on the seas using this unusual method of transport.

Every country around the world celebrates its dead in some way. Halloween is one of these celebrations. Effectively it's a Christian hijacking of the older Samhuin festival, one of the festivals that form the eight-spoked **Wheel of the Year** in the pre-Christian Celtic world, the cross-quarter day that marked the feast of the dead. A night of the living dead is celebrated in all parts of the world at about the same time, a symbol of the end of the **harvest**, the "closing down" of the year, and a time of **death**. It was the traditional time when the animals were brought in for the winter, and so it seemed appropriate to welcome the dead back, too. Bonfires were lit at this time in order to guide the dead back to the world of the living, and bells were rung.

This is the time of year when the **veil** between the worlds of the living and the dead is at its thinnest, the ancestors are honored and their spirits are believed to be able to communicate with the living more easily now than at any other time. Divination, in the form of necromancy, séances, etc. is likely to be more effective now than at any other time too. There are certain rituals that guarantee entry into the other world. One of these is to find a tumulus or similar place that has fairy associations, and run **nine** times around it.

The home is traditionally decorated with things that are intended to scare away the **demons** that abound at this time; however, these items often look pretty demonic themselves. Because it is the time of the pumpkin harvest, the large **orange** vegetables are hollowed out and have faces cut into them that are lit from within by **candles**.

Sometimes, Halloween is called Nutcrack Night. The nut harvest is at its peak so it is natural that nuts, themselves symbolic of promise and fertility, should be used in a ritual to determine a future lover. Nuts are named after the eligible people and placed on the **fire**. The first one to crack in the heat of the flames signifies the lucky future partner. **Apple** bobbing, too, is a popular pastime at this time of year; apples, of course, signify the Underworld. The practice of "trick or treating" is an American invention and reflects the idea that the normal rules are suspended for the night.

HARVEST

The gathering in of the year's crop and the subsequent propitiation of the Gods to ensure the success of the next is a custom that is common to all peoples, whether the harvest is **animal** (the hunt) or agricultural. Even the bringing of greenery into the home during the winter season is a harvest ritual of sorts, meant to welcome the start of the growing season. The Bible uses the analogy of reaping and sowing to mean the gathering of a harvest in a more metaphorical sense on a par with the Eastern concept of karma, or cause and effect.

Some of the more grizzly aspects of the propitiation of the Gods of the Harvest is explained in Part 1 (see **corn dolly**). Another harvest curiosity is the tale sung of John Barleycorn, the personification of the very important **barley** harvest as well as the generic Spirit of Nature that is also symbolized by the **Green Man**.

The first verse of an early English version of the song goes as follows:

There was three men come out o' the west their fortunes for to try
And these three men made a solemn vow, John Barleycorn must die
They plowed, they sowed, they harrowed him in, throwed clods upon his head
And these three men made a solemn vow, John Barleycorn was dead

Because barley can be eaten, as well as brewed to make alcohol, it's a symbol of earthly sustenance as well as spiritual pleasures. However, all the processes that the barley undergoes symbolize different aspects of torture. There are close analogies to the torment, death, and subsequent resurrection of John Barleycorn and the story not only of Christ's resurrection but also of the sacrifice of **Hiram Abiff** in the legend of the Freemasons, whose sacrifice in the name of honor and the greater good rendered him immortal. Effectively, John Barleycorn suffers and dies, but his death means that bread (symbolic not only of material but of spiritual substance, as witnessed in its transubstantiation into the body of Christ) can be made. Like Christ, John Barleycorn dies for mankind, but can look forward to rebirth in the spring.

KISS

A kiss can be a symbol of erotic love, or a symbol of union. The Romans defined three different types of kiss: the *osculum*, or the kiss on the cheek; the *basium*, or kiss on the lips; and the *suavium*, the deep involved kiss, or colloquially the snog, of lovers. To kiss someone means to mingle not only **saliva** but also **breath**, which itself is akin to the spirit of life.

It's no coincidence that immediately after the marriage vows are taken, the celebrant tells the bride and groom that they can kiss. The mingling of their breath symbolizes the fact that the couple breathe the same **air**, a sign of the union of their **marriage** in a physical and spiritual sense.

In the story of the Sleeping Beauty, the sleep symbolizes the innocent state of the Princess who is awakened, not only literally but sexually too, by the kiss from the Prince, who has penetrated symbolically thorny thickets to find her.

Kissing the ground is a sign of affection towards, and union with, a territory. In Christian services, the Kiss of Peace is a sign of recognition that might take the form of a kiss or a handshake. Kissing the **feet** is a sign of respect and obeisance.

Kisses can be used as a symbol of greeting, or alternatively used to say goodbye. Kissing a religious icon shows loyalty and respect; kisses are also used for good luck, for example, the gambler who might kiss the dice before throwing them.

In the Bible, the kiss that Judas gives Christ is a sign of betrayal, immortalized as the Judas Kiss. The Kiss of Death means the final blow, an action that can destroy something or bring it to the end. In the *Harry Potter* books, this is the name given to the terrible spell cast by the Dementors, who kill their victims by sucking their **souls** out of their **mouths**.

The Kiss of the Mafia, sinisterly, means death, and the kiss of the Devil means eternal damnation.

LUPERCALIA

Although much of what we know about ancient festivals and celebrations is speculative, there are some definitive facts about the Lupercalia

The festival predates the founding of Rome in the eighth century BC, a survival of a time when the site of one of the major cities of the world was nothing but a wilderness of hills populated by **wolves**, where shepherds constantly struggled to save their flocks from these predatory creatures.

Any creature that is feared is also revered, worshipped in an attempt to appease the collective spirit of the animal. Therefore, the wolf, which posed a great threat to man and beast, was deified in many parts. The God Lupercus was known as "the one that drives out the wolves," and so there was an element of the festival that was literally about driving the wolf from the door. Lupercus is also identified with Faunus (Pan), the God of Shepherds. Later, the wolf would reappear as a protective symbol in the legend of the founding of Rome; a she-wolf suckled Romulus and Remus in a cave on the Capitoline Hill.

Lupercalia traditionally took place on February 15, with the intention of purifying the city by driving out evil spirits and **demons**, therefore bringing the compounded benefits of fertility and good health. It was also called the Februa, from the Latin word meaning "to purify"; this in turn gives us the name of the month.

The festival celebrants were priests called Luperci, the "Brothers of the Wolf." The Luperci wore only the skins of **goats**, in common with Faunus. Priestesses made cakes from the grain **harvest** of the previous year and brought them to the Lupercal Cave on the Palatine Hill where the ritual sacrifice of two goats and a **dog** was the first item on the agenda. These sacrificial animals were called Februa. Their **blood** was smeared on the foreheads of two of the Wolf Brothers, who were meant to laugh, and the sacrificial knife washed with wool soaked in **milk**.

After the sacrificed animals had been cooked and eaten in a shared feast, the Brothers dressed themselves in some of the goatskin and hacked the rest into strips. Then they ran around the walls of the town, using the bloody thongs to lash the girls that lined the route; since goats were a powerful symbol of sexuality and fertility, the women hoped to absorb these qualities. It is possible that the word *lupercalia* owes its origins to the phrase "*luere per caprum*," meaning to "purify by means of the goat."

When the Romans invaded Europe, they brought some of the Lupercalian rites with them. One of these customs was a sort of love lottery in which the young men pulled the names of available girls out of a box. The pair coupled up for the duration of the ceremony, perhaps longer. Obviously, the wildly pagan aspects of the Lupercalia simply did not fit the requirements of the freshly minted Christian faith, and so in AD 496 the Pope outlawed the festival, installing St. Valentine as the patron saint of lovers and inaugurating his feast day on February 14, **Valentine's Day**. Many of the aspects of the ancient festival of Lupercalia were absorbed into the new religion, albeit in a highly diluted form.

Marriage

Marriage, in the greater scheme of things and particularly in **alchemy**, can represent the union of two opposing principles, primarily that of male and female. For Christians, the marriage of a man and a woman also symbolizes the union of the believer with the Church.

This idea, that a marriage can signify the union of a human being with his or her God, is extant in many different cultures. The Catholic nun is called a "Bride of Christ." In the ancient cultures of Greece, India, and the Orient, temples were dedicated to the practice of sacred prostitution, part of an antique fertility ritual wherein sexual intercourse, a "sacred marriage" was practiced for a religious purpose. In Hebrew, the word for "harlot" originally meant the same as "shrine prostitute," effectively, a holy woman. Times have changed.

These days, a wedding between a man and a woman is packed with symbolism, some of which is sacred, some more saucily secular. The **veil** worn by the bride, lifted by the groom, not only symbolizes the removal of her virginity but her introduction to a new state of being. The shared cutting of the cake, the knife held by both bride and groom, is another phallic allusion. The wedding **ring** is a symbol of eternity.

In neo-pagan wedding ceremonies, such as the handfasting, the symbolism of tying the **hands** together speaks for itself.

Mystery cults

The word "mystery" comes from the Greek *musterion* or from the Latin *mysterium*, and means, quite literally, "secret doctrine" or "secret rite." The only people that could be a part of such rites were the *mystes*, the "initiated ones." Effectively, **Freemasonry** is a mystery religion; for many, so is Wicca. However, all major religions have their inner sanctum of arcane knowledge. In Judaism, for example, this is the **Kabbalah**.

In the ancient world, the mystery cults were those whose secrets were closely guarded, and forbidden to the public. Members that were privy to their inner workings of these cults formed an elite, the inner sanctum, and generally the secretive nature of these groups meant that new members could be accepted into them if vouched for by existing initiates. The nature of the mystery cults meant that there was a lack of any written material or scriptures describing their workings, their secrets passed on orally as the more appropriate way for the "Arcanum," or secret wisdom, to be preserved.

The lack of definitive information about the ancient Mysteries has made them a continuing source of intrigue. The worship of the Goddesses **Isis** and Cybele were mystery cults, as were the Orphic mysteries, the Mithraic mysteries, and the **Eleusinian mysteries.** The inner sanctum of the **Ka'aba** at **Mecca** is reserved for the mysteries of Islam.

Naming

A **name** carries with it great magical power, since the word itself contains the essence of the person it belongs to. Therefore, the naming ceremony is an important rite of passage everywhere in the world, whether it is viewed as religious or secular; effectively, a name is an identifying symbol that someone will carry about with them, generally, for the rest of their lives.

There's a general superstition that a child without a name is somehow vulnerable, susceptible to being kidnapped by the **fairy** folk or similarly mischievous spirits. This is because the name is also a part of the **soul**, and therefore to have no name is somehow to have no soul either.

The Hindu naming ceremony is one of the most important rite of passage ceremonies. It's usual for the **numerology** of the child's name to be carefully calculated to harmonize with its date of birth.

Naming ceremonies that happen later in life—as in the Catholic confirmation ceremony—mark a deeper allegiance to the faith by the addition of a name that has meaning to the faith. The confirmation ceremony is just that; the candidate confirms the promises that were made by his parents or guardians at the time of the first naming ceremony (usually called a Christening within the Christian Church). People who join other faiths or cults later in life might undergo a renaming ceremony, as a way of wiping out the old personality in favor of the new one.

It's not just humans who have names, though. The naming of a boat is considered to be very important, too, since the vessel will be responsible for the safety of its occupants. In particular, the renaming of a boat can be fraught with danger, as to change its name risks incurring the immediate displeasure of the Gods of the **elements**. However, if it is essential, then first of all every single trace of the old name must be purged, wiped out, painted over, or otherwise destroyed. Then, a libation made to **Poseidon**, who is said to know every single vessel on the **seas**. The new name needs to be given immediately afterwards, again with due obeisance to Poseidon and the Gods of the Four Winds.

Passover

The festival of Passover commemorates a crucial moment in Jewish history, effectively marking the birth of the Jewish nation as the Children of God.

The Book of Exodus in the Old Testament describes how God sent the final and most terrible plague to Egypt, whereby every single firstborn male—human and animal—was killed. No-one was spared, not even the pharaoh's family. The Israelites were instructed to smear their lintels with the blood of a sacrificed **lamb** so that the Angel of Death would "pass over" their houses, so sparing their children. The name of this sacrificed animal, the Paschal Lamb or Korban Pesach, could provide an explanation for the name of the feast. The other explanation is the "passing over" by the Angel of **Death**.

Inside their protected houses, the Israelite families ate the meat of the sacrificed lamb while outside the terrible plague raged. The next day, as God had predicted, the appalled and saddened Egyptians told the Israelites to leave.

Passover is a spring festival, intimately linked to the Christian festival of **Easter**. It takes place over seven or eight days, timed to begin on the fourteenth day of the month of Nisan, usually sometime in April. Before the holiday begins, every scrap of "leavened" **food**, or food that has fermented, biscuits, cakes, **bread**, whisky, are removed from the house.

The first and last two days of Passover are holidays; no-one works, families spend time together and share special meals. The most important of these meals is the Seder, eaten on the first night of the festival.

Seder

The ritual foods of the first night of the Passover are laden with symbolic meaning, effectively a reminder of two aspects of the story of the Exodus from Egypt—slavery and freedom. Before midnight and the advent of the plague, the Israelites were slaves; after midnight, however, they were free.

There are seven symbolic foods that serve as reminders of this time:

1. Maror and Chazeret: These are bitter-tasting herbs that symbolize the bitterness of slavery. Maror means "bitter," and horseradish, endives, or **dandelion** leaves might be used. Chazeret itself is a particularly bitter leaf.
2. Charoset: A crumbly mixture, made of chopped nuts, grated **apples**, and cinnamon. It symbolizes the mortar used in building the Egyptian storehouses.
3. Karpas: Cooked vegetables, dipped into **salt water**; this water is a reminder of the tears shed by the Israelite slaves and the

dipping is symbolic of royalty and the newfound freedom of the Israelites.
4. Z'roa: Roast lamb, symbolic of the paschal lamb.
5. Beitzah: A roasted **egg**, that was an offering made in the Temple at Jerusalem.
6. Matzoh: The final ingredient is a plate of matzoh, a special type of unleavened bread. Because no fermented food can be eaten during Passover, the dough of this bread is allowed to sit for no longer than 18 or 20 minutes so the fermentation process cannot take place. During the entire holiday only unleavened bread is eaten; as well as being a reminder of the first bread eaten by the early Israelites, unleavened bread symbolizes humility, since it is not "inflated" in any way.

In addition, the second part of the meal requires four glasses of **wine** or grape juice to be drunk. These four drinks symbolize the four promises made by God to his people: "I will bring out," "I will deliver," "I will redeem," and "I will take."

RAMADAN

For Muslims, Ramadan is a time of physical and spiritual detoxification, a focus for contemplation and reflection that includes **fasting** as a significant part of the process. The word Ramadan refers not only to the religious observances that take place but is the name of the ninth month of the Islamic year.

The Islamic calendar is a lunar one, and the beginning of a month comes when the crescent **Moon** is first sighted. Thus the timing of Ramadan appears to vary from year to year to followers of the solar calendar system.

The month itself is a particularly propitious time, the most important in the Islamic year, since the great adversary Satan and his demonic helpers are said to be locked away by God during this time, incapable of wielding evil influences upon humankind; any malice in thought or deed during Ramadan is the direct responsibility of the person. Most significantly, it is during this month that the Qu'ran was revealed to Mohammed.

The combination of prayer and **fasting** bring about renewed clarity and calmness, unifying body, mind and spirit in the quest for self-improvement and attaining closeness to God. Because the entire Muslim community is involved in the ritual practices and observances of Ramadan, there is a great spirit of unity and moral support as old grudges and arguments are forgotten in the mutual quest for enlightenment.

The first prayer of the day for Muslims during Ramadan comes before dawn. The fourth and final prayer comes at sunset when the daily fast is broken. This results in more activity during the hours of darkness; markets and restaurants stay open later at this time of year in areas where there are large Muslim populations. Sexual abstinence is also practiced during the hours of fasting. Muslims concentrate on the teachings of Islam (for example rereading the Qu'ran over the period) and put great efforts into doing good deeds, elevating their thoughts and actions accordingly. The concerns of the material world take a back seat in favor of the spiritual.

Ramadan is the time for charity and sharing with those less well-off. A tax called a Zakaat, a percentage of unused wealth, is calculated and levied at this time; effectively the Zakaat is a charitable donation.

The fasting period of Ramadan ends when the next new crescent moon appears in the sky. The day following is a feast day; everyone wears new clothes, and families and friends spend the day together.

SATURNALIA

Important ancient festivities are often absorbed into other cultures, and the customs of the Saturnalia have contributed greatly to the way that we celebrate **Christmas** today. For Romans, the Saturnalia was such fun that they took its customs with them wherever they settled.

Here is an account from Seneca, written in AD 50; it might remind you of something.

It is now the month of December, when the greatest part of the city is in a bustle. Loose reins are given to public dissipation: everywhere you may hear the sound of great preparations, as if there were some real difference between the days devoted to Saturn and those for transacting business.

In possibly a very early example of "bah, humbug," Seneca later complains that "the whole mob has let itself go in pleasures."

Originally a feast of dedication in the temple of Saturn in his guise as the God of Crops and sowing, the event took place on December 17 after all the fall planting had been done, although it soon extended for a whole week despite the attempts of various authorities to restrict it. The ropes that bound the **feet** of Saturn's statue for the rest of the year were untied on this day, a symbolic act accompanied by sacrifices that liberated the God, who later became personified as Old Father Time, the bent, robed figure whose sickle "chopped down" the **harvest** of passing hours.

The Saturnalia was a time for the relaxation of the usual rules. Informal **clothing** replaced the toga; gambling was legal, and excessive consumption of **food** and drink was the norm. Everyone, including slaves, wore an item of clothing called a *pileus*, the **headgear** of a free man. Additionally, the masters served one particular banquet to their slaves in a carefully constructed role reversal that would be echoed later in Scotland and other parts of the UK in a ceremony called the Lords of Misrule. At the original Roman banquet, Saturn was present as an effigy or statue and the feast a riotous occasion.

The gifts that we exchange at **Christmas** today were originally a part of the Saturnalian festival. There is a series of poems dating from the first century that describes these gifts, which were diverse. The stanzas mention combs, writing tablets, perfumes, sausages, **books**, and even **parrots**.

Homes and public places were decorated with greenery in honor of the deity of crops and vegetation and as a symbol of the hopes for a fertile year to come, another custom that has endured through the years as part of the Christmas celebrations.

Valentine's Day

The ancient rites of **Lupercalia** cast a long **shadow** down the centuries and lingered on long after the introduction of Christianity. However, most aspects of this festival were dangerously pagan for the zealously reformist early Christians, who needed something that was more aligned to their Christian values and morality to take its place.

The original Valentine was an amalgamation of two or three different men, all named Valentine, and all martyred to the Christian cause; one of them was either martyred or buried in Rome on February 14. However, a certain amount of "spin" was necessary to make St. Valentine fit convincingly as a replacement for the existing Lupercalian excesses. A story was put about that Valentine defied the Emperor Claudius' decree that fighting men should not have sexual relations in case their strength was sapped. The Emperor was not in favor of the new religion and to be a Christian at this time was hazardous to the health, but Valentine continued to proselytize despite the sentence of **death** that hung over the heads of anyone caught doing so. Later, he presided over illicit Christian weddings. According to another legend, prior to his execution, he fell in love with the jailer's daughter and left her a note with the words "from your Valentine" written on it.

Part of the Lupercalian festivities included the young men drawing lots for available young women; these couples then spent time together during the festival, with sex the main agenda. The Church invented a lottery, too, although it was a slightly tamer version.

People pulled the names of various Christian saints out of the hat, and then attempted to emulate these worthies for the rest of the year. Understandably, this custom failed to excite people's imaginations as much as its saucier forerunner and drawing lots to put couples together started again in the fifteenth century, a sort of medieval version of speed dating, except faster, although its intentions were supposedly more innocent than those of the Lupercalia. Despite this, it proved very difficult to suppress the memory of the Lupercalia, and today the Church rarely celebrates St. Valentine. However, as a secular celebration of love and romance Valentine's Day is a great success. The **heart**, as the major symbol of love, is seen everywhere at this time.

The small slips of lottery paper that had the names of the girls written on them effectively inspired the Valentine's Day cards that are such a massive business today, and which tradition decrees should be sent anonymously. It is the second biggest card-sending time of the year after **Christmas**, so the original saints would probably be pleased that people remember them, despite their apparent abandonment by the Church.

WASHING

When it's removed from being an everyday routine, washing or rinsing the hands is symbolic of purification by **water**, an act which takes place before and after a priest carries out an act of worship or, formerly, a sacrifice. Shakespeare's Lady Macbeth has hallucinations of **blood** on her hands that she can't remove; her inability to wash away the blood is symbolic of her guilt. When we speak of "washing our hands" of something we mean that we have completed something and can put it behind us. When, in the Bible, Pilate washes his hands after making the decision to execute Christ, he does so to purify himself, as a visible sign of absolution from his own actions. Arguably, the need to carry out this ritual in such a public way might be seen as an admission of guilt. Therefore, this small ritual can also signify a dubious refusal for the responsibility of a decision.

Baptism is another form of ritual washing. The water of baptism symbolizes forgiveness, regeneration, rebirth, and purification. Full immersion in water makes everyone equal, almost the equivalent of being naked.

WHEEL OF THE YEAR

Reference is frequently made to the Wheel of the Year, particularly among Druid, Wiccan, and other neo-pagan groups. Effectively, the **Wheel** of the Year is the name given to the continual cycle of festivals that take place during the course of the year.

The symbolism of the wheel reflects perfectly the cyclical movement of the seasons and the orbits of the stars and planets. The seasons of human life are reflected in the same way, its key events corresponding to the changing seasons.

The names of some of these eight festivals vary according to the tradition, although all mark key moments in the year. Also, the festivals have been adapted to encompass, for example, Christian beliefs, but generally the spirit and substance of them remains relatively unchanged. It's interesting to see how the same conceptual marking of time takes different forms wherever people happen to be around the world marking the planting and harvesting of the crops, the solstices and the equinoxes.

Here, then, is a Wheel of the Year drawing some parallels between the ancient festivals and the newer Christianized interpretations of them.

MONTH	FESTIVAL	FAITH	MEANING
February 2	Imbolc	Druid/Wicca	For the Scots, the ancient start of
	Candlemas	Christian	the year; new beginnings
March 20/23	Ostara	Wiccan	Spring equinox
	Alban Eiler	Druid	Spring equinox
	Easter	Christian	Death and resurrection of Christ (a moveable feast, sometimes held in April)
May 1	Beltane	Druid/Wiccan	Blossoming, fertility
June 21	Midsummer solstice/	Wiccan	Height and mid point of year
	Alban Heruin	Druid	
August 1	Lughnasadh	Druid/Wiccan	Marriage, harvest, sacrifice,
	Lammas	Christian	baking of the first loaf
Sept 23	Mabon	Wiccan	Autumn equinox
	Alban Eleud	Druid	
Oct 31	Samhuin	Wiccan/Druid	Union of the two worlds, death
	All Hallows Eve	Christian	
Dec 21	Yule	Wiccan/Druid	Winter solstice; the turning of
	Alban Arthuan	Druid	the year, death and birth of the Sun
	Christmas	Christian	Birth of Christ

Part Eleven

THE NATURE OF THE DIVINE

THE ULTIMATE SYMBOLIC EXPRESSION OF HUMAN POTENTIAL

Putting aside the notion of a single Supreme Being for the moment, it seems logical to suppose that the vast pantheon of Gods and Goddesses from all cultures and societies are an extrapolation of human potential, yet another way that we've discovered of defining the Universe and our place in it, projecting our own qualities into the **sky**, and the landscape around us, and amplifying these qualities into divine beings.

When we consider how much time our ancestors must have spent gazing up at the Heavens—from whence appeared the rain and **Sun** to nurture the crops they depended upon—it's not really surprising that many of our Gods and Goddesses emanate from the sky. All the **planets** of our solar system have the **souls** of the immortal personages that share their names. Other aspects of the natural world are deified, too. Animistic religions believe that every **tree**, rock, **mountain**, and body of **water** has its presiding spirit. Many of these old Gods were absorbed into the Christian faith as saints, since a mul-

titude of different Gods was at odds with their one jealous God. The ones that were impossible to absorb were, quite literally, demonized, turned into malevolent, ungodly beings. Pan, for example, the powerful Nature God venerated for thousands of years, bears a distinct resemblance to the Devil.

Our Gods represent archetypes and work on two levels. They not only manifest inside us, but we also project ourselves onto them as external phenomena. In the movie *Castaway*, Tom Hanks' character, Chuck Noland, stranded on an island, finds a volleyball in a box, and after an accident in which Chuck cuts his hand, the imprint of the **blood** forms a "face" on the ball. The volleyball becomes an icon, personalized with a character that is even able to "remind" Chuck of the whereabouts of a coil of rope. Our ancestors similarly projected characters and thoughts onto the effigies of their Gods.

The adventures and escapades of many of our deities read like the biographies of cartoon superheroes. They walk on water, they fly, they hurl thunderbolts about in the Heavens, they can shape-shift into **animals** and **birds**. It's notable, too, that the qualities of the Gods repeat themselves in characters from different cultures. The great multi-talented divinity that the Ancient Egyptians called Thoth, for example, appears in the Celtic myths as **Lugh**, in Greek mythology as **Hermes**, and as **Mercury** for the Romans.

While the Gods might be symbols in themselves, some of the objects or animals that they are associated with tell us about their talents. The Goddess of the Hunt carries a bow and **arrow**, the Goddess of the Harvest her sheaf of corn. **Athena/Minerva**, the Goddess of Wisdom, appears with the **owl**, whose large-eyed appearance and access to the hidden places of the night means that the bird itself has access to hidden or occult information. **Wings** imply communication between man and the Heavens.

Many deities have jurisdiction over the **elements** and the weather as well as features of human endeavor that have a life-or-**death** element, such as fishing, the hunt or the **harvest**. Therefore, it was important to keep these beings happy, something that was achieved by ritual obeisance and sacrifices. The influence of our divinities is far reaching and informs a great deal of our language and our culture, infiltrating fictional characters, brand names, art, literature, and film. Our Gods also inspire allegiance, becoming leaders of tribes or other groups, for example the Shivaite of the Hindu faith.

Let's go back to the sticky subject of that Supreme Being. Overriding all these divine superpowers is the idea, for many, of a universal spirit, a pervading life-force that we are all a part of and that is a part of us. For the purpose of argument, we'll call it The Thing. The problem starts when we start to give The Thing a name, because then the very Thing that cannot be compartmentalized becomes segregated by the nuances of language, even ascribed a sex as either "male" or "female," mother or father. The idea is that The Thing is beyond personification, and yet we personify it and put words into its mouth; in the Book of Exodus, God is quoted as saying "I am that I am."

Yet we constantly find references to a nameless God. The Celtiberians, who lived in north-central Spain and northern Portugal both before and during the time of the Roman Empire, went out every full **Moon** and danced in front of their doors in homage to this nameless God. Like the Celtiberians, the Aztecs also worshipped a God that was so powerful as to be beyond having a name that we could comprehend. Inasmuch as names carry great power, the fact that there are either many names of God, or none at all, is a reminder of the paradoxical nature of a concept that wordy descriptions only serve to confuse even further.

There is no need for there to be a massive divide between the worshippers of many Gods, and those who believe that only one God should be venerated. In the Hindu pantheon, for example, it is very clear that the many Gods of this faith are separate aspects of the One; all parts of a mosaic that reveal the bigger picture to the observer who is able to stand back far enough to see it. Essentially, worshippers of more than one God fall into the category of pagans, a word whose origins are quite innocuous, coming from the Latin *paganus*, meaning "villager" or "rustic."

* ✳ *

It's been very difficult to choose which Gods and Goddesses made it into this section since there are a vast number to choose from. In the end, we decided to try to include a representative sample of the best-known deities from all over the world that reflect some of the generic aspects of certain cultures.

THE TRIPLE GODDESS

Pagans, Wiccans and New Age affiliates often refer to the Triple Goddess, but what exactly does this mean? The idea is ancient, appearing in translations of Egyptian magical papyri, but was really popularized after the publication of Robert Graves' *The White Goddess* at the end of the 1940s.

It's not uncommon for the Goddess to appear as a triad. The **Fates** of Greek myth and the Norns of Norse legend fall into the category. Alternatively, one deity can appear in three aspects; perhaps the best-known example is the Goddess **Hecate**, who appears as maiden, mother and crone. Selene, the **Moon** Goddess, appears in **three** aspects that reflect the phases of the Moon: new, waxing/waning, and full. You might think that should count as four aspects of the Moon, but the waxing/waning part counts as one because it is the idea of change, as opposed to the seeming stasis at either end of this process. The Moon is seen to be a female energy exactly because of this mutable nature.

The ancient origins of this threefold idea are reflected in the triple aspect of the Christian male deity, the Father, the Son and the Holy Ghost.

THE AMERICAS

AZTEC DEITIES

Huitzilopochtli

Coatlicue

In a similar way to **Native American** Gods, the major Mexican Gods belonged to the directions; their domiciles were in the **four** quarters. In the north lived Tezcatlipoca, in

the south Huitzilopochtli, in the east Tlaloc, and in the west, Quetzalcoatl.

The most important of these Gods, arguably, was Huitzilopochtli, the great Warrior God whose name meant "The **Hummingbird** that Comes from the South," or "from the Left," a euphemism for the Underworld, and associated with the element of **fire**. His ferocity meant that he was the subject of much worship; the figure of a giant **hummingbird** appears in the figures of the **Nazca Lines**. This God was born fully armed and immediately avenged all those who had believed that his mother, Coatlicue, had become pregnant by dishonorable means; in fact, Coatlicue, like the Virgin Mary, was extremely pious. One day while she was sweeping the **temple**, an archetypal symbolic "message from the Gods" fell on her head in the form of a small bundle of hummingbird **feathers**, and shortly afterwards she realized that she was expecting a child, its divine provenance assured.

Coatlicue herself is an important personage within the Aztec pantheon. Her name means "Mother of the Gods," a fitting title for a Goddess that gave birth to the **stars** and the **Moon**. Wearing a skirt made of **serpents** and a necklace of human **hearts** and **skulls** that she might have borrowed from Kali, the great Indian deity, Coatlicue is the great Earth Goddess who, again like Kali, is the creator as well as the destroyer.

The three other Gods of the elements and directions have equally exotic stories. The northern God, Tezcatlipoca, was the **Sun** God, the positive aspect of whom was that he ripened the harvest, the negative that he also brought drought. Appropriately, Tezcatlipoca sometimes appeared as a **shadow** or as a **jaguar**. At night, he stalked the earth in a **gray** cloak.

Tlaloc, the eastern God, governed the **mountains** and **water** in all its forms. He watered the earth with four vast jugs of liquid, and each of these jugs symbolized the different aspect of the seasons: growth, blight, frost, and destruction. Tlaloc was the deity to whom most sacrifices were made. Horrifically, babies were purchased in order to be killed in his honor. The babies were cooked and eaten by the priests. The more the babies and children wept, the better the sacrifice was considered to be.

The western God, Quetzalcoatl, is personified as a **snake/bird** and, like the Greek God **Hermes**, has many talents. He was patron of every art and craft and the inventor of metalworking, a civilizing influence on humankind. Quetzalcoatl decided to leave his people, driven out by other Gods. He burned his house and hid his treasure and headed east into the rising **Sun**, promising to return. When the Spanish invaders appeared in the Aztec lands, wearing glittering breastplates, they were hailed as the returning Quetzalcoatl and the Emperor Montezuma welcomed them with gifts. One of these gifts included the famous snake mask, made of precious **turquoises**.

INCA/PERUVIAN DEITIES

Prior to their conquest by the Incas, the Peruvians of ancient times had a totemistic religion, worshipping **animals**, **plants**, and stones whose names they also took. This animal worship even extended so far as to suppose that animals were their God-like ancestors. Their protective spirits were called Huacas.

The Incas brought with them a worship of the **Sun** that replaced the earlier totemistic beliefs. The Sun God, Apu Puncha ("Head of the Day") was the ancestor of all Incas, and had a human form with a flaming golden **halo**. The **Moon** Goddess, Mama Quilla, was the wife of Apu Puncha. Like her husband, she was represented as a human figure with a **silver** halo, like moonbeams. Her main role was as the protector of married women.

Other heavenly divinities that surrounded the Sun God and the Moon Goddess were the **rainbow**, Cuycha, and Catequil the deity of thunder and lightning, his sling and mace echoing the traditional weapons of storm gods. Children were sacrificed to Catequil and twins were venerated, believed to belong to him.

In contrast to other cultures, the planet **Venus** was personified as a masculine deity, advisor to the Sun and the protector of girls and the Moon Goddess. All the other planets were the handmaidens of Mama Quilla. The Pleiades was the most respected constellation since it was the great crop-protector.

The **Earth** was personified as the Great Mother, Pachamama; so no difference here from many other belief systems.

Native American
Deities

Manitou

It is not possible, here, to take more than a cursory glance at some of the deities that belong to some of the many Native American peoples. However, there are overarching tenets that seem, largely, to apply to all tribes.

One of these notions is that of a universal presence, a sexless all-pervasiveness that is similar to the One God or Brahman in Hindu belief. Called The Great Spirit, this largely benevolent Supreme Being governs the Happy Hunting Grounds, a place similar to the Christian concept of Heaven. Indeed, the underlying idea of the Great Spirit meant that the notion of a single, paternal Christian God sat quite comfortably with many tribespeople. There is even a legend of the Great Spirit's gift of a set of inscribed stone tablets similar to those given by God to Moses.

Native American beliefs are essentially animistic; that is, they believe that every aspect of the natural world has its own spirit, sometimes called the Manitou. **Totem poles** are the personification of this idea. A key idea, for the Hopi and Pueblo, is the existence of Kachina, the "life bringer." A Kachina can be a physical object or being as well as a concep-

tual idea of a "life bringer." A Kachina has its own spirit; a poor analogy would be to say that the "Christmas Spirit" is a kind of Kachina. Kachinas are honored with dolls that are used to explain the concept to children, in songs and dances, and are personified as Kachina masks.

Here is a brief look at some of the deities of the Native American pantheon.

Iyatiku is a Corn Goddess of the Pueblos. Like **Demeter** she emerges from the Underworld, the place from which all of humankind is also born, underlining her aspect as an icon of fertility. The **food** that she provides sprouts from pieces of her **heart** that she plants across all **four** quarters of the world. As befits a Mother Goddess, a **cave** or cavern is included among the symbols that represent her.

Muut belongs to the Cahuilla culture, and is the Goddess of **Death**, personified as an **owl**. The Cahuilla saw death as simply a necessary part of life; as such Muut is a benevolent deity who guides **souls** into the Afterlife.

Originally a deity of the ancient Hopi Indians, **Kokopeli** is a Fertility God, encompassing the very embodiment of the creative force. He's portrayed as a dancing, shock-headed figure. Earlier, less-sanitized versions of Kokopeli portray him with a prominent **phallus**, symbol of the male creative force that is echoed in the flute that he plays. Sometimes feared by young girls because of the babies he distributes from the sack on his back, Kokopeli similarly organizes the reproduction of **animals**, in particular those that are hunted.

The magical power of Kokopeli's musical abilities is renowned. With his flute, he can chase away the **winter** and herald the **spring**, as well as calling on the fructifying rains. He has been around for a long time—the first effigies of Kokopeli date back to 1000. Latterly, he has enjoyed a resurgence in popularity, dancing his way across T shirts, baseball caps, and other souvenirs of Native Americana.

The Horned **Serpent**, which goes under numerous other names, is a key God in Native American mythologies, venerated in the landscape at the **Serpent Mound**, for example, as well as in innumerable pieces of rock art and cave paintings.

ASSYRIA/BABYLONIA

ISHTAR

This intriguing Babylonian/Assyrian Goddess appears under different names. She is Astarte and Inanna, too. She shares many of the attributes of the later Goddess of Love, **Venus/Aphrodite**. *The Larousse Encyclopaedia of Mythology* describes her as "the divine personification of the Planet Venus." Like Venus, she is called the "Goddess of the Morn and the Goddess of the Evening," because of the appearance of the **planet** on the horizon at both times of the day. The popular image of Ishtar is of a rotund little statuette, naked and wide hipped, offering her **breasts** in her **hands**.

In common with other divine beings, Ishtar's parentage is debatable. As the daughter of **Sin**, the **Moon** God, she is a Goddess of War. However, as the daughter of Anu, the Supreme **Sky** God, she is the Goddess of Love. Despite her fearsome temper, Ishtar inspired sexual desire in all creatures, encouraging procreation. It is interesting to note that Venus' origins are as a Goddess whose cult worship encompassed prostitution; Ishtar's city, Erech, was called "the town of the sacred courtesans." It's as well to remember that the priestesses of the temples that carried out "sacred prostitution" as a profound fertility rite were deeply respected, and the word "harlot" means the same as "shrine prostitute" or "holy woman."

Ishtar had numerous lovers but none of them seems to have benefited from the relationship; she was cruel and fickle, quickly abandoning her mate as soon as she tired of him. The Epic of Gilgamesh describes how her love caused the death of Tammuz, the God of the Harvest. This story echoes the later tale of Aphrodite, who similarly mourns the loss of her lover Adonis; however, the grief of neither Goddess lasts very long. This story, in which Ishtar descends into the Underworld to find her dead lover, includes an episode where she goes through **seven** gates and loses one item of apparel at every gate. She has to give up every item of **jewelry** from her **crown** to her **girdle**, and then her dress, until she stands naked before the Queen of the Infernal Regions, Ereshkigal, who then promptly locks her up. Back on Earth there is great distress, similar to the despair felt when **Demeter**, the Greek Corn Goddess, abandons her duties and goes to look for her daughter **Persephone**, trapped in the Underworld. Ishtar is rescued with the intervention of the God Ea; sprinkled with the **waters** of life, returning through the gates she retrieves her belongings and arrives back on Earth fully dressed. In common with stories of other deities, this tale speaks of death and resurrection.

Ishtar, as a Goddess with highly charged sexual appetites, was demonized by the Christian faith, which vilified her as the Whore of Babylon and the Mother of Harlots, despite the fact that she was worshipped in Jerusalem, and called the Queen of Heaven.

Shamash

The word Shamash means "**sun**," and it is the name of the Akkadian solar divinity who was possibly the most important of the Gods. Interestingly, Shamash is described as the child of the **Moon** God, Nannar, also known as **Sin**. This indicates the prominence of the Moon over the Sun, which was the case in numerous ancient societies, especially those that were nomadic since the changing phases of the Moon were far more informative about time and place than the more regular Sun. It was only when people had started to settle down to a more fixed, agrarian way of living that the Sun became prominent.

Some aspects of Shamash's life are the stuff of science fiction. He makes his appearance every morning after the giant **scorpion**-men that defended the **mountains** of the East open the great folding door through which the God enters. He then ascends to the top of the mountain where Bunebe, his coachman, awaits with the chariot that carries the God across the skies until he exits in the West via another pair of gates and descends to the depths of the **Earth**.

The quality that Shamash is best known for, as well as his courage and vigor, is that of justice. As the Sun brings physical light to the world, so Shamash chases away the **shadows** of injustice and makes crime impossible, therefore clarifying the truth. Shamash could also dispense with **demons** as he dispensed with the darkness. These demons took the form of illness or misfortune. Shamash was known by the epithet of "Judge of the Heavens and the Earth." He often appears seated—always the posture of a very important God—holding a **scepter** and a **ring**.

Another of Shamash's talents was divination. He could tell men what was going to happen in the future via a soothsayer, who would make sacrifices to the God and then determine future events by analyzing entrails, or perhaps examining the patterns made by oil poured on **water**.

The Hebrew word for sun is *shemesh*. The central **candle** of the **Menorah**, used to light the other candles, is the Shemesh candle.

Sin

The **Moon** God of the Assyrian pantheon, Sin is one of a triad that includes his children **Shamash** the **Sun** God, and **Ishtar**, the divine personification of the planet **Venus**. That the Moon is here seen to be the father of the Sun is because, during the time of his worship, the people were nomadic, and the movements of the mutable Moon were more informative than the constancy of the Sun. Effectively Sin embodies the idea that light emerges from darkness.

Sin was also called Nannar, and took the form of an old man with a dark **blue beard**, the same color as **lapis lazuli**. He traveled in a barque the shape of the crescent moon; this might be the tenuous origin of the "man in the Moon" notion.

Because he brought light to the night sky, Sin was seen to be the enemy of evildoers. Because of this, he was continually under attack by the dark spirits. The solar eclipse was explained in this way. Sin's wisdom was such that at the end of the month all the other Gods came to consult him, bringing their problems for him to solve.

Celtic Divinities

What we know of Celtic beliefs comes down to us from written accounts preserved since the Middle Ages, and in some of the descriptions of the Romans who invaded the Celtic territories. The landscape of the Celts extended through a large area and included parts of Spain and France as well as southern Britain, including, of course, Ireland and Wales. This Celtic landscape is still liberally sprinkled with evidence of the old beliefs; their earthworks and burial mounds are significant symbols in the landscape themselves. The **Horned God**, Cernunnos, is a major Celtic divinity, as is Dagda.

Dagda

Dagda, a deity from Ireland, was the Father of all the Gods, written about in the stories of the Tuatha de Danaan, "The People of the Goddess Dana." Dagda was not one of the most attractive Gods; he appears ugly and pot-bellied, wearing the rough clothes and rude sandals of the peasant. Dagda carries a club so colossal that it drags along the ground making furrows and dykes. Dagda's other great tool was a magical **cauldron** that never emptied; this cauldron appears time and time again in myths, and one of its symbolic meanings is of eternal life. Dagda is a Fertility God, and in common with other Gods had to undergo a challenge. His was a curious one. He had to eat a vast quantity of porridge that appeared in a crater. This happened on November 1, the time of the greatest feasts of the year, the old New Year that coincides with **Halloween** or **Samhuin**. One of Dagda's more attractive skills was as a harpist, the beautiful tunes he plays orchestrating the turnings of the seasons.

Horned God

There are several different interpretations of the symbol for the Horned God, one of the better-known being the "upside down" **pentacle**. The uppermost two points do look a little like horns. The manifestations of this ancient deity are many: Cernunnos in Celtic tales, the Greek God Pan, the Egyptian Aamon. With the coming of Christianity, the old pagan horned Gods were lent a more sinister image than their previous reputation as the male aspect of the nature God. The Horned God was turned into the Devil.

Lugh

One of the major Celtic Gods, when Lugh asked to become a member of the celestial elite called the Tuatha de Danaan he was asked what skill he could contribute. When he replied that he was a carpenter, the response was there was a carpenter already. Therefore, Lugh volunteered his services as a smith; again, the Tuatha already had someone with this skill. However, the persistent Lugh put all his cards on the table and offered his talents as a warrior, harpist, historian, poet, and sorcerer, all skills that underline the multi-talented nature of this God. In this, Lugh has close parallels with **Mercury/Hermes/Thoth**. There was no single person in the Tuatha with all these skills so Lugh was admitted.

A more advanced and sophisticated God than **Dagda**, he had more elegant tools than the other God's giant club. Lugh had a spear and a sling. Lugh was a God of Light, a solar deity whose immortality has been assured in place names such as Lewes, on the south coast of Britain, and even in England's capital city London. Lyon and Loudon in France, and Leiden in the Netherlands, also show the importance of the God. Lugh is honored with the festival of **Lughnasadh** at the beginning of August, which later became absorbed into Christianity as Lammas. Lughnasadh marked the beginning of the **harvest**, a time for weddings and handfastings. In modern Irish, the God gives his name to the month of August, La Lunasa.

RHIANNON

Rhiannon's name derives from Rigantona, which means Great Queen, the same meaning as the **Morrigan**.

The Welsh/Celtic Goddess is aligned so closely with the Roman Epona that it is likely that they are one and the same. Both are associated with **horses**, underlining the ineffable importance of the creature.

Rhiannon first appears in the Mabinogi, the Celtic hero-myths. She is introduced as a beautiful woman, dressed in a golden gown, seated on a snow-**white** horse. Pwyll, the hero, tries to catch up with her but this proves impossible despite the seemingly relaxed pace of Rhiannon's horse and the speed of his own mount. Eventually he calls out to her, and she stops to speak. It seems that she's been promised to another but is handily in love with Pwyll, so they prepare to marry. The labyrinthine tale that follows, which in the original Celtic tradition would have been passed on orally rather than written down, involves magic, shape-shifting, and the birth of a son that disappears. The **six** women who were meant to be taking care of the child panic after his disappearance, and squarely frame Rhiannon. When she awoke, she was daubed with the **blood** from a puppy and surrounded by its **bones**. Rhiannon is accused of eating her baby, and despite her protestations, she is punished, forced to tell her story to every passing stranger and to carry them on her back if necessary; Rhiannon is changed into a horse.

As well as horses, Rhiannon is also associated with otherworldly birds, and inspired the Stevie Nicks song "Rhiannon." The Birds of Rhiannon sing so beautifully that they not only send the living to sleep, but also raise the dead. Both horses and **birds** are psychopomp creatures, that is, they conduct the **souls** of the dead on the journey to the Underworld.

There is a white horse carved into the landscape at the Iron Age hill fort of Uffington, in south-east England. It may be that this horse was carved into the landscape in honor of Epona/Rhiannon.

CHINA

THE EIGHT IMMORTALS

Strictly speaking, the Pa-Hsien or Eight Immortals of Taoist Philosophy are not really Gods, but have attained God-like status because of their adherence to the principles of the faith. It is indeterminate whether these people were real, but whatever the case they have achieved legendary status. Effectively, they are spiritual role models who are often to be seen with the God of Long Life.

In no particular order, here are those Eight Immortals.

2. Ts'ao Kuo-ghiu: A pupil of Han Chung-li, who nevertheless does not follow his master's dress sense. Ts'ao Kuo-ghiu appears dressed as a mandarin.

1. Han Chung-li: A very old man, of reckless appearance. He instructed one of the other immortals, Ts'ao Kuo-ghiu.

3. Chang-kuo Lao: Not much is known about this old man, although his **donkey** also seems worthy of veneration. It could travel colossal distances in the course of only one day, and when it wasn't needed any more it could be folded up like a piece of paper.

4. Lan Ts'ai-ho: Recognizable by his **feet**, one of which is bare while the other is shod. A street-singer who apparently was carried up to heaven by a **stork**, Lan Ts'ai-ho wears tattered clothes.

5. T'ieh-kuai Li: A pupil of the sixth-century BC philosopher poet Lao-Tzu, when T'ieh-kuai Li was meant to join his master in Heaven, only his **soul** went, leaving his body behind. He instructed his pupil to guard the body carefully for **seven** days, at the end of which, if his soul had not returned to reanimate it, it should be burned. However, on the sixth day, the pupil's mother fell ill, and so in his need

to leave he burned the body a day early. Li's soul returned the next day and we can only imagine the consternation he felt at discovering that his body was reduced to a pile of smoldering ashes. He was forced to find another host quickly, and chose the corpse of a beggar that had died from starvation. Therefore, Li appears as a beggar, leaning on an iron crutch and with a large cooking-pot on his back.

6. Ho-Sien Ku: Ho-Sien Ku ascended to Heaven in full daylight. She appears as a beautiful young girl with a **lotus** flower.

7. Han Hsiang-tzu: He appears as a young
man in the clothes and headgear of a
noble.

8. Lu Tung Pin: The Immortal that we have
the most information about. He apparently likes to wander about the world
looking like an ordinary person, reward-
ing the good and punishing the bad. He
helped convert Ts'ao Kuo-ghiu.

One of the best-known stories of Lu is called
"The Dream of the **Yellow** Sorghum." When
he was a student, he stopped at an inn and met
one of the Immortals in disguise. After their
conversation, he slept deeply, and had a vivid
dream in which he saw the rest of his life
mapped out; many successes and accolades
were due to him, but in the end, he saw
himself dying a pauper, killed by a bandit.
After the dream, Lu renounced the world and
took on the Taoist faith.

EGYPTIAN DEITIES

The ancient Egyptians had many Gods, many of them hybridized humans/**animals**. Animals themselves were deified and accorded due reverence, the more dangerous the animal the greater its worship. The **Crocodile** God, Sobek, for example, had its own city, Crocodilopolis. The pharaoh was also considered to be as one with the Gods, and was deified after his death.

The **nine** Gods of Eliopoulos, the City of the **Sun**, were Atum, Geb, **Isis**, Nut, **Osiris**, Nephthys, Set, Shu, and Tefnut.

ISIS

The Greeks rendered the name of the Egyptian Goddess Eset as Isis. She was considered the supreme Mother Goddess, parent of all the other deities. As such, she personifies all the qualities of the other Goddesses.

Both the sister and consort of **Osiris**, her contribution to the civilization of Egypt was to teach spinning, weaving, and the grinding of corn to the women, and the art of healing the sick to the men. She also introduced the idea of **marriage** and therefore domesticity. This would make it appear that, like the Roman Hestia, Isis had started out her journey as a Goddess of the Hearth, but in a legend that reinforces the power of the knowledge of a magical **name**, when she learned the secret name of the **Sun** God, Ra, she became his equal. Drops of her **blood** gave life to every living creature in the Universe. The **Ankh**, a magical symbol of rebirth, belongs to Isis. Her name has been used in tandem with **mystery cults** and secret organizations—the Fellowship of Isis, for example.

The fame of Isis spread far and wide and was not restricted to Egypt. Her influence even extended as far as the Rhine. She was called, like Mary the mother of Christ, the **Star** of the Sea. However, in the sixth century AD her temple at Philae was turned into a Christian church. Like the **Eleusinian mysteries** that celebrated the Goddess **Demeter**, elaborate festivals were held in honor of Isis that similarly taught initiates the secrets of death and rebirth.

Isis brought another great revelation to mankind. This was the art of embalming, and therefore of eternal life. When his brother cut Osiris' body into **fourteen** parts, Isis painstakingly reconstructed the body. The only missing part was his penis, which had been devoured by a **crab**. Thereafter, this creature was cursed in Egypt.

OSIRIS

Again, the Greeks have given us the most familiar name of one of the most important Gods of Egypt, Ousir. Initially a God of Nature, Osiris is identified with other Gods who die and are reborn again. Egyptians worshipped him as the God of the Dead, which helps explain the fascination with all things morbid. As with other mighty Gods, his power is indicated in the sheer number of his **names**. More than a hundred are listed in the Egyptian Book of the Dead.

Osiris was the eldest son of the **Sky Goddess**, Nut and the Earth God, Geb. His grandfather was Ra. His sister, **Isis**, was also his queen; thus the pair symbolizes the perfect union of male and female energies. Osiris proved a civilizing influence, teaching his people the arts of agriculture and dissuading them from cannibalism. His ways were gentle and just, a lover of **music** who invented two different kinds of flute. Osiris' power spread far and wide, his civilizing influence having a profound effect throughout Asia.

There was a cloud on the horizon, though, in the form of his jealous brother, who assassinated him. We have already explained how Isis painstakingly reconstructed his body. Osiris manifested in numerous animal forms; Onuphis, the **bull**, the **Ram** of Mendes that inspired the curious tale of the **Goat** of Mendes, and in the Benu **bird** which has similarities to the **phoenix**, also a bird of death and resurrection. Osiris was celebrated in his own **mystery cults** that, like the **Eleusinian mysteries**, instructed its acolytes in the secrets of death and rebirth.

ANUBIS

This Egyptian God has close parallels with **Hermes**, whose ubiquity is reflected in different Gods from cultures all over the world. This close association would see the God later renamed Hermanubis. Like Hermes, Anubis also has the **caduceus** as his attribute.

Anubis symbolizes his status as a conductor of **souls** by his **head**, which is that of a **jackal**, a creature that is also a psychopomp. Anubis presided over the process of embalming, considered essential if the soul were to have any form of life after death. Funerary prayers and offerings were made almost exclusively to Anubis.

Anubis had been abandoned by his mother, Nephthys, and was adopted by **Isis**. Isis, **Osiris**, and Anubis shared the same father, Ra, the **Sun** God. When Osiris died, it was Anubis that invented the funeral rites and the all-important process of mummification. Known as the "Lord of the Mummy Wrappings," Anubis also had the ability to take the hand of the deceased and guide them towards the judges who then weighed his soul.

GRECO-ROMAN DEITIES

Mount Olympus, in Greece, is a sacred **mountain** archetype and the home to the mighty beings that are called, collectively the Olympians or the Dodekatheon (twelve gods). **Twelve** is, of course, a sacred number belonging not only to the number of solar months in a year but is also the number of fulfilment. So, who were this divine dozen? Although there were more than twelve beings that lived on top of the mountains, the twelve principle ones are:

2. Hera: The Mother. Consort of Zeus, Queen of the Gods, personification of the maternal aspect, ruler of **marriage** and motherhood.

1. Zeus: The Father. Like **Odin**, a God of Thunder and King of all the Gods; his kingdom, the **sky** itself. Dispenser of justice, his word is law.

3. Poseidon: The mighty God that rules over the **Sea**. Also has dominion over **horses** and **earthquakes**.

4. Ares: Not to be confused with **Aries**, Ares is the God of War and bloodshed. The two are sometimes confused, though, especially since **Mars**, the planet of war, rules the astrological sign of Aries.

6. Hephaestus: Ruler over **fire** and forges, Hephaestus is the blacksmith of the Gods, making magically empowered weapons.

7. Aphrodite: Goddess of Beauty, love, and sexual desire.

5. Hermes: The Messenger of the Gods, whose distinctive attribute is his winged sandals and the **caduceus** he holds. Scribe and recorder to the Gods.

8. Athena: Goddess of Wisdom, often accompanied by an **owl** as a sign of her sagacity and access to occluded information.

10. Artemis: Goddess of the Hunt, often depicted with a quiver of **arrows** and a bow. Artemis is also the **Moon** Goddess and the Goddess of Virgins.

9. Apollo: The glorious **Sun** God, governor of light, **music**, poetry, and beauty.

11. Demeter: Goddess of the Harvest, agriculture, and fertility.

12. Hestia: Goddess of the Home and the hearth.

The family relationships of these Gods are labyrinthine. Zeus, Poseidon, Hera, Demeter, Hestia, and Hades were all siblings. Hades, as God of the Underworld, does not figure among the Olympians although he is of course a key God; his realm is the world of the of her time with the other Gods but also belongs to the Underworld where she spends **four** months of the year. Hermes, Hephaestus, Artemis, Apollo, and Ares are children of Zeus by various mothers. Athena was born from the forehead of her father Zeus, and Aphrodite was born from the castrated **phallus** of the sky that existed prior to the Creation.

The Romans adopted many of these Greek Gods and their qualities, adding them to their own deities to form a Greco-Roman pantheon. The table below shows the Greek deities with their Roman counterparts:

GREEK	ROMAN
Zeus	Jupiter
Hera	Juno
Poseidon	Neptune
Ares	Mars
Hermes	Mercury
Hephaestus	Vulcan
Aphrodite	Venus
Athena	Minerva
Apollo	Apollo
Artemis	Diana
Demeter	Ceres
Hestia	Vesta
Hades	Pluto
Persephone	Proserpina
Dionysus	Bacchus
Eros	Cupid
Chronos	Saturn
Coelus	Uranus

DEMETER/CERES

The cereals we eat as part of our breakfast take their name from the Roman Goddess Ceres, whose Greek counterpart is Demeter. It was this Goddess who gave mankind the secrets of agriculture, a pivotal skill that has had a profound effect on human kind, the cultivation of **plants** itself a perfect symbol for a different kind of cultivation as man made the transition from savage to civilized.

Any deity who has jurisdiction over the crops and fertility understandably holds immense power, and the worship of Demeter was the primary focus of the **Eleusinian mysteries** that celebrated the profound secrets of death and rebirth. The winter season was explained, lyrically, as signifying Demeter's journey to the Underworld to seek out her lost daughter, **Persephone**; during this time, she neglected her earthly duties and so all the plants and vegetation disappeared.

The cereal and grain crops, which were this Goddess's gifts to humankind, gave us **bread**, a staple item that nourishes on two levels, spiritual and material.

HECATE

Hecate is the great Greek Queen of the Underworld and the **Moon** Goddess who is often among those that are referred to as the **Triple Goddess**. Famously, Hecate is also the Queen of the Witches, and has two opposing aspects. She is the benevolent Goddess that brings prosperity, protects man at **sea** and ensures that farmers and sailors reap a bountiful **harvest**. However, she also has a terrifying, demonic aspect as the Goddess of the Dead, associated with **ghosts** and nightmares, mistress of sorcery, and summoned by incantations.

As well as personifying the **three** phases of the Moon's cycle (waxing, waning, and full) she also embodies the three parts of the Universe; heaven, hell, and earth. As befits the Sorcerer Queen, Hecate rules over spells, charms, and enchantments; she sends **demons** down the earth to torture men; she haunts **crossroads**, graveyards and tombs, often appearing with her pack of hellhounds. Symbolic of the dark side, Hecate is also a symbol of the subconscious mind, the hidden depths that are full of fear and swarming with monsters.

HERMES/MERCURY

Hermes appears in a number of guises, as befits a God with trickster tendencies. His talents are numerous, his attributes diverse. His Celtic equivalent is the God **Lugh**, who is referred to by Caesar as "the inventor of all arts and crafts." He also appears as Thoth, the great Egyptian God that invented writing and was the scribe of the Gods as well as the judge of the human **soul** and mediator between man and God. In yet another guise, there are parallels with the great **angel** Metatron. The word "Mercury" shares its root with *mercator*, "merchant," indicating his interest in marketing and trade.

The most immediately recognizable symbol that belongs to Hermes is his winged sandals, indicating swift movement and the powers of flight. This makes him an effective messenger of the Gods. Originally he moved between **Zeus** and the Gods of the Underworld, **Persephone** and Hades, so was able to move easily in and out of different worlds, the world of the living and of the dead; he is also a God of the Dead. In his guise as the ibis-headed Thoth, he is also the patron of science and literature, inventions, and wisdom. His trickster skills make Mercury the God of Thieves, too. Communication of all kinds belongs to this God, his image used, for example, by telecommunication companies.

This versatile deity also appears as Hermes Trismegistus, the founding father of **alchemy**. The magical gifts that Hermes Trismegistus brought to humankind include the divinatory arts as well as **music**. The great **Emerald Tablet** that is the cornerstone of the Great Work in Alchemy is a riddle, written in such an oblique way that it has several interpretations. It is said that Mercury brings our attention to great mysteries, but also gives us the means to unravel these mysteries. In Greek myth, Hermes made the first lyre, constructing it from the shell of a **tortoise** and using the guts of a sacrificed **bull** for strings. He also made the first flute, which he swapped with Apollo for lessons in magic as well as a golden **caduceus**, another of his attributes.

Iris

One of the minor Greek Goddesses, Iris is in many ways the female equivalent of **Hermes**. As messenger of the Gods and particularly of Zeus and his wife Hera, whenever she had to come down to Earth from Mount Olympus, it was necessary for her to assume human form; in her God-like appearance, however, she has golden wings, wears a tunic and her defining **rainbow**-hued veil or cloak that billows in the breeze. Like Hermes, she also has wings on her sandals and could travel with ease between the worlds of the living and the dead. Sometimes, Iris used the **arc** of the rainbow as a means of traveling down to Earth. This is one of the most beautiful celestial phenomena, so it isn't surprising that our ancestors saw the rainbow as a sign of communication with the Gods, and expected a message from Iris to follow its appearance. Iris is a benevolent, helpful Goddess, also acting as a sort of maidservant and attendant to Hera and never shirking her duties. She has initiative, too; she attends to the **horses** of other Gods when they return to Olympus, unharnessing them and feeding them with **ambrosia** and nectar.

The beautifully iridescent **iris** flower was named after this Goddess.

Janus

Many deities from one religious discipline will have a counterpart with very similar attributes in another. However, Janus, a Roman God, appears to be unique although there is a link between him and the Greek God Chaos. As the God of **Doorways**, Janus' defining feature is that he has two **heads**. As well as this distinction, he also carries a **key**, to lock and unlock the doors and gates he guards, and a stick to drive away anyone who had no right to cross the threshold.

Because he is the God of Gates, Janus is, by extension, ruler of arrivals and departures and of communication. He is also God of Beginnings and has jurisdiction over the daybreak, effectively allowing the **Sun** to enter through the eastern gate of the **sky**. At the time before the creation of the Universe and all the **elements** were a formless mass, Janus was called Chaos; after their separation and the coming of order, his name changed to Janus, but he still rules the time of transition. The month of January was named for Janus, who looks back to the old year and forward to the new. Janus also inspired the title of janitor, the earthly ruler of **doorways** and corridors. He was honored on the first day of every month.

Persephone / Proserpina

Persephone is one of the Underworld or chthonic deities, the consort of Hades, its King. She is the daughter of the Harvest Goddess, **Demeter**. Before she was kidnapped and carried off into the Underworld, Persephone was named Kore or Cora, meaning "the maiden." She appears in some accounts as the daughter of Zeus and Demeter but occasionally **Styx**, the nymph of the underworld **river**, is named as her mother.

Accounts of Persephone's story vary. According to one, she was gathering **flowers** in a field when the ground beneath her feet opened up and she was abducted by Hades. Demeter abandoned all her duties in order to look for her daughter. During her time in the Underworld Persephone was induced to eat a seed from the **pomegranate**, itself a symbol of fertility and sexual awakening and a euphemism for the loss of her virginity. However, because she had broken the obligatory fast that should be observed by those in the Underworld, she was tied to Hades, and when her mother found her again she had to promise to spend part of the year with him. Persephone, therefore, is symbolic of seasonal change.

The symbols attached to Persephone that allow us to recognize her are the pomegranate, the **bat**, and the **narcissus** flower. Worship of Persephone was a key feature of the **Eleusinian mysteries**. Incidentally, **fairy** tales also advise against eating anything from fairyland, since by accepting such **food** the person is trapped there.

THE HINDU PANTHEON

The system of Hindu deities is vast and complex, a multi-layered society of Gods and Goddesses that encompass a colorful spectrum of personalities. The concept of karma, the rule of cause and effect based on cosmic harmony and balance, is fundamental to Hinduism. The deities themselves are either aspects of the Supreme Being (Brahman), or more personalized, human representations of it (Bhagavan), or otherwise they are Devas, powerful in their own right. The stories of the Hindu deities are many and varied, and to confuse matters even further, each has different aspects of his or her divine self, such as appearing with, or riding on, an **animal**, when the beast becomes the "vehicle" of the God.

The Brahman has three aspects. As the creator, it is Brahma. As the preserver, it is Vishnu. As the destroyer, it is Shiva. Each of these three aspects has aspects of its own, but all comes back to one Supreme Being that has neither gender nor age: Brahman. Having said that, the Gods and Goddesses themselves are distinctly gender affiliated. The male Gods are called Devas, the female Goddesses Devis. Use of this epithet for humans acknowledges the divine being within. The Devas and Devis appear in the paintings, art, and statuary that thickly cluster all manifestations of Hindu culture.

Hindus affiliate themselves to the aspect of the Supreme Being that most appeals. Notwithstanding, there's a mutual respect for all the Gods and for people's right to choose.

Sometimes, Gods take on human form in order to assist humanity in some way. These beings are called Avatars, and in many ways equate to Christ who similarly came to Earth to help mankind toward ultimate enlightenment and the journey to God. In contrast to Christianity, where Christ is believed only to have come to Earth the one time, in Hinduism the Avatar can reincarnate repeatedly, as and when necessary. One of the most famous Avatars is Rama; the stories in the Ramayana are about his adventures, and the Bhagavad Gita is the collected spiritual wisdoms of Krishna, the Avatar of Vishnu.

Each of the Devas or Devis has a particular attribute that identifies it, and gorgeously elaborate stories explain these attributes. **Ganesh** is the popular **elephant**-headed God that removes obstacles, and Lakshmi is the Goddess of Good Fortune, often appearing in shops and business places and attracted into the home by the elaborate rice powder **rangoli** drawings at the threshold of houses. **Sarasvati** is the Goddess of Learning, inspiring students and teachers alike.

It is true to say that these divine beings and their attributes are symbols of man's own qualities and an excellent way for human beings to focus on their skills, a way of externalizing what is within and a means of focus. Psychologically speaking Hinduism is a very clever system designed to bring out the best in people. Ramakrishna, the Hindu saint, studied many other religions including Islam and Christianity, and wisely observed that "the truth is One; the wise call it by various names."

GANESH

We've already mentioned Ganesh as the remover of obstacles. Although Ganesh is also the deity of intelligence and wisdom, the obstacle-removing ability makes him one of the most popular Gods of the Hindu pantheon. It's worth remembering that Ganesh can also place obstacles in the way of people as a form of education. But how did he come about his curious hybrid appearance? There are several versions of the story.

As guardian of the gate of his mother Parvati, in his enthusiasm to do his job properly, one day he tried to prevent Shiva, his father, from entering. The result was that the young man's **head** was cut off. Shiva decided that the head of the first passing **animal** should replace his son's human head. This animal happened to be an **elephant**. Ganesh was restored to life with the addition of this unwieldy head, and given his name, which means "elephant head." Ganesh sometimes appears standing on a **rat** or a **mouse**, an unlikely "vehicle" that was given to him by a contemptuous **demon**. However, the mouse itself is a symbol. The word "mouse" comes from the Sanskrit *musaka*, which means "thief," because mice steal valuable grain. The mouse itself, therefore, is an obstacle that needs to be overcome.

KALI

Kali, as the Hindu Goddess who is not only a protector and a loving mother but also a vengeful destroyer, has parallels with **Hecate** from the Greek pantheon.

Kali is instantly recognizable; her name means "dark," and her appearance is quite fearsome. She appears with dark **blue** or **black** skin, long disheveled tresses of black **hair**, furious **red** eyes, sharp **teeth**, a protruding **tongue** and her distinctive necklace of human **skulls**. Sometimes she wears a skirt made of human **arms**. She herself has **four** (or sometimes ten) arms; in common with other divinities that have supernumerary limbs or heads, this signifies superhuman powers. Kali is often depicted standing over a corpse. In each of her four hands, she carries a sword, a severed **head**, a **trident** or *trishul*, and a *kapala* or skull cup that catches the **blood** from the head.

Like Hecate, Kali frequents the places of the dead, cremation grounds in particular.

Her consort Shiva, who is also associated with these places, has his skin colored **white** from the ashes of the corpses. His pale skin contrasts with the **black** skin of Kali, the two contrasting shades a reminder of opposing forces. As befits a Goddess with such frightening associations and with a reputation for violence, Kali is treated with awe, respect, and not a little fear. She symbolizes **death** as well as salvation. In her more benign aspect, however, she appears as a smiling figure, hands raised in the boon-giving gesture, young, generous, beautiful, and maternal.

In Tantric practices, Kali is revered as the most powerful of Goddesses, and has her own meditation symbol or **yantra**, featuring in the center of the inverted **triangle** or **yoni** symbol. She is held to be the divine essence of the Mother Goddess, the highest reality and the female element, known as Shakti. Her universality means that she rules over all **five** of the **elements**.

To come face-to-face with Kali is to face the reality of death, and all the symbolism of this Goddess acts as a reminder of the need to come to terms with this reality.

SARASVATI

Sarasvati is the wife of Brahma, the God of Gods who created the world. The Goddess of Wisdom, knowledge, and **music**, Sarasvati often appears with a stringed musical instrument called a vina. She is also identified by her beauty and her **four arms**, the supernumerary limbs, themselves symbols of power, also represent the four aspects of learning: intellect, mind, ego, and alertness.

Sarasvati, as befits a feminine deity, is a **water** Goddess and was in ancient times also personified as a river that bore her name, which is now dried up. A **swan** sometimes accompanies Sarasvati. This **bird**, if offered a mixture of **milk** and water, would select only the milk, therefore symbolizing discrimination. Adherents to the Sarasvati cult make offerings of **honey** to their Goddess, because honey is synonymous with perfect knowledge.

Sarasvati gave a great gift to humanity—the **alphabet**.

INUIT GODS

Eskimos call themselves Inuits after the Innua, the spirits that they believe animate every single aspect of nature; the **sea**, the **air**, pebbles, rocks, **animals**, vegetation. These spirits can become the guardians of men, like the familiar of the witch, a **totem** animal that eases our passage through life, offering guidance and encouragement.

SEDNA

One of the most important deities of the Inuit is a **Sea** Goddess called Sedna. Sedna's appearance is fearsome; she is a one-**eyed** giantess with dominion over all marine creatures, and given the Inuit reliance on the seas for their livelihood, Sedna's power is appropriately great. There are several myths about Sedna, but whatever the version they all come back to one thing—the almighty row that she had with her father, the Creator-God Anguta,

which resulted in her death and resurrection as a superhuman being.

One explanation for this infanticide is that, unable to find a man that was good enough for her, Sedna married a **dog**, thus attracting the ire of Anguta. However, here's an alternative explanation: unsurprisingly, given that she was a giantess, Sedna was a hungry child, and spent much of her time eating. In a fit of the midnight munchies she even chewed off her sleeping father's **arm**. Anguta was naturally extremely irked, and threw her over the side of his kayak, successively lopping off her **fingers** as she clawed at its sides trying to save herself. These fingers turned into sea creatures, in particular the **seals**, **whales** and walruses beloved of Inuit hunters. Sedna herself sank to the bottom of the ocean and became its residing deity. It's vital that hunters and fishermen keep Sedna happy, because otherwise she expresses her wrath via the weather.

JAPAN

The pantheon of Japanese deities is vast. Antiquated texts speak of the "eight hundred myriads of Gods," a figure that doesn't seem unreasonable given that every village, every stone, every **tree** has its own **spirit**, an aspect of the original animistic religion, Shinto.

AMERATASU

The **Sun** is frequently portrayed as a male deity, but one of Japan's key deities is the Sun Goddess, Ameratasu. Believed to be an ancestor of the Imperial Family that also reflects the glory of the Sun, Ameratasu's main shrine is at a place called Ise, although for many years her "residence" was in the palace of the Emperor. Her removal was something of a political event, since Ameratasu's priestesses could question the authority of the Emperor, an instance of a classic clash between church and state. The shrine at Ise has been rebuilt several times but always as an exact replica of what went before, a living example of ancient architecture.

This shrine is home to flocks of **roosters**, the symbol of the Sun not only because they are among the first **birds** that greet it every morning at dawn but because of their **rainbow**-colored cockscomb. The **temple** also contains the sacred **mirror** that belongs to Ameratasu. It's believed that the spirit of Ameratasu enters this octagonal mirror in order to communicate with mankind. Legend also states that this mirror was used to draw the Goddess out of the **cave** where she was hiding.

SLAVIC DEITIES

The Slavic pantheon is colossal; each tribe had its own deities and the geographical area of the entire race stretched across a vast area, from the Black Sea to the Baltic. Incoming Christianity wiped out many traces of the major Gods, and so the information we have is sketchy. The major God, the **Sky** God, was called Svarog. Pagan Slavs revered the actual sky as a divinity. Svarog means "bright and clear" and has Sanskrit origins.

THE DOMOVOI

Whereas the major Gods of the Slav pantheon were crushed under the grinding wheels of Christianity, many of the minor, rustic Gods managed to slip the net. The Domovoi (from the same root as the word "domestic") were the main household Gods of the Slavs. The actual name of each home's deity was never mentioned, and he was instead referred to as "the grandfather", or some similar epithet. His appearance varied: he could disguise himself as a bundle of hay, for example, or as a creature covered in silky fur with horns and a tail.

The provenance of the Domovoi has parallels with the mythic creation of **demons**. When the Supreme Being of the Slavs, Perun, made Heaven and Earth, some of the other celestial beings revolted against their leader, and were promptly cast out of Heaven. Some fell into the **forests** or **streams** and retained their demonic character. The ones that fell

into houses stayed there, rendered benevolent by their association with mankind.

Each Domovoi seems to have become attached to a family, and if the family moved to a new house then the wife would attract the Domovoi into it by placing a piece of **bread** under the stove. The Domovoi gave notice of important events in the life of the family.

PERUN AND VELES

The most important God, the Supreme Being, was Perun. His name is mentioned more often in the historic records of the religion as the God of Thunder and lightning, Lord of all the other Gods. In this, Perun equates to the One God of the Christians. So fearsome and powerful was this God that people painted thunder marks of the roofs of their houses to protect them from the devastating weapon.

Perun's counterpart, Veles, equates to the devil. Where Perun appears at the top of hills, effectively in the Heavenly realms, Veles appears in the lower depths, often near a **river**. And whereas Perun is God of Thunder, hot and dry, Veles is the opposite, ruling the damp and cold area among the roots of the **World Tree**.

Veles also has parallels to Pan. Like this Greek deity, Veles is the God of Shepherds, and is closely associated with magic and the occult. The enmity between these two Gods is far reaching. The **Sun** was considered to be

Veles' wife, for example, and when she disappeared over the western horizon every evening it was supposed that she had absconded to spend an adulterous night with her husband's enemy. Another school of thought held the opposing view, that in fact she was actually married to Veles, and her appearance in the east every morning meant that she had been kidnapped by Perun.

NORSE/TEUTONIC PANTHEON

Interestingly, the Gods of Norse/Teutonic mythology were never really considered as being immortal, but were humans with super powers. There were two tribes of Gods: the Aesir, or ferocious Warrior Gods, and the Vanir, deities of a more peaceful and benevolent disposition. The two tribes unified to fight the Giants.

FREYA

Freya was so lovely that she was the constant source of attention from the other Gods. As befits a person of such beauty, Freya ruled over love, fertility, and beauty. She was also the leader of the **Valkyries**, and as such she escorted fallen warriors back to the banqueting halls of Valhalla.

Freya was particularly fond of lovely things. Once, when she found four dwarves making a gorgeous **necklace**, her desire to possess it was so great that she readily agreed to sleep with all of them in return for it.

She can be recognized by a small falcon, which often accompanies her. She also had a cloak of **feathers**, which enabled her to fly.

WOTAN/ODIN

Wotan/Odin is the chief God of the Scandinavian pantheon. His attributes are numerous and seemingly conflict with one another; he is not only God of War and **death**, but also of poetry, prophecy, and of victory. His name comes from the same root as *wuten*, which means "to rage," and the idea of this fury surrounds the God. He is the God of Thunder, heard on stormy nights raging in the **sky** with his army of slain soldiers. Wotan was the God invoked by the Saxons and the Angles when they invaded Britain in the fifth century, and his influence was all-pervasive.

How do you recognize Wotan? To humankind, he often appears in the guise as a simple traveler, wearing shabby **clothing** and a wide-brimmed hat. However, when he appears in his true form he is a magnificent sight. He rides Sleipnir, his ultra speedy **eight**-legged **horse** that can gallop across **water** as though it were solid earth, and he is accompanied by two **ravens**, Hugin and Munin (Thought and Memory), who report back to him every evening the events in the lives of men. As if all this were not remarkable enough, Wotan has only one **eye**. He gave away the other to Mimir, the **demon** that lives in among the roots of Yggdrasil, the **World Tree**, in exchange for a drink of **water** from the well of wisdom that sprung up from the base of the tree.

Wotan is eloquent, speaking in verse. Like **Mercury** whom the Romans likened him to, he brought language to his people, apparently dangling upside down in a **tree** for **nine** days and nights, pierced with his own spear, in order that he should learn the secrets of the **runes**. This curious ordeal was akin to a shamanistic rite of passage that would guarantee his own resurrection. Wotan rules the same day of the week as Mercury, too—Wednesday (Wotan's day), which equates to Mercredi (Mercury's day) in French, of course.

Wotan rules over Valhalla, the Hall of the Slain, where dead warriors are brought by the **Valkyries**, under the command of their leader **Freya**, in order to prepare themselves for the final battle, Ragnarok, which will mark the end of the world.

NEW ZEALAND AND AUSTRALIA

JULUNGGUL

Also called Kalseru, Julunggul belongs to the Australian Aboriginal pantheon, and is the **rainbow Serpent** Goddess of Fertility who oversees the maturation of boys into men. The Aboriginal culture is the oldest on **Earth**, dating back 65,000 years, and the belief system itself is called Dreamtime. Dreamtime explains how the cosmos was made and how everything came into being, and its influence resonates throughout all parts of the world, not just in the Aborigines' lands. Julunggul resembles other serpent deities, including Owa in the Yoruban tradition and Damballah in Voudon. As well as the talents described above, she is believed to have created the landscape itself and is the embodiment of **water**.

RANGI AND PAPA

Many of the myths of the Maoris draw upon the relationship between the **sky** and the **earth**, and this is reflected in the stories of Rangi, the Sky God and great father of mankind, and Papa, a Maori word meaning "earth floor," the Earth Goddess and great mother, Rangi's wife.

Rangi was in love with Papa, and descended to her in the time before the Universe was created. Their passionate embrace meant that all their children were forced to exist squashed into the claustrophobic, dark space between them where nothing could grow because there was simply no space. Their children had several ideas about how the situation should be alleviated, including suggestions of killing them (from Tumatuenga, the most hotheaded). However, the problem was solved by his brother Tanemahata, the God of the **Forest**. He made life bearable for his siblings by simply separating his parents. He achieved this by lying on his back and pushing upwards with his strong **legs**.

VOUDON

Many of the deities of the Dahomey people of Africa, from Benin, appear in the Voudon religion, which is an amalgam of beliefs from West Africa with Christianity. One of Voudon's creation myths shares similarities with the idea of the creation of the world in Judaism and Christianity, but whereas the Abrahamic God apparently needed **six** days to create the world, the primary Dahomey deity, the androgynous Mawu Lisa, needed only **four**. On the first day the world was made; on the second, all plant and **animal** life were brought into being. On the third day, humans were given intellect and languages; and on the fourth day, the far-sighted God created technology.

In Voudon, there are many different loas, or spirits that have attained a God-like status. These loas are able to possess the human **body**, which is the aim of many of the trance-inducing ceremonies of the faith. The spirits split into two categories: the Rada, who offer protection and guidance and are generally seen to be quite benevolent; and the Petro, who are less forgiving, and more associated with the darker side of Voudon magic. Each loa has aspects of both in its personality.

ERZULIE FREDA DAHOMEY

Erzulie is a family of such loa spirits, with Erzulie Freda Dahomey being a very "girly" sort of entity, much concerned with romance, dancing, **flowers**, beauty, and love. Often portrayed wearing three wedding **rings**, one for each of her husbands, Erzulie Freda Dahomey is further identified by the **heart** symbol and by the feminine colors of **gold** and **pink**. Erzulie Freda Dahomey is the embodiment of the feminine spirit, which means that she also has a dark side, the Petro side. Balanced against her coquettish playfulness is an aspect that is lazy, jealous, and spoiled. In this aspect she is depicted with a child in one **arm** and holding a knife.

FURTHER READING

Allcroft, A. H., *The Circle and the Cross*, Macmillan, 1972

Allen, P. M. (ed.), *A Christian Rosenkreutz Anthology*, Rudolf Steiner Press, 1968

Ammer, Christine, *Seeing Red or Tickled Pink – Color Terms in Everyday Language*, Signet, 1992

Andrews, Ted, *Animal Speak*, Llewellyn, 2000

Attenborough, David, *The Private Life of Plants*, BBC Books, 1995

Bahn, Paul G., *Tombs, Graves and Mummies*, Weidenfeld and Nicholson, 1996

Baker, Gordon and Morris, Katherine, *Descartes' Dualism*, Routledge, 1996

Baker, Margaret, *Discovering the Folklore of Plants*, Shire Publications, 2001

Barber, Theodore Xenophon, PhD, *The Human Nature of Birds*, St Martin's Press, 1993

Bardens, Dennis, *Psychic Animals*, Barnes and Noble, 1996

Barker, Cicely Mary, *Meaning of Flowers*, Frederick Warne, 1996

Baxter, Ron, *Bestiaries and their Users in the Middle Ages*, Sutton, 1998

Bayley, Harold, *The Lost Language of Symbolism*, vols 1 and 2, Random House, 1996

Becker, Udo, *The Continuum Encyclopedia of Symbols*, Continuum, 1992

Beer, Robert, *The Handbook of Tibetan Buddhist Symbols*, Serindia, 2003

Bell, R. C., *The Boardgame Book*, Marshall Cavendish, 1979

Benson, Elizabeth P., *Birds and Beasts of Ancient Latin America*, University Press of Florida, 1997

Bernbaum, Edwin, *Sacred Mountains of the World*, Sierra Club Books, 1992

Bhavanani, Dr Ananda, *Yantra: The Mystic Science of Number, Name and Form*, ICYER, 1995

—, *Yoga 1–10*, Satya Press, 2006

The Holy Bible, Authorised Version, Collins

Birren, Faber, *Color: From Ancient Mysticism to Modern Science*, University Books, 1963

Bishop, Peter, *The Myth of Shangri-La: Tibet, Travel Writing and the Western Creation of Sacred Landscapes*, Continuum, 1989

Bord, Janet, *Fairies: Real Encounters with Little People*, Michael O'Mara Books, 1997

Brand, Stewart (editor emeritus), *The Whole Earth Catalogue*, Point Foundation, 1986

Bridges, Marilyn and O'More, Haven, *Markings: Sacred Landscapes from the Air*, Aperture, 1990

Brunton, Paul, *The Hidden Teaching Behind Yoga*, Rider, 1969

Buckland, Raymond, *Signs, Symbols and Omens*, Llewellyn, 2003

Budge, E. A. Wallis, *The Book of the Dead*, Routledge and Kegan Paul, 1974

—, *An Egyptian Hieroglyphic Dictionary*, Dover, 1978

Burton, Richard (trs), *The Arabian Nights*, Routledge and Sons, 1877

Bushnaq, *Arab Folktales*, American University in Cairo Press, 1986

Butler, W. E., *Magic and the Qabbalah*, Aquarian, 1968

Caldecott, Moyra, *Myths of the Sacred Tree*, Destiny Books, 2003

Campbell, Joseph, *The Hero with a Thousand Faces*, HarperCollins, 1993

— *The Masks of God, Occidental Mythology*, Penguin, 1964

— (ed.), *Spirit and Nature*, Princeton University Press, 1983

Camwell, Charles, *Aleister Crowley*, University Books, 1962

Carmichael, Elizabeth, and Sayer, Chloe, *The Skeleton at the Feast: The Day of the Dead in Mexico*, British Museum Press, 1991

Carr-Gomm, Philip, *In The Grove of the Druids*, Watkins, 2002

— (ed.), *The Druid Renaissance*, HarperCollins, 1996

— and Carr-Gomm, Stephanie, *The Druid Animal Oracle*, Simon and Schuster, 1994

Carson, David and Sams, Jamie, *Medicine Cards*, Bear and Co, 1988

Cassy, Rob, *The Ultimate Language of Flowers*, Abson Books, 2000

Castaneda, Carlos, *The Teachings of Don Juan: A Yaqui Way of Knowledge*, Penguin, 1990

—, *A Separate Reality: Further Conversations with Don Juan*, Pocket Books, 1999

Chadwick, Henry, *The Early Church*, Penguin, 1967

Chambers, Robert, *The Book of Days*, Chambers, 1864

Chardin, Teilhard de, *The Phenomenon of Man*, Harper and Row, 1961

Chetwynd, Tom, *Dictionary of Symbols*, Thorsons, 1998

Cheung, Theresa, *The Element Encyclopedia of the Psychic World*, HarperElement, 2006

Chjenciner, Ismailov and Magomedkhanov, *Tattooed Mountain Women and Spoonboxes of Daghestan*, Bennett and Bloom, 2006

Cirlot, J. E., *A Dictionary of Symbols*, Routledge, 1990

Clark, Hugh, *A Short Introduction to Heraldry*, John Walker, 1810

Conway, David, *Magic: An Occult Primer*, Jonathan Cape, 1972

—, *Secret Wisdom: The Occult Universe Explored*, Aquarian, 1987

Cooper, Jason D., *Using the Runes*, Aquarian, 1987

Cooper, J. C., *An Illustrated Encyclopaedia of Symbols*, Thames and Hudson, 1982

Cooper, Robert L. D., *Cracking the Freemason's Code: The Truth about Solomon's Key and the Brotherhood*, Rider, 2006

Cope, Julian, *The Modern Antiquarian*, HarperElement, 1998

Cos, Ian, *The Scallop*, Shell Transport and Trading Company, 1957

Crowley. Aleister, *Magic in Theory and Practice*, Routledge and Kegan Paul, 1973

Crystal, David, *The Cambridge Encyclopedia of the English Language*, Cambridge University Press, 1995

—, *How Language Works*, Penguin, 2006

Cunningham, Scott, *Encyclopedia of Magical Herbs*, Llewellyn, 2000

Dames, Michael, *The Silbury Treasure*, Thames and Hudson, 1976

Dasgupta, S. N., *Hindu Mysticism*, M. Barnarsidass, 1976

David-Neel, Alexandra, *Magic and Mystery in Tibet*, Souvenir Press, 1967

Davies, Owen, *Witchcraft, Magic and Culture, 1736–1951*, Manchester University Press, 1999

Davis, Stephen, *Hammer of the Gods*, Pan, 1995

De Roas, Stanislas Klssowski, *The Secret Art of Alchemy*, Thames and Hudson, 1973

Deacon, Richard, *John Dee: Scientist, Geographer, Astrologer and Secret Agent to Elizabeth I*, Frederick Muller, 1969

Dick, Philip K., *Do Androids Dream of Electric Sheep?*, Orion, 1999

Dobbs, B. J. T., *The Foundations of Newton's Alchemy*, Cambridge University Press, 1969

Douglas, David, *Atlas of Sacred and Spiritual Sites*, Godsfield, 2007

Drury, Neville, *The Watkins Dictionary of Magic*, Watkins, 2005

—, *The Dictionary of the Esoteric*, Watkins, 2002

Eitel, Ernest J., *Feng Shui: Science of Sacred Landscape*, Synthetic Press, 1993

Eliade, Mircea, *The Forge and the Crucible*, Rider, 1962

—, *Yoga, Immortality and Freedom*, Princeton University Press, 1969

—, *From Primitives to Zen*, Collins, 1979

—, *The Sacred and the Profane: The Nature of Religion*, Harcourt, 1987

—, *Symbolism the Sacred and the Arts*, Crossroad, 1988

—, *Shamanism: Archaic Techniques of Ecstasy*, Penguin, 1989

—, *Images and Symbols: Studies on Religious Symbolism*, Princeton University Press, 1991

—, *Rites and Symbols of Initiation*, Spring Publications, 1994

Epes Brown, Joseph, *Animals of the Soul*, Element Books, 1997

Evans, I. O., *The Observer's Book of Geology*, Frederick Warne, 1971

Fakhri, Majid, *The Qu'ran: An English Version*, Garnet Publishing, 1997

Farid ud din Attar, *The Conference of the Birds*, Penguin Classics, 1984

Feininger, A., *Form in Nature and Life*, Thames and Hudson, 1966

Finlay, Victoria, *Colour: Travels through the Paintbox*, Hodder and Stoughton, 2002

Fletcher, Alan, *The Art of Looking Sideways*, Phaidon, 2001

Folklore, Myths and Legends of Great Britain, Reader's Digest, 1973

Fontana, David, *The Secret Language of Symbols*, Pavilion, 1993

Fraser, J. G., *The Golden Bough*, Macmillan, 1957

Frutiger, Adrian, *Signs and Symbols: Their Design and Meaning*, Studio Editions, 1989

Fulcanelli, *Les Demeures Philosophales* (The Dwellings of the Philosophers), Archive Press and Communications, 1994

Gambutas, Maria, *The Language of the Goddess*, Thames and Hudson, 1989

Garai, Jana, *The Book of Symbols*, Lorrimer Publishing, 1973

George, Andrew (trs), *The Epic of Gilgamesh*, Penguin Classics, 2003

Gibson, James J., *The Perception of the Visual World*, Boston, 1950

Gilbert, R. A., *The Golden Dawn: Twilight of the Magicians*, Aquarian, 1981

Gimbel, Theo, *Healing Through Colour*, C. W. Daniel, 1989

Gleick, James, *Chaos: Making a New Science*, Sphere Books, 1988

Goblet D'Alviela, Count Eugene, *Symbols, Their Migrations and Universality*, Dover, 2000

Gombrich, E. H., *Art and Illusion*, Phaidon Press, 1956

Gorman, Peter, *Pythagoras: A Life*, Routledge and Kegan Paul, 1979

Grant, John, *The Book of Time*, Westbridge, 1980

—, *A Directory of Discarded Ideas*, Corgi, 1983

Grant, Michael (ed.), *The Birth of Western Civilisation*, Thames and Hudson, 1964

Graves, Robert, *The White Goddess*, Faber and Faber, 1960

Green, Martin, *Curious Customs and Festivals*, Countryside Books, 2001

Greenspan, Stanley I., and Shanker, Stuart G., *The First Idea, How Symbols, Language and Intelligence Evolved from our Primate Ancestors to Modern Humans*, Da Capo Press, 2004

Greer, John Michael, *The Element Encyclopedia of Secret Societies and Hidden History*, HarperElement, 2006

Guaqelin, M., *Astrology and Science*, Peter Davies, 1969

Hall, Judy, *The Crystal Bible*, Godsfield, 2003

Hall, Manly P., *An Encyclopaedic Outline of Masonic, Hermetic, Qabbalistic and Rosicrucian Symbolical Philosophy*, The Philosophical Research Society, 1977

—, *Lectures on Ancient Philosophy*, The Philosophical Research Society, 1984

—, *The Secret Teachings of All Ages*, The Philosophical Research Society, 2006

Hamon, Count Louis, *The Cheiro Book of Fate and Fortune*, Hamlyn, 1980

Harris, Rosemary, *The Lotus and the Grail*, Faber and Faber, 1974

Harris, Sam, *The End of Faith*, Norton, 2005

Harwood, Jeremy, *The Secret History of Freemasonry*, Lorenz, 2006

Hays, H. R., *The Dangerous Sex: The Myth of Feminine Evil*, Methuen, 1964

Heggie, D., *Megalithic Science*, Thames and Hudson, 1981

Heilmeyer, Maria, *The Language of Flowers*, Prestel, 2001

Henrikson, Alf, *Through the Ages*, Orbis Publishing, 1983

Highfield, Roger, *Can Reindeer Fly? The Science of Christmas*, Phoenix, 2001

Hitching, Francis, *Earth Magic*, Cassell, 1976

Homer, *The Odyssey*, Penguin Classics, 2003

Hoyle, Fred, *The Nature of the Universe*, Basil Blackwell, 1950

Humphreys, Christmas, *Buddhism*, Penguin, 1983

Hunter, Jeremy, *Sacred Festivals*, MQP Publications, 2002

Hutton, Ronald, *Stations of the Sun: A History of the Ritual Year in Britain*, Oxford University Press, 1996

Huxley, Francis, *The Way of the Sacred*, Bloomsbury, 1989

Illes, Judika, *The Element Encyclopedia of Witchcraft*, HarperElement, 2005

Innes, Hammond, *The Conquistadors*, Collins, 1969

Jackson, Robert, *The Alchemists*, Weidenfeld and Nicholson, 1997

Jackson, James P., *Biography of a Tree*, W. H. Allen, 1979

Jaynes, Julian, *The Origins of Consciousness in the Breakdown of the Bicameral Mind*, Houghton Mifflin, 1976

Jones, Steve, *In the Blood: God, Genes and Destiny*, HarperCollins, 1996

Jones, W. H. S., *Hippocrates*, Heinemann, 1923

Jung, C. G., *Spiritual Symbolism*, Routledge and Kegan Paul, 1971

—, *Man and His Symbols*, Aldus, 1979

Kallir, Alfred, *The Psychogenetic Source of the Alphabet*, Clarke, 1961

Kaplan, Stuart R., *Tarot Classic*, Hale, 1974

Karagulla, Shifica and van Gelder Kunz, Dora, *The Chakras and the Human Energy Fields*, Quest Books, 1989

Kenton, Warren, *Astrology: The Celestial Mirror*, Avon, 1974

King, Francis, *Magic: The Western Tradition*, Thames and Hudson, 1984

Knight, Gareth, *A Practical Guide to Occult Symbolism*, Helios, 1964

Knioght, Sirona, *Celtic Traditions*, Citadel Press, 2000

Koestler, Arthur, *The Lotus and the Robot*, Hutchinson, 1964

Kozminsky, Isidore, *Numbers: Their Meaning and Magic*, Rider, 1912

Kushner, Lawrence, *The Book of Letters: A Mystical Hebrew Alphabet*, Jewish Lights Publishing, 1994

Lamy, Lucy, *Egyptian Mysteries*, Thames and Hudson, 1989

Lang, Andrew, *Myth, Ritual and Religion*, vols 1 and 2, Random House, 1996

Larousse Encyclopaedia of Mythology, Readers' Union/Paul Hamlyn, 1961

Larousse Encyclopedia of the Earth, Paul Hamlyn, 1961

Lawrence, Elizabeth Atwood, *Hunting the Wren*, University of Tennessee Press, 1997

Lee, Catherine, *The Language of Flowers*, Ryland, Peters and Small Ltd, 2007

Legeza, Laszlo, *Tao Magic: The Secret Language of Diagrams and Calligraphy*, Thames and Hudson, 1987

Lehner, Ernst, *Symbols, Signs and Signets*, Dover, 1950

—, *Alphabets and Ornaments*, Dover, 1952

—, and Lehner, Johanna, *Folklore and Symbolism of Flowers, Plants and Trees*, Dover, 2003

—, *The Big Book of Dragons, Monsters and Other Mythical Creatures*, Dover, 2004

—, *Medicinal and Food Plants*, Dover, 2005

Leland, Charles, *Aradia or the Gospel of the Witches*, London, 1899

Lethbridge, T. C., *Gogmagog: The Buried Gods*, Routledge and Kegan Paul, 1957

Liungman, Carl G., *Dictionary of Symbols*, Norton, 1991

Lloyd Jones, Hugh, *Mythical Beasts*, Duckworth, 1980

Lommel, Andreas, *Masks: Their Meaning and Function*, Ferndale Editions, 1981

Lurker, Manfred, *The Gods and Symbols of Ancient Egypt*, Thames and Hudson, 1980

Mabey, Richard, *Beechcombings: The Narratives of Trees*, Chatto and Windus, 2007

Mackay, Charles, *Extraordinary Popular Delusions and the Madness of Crowds*, Wordsworth, 1995

Macneice, Louis, *Astrology*, Aldus, 1964

Mathers, S. L., *The Key of Solomon the King*, Routledge and Kegan Paul, 1972

Matt, Daniel C., *The Zohar* (Fritzker edition), Stanford University Press, 2007

McKenna, Terence, *Food of the Gods*, Rider, 1992

Meadows, Kenneth, *Earth Medicine*, Element Books, 1989

Meyrink, Gustav, *The Golem*, Dedalus, 1991

Michell, John, and Rickard, Robert J. M., *Phenomena: A Book of Wonders*, Thames and Hudson, 1977

Miller, George A., *The Spontaneous Apprentice* (Children and Language), Seabury, 1977

Milner, Edward J., *The Tree Book*, Collins and Brown, 1992

Mokkar, Mohan, *Reiki Magic*, UBSPD, 1999

Molyneux, Brian Leigh and Vitebsky, Piers, *Sacred Earth, Sacred Stones*, Duncan Baird, 2000

Murray, Margaret, *The Witch Cult in Western Europe*, Clarendon Press, 1921

Neugebauer, Otto, *The Exact Sciences in Antiquity*, Dover, 1969

Nichols, Ross, *The Book of Druidry*, Aquarian, 1990

Nicholson, R. A., *Studies in Islamic Mysticism*, Cambridge University Press, 1921

Nicholson, Shirley, *Shamanism*, The Theosophical Publishing House, 1987

Nozedar, Adele, *The Secret Language of Birds*, HarperElement, 2006

Okley, Judith, *The Traveller Gypsies*, Cambridge University Press, 1983

Olsen, Brad, *Sacred Places Around the World*, Consortium of Collective Consciousness, 2004

Page, T. E., and Eichholz, D. E., *Pliny: Natural History*, Loeb Classical Library, Heinemann, 1962

Paine, Sheila, *Amulets*, Thames and Hudson, 2004

Pakenham, Thomas, *Remarkable Trees of the World*, Weidenfeld and Nicholson, 2002

Palmer, Jessica Dawn, *Animal Wisdom: The Definitive Guide*, HarperElement, 2002

Palmer, Martin, *The Sacred History of Britain: Landscape, Myth and Power – The Forces that Have Shaped Britain's Spirituality*, Piatkus, 2002

Palsson, H. and Edwards, P., *Seven Viking Romances*, Penguin, 1985

Parker, Derek and Julia, *The Power of Magic*, Mitchell Beazley, 1992

Parker, Julia, *The Astrologer's Handbook*, Guild Publishing, 1985

Paterson, Jacqueline, *Memory, Tree Wisdom*, Element, 2002

The Penguin Dictionary of Symbols, Penguin, 1969

Pennick, Nigel, *Magical Alphabets*, Weiser, 1992

Perry, Francis, *Flowers of the World*, Hamlyn, 1972

Peterson, Joseph H., (ed.), *The Lesser Key of Solomon*, Weiser, 2001

Philpotts, Beatrice, *Mermaids*, Russell Ash/Windward, 1980

Pickering, David (ed.), *Cassell's Dictionary of Superstitions*, Cassell, 2002

Rackham, Oliver, *The Last Forest*, Dent, 1989

Radford, E. and A. M., *Encyclopedia of Superstitions*, Book Club Associates, 1974

Radhakrishnana, R. (trs), *The Bhagavad Gita*, Allen and Unwin, 1954

Rahula, Walpola, *What Buddha Taught*, Gordon Fraser, 1978

Ralls, Karen, *The Knights Templar Encyclopedia*, New Page Books, 2007

Rankine, David, *Crystals: Healing and Folklore*, Capall Bann, 2002

Redgrove, Peter, *The Black Goddess and the Sixth Sense*, Bloomsbury, 1987

Regardie, Israel, *The Tree of Life*, Aquarian, 1975

Richardson, Phyllis, *New Sacred Architecture*, Laurence King, 2004

Rinzler, Carol Ann, *The Wordsworth Book of Herbs and Spices*, Wordsworth, 1990

—, *The Wordsworth Dictionary of Medical Folklore*, Wordsworth, 1994

Riva, Anna, *Secrets of Magical Seals*, International Imports, 1975

Roud, Steve, *A Pocket Guide to Superstitions of the British Isles*, Penguin, 2004

Rowland, Beryl, *Animals with Human Faces*, Allen and Unwin, 1974

Rowling, J. K., *Harry Potter and the Deathly Hallows*, Bloomsbury, 2007

Russell, Bertrand, *The History of Western Philosophy*, Allen and Unwin, 1969

Scot, Reginald, *The Discoverie of Witchcraft* (1584), reprinted by Dover, 1972

Scott, Sir Walter, *Anne of Geierstein*, Adamant Media Corporation, 2000

Sepharial: The Book of Charms and Talismans, Foulsham and Co (no date)

Shah, Idries, *Oriental Magic*, Paladin, 1973

—, *The Sufis*, Octagon Press, 1999

Sharper Knowlson, T., *The Origins of Popular Superstitions and Customs*, Werner Laurie, 1930

Shaw, Eva, *The Wordsworth Book of Divining the Future*, Wordsworth, 1997

Shermer, Michael, *Why People Believe Weird Things*, W. H. Freeman, 1997

Shesso, Renna, *Math for Mystics*, Weiser, 2007

Skinner, Stephen, *Sacred Geometry*, Gaia, 2006

Smith, Andrew, *Moondust*, Bloomsbury, 2005

Smith, Huston, *The Illustrated Guide to World Religions*, HarperCollins, 1994

Spence, Lewis, *The Illustrated Guide to Egyptian Mythology*, Studio Books, 1996

Spencer Neil, *True as the Stars Above: Adventures in Modern Astrology*, Orion Books, 2002

Steiner, Rudolf, *Occult Science: An Outline*, Rudolf Steiner Press, 1969

—, *Manifestations of Karma*, Rudolf Steiner Press, 1989

—, *The Fourth Dimension: Sacred Geometry, Alchemy and Mathematics*, Anthroposophic Press, 2001

Stone, Merlin, *When God Was a Woman*, Harvest Books, 1976

Storm, Hyemeyohsts, *Lightningbolt*, HarperCollins, 1977

Strange Stories and Amazing Facts, Reader's Digest, 1980

Streep, Peg, *Sanctuaries of the Goddess: The Sacred Landscapes and Objects*, Bullfinch Press, 1994

Stuart, Malcolm (ed.), *The Encyclopedia of Herbs and Herbalism*, Macdonald, 1979

Sun, Howard and Dorothy, *Colour Your Life*, Piatkus, 1998

Svenek, Jaroslav, *Minerals: A Field Guide*, Artia, 1987

Symonds John, *The Great Beast*, Frederick Muller, 1951

Talbot, Rob, and Whiteman, Robin, *Brother Cadfael's Herb Garden*, Little, Brown and Company, 1988

Taylor, Thomas, *Eleusinian and Bacchic Mysteries*, Kessinger Publishing, 1993

Thom, Alexander, *Megalithic Lunar Observatories*, Oxford University Press, 1971

Thomas, Keith, *Religion and the Decline of Magic*, Penguin Books, 1973

Thompson, C. J., *The Lure and Romance of Alchemy*, Bell, 1990

Tomkins, Wilma, *Indian Sign Language*, Dover, 1929

Treasures of Britain, Reader's Digest, 1968

Tressider, Jack, *1001 Symbols*, Duncan Baird, 2003

Uyldert, Nellie, *The Magic of Precious Stones*, Aquarian, 1989

Valiente, Doreen, *An ABC of Witchcraft Past and Present*, Robert Hale, 1973

—, *The Rebirth of Witchcraft*, Robert Hale, 1989

Vitaliano, D. R., *Legends of the Earth: Their Geological Origins*, Indiana University Press, 1973

Von France, Marie-Louise, *On Divination and Synchronicity*, Inner City Books, 1980

Wade, David, *Symmetry: the Ordering Principle*, Wooden Books, 2006

Waite, A. E., *The Holy Kabbalah*, University Books (undated)

—, *The Brotherhood of the Rosy Cross*, Rider, 1924

—, *The Secret Tradition of Alchemy*, Rider, 1929

—, *The Pictorial Key to the Tarot*, Paragon, 1993

Walker, Barbara G., *The Woman's Dictionary of Symbols and Sacred Objects*, HarperSanFrancisco, 1988

—, *The Woman's Encyclopedia of Myths and Secrets*, HarperSanFrancisco, 1988

Wallace Murphy, Tim, *Cracking the Symbol Code*, Watkins, 2005

Walters, Raymond J., *The Power of Gemstones*, Carlton, 1996

Watkins, Alfred, *A Ley Hunter's Manual: A Guide to Early Tracks*, Turnstone Press, 1983

Watson, Lyall, *Supernature: A Natural History of the Supernatural*, Hodder and Stoughton, 1973

Watterson, Barbara, *Gods of Ancient Egypt*, Sutton, 1996

Wells, David, *The Penguin Dictionary of Curious and Interesting Numbers*, Penguin, 1986

Westwood, Jennifer (ed.), *The Atlas of Mysterious Places*, Weidenfeld and Nicholson, 1987

White, T. H., *The Book of Beasts*, Readers' Union/Jonathan Cape, 1956

Wilhelm, Richard, *I Ching or Book of Changes*, Arkana, 1989

Websites

www.dharma-haven.org (for digital prayer wheels and the correct pronunciation of the 'om mani padme hum' mantra)

www.druidry.org (the site for the Order of Bards, Ovates and Druids)

www.folklore-society.com (fantastic links to similar organizations all over the world)

www.jstor.org (online academic papers)

www.rosslytemplars.org

www.bnhs.org Bombay Natural History Society (their journal is an invaluable resource)

Illuminati Cipher and Alphabet of Daggers fonts courtesy of Nu Isis

INDEX

Leviathan Cross 117
marriage 597
melusine 313
mercury, sulphur and salt 436, 443, 446
Monad 130
ouroboros 134
pentagram 139
Philosopher's Egg 68
phoenix 316
quintessence 488
rebis **145–6**
Red Stone 54
rose 377
salamander 318
Seal of Solomon 84
Serpent Cross 155
seven operations 140–1, 245, 490
skull symbolism 574–5
Smaragdina Tablet **158–9**
Star of David 152–3
symbols **11–12**
and Tarot 165
tortoise 297
V.I.T.R.I.O.L. **195**
wheel 200
wolf devouring dog 270
World Tree 386
see also Philosopher's Stone
Alcyone 331
Aldebaran 209, 462
alder **387**
alectorius **416**
Alexander VII, Pope 471
Alexander the Great 11, 158
Alfheimr 306
Algeria 370
Ali 276–7, 282
Alice in Wonderland (Carrroll) 265, 370
All Seeing Eye 7, **12–13**, 88, 242, 547, 556, 557
Great Seal of the United States 194
almadel 13
almond tree **387–8**
almonds 17
Alpha and Omega **511**, 522
alphabet 631 *see also* secret scripts and ciphers
alphabet of arrows **528**
alphabet of daggers **528**
alphabet of Honorius *see* Witches alphabet

altar **13**, 33, 237, 453, 456
Court of the Priests 475
Pole Star orientation 244
square form 6
vervain 383
Amalthea 58, 276
amandinus **416**
amaranth **346–7**
Amazons 114
amber **416–17**
ambrosia **76–7**, 627
Ameratasu 116, 129, **633**
American Revolution 398
amethyst 414, **417–18**
amiante **418**
ammolite **418**, 431
ammonites 445
amrita *see* soma
amulet **13–14**, 36, 38, 71, 105
Abraxas Stone 8
almadel **13**
amber 416
apotrope **18**
ash wood 389
bear claws/teeth 259
bulla **30–1**
celestial script 529
chnoubis **38**
cimaruta **39**, 378
cornicello **58**
dreamcatcher **66**
fly 273
Four Sacred Creatures **273–4**
frog 274
hematite 431
jasper 433
lapis lazuli 434
lion 282
malachite 436
manaia **120**
Mjolnir **129–30**
nazar **131**
nine gemstones 491
omamori **132**
palad khik **135**
peony 374
peridot 440
quartz 441
red string **146**
rowan cross 408
rubies/garnets 53
stags horn 294
troll cross **190**
tsa tsa **190–1**

writing of the Magi 545
Ana 575
Analuf, King 458–9
anathema 26
"Ancient Mariner, The" (Coleridge) 325
Ancient Order of Druids 472
Anderson, Hans Christian 314
Andes 236, 330, 463
Andrew, St 149–50
anemone **347**
angel/s 70, 76, 79, 141, 200, 241, 244, 247, 298, **300–1**, 304, 461, 489, 528, 572
Enochian script **530–1**
summoning 523
see also Gabriel; Metatron
angel's trumpet *see* datura
angelica **347**
angelical script **528**
Angelus Silesius 68
angle of the compass **84**
Anglo-Saxons 103, 290, 338, 350, 392, 397, 411, 543, 582–3, 637
Anguta 632
animals 9, 256–99, 619
bezoar stones 299, 339, **418–19**
fantastical 300–23
language 153
struck by thunderbolts 248
see also fauna
aniseed 16
ankh **14**, 42, 113, 182, 191, 534, 580, 619
ankle **549**
Anne of Geierstein (Scott) 438
ant **257**
Antares 216
antimony *see* Gray Wolf
Antony, St. 182
Anu 612
Anubis 256, 270, 279, 299, **620–1**
ape *see* monkey
aphrodisiacs **15–18**
aquilegia 348
betel nut 350
chocolate **18**, 77
ginseng 354
honey **18**, 79
hoopoe entrails 330
mandrake 369
nettle 372
pearl powder 440
pomegranate 407

THE ELEMENT ENCYCLOPEDIA OF SECRET SIGNS AND SYMBOLS

cube **62**, 483
  and cross 117
  Ka'aba 461
Cuchulain 270, 299, 550
Cupid 329, 337, 437, 489, 558
Cups 166, 168
Cuycha 609
Cybele 57, 282, 597
cycle of life **206**
cypress **396**
Cyprus 422
Cyrus II 474

Da Vinci Code, The (Brown) 468
Da'wah **515**
daffodil 359, 371
Dagda **614**
daisy **352–3**
Dalai Lama 4
  fifth 341
Dame Aux Camellias, La (Dumas) 351
dance **584–5**
  bees 260
dandelion **353**
Darjeeling 196
daruma **63**
date palm 316–17, **396**
datura **353**
David, King 234, 474, 529
Davidian alphabet **529**
dawn **252**
day **252**
Day of Judgement/Last Judgement
  302, 336, 384, 419, 475
Day of the Dead 574, 587
Dead Sea Scrolls 229
dearinth **63**
death **585–7**
  jet association 433–4
Death Tarot card **176**, 494
Dee, John 11, 130, 157, 459, 511, 521,
  523, 528, 530
deer **269**
  Three Senseless Creatures 296
deities 605–39
  ambrosia 76
Delphi 132, 324, 328, 402, **456–7**,
  548, 570
Delphic Oracle 271, 457, 482
Demeter 170, 238, 257, 287, 352, 354,
  375, 590, 591, 612, 624, **625**, 627,
  628 *see also* Ceres
demon/s 273, **303–4**, 626, 634
  Abraxus 8

almadel 13
conjuring 105, 153, 438
dispelling 26, 182, 523, 552, 578
exorcism 436
goblins 310
imps 312
incubus **312–13**
possession 511
Ramayana 587–8
repelling 418, 434, 440, 595, 596,
  613
succubus **319**
see also Asmodeus
Demophon 388
Dendera 213
Denmark 335
Derg Corra 91
Descartes, René 575
desert 264
Devil 373, 560, 578, 614
  animal associations 266, 274, 275,
    281, 286, 294
  bird associations 326, 331–2
  cross dispels 93
  at the crossroads 61
  Goat of Mendes 81
  green association 50
  inverted cross 103
  red association 54
  as serpent 298, 327
  666 503
  trident 233
Devil Tarot card **177–8**, 495
Devil's Chord 519
Dharma wheel 21, **64**
diagonal **7**
diamond 105, 413, 414, **423–5**,
  491
Diana 19, 59, 210, 217, 265, 277 *see
  also* Artemis
Diana Nemorensis 251
Dionysus 80, 252, 262, 271, 274, 318,
  332, 357, 383, 417, 429, 577 *see also*
  Bacchus
Dioscordes 15
directions **253–4**, 487
  eight 368, 490
  and Chinese elements 226
  ten 196
  Tetraktys 183
Discordianism 498
Divine Principle, The 192
Diwali 581, **587–8**
djed **65**

djinn 229, 265, **304**
Doctrine of Signatures 15, 59, **344–5**,
  385, 414, 433, 444
Dodona 251, 326, 385, 404
dog 168, 257, **269–70**
  black 48
  Heracles' 52–3
  Moon Tarot card 179
  and peony root 374
  wild 279
Dogon people 73, 498, 560
  granary **457**
  Konoga masks 123
Doldrums 234
dolmen 65
dolphin 244, **271**
Dome of the Rock **475**, 489–90
Domovoi **634**
donkey **271–2**, 616
doorway **65**
  decorated dots 3
  Janus 627
  mezuzah **127–8**
  Passover blood 10
  rangoli 145
  St. John's Wort 379
  torii **187**
  vesica piscis 6, **197**
dorje 67, 196
dot/s **3**
  awen 23
  question mark 144
  quintessence 144, 146
  swastika 164
  Tetraktys 183
  Theosophical Society emblem 185
  vajra 195
  yin-yang 203
Double Happiness **65–6**
double-headed eagle **304**
Douglas fir **399**
Douglas, David 399
dove 281, **326**, 328
  columbine 347
  fleur de lys 74
  Holy Spirit symbol 256, 326, 556
  Noah's Ark 335, 405
  US symbol 194, 348
dowsing 198, 401, 408
Dracula (Stoker) 129
dragon 216, 279, 300, **305**, 313,
  469
  carries the Universe 296
  Chinese Imperial symbol 493

Eostre 68, 276, 367, 588–9
Ephesus 74, 259, 314, 553
Epic of Gilgamesh 394, 612
Epona 279, 615
equinoxes 205, 337 *see also* spring
    equinox; vernal equinox
Erda 228
Eris 498
ermine 95, **272**
Eros 19–20, 339
Erzulie Freda Dahomey 198, 349,
   639
Eskimos
  bull roarer 30
  see also Innuit
Estonians 244
estrogen 18, 68, 589
Esu 61
ether 224
  black egg 182
  gemstone correspondences 429
  head 547
  platonic solids 452, 453
  see also quintessence
Ethiopia 118, 465, 562
Etruscans 39, 115, 199, 480
Eucharist 78, 80, 592
Eureus 234
Europa 262, 267
European Union 493
Euryale 246
Eurydice 398
Evangelists 256, 487
  symbols **70–1**, 110, 183–4, 327
Eve 304, 327 *see also* Adam and Eve
Eveleigh, David 460
Everest, George 237
Everest *see* Chomolungma
evil eye **71**
  protection 18, 105, 112, 131, 146,
    148, 330, 414, 415, 420, 423, 430,
    436, 438, 449, 475, 557, 563, 572
excommunication 26, **592**
Exodus 19, 420, 598, 606
exorcism 349, 425
eye/s **556–7**
  antelope 275
  of Buddha 20
  cowrie shell 59
  daruma 63
  four-eyed jackal 280
  gemstone cures 434–5, 443
  "green-eyed" 50
  hyena 279

mirror of the soul xv, 129, 556
opal association 438
owl 333
protective 18, 19
wisdom symbol **200–1**
see also evil eye; third eye
Eye of Horus 13, 33, 547, 557
Eye of Providence 13
Ezekiel 183

fairy/ies 50, 252, 300, 303, 320,
  306–7, 370, 387, 397, 401, 408,
  426, 447, 464
fall 252
Falun Gong symbol **71**
Faro 248, 382
farohar **71–2**
fasces **72**
Fascism 72
fasting **593**, 599
  Lent 500, 589, 593
Fates 34, 112, 253, 293, 306, **307**, 437,
  486, 532, 558, 606
Father Christmas 41, **307–8**, 583
Fatima 577
fauns 556
feather/s **72–3**, 125, 168
  air symbol 72, 233
  cloaks 636
  dreamcatcher 66
  duck 327
  eagle 280, 328
  farohar 71
  goose 329
  headdress 44
  heraldic crest 95
  hummingbird 330, 608
  Immortals 200
  ostrich 72, 150, 332, 566
  parrot 334
  prayer stick 142
  shamanism 45, 72–3, 320
  swallow 417
  swan 73, 338
  turkey 340
  vulture 341
  white 55, 321
  woodpecker 341
  wren 342
  Zoso symbol 222
feet *see* foot
female genitalia
  aphrodisiacs **17**
  scallop shell 150

see also clitoris; vagina; vesica piscis;
  vulva; yoni
Feng Shui 65–6, 129, 134, **253–4**
fennel 18, 185, **353**
ferret *see* weasel
fetish **73**
Fibonacci sequence 452, **483**
fifteen **495**
fifth element 204
  Tattva 182
  see also ether; quintessence
fifty **501**
  prayer beads 142
fifty-six **501**
fig leaves 40, 87, 291, 398
fig tree **398**
figs 17
  "fico" gesture 563
figure of eight *see* infinity symbol
fingernails **557–8**
  Venus' 437
fingerprints **558**
Finland 298
Finno-Ugric people 259
Finns 244, 289
fire bringers
  fennel 353
  porcupine 288
  swallow 337
  woodpecker binger 341
  wren 342
fire deities *see* Agni; Huitzilopotchli;
  Hephaestus
fire element **235–41**
  athame symbolic 22
  blood symbolic 551
  Chiah 109
  five element theory 226
  flint association 426
  garuda rules 273
  gemstone correspondences 429
  goat symbolic 276
  gold association 429
  gorse association 354
  hands synonymous 547
  hedgehog inventor of 277
  holly ruled by 401
  horse belongs to 278
  lion symbolic 184
  masculine 33, 233, 236
  Masonic system 227
  opal contains 439
  phoenix reborn 316
  platonic solids 452, 453

tenth state 492
thumb 565
tilaka **185–6**, 235
tortoise 296–7
unruly hair 561
wheel 199
World Egg 68
Yab Yum **202**
yantra **203**
hippogriff 311
hippopotamus **278**, 302
Hiram Abiff 82, **85**, 386–7, 469, 594
HIS **101**
His Dark Materials (Pullman) 303
Hitchhiker's Guide to the Galaxy
(Adams) 500
Hitler, Adolf 160, 164, 206, 248, 503,
505
Hittites 304
hobgoblin **312**
hobo signs **514–15**
Hofburg Spear 160
Hogan **460–1**
Hole 401
Holiday, Billie 49
Holland 74
holly 357, 370, **401**, 583
Holly King 401
Holtom, Gerald 138
Holy Communion 76, 347
Holy Grail xi, **93–7**, 159
Holy of Holies 525, 567
Holy River 206 *see also* Ganges
Holy Spirit 234, 235, 326, 556
Holy Trinity 6, 13, 136, 137, 189, 352,
367, 380, 486, 607
homeopathy 219
Homer 231, 232, 238, 266, 303,
315
honey **78**, 501, 631
aphrodisiac **18**
Honorius of Thebes 545
hood **44**
hoopoe 240, **329–30**, 331
Hope Diamond 424
Hopi Indians
Kachina masks 123, 610
Kokopeli **113**
man in maze **119–20**
stag 294
swastika 164
umbilical cord 579
horizontal line **5**
Horned God 294, **614**

Horned Serpent 611
horned shaman **97–8**
horns 177
Aries 208
goat 275, 563
stag 294
Taurus 209
unicorn 320
Horns of Odin **97**
horse/s 8, **278–9**, 253, 615, 627
burial 294
Chariot Tarot card 172
Sagittarius 217–18
Seal of Knights Templar 154
turquoise charm in manes 449
Valkyrie as 321
see also Buraq; Pegasus; Sleipnir
horse spirit (pooka) **317**
horse hybrids
centaur **302–3**
hippogriff 311
horseshoe **98**, 431–2
Horus 193, 264, 547, 557
Ho-Sien Ku 617
hot cross bun 35
hourglass **98**, 471
Huang Di 239
Hubbard, L. Ron 151
Huitzipotchli 161, 330, 464, 608
Hulinhjalmur **100**
hummingbird **330**, 464, 608
Hundred Years War 563
Hungary 579
Hunza people 427
hyacinth **356**
hyena **279**, 391
Hygiea 140, 292
Hymanaeus 568
hymen **568**

I Ching **99**, 134, 384–5, 481, 489,
490
Ibn Hayan, Jabir 195, 495–6
Iceland 318
stave symbols **99–100**
Ichthys 61, 272
Ichthys wheel **100**
Idun 388
IHS **101**
Iliad 375
Illuminati 13, 194
ciphers **534–5**
Illuminatus trilogy (Shea and Wilson)
498

Immortals 200, 241, 249, 258, 296,
354, 355, 370, 406, 407, 411, 505,
573–4, **616–18**
imp **312**
Inari 274, 376
Incas 373–4
coca 352
deities **609**
jaguar 280
lizard 283
rainbow fear 249
incense **101**, 519
incubus **312–13**
indalo **101–2**
India 74, 102, 135, 147, 336, 381, 465,
480
alchemy 11, 436
almonds 388
angels 301
banyan meetings 391
barley 349
betel nut 350
bezoar 418
bird augury 324
caduceus 32, 292
chess origins 37
colors of the rainbow 249
cow/ox 79, 256, 267, 287
cremation 586
dance 584
Diwali **587–8**
fig invocation 398
garuda 315
goat 276
Green Man 91
hair customs 562
hemp 355
Holy Rose 377
Konark temple lodestone 435
labrys 114
lotus 368
"mankolam" 134
mehendi **125**
milk tree myth 79
Mogul palaces 508
monkey 285
onyx 438
owl 333
phoenix period 316
Pole Star 244
rangoli **145**
red for weddings 53
rock temples 229
rudraksha bead **148**

long nose 571
magpie 332
mantis 284
mermaid 314
monkey 285
Mount Fuji **240–1**
nipple plasters 570
No Theater masks 123
owl 333
passion flower 374
paulownia 406
peach tree 406
rice 376
seven 490
tabasheer 446
tea ceremony 381
torii **187**, 251
tortoise 296
umbilical cord 579
whale 298
Japanese Buddhism
five directions 488
Jizo **106**
jasper 191, 282, 414, **433**
Jefferson, Thomas 535
Jerusalem *see* Temple Mount; Temple of Jerusalem
Jerusalem Cross **104**
jet 105, **433–4**
jewelry **104–6**
  amulets **13–14**
  Celtic knotwork **36**
  labrys 114
Jewish tradition
  acacia 386
  agate 415
  Ark of the Covenant 19
  beard 550
  burial 586
  cedar 394
  Chai 515
  circumcision 560
  citrus fruit 396
  date palm 396
  dreidel **66**
  fasting 593
  head shaving 562
  Jerusalem 474
  Khamsa 92
  kidney 568
  lamb 281
  Luz 49
  Menorah **126**, 387–8
  Metatron 127

mezuzah **127–8**
Name of God 520, **525**
Ner Tamid **131**
19-year cycle 497
Passover **598–9**
philtrum 572
shofar **156**
sixty 501
skullcap 44
Star of David 153
thirty-six saintly people 499–500
Torah **186**
  see also Gematria; Kabbalah;
    synagogue; Temple of Jerusalem;
    Tetragrammaton
Jews
  Nazi persecution 56, 153
  transmuted souls 331
Jizo **106**
Joan of Arc 567
John, gospel 160
John Barleycorn 594
John the Baptist 90, 264, 379
John the Evangelist 70, 71, 90, 110,
  184, 327, 456
Johnson, Robert 61
Jolly Roger **157–8**
Jonah 298
Jones, John Paul 222
Jonson, Ben 338
Joseph (Old Testament) 51
Joseph, husband of Mary 271
Joseph of Arimathea 93, 161, 400, 459
*Journal of the Bombay Natural History
  Society* 250
Judas Iscariot 56, 493, 595
Judgement Tarot card **180–1**, 497
jujube **402**
Julius Caesar 253, 329, 333, 626
Julunggul **638**
Jung, Carl 97, 121, 154, 158, 200, 488,
  573
Jung and His Symbols (Henderson) 324
Jung and Tarot (Nichols) 166
juniper **357–8**
Juno 211, 219, 346
Jupiter (God) 467 *see also* Zeus
Jupiter (planet) 174, 571
  and tin 12, 153, 444, 447
Jurassic Park 417
Justice Tarot card **173**, 491, 493

k in magick **517**
Ka 24, 558

Ka'aba 6, 62, 244–5, 419, 461–2, 597
Kabbalah 25, 32, 69, 83, **106–10**, 150,
  205, 228, 265, 386, 418, 484, 492,
  521, 529, 562, 597
  enneagram **70**
  Hebrew alphabet **109–10**, 532
  inverted heart 567
  Merkabah **126**
  numbers 479, 484, 493, 495, 497,
    498, 499, 500, 503, 517
  Nun 494
  pentagram 139, 140
  planetary correspondences 244
  red string **146**
  Sefer Yetzirah symbol **154–5**
  Shema 156
  and Tarot 107, 165
Kachina 610
Kaf **239–40**
Kailash, Mount **237–8**, 368
Kalachakra Seal **517–18**
Kali 106, 152, 262, 280, 501, 566, 578,
  608, **630–1**
Kalpa Tree 414
Kama 334
Kama Sutra cipher **535–6**
kamea 119, **518**
Kami 241
kapala **110**
Kelley, Edward 528, 530
kelpie **313**
Kepler, Johannes 453
kerub **110**
key (clavicle) 14, 39, **110–11**, 627
  to the door 111, 497
  see also crossed keys
Khalsas **45**
Khamsa *see* Hand of Fatima
Khanda **111–12**
Khepera 211, 289–90
Khirka **40–1**
Khu 558
kidney **568**
  stones 426
kingfisher **330–1**
kiss **594–5**
knee **568**
knife *see* athame; boline
Knights of St. John (Knights
  Hospitallers) 183, 379
Knights Templar xi, 117, 455, 526
  Abraxus 8
  alphabet **536**
  Baphomet 25

Luz (Blue City) 50
lycanthropy 322
lynx **283–4**
 urine 284, 416

Ma'at 72, 150, 214, 215, 222, 332,
 434–5, 557, 566
Mab 307
Mabinogi 615
Macarthur, Ellen 232–3
Mag Ruith 199
Magen David *see* Seal of Solomon
magic
 incense 101
 pentagram 139
 and red ochre 53
magic circle 4, 22, **118–19**, 442
magic knot 119
magic seal 119
magic squares 499, 503, **504**
 kamea 504, **518**
magical name **518**
Magician Tarot card **168–9**, 485
magician, signs of **119**
magnetite 435
magpie **331–2**
Mahabharata 335, 593
Malachim alphabet **536**
malachite **436**
Malaysia 59, 418
male genitalia
 aphrodisiacs **17**
 see also lingam; penis; phallus;
 testicles
Mali 332
Mallory, George 236
Maltese Cross *see* Templar Cross
Maltwood, Katherine 459
Mama Quilla 609
man in the maze **119–20**
Man Who Would be King, The 507
manaia **120**
manate 314
mandala 21, 58, 71, 115, **120–1**, 145,
 238, 368, 377, 454, 473, 487, 517
mandorla 197
mandrake **368–9**, 374
Maneki Neko *see* beckoning cat
Mani stone **518–19**
manikin **121**, 393
Manitou 610
manji **122**
mankolam *see* paisley
manna 19, **78**

mantis **284**
mantra 141, 417, **519** *see also* Aum;
 Om Mani Padme Hum
Maoris
 deities **638**
 jade 433
 manaia **120**
 placenta burial 572
 ritual scarring 38
 tree fern in art 160, 452
Marie Antoinette 424
Mark of the Beast **122**
Mark of the Bustard **122–3**
Mark, St. 70–1, 110, 183, 213
marriage **597**, 619, 622
 two butterflies 263
 see also weddings
Mars (God) 279, 341, 383, 431, 467
 see also Ares
Mars (planet) 53, 571
 rules Aries 208
 and iron 12, 153, 432, 444
Martin, St. 40, 233
Mary Magdalene 281, 379, 468
Mary the Virgin 48, 59, 74, 142, 147,
 150, 214, 271, 280, 297, 320, 326,
 328, 342, 358, 377, 380, 384, 454,
 556
 Miraculous Medal **128**
mask **123**
 Lion Dance 282
Masonic alphabet *see* Rosicrucian
 alphabet
Masonic apron **87–8**
masons' marks *see* stonemasons'
 marks
Mason's square 83, **84**
Materia Medica 415
Mather, MacGregor 33
Maths for Mystics (Shesso) 516
Matthew, gospel 154
Matthew, St. 70, 110, 183
Mawu Lisa 639
May Day 415
Maya 46, 230, 293, 484
Mayans
 balche 391
 bat 258
 bird augury 324
 calendar xvi–xvii, 285
 chocolate 77
 destruction 449
 five 488
 jackal 280

night, death, and darkness symbol
 253
 ten 492
 thirteen 493
 tortoise 296
 turkey 340
 twenty 497
 world end predictions 211
 zero (snail shell) 161, 292, 484
maypole **123–4**, 385, 392
maze **124**, 284
 Green Man 124, **459–60**
 man in **119–20**
mead **78**
 magical 97
Mecca 6, 62, 73, 112, 326, 338, 419,
 454, **461–2**, 474, 490, 586
Medici, Catherine de 77
medicine wheel/s **125**, 199, **462–3**
meditation 113, 120, 125, 126, 203,
 238, 511, 554
Medusa 292, 309, 561
mehendi **125**, 356
Mela, St 549
melusine **313**
Menebuch 277
menhirs 132, 201, **463**
Menorah **126**, 387–8, 613
 Messianic Seal 126
menstrual cycle 243, 473, 551
Menthe 18
Mercury (God) 31, 467, 606, **626**, 637
 see also Hermes
mercury (mineral) 222, **436–7**
 alchemy 117, 155, 436, 443, 446,
 487
 and Mercury 12, 153, 444
Mercury (planet) 571
 rules Gemini 211
 and mercury 12, 153, 444
Merkabah **126**
Merlin 313
mermaid 291, **313–14**, 318
Merope 246
Meru, Mount 49, 196, 236, **238**, 368,
 413, 460, 518
Mesopotamia 32, 73, 110, 152, 156,
 177, 312, 476
 tree of life **126**
 Zodiac 204–5
Messianic seal **126–7**
metals
 alchemical transformation 10–11
 minerals, metals and gems 413–49

camel 264
cat 265
diamonds 424
magical breath 553
Maskhara sect 123
phoenix period 316
swallow 338
thumb rings105
yellow dog 270
Zodiac 208, 209, 210, 211, 215, 217, 218, 219, 220
Persian rugs **140**
Perun **634–5**
Peruvian Indians
bezoar 418
deities **609**
emerald "ripening" 425
Peter, St. 2, 103, 111, 136, 336, 341, 470, 471
peyote 345, **375**
phallic symbols
broomstick 30
djed 65
pine cones 407
trees 548
phallus **571–2**, 578, 579, 610, 625
amulets 294
fire symbol 235
phenylethylamine 18
Philip II of Spain 352
Philosopher's Stone 10, 54, 79, 91, 97, **140–1**, 153, 195, 429–30, 487
philtrum **572**
Phoenicians 68
phoenix 235, **316–17**, 309, 328, 620
Four Sacred Creatures **273–4**, 297, 305
Phrygians 57
phurba **141**
Phyllis 388
phyllomancy 385, 412
Pictish swirl script **538**
pig **287–8**
Three Poisons 336
pigpen cipher **538–9**
Pillars of Wisdom 461
pine 251, 348, **407**
pine cone 185, 353, 407
pink **52**
alectorius 416
candles 34
coral 423
lotus 368
rose 377

piropholos **440**
Pisces **220–1**, 273, 549
pixie/s 252, 303, 305, **317**, 556
placenta **572**
places of pilgrimage **453–77**
Plains Indians 337, 514, 552
calumet **33**
planetary (magical) metals 26, 67, 69, 116, 152–3, 245, 422, **444**, 447
alchemical symbols 12
planets 47, 130, 243, **245–6**, 413, 605
alignment 462
color correspondences 476–7
and gemstones **428**, **447**
Hebrew alphabet 109, 532
magic squares 119
mounds on palm 571
Pythagoras' beliefs 483
seven traditional 8, 67, 69, 462, 476–7, 489
and Zodiac signs 207
Plant, Robert 222
plants 9, 345–85, 625
as tools of transition **345**
Plato 6, 105, 129, 230, 355, 413, 423, 481, 485, 573, 590
platonic solids 62, 181, 224, **452–3**, 483
Pleiades 69, 609
Pliny the Elder 15, 284, 297, 301–2, 355, 418, 421, 435, 439, 441, 447, 448
Plough 244
plum tree 348, **407**
Pluto (God) 18, 397
Pluto (planet)
rules Scorpio 217
point within the circle **89–90**, **163**
Pole star 24, 69, 162, 164, **244–5**
Polynesia 98
pomegranate 344, 410, 427, 590, 628
pomegranate tree **407–8**
Pontius Pilate 602
Pontos Riscados **521**
pooka **317**
poplar 231
poppy **375**
porcupine **288**
porpoise *see* dolphin
Poseidon 188, 233, 238, 246, 262, 291, 315, 327, 405, 598, 622, 624 *see also* Neptune
Potter, Beatrix 527
prayer flag **141–2**

prayer stick **142**
prayer string **142–3**, 148
prayer wheel **143**, 519, 521
Presley, Elvis 14
Priapus 547, 572
primrose **375–6**
Prometheus 353, 569
Proserpina *see* Persephone
Protestantism 124, 551
Proteus 291
Pseudo Dionysus the Aeropagite 301
psychedelic plants **345**
Ptolemy 205
Pueblo Indians 327, 340, 341, 449, 610
Zia Pueblo sun symbol **204**
purple 19, **52–3**
costliness 417
Imperial 47
Suffragettes 47
pyramid texts 529, 534, **539**
Pyramids (buildings) 237, 451, **467–8**, 523
burial 229, 468, 586
Mexican 242
pyramid (shape) 235
All Seeing Eye 12
Great Seal of the United States 194
obelisk 465
Tetraktys 183
Pythagoras 78, 82, 89, 129, 139, 183, 452, 467, 481, **482–3**, 484, 488, 492, 519, 547
Pythagoras Y **202**
Pythagoreans 485, 486, 487, 488, 490, 491, 492
Pythia 457

Q *see* quintessence
Qedeshet 273
Qi Gong 71
Qu'ran 26, 46, 112, 234, 293, 324, 329, 336, 427, 462, 488, 500, 509, 593, 600
quartz 441
Queen of Sheba 18, 329, 331, 425, 501
question mark **144**
Quetzalcoatl 161, 608, 609
quicksilver *see* mercury
quintessence 3, 29, 109, **144**, 146, 164, 184, 488

Ra 90, 193, 242, 327, 351, 410, 447, 448, 465, 619, 621

Rudra 284
rudraksha bead **148**
Rudston monolith 463
rue **378**
  weasel's knowledge 297, 302
rule 39, **86**
Rumpelstiltskin 520
runes 29, 175, 264, 524, 537, 637
  bind 523, 544
  gar 91
  Icelandic stave symbols **99–100**
  sig 27, 28, 248, 544
  valknut 196
runic alphabet **540–4**
Russia 68, 299, 304, 321, 562, 589
Russian Orthodox Church 143

sabbats 61, 279
Sacred and the Profane, The (Eliade) xi, 230
sacred geometry 37, 68, 75, 79, 139, 197, 380, **451–3**, 483, 503, 519, 532
Sacred Heart **149**, 567
sacred thread (Poonal) 42
Safekh 406
saffron (color) 45, **54**, 352
saffron (spice) **378**
saffron crocus 47, 54, 352
Saga of Eric the Red 264
sage **378**
Sagittarius 20, 205, **217–18,** 302
Sahu 558
salamander 303, 310, **317–18**, 320
salicylic acid 412
saliva **572–3**
salmon 253, **289**, 400
Salome 379
salt **442–3**
  alchemy 117, 436, 443, 446, 487
  protective power 118, 442
Saltire 136, **149–50**, 158
  heraldry 95
Samhuin 216, 310, 317, 388, 397, 411, 587, 595, 602, 614
Samoyed people 244
Samson and Delilah 561
Samurai 25–6, 186, 284, 350, 358, 394
sandalwood paste 186
sandalwood tree **409**
Sanskrit 20, 67, 113, 117, 120, 142, 164, 181, 185, 195, 201, 203, 211, 218, 235, 334, 405, 438, 472, 517

Santiago de Compostela 244
sapphire 49, 414, 434, **443**, 491
Sarasvati 142, 269, 509, 629, **631**
sardonyx 437–8
sash 42
Satan 188, 258, 302, 318, 462, 600
Satanism 2, 25, 138
  inverted cross 2, 103
SATOR Word Square 504, **521–2**
Saturn (God) 151, 218, 435, 467, 583
Saturn (planet) 571
  rules Capricorn 218, 222
  and lead 12, 153, 435, 444
Saturnalia 308, 401, 583, **600–1**
satyr/s 275–6, **318**, 556
scales **150**, 173
  Libra 215
scallop shell **150**
Scandinavia 250, 310, 313, 332, 342, 386, 388, 403, 540
scapegoat 276
scarab 211, **289–90**
scepter 22, **151**, 169, 170, 198, 613 *see also* shaku
Scientology Cross **151**
Scientology Symbol **151**
Scorpio 204, **216–17**, 246
scorpion **290**, 505, 613
  Scorpio 216, 246
  stings 426, 449
Scotland 74
  boar stones 261
  kelpie 313
  Lords of Misrule 601
  magpie 332
  paisley 134–5
  Saltire **149–50**
  selkie 318
  Stone of Destiny **445–6**
  thistle 381
  see also Rosslyn Chapel
scrying 49, 62, 129, 419, 444, 530
scythe 44, **151**, 210
seal **290–1**, 632
  kelpie 313
  selkie 318
Seal of Knights Templar **153–4**
Seal of Shamash **152**
Seal of Solomon 84, 138, **152–3**, 168, 184, 195
  Chartres labyrinth 115
Seal of the United States *see* Great Seal of the United States
seals **522**

seasons **251–2**
  alchemical symbols 11
  and elements 226
Second World War 55, 56, 60, 161, 206, 335, 459, 515, 527, 530
Secret of Hermes *see* Smaragdina Tablet
secret scripts and ciphers 527–45
Seder 599
Sedna **632**
Seed of Life 75, **154**
Sefer Yetzirah 108
  symbol **154–5**
Selene 350, 606
Selket 290
selkie 291, **318**
Semang people 568
semen 552, **573**, 577, 583
  fig sap 398
  mandrake 368
  mistletoe 16, 369
Seneca 249–50
Sengen 240
Sephiroth 108–9, 140, 167, 386, 492
septagram *see* Elven star
sequoia **409**
serpent/snake 265, **291–2**, 299, 304, 305, 327, 460
  aaskouandy 8
  adder stone **414–15**
  Aesclepius wand **9**
  bites 426, 444, 449
  Cagliostro Seal **32–3**
  and eagle 327
  forked tongue 202, 292, 578
  Furies 309
  Garden of Eden 327, 549, 578
  and garuda 309
  protection from 290, 354, 372, 434, 590
  snake stone **445**
  St. Hilda's stones **445**
  Three Poisons 336
  Uraeus 43, **193**
  see also caduceus; Horned serpent; Kundalini serpent; ouroboros; Quetzalcoatl; rainbow serpent
Serpent Cross **155**
serpent hybrids
  basilisk **301**
  chimaera **303**
  chnoubis **38**
  wyvern **322**
Serpent Mound 292, **469–50**, 611

Triratna (Three Jewels of Buddhism) 142, **189–90**, 486
Triregnum (Triple Crown) 43, **135–6**, 171
Trishul 23
triskele **190,** 277, 568–9
Trithemius, Johannes 138, 545
troll cross **190**
Trulli **475**
Ts'ao Kuo-ghiu 616
tsa tsa **190–1**
tsunami (2004) 247
Tuatha de Danaan 614–15
Tulasi 349
Tungu people 570
tunic 46
turban 45
turkey **340**
Turkey 358, 429
  Attis 582
  double-headed eagle 304
  ladybird 280
  nazar 131
  St. Nicholas 308
  whirling dervish 161
Turks 60
turquoise **448–9,** 609
turtle *see* tortoise
Twelfth Night 395
twelve 193, **493,** 622
twelve-pointed star 154–5
twenty **497**
twenty-five **499**
twenty-four **499**
twenty-one **497–8**
twenty-three **498–9**
23 499
twenty-two **498,** 550
twilight **252**
two **485–6**
  Kabbalah 108
Two Golden Fish 20
Two Mistresses 193
Tyet (Knot of Isis, Blood of Isis) **191,** 433
Typhon 278, 494

Uanaji 349
Udjat *see* Eye of Horus
UFOs 464
ultunda stone 441, **449**
umbilical cord **578–9**
Umbraculum **137**
undine 303, 310, 320, **320**

unicorn 95, **320–1**
  Four Sacred Creatures 305
unicursal hexagram **191–2**
Unification Church symbol **192–3**
United Kingdom *see* Britain
United States 88, 308, 465, 469, 494
  Depression 514
  dollar bill 12, 87, 153, **194–5**
  dove symbol 326, 328, 348
  Dutch Elm disease 397
  eagle symbol 194, 326, 328, 340
  Great Seal 12, 13
  Liberty trees 398
  snake handlers 291
  yellow for cowards 56
Upanishads 386, 460, 593
Upkar 512
Uraeus 43, **193**
Uranus
  rules Aquarius 220
Urim and Thummim **193–4**, 421
Ursa Major 244, 258
Ursa Minor 258
Uther Pendragon 305
Utzon, John 451

vagina 16, **579**, 580
  dentate 569, 579
  lotus flowers 407
  succubus 319
  see also vesica piscis
vajra 24, 26, 67, 153, **195–6**, 248
Valentine's Day 20, 567, 596, **601–2**
Valhalla 241, 321, 636, 637
valknut 189, **196**
Valkyrie 277, **321**, 335, 636, 637
vampire **321**, 573
  rowan stake 408
  silver bullets 444
vampire bat 258
Vanir 637
Varahi 288
Varanasi 231, 454
vata tree *see* banyan
Vatican City 135, 136, 470
Vedas 272
veil 42, **46**, 169
  between the worlds 231, 587
  clouds 247
  hymen 568
  Sancta Camisia 455
  see also Maya
Veles **634–5**

Venus (Goddess) 140, 150, 371, 376, 422, 437, 467, 489, 612 *see also* Aphrodite
Venus (planet) xvi–xvii, 140, 571, 609
  and copper 12, 153, 422, 444
  Ishtar personifies 613
  rules Taurus 209
vermilion (mercuric sulphide) 55
vernal equinox 221
vertical line **4–5**
vervain **383**
vesica piscis **197**
  almonds 17
  cave mouth 228
  fish 272–3
  Flower of Life 74
  lozenge 6, 94
  Magic Knot 119
  Messianic seal 126
  myrtle bud 371
  Seed of Life 154
  spirit enters matter 65, 579
  Tripod of Life 189
  triquetra 189
  World Tarot card 181, 498
Vesta 218
Victoria, Queen 433, 439, 584
Victory Banner 21
Vietnam 99, 261, 293, 298, 350, 407, 561
Vikings 196, 241, 335, 381
vine 91, 185, **383**, 469
  and elm 398
violet (color) **54–5**, 177, 494
  sixth chakra 54, 55, 555
violet (flower) **384**
Virgil 250, 322
Virgo **213–14**
Vishnu 79, 164, 186, 233, 261, 272, 282, 285, 296, 309, 349, 391, 486, 511, 559, 629
Vision and the Voice, The (Crowley) 528
V.I.T.R.I.O.L. **195**
Vitruvian Man 548, 570
volcano **240**
Voodoo Doll *see* manikin
Vortunna 199
Voudon
  asson **22**
  cha cha **36**
  deities **639**
  invocation 517
  ritual dancing 585